Patrick Sellar and the Highland Clearances

People always complain about muck-raking biographies, saying 'Leave us our heroes'. 'Leave us our villains' is just as important.

Alan Bennett[1]

Patrick Sellar and the Highland Clearances

Homicide, Eviction and the Price of Progress

Eric Richards

Polygon at Edinburgh

© Eric Richards, 1999

Polygon at Edinburgh
An imprint of Edinburgh University Press Ltd
22 George Square, Edinburgh

Typeset in 11/13 pt New Baskerville
by Hewer Text Ltd, Edinburgh, and
printed and bound in Great Britain by
The Cromwell Press, Wiltshire

A CIP record for this book is available
from the British Library

ISBN 1 902930 14 2 (hardback)
ISBN 1 902930 13 4 (paperback)

The right of Eric Richards to be
identified as author of this work has
been asserted in accordance with the
Copyright, Designs and Patents Act 1988.

Contents

To the memory of Monica Clough, 1922–1999
and
Paul Bourke, 1938–1999

List of Maps and Plates

– Maps –

1 Sutherland in 1820.
2 Sellar's farms in 1814 and 1831.

– Plates –

1 The young Sellar (courtesy of Christopher and Valerie Lang of Titanga, Victoria).
2 Sellar in his prime. From a painting by Sir David Macnee, 1851 in E. M. Sellar, *Recollections and Impressions* (Edinburgh and London 1907). *Print courtesy of the Trustees of the National Library of Scotland.*
3 Mrs Sellar (1793–1875) (courtesy of Christopher and Valerie Lang of Titanga, Victoria).
4 William Young Sellar (1825–1890), son of Patrick Sellar (courtesy of Christopher and Valerie Lang of Titanga, Victoria).
5 Patrick Plenderleath Sellar (1823–1892), son of Patrick Sellar (courtesy of Christopher and Valerie Lang of Titanga, Victoria).
6 Thomas Sellar (1820–1885), son of Patrick Sellar (courtesy of Christopher and Valerie Lang of Titanga, Victoria).
7 Elizabeth Leveson-Gower, de jure Countess of Sutherland, Duchess/Countess of Sutherland (1765–1839) by George Romney (with permission from the National Portrait Gallery, London).
8 George Granville Leveson-Gower, First Duke of Sutherland (1758–1833) by Thomas Phillips (with permission from the National Portrait Gallery, London).
9 Sir Paul Strzelecki (1797–1873) by permission of the State Library of Victoria).
10 James Loch (1780–1855) (with permission from the National Portrait Gallery, London).
11 Stewart of Garth, Major General (1772–1829) by S. W. Reynolds after J. M. Scrymgeour (with permission from the Scottish National Portrait Gallery, Edinburgh).
12 Dunrobin Castle (with permission from Lord Strathnaver, Dunrobin Castle Limited).
13 Photograph of Patrick Sellar towards the end of his life (courtesy of Christopher and Valerie Lang of Titanga, Victoria).
14 Portrait of Patrick Sellar (courtesy of Justice Robert Fisher of Hahndorf).

Preface and acknowledgements

Patrick Sellar has been dead for almost 150 years but his extraordinary notoriety in Scottish history shows no sign of abating. He continues to personify the worst abuses of the Highland clearances and attracts the severest hatred among passionate critics of the landlord interest. Sellar occupies a position in Scottish history analogous to that of Captain Boycott in Ireland; he has even been likened to Heydrich, an exterminator of the Jews in this century.

Despite the continuing interest, even obsession, with Sellar there has been no previous biography. Though he is the most controversial figure in the unhappy history of the modern Highlands there has been no study of the man, his motivations, his methods, his milieu and his career. Until now, little has been known of this man so reviled. For the most part, the great controversy that swirls about Sellar has been fed from the deep wells of Highland folklore, song and fiction, and later reminiscences, often drawn from subsequent political agitation. This is mainly to be explained by the lack of direct documentation of Sellar – he left no personal archive on which to base a biography. His life must be reconstructed from dispersed and indirect sources which are fortunately abundant. But the written record of the people evicted by Sellar is much sparser, and they are seriously disadvantaged in the narrative of the clearances. This will always be a problem in Highland history.

The greatest interest in Patrick Sellar flows naturally from his role as the man who cleared large numbers of small tenants from northern Sutherland in 1814–15, and then became embroiled in raging conflict and a sensational trial for murder, in Inverness in 1816. This inevitably occupies the central chapters of his story. But Sellar was also a substantial agricultural entrepreneur in his own right, a man of the agrarian revolution. He was, more arguably, a representative product of the Scottish Enlightenment and the Age of Improvement. In this biography I depict him in each of these guises. I have set him in his place and times, in his social context, and in the economic history of the Highland Revolution. His psychology and motivations are laid out as well as the documents can yield. The book is also written in the belief that people should know what they hate, and understand the object of their vilification.

The structure of this biography is mainly chronological but begins midway through Sellar's life. It starts with the events of April 1816, by which time Sellar had reached his maturity and was gripped by the greatest crisis of his life. This unorthodox start is designed to establish the central motif and themes of the book which provide continuity of focus for the subsequent chapters. At the end I return directly to the organising theme, and to the question of 'Sellar's tears', both in terms of his emotions and in the sense of ripping the fabric of the old society. On several occasions through the book I re-set the background to Sellar's life. Otherwise the structure follows the course of Sellar's life.

This is also economic biography, because Patrick Sellar was an innovative entrepreneur at the sharp edge of the Industrial Revolution. There is special interest in the mental world of this Edinburgh-trained lawyer and capitalist as he confronted the vestiges of the feudal Highlands, and as he forced through the modernisation of the region. He was *homo economicus* at the centre of the great structural changes which overwhelmed the Scottish Highlands in the age of the clearances. Sellar, in other words, was a vehicle of change, and in his life we can see exposed the mechanisms of economic growth in early nineteenth-century Scotland.

The purpose of this biography is not rehabilitate Sellar but to exhibit the circumstances that gripped his mind and defined the actions for which he was finally accounted responsible. It is intended to extend not diminish the tragic cast of his life and its significance. Ultimately Sellar's career is about the distribution of costs and benefits in a regime of coercive economic growth.

Patrick Sellar was highly articulate and exemplified the entrepreneurial mentality of his day. He expressed himself in robust, vivid terms, often heightened by powerful metaphor with an earthy turn of phrase. This makes him an excellent spokesman for those urgent forces which reshaped economic life in the critical decades of British industrialisation. By contrast, the records of Sellar's domestic life are thin, and this robs the study of an important dimension; nor is there much evidence of his upbringing. These lacunae are well compensated by the rich record of his thinking processes. Few men were so transparent in that age, and the mind of the clearer and the entrepreneur is fully exposed in this study. His life is a commentary on the price of progress on the edge of industrialisation.

– ACKNOWLEDGEMENTS –

Information about Sellar is dispersed in several collections listed in the Bibliography. Some of these have become available only in the last few years and some of the archival collections have only recently been catalogued. This occasionally makes precise referencing difficult and subject to change. A great deal of the material used in this biography derives from estate papers which possessed their own chronological and alphabetical systems; thus, most correspondence can be retrieved through modern archival citation or the original arrangements. In the early chapters, wherever possible, I have cited documents from the Sutherland Papers, excellently selected and edited by Professor Adam, usually in tandem with other material from the same source and elsewhere.[1]

I have collected material on Sellar over many years, and in the process have accumulated many debts. Most especially I have received help from Mrs Monica Clough who introduced me to Strathnaver, Westhill, Burghead and the west coast of the northern Highlands, and has been a warm friend since we both started at the new University of Stirling in 1967. My second debt is also Scottish: to Dr Malcolm Bangor-Jones who has great knowledge of the history of Sutherland and has been exceedingly generous to this long-distance fellow researcher.

I wish to express special thanks to a succession of archivists at the Staffordshire Record Office, most recently Ms D. M. Randall who arranged for copies of Sellar material to be sent to Australia. My thanks are also due to the librarians and archivists of the National Libraries of Scotland and Australia, in Edinburgh and Canberra respectively, the Flinders University Library, the Scottish Record Office, the Highland Regional Archives in Inverness, and to Mr G. A. Dixon of the Central Archives of Stirling, and librarians in Wick and Elgin. Among private papers relating to Sellar, I was thrilled to find fragmentary evidence of Sellar in Australia, and particularly some rare portraits of the man in the possession of Christopher and Valerie Lang, at Titanga, Lismore, Victoria, Australia. These are published for the first time in this book. Other portraits and papers were kindly provided by Justice Fisher of Adelaide, with advice from the late Mrs Pat Fisher of Hahndorf, Mrs

Jock Pedlar in Adelaide, and Mrs Dorothy Richardson. Michael Findlay at the Otago Settlers Museum helped me with illustrations. For references I am grateful to Dr Douglas Lockhart of Keele University, Miss M. W. Grant of Golspie, Associate Professor Peter Howell and Dr Robin Haines at Flinders University. I also record my thanks to Lady Davinia Loch, of Westbury, Wiltshire, Professor Duncan Poore, and Ms Joanne McNeill. I have benefited from conversations with Dr Margaret Steven, a rare Australian scholar of Enlightenment Scotland and its offspring. Mr John Davey and Professor Donald Meek gave particular assistance in the final phases of preparation. I am always in debt to my sister Marian Richards, and the company of my father, on my research expeditions from Shropshire.

The manuscript has benefited from the advice of Ms Ann Herraman, Dr Robert Fitzsimons and, most enduringly, of Dr Ngaire Naffine. Thanks also go to the Research Seminar in the History Department at Flinders University in Adelaide which first heard about Sellar's tears. The Australian Research Committee and University Research Board at Flinders provided funding and I have benefited from visiting fellowships in the History Program of the Research School of the Social Sciences at ANU, Birkbeck College, University of London, and the European University Institute in Florence. None of the people who have helped with this book carry any blame for the interpretations left in its pages.

Eric Richards
Brighton, South Australia

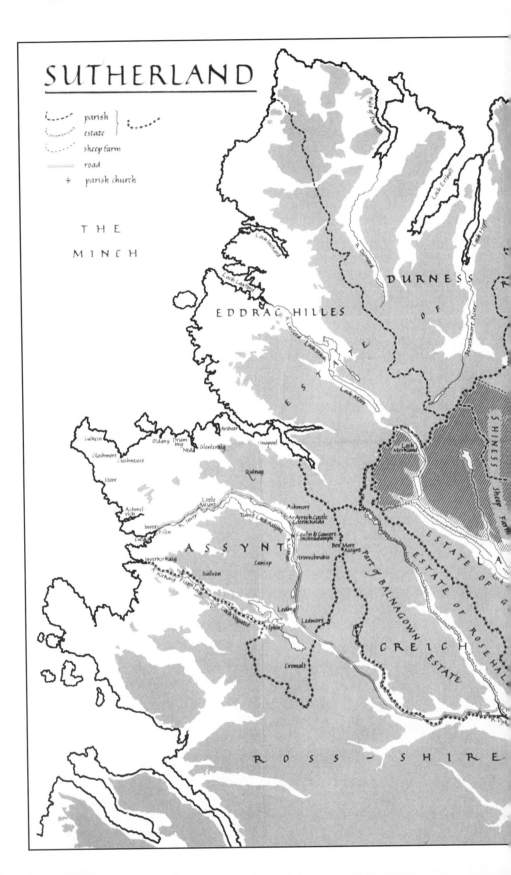

SUTHERLAND

parish
estate
sheep farm
road
+ parish church

THE
MINCH

DURNESS

Kyle of Durness

Loch Eriboll

Loch Hope

R. Dionard

Strathmore River

EDDRAC HILLES

Loch Inchard

Loch Laxford

R. Laxford

Loch Stack

Loch More

SHINESS Sheep Farm

Loch Merkland

ESTATE L A

ESTATE OF G

Ardvar

Culkein
Oldany
Drumbeg
Nedd
Glenleraig
Unapool

Clashmore
Clashnessie

Stoer

Quinag

Achimore
Little
Assynt
Tubeg
Loch Assynt
Ardvreck Castle
Lcierachalada
Coulin & Cam ore
Inchnadamph
Ben More
Assynt

Achmelvich
Inver
R. Inver

Inver Filin

Cula

A S S Y N T
Loum
Stronechrubie

ESTATE OF ROSEHAL

Inverkirkaig
Suilven
Canisp

R. Kirkaig
Flagn Lsg

Part of BALNAGOWN

ESTATE OF G

Loch Veyatie
Elphin
Ledbeg
Ledmore

C R E 1 C H
ESTATE

Cromalt

R O S S - S H I R E

R. Oykel

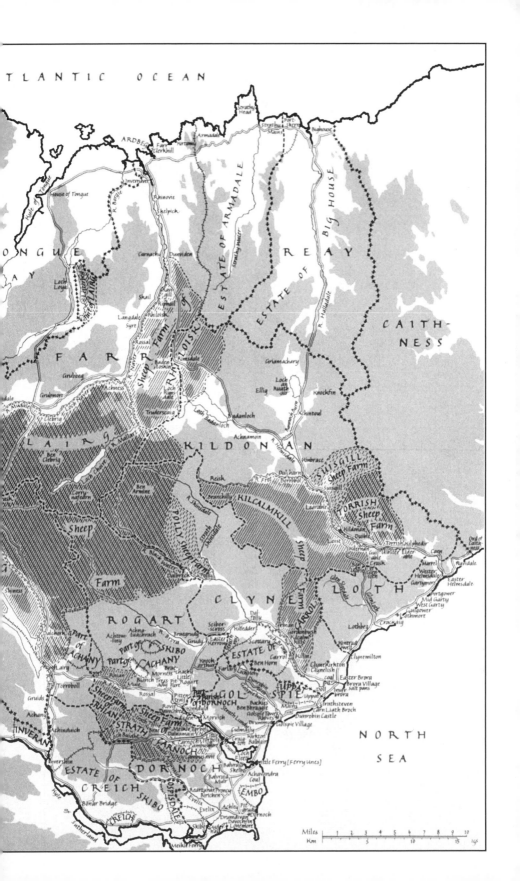

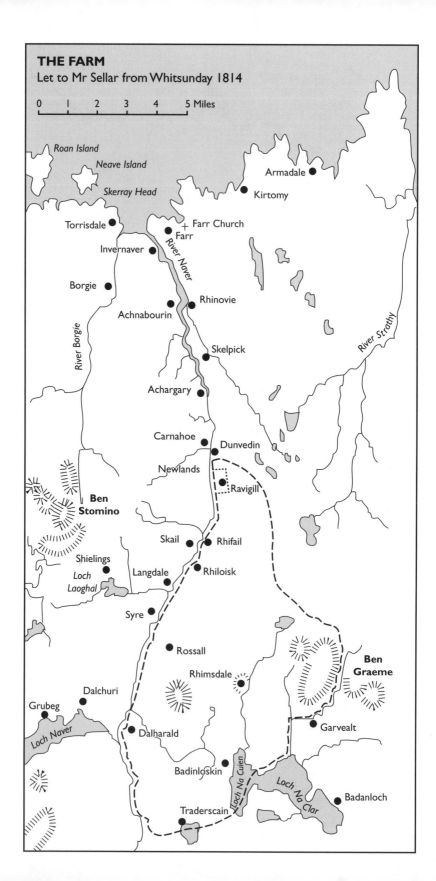

THE FARM
Let to Mr Sellar from Whitsunday 1814

0   1   2   3   4   5 Miles

Roan Island
Neave Island
Skerray Head
Armadale
Kirtomy
Torrisdale
+ Farr Church
Farr
Invernaver
River Naver
Borgie
Rhinovie
Achnabourin
River Borgie
Skelpick
River Strathy
Achargary
Carnahoe
Dunvedin
Newlands
Ravigill
Ben Stomino
Skail
Rhifail
Shielings
Rhiloisk
Loch Laoghal
Langdale
Syre
Rossall
Rhimsdale
Ben Graeme
Dalchuri
Grubeg
Garvealt
Dalharald
Loch Naver
Badinloskin
Loch Na Cuien
Loch Na Clar
Badanloch
Traderscain

CHAPTER 1

The Tears of Patrick Sellar

– TEARS IN THE DOCK, 1816 –

At 1:15 on the morning of Wednesday, 24 April 1816 in a crowded courtroom in the Highland town of Inverness, Patrick Sellar, a sheep-farmer and estate agent, shed tears. The circumstances of this emotional collapse were remarkable. Sellar was a man of granite, the personification of calculating realism, a man reviled for his persistent inhumanity towards the poor Highlanders of Strathnaver in Sutherland, the most northerly part of the Scottish Highlands. Patrick Sellar was already an object of hatred in the county. His name would become a byword for ruthless avarice and he was always to be ranked near the top of the enemies of the Scottish people. His reputation and his tears made an unlikely combination.

Sellar's tears were suddenly released after fourteen hours during which he had stood trial in the Inverness Circuit Court. Until that moment he had displayed little emotion. He had been charged with a catalogue of atrocious crimes, the most serious of which was that of 'culpable homicide', perpetrated during a series of evictions in 1814 over which he had personally presided. He was alleged to have deliberately set fire to the house of a tinker, knowing that a very old sick woman was inside and in peril. The woman was rescued, but her blankets were singed and she died of the shock. Nor was this an isolated case: Sellar had destroyed mills, houses and pastures as he cut a swathe through the old Highland communities deep in the high valleys of the Strathnaver. There were also wider allegations that he had caused the deaths and injuries of several other people. Moreover it was alleged that these acts of gross inhumanity were executed for his own personal gain.[1]

Sellar was a thirty-four-year-old bachelor sheep-farmer and factor

– 1 –

(that is, agent or manager) on the great estate of Sutherland which belonged to the Countess of Sutherland and her enormously wealthy English husband, Lord Stafford. They were in the middle of re-shaping the entire estate – virtually a Highland empire, a *latifundium* of almost a million acres. The policy involved the removal and relocation of the inland peasantry to newly prepared settlements by the coasts. Meanwhile the huge interior tracts were entirely redeployed for commercial sheep-farming, which had become extraordinarily prosperous on wartime wool prices. Sellar himself was required, with his evicting party, to shift the people to their new coastal territories, thereby releasing the land for the sheep-farmers. The great change in the uses of the Highlands had been in train for several decades in the south of the region. The accelerated expansion of sheep-farming across Sutherland had begun in the previous three years.

Sellar was a sheep-farmer on his own account as well as agent to the estate and this complicated his role. In this dual capacity he had taken possession by lease of large tracts of the Strathnaver district in the spring of 1814. In exercising his legal rights of removal and ejection, it was alleged, he committed acts of unspeakable terror against the old occupiers. Eventually the people were stirred to protest and the confrontation culminated in the long-delayed and well-publicised trial in Inverness in April 1816. Sellar became the centre of attention, the symbol of the clearances at large, and the particular target of prosecution. The events in Inverness brought the conflict into exquisite focus. The old way of life, still partly communal and even feudal in form, was pitted against the capitalist intruders, many of them from the south of Scotland and northern England. Sellar was on trial but the entire policy of economic revolution – subsequently called 'the Highland Clearances' – was also, by extension, on trial.

The pursuit of Sellar had begun at least two years before and the trial had been postponed and delayed several times. Sellar was said to have been so unpopular in Sutherland that, even as far south as Inverness, he would be in physical danger if he showed his face in public. In fact he resisted the idea of transferring his ordeal to Edinburgh. There was a degree of exultation reported in Dornoch (county town of Sutherland) when Sellar was first arrested and gaoled in May 1815. Newspapers in London conveyed the sensation and declared his guilt repeatedly in the months prior to the trial. It was said by one journal that 'Botany Bay was too good for him' and that he would therefore hang. Sellar, and the policy that he so perfectly and publicly symbolised, would be routed by the law itself.[2]

The trial before Lord Pitmilly and a jury of twelve gentlemen from the Highlands (but not from Sutherland for fear of contamination from the widespread agitation in that county) began at 11 o'clock on the morning of Tuesday, 23 April 1816. There was a large number of witnesses assembled for both sides, from the people of Strathnaver and from the clearers, and a battery of counsel. The courtroom was full. In the ensuing proceedings, Sellar's character and the details of the evictions over which he had presided were subjected to minute investigation and cross-examination. Sellar sat through the recitation of evidence – much of it alleging grotesque improprieties against defenceless and aged sub-tenants in Strathnaver – apparently without any show of feeling. Hour by hour the case against him weakened: witnesses were refused; evidence was shown to be contradictory; Sellar's character was revealed by respectable testimony to have been unblemished over his entire lifetime.

Eventually, well past midnight, the jury was asked to produce its verdict. The result was a total triumph for the besieged sheep-farmer, 'a complete exculpation' and 'contrary to the most sanguine expectations of his best friends', a unanimous vindication of Sellar's reputation and, specifically, a fulsome affirmation of his actual humanity and benevolence during the course of the removals. In the short time remaining after the announcement of the verdict, Judge Pitmilly took the unusual course of heavily underscoring the verdict of the jury. He expressed great sympathy for the accused sheep-farmer who, he indicated, had been traduced most despicably by evil elements who had wickedly conspired among the naive Highlanders to ruin a good man, Patrick Sellar.[3]

The verdict was, therefore, decisive. Even the opposing counsel concurred and offered the spontaneous observation that any absent witnesses could not have made the slightest difference to the inevitable verdict. Inevitable or not, the dramatic conclusion to the proceedings caused Sellar, at last, to show emotion. The Countess of Sutherland's confidential representative reported the trial and its climax thus:

> It lasted 14 hours. Sellar bore up very well but when the Verdict was pronounced, he burst into tears which had a great effect on the audience.[4]

This man of iron will and the greatest rationality was thus reduced to emotional catharsis, his face crumpled with the extraordinary intensity of the moment. It was the most dramatic moment of his life, a turning point for him and for the Highlands.

That Sellar finally broke down in tears at this moment is understandable. He had just been saved from the noose or, at best, transportation to Australia. His tears may have represented a sensitive heart rarely associated with his name. Sellar's relief at the verdict may have exposed greater fear and doubt about his fate than he had shown before the trial. He had been pursued like a wounded stag for many months. He may have had less confidence in the court and the Highland establishment than his enemies had implied. Whatever it signified, these were certainly one man's tears in the vale of tears and trauma associated with Strathnaver and the Highlands at large in the age of the clearances.

Tears recur throughout the history of the Highland clearances, though rarely among the bailiffs and the factors. The poetic and pictorial account of the evictions, in the Highlands as elsewhere, commonly depicts distraught victims in tearful breakdown.[5] Such scenes were repeated across the Highlands and tears certainly flowed in Sutherland when, between 1812 and 1821, many thousands of small farmers and cottars were removed from their inland townships. Old ways of life were eliminated; houses and entire townships were destroyed. It was a transformation associated with profound emotional disturbance, and all wrought in the name of economic progress or, as Sellar would have said, of 'Improvement'.

The beautiful but empty lands of Strathnaver, after the clearances, possessed the power to move visitors. The pathos of the scene conjured up images of blameless despair. One of the later champions of the Highlanders, an eloquent advocate of land reform and the restitution of the land to the people, was John Stuart Blackie, the somewhat eccentric professor of Greek at Edinburgh University. On a visit to the Strathnaver clearance site in the early 1880s Blackie broke down in tears at the memory of Sellar's infamous deeds in 1814. He published a passionate attack on Highland landlordism and against the long-dead Sellar in particular. Thomas Sellar, eldest son of Patrick and successful merchant in England and America, regarded himself as guardian of his father's reputation. His father had been innocent of the charges against him and had brought progress to the northern Highlands. Thomas Sellar repudiated Blackie's account as malicious and absurd. He was especially pleased to point out that Blackie's tears were not only ridiculous and unnecessary, but that they had been spilled on the wrong side of the river.[6]

– Reputation –

Patrick Sellar became a totemic figure in Scottish history, a figure of vilification, the strength of which has shown extraordinary stamina into the late twentieth century. His enduring infamy into the present is remarkable. For instance, in the summer of 1994, in a pub in Helmsdale, I was assured that Patrick Sellar's was the only grave in the Croy churchyard on which grass refused to grow. And at Elgin Cathedral where, in fact, Sellar and his family are buried, the curators were nervous of further desecration of the gravestones. Popular vehemence remains so powerful that his trial 'might have taken place in the past few weeks'. Sellar is regarded as 'one of the nastiest fellows in Scottish history'.[7] In the literature of the Highland clearances, Sellar's name is often used to evoke images of extirpation, genocide and even of the Holocaust. Ian Grimble likened Sellar to Heydrich who infamously purged Prague of the Jews in the 'Final Solution'.[8] In Scottish, English and overseas newspapers, Sellar reappears at irregular intervals (often accompanied by the first Duke of Sutherland and his wife) as objects of retrospective detestation. Patrick Sellar commands attention as the focal point of many issues in the Highland tragedy and, it will be argued, more widely in the account of economic revolution in its broadest context.

Sellar was not cross-examined at his trial and was, therefore, uncharacteristically silent. He was, in normal circumstances, a man of many words. He wrote a large number of letters over many decades, often with great emphasis, underlining much of his own prose for effect to such a degree that it is easy to imagine that he spoke also in italics. In his own correspondence, Sellar represented himself fully on all the issues which dominated his life, including the circumstances which surrounded his trial. He was highly articulate and offered a continuous commentary on his life and times. Sellar's is a case of remarkably good self-documentation. This is fortunate because his reputation – usually as a *bête noire* in modern Scottish history – is, in general, poorly based.

Sellar's reputation in the mind of modern Scotland is mainly founded on second-hand, indirect and retrospective accounts, sometimes given the extra gloss of fiction or poetic licence. He figures in the imagination – in poems, plays and novels – much more than in the documentary record. Though his own personal and family archive seems not to have survived, he remains one of the better-recorded men of his times. He was not, however, especially conscious of posterity and appears not to have preserved his own papers.[9] Fortunately, enough of his writing exists among the interminable correspondence he conducted with others to allow the re-construction of his life and mental world without recourse to imaginative extrapolation. There was a transparency in Sellar's personality which exposed the entire cast of his thinking on all the central activities in which he was involved. Sellar's melodrama can be retold from fresh evidence.

The Inverness trial in 1816, inevitably, dominated Sellar's life and his reputation. But Sellar lived for another thirty-five years and continued to make his mark on the Highlands. Much of his intellectual energy was spent coping with his unwelcome reputation and combating the recurrent eruptions of public antagonism which disturbed his domestic peace. Sellar was never cowed by his enemies, never at bay as 'the enemy of the people', and this pachydermous side of his personality also invites attention. He defended his reputation with great vigour in the face of recurrent provocation which would have mortally damaged a more sensitive soul.

Sellar was a considerable entrepreneur in his own right – indeed it was in this role that he collided with the people of Strathnaver. As innovator and man of business he ranks high in the annals of Britain's agricultural revolution. Working within the framework determined by the great landowners, Sellar became a leading figure in the movement which transformed the productivity of the Highlands of the early nineteenth century. He merits comparison with the great captains of industry who performed a parallel task in other sectors of British industrialisation. Sellar carried the torch of economic change into one of the most remote regions of the British economy. He was an active agent in the great process which made Britain the most productive economy the world had seen. He was an exemplar of the widening scope of the expanding economy – as a conduit of the latest technology, as mobiliser of markets, as generator of capital, as a source of new wealth, income and efficiency in one of the least responsive corners of the British economy at the time of its decisive transition to industrialisation.

One of the reasons that Patrick Sellar was least likely to spill tears in public or private was that he adopted the persona of the rational and unsentimental man of his times. Sellar gave voice to a rigorous view of the world which had become influential by the time of the Napoleonic Wars. It placed great emphasis on the pursuit of rationality and efficiency as the true marks of progress and civilisation. In a word, it was the pure mentality of 'Improvement', but with a Scottish accent.

Highly tendentious in its perspective on the world, it placed the highest value on economic advance and the raising of standards of material and moral life. It required the elimination of old ways, frequently derided in a single word, 'feudalism'. It was an ideology of calculating rationalism and it helped drive the vehicle of economic change with greater urgency and direction than ever before.

Sellar was among the most outspoken and demonstrative advocates of this re-interpretation of the world about him, in part because he came into such diametric and dramatic confrontation with the forces that he regarded as inimical to the progress of rational improvement. Sellar, indeed, was a perfect specimen of those cultural and intellectual changes that surged so spectacularly in Scotland at the end of the eighteenth century. He was a product of the Edinburgh version of the Scottish Enlightenment. The formation of his psyche and his intellect are central in this story, above and beyond his narrower reputation in the Highlands. Since Sellar was so articulate and voluble in expressing his view of the world, he was able to exemplify the Enlightenment intellect in practice as well as in theory. Here was the man, thoroughly tutored in the classic texts of the Enlightenment, trained in one of its greatest centres in the decade of its greatest influence, who then pursued profits and progress in the real world of economic reconstruction. Sellar was an 'Improvement Man', in the most testing context of the time – where the ideas of the mentors and the philosophers confronted realities of soil and society in the feudal Highlands. In Sellar's story, the ideas of improvement were brought face to face with the recalcitrant world of the *ancien régime*. This was precisely how Sellar perceived the strains of his own life.

– THE SHAPE OF SELLAR'S LIFE –

The story of Patrick Sellar began in Moray in the northeast of Scotland. His career as lawyer and estate agent predated his emergence as a great capitalist sheep-farmer in the northern Highlands. His energetic pursuit of profit and progress started with his entry into mercantile enterprise in Elgin. In 1809 his energies and enterprise were largely redirected to a quite different milieu, the aristocratic landed estates of the Countess of Sutherland. He then threw himself into the great improvement plans which had been designed to drag the Sutherland estate from its feudal backwardness into the new world of capitalistic growth and economic security. In the middle of this dislocating transformation Sellar graduated into sheep-farming on his own account: he seized the moment and committed his capital to the new sector of the economy. This placed him at the very centre of the controversies that whirled about the Highland clearances.

From 1809 several themes dominated Sellar's story. Most prominent were his unhappy dealings with the people of Sutherland at large and Strathnaver in particular. The rising conflict erupted into riot and resistance and then focused directly on Sellar himself. The genesis and form of this hostility marked the first years of his work in Sutherland. His trial in 1816 was the climax of this challenge to authority. Sellar's story exposes not only the anatomy of the conflict but also the way in which Sellar responded to the crisis. His own personality attracted antagonism like a magnet, and this is to be counted in the passion and solidarity that he aroused among his many enemies. His reactions to his vanquished foes consumed much of his time in the immediate aftermath of the trial.

Meanwhile, through the middle years of his life, Sellar performed, with great success, the function of entrepreneur, ensuring that the benefits of greater efficiency reached the furthest outposts of British industrialisation. He was also raising a large and achieving family, his sons endowed with the best education available and imbued with Sellar's own version of early Victorian values. Sellar was himself highly commercial in outlook and yet pursued his enterprise within the framework set by the great aristocratic estate and its traditional assumptions. Consequently, much of his story is about his relations with a landlord who, by definition and tradition, was beyond his class and answered to different priorities. As a practical farmer, Sellar faced the opportunities of the new agriculture with enthusiasm and exper-tise; but he had also to cope with the perils of economic fluctuation in the difficult decades between 1815 and 1840. He wrestled with the great social and economic issues of his day – from the problems of technological progress to those of social breakdown, including the questions of poverty in the midst of progress and overpopulation, and those of widening competition in the rural sector, as well as political instability in local and national affairs.

At the time of his death, his view of the world was generally triumphant. Sellar had become a Highland laird in his own right; he had established a dynasty of successful Sellars; his sons moved in the best social, political and intellectual circles of his day. The Sellars rubbed shoulders with the Gladstones, with Tennyson, Herbert Spen-cer, Benjamin Jowett, George Eliot and the richest commercial fa-milies of Glasgow and Liverpool. The Sellars emerged as a thriving

Victorian family, wealthy, respectable, well-connected and influential. Sellar's life had been capped with success. But, of course, it was success bought at a price. Public controversy continued to reverberate over Sellar's role in the clearances. Questions about the price paid by the people of the Highlands continued to cloud Sellar's reputation, even beyond the grave.

– SELLAR AND PROGRESS –

Patrick Sellar was the most conspicuous instrument in the deliberate root-and-branch destruction of an old society. He was in total accord with landlord policy, but he gave it muscle and determination. Partly by his own provocation, Sellar became the target of the popular odium and abuse of the people who were directly affected by the changes in Sutherland. They indeed pursued him to the point at which he feared for his life. He became the focus of a sophisticated campaign which, among other meanings, demonstrated the power which even the weak can gather and bring to bear on an adversary. Long after his death Sellar remained the target of condemnation by those who, by extension, identified with Sellar's original assailants in 1814–16.

Economic development, past and present, is full of such turmoil. The path of economic transformation commonly entails severe disruption to communities which stand in the way of change. Sellar's case was an extreme and melodramatic version of the general tension which resides at the centre of the process of economic development. Yet most entrepreneurs and most agricultural innovators are able to pursue their enterprise without provoking universal condemnation. Few face allegations of murder. Sellar's collision with the resident people of the Highlands was more frenzied than was common in the story of British industrialisation. The restructuring of the Highland economy (which made it vastly more responsive to the wider requirements of British industrialisation) was a cataclysmic shift in the foundations of life. It required literally the dislocation of the people of the Highlands. The Highland clearances imposed unprecedented changes on the people – relocating them and rendering many of them redundant, perplexed, terrified and angry. It was small wonder that a popular reaction was roused.

Sellar's confrontation with the Highlanders has many parallels in agrarian history. His attempt to impose total and immediate change on the Highlanders of Sutherland was replicated by others in different degrees (though usually with less publicity) across the region from

1780 to 1880. It echoes also in other agrarian worlds. In England, evictions designed to make way for sheep-farming and other forms of stock-raising caused conflict and outrage over several centuries. The introduction of new crops and farming methods was, almost by definition, highly disruptive. People were forced to move, to uproot, to respond to the needs of economic reconstruction as defined by landlords, agrarian experts or, more anonymously, by general market forces. Even the introduction of new machinery or field systems threw agricultural society into conflict as, for instance, in the Captain Swing episodes in England at the end of the 1820s. In Ireland and Wales agricultural change imposed, at different times, equal demands for relocation of the rural populations. It is a commonplace of the agricultural record that change upsets rural society and generates obstinate non-co-operation and, less often, active resistance.

Industrial change tended to be less immediately dislocative. The new industries of the late eighteenth and early nineteenth centuries were more concentrated geographically and their establishment required relatively little displacement of resident populations. Moreover, industry in its new settings, such as the cotton and woollen installations of the first decades of industrialisation, grew by attracting new 'settlers' to their own locations, for example in the remote valleys of Lanarkshire and Derbyshire. New industries, setting up either in rural or urban settings, placed incentives in the way of immigrants to accept employment. The usurpation of territory by industries in towns was relatively gradual and usually ate away at the fields, little by little, over generations without bringing instant displacement to large resident communities. Eviction was less widespread.

More analogous with the impact of the clearances was the trauma created by the later construction of railways into towns which had already expanded in the early phases of industrialisation. Great swathes of old tenements were eliminated in the name of transport efficiency as the railways forced their iron ways into the centres of urban population. The raw inner bodies of urban life were suddenly exposed and large numbers of people ejected. Slum demolition had similar consequences in later decades of economic change. In some ways these changes aroused less social antagonism and outrage than events in remote agricultural societies, which is puzzling.

A more exact comparison of the impact of sheep-farming in the Highlands may be made with modern economic development in the Third World, where similar clashes of the old and the new occur with alarming consequences. Sheep-farming, as Patrick Sellar himself always emphasised, demanded the eviction of practically all human life from the straths and mountains of the interior. Only then could sheep occupy the empty space, and the straths be converted to new scientific rotations of land use. In the late twentieth century similar forms of headlong acceleration of economic growth have occurred in distant parts of Asia and South America, often in the name of cheaper raw materials and a faster rate of economic growth to sustain rapidly rising populations. Modern development frequently demands the dislocation of peasant communities. Thus the creation of modern hydro-electric schemes in remote parts of Malaysia or the Philippines have required the removal of communities and the submergence of their lands. Flooded with water rather than sheep, entire valleys in twentieth-century India and Indonesia have been evacuated for the requirements of electricity for industry, and severe social disruption will undoubtedly be caused by the diversion of the Yangtze in the twenty-first century. The resident people are sacrificed, usually left stunned and helpless in the face of government decrees and the bulldozers. The plight of these people has often attracted sympathetic humanitarian concern in the West. The scale and intensity of criticism is rarely diminished by the provisions made for the people displaced, either by the developer or the government. Echoes of Patrick Sellar and the Highland clearances continue to reverberate in the annals of modern economic development in the Second and Third Worlds.

The cataclysmic destruction of rural communities is, in reality, the less common form of agrarian change. Agrarian communities are more usually dislocated less sensationally by the more gradual, but no less decisive, operation of market forces. In the normal course of events, the rise in effective demand for certain commodities works through the market mechanisms to create powerful incentives to new forms of production. The range of examples in economic history is practically infinite. The expansion of demand for cotton, timber, sisal, flax, wheat, meat and even mining products has repeatedly shifted production in an imperative fashion which ultimately affects the communities of the producers, who are sometimes left dazed by the speed and impact of the changing economic horizon. The consequences of the explosive expansion of wool-growing on communities of Aborigines in mid nineteenth-century Australia provides a direct parallel with the earlier consequences for the Scottish Highlands. It is a generic phenomenon in the great catalogue of economic development, past and present.

– THE MEANING OF PATRICK SELLAR –

The life of Patrick Sellar is, therefore, emblematic of larger phenomena. His tears and his personal conflict in Strathnaver have wide implications. Sellar was certainly instrumental in rendering the Highlands of Scotland greatly more productive than ever before. His 'Improvement' created wealth and resources which made life more sustainable for more people than ever before. This was the ultimate and immediate cause and justification of the clearances. But the costs of economic change, the trauma of economic revolution and the moral outrage of the devastated Highland communities which stood in the path of the changes must all appear on the other side of the balance sheet. Sellar's story relates directly to these abstract propositions but sets them in a tangible world of the Highlands in which emotions boiled over under the immediate pressures of economic progress.

There was, consequently, a tragedy set in the heart of economic progress: an inner conflict which was resolved at the expense of the weakest parties. Sellar was part of the particular Highland tragedy in an age in which the neither the traditional social guardians nor the state saw a clear need to intervene, or to mitigate the consequences of sudden economic change.

The lion's share of Sellar's life was devoted directly to the implementation of such changes and it exemplifies all these tensions. He conducted his own contest with the forces of resistance and expressed an almost continuous commentary on the process throughout his life. Sellar always took the greatest pains to assert his own views. In the process, less directly, there was a parallel uncovering of the response of those about him – on the one side that of the disturbed peasantry and their spokesmen, and on the other, the landlords and the ideologues of improvement itself. It was a variant of the endless problem of inducing economic progress at the expense of a status quo.

Sellar had the ability to absorb an argument and then develop it and take it to its logical extreme which often then carried him beyond the mainstream from which the idea had derived. He thought many of his contemporaries lacked the courage of their own logic. Sellar was a correct man, a stickler for the legal forms. He was forthright, blunt, coarse, raw, clumsy and sarcastic. Many of his contemporaries agreed with his train of thought but recoiled from his mode of expression. Sellar himself could not comprehend the rancour and controversy his words and deeds provoked.

The tears of Patrick Sellar were a demonstration of one man's distress and relief at his own deliverance. They were also, by extension, tears for the human tragedy implicit in the clearances and, further, for the bitter requirements of economic progress in general. Sellar was full of complicated effusions on this question, essentially because he was torn between goodness and avarice, between progress and stagnation, between the past and the future. When his tears subsided he faced his enemies with renewed resolution.

CHAPTER 2

Elgin Days, 1780–1809

– A LIFETIME OF IMPROVEMENT –

Patrick Sellar was born in Elgin in December 1780 and he returned to the same town to die almost seventy-one years later. Though he lived most of his adult years in Sutherland and later developed an affection for Morvern in Argyll, Sellar remained true to his Morayshire roots. He rarely ventured further south than Edinburgh. In later life he made a few excursions to the borders and northern England but his knowledge of the southern kingdom came mainly from his dealings with wool merchants and stock-farmers. He knew London hardly at all. He was a northern Scot, first and last.

Between Sellar's birth and his death in 1851 Britain changed decisively, even in its most northerly extremities. In 1780, Scotland was North Britain, an outer region of the United Kingdom. It was not an industrial, still less an urban, country. Britain was losing the American colonies, the King's illness would soon render his government unstable and, within a few years, the Cabinet would be presided over by Pitt the Younger, hardly a man yet out of his teens. Wealth, as always, was narrowly distributed across society and many people believed that the nation's population was static or even declining. Most of the British Isles was by now able to produce a reliable supply of food for the majority of the inhabitants, but the shadow of famine still stalked some parts of the land – in 1743–4 Ireland suffered disastrous hunger that killed a high proportion of its people. Two years after Sellar's birth there was a severe shortfall in the harvest in his own region, which left an indelible mark on the public mind. It would be remembered with fear for several generations to come. Pre-industrial poverty was everywhere and contemporaries, like all men before them, sought ways and means of deliverance from want; they sought a formula for progress. Four years before, Adam Smith had published his *Wealth of Nations*. The intellectual life of Edinburgh, Glasgow and Aberdeen had stirred into a remarkable ferment. Philosophy and practicality were joined and new ideas for economic advancement flowed to the most distant parts of the British world. New forms of industry were erupting in many parts of the kingdom, often in remote rural places, a few on the fringes of the Scottish Highlands.

At the time of Sellar's death, in 1851, Britain could celebrate its triumph as the first great industrial power, with a global naval hegemony and a resurgent empire. It was the year of the Great Exhibition and Britain was united. Its intellectuals were the arbiters of thought and progress across much of the world. In Sellar's lifetime the nation had industrialised, had won a prolonged continental war against France, had created a great formal and informal empire of settlement and trade, and had reached a *modus vivendi* with its lost colony, the United States. British wealth was now accumulating so rapidly that its beneficial effects were percolating down even to the lower echelons of society. The Industrial Revolution had begun to transform not only the productive habits of the British people but also their consumption horizons. Starvation of old was in retreat – with the monumental exception of Ireland and a few districts of the West Highlands which seemed to go backwards as the nation advanced – and the productivity of the economy was beginning to reflect in the welfare of the masses. It was a lifetime of accelerated change in every dimension of the nation's existence.

In the span of Sellar's life the population of Britain, astonishingly, almost trebled. Great new cities such as Manchester and Liverpool had grown like mushrooms; older ones like Glasgow and Belfast rapidly burst their seams with new people. Even more remarkably, the average income per capita almost doubled in the same period – there was more bread, more beer, more shoes, more warmth, more defence, more books, more of practically everything. Historians, and contemporary witnesses in the 1850s, recognised that, in Sellar's own lifetime, the country had witnessed 'the central event of its modern history', namely industrialisation. In a nutshell it meant that 'The average worker was a great deal more productive that he [*sic*] had ever been before.'[1]

This economic drama was expressed most visibly in the production and export of its manufactured goods, in cotton, woollens, iron, ships and locomotives especially. The cost of production of cotton fell to an eighth of its 1780 level; transport costs fell by two-thirds with the introduction of canals and then further still with railways and steam navigation. But the revolution was also manifested in the constructions of the country, its buildings, factories, roads and railways, villages and cities, bridges and urban housing, lighthouses and aristocratic palaces. It was, however, an increasingly urban phenomenon, seeming to leave the countryside behind.

Yet everyone acknowledged that the role of agriculture was fundamental. The farmers of mainland Britain had also been revolutionary in Sellar's lifetime. Farm production increased throughout the last decades of the eighteenth century. British agriculture fed and clad the nation at war with Napoleon for virtually twenty-five years, and then sustained all the vastly increased and more urbanised population to the middle of the next century. In effect, the rural achievement ran parallel with those of commerce and industry. New techniques of cultivation and breeding, and the more efficient use of land, labour and capital, dramatically enhanced the output of British soil. It was a complicated success story with a hundred contributory elements, not least the risking of more capital, the coordination of markets and the rationalisation of field systems, of ploughing and harvesting. But mostly it was a case of better technology, a cleverer use of resources with new crops and the better breeding of livestock. In 1851 British agriculture still fed almost all British mouths. The labour force in British agriculture grew only a little until the mid-century and then began its absolute decline, at different rates in different regions. In abstract terms, the achievement of British agriculture was to feed and clothe almost all the British people (who were trebling in their number) while drawing upon a relatively static or falling labour force. It meant that rural Britain retained very little of the national increment of population growth in the great demographic revolution across the country. This was a fundamental fact of British economic and social existence during the life span of Patrick Sellar.

The experience of the rural regions was varied – most dramatically different between the southeast of England and Scotland and the west of Ireland. The Scottish Highlands had a mixed experience. In 1780 much of the region faced inwards, most of its people living relatively precarious lives with a large dependence on local subsistence production. The region exported black cattle and illicit whisky to southern markets but little else. Living standards were low by any reckoning and the interchange with the rest of the world was still scant. By 1851 much of the Highlands had been converted to sheep production with a fringe of semi-subsistence crofting and some fishing enterprise in a few locations such as Wick and Helmsdale. But meanwhile the Highlands

had contributed decisively in the supply of raw wool to British manufacturing, to the great mills of Yorkshire. For many decades the
Highlands were able to supplement and then replace imports of the
raw material of a vital industry. The region also provided meat to the
southern markets as never before, and the region began importing in a
much more varied pattern too. And, throughout, the population
revolution had swept over the Highlands; many left the region but
the total population of the Highlands continued to rise, if slowly, until
1851. Even where the introduction of sheep had caused most outrage,
in Sutherland, the population was much greater in 1851 than it had
been at the time of Sellar's birth. The Highlands were, therefore, fully
committed to the logic of industrialisation. Sellar was its most enthusiastic convert and proselytiser.

– MORAY IN THE 1780s –

In the making of Patrick Sellar it is not difficult to read into his
immediate origins and his upbringing a quite precise combination of
influences which brought forth the man: his rationality, his deep
respect for the law, his deference to the established institutions of
the land, his risk-taking and enterprising spirit and, most of all, his
belief in progress and profits. He was, from start to finish, a provincial
on the make. Locality, parentage, education, religion, the models
about him and the opportunities that presented themselves, each
moulded the boy and the man. He was raised to the idea of upward
mobility and the need to grasp each chance of advancement. The
Sellars served the old world but also sought to make the new. They
responded to opportunity, and created conditions for progress. But
they insisted on the stability of society and always expressed profound
respect for the oldest of its institutions. This was a tension at the centre
of Sellar's own personality but it was also a tension characteristic of his
age, and especially of his own region.

Sellar was a man of the Elgin, on the remote northeast shoulder of
the Scottish mainland on the Moray Firth. In the 1780s, it was a world
of small provincial towns, of narrow horizons and country estates.
Wealth was tied up in agriculture, with a rim of commerce and fishing.
Most economic and political power was concentrated in the hands of
large landowners who generally delegated their business to their
lawyers and agents who were, therefore, the vital business cadre of
this society. Elgin was a provincial mercantile and legal centre, but it
was far from the influences of Edinburgh and London. It was distant

even from Aberdeen, though the merchants of Moray traded up and down the eastern coast. It was far to the north but not part of the Highlands: it was a marches country between the lowlands and the Highlands.

More important for Sellar's own future, Moray emerged as a favoured land for agricultural experimentation and development. In the decade of his own birth, Moray became an outlier of the Improvement movement, 150 miles north of its main Scottish centre, in the Lothians. It was mostly a low-lying coastal county which responded well to high grain prices and new investment. Moray, especially along the rich flat cereal lands around Elgin, was more progressive than the rest of northern Scotland in its receptivity to agricultural change. It was the focus for advanced agricultural and commercial production in the region, a springboard for further development from the south of Scotland. Sellar's own family was closely involved in the great movement to transform the agriculture of the northeast between 1760 and 1800. As we will see, one of Sellar's own grandfathers was ostensibly a victim of the local revolution in agriculture, but his son (Patrick Sellar's father) became a muscular enforcer of the same process. Moray was an island of advancement, of modern thinking, on the fringe of the most resistant, indeed recalcitrant, region in the British Isles.

Sellar's own personal world was extended from Elgin, where he was educated at Elgin Grammar School, first to Edinburgh for his education. But in his maturity he remained essentially a well-educated provincial Scot, lowland by origin, exposed at a critical time to the Scottish version of the Enlightenment. He seems never to have regarded his provinciality as a disadvantage, perhaps because he found ample rein for his talents within his own land. He became extraordinarily responsive to the opportunities which blossomed in the northeast and north of Scotland at the end of the century. From this narrow world he eventually voyaged not south but north, to the remotest districts of the Highlands where he was always regarded as an outsider, a southerner.

– THE SELLARS –

Patrick Sellar's father was Thomas Sellar who was thirty-five when his only son was born. He was a successful Elgin lawyer, a provincial bourgeois who became a respected and influential figure in the local community. Thomas Sellar was born in 1754 in New Keith, son of a

Banffshire stonemason who was able to send Thomas Sellar to Edinburgh to study law. The Scottish universities were 'more accessible than those elsewhere and it was not rare for sons of modest families to attend and to proceed to middling professions – to modest clerical careers' and this was the path taken both by Thomas Sellar and his son Patrick in the 1770s and 1790s respectively.[2] After his training as a solicitor, Thomas Sellar returned north and worked for a time as clerk in the office of John Innes of Leuchars, Writer to the Signet. His grandson remembered being told that 'the Morayshire proprietors felt the want so much of a good lawyer in Elgin that they sent their Edinburgh agents to send up "one honest lawyer" ', and Thomas Sellar was selected.[3]

Sellar quickly became the leading solicitor in Elgin, serving the main landowners in the district, especially the Seafield estate. He came to be known as 'Trusty Tom'. He provided prompt and efficient legal services at a time of accelerating agricultural change. As profits rose, so there was a greater turnover of estates, greater investment in improvement leases and the induction of new tenants. For twenty years Sellar was also Procurator-Fiscal of Moray. He had come a long way from his own father's humbler origins in Banff.

Patrick Sellar's mother was Jane Plenderleath, daughter of a Dalkeith minister. She met Thomas Sellar while he was a student at the University in Edinburgh in the 1770s.[4] Jane Plenderleath became a fervent Wesleyan, and John Wesley, on one of his many journeys through the kingdom, visited Elgin in May 1784 and was a guest at the Sellar household. Wesley reported in his *Journal* that he had spent an 'agreeable hour' with 'the daughter of good Mr Plenderleath, late of Edinburgh'. On his 1784 visit to Elgin he addressed a great crowd, exhorting his listeners to 'seek the Lord that he may be found.'[5] Patrick Sellar was then three or four years old and his mother brought her only son to the great preacher who placed his hand on Patrick's head and blessed him. Such a blessing the child may have needed more than most because his mother died when he was six. Patrick Sellar was mainly brought up without a mother in a household dominated by men. The influence of Methodism seems to have waned after his mother's death and he became increasingly Presbyterian and orthodox in his faith.

During the course of his life, Patrick Sellar referred only infrequently to his parentage though he always expressed proper respect for his father who was clearly a model for his own career. The story of his paternal grandfather, however, he often used as an object lesson in social improvement under duress. Several decades later, when his own life was full of turmoil, Patrick Sellar took pleasure in recalling the rise of his own family. His father's father had lived as a small Highland cottar in the hills of Banff and was removed by an improving landlord, spilled off his holding to make way for a better use of the land. Sellar told the story of his forbear as a moral tale – nothing better could have happened to his grandfather who was thereby forced to move (probably to New Keith) and to adjust creatively to the new world. The removal, or clearance, from inland Banffshire, had set the family on the road to Elgin. The dislocation had been therapeutic. It was, for Sellar, a classic story of vigorous disruption in society imparting a healthy jolt which had stimulated a poor family to make a better way in the world.[6] One of the themes of his tendentious adult conversation was the rise of great men from poor origins.[7] The positive power of upheaval was his recurring theme. Patrick Sellar, as the only child, was brought up in a household in which expectations of self-improvement were deeply entrenched.

Thomas Sellar's commercial business was more directly formative in the making of his son's career. Patrick Sellar was apprenticed in a ferment of improvement, frequently competitive and radical in form. His father's work involved large investments in drainage, new farm buildings and the comprehensive rearrangements of farm lands which were likely to extend and intensify production, especially on the cereal lands. Landowners and their advisers learned from each other and copied successful methods applied elsewhere. One of the most widespread innovations of the time was the creation of new villages as nodes of progress and rising rents on previously under-utilised lands, sometimes associated with nascent small-scale industry such as weaving, straw-plaiting or spinning.

Between 1725 and 1850, new villages were created in many parts of Britain, 400 of them in Scotland. This change was evident in the north of Scotland mainly from the 1780s. New villages had several vital advantages: they concentrated the rural population, generated new enterprise and facilitated the release of estate lands for much more rational usage. New villages allowed the creation of great new highly-capitalised farms and gave asylum to the small holders who had stood in the way of rationalisation. The creation of villages, often involving quite heavy investments as well, made possible a return on capital in each dimension of agrarian change. The villages themselves could yield good profits by way of rising rents. It was a mechanism by which a locality could cope with a rising population while its entire agricultural structure was transformed. The system was designed to regularise agriculture, increase rents and accommodate a rising population in new economic structures. Mostly they gathered people from a small radius.[8]

Landowners became eager to board the great pantechnicon of improvement. The village system became a goal, a panacea even. Many landlords remodelled their estates, hoping to attract tenants to develop the lands, spawn industry and enhance rents, and sought to *increase* the size and density of the estate population. It was part of the disruption of rural life, but carried with it an air of benevolence since it was frequently welcoming of population. This was most likely the way that Patrick Sellar's own grandfather had arrived at New Keith a generation before.

The village idea reached the Highlands late in the piece, but then accelerated rapidly. Between 1800 and 1819 forty-eight new villages were planned in the Highlands and Islands – more than in the entire previous century and many more than in the following thirty years.[9] The Highlands were catching up.

Thomas Sellar was already involved in all these varieties of rural engineering when he sent his son to Edinburgh to study law at the feet of the men whose university was reaching the zenith of its prestige. Sellar was a student when the teachings of Adam Smith and Dugald Stewart were becoming the dominant ideology. He rubbed shoulders with some of the most illustrious names of the Edinburgh Enlightenment.[10] It was a rationalist, progressive milieu which set the framework for so much energetic recasting of the world during the coming era of industrialisation. Patrick Sellar imbibed these doctrines as readily as he had the Bible which figured prominently in his father's household. It was a potent brew which entranced his mind; it formed his attitudes and his assumptions to such a degree that, in adulthood, he could scarcely express himself without betraying these intellectual roots.

Patrick Sellar's education as a lawyer did not diminish his passion for the farming life which had been set from his boyhood. In December 1831, Sellar reminisced jocularly about the new education being afforded to the sons of farmers at the turn of the century. He conjured up the rise of rural science and the division between the old and new schools. He regarded himself as a new man of science, the practical product of the Enlightenment:

> In the first years, in which I indulged a passion for farming, there was
> perceptible, a difference in opinion, betwixt the young men who had Just
> come home from College, and the punch-drinking, Joyous old farmers,
> whom the Glorious prices of 1800, 1, 2, 3, 4, 5 and 6 had enabled to bestow
> on their sons, a better Education. The latter dealt in such pithy sayings as
> this 'a weel filled dung cart gangs afore a gude Crop' – 'Breeding gangs a in
> at the mouth' etc etc. The former desired to see, assigned, a complete and
> satisfactory reason, 'why a black hen laid a white Egg'.[11]

Sellar rejoiced in the new age of rural science which had emerged out
of college learning.

While Sellar studied in Edinburgh his father's law practice prospered. In the 1790s improvement in the Firthlands of Moray moved up
several gears. Thomas Sellar was involved in 1799 with plans for new
villages on the Seafield estate at Kirkmichael, Milton and Carrachan.
Sellar recommended that they should be 'set in Lotts in a scattered
Village as [is] frequently to be seen in England.'[12] Lots, essentially,
were small plots of land rented out to new village settlers on improvement leases – that is, minimal rents in the first few years to encourage
reclamation, rising as productivity increased until the landlord was
reaping much higher returns on the change. It would increase
productivity, absorb the rising population, release wide acres for larger
farmers and yield good returns on invested capital. It was a pole of
growth in an age of agricultural optimism, at a time when a landlord
could reap rising returns from a denser population on his estate.

Thomas Sellar's Elgin office also provided a degree of informal
training for up-and-coming young factors of the Seafield estate and
beyond. He trained John Fraser, Cosmo Falconer and Robert Mackid.
The same form of apprenticeship was undertaken by Patrick Sellar in
his father's office when he returned from Edinburgh.[13] It provided a
distinctive environment in which Patrick Sellar sharpened his talents
against the competition of other equally striving young males in his
father's office. As late as November 1815 the elder Sellar was still
providing advice to the Seafield estate and he was often concerned
with removals. It was a time of dreadful frosts and Sellar spent much of
his energy protecting the sheep at Castle Grant from the ravages of
dogs.[14] Patrick Sellar was to be similarly challenged when he entered
eventually the sheep economy in Sutherland. His father had taught
him about poachers and how to deal with lawbreakers at large.

Other Moray estates came within Thomas Sellar's territory. One was
called Westfield which was to play a large role in the family's destiny for
several generations. Westfield was a small but promising estate on the

flatlands slightly to the of west of Elgin. It was owned by the last of the Dunbars of Grangehill until sold to Sir James Grant in 1769. It was subsequently resold to James Robertson, a London merchant in 1774, and then sold again in 1781 to Francis Russell of Blackhall, an Edinburgh advocate. In 1798 Westfield was valued at £488. It was a substantial arable property crying out for renovation. The district was tenanted by small occupiers who lacked capital sufficient to 'set them out into the world'. A contemporary observer said that such small tenants simply lacked the basic initiative to adopt 'the modern improvement of husbandry'. Sellar helped to drag the estate into the new mould of improved agriculture, which probably entailed some loss of the smaller tenants.[15]

Patrick Sellar recollected that his father, as factor of Russell of Westfield, had devised a remarkably swift way of resettling the existing estate population on previously unused land within the estate. His method was especially associated with tree planting, and was achieved with little expense to the heritor (that is, the proprietor).[16] It was also a controversial style of social engineering and the cause of widespread tension within local society. Having moved the incumbent cottagers of the estate off to more convenient sites, Russell of Westfield died leaving his estate in his widow's hands. Despite the earlier improvements and the enhanced rents, the estate quickly ran into financial trouble and was advertised for sale in 1806.[17] Eventually, in July 1808, Westfield at last found a buyer – Thomas Sellar himself who thereby rose smoothly into the ranks of Elgin landowners.[18] He became a proprietor in his own right in a move which carried the suspicion of lawyerly opportunism, the adviser turning proprietor as the main chance offered itself.

'Trusty Tom' was now the gentleman, styled 'Sellar of Westfield'. His son, Patrick, had already joined the business in 1803 and succeeded his father as Procurator-Fiscal in Moray for the years 1806–10. Nevertheless, though a legal career beckoned Patrick, 'like his father [he] preferred agricultural pursuits to following the legal profession'.[19] It was at Westfield that both Sellars were able to practise their own style of improvement, to accelerate the changes undertaken at a more sedate pace previously set by Russell before them. In these few years, an immense extent of hedges with belts of wood was planted, the fields were remodelled with small holdings done away with, and the estate rejigged into four farms.[20] In May 1812, Thomas Sellar advertised his farms at Westfield for lease, stating, 'Reasonable encouragement will be given to substantial and improving tenants for making inclosures'. It was an unambiguous signal of his intentions and priorities.[21]

As improvement fell upon the community at Westfield, the resident people were set adrift, in the manner of Sellar's own grandfather in Banff several decades earlier. Though some of the people may have been employed in the expanded labour force, the benefits largely accrued to the capital-intensive farmers who now reaped bigger harvests than the old system had ever dreamed of. There was a substantial building on the estate, Westfield House, later described as 'a plain country residence, two storeys high, to which several additions have at different times been made.'[22] It remained in the family until its sale in 1862, a decade after the death of Patrick Sellar.

Thomas Sellar was one of the mainly unsung managerial corps of the agricultural revolution. Such men were indispensable to aristocratic and gentry landowners. The Sellars, father and son, were especially notable because they combined their legal practice with a command of the financial and technical requirements of the new agriculture, and they maintained their own entrepreneurial urgency. Their location in Elgin was fortunate since the northern Highlands soon offered a further outlet for their well-honed enterprising spirits.

– ENTER WILLIAM YOUNG –

The Sellars came into association with another remarkable local figure, William Young (1764–1842), with whom they entered a consortium of local business interests whose object was to create a new port at Burghead to serve the transport demands of the region. It was a connection which was fateful for Patrick Sellar's fortunes over the following twenty years.

William Young was sixteen years older than Patrick Sellar, less well-educated in a formal sense, but much more experienced in agricultural improvement than the man with whom he would be inextricably linked in their subsequent work in Sutherland. Young had achieved extraordinary success and local fame for his practical methods of land reclamation, estate reconstruction and sheer creative enterprise in the low-lying lands of the Moray Firth. Looking back over Young's life in an obituary in 1842, the *Aberdeen Journal* remarked:

> We think it will be readily admitted that he has few, if any, equal to him in Morayshire for talent, intelligence, and active enterprise.[23]

Young began his career modestly as a small farmer and corn merchant specialising in the supply of oatmeal trade to the Strathspey district.[24] His success in the gale of improvement in Morayshire derived primarily from his ability to drain previously useless boggy lands and rapidly convert them to grain-producing model farms. Young also developed a variant of the village system driven on by rising prices. For instance, in the parish of Duffus much of the land, once it was drained, became remarkably fertile. According to a contemporary enthusiast, the local people presented no problem to the agents of change, for 'although poor and depressed, [they] are not querulous, they are peaceable and well disposed'. The resident proprietor, Archibald Dunbar, lacked funds for improvement and therefore depended on capital and initiative from other sectors of the thriving local economy, notably the grain trade and the more successful farmers, including William Young himself.[25]

William Young solved both the financial and the technical problems in these situations. For instance, he rented the farm of Inchbroom by Loch Spynie from the Earl of Fife. Young accepted a bargain lease in 1800 from the Earl which required him to spend £1,000 on drainage at the lake in return for rent-free occupation for nineteen years. This was a classic improvement lease. The work began in 1802 and, despite great technical problems, by 1804 'several hundred quarters of grain were reaped from off the ground' which, only a year before, had been under water.[26] The work at Spynie created employment, entailed digging a canal to the sea and inaugurated production where none had been seen before. It was a most impressive demonstration of the power of improvement and capital investment for the benefit of the entire community. Young possessed a rude appetite for agricultural challenges. He emerged as a dynamic agricultural entrepreneur, snapping up opportunities, creating villages and new settlements, multiplying productivity, and generating economic growth. He was able to juggle agricultural progress, increased rents and the retention of the original population in repeated miracles of improvement. In addition, his own business widened to trading in limestone and corn, imported iron and the development of fishing villages, often drawing on his own capital.[27]

William Young was the man with answers, a specialist whose opinion was sought, a man who had demonstrated by example the potential of enterprise across the northeast of Scotland.[28] The most impressive aspect of William Young's endeavours was his demonstrated capacity to transform rural communities, raising output dramatically, redeploying the local population and increasing rents. His reputation was confirmed by the improvement propagandists of the day and it was little wonder that he impressed local proprietors who sought advice and assistance. He was also prepared to risk his own accumulating capital, the most convincing sign of confidence and practicality.

Young's winnings were considerable. He had begun his career in business at seventeen when his father died leaving him £200. By 1806 he was worth £20,000, 'besides having given several thousands to my friends.'[29] His improvements at Inverugie increased the value of the estate to £25,000 and he owned rental property worth £1,800 per year. His financial success gave him a degree of independence over his employers and he made it clear that he was not beholden to them. Young died in 1842 worth £35,000.[30]

Both William Young and Thomas Sellar were, therefore, influential players in the fundamental changes which overtook the coastal lands of Moray in the years at the turn of the century. Agricultural output was greatly increased as the rural society was transformed. The population of the county increased from 4,534 in 1793 to 6,130 in 1831, but the people were increasingly relocated in towns and villages. Young had earned a brilliant reputation, technical and financial, and there was no reason to doubt the substance of his enterprise.

There were, however, local critics. It was later pointed out, for instance, that in the parish of Spynie the number of farms fell from sixty-eight to thirty-eight in the years 1800 to 1809. In Drainie three-quarters of the tenant families had left by 1835. Wartime speculative tendencies, it was claimed, had encouraged the introduction of 'men without capital' bidding excessive rents for Morayshire farms. When prices sagged after 1815, many of these men fell bankrupt and capital went to waste.[31] Moreover, the social effects had been painful to the community and had created great dislocation. Young's own reputation, however, seems not to have been tarnished by such criticisms. His most important individual enterprise, at Hopeman, was an unambiguous triumph.[32]

– THE BURGHEAD PROJECT –

The most spectacular and speculative enterprise in the Moray region was the redevelopment of the port of Burghead. This project brought William Young into close association with Thomas Sellar and his son Patrick; all were members of the Morayshire Farmers' Club. Patrick Sellar was secretary of the club and later, in 1809, he advocated the introduction of merino sheep to the district as well as new agricultural implements. Eventually the association of Young and Sellar at Burghead provided the link with the great northern realm of Sutherland, across the Moray Firth.

Burghead, in the 1790s, was a small fishing settlement located on a rocky promontory jutting out into the Moray Firth. The coastline between Inverness and Peterhead possessed few ports and the vigorous growth of agricultural output had not been matched by the transport facilities of the region. Moreover, especially in wartime, there were military and naval arguments for a new port in the district. Burghead's location provided shelter behind its rock, but its harbour was of limited use. It needed an extended breakwater. Its ancient Roman ruins suggested centuries of slumber. Now Burghead was about to be gripped with 'improvement'.[33]

In 1795 Sir Archibald Dunbar took control of the promontory, intending to create a 'deep, capacious and safe harbour' at Burghead.[34] Little immediate progress was achieved and there were serious difficulties with the capital costs. In 1802 the engineer Thomas Telford was asked about the possibility of interesting the government in the purchase and development of the port.[35] Important links with the Caledonian Canal had been canvassed. Telford said:

> It appears to me well calculated for a harbour for small vessels and might be made useful for the Country and Coasting Trade – but I do not imagine the Government have any intention of becoming purchasers.[36]

Soon however Telford was able to report that a new solution was emerging, though it was not yet equal to the scale of the task required. The Duke of Gordon and a group of Elgin gentlemen had formed a consortium to buy the land at Burghead 'for the purpose of constructing a safe Harbour for trading vessels.' Telford was full of praise for the venture: 'The work is going on with spirit, but the subscribers find their capital of £10,000 will fall short of effecting their purpose, and that without further assistance their efforts will be thrown away.'[37]

The consortium, a nice cross-section of old and new money in the region, an alliance of aristocracy and bourgeois in the new age, was evidently a device for raising the capital for the great patriotic plan to redevelop the Burghead site. The consortium soon outspent its assets and this induced a grant of £2,000 from the government in recognition of the military and naval potential of the new port. The legal papers of the new association were drawn up by Patrick Sellar in one of the earliest surviving documents to bear his signature. The construction work proceeded by degrees and as early as 1808 new feus (that is, leasing arrangements) were being advertised 'to mercantile and seafaring people, and such as may incline to build for pleasure, or the convenience of sea-bathing'. It was an ambitious exercise in village reconstruction, well beyond the average in northeast Scotland. It encompassed a new town and a new harbour, set in a regular grid plan (employing a pattern of the Edinburgh architect, Robert Burn) with its streets named after the investors. It required the demolition of the old town before the new port could rise in its place. The old fishing village and its inhabitants had to be shifted: 'The village was rooted out, and re-built to a plan which gave regular streets.'[38]

When the Burghead capitalists memorialised the committee of the House of Commons in May 1806 they made a decisive point about the changes that were transforming the region. Twenty years before, in March 1782, famine had racked the entire country: it was a time of blizzards, when the cattle were desperate for feed, when the harvest was so late that women stood with their sickles in their hands among the drifting snow and only empty straw was reaped. Hunger had stared people in the face and relief was required across the entire northeast. Now, in 1806, in dramatic contrast, the economic imperatives were at the polar opposite:

> In the winter of almost every year it happens, that while grains [are] selling [at] very high prices in London and south country markets, the grain in this country is detained in the Granaries until prices have fallen, to the injury not only of the Heritors, Farmers, the County at large, but of those places, also, which might otherwise have very considerable supplies in times of dearth.

The consciousness of market imperfections was high; wartime inflation and intermittent bread shortages across the nation added to the credibility of the Burghead project which, claimed the consortium, was

> activated chiefly by motives for the public good, relying also upon public aid when that could be conveniently afforded them, stept forward and made a purchase of the property, for the purpose of erecting a commodious Pier and Harbour therat.

Alexander Gildaire, an Aberdeen engineer, undertook the work and by July 1807, sixty masons and labourers were employed and the expenses reached £10,000.[39] In May 1808 the harbour was declared finished.[40] Its construction was a triumph and required only minimal maintenance over the following sixty years. It opened new market opportunities in the locality. For instance, in March 1809, Patrick Sellar began negotiating through the Farmers' Club in Elgin for a partnership to initiate an enterprise at Burghead to cure and salt beef and pork for southern markets. As Sellar put it, 'The inhabitants here can't consume the cattle they fatten; and they cannot fatten the Cattle they ought to do for want of consumption.' He took a £20 share in the scheme which was made feasible by the new harbour facilities.[41]

Nevertheless operating problems soon emerged at Burghead which eventually caused the undoing of the consortium that had brought the ambitious construction to fruition. A mistake in the original documentation (which may have reflected on the professional competence of Thomas Sellar, as lawyer) robbed the projectors of power to levy shore-dues and this caused disappointing revenues over the first ten years of operations.[42]

Profits at Burghead were less lucrative than the partners in the consortium had anticipated. According to Patrick Sellar, the management of the herring fishing out of the new harbour was 'bungled'. It was not surprising that the partners' interest in the project began to wane. Several of them, in any case, were dead by 1817 – King and Fortheath had gone, and the death of Thomas Sellar in 1817 left his share in the hands of his sheep-farming son, Patrick. The remaining partners resolved to discontinue their interests in the venture and the entire infrastructure was bought out by William Young (recently returned from Sutherland) who had decided 'to complete the improvements at his own risk'.[43] Young embarked on a new phase of development at Burghead which entailed new capital expenditure, especially on the facilities for the herring fishery, with new salt cellars, stations and accommodation.[44]

Young made a success of Burghead which, in 1835, was described as a developing place.[45] It was receiving 400 vessels per annum and serving a regular trade with Leith, London, Aberdeen, and Liverpool. By then Young had achieved the original purpose of the enterprise – that of establishing a regular steamship trade between the Moray Firth, Aberdeen and London, importing commodities such as coal and general goods, and exporting grain, cattle, sheep and other country produce of the local hinterland. Burghead was also developing a tourist role: 'A daily post and carriers to and from Elgin, comfortable lodging houses, and pleasant sea walks, add to its advantages as a watering place.' As a herring station Burghead had succeeded and in 1839 the business continued to flourish despite difficult times.[46]

Young was celebrated as one of the 'foremost men of progress in the north of Scotland'. He had left his mark in the many different locations – including, as we shall see, in Sutherland. About the town of Elgin he had made 'many beautiful improvements' above and beyond his renowned agricultural and transport developments. As well, 'in private life Mr Young was greatly beloved by his relatives, and highly respected by all. Social, hospitable, and full of anecdotes, his conversation was both instructive and amusing.' It was a life of achievement, a life much honoured in the annals of Morayshire improvement.[47]

Young, through these years, had become close to Patrick Sellar. In 1817, indeed, Sellar married Young's niece, Ann Craig (1793–1875).[48] They raised a large family and the eldest of several sons was named William Young Sellar after his great uncle. The Sellar family remembered Uncle William Young as 'a very clever man, and very plain-looking, judging from a portrait owned by his devoted niece, Mrs Patrick Sellar.' The uncle died a wealthy bachelor in 1842 but the Sellars were not best pleased with the distribution of William Young's fortune. He left it all, including the Burghead property, to his nephew on the Young side of the family. The Sellar nephew, who had been named after him, was the only other recipient. He inherited £20 with which 'to buy books'.[49]

– TROUBLE AT BURGHEAD –

A cloud was left hanging over the Burghead venture. In 1818, when William Young had taken over control and possession of the port from the remains of the original consortium, there had been an unpleasant controversy among the partners. The propriety of the business behaviour of Young and Sellar was directly questioned. It was at a time when Sellar was also much entangled with other legal and factorial work in both Moray and Sutherland. The Burghead controversy was as much about ethics as legality.

The manoeuvres surrounding the sale of Burghead to Young were certainly odd. A sketch of the circumstances requires a brief movement forward in Sellar's story. There had been a flurry of change in the previous two years. Sellar himself had been through the trauma of his Inverness trial and had emerged as a great sheep-farmer in Sutherland. He had married Ann Craig and inherited Westfield from his father,[50] as well as the interest in Burghead. In Sutherland, both Sellar and Young had by then been disengaged from the management of the Sutherland estate; Young was selling off his interests in the great agricultural improvements at Hopeman. In the midst of all this, Sellar first bought Burghead and then passed it over to Young in a somewhat complex and circular set of transactions. It was this stratagem which led to extremely angry recriminations from one of the remaining Burghead partners, Peter Brown of Linkwood, who, in effect, accused Sellar of chicanery in the changeover.[51]

Brown alleged that he had been manipulated by Sellar who had connived with Young to deceive and diddle the remaining partners. Brown angrily told Sellar he had cheated the partners but 'the Plot is blown'. Brown declared that Sellar had tricked him into delaying the sale of his own interest in order to reap a better price which never eventuated.[52] And thus Young gained Burghead at a bargain price to the disadvantage of the other partners.[53]

The truth of the matter is not clear. The consortium had certainly been disappointed at the financial returns on their capital. Sellar argued that the enterprise would continue to be unsatisfactory unless further improvements were undertaken requiring, of course, further capital outlay. Whatever the thinking of the group, it was decided to put the venture up to auction (roup), which attracted very little interest. Sellar, seeing that the bids were very low, and without any prior expectation, openly offered £7,200. This was declined by the partnership. Sellar was then offered the property for £8,000, which he publicly refused. Subsequently he was invited to renew his original offer, which he did, and the matter was settled.[54] The intervening understandings are not known but Sellar, it became clear, had been acting covertly on behalf of William Young.

Sellar was roused to a fury by Brown's accusation of crooked dealings. He retorted that the transaction had been plain and simple. None of the other partners had complained. With a characteristic rhetorical flourish, Sellar asked his accuser: 'Were the Duke of Gordon, and Archd Dunbar [two other partners] also fools? or Children? and I was a sharper?' The fact that Sellar had bought the property on behalf of Young – whom Colonel Grant in any case, considered the fittest person for the enterprise – was entirely immaterial, said Sellar, inflamed by the accusation. He pointed out bluntly, 'Nor have you or they a right to enquire why I bought it, or what are my views regarding it, provided I pay the price, which certainly, I intend punctually to do.'

Brown was neither placated nor cowed by Sellar's indignant defence. He was far from satisfied with Sellar's response. Sellar had duped him by his 'uncandid conduct'. Sellar and Young had plotted the outcome, 'conniving together to get the property on their own terms.' Sellar again dismissed Brown's accusations and told Colonel Grant that 'one sometimes meets in this world with Boobies [lowest in the class of children in school] who are come too soon from School and whose folly and impertinence is beneath contempt.' He felt impervious because the entire matter had been conducted publicly.[55]

These vitriolic exchanges may have been a random collision of business personalities. But Sellar tended to attract strong reactions. In his business dealing he was undoubtedly an opportunist with little instinct or taste for diplomacy. He was a man who made money, probably in a strictly correct manner; but he also often made enemies where conflict could have been avoided. He always drove the hardest bargain and was always prepared to take a commercial negotiation to the brink.

Sellar always attracted trouble. But, in 1818, he had triumphed and as we will see in following chapters, he had set his assailants – in Strathnaver and in Burghead – to flight. At this point in the narrative we return to the origins of Sellar's critical association with the northern Highlands.

– Looking north in 1809 –

Between the inauguration of the new facilities at Burghead in mid 1809 and their sale to Young in 1818, was a decade of excitement and turmoil in the lives of Young and Sellar. In these intervening years they achieved enduring infamy in Sutherland – a territory which, on a clear day, they could see twenty-five miles northwards from Burghead across the Moray Firth.

In early 1809 Patrick Sellar had been involved in legal work for various estates and was engaged in lengthy negotiation with George MacPherson Grant at Ballindalloch Castle. Sellar reported that he had pursued a certain Robert Gordon and boasted that he could easily have 'dished him', but Sellar's friends had persuaded him against destroying the person in question: 'I am satisfied that had I acted upon my own ideas I would only have ruined the man and his family without benefiting myself.' Sellar was involved in many contentious legal cases, especially over the recovery of road money from recalcitrant proprietors, and the removal of tenants for clearing landlords. He enjoyed the exercise of power over his business opponents and savoured telling his associates about his triumphs.[56] He proclaimed his reputation for rigour. MacPherson Grant was a close adviser to the Stafford family in Sutherland and was soon to be instrumental in bringing Sellar and Young to the notice of the greatest landowner in the Highlands.

The fateful connection began in the summer of 1809 as a direct consequence of the Burghead project. The original thinking of the venturing consortium had been to connect their expensive new facilities with new road systems pushing northwards – in addition to the shipping links with Aberdeen and the ports to the south. A regular shipping link to remote Sutherland also emerged as part of the transport logic. To this end 'a decked Sloop of 40 tons [with] as small state room [and] a hold adapted to the conveyance of horses' to Sutherland was described a dozen years later by Patrick Sellar himself:

> Mr Young and I, and several other Morayshire men embarked, to see this *terra incognita* [i.e. Sutherland]. We came to Dunrobin Bay in a beautiful morning, a little after sunrise; and I shall never forget the effect produced upon us by the beauty of the scenery – the mountains, rocks, wood, and the castle reflected on the sea as from a mirror.

It was on this arcadian morning that, as G. A. Dixon puts it, 'the spirit of successful Morayshire Improvement was directed at the unimproved vastness of Sutherland.'[57]

The Moray Firth now became a springboard for further development in the most northerly part of Scotland. Young and Sellar represented the most dynamic edge of the astonishing urgency of economic change in the first decade of the new century. They had both cut their teeth, served their apprenticeships, on the responsive flatlands around Elgin where rich returns had been reaped by capital and entrepreneurship. Young had a proven reputation; Sellar possessed an Edinburgh law training and a sharp mind for business. Sellar, still in his twenties, had more to prove than Young, more ground to make up. They converged on Sutherland at the peak of Young's prestige as agricultural adviser. Sellar was full of energy.

CHAPTER 3

Colonising Sutherland and the Dazzling Plans of 1809

– THE NEW DAWN –

The voyage of the Moray packet from Burghead to Dunrobin Bay carried William Young and his partner's son, Patrick Sellar, to Sutherland for the first time in June 1809. The two Morayshire business men intended to create a new trade, reconnoitre the ground and look about for new commercial opportunities. According to Sellar's own recollection, sixteen years later, he arrived in Sutherland only vaguely conscious of the unpleasant changes which had been sweeping across the Highlands in recent decades. In 1820, Sellar recollected his feelings on his first approach to the Highlands as he disembarked in Sutherland. He painted himself as an innocent, gripped by the popular ignorance of the time. He was filled with

> the belief that the growth of wool and sheep in the Highlands was one of the most abominable and detestable things possible to be imagined [and] . . . that the inroads then making on the ancient habits and manners of the children of the Gael were cruel and impolitic in the extreme.[1]

If this were an accurate representation of Sellar's views in 1809 there was no whiff of it in his correspondence at the time of his introduction to Sutherland. Young and Sellar soon found extraordinary scope for their talents in the northern county. Eventually, they were drawn into the greatest sheep removals the country had ever seen.

The arrival of the Moray packet was a literal linking of the latest region of improvement, the Moray Firth, with the largely unchanged territory of the northern Highlands. The extension of transport innovation prised open a resistant periphery of the British Isles. The Highland region was among the last bastions of the *ancien régime* of the economy: when the forces of change finally penetrated the region, the impact was devastating. There was minimal readiness, least of all in Sutherland, for the impending changes to the fundamentals of life. Undoubtedly there had already been a growth in emigration, an increase in rents and more commerce with the outside world even before Culloden. But most of the Highland communities assumed that life could continue undisturbed. Preparations in the minds of the people were slight. Meanwhile – and certainly from the 1790s – pressures were accumulating, ready to flood the straths with new ideas and a new economic system. The advent of William Young and Patrick Sellar at Dunrobin was the signal for an acceleration of structural change, for a far greater determination to impel the district into the new age. Young and Sellar exposed the full potentiality of what they regarded as virgin territory to enterprise and improvement. Sellar, characteristically, believed that they were also the carriers of 'civilisation'.

By the end of 1809 the two Moray men had captured the ear of the owners of the great Sutherland estate and then became critical advisers – not unlike modern economic consultants – to exert a guiding influence on policies which were dominant during the next great sequence of clearances in the northern Highlands. They soon offered dazzling plans to owners who were themselves already hungry for rapid change to the entire structure of the economy.

It is possible to exaggerate the conflict inherent in the convergence of the world represented by Young and Sellar and that of the old Highlands. Shifts in Highland society over the previous century had slowly edged the region towards modernisation. The process was sanctioned and reinforced by governments in London. In some respects, the Highlands already possessed remarkably cosmopolitan connections – most notably with the precocious emigrations of thousands of Highlanders across the Atlantic from the 1720s onwards. And there were other long-distance movements of its people with the cattle trade to the south, in the lowland labour markets and into military service. Nevertheless, when the moment of penetration from outside arrived, the shock was severe. Young and Sellar sought to bring order and improvement to what they regarded as the primitive world of the Highlanders. Almost all the resident people of the old estate took a diametrically opposite view. It was, therefore, a recipe for conflict.

At this point it is necessary to register the state of the northern realm of Sutherland immediately before the arrival of the Burghead Packet in 1809.

– THE COUNTESS AND THE STAFFORD FAMILY –

The Sutherland estate was owned by Elizabeth, Countess of Sutherland (1765–1839). She had inherited the estate as an infant in 1766, and the estate occupied the lion's share of the county of that name. It was administered on her behalf by Tutors until her adulthood. Even before her birth, there had been efforts to transform the estate, to increase its very low rental and to introduce modern agricultural methods. In 1767 the guardians of the Countess began to consider means of introducing commercial sheep-farming.[2] There were substantial 'removings' (that is, the clearing of the small tenantry to make way for new pastoral holdings) in 1772, and there were also efforts to dislodge the old leaseholder (tacksmen) class in the same decade. Signs of accumulating population pressure were evident across the estate.[3] There were recurrent serious food shortages and well-publicised exoduses of emigrants to North America, even before the Countess was born. Already in the west, in Assynt, most of the people were living along the coasts. Estate managers contemplated the idea of new fishing villages to accommodate more of the interior population. But the Sutherland estate, though rich in acres, was extremely poor in capital. Most of the early initiatives at development were still-born and the estate remained hamstrung by its capital deficiency.

The rapid rise of commodity prices (especially of wool) from the 1780s created new opportunities for advance in the northern economy. This generated its own tension. But there were two other constraints. In the first place, the estate was tied up with old-fashioned leases which prevented the landlord from initiating wholesale change. Most of these leases did not fall in until the first decade of the new century. Just as important was the disposition of the resident population. Much of the population was located in the interior glens of the estate, following a mixed cattle/tillage regime and thus standing in the way of capitalist pastoralism on the more extensive scale adapted to sheep production. In addition the local population was increasing rapidly and appeared to be making virtually no progress towards greater self-sufficiency or a better division of labour. The common people repeatedly fell victim to famine, looking to the landlord and their own communities for relief in times of harvest shortage. Their rent payments fell behind, and the potential of the land was not being realised in any sense understood by improvers. There were recurrent food crises in Sutherland (for instance, in 1782–3, 1807, 1811 and 1816–17) and during these times the estate imported emergency supplies of food which the landlord alone was equipped to manage. It was in these times that the most urgent and cogent arguments were bruited for radical change.[4]

The extent and severity of famine in the pre-clearance Highlands became a matter of controversy in later generations. In 1845, even within the Sutherland estate management, there was genuine argument about the level of welfare that used to prevail in the traditional communities in the old days. One estate adviser, MacPherson Grant, recollected his very first memories of the county in 1808 when there had been dreadful weather and floods and he had been unable to obtain feed for his horses, even at Dunrobin. He remembered:

> The cattle on Sutherland were that Spring dying from scarcity of Provender . . . and this is the condition to which your morbid Philanthropists of the present day refer as the days of comfort for the wretched Highlanders![5]

In that year the Countess of Sutherland told her husband, 'The state of the country is such that many lives would have been lost if Falconer [the factor] had not adopted the measures he has', referring to the importation of corn from Peterhead at great cost, which, however, would be retrieved. The incidence of famine gave urgency to her plans for the transformation of the estate. Throughout his life, Patrick Sellar invariably emphasised the famine-prone state of Sutherland before 1809.[6]

Famine and poverty were part of the Highland paradox. The perceptions of the people most affected, those of the interior straths, were rarely recorded. But we know that there was a quasi-biblical alternation of conditions in the Highlands. There were good years and bad. These seasonal and recurrent variations of the harvest produced contradictory accounts of the actual condition of the people of the region. This was especially true of Strathnaver, in Sutherland, which often flourished in ostensibly paradisiacal circumstances of rural contentment, a beautiful place for a large population and a poetic culture. There was, for instance, a report by Benjamin Meredith in 1810 which spoke of the relative ease of the people in the traditional cattle economy. Yet Meredith also believed that the Strathnaver people would benefit from removal and resettlement – so that they 'would be much bettered to what they are at present [sic].'[7] Such contradictory accounts had a special resonance for Strathnaver. This was a district later cleared by Patrick Sellar in the most controversial circumstances. It was in Strathnaver that the people mounted the greatest resistance to the estate management. For their part, the improvers believed that the people of Strathnaver should be cleared for their own benefit. The conflicting perceptions of past, present and future compounded the essential paradox.

The destiny of the Sutherland estate changed radically in 1785 when the Countess of Sutherland married the English aristocrat, George Granville Leveson Gower, born in 1758. Accompanied by his young wife and first child, Lord Gower served as British representative in Paris at the time of the French Revolution and was lucky to escape France without injury. He succeeded his father as Lord Stafford in 1803 and, in the same year, inherited much of the estate of his uncle, the widely famed Duke of Bridgewater. In the year of his own death, 1833, he became the first Duke of Sutherland. His wife outlived him by nine years: she was known (sometimes confusingly), over her lifetime, as Lady Sutherland, Lady Stafford, the Marchioness of Stafford and then Duchess/Countess of Sutherland until she became the dowager of that title.

The alliance of Lady Sutherland with the Stafford family brought together an exotic combination of Highland acres and English in-dustrial wealth. The most unmodernised remote corner of the British Isles became interlocked with the most dynamic sector of its most advanced region – Lancashire and the West Midlands. The Stafford estates were located in Shropshire and Staffordshire (at Lilleshall and Trentham) and were becoming local models of best agricultural practice yielding good rents. They also contained coal pits and iron-works which were developing swiftly from the 1780s. This was a solid basis for any aristocratic family, by any standard, but it was greatly reinforced by a brilliant marriage, with the addition of one the glories of industrial England – the golden profits of the Bridgewater Canal. By the terms of the Duke of Bridgewater's will, the profits, unencumbered and without responsibility, were pumped year after year for three decades into the pockets of his nephew Lord Stafford. This yielded a huge free income to the family and some very large parts of his fortune ultimately went to finance the Liverpool and Manchester Railway, again generating a large income from the late 1820s.

Lord Stafford decided to channel a very large proportion of his extraordinary wealth to the unimproved northern realm of Suther-land. His wife, no doubt, encouraged this great cross-subsidisation from England to the Highlands. Between 1803 and 1816 alone, Stafford received £903,622 of clear income from the Bridgewater Canal. It was the most extraordinary golden goose in British industrial history, and continued to produce its wealth until 1833 when the returns were diverted to Stafford's second son. Meanwhile, mining and agricultural rents rose on the English estates and Stafford's strategic investment in railways also became astonishingly lucrative. The Marquess of Stafford was the richest man in Britain and his marriage linked the most advanced sectors of the British economy with one of the most challenging and backward outposts.[8]

Thus the financial strength of the Sutherland estate in the Highlands had nothing to do with its current income capability. The vast inheritances of 1803 were the key to the subsequent transformation of the impoverished and capital-starved Sutherland estate. It was the font of the great capital outlays which accompanied the Sutherland clearances, and the source also of the purchase of new territory across the county. The Sutherland estate behaved like a great pike, powerful enough to eat up smaller estates on its borders when they became vulnerable to takeover. In the following fifty years the Sutherland estate swallowed most of the smaller estates in the county.

– INITIATING CHANGE –

During the first decade of her marriage to Lord Gower, until he succeeded to his phenomenal inheritances in 1803, the Countess was limited to modest plans for the improvement of her northern realms.[9] Schemes for improvement, usually in the form of large pastoral development, had been initiated during the Countess's minority but accomplished little. A blueprint for the Sutherland estate had been prepared in 1785 which proclaimed, as its first principle: 'Sheep Farming in the Highlands, not Incompatible with Population'.[10] This was the dream which resided in the mind of the Countess of Sutherland for over twenty-five years. Cheviot sheep had been introduced into neighbouring Caithness by Sir John Sinclair in 1791 at Langwell, and flocks had entered Armadale in 1794.[11] Throughout the 1790s sheep-farmers made increasingly seductive offers for lands on the Sutherland estate.[12] A sense of impatience was evident in that decade when the Countess possessed the will and the energy to embark on changes but lacked the means. But in 1799, new plans for removals on the estate were ordered by the Countess. She announced that there would be 'a considerable thinning' of the interior population in the west of the estate. It was part of a plan to consolidate grazing farms and to create a new fishing village in Assynt which would accommodate small tenants dislodged in the process.[13]

The 1799 announcement indicated the tendency of the Countess's thinking, even though little sheep-farming had been developed before the end of the century. It has been described as 'the first halting step' towards large-scale development of the estate. But there was clearly another dimension to the 1799 policy. The Countess referred to the traditional expectation that her tenants would respond with enthusiasm to the wartime needs of the military.[14] In the event, she had been deeply embarrassed by the poor response to the call from the regiment. She remarked angrily that if regimental recruitment were so poor then the people 'need no longer be considered a credit to Sutherland, or any advantage over sheep or any useful animal'. The Countess's annoyance was prompted by the slow pace of both recruitment and improvement, and this perfectly captured the ambiguity of the landlord's expectations in times of radical change. The traditional understanding was that military service gave the small tenantry security for their lands. It was a principle hardly compatible with the rationalisation of land use.[15]

The Sutherland estate, in financial terms, was in modest surplus by 1799. However, it was not generating sufficient investible funds to float major experiments. For ten years, the Countess and her English husband had contemplated radical change on the estate. In the following ten years, especially from 1803 when Lord Stafford inherited his great fortunes, they began introducing new capitalistic farmers and the new breeds of commercial sheep; they began to shift small tenants to the coast; they started new settlement schemes on the village model; and they had already witnessed the departure of many of their common people to the south and to America. They made imperative and increasingly anachronistic demands on the tenantry to yield their young men for the regiment in the crisis of war. But the pace of change was slow and the patience of the Countess, now Lady Stafford, was fully stretched. She wanted swifter and more certain progress. She wanted no less than a revolution in the north.

At the same time, the population of the Highlands had increased at an unprecedented rate, even in the most remote locations. The scale and intensity of the population growth did not become apparent until Sir John Sinclair, and the first national censuses, exposed the numbers involved. Fear of famine and the persistence of extreme poverty and vulnerability were perennial problems in the Highlands. In the main, the community tolerated such levels of human suffering as inescapable. Indeed until about 1810, Highland landlords were anxious to prevent people migrating from their estates to the lowlands or North

America. Emigration was intermittent in many parts, helping to put off any severe worsening of Highland poverty. But the recurrent distress of the people reinforced the prevalent idea that the Highlands were backward and justified radical economic restructuring. This, at least, was the view of many landlords and their advisers.

In 1807, the eldest son of Lord and Lady Stafford, Lord Gower, came of age and it is clear that his mother intended that he should become increasingly involved in the affairs of the northern estate. When Gower left Oxford in 1805, he was intensively briefed on the future of the Highland estate. His mother remarked to him, 'I hope you will be still more personally interested in the consequences of these arrangements than I shall be'.[16] Gower's position was significant. As eldest son he was heir to all the properties of both his parents in the north and south. However, there was a catch. The 'Bridgewater Millions', by the terms of the original will, were destined to descend not to Gower but to his younger brother, Lord Francis. There was a good chance that the younger son would become wealthier than Gower, which was dynastically embarrassing and unacceptable. Hence, beyond all ideas of bringing civilisation and improvement to Sutherland, there was always the plan to raise its value so that its income would place Gower ahead of his younger sibling.[17] This was the tortuous family context which saw profits (generated in Lancashire and the north of England) dispatched to the mountains and bogs of the northern Highlands. The young Gower was inducted into the management in Sutherland where he was also Colonel of the Volunteers. The Countess herself visited her northern realms frequently and made key decisions during her visits in the summer seasons of 1802, 1805, 1808, 1810, 1812, 1813, 1814, 1815 and 1816.

The new wealth inherited by Lord Stafford in 1803 solved the capital deficiency of the Sutherland estate. But three continuing problems hung over the Countess's plans which had been in her mind since she had reached adulthood. One was the spider's web of wadsets and tacks which impeded the reorganisation of the estate;[18] the second was the recurring lack of resolution among the Countess's managers; the third was the obdurate response to any suggestion of change among the existing tenantry on the estate. To this triple problem, all effort was addressed between 1803 and 1809.

The Sutherland plan was designed to eliminate tacksmen and subletting, and land was denied to those who did not contribute to the recruitment of the family regiment during the war. As recently as 1799, these policies provoked protest and resistance among the tenantry which, in turn, caused anxiety among the estate managers.[19] The tensions were especially inflamed in wartime when the estate displayed a vindictive attitude to recalcitrant and uncooperative tenants, notably in relation to recruitment. The factor, however, told tacksmen:

> The number whose failure in spirit and loyalty must subject them to be removed from the Estate will be found very small. [20]

Nevertheless the threat was transparent. The poor level of response to the needs of the recruitment caused irritation in the management of the estate. The factors regarded estate management as a continuing battle against the uncooperative. Rents were raised in 1799 and the demarcation of prospective sheep-farms proceeded.

In July 1805, Lady Stafford declared that the estate would take

> the lower People out of the hands of the Tacksmen, by not allowing the latter to subset, but on the contrary for the little parcel of land allotted to the small Tennents they will pay to us what they now pay to these Taxmen which is lost to us, or if they pay still less, the estate will yet be increased by a third or fourth proportion of the whole and the People happy and contented.[21]

In 1802, a new factor, Colin Mackenzie, was appointed. New enterprises were set afoot. At the same time the earliest large-scale rearrangements of farms to accommodate the capitalistic sheep-farmers were organised. Some of the new farmers were drawn from the old corps of local tacksmen; others flowed in from regions to the south. In 1803, Corryfearn was leased,[22] following the introduction of cheviot sheep into Keodale and Glendhu on the adjacent estate of Reay in 1802.[23] In 1805, David Campbell was required to draw up a schedule of lands to be converted to sheep-farms. It was, essentially, a timetable for clearances. But he was slow to activate this programme. In 1805, the famous sheep-farming partnership of Atkinson and Marshall brought 3,000 sheep from the south and they offered to treble the rents in their new operations in 'The Great Sheep Tenement' in Lairg (Whitsunday 1807) which caused the relocation of small tenants to Strathnaver, Dornoch and Golspie.[24] There were problems with resettlement from the start but in 1808 Suisgill and Kildonan farms were also made over to another new tenant, Houston. The sheep-farms replaced the old cattle economy. The native sheep proved extremely vulnerable to the severe weather of 1807–8 (when they almost all died of rot and scab) and this accelerated the introduction of new breeds.[25]

The Stafford family were evidently conscious of the dangers entailed in their plans for reconstruction. Similar, though less comprehensive, schemes had already been introduced into other parts of the Highlands. The Staffords made no bones about the dislocation, upheaval and likely unpopularity of the changes. Within the Stafford family, and among its Highland managers, there was a continuous internal dialogue. They discussed between themselves the feasibility of the great changes and how the revolution could be achieved and enforced without inhumanity. As Colin Mackenzie put it in 1804:

> Our Constituents were always tender of the people and will not be less so now but it will be a blessing to a great proportion of them to be taught a new and improved application of their industry and labour.[26]

He voiced the blithe expectations of the management even in the early phases of the change. Spots along the coast were then being identified which 'would be excellently calculated for little settlers.'

In 1805, Lady Stafford herself used similar language. She was undoubtedly the driving force and insisted that the new plans would be executed 'with the proper degree of firmness'. But it was vital 'not to disband the People [that is, the small tenantry]'. She specifically declared that she did not want to cause an outflow of emigrants from her estate. But she noted also that the relocation plans would provide an excellent opportunity 'to get rid of them in case[s] of bad conduct', which implied a combination of planning and social control at a new level.[27] She did not wish to drive the people 'to the wall for a little more money'. That would not be 'pleasant'. Nevertheless she spoke warmly of the increase of rents, which was the assurance she gave her husband, the man providing the capital. She also told Lord Stafford that he was personally very popular among the tenantry, rather suggesting that he needed reassurance on the question even in 1805. But, in reality, 'the Highland spirit', in the shape of clanship and vassalage, was already in disrepair.[28]

– NEW PLANS, 1805–9 –

In the summer of 1805 Lady Stafford gave her husband (who often remained in England as she sallied north to the Highlands) detailed accounts of her current plans for Sutherland. She said that neighbouring Caithness was more advanced because it had more contact with the south through its superior trading links. She reported that many complaints had been received against the tacksmen,[29] and her 'decent and good-looking Tenantry' were full of 'universal joy' at the prospect of becoming direct tenants of the landlord. The sub-tenants, under her plans, would pay less rent and the landlord would receive more: she expected 'an amazing increase' of rent. She added that 'the attachment of all ranks here seems as fresh as it ever could be.' She was utterly determined to eradicate the tacksmen and was perfectly clear about the impact of the new sheep-farms: 'Some people (indeed a good many) must inevitably be tossed out which makes all eyes turn the more towards the Harbour or at Kilgower and the fishing village.' She had asked Thomas Telford to examine the possibilities. And there were 'waste lands that will not do for sheep where we propose to allot for a certain rent a House and an acre to a Family, the men will go to work in the south and return to their families in winter which will introduce Industry and bring riches into the country.' Her main fear was that she would bore her husband with so many details.

Two days later, she again referred to 'The Plan I mentioned of accommodating People driven from their present dwellings by the Sheep Farms which are in train'. Much of their immediate difficulties would be cushioned by the availability of employment on the new roads being constructed, and would 'in time accustom them to gain their livelihood by regular labour.' She was finding the operations personally exhausting, but remarked to her husband in London: 'Considering what a large concern this is, and how many people totally depend upon the regulation of it, I think even a little sacrifice in that way becomes a duty.' She also identified an ancillary advantage in placing the tenantry in villages which would 'have the Inhabitants in some degree in our power in case of bad conduct.'[30]

The programme became increasingly ambitious. In 1805, plans for a new village at Golspie had been set afoot, and there were further installations at Culgower and Helmsdale along the east coast. But such a programme, with its inevitable and fully anticipated social turmoil, required skilful and vigorous orchestration and Lady Stafford became repeatedly dissatisfied and frustrated by her current agents and advisers. David Campbell had been appointed in 1802, but departed in a cloud of criticism in 1807. The financial accounts of the estate were in poor condition and Cosmo Falconer, an Edinburgh lawyer who had trained with Thomas Sellar in his Elgin office, was appointed. The factor's role on the great Sutherland estate was described by Henderson, the contemporary Agricultural Reporter: the factor not only collected the rents, 'but, with the proprietor's consent, grants leases and removes tenants; he holds Baron-Baillie Courts to settle petty disputes between the tenantry; acts as Vice-lieutenant of the county, and is a leading man at all county meetings.'[31] His was a powerful and vital position in the estate, especially where the landlord was away for most of the time.

Falconer was made responsible for a further acceleration of the policy and the scale and gravity of the operations was heavy on the minds of all the managers involved. The question of rents loomed large. The estate was looking for 'a very large Augmentation of the Rent Roll' during the period through to 1814.[32] In 1806, Colin Mackenzie had observed that the estate could be let for £20,000 immediately 'but this is evidently impossible without <u>sweeping away</u> what at present is a <u>Superfluous</u> population.'[33] This was the crux of all the thinking – making the estate pay its potential while reaccommodating the population in a productive and humane fashion. It was the object of all the social engineering from the start. The people's minds would have to be converted as the scheme was gradually brought to fruition. As Colin Mackenzie put it:

> Any attempt at an instantaneous change would fail and only involve the bulk of the people in misery and Ruin.

The hazard of the change could hardly have been expressed more clearly. In June 1807, Mackenzie thought it was

> not at all impossible to overcome the prejudices of the People when Schemes of radical improvement are set a going and when the requisite Measures are steadily and dispassionately pursued for Accomplishing them.[34]

The pace of the changes was always the central issue. In July 1807 Falconer was making further plans to incorporate much of Lairg 'in the Sheep Ranges' and 'the institution of the Villages on the coast'. Estate advisers remarked on the slowness of Falconer's progress, but noticed that the whole estate would be out of lease by 1813 or 1814, at which point

> the change of system, the introduction of roads, the institution of villages and other consequent improvements would render Sutherland so very different a country from what it is now so that your Ladyship might very reasonably expect a very handsome augmentation to the Rent Roll.[35]

In 1808 the estate felt it necessary to issue a 'flat denial' to newspaper reports that Lady Stafford was removing her 'fair tenantry'.[36] Throughout 1809 sheep-farms were advertised in Sutherland for entry in the next few years, for instance at Culgower and Wester Garty, 'subject to reservations for the accommodation of settlers upon Wester Garty, in the event of a Fishing Village being established.'[37] This indicated the provisional status of plans for reception at this time.

All the improvers in the estate management gave eloquent testimony to the need for humanitarian concern during the planned transformation. They knew, and emphasised, the enormity of the plans being hatched by the Countess. By 1807 the policy was set: it was described as 'the system of turning the interior tracts of the country into Sheep Walks as a natural and prudent means of improvement'.[38] A question at issue was whether the landlord should continue to worry about emigration from the estate – and the advice in 1807 was to give the people the offer of accommodation; but if they declined the offer and instead emigrated, then that was their choice and not a matter of special regret to the estate.[39] As for Lord Stafford, his first requirement was said to be 'the happiness of the people of this Estate'.[40]

Beyond family considerations there were still wider pressures and incentives at work in the northern Highlands. One was the urgency to increase wool output, as expressed in prices and the competitive bidding for land. Sheep-farming had been spreading north for two decades, profits were swelling and demand was ostensibly insatiable. The demand for other commodities was also buoyant – several decades of inflation had given great confidence to the idea of development and investment in the north. Kelp, fishing and linen manufacture, in particular, had expanded, notably at locations along the east coast. Even the old cattle industry of the Highlands was benefited. But relative commodity prices gave wool a large comparative advantage. Sheep-farming was obviously the most lucrative direction for investment and change.

– INADEQUACIES OF MANAGEMENT –

The earliest efforts to revolutionise the Sutherland estate (between 1803 and 1809) had been hesitant and poorly coordinated. The hesitancy was partly a consequence of management. The existing estate factors were perhaps less well-educated and capable than was required for the task. Cosmo Falconer was the key person. He attempted to reconstruct part of the estate. This inevitably entailed removals and the relocation of population. But Falconer was much impeded by the refusal of the people of the estate to cooperate. In 1807–9 he had attempted to abolish sub-tenancies and destroy the authority of the tacksmen. The assault on the middle ranks of local society was a hazardous strategy for the Sutherland management.

In February 1808 there was a famine crisis too, the first major episode since the evil days of 1782–3. The estate was mobilised for famine victualling, a form of relief which quickly damaged the estate's revenues. Costs spiralled and rents fell. There were also difficulties in the implementation of removals: Falconer was unable to persuade the small tenantry to resettle on the muirs. There was resistance by 'the People of the lowest class', opposition among the tacksmen and many signs of turmoil even though the estate plans were piecemeal and still relatively modest in scale. The symptoms of disaffection included emigration, a sullen refusal to comply and the petty delaying of responses to commands from the estate officials. Falconer had been unable to impose his authority, or to impart enough resolution, to satisfy the wishes of the Countess. She craved stronger management.

By 1809 the intentions of the Countess were unambiguous. She was the driving force behind the plans. Her husband took an intelligent interest but was a distant source of capital rather than a maker of the policy. Lord Stafford was given clear accounts of the developments but took the back seat. He was a man of diminishing vitality, his health was weakening and his eyesight deteriorating. He was increasingly silent in conversation, while his wife became more assertive and directive in the affairs of the family estates.[41]

Under Falconer's slow-moving and nervous control the Countess's estate plans were stalling. Her hunger for new advice for the future of her estate and for men capable of achieving its transformation must have been an open secret in the north. Lord Gower was too young and insouciant for the heavy administrative work involved. At this critical moment in the evolution of the Sutherland plans, the packet from Moray arrived in Dunrobin Bay in June 1809, carrying Young and Sellar.

As we have seen, William Young possessed an exciting and proven record for large-scale and diversified improvements already well-publicised in the northern community of landowners. Patrick Sellar was then a lesser figure, a young lawyer with experience in the improvement of his father's estate at Westfield. Sellar was an implementer, an enforcer, and would be a foil for Young the instigator, the creative planner, the visionary with practical experience. Their first voyage to Dunrobin was a reconnoitre but it was quickly followed up with direct communications between the Moraymen and the resident Sutherland factor, Falconer. Soon Lord Gower was drawn into the discussions and was evidently much excited by their enthusiastic ideas.[42]

The next step in the relationship was by correspondence with the

Countess in London and further visits to Dunrobin Castle by Young and Sellar. They were astonished at the opportunities revealed along the eastern coast of Sutherland. To prove their seriousness they soon made a very competitive offer (in Sellar's name) for the large improving farm of Culmaily in the southeast of the estate, but this negotiation was linked with a stream of gratuitous advice about the general improvement of the estate along the seaboard.

This convergence of the Moray improvers with the Stafford family spanned the second half of 1809. There were excited letters between the Moray Firth, Dunrobin Castle and Cleveland House, the Stafford's residence in London. In July 1809, Lady Stafford had reported receiving 'a very advantageous offer in the way of improvement and a new system' for the farm of Culmaily from Young and Sellar. Their interest was strongly seconded by George MacPherson Grant who vouched for the characters of the two Moraymen. The Countess was immediately impressed and remarked that it was of the 'greatest advantage to get these people' as tenants on the east coast of her estate. She made positive moves to persuade the sitting tenant at Culmaily, Colonel Sutherland, to make way in favour of the Moraymen. They must receive 'reasonable terms', she said.[43] Colonel Sutherland, a tacksman and one of the traditional leaders of local society, took umbrage and was not immediately cooperative. The eventual arrangement became a matter of friction as soon as Young and Sellar started operations.[44]

Lord Gower was also impressed by the infectious enthusiasm of Young and Sellar. In the spring of 1810 he took his parents to Elgin and Inverugie to meet William Young and he joined them again in Sutherland. Young, by then, had captured the ear and gained the confidence of the Countess. But the first step in the courtship had been Culmaily. Culmaily was not a Highland farm but a substantial 300 acres of low-lying terrain (with pasture) not far from Golspie, arable land which had been partially improved before Sellar and Young arrived on the scene. Neighbouring Morvich had already been improved. Culmaily was part of a group of large farms recently established for progressive farming by larger capitalistic tenantry. Kirkton had been taken over by Robert Mackid and Drummuie by Captain Robert Sutherland.[45] They all required the displacement of small tenants in order to reap economies of larger-scale enterprise. The new Culmaily lease was signed for twenty-one years and was witnessed by Robert Mackid. It specifically forbade subtenants and assignees.[46]

The men from Moray made the offer for Culmaily in Sellar's name, his first formal transaction with the estate. The lease addressed the two key priorities in the mind of the Countess. The first consideration was rent: Sellar and Young were prepared to pay a rent markedly higher than those currently prevailing in the district, and 25 per cent higher than paid by the adjacent tenants, Mackid and Sutherland. It was a level of rent also higher than the current inflation. This was a gesture which no doubt alarmed all local tenantry since it was bound to create pressures on themselves. The offer of higher rent was, of course, also an earnest of the intention of Young and Sellar to increase the productivity of the land by bringing to it the benefits of modern techniques.

The second consideration was the improvement of Culmaily. The new tenants promised to change agricultural methods radically, while also resettling the existing small tenants who would be dislodged by their improvements. This was a critical problem for Culmaily and also for the Sutherland estate at large. Sellar and Young possessed the capital and the reputations for improvement to make their offer credible and extremely attractive to a landlord who had endured endless frustration with her estate for almost two decades. Indeed, in April 1810, the arithmetic of their plan of improvement became clearer. There were, in fact, 253 people on the farm but the plans were based on the retention of only forty of them. The rest, that is 84 per cent of the population, would be placed elsewhere. They would go to Achavandra or Skelbo where, averred Young and Sellar, they would certainly be a 'treasure' to themselves and the scheme itself when they were employed in the industries to be established there.[47] The Culmaily farm would become a microcosm of the changes impending across the Sutherland estate, entailing radical change and the reaccommodation of the displaced people on 'lots' and in new modes of employment.

Their plan was comprehensive and included the establishment of small domestic industry among the resettled small tenantry. There would be mills for threshing and a lint mill which would serve their own needs and also those of 'all our Sutherland neighbours'. Sellar and Young simply could not understand why flax was not already grown in the county since it would form the basis of a linen industry and bring employment and income to the people.

The Sellar/Young plan for Culmaily was, of course, a replication of methods they had both employed successfully in Moray. It also constituted an exciting anticipation of what could be done for the rest of the Sutherland domain, a model of improvement for Lady Stafford's keen contemplation. Sellar and Young addressed each vital need in her receptive mind. They were now prepared to invest in the very territory that the Stafford family wished to transform and whose aspirations had been frustrated and thwarted over the previous decade.

The Moraymen promised better rents at Culmaily, more cultivation, the rearrangement and reaccommodation of the people, new employment, drainage and manufacturing. All this would be done with benevolence and would provide a 'demonstration effect' to the backward Sutherlanders for their emulation. It required a new division of labour and use of the land. At the outset, the plan was premised on two radical propositions. One was the explicit conversion of the small tenantry into a proletariat – the people would become 'good labourers' and they would be much the better for their changed status.[48] The people, said Young, would become 'labourers and mechanics'.[49] Second, a sharp wedge would be driven into the society of the eastern coastlands – the structure of subtenancy would be abolished in one fell swoop. The old tacksmen class would be extinguished. Already this policy had created tensions with the management of the estate. Lady Stafford was aware that her factor was unpopular with 'the Gentlemen', that is the tacksmen of the estate. But, she said, 'he understands managing the common People . . . the People and things [sic] seem to flourish and to be happy and contented'.

Relations between Sellar and his new neighbours at Culmaily was a critical matter and would colour his entire career on the estate. Most significant was Robert Mackid, also a lawyer and improving capitalist farmer from outwith the estate. Mackid was thirteen years older than Sellar. He had been educated at King's College, Aberdeen, in 1785–7 and then served a legal apprenticeship in Thomas Sellar's practice in Elgin before he became a notary in Edinburgh in 1791, serving as a clerk in a lawyer's office. Thus Mackid probably knew Patrick Sellar as a child. Mackid then served as a clerk in Fortrose and became a procurator in the sheriff court of Ross and Cromarty. In 1806 he moved to Tain and developed his legal practice. In September 1806 he was appointed a sheriff-substitute in Sutherland, where his name had been suggested by William Mackenzie, family lawyer to the Staffords. Mackid received his commission from George Cranstoun, Sheriff-Depute. But Mackid continued to divide his time between Tain and Sutherland, and he also did work in Cromarty. In September 1807 he started to devote himself exclusively to his Sutherland employment and he moved to his new residence at the substantial farm of Kirkton in mid-1809, just before Sellar's own appearance in the county. Mackid set up as a large farmer in Sutherland on one of the newly consolidated properties which he had examined with the assistance of an experienced south country farmer in late 1808. This property was Kirkton. Mackid began to devise plans for grandiose buildings estimated to cost £1,500, but the estate resisted his plans on the grounds that the landlord would become liable for excessive compensation if it failed.[50] He nevertheless proceeded with a very substantial new construction at Kirkton.

Culmaily, as we have seen, was mainly in the hands of small tenants and some of it was marshy and undeveloped. When Sellar and Young set up plans to introduce a flax mill on the Culmaily farm, they ran into objections from neighbouring farmers, including Robert Mackid who believed that it would create the danger of flooding on his adjoining farm at Kirkton.[51] Operations at Culmaily were also obstructed by the continuing resistance of the wadsetter Colonel Sutherland who would not budge from neighbouring Morvich. Sellar and Young paid higher wages to the labourers they employed on their drainage works; they also, to the fury of local suppliers and tacksmen, supplied meal at lower than prevailing rates.[52] The Moraymen thus immediately locked horns with their neighbours. Nevertheless the 'Agricultural Reporter', Henderson, in 1811 was already able to testify to the technical excellence of their operations at Culmaily which included 'a handsome dwelling house, a commodious square of offices and houses', a grist mill, a thrashing machine, and draining, which was associated already with great increases in the output of potatoes, oats and wheat.[53]

As soon as Sellar began his operations at Culmaily, he quickly discovered that it was 'not at all agreeable to the Gentlemen resident there'. He instantly trod on their toes.[54] In mid-November 1809, he gave Gower a full account of his current thinking about radical change in the context of Sutherland. This was his most elaborate exposition of how he thought a cottager would live as a proletarian in an improved regime, that is 'how the cottager [contrived] to live on from two to four acres of new Ground.' Under the new village scheme the people would progress by stages; cottagers would start with two to four acres of new ground:

> The cottage completed and the ground dugg are given him, say in March. He sows his crop – a patch of Turnip; another of oats or barley; A little wheat where climate permits; potatoes and some lint. He then goes to wherever work is to be done and money acquired. He returns in October with £8 or £10 in his pocket, and finds his little crop in the yard. He diggs his potatoes;

repairs his cottage, buys a pigg, and makes himself snugg for winter. He buys milk from the nearest farm til he can afford a Cow; which may probably be next season; for if he had been bred a shoemaker or any other Country trade he practices it during winter. He bye and bye sells a litter of pigs, a web of cloth, egg and poultry. He waxes stronger by degrees and improves a few acres of the adjoining moor. One at least, of his boys is educated in Latin, writing, and accompts, by the nearest Schoolmaster, and is sent off to push his fortune as he best can. Whatever climate is witness to his toil the place of his nativity keeps the first part of his heart; he remits money to his parents. If he die he wills his money home. If he lives he brings it to his father's cott.

Sellar pointed out that Robert Burns was the son of a cottager and strongly recommended the poem 'The Cottar's Saturday Night' which, he said, would delight Lord Gower.[55] Sellar also extolled the virtues of mobility and emigration. He knew twenty families in the Westfield district who had been 'enriched by emigrations from their father's or their uncle's house.' He cited the case of the family of Sir William Grant which lived within a mile of Ballindalloch. Their sons had migrated with great success. Sellar had conducted long-distance legal business for family members living abroad, and was especially proud of his Jamaican business dealings for such families.[56]

– THE PROMISE OF FORTUNE –

The first commercial voyage of the Burghead packet in August 1809 yielded an immediate profit which, wrote Young and Sellar, 'augurs well for her success when the communication is better known.' In their copious correspondence with Lady Stafford they diagnosed the problems of her estate, implicitly offering solutions, increasingly adopting an informal role as consultants to the estate. Time after time they emphasised that 'the poverty of the people was occasioned by the misapplication of their labour and the mismanagement of the soil.'

Sellar usually assumed the lead in these discussions. He was a more natural and prolific penman than Young who tended to brevity. Sellar wrote like an improvement ideologue touched with a messianic faith in the cause. The common people of the estate, he said, were impoverished because they knew too little of the division of labour and new methods of cultivation. They did not understand the power of the market. These precepts applied to all aspects of their common lives and the best example was the continuing reliance of the people on peat: the typical Sutherlander spent the best quarter of the year digging peats rather than cultivating crops such as turnips as winter feed for their cattle. Horses were used to carry the peat but the same horses ate all the available fodder in the winter months. Hence, the common Sutherlander was compelled to buy in various goods at punitive prices and inevitably fell into debt. If a regular supply of coal were inaugurated this chronic problem would cease. As Sellar said:

> Thirty years ago Moray used peats as the Sutherlanders do now. They did not practise alternate husbandry. They had not the time for it. Now coals are brought in at 5 ports and the face of things is changed.[57]

Young and Sellar conjured a vision of Sutherland. It was a beautiful, but utterly neglected, county, and a century behind Moray. The people were idle, backward and appallingly impoverished. They were ignorant, they obstructed efforts at progress and they execrated the new sheep-farmers from the south. By 1809 many of the sheep-farms of the future were already demarcated in the estate plans.[58] Farms were being advertised in July 1809, with specific reference to the resettlement villages already in preparation. But Sellar and Young were not at this stage concerned with sheep-farming. They were coastal improvers who identified great opportunities on the narrow tracts of land which fringed the main mountain mass of the estate.

Their advice entailed a growing and comprehensive indictment of the resident people. They were a deadweight on the estate and its improvement. They paid rents less than a quarter of the true value of their lands. They damaged the soil. The tenantry were gripped by 'established habits' and, for any progress to be made, these habits had to be 'broken through'. The ruinous system had followed 'from father to son through all generations. People wedded to such immemorial customs are with difficulty led into a new tract.' Their recommendations entailed a terrible imperative: 'They must see to believe'. Culmaily would be a model demonstrating the benefits of progress and change, and other improving tenants would be attracted to the estate by the example.

Young and Sellar soon offered to extend their operations along the coast and they could pay the proprietor 'double the present rent at our entry':

> Quadruple it when our improvement is made and we have tasted somewhat of the benefit of it. Say in ten years and pay eight rents when we have benefited still further – say in another ten years. Thus £60 for the first period of ten years, £120 for the second ten years and £240 for the third period – thirty years in all. We should profit more by this farm than any other tenant, for we calculate that the tenants in the interior seeing our flax growing –

and floating down to Culmaily miln, and having the profit explained to them would immediately follow our example, and our miln would, in this case, pay beyond calculation.

It was an enticing prospect. To the Stafford family it demonstrated the possibilities of the coastal lands, not merely for Sellar and Young, but for the country at large, for resettlement.[59]

In September 1809, Sellar and Young spent ten days in southeast Sutherland, between Culgower and Skibo. Out of this visit came the most thorough statement of their view of the county and its prospects. They were 'pleased beyond measure with the beauty of the country, its susceptibility of improvement and the disposition of the people to get forward'. The last remark was a surprising contradiction of their previous condemnations of the people of the estate. The organisation of the estate, however, was profoundly deficient. The poor people laboured under awful disadvantages. They were 'without education skill or capital' and they cultivated the soil in the least efficient manner possible. There was practically no division of labour among them – no tradesmen, manufacturers or labourers because they were primitive, self-sufficing peasants. They had to import 'every piece of mechanism or manufacture wanted . . . yet nothing is exported by them in exchange for the wealth of other countries'. The landlord's benevolence had coddled them in their inefficiency, especially in times of dearth:

> They cannot raise provisions for their [own] consumption, insomuch that they must have perished but for your Ladyship's bounty. Their unavailing efforts to perform that for which they are not fitted had damped and depressed their industry. Your Ladyship had lulled asleep their care . . . they have sunk into despondent security.

The solution, emphatically, was not to rid the country of the population. The people were appallingly poor, but there was no question of Sutherland being overpopulated. Rather, the labour of the people was simply misapplied. Population was a great strength, declared Sellar and Young. There was still an anti-Malthusian strain in their thinking at this time. The idea of excessive numbers was wrong:

> This, with great deference, must be mistaken, for England, although less fruitful and more populous, is richer than Spain; and it is so, only because it is more populous, and because every nation pays tribute to the well directed industry of its people.

Hence the people of Sutherland were a great asset. It was now essentially a matter of directing them into industry, in every sense, and encouraging their division of labour. They would be like the Israelites, led from Egypt into the Promised Land.[60]

These recommendations were so far confined to the coastal lands of the country, to agriculture and industry and the new division of labour. Sellar and Young assumed a basic 'pliability' of the people who needed only be shown a light for their conversion. There was a curious absence of reference to sheep-farming in these discussions: Young and Sellar were advising the creation of a new economy for the displaced people of the interior. The sheep-farms could look after themselves. Yet it is inconceivable that the astute Moray improvers did not connect their ideas for the coastal transformation with the larger question of sheep clearances. Villages would absorb the interior population in productive employment on the coastal margins of the estate and this would obviously provide the perfect complement to the further progress of sheep-farming in the interior. The fate of the people who were displaced by sheep-farming was the central problem for any Highland proprietor sensitive to the welfare of his or her small tenantry. Lady Stafford located this problem at the centre of her own priorities.

In October 1809, William Young arranged for an architect and engineer from Moray to examine Achavandra and Golspie, indicating that he was already taking part in the planning of the centrepiece of the changes. As R. J. Adam observes, 'Young did not invent these plans: he was, however, the first person to appear on the scene with the capacity to give them real impetus.'[61] New farms created at Achavandra were designed to accommodate small tenants, and twenty were resettled there by 1812. Falconer, nevertheless, had experienced difficulty getting the plans forward; there was even a problem in getting labour to prepare the lots and men were brought in from distant Strathnaver.

In November 1809 Patrick Sellar announced that he would move permanently to Sutherland 'to push our plan with vigour'; he and Young had meanwhile moved to acquire the additional lease of the Morvich farm which also required the removal of small tenants.[62] They planned to lay the groundwork of flax and woollen mills. They advised against a deep-water harbour because the trade did not warrant the expense, but spoke of possible exports from Sutherland, including cloth, flax, yarn, and cured provisions. The two informal advisers looked forward to Lady Stafford's next visit in the coming spring: 'When on the Spot your Ladyship will see the scene of action; ascertain facts, discuss what may be for or against each idea; and Judge better, than by correspondence, what is proper to be done.' They defined the great problem as the 'habits and prejudices of the people'. Sellar and Young complained that 'They will adopt nothing new <u>until they see it is done successfully by others.</u>' Until then no revenue could come from 'the dry husks of oppressed indigence'. Eventually all would become prosperous and mutually supporting in a proper division of labour.[63] It was pure Adam Smith, the foundation of all improvement.

– CLAMOUR AMONG THE PEOPLE –

William Young, fresh from his resettlement successes in Moray, gave his *imprimatur* to the plans for equivalent lands in Sutherland at Achavandra on the coast between Dornoch and Skelbo. This was a pilot scheme for the Sutherland estate, already launched under the aegis of Falconer and Gower. It involved the sequential development, out of previously barren moorland, of plots of arable land to which labour was applied. At first rent was low, then rising as the improvements took hold. At Achavandra, wrote Sellar and Young, a very good 'haven' was being created as a retreat for people displaced by improvements, as well as for fishermen. 'The fertile soil of Achavandra could provide food for the <u>first</u> settlers, and the extensive moors behind, which court to be planted and improved [and], will afford them employment while they bring forward their families.'

This was progressive improvement in the most approved and economical manner, and it was similar to Young's successes in Moray where, within a few years, he had

> settled nearly 300 souls on a spot at Inverugie which when he began, was perfectly barren; and a considerable tract of ground near the village is, in consequence of their industry, (in a great measure) risen in rent from something like 2/6 to nearly £3 per acre.

Achavandra was designed to receive people from the interior dislodged by sheep-farming. These were the refugees created by the clearances. But there had been problems concerning the malleability (or 'pliability' in Sellar and Young's phrase) of the people for whom the plan was devised and on whose labour and cooperation it all hinged. A programme of removals had been arranged and advertisements for the sheep-farms were already in the Scottish press. The timing of the programme depended on the creation of new facilities on the estate for the reception of the displaced people. At no stage did the estate at this time consider the possibility of ejecting the people. This was not part of Lady Stafford's thinking.

The Achavandra experiment, under Falconer's direction, ran into serious problems during the first attempt to resettle displaced tenantry on the muirs. This coincided with the second visit of Young and Sellar to Dunrobin and was clear-cut evidence that the people were resistant to the policy designed to reconstruct the estate economy. The people had been offered plots at Achavandra – advertisements were displayed, terms announced, the ground prepared. The estate was committed to readying the muirs for their arrival. On two scores there were immediate difficulties. One was persuading the people to come to Achavandra; the other was the preparation of the ground. In September 1809, Falconer reported, disconsolately, that of the people scheduled for removal 'none of them would accept the offer' of muirland. They would not submit to the plan for their resettlement. There had also been conflict over the amount of building assistance to be given to the new settlers: Falconer said they had plenty of stone and timber for their new cottages and needed no further help.

The people were bridling and uncooperative. Falconer had provided 'a tolerable accommodation for the whole' but the response had been very poor. Now Young and Sellar had introduced additional plans for accommodating such people which would 'endeavour to force them into work'. But the people, said Falconer, were congenitally idle and 'only a determined plan will drive them to a change, and you cannot help if they leave the estate, if they obstinately resist any endeavour to connect them with work'. These were unmistakable symptoms of sullen opposition. Similar passive resistance had marked earlier removals on the Sutherland estate and in other parts of the Highlands as change was introduced into the glens and straths. Falconer was thoroughly jaundiced against the people who were, to an equal degree, stubborn or worse.

There was also evidence of emigration which, in the context of the time, gave the appearance of rejection and desertion. Most Highland landlords still feared and resisted the loss of population from their estates. Falconer said that, though none of the people recently removed had emigrated, others had taken

a freak into their heads to leave the country because they foresaw that they had not chance of possessions, did they remain, and there was a sort of discontent among them and also a stirring up by some disaffected persons which led to the embarkation.

Falconer thereby identified key signals of trouble: discontent, anticipatory emigration, a society in a stir and disaffection. In this fraught context, the estate plans in turmoil, Sellar and Young now offered their well-sought but gratuitous advice. Falconer was weary of the whole matter (though he had been in the factorship only a short time). He said that it did not matter much if the people went to America. In this Lady Stafford almost certainly continued to disagree. She regarded her factor's attitude as defeatist.

Falconer's pessimism contrasted dramatically with the enthusiasm of Sellar and Young. The ideas of the men from Moray addressed the critical question of accommodating the removees, evidently the most important single problem facing the estate and probably the greatest weakness in all the efforts to reform the Highlands in the age of the clearances. Falconer may already have been at the end of his tether on this very question. He was aware of the new ideas of Sellar and Young and appreciated their scale and expense. New fishing villages would be splendid, he agreed, but they would take much time to establish. Meanwhile the comprehensive 'removings' ought to be postponed. Their idea for spending substantial capital to employ removees on trenching at Achavandra would be equivalent to buying a small estate. It would create employment 'to the useful inhabitants' and, he added bitterly, it 'would at least shut their mouths against the clamours and prevent a plea of hardship'. Falconer could see little other than trouble for the estate plans, but he was not prepared to criticise the enthusiasm of the Moray men.

Young and Sellar, either oblivious of these difficulties or disregarding them as temporary hitches, continued to ply their special brand of optimism. In November 1809 Young again affirmed the potential of 'the improvable moors' at Achavandra. Intensive agriculture, plenty of wage labour and new cottages – helped by initial bounties – would demonstrate the new world of opportunity awaiting the people of the interior:

> However much it may astonish present inhabitants, I know that what may be cultivated and that advantageously on the finest soils in Sutherland, I scarcely see a boll that is the grain which would enrich the country and from which money, not intoxicating liquors, is to be got.

Young admitted that it might be necessary to 'stigmatise the slovenly', but the people would undoubtedly be happier on the coast and this, he kept repeating, was the ruling passion of the Stafford family – that is, 'the comfort of the people'.[64]

So far as Young and Sellar were concerned, the transition was not problematic. Secure, productive employment in a diversity of activities on the coast would arise; the desperate poverty, inefficiency and squalor of the inland peasantry would come to an end; famine would become historical. Sellar and Young recognised no tension in the required shift in status that faced the people when offered this new world of efficient commercial employment, that is, the exchange of peasant status for proletarian. Before their influence became decisive, it was already becoming evident that the people themselves were, at best, resistant. Some were already departing in advance of the much anticipated changes. These were the seeds of conflict which eventually placed Sellar in the shadow of the gallows.

− Falconer undermined −

In the last months of 1809, the advice of Sellar and Young shifted into a new gear which coincided with the swift undercutting of the existing and irresolute estate management of Cosmo Falconer. As early as August 1809, Sellar had made typically feline remarks which were certain to undermine the factor: 'We are well acquainted with Mr Falconer's good worth and Good Sense; but it is a weakness attending human nature, zealously to prosecute our own schemes rather than those which may be somewhat suggested by others, and it was a sense of this, and of the necessity of Mr Falconer feeling himself thoroughly at the head of affairs' that Mr Young made suggestions directly to Lord Gower.[65] Having taken a foothold with their own plan for Culmaily, they graduated towards a master plan for the entire rebirth of the coastal economy.

Young was clearly leading the advice proffered to the Stafford family. Sellar was the junior partner. But Sellar evidently commanded Young's confidence, perhaps in recognition of his legal expertise and his writing abilities. Sellar's distinctive imprint is identifiable in their rush of letters to the family. Young himself possessed an impressive range of business connections in Scotland and beyond, and could raise prospects of employment in many parts of the economy – from mining to fishing, from cotton manufactory to limestone supplies. He saw Sutherland as 'a new colony' with the greatest potential and one in which the natives could well be 'brought forward'. The marvellous attraction of his and Sellar's proposals was that they seemed to guarantee the reconciliation of the great contradiction in the emerging Highland economy: the coexistence of sheep-farming with the welfare of the existing population. The men from Moray repeatedly returned to Lady Stafford's avowed desire to succour the people. Large-scale investment by Lord Stafford in the infrastructure of the new economy would attract diversified development to the coast: the people would be retained and their future happiness secured. Their vision in 1809 was an embellishment and extension of the somewhat embryonic and unconvincing plans of the previous regime in the Sutherland management.[66]

– FALCONER UNDER SEIGE –

Though Cosmo Falconer nodded his assent, somewhat sceptically, to the increasingly grandiose suggestions of the Moray men, he advised great caution. Falconer was aware of the success of Young's fishing village at Inverugie. It would be feasible in Sutherland, but he warned: 'Such a change cannot be expected to be the work of a year. However, being begun, less could be said for the people if they allowed their prejudices to carry them away from the Estate.' This was a central point, but he advised that if the experiment was to be made, then the impending removals would best be postponed until the experiments were tested. His hesitancy and scepticism were transparent.[67] In October 1809 he had remarked: 'Nothing but work and plans for work to employ them, can meliorate the situation of the poorer classes and redeeming land by trenching seems a very probable plan to adopt for payment.' He was sceptical of Achavandra, but thought the plan for Kintradwell might succeed.[68] He said, in a mood of deepening pessimism, that if the Achavandra experiment failed, then the removals would have to be postponed. It was the very last type of advice that Lady Stafford wanted to hear.

It must have been obvious to Falconer that his own position would sooner or later become untenable. Indeed Young and Sellar were brutally frank about his failings. Having built up their visions of a new Sutherland – quadrupling rents, liberating the common people from the age-old slavery of peat-digging, the establishment of manufactories and the revolutionising of agriculture, and the creation of a new seaport, all this being imprinted by November 1809 – they pointed to the inadequacy of Falconer's management which stood in the way of a realisation of these splendid ideas. Young and Sellar said candidly that Cosmo Falconer could not possibly accomplish the scale and sophistication of plans that were now envisaged. He was blamed for the poor progress on the estate. He was personally and professionally ineffectual.

Three months later Patrick Sellar wrote to Lord Gower a further litany of criticisms of Falconer which seemed pregnant with premonitory meaning. Falconer, he remarked, had 'not bargained with the tenants' to persuade them to take up the coastal lots which had been prepared for their accommodation. More forcibly, and in characteristically italicised thinking, he added that 'we must carry through the plan, and if your Lordship give the fiat I shall pledge my head we do the business.' Most of all, he said, 'Mr Falconer has not properly courted the people.' Sellar, in these chillingly prophetic words, was evidently on the point of offering his own services where Falconer had failed.[69]

Falconer was under assault, indicted for his inability to carry through the plans for the resettlement of the small tenantry, which was the most difficult single issue in the general plan for the transformation of the estate which Sellar and Young were to expand dramatically. Sellar and Young believed that Falconer had been derelict in his duty to provide adequate facilities for the reception of removees from the interior. They even suggested that he had been, in some way, responsible for the large number of 'fever deaths' that had occurred in the county in May 1810. At Culmaily, the wright had made sixty-five coffins in great haste to deal with the emergency. Falconer, typically, had botched the arrangements:

> Where nature cannot provide food for the numbers, she sometimes suits the numbers to the food. The inhabitants who formerly occupied the extensive sheep walks in the interior are crammed, we understand, into hamlets there, without any new tract being pointed out for their industry, and wanting, we fear, the full supply they formerly engaged on their boundless pastures – depression, sloth, filth, are the consequences – disease follows; contagion spreads, and where all are predestinarians careless of precaution, and little medical aid is to be procured, it is not wonderful that much mischief is done.

Later, in the same year, Sellar alleged that Falconer had been guilty of commercial sharp practice for his own benefit and against the interests of the people and the landlord. Falconer, he claimed, had forbidden a storekeeper from selling meal until Falconer had sold his own stock even though the storekeeper was in the service of the Stafford family.[70]

This was a savage indictment of Falconer. The allegations owed more to Sellar than to Young. The invocation of the new Malthusianism, combined with high moral indignation, bore the hallmarks of Sellar's particular intellect. Nor was he able to contain his sarcasm towards the religious faith of the people. Sellar's scorn for the old Highland system was total.

The Stafford family was not simply bedazzled by the shining re-commendations and enthusiasm offered so freely, and with such optimism, by the experienced men of Moray. Young and Sellar spoke Lady Stafford's own language and their advice fitted her own plans perfectly. Two years after her first encounter with the Moray men, Lady Stafford announced her delight with the arrangement which they had just reached. As she told her regular confidant, Walter Scott, she was full of expectation from 'our Scotch Factor':

> I have great hopes at present from the abilities of this Mr Young, of considerable improvements being effected in Sutherland and without routing and destroying the old inhabitants, which contrary to the Theories respecting the matter, I am convinced is very possible.[71]

Few in the Highlands believed that sheep-farming could be halted. Young and Sellar, Lady Stafford announced, could make the new system operational without 'routing and destroying the old inhabitants'. This was the crux of the matter. The improvers from Moray told the Staffords precisely what they were so eager to hear.[72]

CHAPTER 4

The Installation

– THE EYE OF A NEEDLE –

In the winter of 1809–10, Sellar and Young organised their own operations at the Culmaily farm in Sutherland. But there were now larger possibilities on their new horizons. They continued to ply the Stafford family with enthusiastic advice about the improvement plans for the great estate which were moving too slowly for their desires. With each communication, the influence of Young and Sellar grew. They soon began to overtake Cosmo Falconer as the cental instrument in the revitalised policy. Falconer, with some dignity, bowed to the inevitable, though he was, in the process, deeply humiliated.

While the subversion of Falconer developed through 1810, Sellar continued his legal practice in Elgin.[1] Landed proprietors in his own district employed him to collect rent, summons rent defaulters and, increasingly, to order and execute removals. He took instructions from estate factors and their lawyers and implemented the least popular aspects of estate policy. In March 1810, he enforced removals on the Invershie estate, summonsing rent defaulters and wrestling with tenants' rights where a landlord wanted immediate access. Sellar was cutting his factorial teeth very effectively. He was also heavily involved in the highly contentious business of road construction. The implementation of the Road Fund in the Highlands generated endless legal controversy between Highland landowners over their responsibilities and financial contributions. Sellar was severely critical of prevailing political attitudes and *mores* and he ventilated some of his opinions to William Young in Spring 1810. Of a local road project, he remarked: 'It is heart-breaking to see now that this most beneficial measure has been thwarted'. More generally, he said that 'Even in this cold latitude', thinking people possessed 'a firm attachment and loyalty – to their last shilling'. But, like himself, they were equally passionate in their 'detestation towards the placemen and obsequious beef eaters [*sic*], who are the only formidable enemies of their Country . . . The cause is John Bull versus sinecure places.'[2]

Sellar maintained a prolific correspondence at this time, usually enlivened by his characteristically robust turn of phrase and frequently critical of society around him. Thus in November 1809 he had denounced the inefficiency of small tenants in Sutherland who wasted their families' efforts gathering peats instead of specialising in more useful kinds of labour. Such misapplied labour led to debt, the tenant quickly becoming oppressed by his circumstances, and 'his children are a dead weight upon him, till taken off by the Recruiting Sergeant'.[3]

As Sellar railed against the enemies of progress, his own affairs were becoming increasingly complicated, not only through his legal practice but through his involvement with his father's heavily capitalised ventures at Westfield and Burghead in Moray (as we have seen in Chapter 2). By 1810 he was also committed with Young to the new operations on the Culmaily farm in eastern Sutherland. He was a man of affairs, corresponding freely with the local aristocracy and now on close terms with the richest and most powerful family in the north. Larger visions in Sutherland were in the offing and the main residual impediment was Cosmo Falconer, of whom Sellar possessed a rapidly deteriorating opinion. His criticisms of Falconer were increasingly severe and urgent and soon became ruthless, but they also presaged the dangers which his own impatience towards the people at Culmaily and elsewhere eventually would pose. The fact that Falconer had already failed in his dealings with the people emphasised the extreme sensitivity of the question. By February 1810, Sellar was virtually assuming that he and Young would replace Falconer, though he remained coy about going over Falconer's head for many months yet.[4]

The critical moment for Falconer arrived in July 1810 when Lady Stafford made her seasonal journey to the north of Scotland. *En route,* she visited William Young at his own estate at Inverugie in Moray. She was greatly impressed with what she saw at Inverugie and reported to her husband: 'We have got acquainted with Mr Young, a grave sensible intelligent man, and I think one of wonderful ability. I wish you could see the farms he has reclaimed from Deserts'. His achievements were palpable: 'I cannot call him an Enthusiast for he is a grave man, but his mind seems totally wrapt up in carrying the same system to Sutherland'.[5] Young had remarked that he could not comprehend why the

Sutherland estate which, under Falconer, 'hardly remits anything', did not yield £24,000 per annum. He had also said that everyone knew that Falconer was 'honest and well-meaning', but he was becoming increasing indolent and immobile, and he 'had no head for general arrangements'. Then, in the next breath, Young alleged that Falconer was wasting money and getting rich at the expense of the family. There was simply no hope of any advance under Falconer. As for Young himself, Lady Stafford told her husband:

> I think you will like him very much, there is so much decency and propriety with such a *connaissance de cause* about him.

Young, in Moray, had obviously enriched himself and all about him. Young had said that there was 'a tide at work which he happened to understand: in short he is a mine of knowledge and practice'. Lady Stafford was impressed by everything she saw in Moray: it was so reminiscent of England and the clean and active people in the south. Young told her openly that he could make Golspie a flourishing place 'which will turn all things upside down, but he says the people will be no disturbance and will put a vast deal of money in our hands.'[6] It was irresistible.

Young and Sellar had already told Lady Stafford bluntly that her great agenda required

> unabating zeal, patient vigilance, conciliating conduct, and continued alacrity in your Ladyship's man or men of business to accomplish them . . . And We, candidly, assure you, that we no more See how these things are to be carried thro' under the present management, than how 'a Camel is to go thro' the Eye of a needle'. We, of course write to your Ladyship <u>in confidence</u>. We should be sorry to have any person think us inimical; for we are far from being so, tho' in saying so much, the execution of which may be attempted, it becomes a duty to dissemble nothing from your Ladyship.[7]

Lady Stafford described William Young to her husband as a '*homo gravis and seriosus*: I try to look wise and grave also and not appear childish and trifling'. Young had remarked that Falconer knew 'but little of Turnips and Mankind'. At this point, in July 1810, Lady Stafford still thought of retaining Falconer, with Young to mastermind the greater plan. She concurred with Young, when he 'says what I have always thought, that you cannot turn poor People however industrious into a bare field and desire them to build houses and settle there'. They needed great assistance in the preparation of the new settlements and would need to be employed as labourers if they were to pay rent.

She agreed that 'the idle' might not choose to accept this and would go elsewhere, and 'that certain widows and old helpless Persons must be suffered to dye out, which occasions the necessity for a change being more gradual.' Thus were the arguments and plans rehearsed in mid-1810 by the owner and her new and energetic advisers.[8]

During the July 1810 visit to Inverugie, Young had comported himself with great deference, but his destruction of Falconer was clinical.[9] In August Falconer accepted the termination of his commission. He would be replaced, at the following Whitsunday, by Young and Sellar who would become the new factorial management. William Mackenzie, the family's legal adviser, described Young and Sellar in the warmest terms and told Lady Stafford: 'They unite together everything calculated to ensure your unqualified approbation.' Their appointment would solve the estate's central problem. This was 'the want of an active and well directed mind to set the whole in motion'. Falconer took his dismissal hard, and when he wrote his valedictory letter, he confessed to 'the tears which have dropt since I took up the pen'.[10]

Falconer conceded that Young and Sellar were 'men of enterprise' and that Young had shown 'disinterested . . . zeal for improvement'. But Sellar, he sharply volunteered, was different. Falconer, no doubt a disappointed man with a chip on his shoulder, now singled out Sellar for special comment. Sellar was:

> A raw inexperienced young man [who] could . . . have no claim to the honour your Lordship and Family have conferred but from the casual connection with the other in an adventure in this Country in which self-interest as on the other side of the water, stimulates zeal.

Sellar had evidently made an enemy already. Both Young and Sellar were so much taken up with their Moray concerns that they 'must be dogged with their own distant Concerns'. The magnitude of the task in Sutherland, Falconer warned, demanded total commitment, including permanent residence.[11]

William Young and Sellar soon took up residence near Golspie, thus confounding Falconer's suggestion that they would lack local connection. Later in the year, Young himself painted a picture of his young colleague. Sellar, he noted, would be most useful in the estate's business and should have extra duties. He told Lady Stafford:

> He is quite a bustler and would do remarkably well among the Fishermen and Kelp makers during the busy Season; and altho' not Agriculturalists, abilities in that way are not wanted. In these places he would be quite in the

Centre of all, and after the Farms are laid out he would only have to improve the shores which I believe suits his turn exactly.

Such duties would allow Sellar to return to Elgin for the winters. Young's advice suggested that Sellar's energies would be best channelled into strictly practical matters.

– The transitional management –

The introduction of the new management was subject to a long transition before the final departure of Falconer at Whitsunday 1811. This itself caused confusion and frustration, especially for Sellar. The original discussions described Young and Sellar in anachronistic terms as 'Joint Chamberlains' and there was a serious lack of clarity about the precise apportionment of their duties. The role of the Sutherland factors, as described by R. J. Adam, was invested with considerable status and clout. The factor was accorded great local autonomy and was like 'a great medieval lord's bailiff' – a substantial figure in local society, mixing on at least equal terms with the large tacksmen, and usually occupying a large farm rented from the estate as part of the contract.[12] William Young was thus appointed 'Commissioner' to carry on 'the progressive improvements' on the estates. In the new regime, he was given primary control.[13] The position gave him specific authority to remove tenants at the expiration of leases. He was explicitly invested with 'sole power and management' with a salary of £750 per annum. He would be 'general manager'.

Sellar for his part, was given precise responsibilities:

> to collect the rents, keep accounts of the expenditure, pay attention to the various rights of the tenants, to their fulfilment of the conditions of their Tacks, to the enforcing of the laws for preserving the plantations and the Game, transactions with Ministers and Schoolmasters, framing Tacks and other writings.[14]

In effect, Sellar was charged with the task of collecting the income of the estate and channelling the funds to Young to provide the means of financing the estate improvements. One of the clauses required them

> to exert themselves to quash all Law suits and quarrels among the tenants, so far as it may be prudent for them to interfere.

Sellar's domain was rent collection and the removal of tenants, accounting expenditure, negotiating with tenants, arranging plantations and game, and conveyancing. Sellar's legal training gave him special experience in arranging estate papers and this was a distinct advantage in the greatly increased legal transactions of the estate.[15] His dealings with the people of the estate, however, were impeded by his lack of Gaelic.[16] Sellar and Young were responsible for distinct spheres, but the line of control was not specific. The managerial arrangement, to the annoyance of the estate's lawyers, was not fully vetted at the time.[17] Sellar's salary was £275 per annum and the agreement was finalised in February 1811, at a time when the two men were hardly able to agree on their own affairs at Culmaily. Young's salary was more than double that of Sellar, which reflected their relative importance in the eyes of the Stafford family.[18] Sellar undoubtedly felt aggrieved about his lower status and his complaints caused great irritation with the family, even before the agreement came into effect.

Sellar was touchy, ambitious and monopolistic by nature. He was not content to accept a secondary role in relation to Young. In any case, Sellar possessed an ingrained tendency to generate bad blood. He fell out with associates at all levels. Thus in 1811 he ran into conflict over his Culmaily lease with the estate's main legal adviser, William Mackenzie. The resultant enmity against Mackenzie was sustained for many years.[19] Similarly, in the first year of his work on the estate, Sellar locked horns with Robert Leith, a tenant in Culgower, over Sellar's right to take seaweed from the beach after a storm. Leith, who leased the kelp rights, sought legal redress but backed down when he realised that Sellar would contest the issue beyond the actual value of the kelp in question.[20] In October 1812 Sellar had a blazing row with a ferryman who had failed to disembark Sellar's horse to Sellar's satisfaction. Sellar thought he had been insolent and wanted him sacked. Young found this harsh, especially since he was an excellent ferryman. Both Young and Mackid had been involved in the episode.[21]

Much more serious was the accumulation of tension between Young and Sellar themselves. It developed almost immediately their new administration began in mid-1811. The disagreement sprang from a demarcation dispute about the extent of their respective responsibilities. Young tried to persuade Sellar to confine his planning advice to his operations at Culmaily, but Sellar resisted the idea. Young remarked, 'until now [Sellar] has been anxious for Farming concerns and has plenty of time to attend them'. Sellar pressed to be involved in the central estate plan, which Young regarded as his own province. Simmering resentment soon broke surface. In June 1811 Sellar was engaged in rent-collecting about the estate. He wrote to Lady Stafford about his collection in Strathnaver in typically tendentious terms: he had been 'endeavouring to find some money to answer Mr Young's demands but with very little success, as the tenants have not yet Sold their Cattle and it is to no purpose to distress them.'[22] Meanwhile he was already strengthening the game-keeping aspect of his work. In the middle of this detailed reporting, he made allegations that Young was trying to displace him from his factorship. Sellar then aggravated the conflict by protesting to Lady Stafford that Young had required him to employ two of his own nephews in his office.[23] In the following month, July 1811, the matter came to the boil. Sellar complained directly to Lady Stafford that he was losing his authority and that the formal agreement was not being honoured. For his part, Young regarded Sellar as too forceful and pedantic in his dealings on the estate.

Lady Stafford was exasperated by Sellar's attitude and was seriously inclined to dismiss him within a few months of his installation. She thought of seeking Sellar's resignation. She wrote, 'Sellar has no sense and perhaps we may be as well without him; it is quite ridiculous that from a jealousy which I see he entertains of Young's nephew that he should go on in this manner'. The squabble, and lack of communication between the two men, was intolerable. She told Lord Gower unequivocally that 'Young is the important person, the other is nothing without him and would never have been there but for him'. She said that unless Sellar accepted the position, they would be better off without him altogether. She saw Sellar as 'a clever writer and accountant, and very zealous, but I should think perhaps at times too much so without direction.' Sellar had to be told that he was 'only subordinate to Young and not an independent Factor'. It was imperative that Sellar be kept 'within bounds'. In July 1811, she unambiguously instructed Sellar that Young was in general control. Yet Sellar persistently questioned this clarification – indeed three times he protested before eventually accepting the directive. All this initial acrimony consumed much time and energy, and soured feelings, at a critical moment in the consolidation of the new agency.[24]

Young emerged triumphant. At the end of 1811, Lady Stafford was assured of the virtues of her new manager by her legal adviser, William Mackenzie, who said, 'he will prove exactly the Character of man who in the present situation of the Sutherland estate could alone bring out quietly the resources it possesses.'[25] But the dispute between Young and Sellar was an unhappy start to the new regime and exposed aspects of Sellar's personality, long before he clashed with the general populace of Sutherland. It also anticipated the extreme difficulties of administering the great plan when the agency itself was divided and ill-tempered about its internal territorial demarcations.

Sellar continued to chafe against Lady Stafford's ruling about his status. His own response to his newly defined functions was little short of operatic. He was now placed, he protested, in a most painful predicament. His work, the detail of rent collection in particular, attracted 'odium' among the people of the estate, yet he was not allowed to exercise his own discretion. He told Young 'that [he] did not come to the Country as his Clerk'. The original agreement had given him much more authority. He besought Lady Stafford to 'save me from this disgrace', that of receiving her orders at second-hand. He assured her that he could look after his own department. As Sellar saw it, he did all the unpopular work of rent collection and removal, while Young spent the estate's income with abandon. A year later, he described himself, with some scorn, as 'the organ merely by which the Family's rents are brought in, and paid away by the decision of others.' His transparent ambition and frustration shone through his letters and his persistent sarcasm irritated all his superiors.[26]

The tension between Sellar and Young was compounded by a new disagreement over the tenancy of the Culmaily farm (together with Morvich). This was originally a joint-venture, but Sellar now demanded a separation. His preference was to take the adjacent farm of Morvich but, with poor grace, he accepted Culmaily in his own name. Culmaily was, in reality, too large for his capital. Sellar was forced to raise credit to stock the farm and he eventually received a large loan from Lord Stafford at 6 per cent interest. This was a critical moment since it tied more closely together the fortunes of Sellar with those of the Stafford family.[27]

Despite internal divisions in the management, the style and direction of the new team was quickly made public. It was clear that Young's grand plan had been accepted, apparently in toto. Young would consolidate and accelerate the sheep system and create a parallel economy for the people displaced. As early as September 1810 he said that Strathnaver was 'only adapted for the Sheep system'.[28] He was emphatic that only a gradual sequence of change would succeed. But 'with sufficient notice to the present occupants to provide themselves, the hardship ought to be less felt'. The anticipation of hardship for the people was openly recognised.[29]

Within a few months, Young had stamped his imprint on local opinion to such an extent that even critics of the sheep-farming culture were lauding the Sutherland system, now clearly to be associated with

William Young. Thus John Henderson, in his *General View of the Agriculture of Sutherland* (1811), was already able to commend the programme which was 'on a scale perhaps more extensive than has hitherto been attempted in the North'. Once more the point was made that the Stafford family was introducing sheep-farming without decreasing the population:

> Situations in various ways will be fixed for the people. Fishing villages in which mechanics will be settled; inland villages with carding machines; moors and detached spots calculated for the purpose, will be found, but the people must work.

Henderson had evidently been well-briefed by the new management: 'The industrious will be encouraged and protected, but the slothful must remove or starve, as man was not born to be idle, but to gain bread by the sweat of his brow.' The language here was that of the improvers and was unambiguously also that of confrontation. If the people did not cooperate in their new design then they would simply be evicted, or left to their own pitiful devices. Henderson gave his *imprimatur* to the Sutherland estate plan which would

> tend most effectively to increase the number, as well as the comfort and happiness of the population of this country; and whilst it will put an end to emigration, sheep-farming may be extended in the interior of the country; thus increasing the wealth and resources in a pecuniary and political point of view.

People and sheep would coexist and emigration would simply dry up.[30]

There was a lengthy delay before Falconer's factorship terminated at Whitsunday 1811 and Sellar, in particular, felt frustrated by Falconer's leisurely ways and his retention of legal responsibility. But the flow of extra funds from Lord Stafford to the new regime was set in motion before its formal installation. Young now controlled the pace, the direction and, indeed, the detailed plans. These soon included coal-mining at Brora, preparations for salt manufacture, and carding operations too – though, Young stressed, this was merely 'a prelude to more extensive manufactures'. Fishing settlements were emerging; cottages were being built to attract fishermen from other parts of eastern Scotland. The settlements would set a model for the local people, encouraged also by the recent favourable shifts in the seasonal migration patterns of the herring shoals whose behaviour was a recurring problem for planners in the Highlands throughout these years.[31]

As the agenda of improvement evolved, and while Young and Gower examined southern models of enterprise, the day-to-day management was left in the hands of Falconer, with Patrick Sellar critical of his every move. Falconer possessed no 'method' and Sellar complained of the 'unsettled state of arrangements' which he said were almost 'crippling my future progress'. As for himself, he told Gower: 'Humbly trusting that if I err, or my zeal exceeds my prudence in any thing my noble employers will state such to me that I may correct it, and avoid mistakes.' He still wanted his functions to be more clearly distinguished from those of Young.[32]

While Falconer 'continues to govern', said Sellar, 'and I want for proper constables, I cannot proceed with effect in checking poaching. Your Lordship will see from the Inverness Journal that I have done everything in the way of menace.' Sellar said he would, meanwhile, 'proceed with a firm hand in the Removings and whatever else comprises our duty.' He was already confronting practical and recurrent problems with the rearrangements, with people claiming rights to the lands, some with 'pretended Tacks [that is, lease agreements] said to have been given' by Falconer. All this complicated Sellar's work. By January 1811, he was organising his own complex lease for Morvich and Culmaily.[33] He had employed a young man from Ballindalloch as a ground officer for Strathnaver, and he was 'perfecting himself in Gaelic', in readiness.[34] Sellar dined with Falconer, who had been obliging, communicative and friendly, but wanted to retain the lease of Rhives, which the factor normally occupied.[35] The same day, Sellar complained that 'the present unsettled state of arrangements here . . . [is] crippling my future progress'.[36] He also said, 'I find Mr Falconer so tedious, and his movements attended with so much difficulty, that I defer further procedure concerning the state of the tenants.'[37] Sellar told Lord Gower that Falconer rarely gave more than six hours a day to his duties.[38] He was fat, lazy and incompetent.

Sellar had pressed Falconer to implement outstanding removals in January 1811. Sellar informed Gower that full factorial authority was required before real progress could be made. He was pushing hard: 'The legal forms of these removings require to be immediately gone through; and as it is, really impossible to attend to them or any thing else while all credentials are vested in the person of Mr Falconer.' Sellar's was the authentic voice of urgency in the improvements. There was no ambiguity or subtlety in his advice: it was imperative that the management 'limit Mr Falconer to his proper duty, which is, the winding up his affairs.' Meanwhile, it was clear that Sellar and Young were, in Sellar's direct language, 'to proceed with a firm hand in the

Removings'. In the same letter, Sellar referred to the impending arrival of a doctor seeking to circulate the Bible among the people, which Sellar described as:

> the pure morality and Sublime ideas which tend in their opinion to the benefit of mankind. When we think back on the days of Martin Luther and think what the circulation of this book has done, to Substitute sense and goodness for the Claims of Bigotry and Superstition, we can scarcely deny our approbation of the patriotism of these gentlemen.[39]

There was iron in Sellar's opinions, a firmness based upon precept and morality. His thinking owed a great deal to the thinkers of the Enlightenment, to Benjamin Franklin, and, of course, to his particular reading of the Bible.

At the same time, Sellar reported, with typical enthusiasm, about the improvement methods being used at Westfield and elsewhere in Moray. He spoke of the progress which had been achieved by Rothie-murchus. Sellar exclaimed that had such a man as Rothiemurchus not taken the high road to improvement he would 'have been a lieutenant in a marching regiment, seeking the employment of such a family as your Lordship's'. Instead, great wealth was being generated by the new ways of thinking in the district. As for Falconer's plans for cottager settlement at Achavandra, Sellar calculated that it would cost £50 per family, £5,000 for 100 families' and 'there are many thousand families to provide for in Sutherland.' He said it would have to be done more cheaply and gradually.

In these initial stages, Young and Sellar were establishing their priorities, amid the general imperatives imposed by Lady Stafford's own radical agenda of change in Sutherland. Certain words recurred in their deliberations. It was vital that the coming removals be undertaken 'with humanity', and that the policy be pursued 'gradually'. Both words had elastic meanings; actions regarded by Sellar as 'humane' and 'gradual' were seen as brutal and precipitate by the defenders of the *status quo* and by the advocates of the people in the inland glens.[40]

– GOOD INTENTIONS –

At Whitsunday 1811, Young and Sellar were in full command of the northern empire of the Sutherland estate. Lady Stafford's plans had matured, and now arrangements proceeded towards a new and much larger round of clearances and the creation of resettlement facilities. William Young was full of confidence.

Emigration, in the context of removals, was always an awkward matter because it indicated a failure of the resettlement promises as well as the resistance of the people to the grand Sutherland plan. It was bad publicity and poor for morale. But Young was robust on the issue. He declared: 'I . . . at present have no fear of emigration from any part of your Ladyship's domains.' Discontented or restless fools might go off the estate, 'but people in general have sense enough to see what is for their interest, and with every reluctancy to labour, will at last follow our plans.'[41]

Sellar, since his arrival in Sutherland, had also been converted to the Sutherland system. Despite his later protestations (that he had despised sheep-farming when he first arrived in the county[42]), one of Sellar's first pieces of advice to Lady Stafford, in August 1809, had been to extol the great potential of merino stock for her estate. He said that 'the great part' of the estate was best suited to wool, its great 'staple'. His conversion to sheep-farming, within a few months of his first exposure to Sutherland conditions, was therefore extraordinarily swift and complete, though he later remarked that it was 'the mildew of 1812 that convinced us of the impolicy of keeping a highland population on land fit only for grass.' His own letters show that he had been convinced of this opinion long before the mildew.[43] But in the first years of management, Sellar was factor/farmer but not yet a sheep-farmer.

By 1811, the blueprint for improvement was complete. The most intensive plans concerned the east coast arable/fishing/industrial complexes, designed to provide accommodation for 'settlers' from the inland. No other landlord in the Highlands had ever adopted such an expensive and elaborate policy to provide for the small tenantry. Though upon a less ambitious scale, development was also planned along the more distant north coast and in the west at Scourie. The seriousness of these resettlement plans was soon to be heavily underscored by major land acquisitions by Lord Stafford. The adjacent estates of Armadale and Strathy were swallowed up in 1812–13, the main purpose being to secure more coastside territory specifically and expressly to cope with the coerced inflow of settlers from the interior clearances. Lady Stafford was pleased with the purchase of the Armadale estate for £25,000 and celebrated the event. Young, though glad to get the new terrain, thought the price had been a shade too high.[44]

In parallel formation were the removal plans for the interior people which eventually entailed the partition of several hundred thousand acres into vast new sheep-farms. The timetable was determined by the expiration of existing leases. The schedule involved lands from Assynt in the west to Strathnaver in the north and to Kildonan in the east. In all these great dislocations, William Young relied on Patrick Sellar to execute the changes. Sellar dealt face to face with the people to be removed. The integrated redevelopment of the inland and littoral economies depended on synchronised timing. In particular, the plans required the preparation of the coastal 'lots' for the resettled people. It also depended on the persuasion and cooperation of the people themselves. This was Sellar's central responsibility which, he claimed, required many tours over the inland townships, which enabled him to know exactly how to deal with the people in question.

Sellar was now thirty years old, unmarried but already established at Culmaily. He was certainly a man of means, invested with considerable authority as a Justice of the Peace and as a factor. In March 1811, Sellar was admitted as procurator and agent before the Dornoch Sheriff Court.[45] He was probably up to his limit in debt, receiving financial assistance from his ageing father and from his legal work in Moray. In the exercise of this authority, especially in the context of the great changes on his Sutherland bailiwick, Sellar expressed a stream of good intentions. He was highly critical of the current state of the people but he was emphatically solicitous in his utterances. In few of his remarks in the early stages can we detect the seeds of explosive confrontation that would eventually mark his dealings with the people. Much of what he said was couched in terms of elaborate benevolence. In August 1810, for instance, Sellar told Lord Gower that honey should be encouraged as an excellent supplement to the simple economy of the common people. He arranged for the distribution of hives among them. With typically heavy emphasis, he remarked: 'attention on behalf of the people to these simple matters is indispensably necessary; and though attended with less glory, possibly they bring more pleasure than the butchery or oppression of thousands of our fellow creatures.' These comments almost certainly expressed a sincere, if condescending, self-belief about his good intentions and benevolent ideals.

Throughout his life, despite extraordinary turbulence and public criticism, Sellar maintained a consistent moral confidence. Moreover, he was, from the start, perfectly aware of the danger of popular turmoil inherent in the impending structural changes in Sutherland. He was remarkably assured that, where others had behaved badly and inhumanely, he (and the Sutherland regime) would be beyond such 'butchery and oppression'. His motives and philosophy were, in his view, pure and entirely rational.[46] More questionable was the matching of his zeal with his patience.

– PREPARATIONS FOR REMOVALS –

One of Sellar's first tasks as factor was to prepare a new account of the estate, virtually a Domesday Book of its arrangements prior to the great new removals. Sellar immediately told Lady Stafford that the prevailing system was an appalling mess, and had been so since 1769. Moreover, the previous factors' papers were generally 'in such barbarous confusion' that his first task was to sort them out. Being meticulous and assiduous, Sellar immediately uncovered every variety of anomaly, irregularity and informality in the prevailing arrangements. The confusion he came upon in the office was utterly anathema to his tidy, probing mind. Inevitably, in the process, he aroused the greatest suspicion and anxiety wherever he pried.[47]

In March and April 1811, Sellar was occupied searching and regularising the existing leases on the estate. His task required a full schedule of properties and the state of the tacks which governed the disposition of the estate, specifically in terms of their prospective improvement. The termination dates of the leases, of course, provided a timetable for 'improvement', a schedule of access for the landlord.[48] It would also chart the removal of the people from the straths, a prospect certain to put fear into the minds of the people. It was an exercise extremely well suited to Sellar's methodical way of thinking, and it yielded a document which was clearly based on the assumption that most of the population possessed no rights whatever to the land, moral or legal. Indeed, every individual report per property on the estate contained the line, 'Matters requiring attention at removal'. At only one point in the survey did Sellar make specific reference to 'the practice of the Country', and this was relevant only to the disposal of moveable property. Sellar believed that existing 'regulations' were unambiguous. The law was perfectly clear that the end of a lease or tack gave the proprietor complete authority to redeploy the land in whatever way she desired.

Radical changes in tenancies had been occurring for more than a decade on the Sutherland estate and large sheep-farms, such as that at Shiness, had already been created in the 1807–8 removals. Sellar's survey of 1811 demonstrated the extraordinary increase of rents that attended such changes. It also documented the erosion of the final remnants of feudal arrangements of the estate, such as the conversion of services to money rents during the time of the Countess's minority.[49] One of Sellar's tasks was to codify the regulations governing small tenants, which he did with his usual precision.[50] The tenantry would henceforth be ruled by regulations; the sloppy ways of the old estate management would cease. His document was unambiguous about procedures on the termination of leases, and his careful register of the leases was designed to provide 'peaceable possession' for new tenants.[51]

By mid-April 1811, Sellar had finalised his great review of tenancies, while Young had prepared lots in many parts of the estate ready for further clearances.[52] Sellar inevitably discovered further extraordinary anomalies in the rentals. His next task was to attack arrears across the estate.

While William Young travelled to England with Lord Gower and Telford to inspect the latest technical advances in mining, drainage and estate management, Sellar further explored the mountains and straths of the vast Sutherland estate. His own commercial instincts were aroused. Sellar was quickly educating himself in the ways of the pastoral economy and, in March 1812, he met Anthony Marshall, one of the great new sheep-farmers. Sellar was clearly impressed by his demeanour, knowledge and acumen: 'He is a sharp clever man, knows every spot in the Country and every point to be attended to in it most minutely, and will not I suspect Give up any thing without very good recompense.'[53] He regarded Marshall as the very model of enterprise and commercial rigour. At this time Sellar began to see the possibilities of sheep-farming as a use of his own capital and energies. Meanwhile all his duties gave him scope for argument and conflict with his neighbours, his colleagues and with miscreants, wherever he could find them.

Before Christmas 1811, Sellar was engaged in collecting rents and arrears, chasing poachers, muirburners and woodstealers. He could not have been popular. Returning from the interior, he reported:

> The Strathnaver people are very bad payers and seem totally inactive, following the business of eating and drinking more than their farms, and there is much need for some new arrangement among them. The greater part of the Young men of Kildonan have been abroad this last summer at the roads and to the public works and their rents have been paid well.

Cattle sales had been buoyant and he expected good rents, but Sellar was highly critical of the persistence of rent payments in kind, which he regarded as the antiquated and barbaric relic of a feudal past.[54]

Another feudal anachronism was Gaelic. Sellar believed that Gaelic was a dying language and an impediment to progress in the Highlands. He said that the working people should not be required to learn the grammar of two languages and it was, therefore, foolish to teach Gaelic in school. All the advances in science were in English only (he took an equally dismissive view of indigenous literature): 'I would therefore suppress the reading of Gaelic, and induce the study of English as much as possible.'[55] Sellar's views were at their most scornful when they touched on the subject of Gaelic and they guaranteed maximum offence among the defenders of the old society and its culture.

The new regime of Young and Sellar began to sweep away the previous system of management and with it many of its unofficial and informal local arrangements. Sellar reserved some of his greatest indignation for the manner in which the estate had dealt with the question of 'the preservation of the Game' which was now his direct responsibility. It was an intensely sensitive matter for the estate and the community. In Dunrobin Glen, for example, the game was repeatedly disturbed by the tenants' dogs. Sellar declared, 'it humbly occurs to me, that it should be cleared of all this.' People, dogs and game were not compatible.[56]

Sellar thus stretched his wings in Sutherland affairs, establishing his authority in all quarters. In early 1812 he was preparing to set up a Sutherland Farmers' Club (on the model of the Moray body of which he was secretary) and he established a library for the collective good. He was heavily involved with the factor's work and was advocating trials with the new merino sheep in the county. He was particularly alert to commercial possibilities, citing the case of a young East Lothian farmer who had settled in the north some twenty years before and 'has made a fortune of some £10,000 by vigilant attention and judicious adventure in farming.'[57]

The scale of the removal plans being organised in spring 1812 was immense and Sellar laboured meticulously at the preparation of the legal papers. He mentioned in March that, 'The number of persons for whom I have prepared and sent Charges for Removal is 836 besides subtenants.' This figure probably related to families and consequently the number of individuals involved would have been a multiple of 836, together with the sub-tenants and squatters (the unofficial population of the estate).[58]

As plans for the dramatic new removals were maturing during 1811 and 1812, the jealousies in Sellar's relations with William Young continued to unsettle their working arrangements. In February 1811, the matter came to a head when they disagreed seriously about their respective participation in the farms at Culmaily and Morvich. Young wanted to extricate himself from the partnership, probably realising that Sellar would be too difficult to work with. During the course of the conflict, Sellar made a number of sharply-worded remarks against Young regarding 'the volatility and sanguine temper of my friend'.[59] He pointedly remarked to Lord Gower that Young and Robert Mackid were involved in some joint timber business, which Sellar had refused to join, and which turned out unsuccessful.[60] In another letter, Sellar again described his partner as 'volatile, sanguine and keen in his conceptions'. With a hint of a sneer, he remarked, 'I could not follow the Quick Succession to his [Young's] ideas'. It is difficult to imagine much warmth remaining in his relations with Young after their disagreement so early in their work for the Sutherland estate.[61]

Further antagonisms between Sellar and Young recurred in April 1812. Sellar undertook the unpopular work of gathering rents and organising removals while Young spent the proceeds in a way which Sellar regarded as prodigal and poorly accounted. Though clothing his reports with embarrassment, Sellar was simply unable to restrain his criticism of his superior.[62] Sellar also declared that he hoped his own zeal would not exceed his prudence, which suggested a certain realistic self-awareness. One of Sellar's main missions, in May 1812, was to apply much stronger prohibitions to illegal distilling on the estate, partly justified, in this instance, by the onset of famine conditions.[63] Sellar complained that he was being held up by Young's indecision. There was a symbolic moment, in February 1811, when he sent Lord Stafford some gold and silver coins which had been picked up in Strathnaver, adding, 'I hope by and bye to become better acquainted with that country.'[64]

The late spring of 1812 was a time of food shortage in Sutherland and it again verged on famine in some parts. As usual, the estate took precautions to maintain the supply of imported meal. Sellar circulated the ministers of the church requesting the numbers of their respective parishioners who might need to be fed following the 'most alarming appearance of Scarcity'. He was critical of the people for being in this position, since they had been warned of the risk in the previous autumn. Now it could only be mitigated by 'every family adopting the most careful economy', together with the suppression of distilling, and by everyone planting as many potatoes as possible. By mid-May, however, Sellar was able to report that 'the snow is breaking up in the mountains and the vegetation proceeding almost visibly.'[65]

– TROUBLE WITH MACKID –

While Sellar conducted much of the harsh work of estate administration and maintained his uneasy working relations with William Young, he also embarked on the most dangerous conflict of his life. Robert Mackid was Sheriff-Substitute of Sutherland, the chief resident law officer in the county. He was also a close neighbour of Sellar in Golspie, where he held the farm of Kirkton. Their respective positions inevitably meant a considerable overlapping of business. Sellar saw himself as the enemy of corruption and lawbreaking at large. He was, therefore, closely interested in Mackid's own professional responsibilities.

The conflict between Sellar and Robert Mackid began to bubble as soon as Sellar delved into the day-to-day details of estate management. Sellar immoderately found fault with Mackid when he uncovered the prevailing *modus vivendi* of the estate. In no time Sellar, his antennae fully extended, detected the acrid air of petty corruption and bad practice. The Road Fund and its administration particularly attracted his attention. The Fund required contributions from heritors and its collection was always a problem. Now it was a shambles. As early as February 1811, Sellar discovered a great backlog in the fund's collections. The responsible local official was Robert Mackid who had been appointed clerk to the JP after the death, by drowning, of his predecessor in August 1809. The mess of inefficiency in the Road Fund was the perfect challenge to Sellar's quest for order. Four-fifths of the funds had not been collected and the situation was 'in the worst state possible'. Sellar suggested that Mackid's commission should be terminated, and he immediately suggested replacements.[66]

At the same time, Sellar emphasised that he had no personal 'feud' with Mackid:

> Mr Mackid the Justice of peace Clerk is blamed, and I know he is indolent, but this was to so many an unpleasant subject that I suppose he has not been pushed to his duty.

Sellar immediately saw himself as the man to push Mackid, remarking to Lord Gower:

> I have fought some battles against corruption with men of Considerable power in Moray . . . and I see nothing in the matter to stagger me.

Sellar was not to be staggered and he smacked his lips at the prospect of reforming Mackid.[67]

Nine days later, Patrick Sellar wrote to Gower telling him about Mackid's personal circumstances: 'The poor man is not in Good Health, and in low spirits'. He had given up a business in Ross-shire for a £90 salary in Sutherland which, together with a small farm, permitted him an idle life. And, instead of building 'a stance of Good offices' he had built himself 'a Castle'. He lived there a life of 'much indolence and inattention'. 'He feels all this; excuses himself concerning the road funds by his numerous engagements in another County, and promising every attention in future.'[68] Mackid was full of excuses about the Road Fund and promised greater attention in the future. Sellar was concerned that his reports would do him great damage, and now retreated from his earlier call for Mackid's dismissal: 'I am fearful that my report bring any severe sentence against him'. Sellar suggested that he take over responsibility to work with Mackid as best he could.[69] This seems to have been acted upon: Mackid, therefore, was lucky to avoid dismissal at this stage.[70]

If Sellar's attack on the administration of the Road Fund was a cause of local embarrassment, his continuing assault on the poaching problem on the Sutherland estate was little less than explosive. On the question of game, Sellar declared that the estate was riddled with 'cunning', by which he meant corruption. He could not see its total eradication until more police became available. They needed men 'who, like me, are independent and indifferent to every consideration there than the good opinion of the [Stafford] family'.[71] The organisation of game on the estate was sullied by 'intrigue'. 'It is all a smuggle,' he concluded. Even the officers who were supposed to prevent these illegalities were corrupted. Sellar reported that he had, himself, already been approached by a local identity 'to be in league with me . . . to do us favours, in return for favours to be done him.' Sellar wanted to attack the corruption by, first, appointing his own man. Sellar named his suspects and drew up a list of poachers.[72] It was at Mackid's office that Sellar began his war against 'the Poachers'. Sellar also set up a prison notice, offering a reward for information about poaching.[73]

Sellar's campaign against poaching was the quickest way to make enemies in eastern Sutherland. He had already uncovered petty corruption at all levels.[74] His attack on poaching quickly harvested some awkward culprits. In April 1811, Sellar reported that he had prosecuted two sons of the substantial tenant, MacDonald of Polly, for dealing in game. They were supplying game to 'Achany's table from this Estate'. Achany was an important figure in the local community, and Sellar's action inevitably implicated Achany, adding to the embarrassment of the situation. Sellar reported: 'I feel some little delicacy too on this score, as he is a freeholder, and hope to get them punished as poachers without any particular allusion to him. If my information be established they ought to be Removed.'[75] With his vigorous and unprecedented vigilance, Sellar now also caught a group of poachers which included the sons of his neighbour, Sutherland of Scibbercross, though he conceded he may have been mistaken. Sutherland eventually became Sellar's implacable enemy but seems to have taken Sellar's apology well at this time. Sellar himself remarked that Sutherland was one of those 'narrow Countries' in which misrepresentation was always likely.

By 1812, Sellar had crossed swords with some of the most influential men of the old tacksman class in Sutherland. It was dangerous work and Sellar underestimated the enemies he accumulated in his hot pursuit of efficiency and legality. He had exposed Mackid as incompetent in the administration of the Road Fund; he had elbowed his way into Mackid's own legal territory; he had taken over one of the best farms in the district and was bent on demonstrating his agricultural superiority over neighbours for whom he showed little more than contempt. Even worse, he had caught senior tacksmen *in flagrante delicto*, poaching from the Countess of Sutherland in the shadow of Dunrobin Castle.

As the great changes on the estate approached their new climax of removals under William Young, Sellar was to discover that Mackid himself was a poacher. Sellar had Mackid in his sights, even though most of the county regarded such poaching as relatively venial. By focusing his attack on Mackid – as exemplar of the old corruption – Sellar made for himself a permanent foe who, despite his reported indolence, would prove most formidable and dangerous in the context of the first round of the Young/Sellar removals.

CHAPTER 5

The New Clearances, 1811–12

In Moray, by his own account, the young lawyer Patrick Sellar had already recorded a series of battles with his assorted opponents. As soon as he arrived in Sutherland he plunged into conflict with practically every party with whom he converged. He was even at odds with his closest colleague, William Young in their business venture at Culmaily, and with his employer, Lady Stafford, over the definition of his functions and, more vexatiously, his status. He was in conflict with his predecessor, Falconer, even before he took over the reins. He quickly ran into headlong confrontation with one of the main legal officers in the county, Robert Mackid, over the road money accounts. Sellar then took it upon himself to pursue all local land holders in default of their contributions to the road fund. Mackid was also to be pursued over the question of poaching, which widened Sellar's confrontation with many parts of the community, including the many customers of the poachers. He assailed the smugglers and also their clients. In each case, Sellar asserted his legal authority to undermine people whom he undoubtedly regarded as enemies of society. Individual tacksmen soon perceived him as a threat to their lands and status. His operations at Culmaily were designed specifically to demonstrate the backwardness of his neighbours. Before long, Sellar would be offside with the entire population – extracting their rents, their debts, their defaults and, finally, ejecting many of them from their lands. He became the universal messenger of fear and thus he was demonised.

In 1810–11, Sellar and Young were about to embark on a series of mass clearances and large-scale resettlements within the Sutherland estate (as well as significant outmigration). The critical moment came at a meeting at Golspie Inn in December 1811, at which the interior lands of Assynt were auctioned off to the highest bidders. At this somewhat bibulous event the fate of the people of that great western district was sealed. It was to be the most extensive and the swiftest clearances so far attempted in the Scottish Highlands, part of one of the most ambitious experiments in social engineering envisaged in the age of improvement.

Before we consider the convergence of sheep-farmers, factors and tacksmen at the Golspie Inn, we need briefly to retrace the steps towards the new phase of the clearances in order to set the events in the perspective of the times.

– Origins of sheepfarming in Sutherland to 1812 –

The first commercial sheep-farming enterprise was attempted on the Sutherland estate at Dunrobin under the aegis of William, Earl of Sutherland, in 1761. His death soon followed and the factors of the infant Countess Elizabeth, his successor, did not extend the venture. John Campbell of Languine reported on the suitability of sheep in Sutherland in 1767, but again without significant result. Malcolm Bangor-Jones has shown that commercialisation ran in parallel in the old parts of the economy. The tacksmen dealt robustly with their under-tenants to increase the scale of both cattle and sheep production in the pastoral revolution.[1] The trend was always towards a reduction of land in the hands of the small tenantry.[2]

The first sustained inauguration of commercial sheep-farming in the county was on the adjoining Reay estate in the 1770s. Significantly this was achieved by a tacksman's son, a former Jamaica planter who returned with his colonial winnings to take up the Balnakeil farm and who introduced sheep from Tweedsdale to the Parph peninsula at Cape Wrath. On the Reay estate, as late as 1787, tacksmen had cleared off their subtenants in the rationalisation of lands for larger-scale cattle-raising. This was, indeed, in advance of the official estate plans for removals for either cattle or sheep on the Reay estate.

The Balnakeil initiative leap-frogged the general extension of sheep northwards which reached the Great Glen a few years later. The general incursion of the new sheep, the Blackfaced variety, reached into southern margins of Sutherland at Strathoykel in the late 1770s with the help of 'southern graziers'. The invasion then stretched across into Sutherland in Criech parish. The initial advance was attributed to the work of Sir John Lockhart Ross (a distinguished naval commander and improver) who brought the Blackfaced sheep from Crawford Moor, and who later introduced new Tweedsdale breeding rams to improve the stock. These early successes attracted more southern farmers, men with capital, seeking cheap leases. In 1781, William Geddes of Tummel Bridge in Perthshire entered Sutherland and faced considerable local resistance to his innovations, suffered thefts of sheep and meal, and was provoked into legal proceedings to protect his enterprise. In 1788, at Rosehall, in the south-east of the county, a new sheep-farm of 12,500 acres was carved out of holdings for Campbell of Languine. This required the removal of 121 families. The farm at Cassley was also cleared to make way for sheep. These early penetrations into Sutherland, in the 1780s, created large new grazing farms let on long leases, and they generated immediate protest among the small tenantry displaced in the process.

The imperial advance of the sheep was, therefore, well established in the county by 1790, though not yet on the great Sutherland estate. Excepting Balnakiel, which eventually went to John Dunlop of Ayrshire, many of the new sheep-farms were taken by local men; the rent of the Reay estate doubled between 1800 and 1809, though it did not rescue the traditional owners from ultimate takeover by the Sutherland estate.[3] Efforts were made, at the time, to diminish the oppressions of tacksmen. But the main motivation of the changes in landholdings was that of greater rent extraction in an age of inflation, thereby taking advantage of the soaring sheep-farming profits.[4]

Andrew Kerr brought Cheviots to the farm of Armadale on the Strathy estate of Lord Armadale in the extreme north of the county. He obtained a nineteen-year lease, which was later passed on to Gabriel Reid, a Northumberland sheep-farmer, who became a great figure in the north. Reid subsequently married the daughter of Mackay of Bighouse and cleared families from Armadale and Portskerra. Meantime George Dempster, often a public opponent of sheep-farming on a large scale, had brought sheep to his Pulrossie estate in 1796, advised by Andrew Thomson of Berwickshire. On the Bighouse Estate, sheep were introduced in 1812 and the rents doubled, this of course being a feature of the entire progression of sheep into the region. Southern sheep-farmers regarded Highland rents as extraordinarily low; Highland landlords were delighted with the new bids for their mountains and straths. It was, in that limited sense, a perfectly rational convergence of landlord and capitalist interests.

It was curious, therefore, that the great Sutherland estate was left behind in the northward march of the four-legged invaders, despite the 'kind of rage for sheep-farming' identified by the Sutherland factor Hugh Rose in 1786. Rose himself was reluctant to introduce sheep during the minority of the Countess. The entanglement of so much of the estate in leases and wadsets constrained estate plans until the turn of the century. In Assynt in the 1790s, sheep were introduced on the farms of several tacksmen who saw opportunities for profits from the remarkable advance of wool and mutton prices. The central estate administrators were alarmed at the disruption caused by these tacksmen, and attempted to curb their actions by establishing a rule that every sub-tenant cleared must be provided with a possession of 'equal rent and value' in the same parish. The entire process was already generating a great deal of low-level conflict while the estate tried to contain the adverse consequences.

There was a quickening of activity on the Sutherland estate by 1801 when lands for sheep-farms were advertised, though still on a small scale. The relatively poor local recruitment for the family regiment in 1799, as we have seen, spurred the Countess towards a more robust attitude to the introduction of sheep. In 1801, the Rubha Stoer district in Assynt was advertised as sheep-farms. In 1802, two Ross-shire proprietors obtained a four–year lease in upper Strathnaver and Lairg for incoming sheep and this brought them into conflict with small tenants at Truberscraig. In 1803, under the special advice of Colin Mackenzie, the new agent from Edinburgh, a more elaborate plan emerged to clear people to the coast in order to accommodate more sheep-farms.

The next major acceleration on the Sutherland estate came with the advertisement in 1806 for the so-called 'Great Sheep Tenement' which overlapped into the parishes of Lairg, Rogart, Clyne, Kildonan and Farr. This huge farm was let to the Northumberland farmers, Atkinson and Marshall, at £1,200 per annum, rising to £1,500 after two years. Another great farm at Suisgill was let to Thomas Houston (tacksman of Lothbeg). In 1808 the farm of Shiness was advertised and let to Donald Matheson, also a former tacksman. The revolution had thus progressed by stages, led by men from within and beyond the county. The disruption entailed in these creations was already massive: 'the Great Sheep Tenement' required the removal of 300 families, eighty of them from Strathnaver. A few were kept on as grasskeepers. Some emigrated to America (one ship with 140 passengers was lost off Newfoundland). Most families were resettled on the north side of Loch Naver and down the strath, and this was accompanied by complaints of overcrowding. In this phase, the Sutherland family attracted criticism for creating coastal congestion and for the inadequacy of the reception arrangements. Moreover, during the factorship of Cosmo Falconer, much of the original momentum was lost. In 1810, Benjamin Meredith was hired to make a survey of Strathnaver and he recommended a great new sheep-farm, with the parallel creation of a village at the mouth of the Naver and small farms in other parts of the strath.

Wool prices in 1809 were six times their level at the start of the French Wars. It was an unmistakable market signal to all prospective suppliers of wool. The Highlands were a region ideally placed to respond to the nation's needs and Patrick Sellar, in particular, was intensely aware of the opportunities. Sutherland was late to respond to the call which, of course, added to the urgency of innovation in the county. Sellar himself was on the brink of entering the sheep economy on his own account, but he did not make his move until the final moment of the wartime boom. Wool prices reached their zenith in 1813, the year of Sellar's induction.

This, then, was the long prelude to the revitalised plans for the swift expansion of sheep-farming across the Sutherland estate, scheduled for 1812–13, now under the management of William Young and Patrick Sellar. By 1812 large tracts of Assynt in the west were already redesignated for lease as five sheep-farms. William Young toured Strathnaver and concurred in the determination that it, too, should be disposed as sheep-farms. On the Sutherland estate (and also in Reay), the landlord's expectation was that the common people would be accommodated in new coastal holdings and would be available for 'fair and lawful wages at kelping or fishing when called upon to do so'. They would become a new proletariat.

– THE ASSYNT CLEARANCES, SPRING 1812 –

In December 1811, William Young arranged a meeting at Golspie Inn for parties interested in the five new sheep-farms to be created in Assynt.[5] Golspie was on the east coast, far from Assynt, and local interests travelled across country to reach the auction. The men from the west said it was their first visit to Dunrobin in nineteen years.

The local bidders were desperate to retain their lands and this led to fierce bidding. Eventually, in the face of great competition, the Assynt tacksmen prevailed. They were said to have 'promised anything rather than lose the land'. It was also claimed that they were 'in that ripe state', that is so agitated, that they did not 'well know what they were doing'. As a consequence they contracted to pay disastrously high rents for which they suffered in the subsequent years. The tacksmen were bound in the new leases to implement removals by their own means; they were also required, by estate regulations, to allow the departing tenants to carry with them all their timbers and to assist them in the building of new cottages. The tacksmen thus agreed to pay hugely increased rents and to execute the clearance of their own people. It was a most satisfactory arrangement for the estate managers.

This fraught negotiation had been a conjunction of the compelling plans of the management and the desperate determination of the Assynt tacksmen to cling on to their lands. Caught between were the common people whose removal now became inevitable. After the tension of the auction, the managers and the tacksmen celebrated. The episode was marked by 'a good deal of fun in the evening' with Gaelic songs from the tacksmen and the singing of 'Auld Lang Syne' from Patrick Sellar – while Young himself regaled the assembly with talk about tups and wethers. Young apologised to Lady Stafford for the entertainment expenses he incurred at the inn, but remarked that he did not wish to appear to treat the tacksmen shabbily at such a time.[6]

As soon as the Golspie agreement had been sealed, arrangements for the clearances in Assynt moved ahead swiftly. The responsibility for the first great removals of the Young/Sellar regime had been delegated to the new leaseholders, men who could exert their traditional authority over the subtenantry. This would be an inestimable advantage in the coming removals. But the timing was not auspicious. Famine stalked the land again, yet this, if anything, gave greater urgency to the policy of resettlement. The 1811–12 winter was severe and William Young reported in April 1812, 'the dreadful season in the North and the consequent effects which may be apprehended from the present almost unprecedented early scarcity of grain.' The weather was appalling and relief shipments were required.[7] Meanwhile the capital works schemes were progressing under Young's optimistic leadership. By mid-1812 these included ambitious plans for coal production at Brora on the east coast. Young's exuberance and enthusiasm were transmitted to Lord Gower who, in a letter in August 1812, exclaimed, 'We hope it will soon give everything a new life. I believe this will become paradise.'[8]

Prior to the Assynt removals, the estate had been surveyed, the leases codified and the timetable established, all mainly organised by the assiduous pen of Patrick Sellar. William Young had inspected the ground, in 1811, and determined that it was best suited for the Cheviot sheep with the development of the coastal arrangements for the people who would thereby be displaced. The latter, he remarked with emphasis, was vital:

> aware as I am that Lord and Lady Stafford will in this and other districts rather sacrifice their interests than that the people should be entirely dispossessed.

He had in mind kelping and fishing. Yet though he talked of the proposed development of Lochinver as the 'Metropolis of Assynt', he described the arrangements in terms of philanthropic sacrifice.

The new removals in Assynt in the spring of 1812 cleared eighty-one families, many of whom gained accommodation in the inland villages of Elphin and Knockan; others descended to coastal townships. In 1812 a farm in Rogart in the east was also created, requiring the removal of a dozen families. Young was nervous and, in February recommended great caution in clearing the sub-tenants of two existing sheep-farmers (Atkinson and Marshall). It would be better, he said, to let them remain quietly until the new sets had been arranged: 'and although they are not tenants of Lord Stafford's still they are natives and the whole blame will be thought on us [sic].'[9] There was a fear of turmoil and publicity in the minds of the clearers. Sellar organised the final papers and was also monitoring the course of the removals.[10] In May, he went to Assynt to 'settle the tennants by the new Arrangements', using boats for part of his travels.[11]

Patrick Sellar was, therefore, directly involved in the removals. His colleague, William Young, was apprehensive not only for the passage of the removals in Assynt, but also for the smaller ejectments in Strathnaver, Kildonan and Clyne.[12] But in April 1812, Sellar was sanguine and reported that Young was in Assynt and that 'he will have settled the people to his mind.' At the same time, the food crisis worsened. Once more Sellar implemented the most unpopular measures during the emergency, and these included directions to church ministers to insist that the people end their illicit distilling and plant more potatoes for the coming season.[13]

Despite high apprehensions, the Assynt removals, negotiated in November 1811 and executed in the spring of 1812, passed relatively quietly and created little apparent dispute. Unhappily no detailed accounts of the events have survived, but there was a general air of satisfaction among the factors. William Young commended the unresisting people of Assynt as sober, industrious and uncorrupted by illicit distillation. Sellar, himself, later said that the peaceful clearances in Assynt were attributable to the fact that the cleared land was earmarked for the existing tacksmen who therefore were on side. Sellar explained: 'The gentlemen who were to receive possession had so much influence over the people, that little or no interference of mine was necessary.' This was uncharacteristically modest of Sellar, but he was making a wider point that the general disposition of the tacksmen was always a critical factor in the history of the clearances.[14]

Young knew that the plans involved proletarianisation for the people removed. Yet some of them, because of their ingrained habits of life, would never become fishermen or kelpers:

> But unprofitable as such a race are the best must be done, and they may be at last useful as roadmakers and labourers at home and in the low Country, in place of, at present wasting their time in Sloth and idleness.[15]

In Young's reports there was already a rising sense of frustration and irritation with the backwardness of the population with which he was required to deal. Preparations continued during 1812, designed to follow the timetable of progress promised by Young and according to the schedule Sellar had devised in his survey of 1811. The next round of clearances would be in Kildonan and in Assynt again, as part of the sequential redeployment of the estate in the grand plan.

Through 1812, the plans matured and, despite religious distur-bances in Assynt, the estate maintained the outward face of peace and progress. Large removals were impending for the following year, but Young's tone remained calm and optimistic. By early 1813, Young was finalising his schemes for removal and resettlement in the parishes of Clyne and Kildonan, the people of the inland territories to be shifted to the northern coasts. He was fully confident of his plans. The northern reception areas, he recollected:

> gave us the command of much coast side where crops are sure to ripen. The sea would have afforded constant supplies of fish both for the people and for export. I had determined to place sixty or eighty families on this and who live at present in the most mountainous part of the estate, and who earn their subsistence not by the ground or any honest means, but as smugglers and I am determined to set off this part of the property to shepherds.

The tone of Young's remarks was shifting also. His entire programme of improvement depended on the cooperation of the people in his complicated plans for their resettlement. If they refused to accept the plans then the estate would be compelled to invoke the law. The capacity of the estate management to prevail in these remote places ultimately depended on either co-operation or coercion.

– A NEW BROOM –

The first removals, in Assynt, may have passed calmly, but a disturbingly discordant note was soon sounded, privately, from within the Sutherland estate administration. It was prompted by the appointment of a new Commissioner to Lord Stafford, James Loch. He assumed a general supervisory control over his new employer's diverse and far-flung business and political interests. Loch's function was to oversee general estate administration, but not to interfere directly in the ordinary management of the individual parts of the great Sutherland empire (which included estates in Shropshire, Staffordshire, Yorkshire, the Bridgewater Canal, political interests in many places, industrial concerns and urban properties in London). Though Loch was appointed in 1812, he did not exercise direct control in Sutherland until August 1816, after Sellar's trial. He was essentially Lord Stafford's personal appointment, his new right-hand man.

Like Patrick Sellar, James Loch was Lowland-born and Edinburgh-educated, and a lawyer. Both were also thirty-two years old, but there the similarity finished: Loch was a smoother and more polished individual. He had been raised in the bosom of one of the most influential families in Scotland, the Adams of Blair Adam in Kinross. James Loch attended Edinburgh University and was a member of the Speculative Society, even as a student. He was further trained at the English Bar, and mixed easily and effectively in the highest political, social and aristocratic milieux in both Scotland and England. Loch was a close associate of Brougham and Jeffrey in the glittering circle of the *Edinburgh Review*. He was trained in rural management and seemed destined for a political career until he rather suddenly took over the challenge of coordinating the great estates and territories of the Marquis of Stafford in 1812. James Loch was an intellectual, a subtle man with great abilities.[16] Among the matters he would manage over the next forty years was the turbulent relationship with his contemporary, Patrick Sellar.

James Loch accepted Lord Stafford's appointment in 1812. At the time, at dinner parties in London and Edinburgh, it was said, rather ruefully, that the Stafford family had turned their thoughts 'entirely to economy and the society of Scotch agents'.[17] Though he mainly concentrated, at first, on Stafford's substantial English estates, Loch was charged with the larger responsibility of coordinating estate finances as a whole. He had already served a thorough managerial and practical apprenticeship on the estate of his uncle, Lord Chief Commissioner William Adam of Blair Adam in Kinross.

Late in 1812, Loch reported, to his uncle, his confidential first reactions to his new career. He discovered that William Young, in addition to his role in Sutherland, had been used in a consulting capacity on the West Midland estates of Lord Stafford at Trentham and Lilleshall. Loch was aghast at the style and tenor of Young's advice. Loch reported to the Commissioner that Young was 'a very first rate Highland improver, a strong-headed intelligent Scotchman, born and bred in Moray beyond which he has never been till he came here'. Young had made it known that

> everything that differed from Moray was wrong and everything was to be improved by the total eradication of the present tenants and the introduction of Scotch tenants. This was I think in some degree approved of, and a vast and immediate rise of rent was and is expected.

Five years later, Loch found himself in the position which required him to defend the entire policy on the Stafford estates in both England and the Highlands. In 1812 he simply expressed his shock and genuine astonishment that 'a tenantry of 200 years standing Mr Young did not consider as deserving attention.'[18]

The importation of Moraymen, southerners and Englishmen into the northern Highlands generated serious resentment. There was evidently a reciprocal resentment on Lord Stafford's English estates caused by the concurrent influx of Scotch tenants, advisers and agents. If Loch were shaken by the 'strong-headed ideas of Young' (and by extension those of Lady Stafford and Sellar),[19] it is scarcely surprising that the people directly affected by these policies eventually reacted with vigour and protest. On the English estates, where the changes would be, by many degrees, less dislocative, there was already a great turmoil of criticism and public outcry. In the Highlands, the physical response was about to erupt during the second round of clearances attempted by the new regime, despite the auspicious start in Assynt in 1812.

CHAPTER 6

'The People's folly':
Kildonan and Assynt, 1813

– WINTER RESISTANCE, 1813 –

The passage of the Assynt removals in 1812 boded well for the next stage in the grand plans to transform the Sutherland estate. The Strath of Kildonan, reaching to the north coast, was scheduled for conversion to sheep-farming at Whitsunday 1813. Now, however, the plan was resisted, even before it was begun, and several months ahead of its implementation. William Young's regime was brought face to face with the recalcitrant and angry people of the interior settlements who stood in the way of the sheep-farmers. The events in Kildonan, in the months of January to April 1813, became a severe test of the resolution of the new management in Sutherland and, by the same token, a measure of the solidarity of the inhabitants to prevent their removal.

Sellar was in the middle of these events as factor and enforcer. A stickler for detail and legality, he had perambulated the estate and warned the affected people of their impending removal and the plans for their resettlement. He served the notices to quit, all perfectly legal. He undoubtedly struck fear into the hearts of these communities. When Sellar was in Kildonan collecting the Martinmas rents, he reported that he had faced serious harassment on account of the forthcoming removals. There was, he sensed, a clear danger of violence in the district.[1]

By the winter of 1812–13, there was, therefore, a heightened awareness of the impending events. The Kildonan trouble would be the most serious resistance to descend on the estate and the more disturbing because the people now acted not only in unison, but also in advance of the imminent removals. They resisted when the valuers inspected the land for prospective farmers bidding for the lease. But the lease was not vacant until the occupying tenants were shifted off

– 93 –

the land. The valuers, therefore, became the first target for the aroused inland communities.

As the events in Kildonan unfolded, in January 1813, Young himself was away on business and he reported in great alarm:

> One of the lots was to be valued in my absence. The natives rose in a body and chased the valuers off the ground and now threaten the lives of every man who dares dispossess them.

Young was outraged and panic-stricken. Sellar was soon at the centre of the eruption and recollected that 'the tumult' was 'occasioned by this proposal for resettlement before the notices could be served'. The obstruction of the valuers was the spark which ignited a succession of more incendiary confrontations between the authority of estate management and the law on the one side, against the collective force of the people on the other.

When the Young/Sellar regime faced the belligerent and coordinated resistance in Kildonan, they confronted people whose lives they claimed would be much improved by the impending changes. Young boiled over with anger. 'Everything I do', he told the new Commissioner James Loch, was 'in a manner at the point of the sword. Both rich and poor (and with very few exceptions) are hostile to every plan for improvement. They are absolutely a century behind and what is worse a great many want common honesty, but,' he declared, 'I had brought them wonderfully forward and had calculated that in two years I should have all the estate arranged.' The extraordinary aspect of Young's remarks was not so much his bewilderment but his assumptions. He believed that his massive plans could be completed within two years and that the people would be assimilated into his own way of thinking. His shock in February 1813 was proportional to the unrealism of his understanding of the world of the Sutherland 'natives'.

Young's reaction was reinforced by Patrick Sellar, who expressed his own anger at the time of the eruption of resistance in Kildonan. 'Such a set of savages is not to be found in the wilds of America', he fulminated, 'and you may believe their conduct is not much disapproved of by many who ought to know better.' He warned, 'the whole country are on the watch to see how the war will end and so act accordingly.' As far as Young was concerned, the collision between his rational, humane and civilising principles, and 'the savages' of the Kildonan interior, was a watershed: 'If Lord and Lady Stafford do not put it in my power to quell this banditti we may bid adieu to all improvement.' James Loch, now in general management of all the

Stafford estates, was not surprised at the outcome (given his reaction to Young's opinions on the English estates), but he and the Stafford family accepted the need for a vigorous response. He thought it might necessitate a show of military force to restore order to the estate.[2]

The valuer, and two of the new sheep-farmers and their shepherds, were chased off the land down the Strath of Kildonan in mid-January 1813. Between 23 and 27 January, Sheriff Mackid investigated the episode at Golspie and then went with Sellar and Young to Strathnaver to negotiate an end to the tumult. On 2 February, they met the assembled people in the Kildonan schoolhouse and attempted to persuade them to agree to a bond of peace. Some of the people complied. Mackid asked the remainder to meet him in Helmsdale on 10 February. But, on the appointed day, more than 100 people from the interior arrived in threatening mood. Mackid tried to arrest some of them, Sellar assisting, but the crowd once more intervened. Sellar announced that the court would be adjourned to Dunrobin Castle. Again the proceedings were prevented by the crowd. There had been some fear of an attack on the castle. Troops were sent for and, in March 1813, Cranstoun and Mackid investigated the events. In the event, no one was brought to trial, possibly because of the intercession of the Stafford family.[3] This, in summary, was the shape of the Kildonan conflict.

It was a spectacular escalation of resistance to the removals which, until then, had been confined in Sutherland to the petty harassment of sheep, shepherds and sheep-farmers. At one point during the events, a small group, including the Sheriff, Thomas Houston, Sellar and Taylor, had set off for Kildonan to collect the bond from the people. They were confronted by a crowd of men, about 150 in all, armed with staves and cudgels, who declared that they would not, in fact, give their bond. They objected to the takeover of the land by the sheep-farmer, Reid. They said that the land at Armadale (recently acquired expensively by Lord Stafford) would not suit them, and they possessed letters which entitled them to their land in return for furnishing men to the 93rd Regiment for war service. Sellar examined these letters and found that the obligation which they contained had expired in 1808. Sellar explained to the people the lapsed status of their documents: 'Their answer was it may be so but we will hold the land until the men are delivered to us again.'

One of the people named in the warrant spoke to the officer 'with Tears in his eyes', saying that he wished to convey a message to Lady Stafford's managers and to the Sheriff. The message was to the effect 'that if any man who came down to Golspy' were apprehended, 'there would be such news of it as never happened in Sutherland before, as there would be three hundred men assembled on that occasion.'[4] The strath was brimming with tears, indignation and resistance. Mackid, in the absence of his superior, Cranstoun, and unable to assert the authority of the law, had been in a high state of alarm. Cranstoun had eventually hurried northwards.

Sellar advocated severe measures against the resistant people; stability and firmness were, he declared, indispensable, to 'speedily put down the spirit of insubordination, by persuasion or force'. And force then should be followed by salutary punishment.[5] Sellar exhibited great *sang-froid* throughout – he was prepared to face the rioters on their own ground, he took the pulse of the events, and he made his feeling clear at all times. He reported that 131 Kildonan men were solid in their resolution to prevent the arrest of the ringleaders:

> They were determined they Said to Stand as one man, in defence of their land and their property. On my endeavouring to point out the Folly of a handful of men pretending to fight against the Laws and Strength of the British Constitution and against 'Common Sense' they said they were Loyal men whose Brothers and Sons were now fighting Buonoparte and they would allow no Sheep to Come into the Country.

In mid-February, Young had received a deputation of the 'malcontents' who were beginning to cool, and the people promised their loyalty if they were allowed to continue on their lands. Young told them that this was out of the question but that Lord Stafford might forgive them, and indulge them with lots at Strathy, if they became peaceable. Young told them that no agreement was possible if they continued to consort with their supporters from Caithness and Strathbrora. This was an indication of wider support for the resistance. At the same time, the rebellious people had written to the Duke of York, with the help of 'some pettyfogging attorney', presumably to plead for the intervention of the government.[6]

It was at this point that Young reached the end of his patience and said that the time had come for the introduction of the militia, or a regiment of the line, to enforce the law. Young was aware of the salutary consequences of military action. In Braemar, only four years earlier, the military had settled a riot without bloodshed. He believed that 'the baleful traffic in whisky' was at the bottom of the trouble. It was vital that law and order be established. If the situation were not quickly resolved, it would deter the introduction of strangers into the county.

Sellar had been at the head of the latest confrontation with the people and his language was predictably stronger. He had not succeeded in making peace with the rioters. They had refused to sign a bond 'and their orators declared that they were entitled to keep possession of their Grounds and would allow no Shepherds to come to the Country'. [7] Sellar quoted the people:

> How could they sign a Bond of Law burrows [that is, security] with respect to men who would ruin them and their families, and against whom they therefore entertained enmity in their hearts?

Sellar calculated that there were fifty 'desperadoes' with about '100 deluded men who walk trembling'. Many of them would prefer to seek forgiveness 'if they dare avow it'. Sellar said that the eyes of other parishes were upon them. There were spies everywhere, looking for any chance of success 'that it might induce a change of Mr Young for some Corpulent Good-natured Gentleman [i.e. in the model of Falconer] who would stay at home, and take things, as formerly.' Sellar said it was imperative to be firm at this stage in order to 'dissipate this confederacy' and to prevent it widening. He expected to recruit a respectable gentleman to put down the resistance, 'and there is good reason to think that the matter Shall be brought to evaporate in Smoke'. He agreed with Young that a show of Military power would avoid bloodshed. He saw it as an opportunity to snuff out all further opposition:

> The presence of the military will at once, and without Bloodshed, extinguish the last Spark, a flame which, <u>if Suffered to remain must increase</u>, and by the damage threatened to property, the Jeopardy into which men's lives are put, not perhaps, by open attack, but by assassination, and the natural timidity of the Shepherds, cannot fail to frighten men from embarking their property in the Country, and thus [essentially?] retarding the improvement of the Estate.[8]

Sellar argued that the rioters should be 'totally suppressed' and the ringleaders brought to Dornoch for condign punishment. He connected some of the opposition to his own efforts to prevent illicit distilling in the district. He favoured the introduction of the full might of the law supported by military force. At the end of January, he reported directly to Lady Stafford:

> I augur a peaceable termination to this mad attempt, which however would certainly have produced serious consequences, had not the most prompt measures been followed to defeat the purposes. I trust that on the shores of Strathy and Armadale this population may be applied to better purposes than smuggling whisky.[9]

Sellar had squared up to the people before the removals. He had set about the elimination of illegal practices. He was determined to reform the entire society and to institute a better community on the new plan. It was already a prescription for confrontation. Sellar was a young man in a hurry, invested with authority over a sullen and potentially mutinous population.

Sellar declared that the riot warranted 'the most exemplary punishment of the offenders, together with the banishment from the estate.' He found a phrase for their behaviour. It was 'the people's folly' which had caused 'decent and innocent men to get involved'. Sellar said that these men would soon demonstrate their contrition by coming forward in a body to 'declare their innocence and abhorrence of the late riots'.[10] His own preference was for 'a Voluntary Resolution'. Failing this, the people should be shown the full majesty of the law:

> We have seen ten times greater risings suppressed and we shall by and bye have [billets?] to be got for 500 men in your quarter, should we not find the business peaceably carried thro. But of this I trust that you will take no notice lest these to be punished should effect their escape, and we depend on your secrecy.[11]

Sellar believed that the billeting of troops would punish the entire community, a sledge hammer to wield on a recalcitrant people.

– OPPOSING INTERESTS –

In mid-February, the events in Kildonan had not been resolved and Sellar eagerly anticipated the arrival of Cranstoun as the full representative of the law in the county. Cranstoun was well thought of in legal circles but did not understand a word of Gaelic.[12] Sellar told Lady Stafford that he expected that Cranstoun's presence would bring

> stability and firmness to our counsels. These will speedily put down the spirit of insubordination, either by persuasion or by force, or both, and then, it will only remain for Lord Stafford and your Ladyship to order such punishment to the ringleaders and such forgiveness to the deluded people, as you may see proper.[13]

Sellar therefore again urged the prompt use of force to restore order to the land. He agreed that the entire future of the improvements was at risk. Continuing resistance would also dissuade strangers from entering the country and check the progress of the estate. A week later, he implored Cranstoun to act effectively to 'proceed firmly with a few of the worst of the Ring leaders, those men, for instance, who want an Embassy to other countries to enlist men.' This was a reference to a bizarre rumour that the rioters were considering a treacherous connection with the French enemy. Sellar was not amused (nor were others) at this time:

> If we treat the matter with [Levity?], the same Comedy or perhaps a tragedy may be performed on the Country at some no distant time, and the impression which such tumults have on the minds of strangers who might otherwise be disposed to Settle in the Country is of itself a serious check to the improvement of the Estate.[14]

Sellar dismissed one of the estate employees whom he had used to serve notices of removal to the small tenantry. He claimed that this man was 'in league against us' and had become 'intentionally negligent' in the course of his work.[15] This spelled a growing polarisation in the community, a sign of the acute tension which the removal policy was now arousing. Reid, the incoming sheep-farmer, was fearful for his personal safety. Reid and Young had retreated to Dunrobin Castle for protection. But Sellar, by contrast, thought that only the sheep stocks were in real danger. He conceded that Reid 'cannot farm in Safety unless many of the Lawless families be put out of the Country.' But he said he felt no personal danger in this 'idle clamour', and it did not alter the fact that the country was naturally fitted for sheep. Sellar was also free of pessimism in this turn of events:

> When it has once been extinguished, there will (as Assynt is arranged) be no chance of any repetition of the offence.

Sellar wanted to demonstrate the power of the law, the sanctity of property and the irresistibility of reason. Young and Sellar were agreed that they faced concerted collective action in Kildonan and that it must be scotched.

Sellar, in a theme familiar throughout his confrontation with the common people of the estate, believed that the Kildonan people were being 'misled by men of better Sense than they possess'. They were men

> who See that they can Get no good old-fashioned bargains on the Estate; provided Strangers, who know home, by better management, to take more value from the Soil are permitted to Compete with them. Not one Gentleman in the Country has offered the least assistance.

This was a telling point which exposed the social fissures created in the process of improvement. The 'gentlemen' of the county, at the moment of trouble, had suddenly made themselves scarce. One of

them had left the county on 'pressing business'; another was 'tormen-
ted' by a severe cold; Clunes was 'confined to bed with a fit of Ague'
which lasted almost three weeks.

The withdrawal of the traditional social leaders of the county was
paralleled by the solidarity of the rest of the community: 'The whole
population feel desirous of Success to the rioters, knowing that they
have a common interest in the Exclusion of Strangers.' Thus Sellar
admitted that the managers and the sheep-farmers were alone. The
social leaders had made themselves invisible in the crisis. They faced
not merely a conspiracy, but the broad opposition of the great mass of
the community. The future of the improvements was at stake. The
management must have an armed force to suppress the opposition
and it must be followed by judicial investigation. The estate simply
could not afford to lose this contest.

For Sellar, there were two essential questions at issue:

> First whether it is most Expedient that this County import Grain for the
> maintenance of idle Smugglers, to export food and Raiment towards the
> support of the British Empire, and second Whether these foolish men can
> be brought to order, there is with Great Deference, room for but one
> opinion; and, [whether] it [can] be proven, to the Satisfaction of every
> liberal and unprejudiced mind, that the removal of these men from
> Kildonan to Strathy, and the Grant of wool and mutton and the mountains
> of Kildonan, are measures calculated to add to the Comfort of the people
> and the Strength of the Country.[16]

Sellar's lengthy tirades exposed the scale and gravity of the resistance
which the people achieved at this time. Sellar put his own twist on the
story. It is also clear that Sellar and his associates were fully aware of the
gravamen of the arguments against their plans. The people were
simply wrong, misled and deluded. They did not know the law, they
did not know what was best for the country and they did not even know
what was best for themselves. In Sellar's view, there was no incon-
sistency of interest between the shepherds, the landlords, the national
economy and that of the community itself.

– THE MILITARY –

James Loch and the Stafford family, far removed from the dramatic
and worrying collision in Kildonan, promptly extended their full
support to Young's ostensibly uncompromising stand against the
resistance. There would be no retreating from the policy, nor from
upholding the law. Loch said it was vital to get the main legal officer in

Sutherland, Cranstoun, to show 'the higher classes' the authority of the law. The Stafford family accepted the idea that its entire policy was at stake. The policy could not conceivably be abandoned. The arrangements were 'just and liberal', and if military aid were required, then so be it.

Amid the turmoil, Young was driven to distraction by the Kildonan people and did not conceal his frustration. The riots had 'deranged' his plans. Early in March 1813, he said: 'A more provoking lawless set of people than many of the Kildonaners never inhabited a civilized Country.' He had arranged for one group to sign a 'penitential paper', but another group was signing petitions of 'the most gross and calumnious untruths'. The latter had declared that Young had said that Switzerland was too good for them; that, Young, Sellar and Mackid had all told them that they would be instantly evicted. This suggests a degree of panic and confusion, as well as a modicum of organisation, among the people. Indeed there was further evidence of coordination; the rebellious community selected a representative, William Macdonald, a former recruiting sergeant of the 93rd Highlanders, to be sent south to London to represent the feelings of the people to Lord Stafford and the Prince Regent as a protest against the removals. He raised a subscription of £20 to fund his journey to London. Sellar referred to the representative, sardonically, as 'the ambassador'. It was also said that if the representations in London failed then rebellion was likely to follow.[17]

Cranstoun belatedly arrived in Sutherland, from Edinburgh, in late February 1813, and stayed with Mackid in his house at Kirkton.[18] Cranstoun intervened and attempted to conciliate the people but few of them were prepared to meet him, perhaps leaving their fate in the hands of Macdonald in London. Meanwhile, Sellar again complained of the lack of solidarity among the gentlemen of the county. Young took an optimistic view, despite his rising temperature: 'The disturbance will soon terminate, it makes an awful noise at present but like the tail of a dog will soon die away.'

Cranstoun reported to Loch from Golspie that the disturbance in Kildonan continued and that he had failed to subdue and placate the people at Helmsdale. Consequently he called in the soldiery in the second week of March 1813, requisitioning 230 rank-and-file troops from Fort George, plus two companies of militia from Aberdeen. Cranstoun was confident that the troops would instantly restore order and that many of the rioters would soon face trial. The tenor of local opinion was clear:

> At present . . . we have threats of resistance and there is certainly a very extensive and well-organised combination among the tenantry, and I fear (as you conjecture) that persons of a better sort may be implicated.

Sellar reported that, as soon as the military was called, the confrontation ceased, the rioters submitted and the soldiery soon returned to their barracks at Fort George.[19] Apparently, the resistance simply evaporated at the sight of the soldiery. Sellar singled out Sutherland of Scibbercross as the leader 'whose brother in London is a very clever desperate Character.' The Sutherlands had used all their energies to generate publicity in the London newspapers, notably by means of the *Military Register* which became a mouthpiece for disaffection against the Sutherland estate for the following seven years.[20] Sellar declared that the events in Kildonan now fully justified the estate policies: 'We therefore feel very easy consciences in discharging our duty in the County', and hence the estate should carry through the plan without delay. The only drawback he now identified was the likely loss of some of the small tenants. It would be carried through 'tho' very likely at the expense (if such be an expense) of a few of the most volatile who may Emigrate to some other country'.

At the end of March Young was able to report the *dénouement* of the Kildonan disturbances. The military intervention had been 'absolutely necessary'; the people were now 'perfectly submissive'; Cranstoun had ordered a thorough investigation. In London James Loch met Macdonald, the people's 'ambassador', who was told that obedience would be demanded. In reality, however, a face-saving compromise had been formulated – the people accepted the demand for obedience and further legal retribution was suspended. Macdonald had spoken 'in handsomest terms' of the gentleman-like behaviour of William Young. By contrast he complained vehemently 'against Sellar and Dornoch Law'. He made specific allegations against Sellar, claiming that he took small sums of money for his own pocket during his rent collections. Meanwhile the sensation in the northern Highlands had reached the London newspapers. Loch embarrassingly found it necessary to re-assure Lord Sidmouth, Home Secretary, that peace had been restored in Sutherland. Gabriel Reid, the incoming sheep-farmer, agreed not to press his right for immediate entry to the lands for the current crop.[21]

As for the allegations made in London against his colleague Sellar, Young rushed to his defence. Young could not possibly believe 'for a moment that he [Sellar] could be capable to extract a single shilling improperly from the people far less to put it into his own pocket'.

There had been similar allegations before. Young believed that the claim was part of an attempt by the people to avoid paying rent. Sellar's rent-collecting duties faced every type of prevarication. Young said that 'Dornoch law' was now very well-administered and he testified to the fact that both Cranstoun and Mackid were performing their duties satisfactorily. Young also took the opportunity to deny Macdonald's opinion of his own popularity: 'I am accused and certainly with justice of All these changes and supposed hardships.' Sellar collected the rents, which Young pointed out, 'I have the cruelty to impose.'[22] As for the benevolence of the entire policy, Young declared:

> The annals of History do not afford prooff of any Proprietor of a Highland estate having done so much for a tenantry.

Sellar was glad to observe the termination of the 'mad attempt' to prevent the improvements. He looked for punishment of a few ring-leaders. He especially looked forward to the time when the interior people would be brought to the shores of Strathy and Armadale where they would 'be applied to better purposes than smuggling whisky'.[23] In the outcome, the Stafford family chose not to prosecute the leaders of the Kildonan riots. Sellar regarded this as a sign of extraordinary weakness in the administration and an incitement to further trouble. He was highly critical of the *dénouement* and believed passionately that the leniency shown towards the Kildonanites, in 1813, created the conditions for his own agonies one year later.

– Selkirk stirs emigration –

At the beginning of April 1813, Young reported that the 'Kildonan people . . . since the Military came have been quiet as lambs, I do not hear a murmur among them.' One of the ringleaders was now 'begging' for a lot at Strathy and admitted that he presently planted very little ground and 'no impartial person could say that he would not be better off on the coast'. Sellar declared that the removal of the people to the coast was indisputably beneficial: 'it must certainly be admitted that the exchange is to be in all respects more favourable for the people.' The main obstacle to the resettlement at the coast was 'illicit distilling [which] induces them to continue where they are.'[24]

Young's preparations for the resettlement of the Kildonan people on the north coast at Armadale proceeded, but a new element entered the scene. This was the intervention of the Earl of Selkirk who was recruiting for emigrants in the Highlands. He sought men for regimental service in Canada, who would then stay on after the war as settlers with their families. This was not entirely welcome to Lady Stafford. Though she could see some advantage in the idea, she knew also that it would reflect poorly on her elaborate plans to provide comprehensive facilities for her tenants, large and small. She explained her intentions to Lord Selkirk. She said that she would not interfere with the question of emigration and remarked ruefully that if she, herself, made any proposals for emigration to America to the people of Sutherland 'they would suspect they had not fair play and that it would defeat its own purpose.'[25]

Young remarked that Selkirk was under the misapprehension that the Kildonan people were relatively wealthy whereas, in reality, few of them had more than five acres, many less than three. As he put it, 'Forty years ago, this Country did not contain half its present population, the farms were moderately large, but the people were under no restriction as to subletting and have frittered away their possessions among their sons and daughters so that they could not now live [even] if Lord Stafford was to give them for nothing.'[26]

By April 1813, Selkirk claimed to have made a list of 580 names for his emigration scheme. Young remarked, 'I have plenty to do without wasting my time in making arrangements for Men who do not seem disposed to avail themselves of the trouble we are taking.' Lady Stafford talked further with Selkirk about his plan to recruit married men from Sutherland to serve in the Canadian Regiment. Lady Stafford regarded this as a foolish idea which would, in any case, have little bearing on realities in Sutherland. 'In short', she concluded, 'I do not see anything more that can be done by us in our offers being rejected and as the People resist by force no one can complain if they are brought to reason by the same means.' She believed that the resettlement arrangements were 'most liberal', but Selkirk told her that 'he could understand that in the state of mind of these people, many wd not accept', and he was prepared to offer them the means of emigration.[27]

Nevertheless, in April 1813, Young was able to report that all the people seemed quiet. Selkirk had created much interest in emigration among the people of Kildonan and Clyne. Young could not understand the reaction which Selkirk had generated in the parish of Rogart where no removals were planned. The people of Rogart had been roused to emigration even though 'not a man had been disturbed' except to improve the lots greatly on a nineteen-year lease.[28] Emigration was evidently stimulated by changes across the estate, whether the people were subject to removal or not. The people were in a stir.

– MACKID VERSUS SELLAR –

Kildonan simmered down as Cranstoun re-established his authority. But, at that very moment, in March 1813, the origins of Sellar's mortal contest with Sheriff-Substitute Mackid (which would culminate in Sellar's trial in 1816) were clearly registered amid the correspondence about the Kildonan events. Sellar alleged that Robert Mackid had been acting 'slily to Mr Cranstoun'. Mackid had become malevolent towards him, claimed Sellar, and it was connected directly to his work as factor among the people of the inland straths. Sellar recollected that, even before the Kildonan tumults, he had been mistreated while collecting the Martinmas rents in the district:

> I was very nearly mobbed by the people to be dispossessed on the subject of the usage they were likely to experience at the ensuing Whitsunday. At the least, their conduct was very threatening, and I think, on my return I gave your Ladyship a hint of what might be anticipated from them, long before there were any suspicions of the extent of the evil. The same people subsequently hounded the Gentlemen employed for your Ladyship off the ground, for the avowed purpose of Shedding the blood because they were in your Employ; and treated Mackid and me with no little indignity when we thereafter went in the beginning of February to Kildonan to receive their Bond to keep the peace.[29]

They had even attacked 'Lord Stafford's own shepherd', 'and threatened to Cutt his throat if he dared to attend his Lordship's flocks at his farm at Craggy.' Sellar had issued eviction notices to tenants in arrear and declared: 'I would apply the same step to every person in arrear whom I found in arms in the same cause'. Sellar had thus felt the sharp end of the Kildonan conflict even before the riot. He had then worked closely with Mackid who was directly involved with Sellar in serving notices on the people. It was during these events that Sellar sensed that Mackid was beginning to subvert the conduct of the removals.

Sellar thanked Lady Stafford for her concern 'for the unpleasant situation of your servants, Mr Young and me, in the late tumults of this Country.' He assured her that they were 'not in the smallest degree of personal danger, nor are our feelings affected by such idle clamour as has been employed to vex us and to keep up irritation in the minds of the people'. He then expatiated on the prudence of providing Alpine plants as 'the food only of sheep (a Creature fitted for clambering over such Ground and <u>clothed</u> by nature for the Climate)'. Without sheep such natural resources were wasted to the world. Moreover, in the ocean the fish were clearly not meant merely to

> dissolve in the deep where they came; while the people of the Country lodged in uncomfortable Cabins in the district <u>which belongs 'of right' to the beasts of the field</u>, lead, in common with their miserable horses and cattle, a life of idleness and starvation by dissipating the other resources and natural wealth of the Country.

The country could not advance until totally changed, 'until the mountains be applied to their natural purpose'.

Sellar's convictions regarding the wisdom of the removal policies had been powerfully reinforced by the riots in Kildonan. 'Whatever clamour inconsiderate people may indulge in, we are satisfied that the public will soon see how unpatriotic Lord Stafford and your Ladyship would be' if they did not follow through their plans. 'Thriftless ignorance and laziness' was the *status quo*; the people must be brought to the coast to gather the fruits of the earth and the ocean. 'In a word they will be convinced what proprietors farther South did progressively in former ages; and when had they not done, Great Britain might now have been some such mighty Empire, as that of Otaheite!'

Thus, to Sellar, the clearing landlords and their agents were simply discharging their duty to the Country, 'by leading some and driving others, and leaving to the Law those who will neither lead nor drive.' The 'most volatile' should best 'emigrate to some other Country.' Sellar said that the introduction of the military had brought peace and calm, and the episode had demonstrated that the Highlanders were 'no more deficient in prudence than in Bravery, nor will they oppose a force which they are unable to resist'. Sellar believed that the rebellious people had been led by the Sutherland brothers, that is Scibbercross and his clever and desperate brother in London who, he believed, were the authors of the damaging letters recently published in the *Military Register*. It was, 'altogether, an attempt to frighten the shepherds and us; They did not dream of fighting against Great Britain.' The people would soon repent and good conduct and industry would then follow.[30]

It was in this sequence of correspondence that Sellar directly alleged that Mackid had fed Cranstoun with malicious allegations against him, and connived to trap him in the minute details of his rental accounts. Sellar explained to Cranstoun that he found it difficult to 'strike the proper medium', but each accusation had to be met. He insisted that he be told all accusations so that he could answer them in detail.[31] Already, therefore, Sellar believed that Mackid was plotting against him and was in league with resistant elements among the small tenantry.

In April, in the aftermath of the riots, Sellar wrote to say that he believed he had become the target of popular obloquy, and was now regarded as the man responsible for the execution of the removals. It was, he said, his main function to 'keep the Tenantry in Check' and therefore he must 'continually [be] upon the alert to find matters of accusation against him. The less Accessible they find him by other means the more sharply will they watch him!' It was a psychological game of cat and mouse. He expected many complaints. Indeed, he said, he was surprised that more accusations had not erupted already.[32] Sellar knew, therefore, that he was marked as the focus of resistance. But he also admitted that he courted unpopularity by his own rigorous interpretation of his duties.[33]

In March 1813, revealing the depth to which relations with the people of the interior had sunk, Sellar had told Lady Stafford that his role as estate factor led to endless accusations against him. He told her, 'I have no fear of death by the hand of any man who will look me in the face; but I am not the less liable to assassination.'[34] Lady Stafford may have regarded Sellar's lengthy tirades as self-dramatisation and typical of the man. In retrospect, Sellar seems to have calculated his situation with some accuracy. Long before his ordeal had taken shape, he had identified himself as a marked man.

Despite his sense of persecution, Sellar was able to assure Lady Stafford that he feared no personal danger. Indeed, in the midst of the turbulence, he was able to find the time and the equanimity to rehearse the arguments in favour of the policy which was now generating such disturbing resistance. They centred on the natural advantage of the region for sheep-farming. It was impossible for the country to reach its 'strength', nor the people to achieve

> comfort until the people be brought from the mountains and placed on the shores, where in the milder climate they may profit by the bounty there afforded them.

He concluded: 'Therefore, whatever clamour inconsiderate people may indulge in, we are satisfied that the public will soon see' the wisdom of it all. He believed that the improvements would soon produce 'pure Gold and Silver from the British mine, of which Mexico and Peru only produce the Resemblance.' It was a flight of the imagination and typical of Sellar's turn of mind.[35]

– RELIGIOUS TURMOIL IN ASSYNT –

Within the Sutherland population, and especially in Assynt, there were currents of popular feeling of which Young and Sellar possessed only slight understanding. In August 1811, Young mentioned a 'schism among the people' related to the intrusion into Assynt of 'Haldanites' (or 'sectaries', as he called them). There was, indeed, a local eruption of ideas of popular evangelicalism, partly excited by Paineite notions, common in many parts of Scotland in these years. The ideas of James and Robert Haldane were regarded by the government and the established church as potentially subversive. In 1799, their supporters were denounced as 'persons notoriously disaffected to the local Constitution of the country'.

The Haldanites sent dozens of lowland missionaries and preachers into the Highlands, spreading a gospel which espoused ideas concerned with the essential 'dignity of man'. Their ideas had widespread exposure. The fervour reached remote Assynt at this time, and built a substantial following which suggested a growing and dangerous turbulence in the district. William Young reported that the local minister had a huge parish to sustain and it was not difficult to imagine that 'the flock [would] go astray' when they were so little served by a minister who was overstretched.[36]

There had been a long record of sporadic resistance to the established church in many parts of Sutherland, expressing recurrent agitation against orthodoxy.[37] In July 1813, the induction of a Moderate new minister was riotously obstructed by the people of Assynt in an episode not ostensibly related to the removals. The connection between the religious and the eviction riots seems to have been achieved through Duncan MacGillivray. He was a licensed preacher in the Heights of Kildonan and was appointed assistant and successor to the ageing minister in Assynt. The parishioners refused to accept him as their minister 'because he had tried to use his influence to persuade the Kildonan people to give up any idea of resistance.' He was believed to be a spy for Sellar.[38] In the event, the church doors were barricaded against the incoming minister and there were fears of serious physical violence.

Young regarded the people involved in the Assynt events in July 1813 as 'blockheads [and] . . . Mountain savages' and he was surprised that there was no loss of life. Young was involved personally since he had accompanied the new clergyman and, together with the new man, had been harassed by the people. The riotous people had, however, disagreed among themselves about whether the factor and the minster should be handcuffed and put out to sea in an open boat. Though they had been much personally humiliated in the episode, Young and MacGillivray had extricated themselves from the danger. The sheriff then began an investigation, but his authority was also at risk: 'The Kildonan riots were a mere nothing to this and the people and some shadow of excuse', remarked Young angrily.[39]

Troops were again readied for dispatch to the Assynt coast and, in August 1813, 160 troops left Leith by sail. But their introduction was countermanded by the Lord Advocate, though more troops were put on alert in Fort George. The situation was complicated by the concurrent fear of American naval incursions off Caithness.

There was great division in the ranks of the law-enforcers and the estate managers before the Assynt resistance was eventually quelled by troops from Edinburgh. The intervention of the military was followed by the prosecution of several parishioners for mobbing and rioting.[40] Cranstoun, Mackid's superior officer, was highly critical of the decision to introduce troops; he believed that there had been too much 'parading of constables being marched up the Country from Dornoch in files'. This, he said, gave the impression of weakness rather than strength. As the Assynt tumults subsided, a number of legal steps followed. In this sequel, at the end of July 1813, Robert Mackid instituted a precognition (a preliminary investigation) of the Assynt riot. Mackid had made an 'extraordinary blunder' in the documentation of the case and had actually altered names of the witnesses on the legal documents. William Mackenzie believed that Mackid should be dismissed.[41] Cranstoun, meanwhile, organised legal action against some of the rioters and arranged for their appearance before the court in Inverness. Mackid had certainly bungled the indictment by altering the official papers and the case was seriously undermined. Nevertheless the case went ahead and three of the rioters were found guilty and imprisoned.

At the end of the Assynt events, there was serious talk of Mackid's dismissal.[42] William Mackenzie reported that Mackid, who used to be very accurate in his legal work and who gave good satisfaction, had greatly disappointed expectations and had become indolent. Yet Cranstoun leapt to Mackid's defence and said that he had been effective for the past six years; he had moved to Kirkton at some personal loss, and he should certainly not be dismissed 'on account of an error of judgment or even a single act of negligence.' Mackid thus survived once more, though it was agreed that any further error would mean his certain dismissal.[43]

– YOUNG AND SELLAR COMPARED –

James Loch visited the Sutherland estate in the summer of 1813 and made a full report on the state of affairs in the management. He quickly developed a good *rapport* with William Young. Young was responsible for the finances. At the end of the year, Loch reiterated his good opinion of Young whose conduct was, he said, 'most confidential and gentlemanlike'.[44] In the course of these *post mortems* with Loch, Lady Stafford remarked that William Young 'had an excellent head for general affairs but in his eagerness to dispatch them I think he has made a bungle' on some matters of detailed execution, notably the coal operations on the east coast. But the attitude of Loch and Lady Stafford to Patrick Sellar had a different tone. Loch discovered that Sellar was mainly responsible for rentals and was the type of person who was best entrusted with detail, such as monitoring methods of road construction and collecting tolls. Sellar, he thought, was a man of 'sharpness and accuracy' who would make people pay and also 'enforced the law strictly'. When Loch finished his long letter, he remarked, 'I have been bit by Sellar and am possessed with the same love of penmanship.'[45]

In October 1813, Sellar wrote to Lady Stafford in typical mode, characterising the old system of 'Tricks and Canting which have hitherto enabled the Tacksmen to oppress the tenantry, and force the tenantry to seek a living, in a manner that damaged the property of every person in contact with them.' The small tenants, he asserted, would be much better placed on the coast with genuine employment.[46] It was such remarks as these that caused both Lady Stafford and Loch to take the view that Sellar overdid his rhetoric. He obviously embarrassed his associates by the acerbity and excess of his expression. As Lady Stafford put it, 'Sellar's language in writing is not good,' by which she meant that he was strident and undiplomatic.[47]

In the interim, the Kildonan removals of 1813 were accomplished without further explosion and the estate managers and Lady Stafford pressed forward with the over-arching plan for removals and development along the coasts. But in late 1813, Sellar ran into another fiery row, this time with the formidable Thomas Telford. Telford was renowned for his short temper and his proprietorial attitude to engineering projects. He clashed badly with the local managers of the great construction work proceeding on the Mound, where 700 men were employed at critical times. Telford took exception to the fact that his own people were not being employed in Sutherland. Sellar explained Telford's fury in terms of the latter's health and eccentricity.[48]

At the end of 1813, Sellar was much gratified by a further mark of favour from the Stafford family. He was now included in the tiny number of enfranchised tenants in the County of Sutherland which the family controlled without serious opposition. Sellar could hardly contain his delight; he was deeply honoured to be entrusted with a vote in the County of Sutherland:

> We could not be more touched with this instance of the confidence so very flattering to me, from the dignity of the Gowers, and the short Specimen of my conduct, on which it was conferred, and it was with great regret we thought it impracticable to attain the honour at present, by reason that my funds were about to be locked up in farming, as my father's are embarked in Burghead harbour, in a farm near Elgin in some roads, and in the property of Westfield near Inverugie for which he has recently paid £19,500, and in the improvement of which he much expends a good deal more.

Sellar's financial limit had been reached and this was circumvented by a substantial loan from Lord Stafford. This was a critical moment for Sellar since it gave him *entré* into the highest rank of society in the county, and also the opportunity to expand his operations in Sutherland as opportunities arose.[49]

– Sellar as sheepfarmer, December 1813 –

Patrick Sellar's fateful entry into sheep-farming on his own account in Strathnaver occurred at another auction for leases conducted by William Young at the Golspie Inn on 15 December 1813. At 'the set' were representatives of the sitting tenants, as well as John Patterson, a sheep-farmer from Caithness. The lands included large stretches of territory in the upper part of Strathnaver, incorporating the farm of Rhiloisk. According to Sellar, his decision was made on the spur of the moment. He had not intended to bid for the lands to be cleared in the following spring, until he saw the weakness of the competing parties. In the upshot, Sellar outbid the current tenants as well as Patterson, but the added competition evidently drove up the final price of the lease.[50] The tenants had offered £250 per annum, but Sellar offered £360, rising to £410 after the first seven years. Sellar contracted to pay double the prevailing rent for parts of Strathnaver, including Rossal.[51] The lease, written in late 1813, included a clause by which the new tenant agreed to 'free Lady Stafford of any claim by the tenants for their timber at my Entry'.[52] Referring to Sellar's successful bid for the Strathnaver leases, Young felt it necessary to assure Lady Stafford that his colleague had been shown no favour in the bidding. Sellar had simply offered a rent greater than those of his competitors.[53]

Sellar thus acquired lands full of the promise of lucrative returns accruing to sheep production. But Strathnaver was also full of people, now reduced to the status of temporary subtenants, whose rents Sellar immediately increased. The lease entailed their removal and this was a matter for urgent arrangement; any delay would prevent the introduction of Sellar's sheep and would cause immediate financial losses on his newly borrowed capital. Sellar warned the tenants of their impending removal and this involved a complicated timetable which allowed some to remain longer than others: the schedule was determined mainly by the availability of resettlement sites for the people to be removed. This was essentially an estate matter, and it was already creating problems. Sellar gave the Strathnaver people traditional notice to quit, and the outgoing tenants had customary rights to the arable land and barns until their last crop was brought in.

Sellar's lease in Strathnaver included all the farms on the east side of the Strath, together with Rimsdale and Garvault in Kildonan, acquired by stages in 1814 and 1816. Young persuaded Sellar to let many of the resident tenants stay on for an extra year to ease pressure on the resettlement facilities. The arrangement involved the intercession of the Reverend David Mackenzie, who explained the plans to the people affected in Gaelic. Sellar met the people at Suisgill, in January 1814, and agreed to give the people half the ground for another year.[54] Sellar subset three-quarters of the tenants of Rossal for £170 per annum. His total initial rent was £200. He prepared meanwhile for the clearance of twenty-eight families from Ravigall, Rhiphail, Rhiloisk, Badinloisk, Rimsdale and Garvault. This was scheduled for Whitsunday 1814, and this relatively small episode was the specific origin of the events which, two years later, culminated in Sellar's trial.[55]

Before these dramatic events began their course, Sellar had already moderated his demands for access to his new sheep-farm. At the behest of William Young, in January 1814, Sellar agreed to compromise his entry into Strathnaver, to delay his operations for several months and, for some of the territory, for considerably longer. This was a substantial concession on his part. Sellar wanted to conduct a census there but this was also postponed. He placed all the subtenancies on an annual basis. The impending removals, part of much larger dislocations of the Sutherland estate's inland populations, were staggered to reduce pressure on facilities. In this phase, the scale of the removals increased and several thousand people were dislocated within or beyond the estate. Young was especially apprehensive about the Strathnaver removals.

– COLLIDING FORCES –

The conditions for collision between Sellar and the world about him were now remarkably well assembled. Sellar had alienated many people on the estate, high and low, but especially in the old society. He had declared war on poachers and illicit stills; he had extracted rents with a new efficiency; and he had issued writs for removal to hundreds of small tenants. He had scorned the farming methods of his neighbours and harried their sons when they took game from the Countess's lands. He had also bid up the price of land in the east and now in the north of the estate; he had humiliated the Sheriff-Substitute and converted him into a permanent and profound enemy. He had thrown himself into all the most unpopular work undertaken by a Highland factor. And now he was to become a sheep-farmer in his own name. By his own account, Sellar was pitted against the most formidable vested interests in the county. The stage was readied for the ultimate contest.

CHAPTER 7

Sellar and the
Strathnaver Removals, 1814–15

– A QUIET START, WINTER 1814 –

The year 1813 had been punctuated by riots in Kildonan and Assynt, and the Sutherland estate administration had been made anxious for the future of its great plans of reconstruction.[1] At the end of the year, however, spirits lifted and a welcome calm seemed to settle on the land. Calm was required because 1814 was to be the year in which the removal and resettlement programme would move forward at a greater pace, and on a scale unprecedented in the Highlands. Young's vision was about to become tangible: hundreds of people were to be shifted from inland Strathnaver to the coasts, and the new works along the coast were to reach their first fruition. He remained anxious for the future subsistence of the people and feared the recurrence of famine.

Meanwhile, Young's right-hand man, Patrick Sellar, had negotiated his own way into sheep-farming. The terms agreed for his 'sett' at the Golspie Inn in December 1813 augured well for Sellar's new venture, though his prospects depended, of course, on the removal of the existing population. Young assured Lady Stafford that all was 'peace and quiet at the Set on Wednesday and the Strathnaver Men who were dispossessed from the Lot which Mr Sellar gets seem satisfied so [far] as I could discover.' Young had planned lots for them at the seaward end of the Strath.

Apprehension resided in the minds of the new sheep-farmers of the estate. They were sufficiently concerned about the threats to life and property (mainly their sheep stocks) that they clubbed together to form a quasi-vigilante body called the *Sutherland Association for the Protection of Property*. Young continued to waver between optimism and trepidation; similarly he oscillated in his view of the future of the common people of the estate. His plans were premised on the retention and resettlement of the interior population. But he increasingly also thought that emigration had an important role in the new context. His thinking was now influenced by the ideas of Malthus, and this was underscored by the recent incidence of near-famine in the northern Highlands. He wanted the government to stop thinking of returning the Cape of Good Hope to the Dutch and, instead, people it with British emigrants. He was thinking of Highlanders in particular. Nevertheless, in the meantime, coastal land was being acquired for the people to be cleared from Strathnaver and elsewhere. The outcome, Young told Lady Stafford, would be a great augmentation of the estate rents from £11,000 in 1809 to £20,000 by the time the Strathnaver and Brora arrangements had been completed.[2]

At the beginning of 1814, Young returned to his own property in Inverugie in Moray, leaving Sellar 'preaching up sobriety and activity in my absence'. Sellar indeed was full of activity at this time, correcting behaviour, collecting rents, distributing meal, preparing his finances for his great new venture in Strathnaver and continuing his farm improvements at Culmaily. Much of this display of activity brought him into conflict with people he regarded as miscreants. In these months he consolidated several of his deepest enmities. The most important was that with Robert Mackid, the Sheriff-Substitute.

– THE COLD OF WINTER –

At the start of 1814 Sellar reported that the frosts and snows had been so severe that the game had been forced onto lower ground. Sellar knew that poaching would become an increased temptation and he ordered enhanced vigilance to counter the possibility. As he put it, 'It is at this season that the greatest mischief is done by the poachers.' One of his men, Nash, apprehended an offender and Mackid, as law officer, was informed. The problem was that Mackid himself was also accused of poaching at that very time. Sellar expressed his astonishment to Lady Stafford: 'Your Ladyship will recollect that I took him over the coals in Spring 1811; and that we passed it over as a thing incredible of a Gentleman in his office.' Thus Sellar registered their gathering conflict over three years.[3]

Sellar could hardly contain his horrified excitement over Mackid's entanglement in the new poaching episode. He had received a report which provided explicit information against Mackid for poaching:

I have not [received] return from McKid for my note, and I fain hope that the information may have been in some degree, incorrect; for nothing could be more mean than for a gentleman to kill a proprietor's Game in the Snow, and without being Qualified by Licence or lease of the landlord. However, the informant, who is one of our Police, has been here tonight offering his Affidavit, and claiming his Guinea; and I suspect Mr Mackid has been very foolish as to run his head into this Scrape.

Sellar eagerly awaited his instructions.[4]

The episode again demonstrated the habitual latitude to the question of poaching on the estate. Mackid regarded the custom of the country in a different light and obviously expected a blind eye to be turned to such misdemeanours. Sellar, by contrast, offered his 'police' special incentives for the capture of poachers, regardless of status.

The poaching episode remained in suspense while Sellar went about the rest of his business. In September 1813, Sellar had boasted that he was collecting the greatest rental in Scotland, possibly the largest in Great Britain, taken over ten parishes. He was finally very pleased with his rent collection despite the weather, and in March 1814 he was in jovial mood reporting the successful result, and now engaged 'in that most excellent comedy called "much ado about nothing".'

Nevertheless, the rent collection had been a great contest with the people because the 'numerous Removals now Going on' encouraged them to do as 'the Egyptians', that is to flit before paying their rents. Sellar had undertaken a great perambulation of the estate, during which his guide lost several toes from the frost. Sellar had served notices of removal affecting some 700 cases.[5] He had been out and about in the worst imaginable weather, deep in the interior straths of Sutherland whence he described his mission in vivid tones. He had encountering blizzard conditions: there had been 'sad fighting to get through the form of the collection. The snow better than a yard deep and the frosts keener than I ever felt.' In many places, in Armadale, Strathnaver and Assynt, none of the tenants or their tacksmen had even bothered to appear for the rent collection. One of his company in the collection party had practically fainted away with the cold while another was so frost-bitten 'that we had difficulty getting him home'. This was his assistant, Roy, who suffered excruciating pain when he ill-advisedly plunged his frozen feet into warm water: according to Sellar, 'they mortified and he has lost the greater part of each [with] much suffering and is lame for life.' Lady Stafford received this intelligence with much melancholy.[6]

Sellar also reported symptoms of opposition from the people, which might well threaten his own imminent entry into the Strathnaver sheep-farm:

> The people of Kildonan who met me at a Shepherd's house in the upper end of the Parish after paying their rents carried home a joint of mutton and some other trifles which they pilfered from the house. The Polly people shewed some indication to riot on the place being Sett, but the Court of Justices having been immediately summoned and an officer sent, to order them down . . . the matter was instantly settled, and there is no chance of any disturbance among any class of the people. I have given the people of Rossal Lott about one half of it at a fair proportion of my permanent rent [of?] 19 years, to assist them in pasture for the first year they have Lotts from Mr Young, and the people of Strathnaver so far as I can learn are all well pleased with what I proposed to them.[7]

There was great consternation brewing among the people and Sellar expected some resistance in the coming removals. After persuasion from Young, and as a gesture of goodwill, Sellar had agreed to a temporary delay of the removal of some of the Strathnaver people. In the months just before his removals, Sellar reported that the people to be affected were in good spirits. He had met them and agreed to allow them special concessions for grazing for an extra year. He concluded that:

> All the people of Strathnaver so far as I can learn are well pleased with what is proposed for them.[8]

In the interim, however, the severity of the weather had caused large losses of sheep stock.

Mackid, caught in illegal acts, decided to write 'a penitential letter, [in which] he confesse[d to] the act of poaching'. Lady Stafford left the matter in suspense while she decided how to resolve the embarrassment and whether to prosecute the poachers, including the main resident law officer in the county. Sellar meanwhile continued to denounce Mackid:

> McKid is a Clever man without sense or principle; if the Country were Clear of him and a moderate honest man in his shoes it would be well.

In February 1814, Sellar promised Lady Stafford that he would not 'rest upon my oars concerning Mackid'.[9]

Sellar's views were unambiguous and no secret from Mackid or the people of the district. But neither Mackenzie, Lady Stafford's legal man, nor Cranstoun, the principal representative of the law in the north, were prepared to bring the might of the law down upon

Mackid's head for the crime of poaching. Mackid, said Sellar, had acted in a manner 'unbecoming to a Gentleman', but Cranstoun probably regarded the crime as a small thing, and was prepared to keep Mackid on. Sellar said that the estate might well come to regret any tolerance of Mackid's crime. It was an extraordinarily prescient thought, early in 1814. Yet, in the same breath, Sellar declared, 'I am, without the Smallest intimacy to friendship, on no bad terms with Mr Mackid.' To suggest that Mackid could possibly be on good terms with Sellar suggests astonishingly blinkered vision on Sellar's part. Mackid could only fear and loathe the man whose naked purpose had been to demolish his professional reputation.

Having roundly denounced Mackid, Sellar typically proceeded to declaim at length on matters of agricultural detail, the renewed frosts and a foot of snow that had fallen. He repeated his faith in turnips and hay, and was persevering with his merino experiments. His sheep were happily coping with the extreme weather. Yet, preying on Sellar's mind was the Mackid problem. Sellar believed that it was foolish laxity not to move against the Sheriff-Substitute, and in later years he looked back on the poaching episode as a turning point in his life. At the time, in early 1814, he experienced a sense of premonition of the retribution which Mackid would eventually extract. He predicted that his enemy was determined

> to take revenge on us by breaches of trust, in which he could keep within the letter of the Law and so do us much annoyance.

In April 1814 Lady Stafford declared an amnesty for a list of twenty-four poachers including Mackid (the only 'Esq.' among them) on the understanding that any further offence would mean instant eviction from the estate. Sellar was alarmed and told Lady Stafford that Mackid had repaid 'your Ladyship and Lord Stafford's indulgence by every little hostility in his power towards me, although without any bad effects.' Sellar was now in a state of high alert about Mackid's likely attempt to damage him personally. Sellar believed that Mackid was desperately attempting to find fault with Sellar's own professional work: 'I have endeavoured to give him no room to Quibble or Trick me. In between 50 and 100 Suits since Xmas he could not, with all his ingenuity find the least flaw, except in one unlucky case for payment of a Rent in Strathrusdale where he got the letter of the Law on his side'. Sellar's work was essentially legal and dealt in matters of petty detail. As a man of great pertinacity, Sellar's professional manner invited challenge, and seemed to welcome disputation.

Mackid and Sellar were patently at loggerheads, squaring up to each other. Both were lawyers and their legal daggers were drawn. It was a dangerous moment for Sellar since he was about to execute his own clearances in Kildonan. Mackid meanwhile was picking over all the estate law suits in search of any legal blunder by Sellar in relation to 'the necessary removings in the Parish of Farr etc.'[10] On the poaching issue Sellar had failed in his effort to bring Mackid to book.[11] It was crystal clear that, in the process, Mackid and Sellar had become mortal enemies. Though Sellar had gained the upper hand, Mackid was capable of great damage. Only three months later, when Sellar was immersed in the great round of removals at Whitsunday, he reported again that Mackid had 'oppressed' the officer who had exposed his poaching offences. Moreover, Mackid had been in Assynt making inflammatory speeches against Young. Sellar once more suggested that the time had come for Mackid's dismissal.

In February 1814, Sellar continued his journeys which extended to Assynt in the far west of the estate whence he reported in typically triumphant terms. It was, he wrote, 'a broken mass of Rocks hurled together, but mixed with fine green pasture.' Stock losses had been small, despite the severity of the weather. He happily dilated on the potential of the alpine plants of the region. Scobie, a sheep-farmer from the old tacksman class, had asked for a delay in his rent payment on the grounds that his sheep were suffering from the effects of braxy, but Sellar scoffed at the excuse:

> The truth is these Assynt <u>Gentlemen</u> have no Skill. They wont expend money in travelling to acquire it, or, in sending their Boys from home; and where they should all be affluent, they are in poverty. They are almost all behind in rents. They should look for some spirited Northumberland or Tweeddale man; make a Cutt in among them and settle him there. Mr Young and I have often tried to Get their boys for a year or two, from them to our farms, and to the shepherds here, but all in vain. They have too much pride and too little industry, or rather too little pride of the sort which a farmer ought to possess.

For Sellar, Sutherland was the 'best stock and wool country in Britain, perhaps in the world'. He cultivated his own contacts in the world of sheep-stocking and was in communication with such influential luminaries as George Tollett, and Morton and Culley, sheep-farmers in Northumberland.[12]

– THE FRENZY OF ACTIVITY: EARLY SUMMER, 1814 –

Though the removals in Strathnaver at Whitsunday 1814 were the most infamous in Highland history, and though utterly central to the life of Patrick Sellar, they are not well documented. The Sutherland estate papers are relatively scant for the few months that surround the events. Nevertheless, there survive enough fragments to capture the context of the emerging drama. Even before the removals were implemented, Sellar had cause to complain of the irresolution of the sheriff officers employed to deliver the removal notices. They were, he fulminated, 'not only ignorant and incapable . . . but extremely lax and irregular in the Execution of Summonses.'[13] These, of course, were the men on whom Sellar and the estate depended for the implementation of the improvement policy, and particularly for the execution of the evictions.

At the end of May 1814 William Young gave a vivid impression of the frenetic pace and great scale of the changes over which he was, at that moment, presiding. He looked forward to what he called 'a glorious summer' of construction and improvements:

> Our present hurry is beyond what any person who is not on the Spot can form an idea of, and I shall for the next 14 days be all together in Straths Naver and Brora where we have at least 430 familys to arrange in different allotments, to double their present rents, and put them in a more industrious way of Life.[14]

He disagreed with James Loch who advocated a more stringent approach to rent extraction, taking the small tenants' side of the argument. Often, he argued, it was difficult for tenants because their income depended on the sale of cattle and it was important not to force them to sell at very low prices. Discretion was required if the factor was to judge their true ability to pay. Blackguards and idlers should be dealt with strictly, 'but the industrious and diligent' needed to be nursed like children. Sellar's rent collections evidently required the exercise of delicate judgement.[15]

It was a time of extreme activity both in the interior (with the removals) and along the coasts (with the resettlement zones and the new ventures introduced by Young). The estate correspondence gives only a hint of the agitation that accompanied these events. The clamour of complaint evidently developed only slowly. Sellar himself received differing and wavering signals from his superiors. Thus, in May 1814, James Loch spoke of giving Sellar instructions 'to be peremptory in the collection of his rents at the different Audits'. It was never good practice to allow the tenants to fall into arrear.[16] Young observed that, but for 'political motives', Sellar would have been more decisive than polite with his removals.[17] Sellar's own removals took place after Whitsunday 1814, and involved only twenty-eight families.

In the second week of June 1814, William Young reported his return from Strathnaver after 'settling about 250 familys on the Banks of the river and seaside without a murmur.' None of the settlers received more than three acres arable, together with pasture for two cows and a horse. Consequently, and in line with Young's grand plan, they would simply have to engage in work on road construction and the fisheries. Young provided a rare detail:

> I fell in with a fine old man in Strathnaver who told me (and I believe him) that he was a Sergt in the Earl of Sutherland's Regt and drove his Coach for 3 to 4 years, his heart seemed full but he asked nothing, and I ventured to say your Ladyship would give him his small Lot 14/- yearly rent for nothing while he lived.

It was a symbolic and revealing moment in the very heart of the clearance.[18]

In July 1814, Lady Stafford was in Dunrobin, and close to much of the energetic activity in the great summer of removal and regeneration, and this may explain the infrequency of letters at that time. At first she was much pleased with the scope and appearance of the changes.[19] She dined with both Young and Sellar and responded to the events unfolding about them.[20] She was especially impressed with Sellar's operations in Culmaily. On 7 July (which was after Sellar's clearance in Strathnaver), she told her husband:

> The Strathnaver People are well satisfied with their double rent, the others are quiet and going on well.[21]

This was a surprising construction: either she was unaware of trouble brewing, or the trouble had not yet accumulated to a level which reached her ears. She simply remarked that the new arrangements were upon the people and that progress had commenced. She believed that her own presence had helped to keep the plans in focus, and she had made sure her factors knew what she expected.

Her exchanges with her managers at this time included what she called

> a *Tête à Tête* with Sellar this morning and [I] have read his rentals – all perfection like Bradshaw's, and as neat.

This was an interesting comparison since R. H. Bradshaw was the clever, but irascible, Superintendent of the Bridgewater Canal, who presided over the great flow of revenues into Lord Stafford's coffers. But he was also extremely headstrong and unpopular with many associates, and even with his beneficiaries.[22] It was at this very time also that Lady Stafford was reading Malthus and remarking that 'He might have said it all in one page. He longs to drown Children but proves that population do what you will, will take care of itself.' [23] And, as usual, Lady Stafford spent some of her sojourn fielding local complaints. For instance, Scibbercross, a local tenant, had complained that the estate managers were ignoring him.

Lady Stafford visited Sellar's farm at Culmaily and described his farming operations as well as his manner of thinking:

> He is busy making hay and is to have it in a large Hayrick in a fortnight. We see his farm in excellent order. He has taken in 24 acres of the large green nobby field above his House, the taking four large stones out Cost £80. He does the other half next year. He made £500 profit last year of his cattle. The Sheep we are to hear more of as we had not time to go back to see the wool. The black Houses are levelled, making manure. The plain is really a very fine sight.[24]

Sellar was omnipresent – even entering the new coal pit, investigating the seams, endlessly proffering advice on every subject.

As Lady Stafford scribbled these frequent confidential reports from Dunrobin Castle, to her husband in the south, she offered fleeting impressions of Sellar the man. She concluded that

> Sellar is an excellent man of business but has not enlarged views, and plagues people with trifles.

She contrasted him unfavourably with William Young who was far better on general matters, was honest and exuded 'good feeling', presumably in contrast to Sellar.

– STRATHNAVER IN 1814 –

It was during these weeks of frantic activity – in May and June 1814 – that Sellar and his clearing party set to work removing some of the people of Strathnaver so that he could take possession of his great new sheep-farm.

Strathnaver, a romantic wide and lush valley stretching from the high mountains deep in the interior of Sutherland, is joined by endless rivers and burns as it runs out into the northern ocean. On a summer's day, it possessed an idyllic air of bounteous nature, a place made perfect for communal rural living. In winter it might feel like the last home of the damned. This was its historical personality also – its alternation of faces, of good times and famine, of sunshine and storm. It supported human life and culture of remarkable distinction and fertility; but it reclaimed life by the savage turns of the seasons. Famine and deprivation certainly stalked this land, even in the first decade of the nineteenth century. It was an anxious society often thrown onto the calculated charity of the landlord who operated as a sort of lender of the last resort, tiding the common people over recurrent food deficits. Nevertheless, an estate survey in 1810, by Benjamin Meredith, described the district as 'upon the whole calculated to support the numbers collectively kept on it, and which are by no means inconsiderable.' Meredith noted that cattle production was the main source of income, but the local economy was also supported by seasonal labour in the south.[25]

Strathnaver had an extraordinary record for its delivery of soldiery to the regiments, especially from the 1770s to the French Wars, during which time five companies were raised, causing some serious labour shortage in the local economy.[26] In 1810, even as the land itself was becoming commercially more valuable, and when the landlord was richer than ever before, the people found they were to be extruded from these lands. They had no stomach for this. They had lived with recurrent deprivation since time immemorial. They were prepared to pay more rent, but they did not seek or want change. They were in a commotion of the collective *psyche* and they inevitably collided with Young's plans. More especially, they were familiar with Patrick Sellar, both as rent collector and agent. Now he emerged as usurper of their lands.

Horace Fairhurst, the archaeologist, provides a telling description of the territory taken over by Sellar. Strathnaver, he wrote, is mainly a wide irregular plateau, rarely rising above 800 feet, and taking the form of an extensive peaty moorland, interspersed with shallow lochs and rocky rounded hills. Beyond are great mountains including Ben Loyal and Ben Hope. The straths are quite broad and Strathnaver 'is a rather shallow, gentle-sided valley', much in contrast with many of the great glens of the central Highlands. Most of the settlements were deep inland in many scattered groupings. For example, Rossal was an island of cultivation in a sea of moors, surrounded by much grazing.[27]

Archaeological evidence demonstrates the continuity of settlement in these higher reaches of Strathnaver since 'relatively ancient times', probably from the early Iron Age, and certainly since medieval times. Henderson, the 'Agricultural Reporter', in 1811 mentioned forty-nine settlements, mostly in Strathnaver. In Rossal, a largish township, there were thirteen families. Fairhurst suggests that the number of settlements in Strathnaver had increased by the 'colonisation of shieling grounds and that this process was greatly accelerated in the later 18th century.' Fairhurst found no evidence of burning at the site, when he excavated it in the early 1960s. There were, however, clear marks of an expansion of arable areas at Rossal at the time just prior to the clearances, 'presumably as a result of land hunger.'[28] The strath was full of substantial settlements in the form of townships with their arable and shielings which had expanded, often with increased potato cultivation, under the impact of rising population. It was not a stagnant community, but it may have become more vulnerable as a consequence of this demographic expansion. Whatever the case, Sellar, as soon as he appropriated the territory, could use the land more effectively, at least in the commercial market sense.

– THE FIRST ALLEGATIONS AGAINST SELLAR –

A month after his removals in Strathnaver, Sellar referred to certain complaints made by 'the Kildonan tenants removed to Strathnaver', though he doubted that the people were actually agreed about the form of their complaints. They asserted against Sellar that they had received insufficient notice; they had suffered from the removal of their timbers; there had been excessive burning of their heather; and barns had been destroyed though the custom of the country required him to leave them for another year. This was the first recorded indication of trouble in connection with Sellar's removals in 1814.

Sellar immediately claimed that the complaints had been instigated by Mackid.[29] He said that he would organise his evidence to counter the allegations. He remarked that, since he entered the service of the Stafford family, 'there is no part of my conduct as your factor, which can cause a friend, I have, to blush, to see the account, [?] printed, and posted on the market Cross.' He had committed his 'heart and soul' to their service, but if they could find a better man than he, then he would be happy to depart. The salary, he said, was of no significance to him. He would rather 'spend £500 a year in this thatched Cottage [Culmaily] with his people and shepherds and cattle and flocks about him, than £5,000 on the best house in England.' It was an odd thing to say, and may suggest that the allegations being made in Kildonan were sufficiently serious to make him think of resigning from the Sutherland management.

Sellar remarked that the common people, both high and low, 'have an uncommon talent for intrigue':

> They never were kept to their text [*sic*] in any one point, until I came among them: no factor I think had the same pleasure in exploring their fastnesses. They have seen no vascillation [*sic*], no slackening in my duty. They have no hope while I am your servant, for they know they cannot cheat me. But they may find a less bustling person in my succession; and, hence, the Stories and insinuations and whispers which they have endeavoured to Convey to your Ladyship, but none of which, I aver, can stand the face of day. This pitiful persecution was transferred to me, from the person of that <u>great man</u> Mr Cosmo Falconer. It will pass from me to my successor; from him to some body perhaps yet unborn, and it will be felt in future ages by those who in telling the Roll of the Noble Family, shall point to your Ladyship.

Sellar then appealed to posterity: those who studied the Stafford family in a future age would be bound to conclude that: 'This Lady lived two hundred years ago, and she did more to bring forward her native country than any that went before her.'[30]

Lady Stafford had already been made aware of the complaints against Sellar. In a devastating, but confidential report to her husband, she indicated that she was perfectly able to imagine that Sellar had transgressed:

> The more I see and hear Sellar the more I am convinced he is not fit to be trusted further than he is at present. He is exceedingly greedy and harsh with the people, there are very heavy complaints against him from Strathnaver in taking possession of his farm, not allowing the indulgence others have always done the first half of the year etc., etc. This is to be examined and I believe it will be necessary to bring him before Cranstoun. He is full of law Quirks and with a good-natured appearance is too much the reverse in conduct, besides having no judgement or discrimination.

In this pen-portrait of Sellar, Lady Stafford seemed to recognise that it was likely that he had been cruel and unbending with the people. But there was no reference to any use of violence by Sellar against the people in this account. Indeed the Strathnaver complaints at this time did not speak of violence by Sellar or his clearers. Nevertheless, Lady Stafford's remarks constituted an extraordinary acknowledgement that she had left the removal of small tenants in the hands of such a man as Sellar.[31]

At the moment that Sellar's capability and judgement was being subjected to intense scrutiny, William Young announced that he wished to take a lesser role on the Sutherland estate. Young declared that, once the current round of improvements had been completed, his role would be much diminished. Lady Stafford was perfectly frank that Sellar could not be thought of as his replacement:

> Sellar I am convinced would not do well, and without raising eternal riots and complaints.[32]

Thus, in July 1814, significant complaints had been voiced against Sellar by the people of Strathnaver. They were sufficiently serious that his employer believed it was a matter for the chief law officer to investigate.[33]

The Sutherland removals of 1814, in reality, had passed with little opposition, even if the equilibrium of the Stafford family had been somewhat disturbed by the emerging complaints against Sellar. But the complaints, though worrying, were not excessively alarming. They scarcely cast any serious shadow over the future of the improvements policy. If Sellar had acted harshly, or had gone beyond the strict limits of the law relating to removals, then he would have to compensate the victims.

Meanwhile the planning continued for further removals in 1815. In November 1814, for instance, William Young celebrated a good fishing season at the new port of Helmsdale and reported the enthusiasm of the local population. Thousands of pounds were now circulating among the people and 'their rage for this traffic is now as great as two years since it was for land.' They were even vying for shares in fishing boats, which was a sign of their enthusiasm for the new resettlement zones which had been provided for their existence on the coast. Other amazing changes were in train, especially at Brora, where coal was being mined under Young's aegis: 'I suppose a more rapid and I sincerely hope advantageous reform was never wrought in any part of the Kingdom.'[34] The tone of Young's remarks was optimistic, though his reference to the people's loss of their land hinted at the psychological turmoil that accompanied his social engineering. In November 1814, there was no suggestion of a crisis in the management.

Sellar, increasingly irritated by the complaints brought against him, hardened his attitude to the local population. In August 1814, he characterised the people as 'a parcel of beggars with no stock, but cunning and laziness':

> Sutherland is a fine country badly stocked. The people have often succeeded against industry – they have wearied out the agents in succession by their Craft and their intrigue and Combination; and altho they are driven at

present pretty much from their original habits the mass requires a great deal of more yeast yet before it shall become leaven. They require to be brought to the Coast where industry will pay, and to be <u>convinced</u> that they <u>must</u> worship industry or Starve. The interior of the Country is clearly intended by Providence to Grow wool and mutton for the Employment and mainte- nance and enrichment of industrious people <u>living in Countries Suited to manufacture</u>. It is part of the territory of 'the beasts of the field' where it was not meant that '<u>man</u> should dwell in Cities.'[35]

In his subsequent interpretation of the evolution of the campaign against him, Sellar thought that the first few months of 1815 was the critical time. The new year witnessed a new sequence of events during which, thought Sellar, the campaign to damage his reputation got out of hand. But at the start of that year the factor's life continued as before. Sellar had collected rents, and there was a celebration of the marriage of the daughter of the Staffords, Lady Charlotte, which was the pretext for much merriment across the estate. Sellar himself attended a dance till 6 a.m., and bonfires were lit across the estate from coast to coast. An ox was roasted for the poor people.[36] But meanwhile the antagonism towards Sellar continued to simmer and then bubble.

Among the people of the inland villages of Sutherland, the removals were a time of extreme turmoil, alarm and anger. But there was little overt resistance. One of the rare voices of these people was sounded in the somewhat formal words of a petition from George Mackay, written in February 1815 from the Heights of Kildonan. His petition was channelled through William Young, who properly passed it on to Lady Stafford. Mackay was an interior tenant who held good cattle grazing land which was in the process of being repossessed in the plan for the settlement of coast side farmers. He was a pre-clearance tenant faced with removal and resettlement, one of the lost stratum of the old Highland life. Mackay remarked that he and his 'predecessors have lived comfortably and happily, under the worthy and ever to be esteemed ffamily of Sutherland from time immemorial'. This was a direct appeal to history and continuity as well as to loyalty. He and his forebears

> brought up ffamilies on their small farms with satisfaction and comfort to themselves, useful members of society, a heroic and able race well calcu- lated for the service of their King and Country. That to annihilate such a Race (while they are at the will, desire and disposal of their esteemed Proprietor), the Petitioner is confident, never was the intention [of the family of Lady Stafford].

Mackay explained his precise circumstances. He had entered his lands fourteen years prior in succession to his father-in-law, at £6 per annum. Since he had undertaken improvements (he made no allowance for inflation), the holding now yielded £20. He was under notice of removal at Whitsunday, 'and thus driven from the place of his nativity in the utmost distress without knowing where to go with his small ffamily'.

Young explained to Lady Stafford that Mackay had actually received a great deal of persuasion to accept alternative land at Brora, but had resisted the idea. Mackay had clearly refused the very notion of Young's plan. Young gave his own feelings about the position facing people such as Mackay:

> When the people in this Country better understand my motives for the changes, they will at last find themselves directed to their own interest although to certain individuals they must occasion a temporary hardship; but no Proprietor can do good by the wreck of his tenantry – it is for their mutual interest that the people should be put into situations where their time is not to be misspent and their Children be brought forward.

Young was obviously aware of the resistance to his plans which he tended to attribute to misunderstanding and ignorance. He would try to educate them to the rightness of those plans.

Regardless of such petitions from below, the main long-term pre-occupation of the Sutherland planners became the future prospects for British agriculture, as peace with France was anticipated. Everyone realised that wartime price levels would not continue at the end of the war with Napoleon. But William Young was confident that the rents set for the sheep-farms in Sutherland would not decline in the new environment, presumably because of the huge productivity gains expected of farmers such as Sellar. Young also believed that the lands crofted out to the re-settled small tenants were well-rented because the people were now engaged in the fisheries and 'will live far better than they ever did, while cottars must starve all very justly'. His belief in the sagacity and economic rationale of the resettlement policy remained undimmed. He expected, in the long run, ('although I may never see it'), that the rental of the entire estate would eventually reach £40,000.[37] He wanted James Loch to come north to see the changes on the Sutherland estate; there was no sign that Young's resolution in the Sutherland plan had been weakened by recent criticisms.[38] Sellar himself took the same view, but expressed it in a much more vigorous form.[39]

– MURDER –

In mid-February 1815, Lord Gower passed on to Sellar the latest complaints from Strathnaver concerning his removals in the previous year. Now, however, the allegations were much more serious, and contained the charge that Sellar had been responsible for the loss of lives, including that of an old woman named Chisholm, as well as certain miscarriages during the 1814 clearance. Suddenly the case against the sheep-farmer/factor had taken on much larger dimensions. Sellar quickly told Lady Stafford, 'The petitioners against me are a few tools employed for a purpose. Mr Cranstoun will settle it and your Ladyship will in time comprehend their story better than you can possibly do at present.'[40]

Sellar immediately declared that he knew nothing of the death of any woman, or of any miscarriage, between Whitsunday and Martinmas in 1814; he was sure that if there had been it was not a result of his 'cruelty'. If his sheep had trespassed, whether it was his fault or not, he would have the loss redressed without delay. He told Gower that the matter should be inquired into by the Sheriff-Depute, Cranstoun, whose investigation he was perfectly happy to answer. Sellar had already been to Strathnaver – to Ravigall, in particular – 'to conciliate the people', and he had given them straw at half price, and 'we made Good friends and understood that what was past on either Side should be forgotten'. To others, he had suggested arbitration, which he understood to be acceptable. He would wait on Cranstoun's advice. This was the first act in a long saga which would run until Sellar came to trial, fifteen months later.

Sellar mused about his future, offering an extraordinary self-analysis:

> I fear I have been bred to too much precision, and possess too much keenness of temper to be so useful in my office as I ought and sincerely wish to be. A man less anxious might better suit the situation and the nature of the people.

This self-dissection was uncannily close to those of some of his most candid and confidential critics, including James Loch, Lady Stafford and William Young. It was a remarkable degree of self-awareness in a man who frequently repeated his errors despite himself.[41]

William Young, who had fielded the Strathnaver petition which had precipitated Sellar's introspection, was instructed to request the intervention of Cranstoun in the dispute. Young was already depressed by the new turn of events:

> I was really in hopes that all this Jarring had been amicably adjusted betwixt Mr Sellar and the tenants and that the Noble Family would never have heard more of it. I wish there is not some incendiary at the bottom of it, however the truth will come out and it is right it shoud [sic].

Young's fear of an 'incendiary' was prescient. But he expected Cranstoun to investigate and produce a final arbitration to settle the matter once and for all. A draft document was readied for the various parties to sign, apparently in terms of damages that would satisfy the complainants.[42]

Sellar now bombarded Lady Stafford with long letters of self-justification which fully exposed his way of thinking. He endeavoured to 'unriddle' the true meaning of the Strathnaver petition. He retold the story of his career into sheep-farming. He had received permission from the Staffords to bid for the Langwell Farm but had been put off by the resident tenant, Robert Gordon. Instead he had bid for the farm at Rhiloisk against the competition of the existing tenants and a Caithness shepherd who had forced his own offer up £60 more than he had expected. 'I know that the Great part of the Ground in question would pay more by Sheep than people.' The sudden success of his bid had been a surprise to Sellar, who found himself 'tacksman of Grounds of which I know little or nothing'. Young had persuaded him to promise the people that he would accommodate them for a year or two until they had made their own arrangements. This promise had been made on 15 December 1813, and Sellar had reached an agreement with the people, on 15 January 1814, about their location; one half would stay and the other half receive resettlement lots from Young; Sellar's sheep would get access by 26 May 1814. The entire removal in Strathnaver, he observed unequivocally, was accomplished according to law.

Sellar asserted that the allegations regarding the tinker, Chisholm, and his mother-in-law were separate from the main arrangement. Sellar related in detail Chisholm's record of bigamy and cattle-thieving. It was a tale of domestic chaos: Chisholm's first wife had threatened him with a gun; the people of the district had wanted Sellar to evict him. Sellar had given clear instructions on this question and it had been agreed that the people of the strath would take care of the old woman. Chisholm's house had been demolished and burned by Sellar's order. But Chisholm had then returned and rebuilt his hut.

As for the old woman in the petition, Sellar claimed that she had died, in the following summer, of old age: 'This is the murder of which I am accused!'[43] He had no knowledge of any alleged miscarriages. On the matter of the incursion of his sheep, he was prepared to recompense the people, regardless of whose fault it was:

> I will not have any of them feel that I am Sharp or contentious about trifles; I entertain no bad passion against the poor man, on account of the trouble which they occasion to me; I am satisfied that I shall be abundantly popular with them when circumstances permitt me to be so, and that your Ladyship will find me to have been as Just and Correct a servant as any that has had the honour of your employment.[44]

In March 1815, Sellar defended his record further, and wrote a long, reasoned justification of his management over the past five years. It was a comprehensive response to the recrudescence and inflation of the accusations against him. His self-justification began with a characterisation of the improvements which he and Young had wrought since they began:

> When we came to the country in 1810 the whole Estate was unarranged and out of Lease; and, in the infinite collection of pence and halfpence from individual tenants on every part of the Estate, on the hearing of their endless disputes and tricks and counter tricks, was really the most [onerous] business. Now, the whole nearly, is set, and under conditions, and in place of 30 people coming (from Assynt perhaps) at thirty different times with one pound or five and twenty shillings each, upon each trifle of which interest, school salary, road money etc was to be calculated and receipt Granted, one man brings or nearly brought to the bringing the whole £30 or £40. In like manner in place of the old good natured policy of winking at poaching etc [. . . we established the . . .] whole police[. . .] and the ground officers etc [?] so much on the alert.

The benefits of these changes, said Sellar, had been decisive. The task of management was now much cheaper and more efficient. Indeed, in his success, he had practically made himself redundant.

Sellar was equally confident of his sheep-farming venture in Strathnaver, now that he was established: 'After three years trial I made I cannot doubt Success, but there has been such an air of ridicule thrown on all agricultural speculations near Caithness, that one is not safe to talk on the subject.' His lambing operations had been extraordinarily productive. He said, candidly, that he no longer needed the Sutherland factorship.[45]

Looking back to 1809, he declared that he had come to Sutherland 'in consequence of a passion for improvement':

> But the duties of my office, which are directed <u>entirely</u> to the restraint and coercion of others, did not indulge their passion and I fondly flatter myself

that by proving myself a good tenant, and an enterprising settler in your country, I may effectively retain the good opinion of the noble family, and enjoy the pleasure of living under them by holding a situation which in this country at so very great a distance from the counsel and guidance of one's Employer, requires a degree of policy and management I do not possess.

This was a typical Sellar ploy in which he hinted that the landlord should be more directly involved in policy, and described himself as a 'settler', frankly defining his work as coercive.

Sellar's elaborate self-justification was prompted, of course, by the new and much more serious petition received in February 1815. Sellar was anxious that Cranstoun should investigate the petition fully and settle the matter once and for all. He wanted the full story thoroughly ventilated:

I am quite sure I have been correct and Just with every person to the fractional part of a farthing, and I have been steady to my duty which was a more difficult matter in the circumstances in which I have been placed. I shall only add that I freely forgive the poor man [and the people's abettors?] and that I think before twelve months pass after the final settlement of the dispute Your Ladyship will have them acknowledge that they were mistaken.[46]

The complaints of the people of Strathnaver against Patrick Sellar indicated a degree of turmoil in Sutherland which was already disturbing the confident thinking of the management and upsetting the equanimity of both Young and Sellar. In February 1815, Sellar was clearly distraught about the attacks upon his reputation among the people. He now anticipated his withdrawal from the management of Lady Stafford's estates to concentrate on sheep-farming. He was uttering thoughts tantamount to an admission that he could not work with the people. But he condemned his accusers out of hand. He thought of resigning from the management when he had completed the 1815 accounts, at which point 'I should then expect any intrigues to cease.' He would fare better as a farmer than as a factor. He had always kept within the letter of the law. He did not conceal his bitterness at his predicament. His transparent deference towards Lady Stafford was mixed with his usual ironies. He believed that the Stafford family were not providing the local management with sufficient support. He was now personally in jeopardy but, he added pointedly, if events turned out for the worst at least the Stafford family will have 'made a fortunate escape'. He was saying, in his circuitous way, that he was becoming a scapegoat.

– THE GATHERING NIGHTMARE –

Sellar's conciliatory words and promises fell on stony ground. In the following few weeks, the allegations strengthened and widened, quickly extending beyond Sutherland and reaching as far as London. Soon Sellar's name was being bruited about Edinburgh and the capital itself. The assault on Sellar had taken on a much more dangerous character. The popular movement became a sophisticated exercise in the use of collective action in a peasant society. The 'weapons of the weak'[47] were now unsheathed. The first effect was to enrage Sellar to a further frenzy of letter writing.

In February 1815 there had been confident talk of an amicable arrangement between 'Sellar and his pursuers'.[48] A submission was drawn up which would have terminated the matter, if both sides agreed. Despite Sellar's willingness to negotiate, the petitioners would not agree.[49] Rather than accept Sellar's offer of compensation, in March 1815, the Strathnaver people declared that they would be satisfied with nothing less than a full legal prosecution against Sellar. They had no wish to enter a submission with Sellar. It was reported (as always, through the filter of intra-estate correspondence) that they believed that 'Sellar had dealt with them so harshly that they now wish the case to be made as public as possible'. A submission would have been a much cheaper and quicker method of testing the case, but the people were taking legal advice. They wanted Cranstoun to examine their petition. One of the people involved, John Munro, said that the people wanted Sellar punished 'in consequence of Mr Sellar's harsh treatment to him and the rest of the Tenants that were ejected at Whitsunday last'.[50]

In March 1815, Sellar wrote a long formal letter to Cranstoun about the complaints that had been levelled against him by the people in the Heights of Kildonan and Farr. Sellar immediately referred to his feud with Mackid over Sellar's protection of game. He once more rehearsed his version of recent events. He pointed out the 'mildewy' character of Strathnaver and its unsuitability for human settlement. The old lease had expired in the summer of 1813. The Staffords decided to lay it out for sheep, and determined 'that the people thus displaced should be provided for along the coast in lots of two to three acres each, enough for the support of an industrious family but sufficiently pinched at the same time to induce to attempt the fishery.' The lands had been advertised for occupation in late 1813 and Whitsunday 1814. It was Sellar's 'unpleasant duty' to remove the people and Young's to provide the lots. Sellar became one of the new tacksmen. He agreed to allow some of the people to stay longer than his lease required to enable the settlement plans to mature.

Sellar then gave his version of the clearance. He wrote that 'peaceable possession' was expected, but the people would not obey the sheriff's order. Sellar 'was obliged to apply for a precept of Ejection.' Promises were repeatedly broken. Eventually the men of the townships disappeared, 'leaving the women to give any satisfaction'; they had plainly hoped to exhaust Sellar, expecting him to return forty miles to the coast 'without doing my duty'. Sellar was not prepared to do this; so he waited patiently till the second week of June, while his flock starved on other ground. He then began to eject the people, family by family. In the process, the houses were demolished. This was achieved by cutting the pins which held the frames of the roof together, a method designed also to prevent repossession. After a few roofs were thus dismantled, the men reappeared and began to cooperate – and by about 25 June, Sellar gained possession of all but a few places at Rhims where there were said to be sick persons. The 'tricks and arts of the people' had been a challenge to Sellar. The losses of sheep-farmers were enormous. Hundreds of sheep were stolen. But Sellar had left barns sufficient for the current crops of the people, one per hamlet. Everybody in the affected communities had wanted Chisholm the tinker/gypsy to be ejected. The tenantry assisted Sellar's party to oust Chisholm on the 13 June. He was paid for his roof timber which was then burned. His was the only house burned in the operation.[51] This was Sellar's version of the Strathnaver removals.

Lady Stafford had received the petition from the Strathnaver people 'complaining of harsh treatment' during their removal by Mr Sellar at Whitsuntide, to which she had replied:

> If any persons on the Estate should receive any illegal treatment, she will never consider it as hostile to her if they have recourse to legal redress as the most secure way to receive the justice, which she always desires they should have on every occasion . . . She will on the present occasion allow such tenantry as have houses to build and [have] been removed at the last Whitsunday 1814 half a year's rent to remove any difficulties under which they may labour.

Lady Stafford's answer was, therefore, placatory and soothing.[52] Sellar later regarded the family's responses to the various Strathnaver petitions as absurdly conciliatory, to such a degree that the people believed that they had won the landlord's support against the factor.

The Strathnaver petition was now in the hands of Cranstoun and the people wanted the matter taken to court for the trial of Sellar on charges which, many months after the events, now included that of murder. In April 1815, an extra, and no less dangerous, dimension was added to the situation facing Sellar and the Sutherland estate by the articles in the *Military Register*.[53] This sustained and well-written denunciation of the whole policy caused the landlord camp realistically to fear that, unless effectively scotched, the question would be channelled straight into Parliament.

In the first week of April 1815, William Young received a copy of the *Military Register*, sent anonymously from London. On the final page he found 'one of the most scurrilous letters imaginable'. It was a full-blooded attack on the Sutherland regime, and on Sellar in particular. Young speculated that the author would be known to the family of Lady Stafford, 'but must have had some aid from the North'.[54] Young was highly indignant and exclaimed that if any of the foul allegations were true, he would be unworthy of his aristocratic employers. He would certainly be able to disprove all the allegations as far as he was implicated. In the heat of the moment, he then declared his own role in the events:

> I came here to do good not evil so as my abilities go, but to harass the meanest person on the estate improperly ought to unfit me for such trust. Lord Gower knows what steps I took about the Strathnaver business which should have satisfied all parties.[55]

Young left the matter there and did not refer to it again in his following few letters. Indeed, while a legal assault on Patrick Sellar was being mounted among the former tenants of Strathnaver, the Sutherland estate managers were engulfed in the next stage of the grand plan for the reconstruction of the coastal economy in the middle months of 1815. Sellar himself continued his experiments with Tibetan goats, merinos and cheviots.[56] Young enthusiastically reported to the receptive ear of Lady Stafford the industrial developments along the east coast and the happy prospect of higher rents. He was at full stretch in the spring of 1815: 'I wish to God your Ladyship and Lord Gower were now here,' he ejaculated, 'so many things claim attention.'[57] The frenzy of activity gripped his every moment. Yet soon, within a week, the atmosphere of progress would be destroyed by a further attack on Sellar.

In the middle of April 1815, Sellar was out on his factorial duties, disregarding the snow storms that raged across the county. In such dramatic weather William Young passed on a copy of the *Military Register*. Sellar promptly concluded that it was the work of the Suther-lands of Scibbercross. He described it as an attack on all improvement: their plans were thus 'violently condemned by desperate men'.[58]

Sellar was highly indignant, and thundered against his new assai-lants:

> There are many men, who determine such points, after the manner of the French national convention – by acclamation. To convince these is im-possible; but, Gentlemen who are pleased to think, cannot, I humbly conceive be at a loss to determine whether there be most humanity in leaving this race of people (as they have been during past ages) to live in barbarous cloth and Filth, breeding men for the recruiting Sergeant, or in driving them, to industry, advancement in civilisation, society, and the consequent comforts of life, possessed by the people of the low Country. If humane . . . to grow (by what is at present lost) wool for the employment of Industrious people and the clothing of those whose country does not produce wool, and to cure and export, to those who want food and some share of that immense body of fish annually offered us by nature.

Such was Sellar's assessment of the true meaning of humanity in such a backward society as that of the Highlands. The humane course of policy was to remove the people from 'the state of Famine, disease and wretchedness, visible in all animals under a highland man's charge, to the comfort, attending care, industry and improvement in rural economy.' He argued that it was necessary to compare the typical man of Strathnaver with the man removed in Morayshire thirty years before (like his own grandfather), or the fishermen of Armadale who had been placed on the coast twenty years earlier. 'Our consciences, on this score, must completely acquit us,' he declared.

Sellar thus confronted the argument for and against economic change, and concluded that there was no room for doubt. In the process, he once more offered the story of his own family as evidence in point:

> My great grandfather was a small tenant removed from a late poor place like Rhimsdale in the heights of Banffshire. The honest man was no doubt cruelly used – he was forced to apply to industry, and to put his sons to business in place of keeping them idly about him. But what do I not owe the proprietor that he had the humanity to drive us to our thrift. I am not superstitious, but, I believe, in my heart, that it is out of the great goodness of providence that he put it into the minds of such great people as Lord and Lady Stafford and your Lordship to force us to what is proper for us, and for the General welfare of every creature unto you.

All the arguments about humanity were separate from the other question, that is whether a proprietor should forfeit £15,000 or £20,000 per annum 'in order that men of peculiar habits may be bred on his Estate to supply the periodical butcheries required in the wars of Europe.' As Sellar put the matter, the old Sutherland estate, under 'turfcutters', had yielded £20,000 less in rent to the landlord than it would pay under the sheep-farmers: 'It is £10,000 even now while we are struggling with the first obstacles to improvement, the prejudices against it, the intrigues employed to thwart its effects.' As for his own conduct, Sellar reiterated that he had been 'in all things honest to the fractional part of a penny, and correct in my duty to the best of my abilities, I wait without flinching, whatever they may next attempt.'[59]

Sellar was waiting for the next blow to fall, while he continued his work as factor and farmer in Culmaily and Strathnaver.[60]

– MACKID EMERGES –

In mid-May 1815, Sheriff Cranstoun, who was mainly absent from the county, at last responded to the petition from the Strathnaver people against Sellar which had been forwarded, via Lord Gower, from Young. Cranstoun authorised Robert Mackid, his Substitute, to undertake a precognition of the complaints against Sellar in Strathnaver.[61] The time was ripe for a full-dress confrontation between the adversaries, Mackid and Sellar, their roles now reversed. The poacher was turned gamekeeper.

CHAPTER 8

Mackid's Precognition
in Strathnaver, May 1815

– EXPECTATIONS –

Robert Mackid, in May 1815, began his investigation into Patrick Sellar's conduct during the 1814 Strathnaver removals. Sellar now openly identified Mackid as his mortal enemy. He was the man who was determined to ruin him and to reverse the great changes in train on the Sutherland estate. He was at a high pitch of anxiety, as was the Sutherland estate administration. The precognition, of course, also raised the greatest expectations among the people of Strathnaver at large, and among the enemies of change across the northern Highlands.

The crisis emerged from the complicated and relatively poorly documented legal procedures undertaken by Mackid in Strathnaver over several weeks in May 1815. Mackid was acting on behalf of George Cranstoun, who had been appointed Sheriff-Depute of Sutherland in 1806, but who continued to live in Edinburgh. His long absences from Sutherland earned him the displeasure of James Loch and William Young,[1] and gave his Substitute, Mackid, unusual rein in the county. A precognition was a preliminary judicial examination of witnesses, an investigation which prepared the initial ground for legal proceedings. It was the first testing of the evidence, not unlike a coronial inquiry in other jurisdictions. But a precognition carried no legal standing of itself; the evidence adduced was not admissible before a court.[2]

Sellar, of course, was himself a much-practised lawyer; he probably regarded his assailant, Mackid, as greatly inferior in legal training and correctness. The greater part of the case against Sellar ultimately turned on the legality and propriety of Mackid's official actions after his original precognition in May 1815. The survival and rediscovery of the papers gathered during the Precognition provides an opportunity to re-examine the case.[3] The status of the evidence derived from a precognition requires caution, not least because it was not directly acceptable to a court; in Sellar's case it was evidence collected in highly controversial circumstances which inevitably cast shadows over its veracity, both at the time and in retrospect.

– THE SEQUENCE OF EVENTS –

The train of events which led to the Precognition was set in motion by the petition against Sellar by the Strathnaver tenants in early 1815. This, as we have seen, listed allegations against Sellar which detailed the deaths of people at the time of the removals and looked to Lord Gower 'to recover their damages'. The petition referred directly to Chisholm's mother-in-law who had narrowly escaped the flames, 'at the risk of the life of her that took her out to a Bothy where she lay on the ground until she expired a few hours afterwards.' Also cited were miscarriages consequent upon the removals. It was said, too, that twenty-nine barns, eight kilns and a mill were pulled down as well as dwellings. The crops of the people had been consumed by Sellar's sheep. The petitioners asked that 'your Lordship will not overlook so many poor and loyal people to be so injured indeed ruined with impunity.' They expressly sought a precognition and legal steps to pursue Sellar. There were thirty-five names attached.

In February 1815, Lord Gower in London, responded to the Petition by saying that it was the Stafford family's wish

> that Justice should be impartially administered. I have sent the Petition with direction to Mr Young that proper steps shall be taken for laying the business before the Sheriff Depute that a full hearing be given to all parties. The Petitioners will therefore be assisted by him, if they desire it, in having the Precognition taken before the Sheriff-Depute according to their petition.[4]

By the end of March, Cranstoun had at last acknowledged the petition and said that if the people of Strathnaver intended to proceed to civil or criminal action, they should direct themselves to the Sheriff Court. If a precognition were required, then Mackid would conduct the process. Thus Mackid was armed with clear authority from his superior.[5]

In early May events took a step further when Mackid, writing from Fortrose, told Cranstoun in Edinburgh that he now believed that Lord Gower positively wanted him to proceed with a Precognition. Mackid sought Cranstoun's advice on this matter: 'I must not shrink from the task . . . and I hope in God I shall be enabled to execute it with candour, justice and impartiality.' Mackid repeated the full litany of charges – which now included fire-raising, reducing the tenants to distress, and setting fire to Chisholm's house which contained money and furniture. But now, 'to add to this dreadful calamity it is alleged that Chisholm's mother-in-law was in the house at the time, and was carried out from the flames at the risk to the Individuals by whom performed this human office. She died a few hours afterwards.' He also referred to several miscarriages caused by the havoc of the removals. Gower received this more detailed and explicit document on 8 May, and responded by telling them that the Stafford family wanted justice upheld. He told Young to present the allegations to the Sheriff-Depute.[6] Consequently, Mackid had clear signals both from Cranstoun and the Stafford family.

Mackid had one further reason to pursue the Sellar affair by means of a Precognition. The necessity, he remarked, was much increased by the circulation of the London newspaper, the *Military Register,* in the north of Scotland and in the south. It was, he said, 'a remarkably nervous and well written paper on Sutherland emigration' in which was detailed, 'with extraordinary degree of accuracy', many of the facts stated in the petition 'although I hope with too high a degree of colouring'. He argued that the magistracy of the country could not ignore such powerful statements in the public prints. Mackid asked Cranstoun for advice, namely whether bail should be taken and whether he should take Sellar's own declaration.[7] Mackid clearly expected that his coming precognition would elicit allegations of atrocities and that these would attract national publicity. He was already anticipating arrests.

The impact of the Precognition was further reinforced, in late May 1815, by a letter sent by John Munro of the Strathnaver tenants, to Andrew Clephane, the Advocate-Depute. The letter detailed 'the many instances of grievous oppression, by which I and a great many of my poor neighbours and acquaintances have suffered severely.' Munro sought justice from Mackid, having found that William Young would not assist the people:

> A number of poor illiterate Tenants, as we are, could have but a small chance of success in this manner, against one who is himself a Lawyer [that is, Patrick Sellar], who has so much power, and that power derived from the Marquis and Marchioness of Stafford, unless some independent person, of ability and interest, would befriend us and take an interest in our case.[8]

Munro claimed that the tenants of Strathnaver had always been loyal and dutiful, and now merely begged for justice. Mackid regarded this document as the essential justification for his Precognition, and he transmitted Munro's letter to Edinburgh on 24 May 1815.[9]

– THE TESTIMONIES –

The precognition was taken in the first two weeks of May 1815 at Bettyhill and several other locations in Strathnaver. By 19 May, Mackid had finished his examinations;[10] he prepared a lengthy document dated 22 May 1815 in which he assembled the testimonies against the men whom Mackid already described as the 'guilty actors'.[11] The precognition contained the evidence of forty witnesses which was set out in a systematic and professional fashion. The witnesses were sworn to their evidence which was also fully witnessed. Many of the witnesses were Gaelic-speakers and their oral evidence was taken through an interpreter. This mediation may have robbed their testimony of some of its *verbatim* quality and there was, indeed, a certain homogenisation of tone in the evidence as recorded.

Mackid collected a great array of evidence from these witnesses over a large district in a short time. Several of the witnesses were illiterate, but claimed that their families had rendered faithful service to the Sutherland estate for over a hundred years. The range of ages amongst the witnesses was great; and some of the people questioned were respectable by any account. David Mackenzie, Minister of Farr, played a conspicuous role during the events, and he too was interviewed. Mackenzie was a literate, Gaelic-speaking servant of the church, well-regarded by the Stafford family and a welcome guest at Dunrobin Castle. Though not an eyewitness to the removals, Mackenzie felt able to declare 'that the clamour of the People in general was loud and violent against Mr Sellar for his harsh and severe treatment of them'.

The testimonies given to the precognition, taken together, indicated that there had been genuine doubt about the 1814 timetable of the removal and the exact date at which the people were meant to decamp from Sellar's leased land. Several of the witnesses alleged that Sellar's shepherds had maintained varying levels of harassment which, among other consequences, had caused the loss of cattle. Sellar had been clearing and firing the pasture lands from March through to June. It was claimed repeatedly that the people's cattle were deprived of pasture, that their potatoes were wasted in the process and that none were left for seed. One witness, who had lived in the district for thirty-five years, was adamant that the practice of the country gave outgoing tenantry the rights to barns and kilns 'until the whole of their crops are completely secure and manufactured'. Sellar had ignored the custom: roof timbers were cut down and furniture thrown into the weather; William Gordon said that his wife had been put out into the open without cover 'notwithstanding her tears or entreaties'. Her cries did not 'soften the hearts of the operators to permit her to secure her furniture – not even a temporary shelter.'

Witness after witness repeated such stories which became a catalogue of atrocity. Cattle had been driven off by the flames of the burning pastures and buildings; the people had been reduced to poverty by the loss of crops, stock and property; furniture had been smashed by the officers before it could be removed. Hugh Grant described the actions of what he termed 'Mr Sellar and his hatchet men'. He remembered 'Mr Sellar's usual cry being, to his Party, to make haste, throw out the furniture, and knock down the houses.' Donald Mackay of Rhiloisk, aged eighty-four, was examined through an interpreter and said he knew the practice of the country well. He too 'fell prey to the fury of the assailants', became ill, and was laid down for four or five days and fed by the people from across the strath, until he recovered from his ordeal. He had crawled to the shepherd Draper's house, but had been turned away without mercy.

Another old resident, a woman of seventy-six, had paid rent to the estate for more than sixty years. She, too, had crawled away from the scene of the hatchet men. The practice of the country had been set at nought, and food stocks and crops had been destroyed. Another resident testified that everyone knew that Sellar was wrong to set fire to the pastures and that he would rue the day; Sellar himself had declared that he would take the risk. Sellar had personally ordered the firing of the houses. Sellar made paltry offers of compensation for their losses.

Among the testimonies were several which claimed explicitly that deaths had been accelerated by the 'cruel and hard-hearted' attitude of Sellar and by his consuming rage for action. William Chisholm claimed that he had an earlier arrangement with Cosmo Falconer to pay five guineas a year for his land at Rossal, and had received no summonses for removal. His mother-in-law was more than a hundred years old and had been bedridden for five years. Sellar had met Chisholm at the Farr mission; he told Chisholm to get out by the next day when his house would be fired. His mother's funeral money was consumed in the blaze. At the moment of the eviction Chisholm said he had been so confused and alarmed that he had not been able to attend to his mother-in-law. She had been carried out with her blankets in flames to a miserable bothy where she expired after two days. Sellar had offered no assistance but 'had stood with his stick lifted upwards, keeping them [the hatchet men] clearly engaged in their work of destruction'. Sellar gave Chisholm six shillings as compensation.

Another witness before the Precognition told of his wife fainting with shock, and falling down in the smoking ruins of her home, accompanied by her eleven-year-old daughter. At Rossal, Sellar had demanded the removal of several old women, a demand which the people had refused, 'in case the poor women die among their hands'. But when the flames were applied, they were rescued at the last moment – the houses were razed to the ground within half a hour. Sellar had given the orders personally. A mother of ninety years had been found stretched out in a miserable bothy, in a speechless and totally insensible state: 'and she was never afterwards heard to utter either a moan or a groan'. She died five days after the events, her blankets burnt in several places.

John Mackay confirmed the Rossal story of the old women at risk as the evictors approached. One of the old women exclaimed, in Gaelic, ' "O the fire" and this when the flames began to approach the bed on which she lay'. Mackay remarked that 'he never saw such an object in his life time, and he hopes in his God he shall never see such another.' The old woman had been 'neither able to move hand or foot, her knees stuck up below her chin and her elbows indented at her side . . . the scene altogether was shocking to humanity.' A tenant from Skalehad had remonstrated with Sellar, who refused to listen and 'said he had the right to do as he pleased, that the timber was all his, and that he would burn it if so inclined.'

Several of the witnesses alleged that Sellar had refused to respond to the pleas made on behalf of the aged and the sick; he would 'not listen to the call of humanity'. In one case 'with fury and rage [Sellar] gave orders that she [a sick woman] might instantly be turned out whatever the consequences might be or that he would order the house to be pulled down about her ears.'

The testimonies constituted a portrait of a people in shock. Sellar's violent assault on their houses and their kinfolk had gripped them with a sort of paralysis, a mute hysteria. William Mackay, for example, had found his wife on the roof of his house trying to save the timbers. She had become speechless, 'shaking like an aspen leaf and her whole frame in a state of agitation'. He thought she was about to die. She was then bled with a lancet and began to revive, but was ill for several weeks. Another woman fell through her roof and was found 'speechless on the floor with her children all crying around her'. She too would have died but for the assistance of her neighbours. She suffered a miscarriage.

Charles Gordon was over seventy years of age and had served for three and a half years as a soldier; he had filled an official role in the parish as regards to oaths, and knew all the rights of tenants. He claimed that the rights of the people to compensation had been ignored. John Munro had lodged complaints with Lady Stafford as early as July 1814, and still there was no redress. Munro had taken the case forward to the official authorities. He himself had made a partial move to the new settlements and had returned to his wife in Strathnaver to find that his property had been demolished in his absence; he had then tried to recover his timbers but had been prevented by violent intercession of Dryden, Sellar's shepherd, who had cut the loads from his horses on Sellar's express orders. Other witnesses said they had not understood Sellar's orders since they were in English.

The precognition proceeded to Langdale where Dryden was interviewed. He agreed that timber had been cut from the horses, and that the people's animals had been poinded. The animals in question were trespassing and 'eating upon his master's grass'. Draper claimed that the people had agreed to the burning of pasture and that he had executed the burnings on Sellar's orders. Another shepherd, John Mackay, said he too had acted on Sellar's orders and those of Dryden in burning pasture and that, in any case, the tenants had agreed to the action. At Brachachy, further evidence was taken, some of it incoherent in the written account; it included denials by tenants that any grass burning had been acceded to; much of it specifically denied the shepherds' claims, which were reiterated in evidence collected at Dalcharn the following day.

– THE EVICTING OFFICERS –

By 19 May 1815, Mackid had finished the main business of his Precognition in Strathnaver, though he had made no contact with Patrick Sellar and had not yet interviewed his shepherds or the officers who made up the removal party. Sellar was perfectly aware of Mackid's investigation and certainly feared the worst from the man he now regarded, not unreasonably, as a very dangerous enemy. His frustrations were compounded by his exclusion from the inquiries; moreover Mackid had refused to receive Sellar's own evidence during the precognition. On 27 May 1815, Mackid received a letter from Sellar saying he was presently at home and expected 'to be informed what crime it is that you lay to my door; and that I am ready to answer any questions which you think proper to put to me relative thereto.'

Rather than meet Sellar, two days later Mackid interviewed Kenneth Murray, Alexander Mackenzie, James Fraser and Alexander Sutherland, the sheriff officers who had been employed by Sellar in the evictions. They testified, in essence, that they had simply followed Sellar's instructions during the removals. As one of them put it, they had acted

> by the orders of the said Patrick Sellar from the dread of whom at the time they durst not Refuse to do anything. That they knew well enough they were doing wrong, and that they never saw the like done before. That it was contrary to what his own free will would have determined and was done solely out of dread of the said Patrick Sellar's authority. Declares it is understood that unlimited obedience must be paid in this County to the Mandate or Command of a Factor. They had been armed with hatchets, some of which had [been] delivered to him by the people from fear of Sellar.

He said that 'his party wrought more like Negroes than reasonable men.' But he said clearly that the old woman at Chisholm's house was removed before fire was set to the house. He was explicit that all the work was done to Sellar's orders: 'None of them durst venture to speak to him for fear of his displeasure and getting an answer from him as he was in such a passion.' Moreover, one of the officers remarked, Sellar had recently briefed him to perjure himself. This evidence was 'freely and voluntarily emitted', and in the presence of witnesses.

Another of the evicting officers concurred in the story of the great destruction of houses directly under the eye of Sellar:

> he contended that all was right under such a man of Law as Mr Sellar, and his being a Factor withal . . . he did what ever was desired without any scruple or dread tho' he was concerned that he was sometimes doing wrong.

He had feared Sellar's vengeance. He declared 'that they were compelled to work like Negroes at all hours . . . Mr Sellar wished the party to be so expeditious in their work of destruction that he would neither give them time to eat drink or take snuff.' He added that Sellar had attempted to have them agree to a particular line of reporting. James Fraser also claimed that he had acted under orders of Sellar and had done things 'which were completely contrary to his inclination'. He said that the danger to Mrs Chisholm was known and the practice of the country had been ignored. This view was repeated by Alexander Sutherland, who acknowledged that he had set fire to houses under orders. He had never seen this sort of eviction before.

Thus the party of evictors gave damaging evidence before witnesses and testified directly to the details of the action. Between them they produced a vivid account of the atmosphere at the moment of removal in Strathnaver – of hatchets and fire and screaming, and everyone afraid of Sellar, in a rage, who shouted the orders. Even more damaging was the sworn evidence that Sellar had subsequently attempted to regularise and perjure the stories before they reached the precognition. The officers all claimed that they simply followed orders. None of what they admitted was necessarily illegal, but it was damning evidence of the madness of the events.[12] It left the indelible spectacle of the removal party, reinforced by the laws and the agent, hacking the houses down, and setting the pastures afire to the sound of protest and the screams of the people. The hatchet men remained fully indemnified by the presence of Sellar. They were ordinary men following orders from a man of unimpeachable authority.[13] Mackid was ready to take the next critical step.

– Sellar in alarm –

Sellar was filled with alarm. He was quickly alerted to the danger of the situation and wrote to the Lord Advocate of Scotland while the precognition was in train to complain of Mackid's proceedings. Sellar said that he was fearful of being ruined by Mackid's 'machinations' and 'his contrivances'. Sellar launched into a loud defence of the policies which he had been implementing and an exposition of the campaign that had erupted against him. The familiar arguments were repeated. Thus, Sellar again asserted that the inland of the Sutherland estate was fitted only for the occupation of stock and was 'never intended for the residence of man'; the coasts were ideal for fishing. Yet the possibilities had been ignored and the people had 'lived in the same degree of civilisation as their fathers had done 500 years ago, altho' in less purity.' Their main employment was to import grain from Caithness to use in illicit distillation in 'their impenetrable fastnesses'. The Stafford family had embarked on '*humane*' improvements – cheviot sheep in the inland zones, people on small lots on the coast, 'pinched enough to cause them to turn their attention to the fishing'. It was humane because 'these barbarous hordes' would have better association, division of labour, and education, and would thus 'advance in civilisation'. In the process, many thousands of pounds were being spent beyond the value of the rentals in such improvements.

Sellar told the chief law officer in Scotland, that the changes on the Sutherland estate had generated 'ill-will' against the Stafford family and 'their doers', and their policy was ignorantly branded as a cruel system:

> Every measure of intimidation as well as artifice and intrigue was employed to thwart it; and when these failed, to calumniate, and to entrap and distress their agents.

He then spoke of his own role in these events. William Young, he explained, was responsible for the arrangement of the reception lots:

> Mine was the more unpleasant one of removing them to their lotts and putting the new tenants in possession; in the execution of which, I had to perform a most difficult task, rendered more so by the circumstance, that of the several farms sett for Cheviot stock, I myself required for the maintenance of my stock, access to one which I had with my employer's approbation become tacksman.

At the time of the removals, Sellar's shepherd had been grossly insulted and comprehensively obstructed. The people prevaricated and made repeated promises to go:

> and the men having at the time all disappeared leaving the women only at home and wearying me out . . . I at length desired the officers read their warrants and do their duty. They pulled down the cabins and the men returned to obey the officers.

Sellar claimed that 'not one hutt or one stick of single hutt on the ground taken possession of by me was burned by any person in my employ.' The people themselves had asked him to get rid of Chisholm because they could not be answerable for cattle and sheep if he stayed.

Sellar then staked out his own allegation of the conspiracy against him, concerted by Mackid himself. Mackid had organised the people to complain against him to the Stafford family; he had been complicit in the anonymous publications circulating in the county, and he had been involved in the petition to the Advocate-Deputy. In all these attacks, he said, 'they have carefully avoided the precise discussion of any charge'. In essence, there was a treacherous plot against Sellar, and Mackid was 'the silent mover of the business.'

Sellar was flabbergasted at Mackid's conduct of the case. He claimed that Mackid had deliberately initiated the precognition in his absence; he had given Sellar no notice of the charges to be raised against him which Sellar could only gather from anonymous prints (that is, the reports in the *Military Register*). It was there claimed that he had torched dwellings and covered the country in one general conflagration. It would be a serious charge against Sellar, 'so heavy as to [inflict?] the punishment of death'. Sellar said he had made no quibble 'to conceal the facts, and evade the law'. He simply wanted the Lord Advocate to know the evidence so that he would understand that he was different 'from the common cast of criminals who come under your cognisance.'[14]

Meanwhile Sellar had written to Mackid requesting a precise statement of the crimes which were being alleged against him. Mackid had made no reply. In the last week of May 1815, Sellar again wrote to the Lord Advocate to say that Mackid had conducted his Precognition in Strathnaver and had refused to grant Sellar a hearing. The precognition, said the agitated Sellar, was bound to be 'a tissue of Misrepresentations against me' because of Mackid's 'ill-will towards me', and because of his manipulation of the Gaelic-speaking witnesses. Sellar had heard, from a gentleman, that Mackid had been saying that he 'would let slip no opportunity to do me an injury . . . to wind a pirn [Scots for a reel or bobbin on which yarn or thread is wound] about my ears'. He had silenced all witnesses who were at all favourable to Sellar. Sellar now pleaded for the protection of Cranstoun or the Lord Advocate against Mackid:

> Mr Mackid must know me to be innocent, but he hopes to ruin my character, and to injure my fortune by subjecting me to odium, trouble and expense.[15]

– SENSATION, 31 MAY 1815 –

Within days Sellar's worst nightmare was fully realised. Mackid concluded his precognition. By the time he had interviewed the sheriff officers, Mackid believed that he had more than enough evidence to warrant the arrest of Patrick Sellar and his assistants, though he had not interviewed the principal figure himself. Sellar made no attempt to evade arrest and made himself available for interview. But, very early in the morning of 31 May 1815, Mackid's officers descended on Culmaily Farm, took hold of the factor-cum-sheepfarmer and despatched him to the County Jail at Dornoch. Within thirty-six hours Mackid had also rounded up four of the sheriff-officers as accomplices in Sellar's eviction, and they too were incarcerated in the Castle.[16]

The details of the drama soon emerged. William Young, in the greatest agitation, reported the crisis to Lady Stafford. He had spoken to Mackid to ask what had happened: 'With a demure [face?] he told me that Sellar must be hanged or at any rate sent to Botany Bay and advised me to have no communication with him.' Sellar had been escorted to jail by two officers and half a dozen constables. Young visited Sellar twice in the jail. Mackid had effectively brought the affairs of the estate to a standstill.[17]

In London the correspondent of the *Military Register* was exultant at the news from the Highlands. Mackid had refused Sellar bail. The pirn was now firmly wound about Sellar, who was trapped by law.

– MURDER! –

The arrest of Sellar was a sensation and Mackid was himself in a state of advanced excitation. He had been galvanised into action and he wrote a remarkable, and ultimately a critical, letter on that day to Lord Stafford, reporting his Precognition and the arrest. It was a document which would eventually figure crucially in Sellar's defence. Writing from Kirkton, he referred to the petition of the Strathnaver people to Lady Stafford in July 1814 and to her response (which said that the family sought only justice in the affair). Mackid told Lord Stafford that he had been prompted to conduct the precognition by a letter he had received from Lord Gower and by instructions sent by his superior officer, Cranstoun: 'I was compelled to enter upon the investigation of the complaints'. He declared, 'a more distressing task I have seldom had to perform'. Mackid then re-iterated the story of the events at Whitsunday 1814:

> It would appear however that Mr Sellar still refused or delayed to afford that redress to the removed Tenants, to which they conceived themselves entitled, which emboldened them to approach Lord Gower with a complaint, similar to the one they had presented to Lady Stafford.

In February 1815, Gower had replied that they could take it to the Sheriff-Depute. Soon after, it had been transmitted to the Sheriff-Depute the Tenants. Cranstoun had delegated the task to Mackid as his Substitute. Therefore Mackid had been given express instruction to conduct a precognition.

> With this view I was induced to go into Strathnaver where, at considerable inconvenience and expense, and with much patient perseverance, I

examined about <u>40</u> evidences upon the allegations stated in the Tenants Petition, and it is with the deepest regret, I have to inform your Lsp that a more numerous Catalogue of crimes perpetrated by one Individual has seldom disgraced any Country, or sullied the pages of a Precognition in Scotland!!!

Mackid than added:

This being the case, the laws of the Country imperiously call upon one to order Mr Sellar to be arrested and incarcerated in order for a trial, and before this reaches your Lsp this preparatory legal step, must be put in Execution.

Mackid expressed his sorrow at the events. He then retailed, in confidence, the charges against Sellar which included wilful fire-raising in circumstances of cruelty '<u>if not murder</u>!!!' Lives had been endangered 'if not <u>actually lost</u>!' The allegations included the demolition of houses, a mill, sheep cots, kilns and 'innumerable other charges of lesser importance [which] swell the list'.[18]

– SELLAR AT BAY –

It was only after his arrest that Sellar was subject to examination by Mackid and the interview was recorded. Sellar was prepared for this moment and presented a nineteen-page document which provided the basis of his remarks. He described himself as the under-factor to William Young, employed particularly in 'the Department of Out-putting and Inputting Tenants' in the new arrangements. Sellar offered his own account of the events from the start. He had arranged for some of the people in Strathnaver to stay on his farm for an extra year and everything had been explained to them in January 1814, determining who would go and who would stay. He had also given an elaborate explanation of the muirburning arrangements. He understood that the people had agreed to his terms and requirements.

The subsequent removals, Sellar declared, were perfectly legal and fully arranged with the people. Chisholm, in particular, was evicted altogether because his neighbours said he was a vagrant, a bigamist, a tinker and a thief. The people wanted him evicted. Sellar said that he had made a present of most of the house materials to the departing tenants and had allowed the people a still longer period for the removals, which he extended into June. Chisholm, however, kept returning and his house was burned down to prevent this happening again. It was only later 'That . . . the ignorant people had been

stimulated by artful and designing men to complain of oppression.'
Only then did the loss of money from Chisholm's house arise. Every-
one had been properly warned off, and Sellar had certainly seen
Chisholm at the Farr Mission.

Sellar declared that he had instructed the sheriff-officers to eject the
tenants and remove the roof of each house, except those in which
families with sickness had been mentioned. Barns necessary for crops
were to be preserved from this order. Sellar had not attended all the
ejectments. The crux was that he had been patient to the human limit
and

> that after repeated promises by the Tenants that they would peaceably obey
> the Sheriff's decreet and after they repeatedly failed in implementing their
> promises the declarant was under the necessity . . . of directing the Officers
> to execute their warrants.

He attended at the start, but after a few ejections and unroofings, he
found that the people 'yielded obedience to the warrant and removed
themselves'. He could not attend all the events. Most people simply
departed. Unroofing was required to prevent further reoccupation
and he was fully within his rights to demolish the houses. He considered himself entitled 'to remove from and to take possession as
entering tenant of all the Houses and Hutts at the term of Whitsunday'; he left the removed tenants in possession of a Barn each and
timbers galore. Such was Sellar's first reaction to his incarceration.

As well as giving evidence before Mackid, Sellar also began his
counter-attack which, while imprisoned, took the form of an 'Instrument of Protest for wrongous Imprisonment and Damages versus
Mackid and other Abettors'. In this action Sellar prepared a document, signed before witnesses, which

> declared and represented that the before mentioned charges of which he
> the accused in the warrant were all False and groundless, originated in ill
> will and malice entertained against him by the said Robert Mackid.

Sellar had offered ample bail but had been denied the opportunity to
attend 'his many important duties of his official situation as Factor . . .
and thereby ruin him . . . in his character and means.' Sellar demanded that Mackid 'should be liable to him . . . in the pains and
penalties of the law for wrongous imprisonment.' This was his immediate response, which he renewed one week later.[19]

Meanwhile news of Sellar's arrest quickly circulated. In particular,
the *Military Register* in London reported excitedly that the people of

Sutherland were jubilant.[20] It now asserted that the tenants had proved 'their case to its fullest extent', that three lives had been lost, that '*The Sheriff was so affected by the detail that he fainted in the corner, overpowered by his own feelings*', and that Sellar had been imprisoned in Dornoch Jail, though there were 'well grounded fears that he would be permitted to abscond'. The 'sorry lines of injustice, tyranny and oppression' in the Sutherland administration 'had been exposed'. The *Military Register,* reasonably enough, claimed its share of the credit for these satisfying developments. Within a week, 'Highlander of Sutherland' reported that Mackid had refused a large amount tendered as bail, and that Sellar's fate was now placed 'in the hands of the law, and of twelve honest men of his country' and he would 'take his trial for his life'. The people of Dornoch celebrated the arrival of long-delayed justice 'with the same warmth they had received the news of Wellington's immortal victory' at Waterloo.[21]

The excitement of the moment depended, of course, on the evidence gathered by Mackid among the common people in Strath-naver. It had been sworn and signed by more than forty people and, without question, formed an eloquent expression of their collective grievances. It was unmistakable testimony to their fear and anger. Sellar's own response to the charges did not question most of the realities of the evictions of 1814: there had been demolition, destruction and coercion. But, claimed Sellar, all was done within the law and with leniency. The real issue was whether Sellar had ordered acts of savagery tantamount to manslaughter against sick and aged people. Against this was the counter-allegation that Mackid and his associates had conspired with the people to inflate their grievances into charges of homicide. The people were certainly aroused against Sellar, and Mackid was burning with hatred for him. But if it was conspiracy it was, so far, extraordinarily well-sustained and articulated among a large number of witnesses. Sellar faced a formidable foe.

CHAPTER 9

Sellar Concussed

– IN JAIL, MAY/JUNE 1815 –

From Dornoch Jail, Patrick Sellar wrote to Lady Stafford on 31 May 1815, the day of his arrest. He was desperate, frustrated and indignant, and he begged for her assistance. The precognition, he exclaimed, had been totally one-sided and undertaken by 'Mr Mackid, my personal Enemy'. Mackid was a man inflamed 'with all the art in his power', and had seized and imprisoned him without giving him opportunity to defend himself:

> His hope is to Concuss me, to ruin my character, by Clamour and to derange my affairs.

Mackid had oppressed him severely. But Sellar had already appointed James Robertson, 'doer for the duke of Gordon', as his legal representative.[1] He had offered three names as sureties for bail: his father, a wealthy uncle and William Young.[2] Yet Mackid had denied Sellar bail. Sellar, in his predicament, appealed to the Stafford family to help 'procure' his 'liberty and a fair hearing'.[3]

The jail records for Dornoch, county town of Sutherland, registered the incarceration of Sellar (and the sheriff officers who had assisted him in the 1814 removals) in minimal detail. In the previous two months there had been only two other prisoners: one had violently resisted an excise officer employed in seizing an illegal still at Kilfedder in Clyne parish; the other was a servant jailed for stealing a sheep from a tenant in Kildonan. Those two prisoners, in contrast to Sellar, represented the typical form of crime and punishment in Sutherland.

The jail or tolbooth was located in the tower of the western part of the ancient castle of Dornoch which had been repaired in the previous year at the expense of the Countess of Sutherland and the Marquess of Stafford.[4] It was, therefore, especially symbolic that Mackid should now utilise these facilities, as well as the full paraphernalia of the law, to assail his targeted enemy, Patrick Sellar.

The Tolbooth entry for 31 May 1815 detailed the extraordinary turn of events:

> Mr Patrick Sellar at Culmaily Factor to the Marchioness and Marquis of Stafford – Incarcerated by warrant of Robert Mackid, Esq. Sheriff Substitute of Sutherland. On a charge of having wilfully set fire to the house of a Tinker in Badiloskin of Rossal in Strathnaver and demolishing the Mill of Rhimsdale both part of Mr Sellar's own Sheepfarm. Committed to jail [betwixt?] the hours of 5 and 6 in the morning.

Sellar, at this point, had evidently not yet been charged with culpable homicide, rather with firing a house and demolishing a mill on his own property, without reference to loss of life. But William Chisholm, the tinker, would soon become the central figure in the case.

Sellar's arrest was a bombshell. After the early morning arrest Mackid quickly stripped Sellar and his assistants of their legal offices in the county.[5] Mackid held Sellar in jail on sufficient minimum charges, reserving the greater allegations for further elaboration. Meanwhile, however, Mackid wrote a letter to Lord Stafford which contained much more dramatic charges, and couched in highly coloured and unguarded language (quoted at the end of Chapter 7). The contents of this injudicious letter were somehow delivered to the local correspondent of the *Military Register*.[6] When the account was published in London it was fallen upon hungrily by the rest of the press, and suddenly Sellar's name became infamous across the country. Such was the sensation that his fate seemed already sealed.

The immediate reaction to the drama of Sellar's arrest among his own associates exposed both anxiety and scepticism. There was no automatic assumption of Sellar's innocence, even among the managers of the estate or among the Stafford family. They were all aware of the larger charges – including murder – which loomed beyond those already presented by Mackid at the time of Sellar's detention.

On the day of the arrest, while Sellar suffered paroxysms of anger and despair in jail, William Young reported the disaster to Lady Stafford confessing that he had been 'more unhinged' by the events than he could effectively express. Mackid, he recounted, had been engaged for some days taking a precognition in Strathnaver. The result of the investigation, Mackid told him, had 'induced him not to accept of Bail but to issue a warrant of commitment.' Young could not predict how His Majesty's Advocate would respond to these events because

Mackid and Sellar conveyed such different accounts: 'The one enlarges, the other palliates the guilt.'

Young assured the Staffords that their estate business would not suffer: 'I know whatever happens that Mr Sellar's books and accounts will be found perfectly correct.' Sellar was a stickler for accuracy and office efficiency and there would be no question marks hanging over the estate accounts. Young had been with Sellar the night before his arrest (of which Sellar must have known in advance) and Sellar had spoken 'of bringing his Clerk to continue their workings in Jail and to give him a mandate for the collection of money'. Between times, Young was looking after affairs on the estate and a message had been sent to Edinburgh to seek the opinion of the Lord Advocate on the question of whether Sellar would be confined in jail until the September circuit of the court. Young could hardly believe that bail would be refused much longer. The postscript to Young's letter was a more urgent and direct expression of his state of mind in this crisis:

> I flatter myself that Your Ladyship may be induced to write down to Edin in favour of Mr Sellar's liberation that he may soon return to his business. My God what an affair this is.[7]

Young repeated specifically and unequivocally the claim that Mackid had said, 'when he was about to commit Sellar that he would *be hanged* or sent to *Botany Bay*.' Young was beside himself with anger at these 'foul' charges:

> All Sellar has done will appear trivial indeed and perhaps unworthy of notice; had the people followed the advice given by me and approved of by Lord Gower to submit all claims for damages to you the ends of justice would have been answered – but this did not suit other men's purposes and such a clamour never [was] raised in any remote country. I should not wonder to see riots worse than Kildonan, for the people believe they are now at liberty to do what they please, and some of them are constantly at me, anent supposed grievances.[8]

The Stafford family remained in the south and their Commissioner, James Loch (in London), was no less distressed by the dramatic news of Sellar's arrest. Loch enjoyed the confidence of his uncle, Chief Commissioner Adam, of the Jury Court in Scotland to whom Loch poured out the Sellar story in decidedly candid terms. Sellar, he said, may have been 'a little hasty in ejecting some Old tenants'.

> He had evidently many Enemies to contend with who will make the most of any act of hasty imprudence which he may have committed, I am afraid he has been hasty.[9]

Since the original complaint had been known in 1814, the action had shifted to 'a criminal prosecution with all manner of atrocious acts'. Cranstoun had instructed Mackid to take a precognition, but Mackid had expanded the charges and jailed Sellar on 'a bailable offence'. Loch stated unambiguously that Mackid was totally unsuitable to undertake a precognition:

> He has no courage, his local prejudices in favour of the people and against the system of improvement adopted by Lord and Lady Stafford quite unfit him to be a judge when the Agent and people are parties.

Loch continued his account to Adam. Mackid had examined the witnesses through an interpreter of his own choice; the witnesses were

> a set of people whose education and rank of life entitle them to little credit unless supported by other evidence. While I state this I am far from thinking that Sellar has not acted hastily and unadvisedly, but that he has been guilty of the crimes (even that of murder) that are insinuated rather than alleged by Mackid against him I totally disbelieve and I look upon them as pure offspring of jealousy and ill nature.

Moreover, Mackid was giving the false impression that the Staffords approved of his procedures. There was widespread dishonesty in Strathnaver and the people would go to any lengths to retrieve their possessions.

Loch added that Sellar and Mackid had quarrelled about game, and Mackid had been convinced that Sellar wanted to take his position as Sheriff-Substitute. In addition, Loch found it necessary to remark that Sellar 'is extremely unpopular both from the situation he holds and his manner of executing it.' Without mincing his words, Loch summed up Sellar's character. He was

> a clever keen Scotch writer, a man full of energy, which activity has necessarily been often called for to enforce very disagreeable but very necessary acts of vigour, added to which he has a quick sneering biting way of saying good things in the execution of his duty which I do not think has made him popular with any body whether in the management of the affairs or otherwise.

Thus, Loch was prepared to accept that Sellar was capable of behaving harshly and injudiciously because such things were in his nature, but he was not a murderer, and Mackid was hopelessly prejudiced. It was a good summary of the views of the Stafford camp at this point and was scarcely a resounding vote of confidence for their imprisoned factor. It was already clear that there would be no united front to defend Sellar, though, of course, the purpose of Loch's intervention was to seek influential opinion to curb Mackid's excesses. Mackid had exceeded his authority by a very long chalk. Mackid's letter to Lord Stafford appeared to condemn Sellar as guilty ahead of any trial of the evidence and was, therefore, according to Loch, grossly improper. Moreover, though Lady Stafford favoured a civil process, Mackid was forcing the people towards a major criminal procedure by inflating the entire matter.

As a coda to his account, Loch reiterated the hurt felt by the Stafford family at the appalling turn of events. They wanted their improvements engineered 'with the utmost regard to the feelings and prejudices of the people', and with ample time for their reaccommodation. Cranstoun had allowed an inferior officer, Mackid, to deal with a sensitive matter. Mackid should be dismissed regardless of Sellar's fate. The Staffords themselves had been placed in an invidious position. They had no wish to protect their factor; on the other hand they did not want the people of Strathnaver to believe that the landlord supported their allegations. Any hint of weakness would only cause the allegations to multiply.

At the time of the precognition William Young had been absent from Sutherland on pressing business with his brother in Morayshire.[10] He admitted that he had been glad to have avoided examination by Mackid.[11] Meanwhile Young reported signs of unruliness among 'the ignorant people'. He was reluctant to go to Edinburgh for fear that 'all order will be at an end'. Even the traditional supply of peat to a local schoolmaster had been truculently refused by six men who, if compelled, threatened that they 'would seek a better country for themselves'. The estate was losing control and the people were increasingly insolent.

Young could see the attack on Sellar being translated into the breakdown of all order, to riots and the loss of control by the estate. The people were in an assertive mood, demanding concessions which were unrealistic but which had been encouraged by Mackid's treatment of Sellar. For himself, Young said that though he was heavily tied up in business he hoped for an examination 'by some respectable person totally unconnected with Sellar'.[12]

– SELLAR FREED, 6 JUNE 1815 –

Mackid refused bail and kept Sellar in custody for a whole week. His decision was overridden from Edinburgh. The news of Sellar's plight had been delivered to the capital (where Sellar applied to the Court of Justiciary for his release), and returned to Dornoch, all within seven days.[13] It was a rapid transit for its day.[14] Immediately on his release from the Dornoch tolbooth, Sellar rushed to Edinburgh to consult his lawyers.[15]

On his liberation Sellar told Loch privately that Mackid had no case against him and that Mackid had acted 'in the most diabolical manner from first to last'. He hoped that an independent inquiry into the business would be instituted. Sellar claimed that none of the Precognition evidence had been taken under oath: 'Mackid knew well they could not swear to what he took down from them. He misled to Kill me by defamations, not by Law.' Going over the critical sequence yet again, Sellar noted that the grounds in Strathnaver were publicly advertised in September to November 1813; the Set had taken place on 15 December 1813; Young and the minister, Mackenzie, explained it to the people in Gaelic and English. The minister had begged Sellar to give them more time to remove, and he eventually agreed to let most of them stay for an extra season. He then readied his business and flocks for entry to his lands in May 1814. Legal notices were served in March. In May, the people still would not go and it became clear 'that I should be a ruined man before they would permitt me to Enjoy it. I took out a warrant for their Ejectment.' He then waited until 14 June before he took possession. Meanwhile his ewes had been dying in Culmaily and the rest were affected by disease which had forced him to sell many of them at one third of their original value: 'Because I suffered all this without a murmur I am not, unfortunately, Considered to be an Injured person'.

Sellar alluded to the awkward question of the state of readiness of the resettlement lots. This had been Young's responsibility. The reception facilities were certainly not prepared early enough. Sellar regarded this as irrelevant because the people refused to move. They had kept 'violent possession' of his land through the first two weeks of June:

> Why? – because they were stirred up to mischief, by a party which has always existed on the estate, and who watch opportunities to harass or annoy the agents – be they who they will – in the hope of getting them turned out.

Sellar, at this moment of crisis, reiterated his faith in the removal system. He recollected again that he had 'long been a passionate declaimer against the only reasonable improvement [for] which the highlands (I may say) are susceptible.' But now the benefits were palpable:

Ask Sir William Grant what his Grandfather was – a Removed tenant! But for the Just views of the proprietor this great man would have been now on a place like Scottany and at a rent of £5 – following two [or] three highland poneys with a cocked bonnet on his head and a Red top to it, and a ragged philiby reaching half way down his leg, afflicted I doubt not by the hereditary itch, which all the Brimstone in Scotland would be tardy to Cure.[16]

Such was Sellar's passionate reaffirmation of his creed on his release from jail.

Sheriff-Depute Cranstoun was placed in an awkward position by the action of his substitute Mackid. He was expected to calm the situation and reinstitute order to the legal processes. At the end of July 1815 he assured Young (who was nervous of personal implication) that 'Mackid had been empowered to precognose [sic]' Young. Cranstoun assured Young that Mackid's investigation would be restricted to the conditions of leases and the situation of the Strathnaver tenants. Young was obviously reluctant. Cranstoun remarked, 'be assured that there was not the most distant idea of inculpating you.' He added, more reassuringly, that Young's own character was widely respected; his evidence was required merely as part of the chain of testimony. From this exchange it is evident that Young thought that Sellar's offences, if any, were trivial, that Young wanted to avoid Mackid at all costs, and that he feared for his own personal entanglement in the case.[17]

Writing from Leith, in early July, Sellar told Lord Gower that he had been talking to legal men, including a person from Ross-shire who had faced similar libels: 'He feels a good deal for my misfortune.'[18] Sellar was anxious that he had incurred the displeasure of Lady Stafford:

> nothing more heavily bore on my mind than the trouble which my misfortunes have given to Lord Stafford, Earl Gower and your Ladyship, and your anxiety lest I should, by any imprudence, have got into a scrape.

Sellar was aware that the entire tone of conversation in the county of Sutherland was against him. There had also been an attempt to poison the mind of the Lord Advocate, and to screen Mackid. Sellar urged Lady Stafford to persuade the Lord Advocate to have him examined by an 'imported' sheriff, from Ross or Caithness. Sellar heard rumours that the Stafford family did not support him, and he pleaded with Lady Stafford to make it clear to the Lord Advocate that they were not actually against him, and that he craved a fair trial before an impartial jury.[19] Sellar was nervous of his support in the Stafford family, and among respectable society across the county.

He was even more nervous of opinion in the press, which he had monitored throughout July. His arrest had been reported, through the *Military Register*, to London and then back to the Scottish papers. Sellar believed that the reports originated in Sutherland itself and, in due time, he expected to 'trounce' the authors and the editors. Sellar waited on developments from Cranstoun, especially in regard to Mackid:

> I shall give myself no peace or rest until I get the whole of this uncommon affair [expiscated] to the bottom and the authors brought to justice. With calmness and assiduity I dont fear to effect this and I trust that if we were once clear of this wretch Mackid, and your Ladyship had soundly[?] talked to some other people, a permanent peace may succeed the troubles which have disturbed us in our duty, of which Mr Young at one time and I latterly very nearly became the victims.[20]

Sellar continued to blame most of the troubles on the Sutherland estate on illicit distilling in the straths. Though under legal assault by 'the people', he continued his factorial duties without respite. In July 1815, he was again pursuing poachers and their receivers and he detected a continuing spirit of resistance in the district. His officer had

> searched only two days; for the people are now so well drilled, that they quickly sent the tidings of his arrival and his business over the whole country. The bark and leather and sticks were of consequence presently put under ground and none was to be found after the first houses searched.

Sellar decided to send further posses of Sheriff-Officers to the scene to hunt more offenders who, he, declared, should certainly be turned off the estate:

> The Proprietor can have not peace or rest until he [can] convince the people that their impressions are erroneous, and that in <u>future</u>, they will do well to <u>think</u> before they allow themselves to be so misled.

These were hardly the words of a man seeking to mend fences with his neighbours or to pour oil on troubled waters.

Sellar declared that he would never become 'querulous'. He had entered Lady Stafford's service, in 1810, 'with a Cheerful heart, [and] I shall do my duty like a man. I shall, when my term comes, become my own master or go to serve a new one, with the same Severity.' He proclaimed that he would always utter the truth regardless of rank. Sellar declared that the Stafford family's 'condescension to the people, misinterpreted and abused as it has been by designing men, has put the people besides themselves.' A proprietor must support the requirements of discipline on an estate. He drew a broader lesson:

The Scotch are very Considerate. Such lessons are not thrown away upon them. And in all countries and people, the dreggs of the national character lay at the bottom of the mass. In the improving, the revolutionising of a highland estate, the ideas which I have ventured to State, apply with much more force, inasmuch [as] it is a most arduous operation, to drive a Stubborn crafty people against their inclinations – that is from idleness to industry, and if the people suppose that they have the Ear of the King against the minister, the thing is impracticable. They will hang to their old habits like a reluctant Swarm of Bees to the mother hive; and he who dares to drive them to their own habitation, shall be <u>stung</u>, in proportion as he is zealous to push them forward.

This was Sellar at his most didactic and, whatever his choice of metaphor, it is unlikely that the Stafford family would have welcomed yet another lecture from their awkward and badgering factor. Sellar cared not at all for his reputation among the common people whom he was prepared to harry until they became fully efficient and properly civilised.[21]

Sellar had heard that Mackid was in daily contact with the people: 'It was thus. Let the Strathnaver people stand by him, and he would lead them as a General would an army.' They had also been incited to refuse to pay interest on their rents because, they said, this money went into Sellar's own pocket (no doubt as part of his factorial agreement); Mackid had advised them to refuse rent payment altogether, even though they were already £5,000 in arrears. Of Mackid, Sellar now remarked:

He is above the Law. I inclose a note of the arrear he owes, and your Ladyship can do with it what you think best.[22]

There was no notion of retreat in Sellar's attitude to the estate and its people. He may have been concussed, but he was already fighting back, and Mackid was his prime target.

– LADY STAFFORD'S VISIT, AUGUST, 1815 –

When William Mackenzie, the Staffords' legal adviser, reported Sellar's release on £100 bail, he commented incisively:

Sellar's conduct has been rash and more keen than necessary but Mackid had brought himself into a serious scrape which will probably end in his dismissal.[23]

Mackenzie thought that Mackid's action had been 'extremely irregular if not absolutely illegal', from the want of a precise statement of the offences charged and the names of the parties injured. Of Sellar, Mackenzie commented, 'it is in every point of view a matter much to be regretted that the factor on the Estate should be in such a situation so destructive of that Appearance necessary to support the Authority vested in him.'[24]

Mackenzie met the Lord Advocate in Edinburgh. The latter took a robust view of the matter: 'His opinion in point of law is that he Sellar is not guilty of Wilful fire raising but is guilty of Culpable homicide and criminal oppression and that a trial must take place.' But the Lord Advocate also wanted an additional investigation to be taken, and for Sellar to be given the opportunity to state his evidence in exculpation. William Young had said that any trial should be held in Edinburgh but the Lord Advocate clearly disagreed, insisting on Inverness, 'and says particular care will be taken to pick a impartial jury'. The indictment was being prepared in the Lord Advocate's office and 'he repeated to me that he considered Sellar's conduct as extremely cruel and oppressive.'[25]

After his stretch in jail Sellar was incensed that the Lord Advocate should continue to take advice from Mackid. The people believed that the Staffords concurred in the action. He again besought them to make their position clearer. He wanted an independent commission to track down Mackid and his conspirators, and to 'Chase him from pillar to post – we will blow him out of the water.' He claimed that the editors of the *Military Register* were already in 'a sad fright', for their gross libel on an innocent man: 'I anticipate some little amusement in trouncing McKid, Dudgeon, these Editors and their informant.'[26]

Between Sellar's arrest at the end of May 1815 and his trial the following year there was a series of legal manoeuvres which were mainly instituted from Sellar's side of the conflict. Several gambits were employed to resolve the issues facing Sellar with the object of avoiding a trial. Already, even before the arrest, more than a year had elapsed since the alleged offences were committed in Strathnaver at Whitsunday 1814. Lady Stafford had, by her own account, previously tried to arrange for the matter to be dealt with by civil process, as a matter of damages which could be arbitrated between the parties. Through the winter of 1814–15 the people of Strathnaver steadfastly refused this resolution.

The stakes had been raised much higher by Mackid's precognition, but there was still hope in the Stafford camp that the matter could be settled with less public gaze and hysteria. Hence, there was delay and prevarication. But this was not the only source of slow resolution. The legal forms had been vitiated by Mackid's own excessive zeal and excitability. His precognition had been, at least in part, botched by irregularities. He had, for instance, conducted the investigation without the Fiscal and without the Sheriff-Clerk. Moreover, the courts moved in slow circulation in the north of Scotland, and the case had to wait its turn. Sellar, never patient, was frustrated by the delays and spent much of the time preparing his defence and venting his rising anger. Yet the most remarkable feature of the long pre-trial saga was the tenacity of the people of Strathnaver who maintained their adamant commitment despite the long delays. They were sustained, at least in part, by the newspaper campaign continuing in the *Military Register*. Sellar believed that he had discovered the source of the conspiracy in Sutherland. It involved Mackid together with Sutherland of Scibbercross, who fed 'the London libellers' with local news. Sellar declared: 'Sutherland and the newsmongers have libelled an innocent man. The root is laid bare for the <u>Stroke of the Axe</u>, and down comes the tree.'[27]

Patrick Sellar regarded the whole sorry business as a concerted campaign against him. To be sure, this reflected a degree of understandable paranoia on his part. But it also reflected an authentic and sophisticated form of protest among the people of Strathnaver, a degree of organisation beyond the usual historical expectations of such a pre-industrial society.[28] The Sutherland family and its advisers did not underestimate this danger; Sellar was menaced, and he feared for his liberty and for his life.

Lady Stafford remained far removed from the scene of the drama until her visit to the Highlands in the late summer of 1815. She had the greatest regard for James Loch's abilities and she hung on his advice. He was 'of infinite use, he is so acute and so sensible and takes so much pains, his law education make him of much service now to us, and his manners besides are so agreeable to everybody that he is quite a treasure here.' Loch was certainly a smooth man compared to Sellar, who upset everyone he encountered.[29] Loch, in his turn, relied on his uncle. In July 1815, Loch told Lord Commissioner Adam, in confidence, that the Staffords had a

> high opinion of Sellar's honesty, and zeal for their service and interest, and the management of the affairs under his charge. Of his discretion and temper in putting the people out, and whether he may have been hasty in some of his Acts, is a different question . . . there is no wish to screen him.

Loch, indeed, wanted a new precognition. This, he anticipated, would help to show the policies of the Sutherland estate in a more favourable light, and help to reconcile 'both the higher and lower people of the country to what had been done and is intended.' The proprietors were sincere and 'Every intention and tenderness were by them intended and shewn.'[30] Adam advised his nephew, Loch, that the most important thing to establish was that Sellar acted 'for his own personal object, and that he had a motive beyond the duty which he owed to his employer.' This, of course, would distance him from the Staffords and Loch. But Lady Stafford continued to utter her clear resolution: 'Sellar should get all the proper assistance and protection we can give him. We must be very firm not to give way in this affair as that would put an end to all things.'[31]

Lady Stafford, who held the reins in the policies governing her northern realms, sent reports back from Dunrobin Castle to her husband Lord Stafford in England.[32] Many weeks had already passed since Sellar's arrest and release on bail. Early in August 1815, she held meetings with ministers in the county. She singled out for special mention the Rev. David Mackenzie, the minister of Farr, whom she described as 'a good looking young man', who was 'sensible, intelligent and gentlemanlike'. Mackenzie, she remarked, merited promotion to the parish of Golspie. Mackenzie told her that 'the people in Strath-naver are excellent people if not misled by those to whom they look up, and . . . he finds it very necessary to preach to them to pay due attention to the nature of an Oath.' There was a real fear that the people believed that the Stafford family was also opposed to Sellar. Lady Stafford believed that the people were now 'all settled and contented'. Mackenzie's remarks hold special significance because he later became regarded as a 'quisling' in terms of the representation of the people during the Sellar affair. Mackenzie had made a most positive impression on Lady Stafford, whose next thought was to set in motion strong action against all poachers, smugglers and anyone else involved in petty corruption. She clearly intended to reassert her authority as landlord.

James Loch, who accompanied Lady Stafford on her northern visitation, agreed that a reassertion of proprietorial pressure was imperative, otherwise all improvement would grind to a halt. Loch had been engaged in comprehensive discussions with Young, Sellar and Mackid and was convinced that the people were 'merely instru-ments in the hands of a few designing tacksmen', who were leading an assault on the entire system of improvement. They were mainly half-pay officers from the military 'who have so long lived upon the [Sutherland] family and considered the estate as their own'. Loch now fully endorsed Sellar's conspiracy theory. He believed that as soon as the people understood the resolution of the proprietor they would 'completely change the complexion of the story'. Then the great work of advancing the civilisation of the country would once more go forward.[33]

Lady Stafford saw Sellar and told her husband: 'From what I have seen and heard I am convinced he is innocent and has been correct and straightforward in what he has done and that the people are *set on* and not so much in it themselves.'[34] As she toured about her estate she was much impressed by Sellar's farm but was also pleased with the appearance of those of his sworn enemies, Mackid and Sutherland, each with great haystacks on display.

Loch examined Sellar's case in August 1815, in company with Lady Stafford, and thought that the whole matter was coming to the boil. Lady Stafford had concluded that the Strathnaver 'people burnt the house [of Chisholm] themselves and not Sellar after all'. Sellar's only fault had been to employ Matthew Short as a shepherd. Short was a man with an unsavoury record as 'a brute', and Sellar had since discharged him. Loch had discovered that there had been a 'subscription and combination among the better sort to effect a demolition of our new system'. It was a collective attempt to reverse the removals, and to reinstate the old ways. The great object for the estate was now 'to find them out' and expose the conspiracy which was currently being replicated by 'both gentlemen and common people' on the nearby estate of Dempster at Skibo.

Lady Stafford fully accepted this diagnosis. She was certain that 'the Upper Ranks' in Sutherland were disgruntled, and 'the Question [was] now whether the Estate is our own or theirs.' The authorship of the articles in the *Military Register* was now obvious, she said, and everything should be done to 'rout him [i.e. Scibbercross] entirely and some others as soon as we can, and a good many of the common people probably, who are all tenants at will. This will probably soon lead to another sheep-farm or two.' She was evidently angry, and in fighting mood. She also wanted a census to prove that the population had actually increased in the time during which the improvements had been instituted. This would prove that the libellers were wrong.[35] She noted, incidentally, that Mrs Mackid had been very unhappy and that she could well understand the feelings of Mackid's poor wife.[36] The entire community was in an agitated state.

Loch felt able to assure Lord Commissioner Adam that the Stafford family had no other desire than that 'justice be done between the parties'. They 'did not wish to protect Sellar if he had done wrong, [but] they as little wish to subject him to the punishment of a trial if there is no proof of his having offended.' Loch assured him again that 'Sellar is a man [for] whose zeal, fidelity, and honesty they have the highest regard, though from the keenness of temper he may have exceeded, in a way not to be defended, his powers and orders.' Loch at this time thought that the Lord Advocate should order a new Pre-cognition.[37] Loch made a telling prediction when he said:

> All the poor people who have hitherto come forward against Sellar as the tools of Mackid and Co will immediately turn around and will completely change the complexion of the story they have been telling. They have done what they have in the full idea that their conduct was agreeable to the wishes of the family and they were to be rewarded accordingly.

Loch thought that the affair would probably not go to trial.[38] Having talked at length to Sellar, he thought the 'people are merely instruments in the hands of few designing tacksmen who sought to undermine the entire improvement system.'

In the following month Lady Stafford responded to another petition from Strathnaver. This was a plea for the reversal of the removals, and made reference to promises made as long ago as 1799, at the time of regimental recruiting, when various leases had been 'sett' in the district. The petitioners claimed that the 1799 document (which Sellar had seen in 1813) established their unlimited tenure. Lady Stafford rejected these claims as nonsense, and summarily dismissed the petition. She reiterated her policy, saying bluntly that the new arrangements would proceed; she scolded her petitioners for neglecting their new lots. By invoking the promises of 1799 the petitioners exposed both their expectations and, as far as the landlord was concerned, their delusions.[39]

At the end of her northern visit Lady Stafford came to the conclusion, which she gave to Cranstoun:

> The fact is that Sellar, though Young believes he was within the letter of the law, was too precipitate and ought or had better have given the people a week or two more to prevent all this noise. The fact is we have suffered a great deal with patience, and have done everything very properly and with great indulgence and consideration.

She was keen to get all this displayed in court if necessary – to bring some light on the matter and to disperse the libels. Sellar had asked her to institute prosecutions in order to bring a halt to further 'clamour'. She remarked, 'I hear there is a great deal [of clamour] respecting Sellar.' Simultaneously she had been advised by her other managers that the estate would be best served if Sellar were brought to trial. On the other hand her son, Gower, was concerned to avoid giving the impression that the estate was about to abandon Sellar.[40]

Cranstoun, the first law officer in the county, recognised the opposition of 'the old set' in Sutherland to all improvement. This opposition had now become focused on Sellar. Lady Stafford had been much impressed by Cranstoun. He had been very agreeable and had assured her that Sellar possessed many good qualities and was strictly honest. Cranstoun also said that Sellar was intemperate and had 'no command of himself, and that he had seen him provoke Mackid, though he had himself no good opinion of Mackid' and thought his letter to Lord Stafford (see above, p. 149) was 'quite disgusting'.[41]

– THE SECOND PRECOGNITION, SEPTEMBER, 1815 –

There had been serious irregularities in Mackid's first Precognition in May 1815, and the charges against Sellar had not been fully stated. Cranstoun had been implored by Sellar to overturn Mackid's work by a fresh investigation. In September 1815 Cranstoun arrived at Golspie and moved to conduct his own precognition. He interviewed the same people Mackid had selected for the first precognition and Mackid was again present at the examinations, while the proceedings were translated by the same interpreter chosen by Mackid. And once more Sellar himself was not allowed to present his own views.[42] Cranstoun concluded that a trial was imperative because of the publicity attending the case. This was an indirect tribute to the power of the campaign concerted by the *Military Register* which had kept the matter warm in the national and local newspapers.[43] The people of Strathnaver may have been frustrated by the repeated delays, but now they were on surer ground; moreover, Mackid had been distanced from the prosecution of the case. Sellar was stymied by the new precognition, and a trial loomed larger than before.

The outcome of the second precognition provoked Sellar to new heights of outrage. As Sellar angrily remarked, Cranstoun had chosen merely to 'verify' the previous precognition – simply checking the evidence given by Mackid's original witnesses. Now Sellar circulated his precise response to each of the accusations.[44] He recollected that the first complaint by the Strathnaver people, promoted by Sellar's enemies, did not reach Lady Stafford until July 1814, several months after the removals in question. The first petition related to heath burning, and the pulling down of houses, and not to the 'more heinous circumstances' which only emerged in the following year. Since Cranstoun had refused to examine Sellar's own witnesses, Sellar now demanded that the case go to trial. Sellar was full of anger, but his demand also suggested a considerable confidence in his case.[45] During these exchanges Sellar conceded unambiguously that he had demolished houses during the evictions and had set them afire.

Sellar, totally incensed by the second precognition, challenged Cranstoun directly to reckon with the evidence he wished to present. He complained again that his own witnesses to the 'Ejectment of the Tinker' had not been called. He had four testamentary witnesses to that event. He named his sheriff officers as well as two others, 'indifferent spectators'. The latter included Donald Macleod a mason, son of William Macleod in Rossal. It seems almost certain that Macleod was the man who, three decades later, wrote *Gloomy Memories*, an utterly condemnatory and very damaging personal account of the Sutherland clearances from which much of the subsequent historical and fictional case against Sellar was to be constructed. As Professor Adam remarks, 'It is remarkable to find Sellar proposing Macleod as a witness on his behalf.'[46]

Sellar's letter to Cranstoun answered, point by point, the charges against him (which now must have included the allegations of personal injury and murder). Sellar had made his own inquiries in Strathnaver. First, he claimed that the young man allegedly injured in the evictions who was reported as dangerously ill in Garvault was, in reality, out of bed, dressed, in rosy good health, and 'had been fox-hunting' on the previous day. Sellar had witnesses to testify to this. The second case concerned an old man of eighty-five years, Mackay by name, who was allegedly turned out barbarously and left in the open for several days. Sellar retorted that there was no such man in Rhiloisk. No one had been forcibly removed from this place, apart from James Mackay Cooper. There had been a man named Mackay who had flitted by his own accord:

> Nota. This <u>infirm</u> old man took the occasion of my imprisonment and subsequent absence in Edinburgh to fell a tree with a hatchet with his own hand and steal it from Langdale. And I have not brought him to punishment lest this too should be considered oppression.

In the third case, Sellar was accused of demolishing houses inhabited by sick people in Rhimsdale. He acknowledged that he had been informed about these people on 8 June, during the 1814 removals. He had allowed them to remain until the 11th, the invalids agreeing to flit by that date. On the 13 they were still *in situ*. At that point Sellar had returned to Culmaily. On 14 June his officers found the people still there, accompanied by many of their sheep and cattle. They were ejected on the 14th and at that point the houses and byres were pulled down, but 'leaving the houses where the sick people were said to be'. Some of the people were still there more than a year later.

The fourth instance concerned a woman who miscarried in Ravigall. Sellar said he had no knowledge of this case. One of the officers said that a woman had experienced a fall, but no request had been made about such a person. The woman who fell had been seen as hale and well, working on a roof. Three widows were still resident, in September 1815, at the original site.

The question of muir-burning, which Sellar did not deny, was a smaller matter. Sellar asserted that muir-burning was, in any case, highly beneficial to tenants. The destruction of barns was a technical legal matter, and Sellar was able to quote Robert Bell's authoritative legal opinion on the status of leases,[47] which confirmed Sellar's legal right to his destructive actions at the time of the removals. Moreover, as he emphasised:

> knowing that they would stay in the Barns in place of going to their allotments and harbour horses and cattle, and Eat my mutton thereon, I considered myself justified in taking possession of them, and I put no hardship on the people.

Sellar also pointed out that harvesting tenants had no use for barns and used ricks instead for their crops. He added, with his usual irony, 'I trust it is not possible that I could in this have acted with any criminal intention.'

At the end of this elaborate recital of his defence, Sellar said that the specific complaint made to Lady Stafford at the end of July 1814 was six weeks after the original episode. He made one of his most cogent points when he claimed that it was virtually incredible that much graver offences (such as murder) would have been withheld at that time. He asked, would his accusers have suppressed 'these more heinous Circumstances now brought against me if such circumstance had really existed'. He hypothesised that the charges had been 'fabricated afterwards for the particular purpose of giving colour to this distressing procedure.' [48]

In late 1815 the Sutherland estate was so anxious for its reputation (and for the future of its improvements) that Lady Stafford communicated with Lord Sidmouth to keep the government informed of events.[49] James Loch prepared a public statement in the estate's defence. It was eventually issued anonymously as a pamphlet at the end of the year.[50] Sellar was too preoccupied with his own dilemma to provide much assistance in its production but, when asked, offered Lady Stafford another stream of angry denunciation of his assailants. The Sutherland estate, he said, was under attack:

> a Junta of persons, with a boldness and impudence, and a dexterity, of which I know no parallel, have attempted to control [the estate] so as to suit their own interests . . . The drift of those conspirators is plain as sunlight. It is to distract Lord Stafford and your Ladyship's plans, to raise the people to disturbance, and to frighten your agents, whereby to stop the new arrangement and increase the rent of the estate.

Sellar's anger was sharpened by continuing thefts occurring on his new farm in Strathnaver. His sheep were being carried off in the middle of the night, in twos and threes. The adjacent land was being misused, to his own disadvantage: 'There is no person on this waste at present except a Highland cattle herd . . . who occupies himself during the winter in smuggling whisky.' Sellar said he could pay three or four times the rent, up to £300, if only he could place his sheep on the land. It was hardly the expression of a man down-trodden by his oppressors.[51]

– THE COOLNESS OF LOCH AND YOUNG –

One of Sellar's greatest frustrations, throughout the prolonged period before his eventual trial in the following year, was the refusal of the Stafford family to provide him with the letter which Mackid had written to Lord Stafford at the time of his arrest in May 1815. This was the intemperate and incriminating document which exposed Mackid's excitement at having cornered Sellar: it proclaimed Sellar's guilt in advance of a full legal investigation. It was obviously an improper communication by anyone claiming to act for the Law.

Sellar repeatedly appealed for the letter.[52] In late October 1815, James Loch again refused Sellar's request, saying it would be wrong to hand over such a document, and also telling him that there was no proof of conspiracy. Loch went further and told Sellar to 'avoid a certain Ironical mode of expression which does you more mischief than you are aware of'. Loch told Sellar that his style was, in effect, too insinuating for his own good. He added, 'The same is the case when you speak of the Highlanders both of the better and the lower ranks.' This was a reference to Sellar's gross and blunt prejudices which he often ventilated in letters and conversation. Loch also told Sellar that he was wrong about the law pertaining to precognitions. He recommended steadfast behaviour and advised Sellar to desist from his tirades of personal denigration. It was severe advice which must have been painful to Sellar in his moment of crisis.[53] Loch in his cool appraisal of the situation was highly critical of Sellar. He offered no sign of support, let alone solace. Loch's attitude accentuated Sellar's sense of isolation; he could have felt little solidarity with the Sutherland estate.[54]

Meantime, William Young carried the responsibility for the progress of the plans, regardless of the Sellar affair. In October 1815, he was in another 'rush of business', especially along the east coast. He reported the general atmosphere on the estate: 'We are all peace and quiet here at present altho still the Highlanders expect to get Peter [*sic*] Sellar tried and they have been told a King's Cutter is to carry him to Leith.' Young said that the *Military Register* was keeping the people in a state of agitation. He was rueful about the turn of events:

> But for the infernal spirits who rouze the poor and ignorant wretches to rebellion merely from Sinister motives this is a most delightful Country and for the means of improvement beyond anything in the north or I believe in Scotland at large.

The advantages of Sutherland were manifest. It possessed coal, clay, lime, rivers with waterfalls, land of every description, manure in abundance and an excellent climate, with roads along the coast which were soon to be extended into the interior. The Sutherland improvements constituted, Young said, a 'subject for the Philosopher as well as the Agriculturalist and Merchant'. However:

> Until the people are made to know their real friends which can only be done by stigmatizing their enemies . . . it is not possible to do their real service.

Young also pointed out that the unfortunate emigrants from Kildonan, who had joined Selkirk's American settlements, had written back from the colony describing their woes: 'They are starving and supplicate their friends to remain contented at home.' He thought it would be excellent to distribute copies of such negative letters among the 'highlanders'.[55] It would help to dampen the influence of the 'infernal spirits who work on the people'.[56]

James Loch was, evidently, keen to create some political distance between the estate and Sellar in the rising crisis. In November 1815, while the Sellar affair remained unresolved, Loch gave Young the clearest instructions. Absolutely no further disturbances must occur during the coming removals and resettlements, and nothing should be done 'to create real or alleged hardships'. Nothing must be hurried. Loch's obvious concern was to avoid a further public airing of the entire policy. He pointed out that Lord Reay had achieved large-scale removals without public aggravation. In the previous year, even the most sympathetic and well-informed observers had suspected that the removals on the Sutherland estate had been too hurried. Young received an unadorned warning from Commissioner Loch in London:

> If another set of complaints should occur, believe me it will make a most serious impression on the public mind even in the minds of those most interested in the improvements and I am most firmly of opinion that it would be noticed in parliament.[57]

Young bridled at some of these remarks and retorted with a flow of heated words which exposed some more elements of the 1814 removals. He said, first, that the Reay Country was simply not comparable with the Sutherland estate since it contained no 'fire brands'. Second, he conceded that the Strathnaver people had certainly received too little notice of their removal; Young declared unambiguously:

> The Strathnaver people certainly got too short notice and should have had longer time to move off I admit it, but the fault was none of mine and had Roy the land surveyor's advice been listened to the thing would not have happened.

Third, the sheep-farmers, especially Sellar, expected too large a financial return and that too quickly, even in the first summer of their leases: 'Our friend Sellar ought to have known this, but dearly he has paid for his rashness.' This was a clear admission of errors of planning and synchronisation at the time of Sellar's clearances, as well as the failure of coordination between the central factor, the surveyor, the under-factor and the tenant. It had been a botch. This exchange showed, with great clarity, that the management was divided and that, in private, they each conceded that serious errors and even oppression had been perpetrated in the 1814 removals. There was little sense of cohesion among the landlord team.[58]

Attempts were made, in late 1815, to raise morale and good feeling among the small tenantry of the Sutherland estate. Thus, in November,

William Young organised to 'sacrifice three or four fat sheep for a feast at Brora' to celebrate the birth of a son to Lady Charlotte, and a dance at Dornoch Castle (which may have given Sellar a *frisson* since he had been incarcerated in that very building only a few months before). Young observed that Sellar was pressing to take over more pasture land from small tenants which, he said, would yield far more rent under sheep. Young was generally optimistic about the arrangements he had instituted: the herring fishing was promising, and so was the cod and ling, as soon as the people began to 'adventure in it'.[59]

At the end of 1815, Young was in a stock-taking mood, now anticipating his own eventual withdrawal from the estate management. In effect, Young said that he had done his main work in Sutherland and that henceforth the estate improvements could be managed simply by 'a good superintendent'. He recollected Mackid's sinister advice 'to cut and run' from the management of the Sutherland estate which he had rejected. It is not difficult to detect a certain tiring in Young's attitude. As for Mackid, Young said he had 'new cause to believe that this law-giver is the author of much if not all which has appeared [referring to the articles in the *Military Register*], and highly as I esteem Mr Cranstoun it is impossible to put up with such a Substitute.'[60]

Young was jealous of his reputation in the county (which contained an implied contrast with Sellar), and remarked to Loch (whose intrusions were not welcomed by Young):

> Really, my good sir, I stand well with Gentlemen of the Country at least I think perhaps as much as any person situated as I am can expect to do.[61]

He declared that not even the Apostle Paul would be able to demonstrate good intentions to 'the people' or convince the writers of the *Military Register*. In one light this was a confession of failure in the propaganda campaign for the minds of the Sutherland people in these years.

Though little is known of the responses of the people of the inland straths to the clearances, Loch reported one striking development in Kildonan. In November 1815, a large meeting of the people had been held to consider an attempt to raise a collective bid for grazing leases. The notion was to outcompete the large farmers who were appropriating the old lands of the people. It was a rational effort, on a collectivist principle, to pre-empt the sheep-farmers in their plans to appropriate the glens. William Young dismissed the manoeuvre out of hand, asserting the improvement orthodoxy that small tenants should confine themselves to crofts along the coast, and leave grazing to the great stock-farmers. He stated flatly, 'it is not possible they can pay the same rent that a Stock Farmer will'.[62]

– The attempt at compromise –

The delay over the Sellar affair dragged on. In London the *Military Register* repeatedly demanded that Sellar be brought to trial without further prevarication, claiming that the defence was attempting to wriggle out of the proper course of justice. It was indeed clear that the Lord Advocate had interceded to induce a compromise, recruiting the Rev. David Mackenzie to arrange arbiters between Sellar and the Strathnaver complainants. Sellar regarded Mackenzie (who was much favoured by Lady Stafford) as one of his many enemies and accused him of leaking the plan to the *Military Register* 'and that the crown lawyers in consequence decided that a public trial was necessary'.[63] While efforts to promote a compromise continued,[64] action on the case against Sellar necessarily hung fire. The people of Strathnaver became the more restive.

William Young received two more ancillary petitions in February 1816. A tacksman in Rogart was desperate about his rent arrears and sought relief: his rent had been contracted two years before at £85, but that was based on prices which had since collapsed. The second petition was from twenty-nine signatories from Bettyhill, calling themselves loyal 'Tennants of the Parish of Farr'. They were also in a distressed and ruinous condition brought on by the fall in prices. They recalled each increase of rent under a succession of factors from Campbell to Young. At one time they had been able to pay, 'Without the Smallest Tincture of Grudge'. Repeated increases had become unbearable and were made worse because 'tennants being collected and cruded together [which] rendered every circumstance of life disagreeable'. Now their cattle prices had halved, almost overnight. Their petition was the authentic voice of the small tenantry living under the whip of adverse market prices. They had also suffered the consequences of unsympathetic landlord-initiated improvements, which simply added to their congestion. Young's economic miracle had not yet brought any alleviation to these people; the price of their main commodity had collapsed.[65]

The petition from Bettyhill had been certified by the Rev. David Mackenzie. Between Christmas and his trial in April, Sellar developed great animus against Mackenzie who, he believed, provided support and guidance to the people of Strathnaver as they prepared for the court case against him. Strathnaver men had been circulating through the straths in Farr and Caithness raising funds, 'begging money wherewith to prosecute me', he reported. Mackenzie, said Sellar, had certified in writing 'the truth of their averrments' for the appeal; he had also sent material to the *Military Register,* including 'a severe philippic against the administration and the administrators of Justice in Scotland'. Sellar was outraged that Mackenzie had countenanced the campaign and had given credibility to the Strathnaver campaign. Sellar was the more indignant because, he told Mackenzie, 'you were in our confidence'.

Mackenzie's position was complicated by the fact that his stipend (which had fallen behind) was paid by the Sutherland estate through Sellar himself. The minister protested his innocence of Sellar's charges and claimed that he had been misrepresented by Sellar's 'antagonists' whom he had refused to supply with character references as witnesses.[66] He declared, 'I have admonished and exhorted the people again and again to have a regard to truth and consistency.' He had been manipulated, and he was sorry for the newspaper misrepresentations of his own position. Shortly thereafter he published a denial letter in the *Military Register* which no doubt materially assisted Sellar's cause. But, throughout, Mackenzie appeared as an ambiguous figure, perhaps compromised by his position between his paymaster and his parishioners.[67]

Sellar dramatised his own situation in January 1815 by likening himself to 'all the reformers' from Luther to Coke who had been confronted with 'errors, frauds and quackery'. Eventually all such reformers prevailed by virtue of 'their unabating zeal and enthusiasm, regardless of ignorant opposition'.[68]

Under the promptings of the Lord Advocate, supported by Lord Gower and mediated by the Rev. Mackenzie, a last attempt at arbitration was attempted between Sellar and the people. It was presided over by Cranstoun or Traill (Sheriff-Depute of Caithness) in the week of Christmas 1815. Despite these concerted efforts, the people of Strathnaver, once more, simply refused the latest offer of arbitration. The case would therefore proceed to trial. But the charges, to Sellar's mounting frustration, had still not been spelled-out, nor had the date or the location of the trial been settled.

The Lord Advocate set in motion the preliminary procedures for a trial in mid-March 1816. At this news, Lady Stafford was not overconfident. She remarked: 'We have only to hope he [Sellar] will come out clear'.[69] Sellar established his defences and his witnesses; his opponents were more dispersed, less well-educated and poorly co-ordinated, even though they had maintained sufficient cohesion to sustain their determination for almost two years. This was a time of increased movement in the county and some of the Strathnaver people had left the estate, some going abroad, some settling in adjacent counties. It was difficult to keep tabs on original witnesses. The people had little money to mount the legal case. Some spoke only Gaelic. There is no direct documentation of their side of the struggle.

– MACKID FIXED –

There was one other vital development at the moment that Sellar was at last arraigned to court. At the start of February 1816, Sellar's lawyer, Robertson, dissuaded his client 'from taking any steps against Mr Mackid at present'. But only one month before the trial, William Mackenzie told Lady Stafford that an arrangement had been sealed with Mackid concerning his resignation as Sheriff-Substitute. MacPherson Grant reported the news and also noted that he had 'every reason to believe that it is finally determined to try Sellar at the next Inverness Circuit. I don't know particulars.'[70]

Grant was exceedingly pleased with 'the arrangement to be entered into with Mr Mackid' who would also relinquish his farm at Kirkton. It was more favourable to Lady Stafford's wishes than they had expected. Grant said that this was 'independent of any benefit from getting Mr Mackid out of the Judicial situation he now fills in the County.' Grant had ensured that strict equity had been preserved and 'that Mr Mackid might have no grounds for asserting that he had either been bribed to give us his Farm or for Alleging that he had been oppressed by being obliged to abandon it on terms injurious to his interest.' These arrangements, which guaranteed the exodus of Mackid from all connection with the county and the estate of Sutherland, were conducted on the eve of Patrick Sellar's trial and suggest that Mackid was less than optimistic about the likely outcome of the coming climacteric.[71] William Young was surprised at the agreement with Mackid. These manoeuvres in March 1816 helped to neutralise Mackid before Sellar's trial one month later.[72]

A neighbouring proprietor and substantial political figure, George Dempster of Skibo, congratulated Lady Stafford on the news that they were likely to get rid of a very great and long complained of nuisance in Sutherlandshire, in the person of Mr Mackid as Sheriff Substitute . . . perfectly convinced as I am that he has been the secret but chief promoter and publisher of all the unpleasant disturbances in the County that have lately attracted so much notice in the Publick.

He said that Mackid had shown him inveterate hostility ever since he was refused a tenancy on the Skibo estate.[73] Dempster's letter suggested a degree of landlord solidarity, and was also evidence of Mackid's alienated status in the county. Against this, however, was the fact that he had risen so high in the legal hierarchy in Sutherland.[74]

– THE TRIAL PREPARATIONS, MARCH/APRIL, 1816 –

Sellar waited for his now imminent trial as impatiently and as volubly as ever. He was, of course, to be tried for crimes which were punishable by hanging or by transportation to New South Wales or Van Dieman's Land, just as Mackid had promised when he arrested Sellar in May 1815. And so Sellar and the people of Strathnaver waited for the law to begin its course. The *Military Register* continued to claim that Sellar would never be brought to court and was being shielded by the landowners and legal authorities. When the trial was at last arranged the speed at which it was instituted seemed to catch some of the parties by surprise.

William Mackenzie said that the Lord Advocate had made every effort to divert the people from a trial. Eventually it had become unavoidable:

> The Indictment of Sellar is in the press but Mr Cranstoun told me he had read it and thought it well prepared and expressed as his opinion that the Lord Advocate had no other course to follow since he had failed to reconcile the private parties.[75]

This outcome had been achieved against the legal odds. It indicated a degree of professional competence by Mackid against his superiors in Edinburgh. It showed the influence of the press led by the *Military Register*. Once the story was emblazoned in the national newspapers, it was much more difficult to avoid a public resolution. Most of all, the calling of the trial spoke volumes for the determination and obduracy of the people involved in Strathnaver, and their anger at Sellar, who had come to personify the reviled improvement policies of the Sutherland estate. The accusers had raised money to pay for legal costs and had recruited support in neighbouring Caithness. This was non-violent peasant resistance in its most organised and menacing form.

Sellar's indictment was published in the second week of March 1816.[76] The charges were:

> CULPABLE HOMICIDE, AS ALSO, OPPRESSION and REAL INJURY, more parti-
> cularly the wickedly and maliciously setting on fire and burning, or causing
> and procuring to be set on fire and burnt, a great extent of heath and
> pasture, on which a number of small tenants and other poor persons
> maintain their cattle, to the great injury and distress of the said persons;
> the violently turning, or causing and procuring to be turned, out of their
> habitations, a number of the said tenants and other poor people, especially
> aged, infirm, and impotent persons, and pregnant women, and cruelly
> depriving them of all cover or shelter, to their great distress, and the
> imminent danger of their lives; the wickedly and maliciously setting on fire,
> burning, pulling down, and demolishing, or causing and procuring to be set
> on fire, burnt, pulled down, and demolished, the dwelling houses, barns,
> kilns, mills, and other buildings, lawfully occupied by the said persons,
> whereby they themselves are turned out, without cover or shelter, as
> aforesaid, and the greater part of their different crops lost and destroyed,
> from the want of the usual and necessary accommodation for securing and
> manufacturing the same; and the wantonly setting fire, burnt, and other-
> ways destroyed, growing corn, timber, money, and other effects, the
> property, or in the lawful possession of the said tenants and other poor
> persons, are crimes of a heinous nature and severely punishable.[77]

The charges related to events on 15 March 1814 and in April and May thereafter. They included damage to many miles of pasture by burn-ing, and were followed by a list of thirty-three witnesses including Mackid and David Mackenzie, William Young and Sellar's two shep-herds. Further detailed charges included the case of Donald McKay, 'a feeble old man of the age of four score years or thereby . . . who upon being so turned out, not being able to travel to the nearest inhabited place, lay for several days and nights thereafter in the wood in the vicinity, without cover or shelter, to his great distress, and to the danger of his life'. There was other vivid detail of fire being set to houses and sick people being dumped on the ground. Some of these episodes resulted in deaths as a result of the sheer recklessness of the proceed-ings and the extreme callousness of Sellar's behaviour at the height of his rage.

Sellar's own reaction to this outcome was characteristically ironic and bitter, in equal measure:

> I am the first man brought to trial for having under the sheriff's warrant
> turned out a tenantry, violently retaining possession, a month after the

Ground had been advertised, five months after it had been publicly set to another, three months after they had got notice to quit, and one month after it had become the property of the new tenant whose payment for it had begun, and thus ceased to exist.

I feel astonishment how it is credible, that I, a man originally of some humble independence and prospects in life, to which was added the honour of Lord Stafford and your Ladyship's confidence, should, without any imputation of insanity, of private interest, of malice, of passion, go furth, in broad day, in prescience of officers and witnesses to commit crimes! I feel confident of acquittal, notwithstanding the perjury to be expected of highland witnesses – the bias of a highland Jury, and the circumstances that Ld Pitmilly who is to be my Judge is brother of the partner of Mr Mackenzie; whose influence, I believe, did at the first foster and bring forward this and similar oppressions against me. I trust the last circumstance is accidental and I rely on the paternal Care of providence who watches over all, guides all human events, and, in the wisdom and goodness of whose decrees, I entertain full and implicit confidence.[78]

By Sellar's own account, he had little faith in either the judge[79] or the jury.

– THE EVE OF THE TRIAL –

Sellar continued to perform his estate work and his farming in the early months of 1816. In March, for example, he expatiated on the emigration issue on which he was highly critical of the government's vacillations. He believed that every official encouragement should be granted to emigrants. He was now a Malthusian on the issue: emigration would afford some temporary relief from numbers and would rid the country of less desirable parts of the population. But it would not cause a permanent diminution of the population, as had been demonstrated by the recent statistics for Sutherland. He added:

> It signifies not one pinch of Snuff to Lord and Lady Stafford, what number of Whisky Smugglers chuse to be off; for, their place must of course be presently filled up by men, who by industry increase the subsistence, and, of course, the numbers of the people.

At the time Sellar was greatly involved in the construction of The Mound at Strathfleet, an enterprise which was punctuated by massive engineering problems and monumental arguments with advisers, including Thomas Telford himself.[80]

Sellar gave the appearance of confidence and normality, but as the trial approached he showed signs of inner agitation. Charles Adam, cousin and consultant of Loch, reported that 'poor Sellar . . . is by no means in a state of mind to give his attention to the great work agoing at the Mound'. By then the trial was only days away. In fact Sellar did not obtain the precise terms of his indictment until two weeks before his trial, Mackid 'having kept it back . . . to the latest day on which it could be served.' This delay reduced Sellar's ability to prepare his case yet, he exclaimed, 'I dont at all fear the result.' He had returned to his father's house at Westfield in Moray to make ready for the trial. With all his documents arranged, he was able to state: 'I am prepared on almost every point.'

Sellar's mind traversed the recent history of sheep-farming and resistance in the northern Highlands. He recalled the famous riots in Ross-shire 'a good many year ago' – in 1792, when two men called Ross had been actively engaged. They had subsequently moved into Sutherland at Uppat, not unlike an infection, he implied. Here they had been involved in the riots of 1813, and were subsequently 'leaders in this conspiracy against my removings in 1814, now in question.' Alexander Sutherland of Scibbercross had also fostered the 1813 riots and published articles in the press, and continued to promote the 'villainous libels 1815 to 1816'. Sellar's counsel in the coming trial would establish 'this connexion of all the riots and conspiracies with each other'. Thus Sellar persuaded himself that there had been a continuity of concerted and conspiratorial resistance from 1792 to 1816, he being now the final target of the campaign. This was the most elaborate version of Sellar's conspiracy theory.

Sellar asked Lady Stafford to furnish him with every other libel relevant to the case: the identification of all his enemies and defamers would also, in the long run, help her estate management as well as his own case. He also asked Loch to send him a complete set of the *Military Register*, assuring him that no one would know. Sellar declared that he hoped soon to be relieved 'of a load upon my mind which for 18 months back has oppressed me into stupidity. I am near bringing these fools to the Jail of their race, I trust.' He had tried to focus on the great engineering problems of the Mound but, he said, his mind was 'too full of my own Story to give any proper attention to any other.'[81]

Lord Moray, one of Sellar's character witnesses, told Sellar to 'implore' Lady Stafford again to release the extraordinary and vital letter written by Mackid to Lord Stafford in June 1815,

> with a view to ruining me in your good opinion. The circumstances of such a letter having been written came to my knowledge <u>legitimately</u> by persons to whom <u>Mr Mackid told</u> the fact.

Sellar asked Lady Stafford to consider him 'as an accused servant entitled to justice to have communicated to him the particulars of such accusation'. The letter was critical to his case, 'not only to vindicate myself, but make Mackid's conduct appear in a proper light to the public'. He claimed that it was direct evidence of Mackid's malice as a magistrate. At the eleventh hour, on the eve of his trial, Sellar was at last given access to the crucial document. On 24th April 1816 Sellar thanked Lord Stafford from Inverness for the letter, remarking, 'We could not refrain from producing it.'

In the days before his trial Sellar remained in Elgin and Westfield gathering his testimonies and preparing his defence. He had engaged expensive and superior counsel. His opponents in Strathnaver were being gathered together: they faced a long journey to Inverness and problems of co-ordination and language too. The Crown prosecution had not been organised until the very last moment, and faced disadvantages in this respect. Mackid was already a broken reed even before the trial. Cranstoun was absent. The trial, earlier expected to be moved to Edinburgh to avoid local prejudices, was now set for Inverness; a jury had been drawn from outwith Sutherland in order to ensure separation from county involvement.

Though Sellar proclaimed his innocence and his confidence, he was a nervous man. Many of those about him were far from completely optimistic about the outcome of the trial. People across the Highlands, within and beyond Strathnaver, were holding their breath for the outcome.

CHAPTER 10

Trial and Retribution

– FOREBODINGS IN INVERNESS, APRIL 1816 –

Patrick Sellar was at last brought to trial in Inverness on Tuesday, 23 April 1816. Almost two years had elapsed since the original removals in Strathnaver. The most serious charges in the long indictment were those of 'culpable homicide'.[1] Sellar was accused of having 'culpably killed' Donald McBeath, an old man in his sick bed, and Margaret McKay, who was ninety years old. The proceedings before Lord Pitmilly[2] began at 10 a.m. and finished after 1 a.m. on the following morning. Sellar was tried before a jury of fifteen 'gentlemen drawn from outwith Sutherland' and evidence, cross-examination and judgement stretched across fifteen hours. No official transcript or report of the trial[3] survived and this has contributed to the persistent questioning of the event as a proper and fair trial of the Sutherland sheep-farmer. The unanimous verdict of the Inverness court in April 1816 was subsequently contested in a hundred accounts of the Highland clearances, both in Sellar's own lifetime and since.[4]

The defence was far from confident of the eventual result of the case. A sense of danger was exposed by one of Sellar's counsel the day before the trial. Henry Cockburn (later a great figure in the Scottish Bar) was, at the time, a junior lawyer and was clearly anxious for his client's case, emphasising the perils he faced as he entered the court room:

> My client P. Sellar had been shamefully persecuted and whatever the result may be he is innocent as innocence itself. The only risk arises from the gross local prejudices which have been indulged against him for two years and which it is difficult even for an honest Jury to get out of their Heads.[5]

– SELLAR'S LEGAL ARRANGEMENTS –

Sellar did not stint on his preparations either in detail or in expense. For his defence Sellar engaged the services of James Robertson on 2 June 1815, almost a year before the eventual trial. The timetable of Sellar's legal moves was documented in Robertson's financial accounts. In June 1815 Robertson recorded that Gower had sent Sellar a copy of an advertisement 'accusing you of having been guilty of murder and other crimes'. In July 1815, Sellar was in daily consultation with Robertson in Edinburgh and there was much correspondence with newspaper editors. In December, Sellar obtained advice from Robertson about statements in the *Military Register*. In late January 1816, Sellar and his lawyer held discussions 'respecting an overture for settlement'. At the start of February 1816, Robertson dissuaded Sellar 'from taking any steps against Mr Mackid at present'. On 11 March 1816, Sellar received notice from the Crown officers 'intimating their determination to bring you at trial at next Circuit.'

Sellar, a lawyer himself, hired the best available lawyers who, in their turn, commissioned the services of solicitors in Inverness, namely Messrs Anderson and Shepherd. On 3 April the young Henry Cockburn was retained by Sellar's counsel. The counsel amassed 75 pages of evidence in their preparation for the trial (Mackenzie reported that Sellar's counsel's brief ran to 400 pages). The total cost, including their attendance at the trial, was £599 13s 8d.[6]

The accounts for the trial, and the associated costs, reveal the tactics employed on Sellar's behalf. Sellar's solicitors in Inverness undertook a great search which eventually harvested evidence from a large number of exculpatory witnesses. These witnesses were dispersed through Sutherland, the Reay Country, Caithness, and Ross, and were only found with considerable difficulty and expense. The solicitors' receipts show payments made to witnesses for Sellar, some signed for with crosses, and included Donald Macleod for Rossal.[7] The total expense on this item alone was £53 15s 0d. Each witness was paid for nine days at 4/6 per day. They also had to be conveyed to Inverness for the trial, and accommodated there too.[8] The solicitors' accounts detailed the cost of 'trouble in this business including Whisky and other entertainment to Ewan and his followers', as well as 'cash paid to same Ewan Chisholm' to ensure his attendance at the trial. Sellar's outlay on this elaborate and difficult detective work and its detail was heavy. All the witnesses were accommodated at his expense.[9]

The evidence of the lawyers' financial accounts showed also the timing of the moves, the overtures for settlement, the raising of witnesses (who were mainly not used), and, especially, the entertainment provided. But the most telling point was Sellar's insistence on bringing forward Chisholm the Tinker and forty-one others, as his witnesses. This was not the act of a man fearful of the testimony of the people, at least on the point of law under which he was charged. In the outcome only a small proportion of Sellar's defence case was employed in the formal proceedings of the trial. It is clear, however, that Sellar's legal preparation was decisive in determining the tactics of the Crown Prosecutor in the conduct of the case against Sellar.

Just before the trial there was tense discussion among the Sutherland advisers about whether anyone from the estate should attend the proceedings. In the event, they decided against an appearance in order to maintain distance from the case, and also to demonstrate impartiality. They also worked to avoid the suggestion of excessive anxiety by Sellar's employer.[10] William Mackenzie was notably pessimistic about the outcome. Only days before the trial he wrote, privately, that the coming trial would reveal that the lots for the removed people had not been ready at the time of the removals. The people were given only two or three days to remove to their future lots and this would look very bad for the estate.[11] Mackenzie said that the readiness of the houses had been Young's responsibility, but Sellar should have known anyway. If oppression was proved this would return to the feet of Young and the surveyor Roy, as well as to Sellar.[12]

The estate was, therefore, decidedly nervous of the outcome of Sellar's trial, and the Stafford family effectively left Sellar to his own devices. Indeed it was not until a few days before the trial that Sellar at last gained access to the vital Mackid letter which seemed to incriminate Sellar's most dangerous enemy.[13] In this letter Mackid had improperly proclaimed Sellar's guilt to Lord Stafford before his prisoner had been tried. The good wishes of the Stafford family were delivered to Sellar as he approached his trial, but everyone in the estate administration had been carefully distancing themselves from him. Their last message was to emphasise that, in the Strathnaver removals of 1814, Sellar had acted as tenant not as factor.[14] They were trying to protect their own backs.

– THE TRIAL –

The wisdom of holding the trial within the Highlands was questioned both by Sellar's friends and his enemies. The *Military Register*, at least, believed there was a plot to hold the trial in Edinburgh to make it difficult to assemble the prosecution witnesses. Sellar himself welcomed the Inverness location.[15] In the outcome there are no accounts of public antagonism to Sellar in Inverness at the time of the trial. The reports in the newspapers gave straightforward accounts of the outcome and the concluding remarks of Lord Pitmilly. The only detailed account of any sort was a substantial pamphlet of sixty-seven pages issued by Sellar's junior counsel, Patrick Robertson, which provided a narrative of the evidence and summaries of the cases made by the lawyers as well as the judge's summing-up.[16] Robertson's *Report* was published within a month of the trial and was probably an attempt to capitalise on the trial, either by the lawyers or by Sellar. It was expressly intended to disperse the 'contemptible lies' suffered by Sellar who had been 'branded with the name of a tyrant, oppressor and murderer'.[17] The account was not publicly challenged at the time of its publication.

The trial began with the reading of the long indictment and then a summary of the Crown case, after which Sellar's counsel immediately rejected all the charges and challenged the prosecution to provide any proof of the allegations. All Sellar's ejectments had been not only lawful but executed with 'great indulgence'. Sellar rejoiced in the opportunity to demonstrate his complete innocence before a dispassionate British Jury. Then, before any evidence was taken, Pitmilly intervened to condemn the recent circulation of publications [no doubt including the *Military Register*] 'as of the most contemptible nature'. Thus Pitmilly's own attitude was made clear to the Jury from the outset.

When the Crown brought forth its first witness, Robert Mackid, an objection was lodged by the defence on the grounds of his 'malice and partial counsel' against the defendant. This was largely based on his self-incriminating letter written to Lord Stafford at the time of Sellar's arrest, produced as a trump card by the defence. At this vital juncture in the trial witnesses were called to test the point, apparently sustaining the allegation. The Crown declared that Mackid had been called only as a witness to establish practice in Sutherland with regard to the rights of outgoing tenants to their barns and arable land. In the outcome Pitmilly allowed Mackid's evidence *cum nota* but he was not called on to provide evidence directly relevant to central charges against Sellar.

The Crown then brought forward Chisholm and his wife who separately described the day of the eviction at Badinloskin, followed by eleven other witnessses for the prosecution. Robertson's *Report* recorded little of the cross-examination of the witnesses. Much of the detail of the precognition evidence was reiterated and there followed vivid accounts of the confusion and destruction during Sellar's evictions. But the detailed testimonies contained transparent contradictions and offered little direct evidence that Sellar had unambiguously and deliberately caused injury to any individual. Even the essential sequence of events was confused in these testimonies. There was no unanimity about the precise whereabouts of Chisholm's mother-in-law at the time of the eviction nor who had responsibility for the fire or for her rescue. Her daughter gave a different story from that of her husband, and subsequent witnesses did not help the case. Though the allegations against Sellar were repeated they did not cohere into a sustained case; the evidence was not marshalled in a way which could conclusively pin any death or injury to any specific act by Sellar or his men. The evidence for the Crown indeed strongly suggested that Chisholm was using his aged mother-in-law as a device in delaying Sellar's eviction order. His wife seems to have deliberately absented herself at the time of the eviction. They disagreed about the loss of £3 in notes. Most of the rest of the evidence was about the destruction of barns, houses and kilns against the custom of the country. The prosecution had called more than a dozen witnesses but others were refused on the grounds that they were 'erroneously described' in the list.

Sellar's defence began with the reading of his long declaration of 31 May 1815 when he was in the hands of Mackid. Then five character witnesses, two sheriff substitutes, two proprietors and a merchant were presented, each proclaiming Sellar's 'character for humanity'. Sellar was, wrote Sir George Abercrombie of Birkenbog, 'a young man of great humanity, and I think him incapable of being guilty of the charges brought against him'. At this point the prosecution decided to drop part of the case against Sellar but the defence counsel insisted on bringing forth its evidence about 'allegations of injury etc, simply as a specimen . . . of what had been the actual conduct of the tenantry during the proceedings.' This was to demonstrate that Sellar had been traduced by his opponents. Sellar, in other words, wanted to use the opportunity to demonstrate his innocence. Defence witnesses were introduced to ridicule previous testimony and to describe the actual events.

The defence testimonies, though designed to absolve Sellar from the charges of murder, conceded most of the story of the events in Strathnaver short of the loss of life. The defence did not contest the basic facts of the ejection and destruction. Sellar and his party had indeed executed the necessary physical eviction and demolition, but had used minimum legal measures only. Sellar had given specific instruction for the men to behave with humanity and to retain a vital number of mills and temporary buildings for the sick and aged. The defence called nine witnesses but 'a vast number of additional witnesses in exculpation' who were in attendance were not called because it was thought to be 'superfluous' to the needs of the case. In effect there was a considerable concurrence between the defence and prosecution accounts which testified to the destruction and hysteria that accompanied the Strathnaver removals. The explosive difference was whether Sellar had caused the deaths of two elderly people and serious danger to the lives of others who stood in the way of his evictions at that time. It was on this difference that the entire proceedings were hinged.

In the final speeches before the court Drummond, for the Crown, conceded that he could not establish culpable homicide. But the serious charge, that real injury was done to the old woman in Badinloskin, remained. So did the destruction of the barns. For Sellar, Gordon especially attacked Mackid and the character of Chisholm and his associates, and asserted Sellar's total innocence. The trial was in reality 'a conflict between the law and the resistance to the law'. On the result of the trial depended all further improvement.

Lord Pitmilly then addressed the Jury, stating the law and summing up the evidence. The only central charge that remained concerned 'the old woman in Badinloskin'. Sellar had destroyed barns but the law was on his side in this matter. Moreover the law said that Sellar 'was entitled to proceed with the ejections.' Pitmilly pointed out that Chisholm's evidence had been contradicted by his wife, though it was confirmed by John Mackay, and then contradicted by Sutherland, Fraser and Burns. Pitmilly told the Jury that if they were unsure they would have to take into account Sellar's character: 'for this was always important in balancing contradictory behaviour'. Pitmilly remarked that there was real evidence of Sellar's regard for the sick and his humane behaviour. His character references did not constitute evidence, but would have weight with the jury. It was a very pointed commentary and left no doubt about Pitmilly's view of the case.

Within fifteen minutes the jury returned with a unanimous verdict of 'NOT GUILTY'. Pitmilly immediately expressed his warm concurrence in their view. Drummond also chimed in, saying that the result would have been the same even if the witnesses 'who were objected to on account of their designations had been examined.'[18] Once the verdict had been announced, Pitmilly addressed Sellar directly with final words, of great solace to the embattled sheep-farmer:

> Mr Sellar, it is now my duty to dismiss you from the bar; and you have the satisfaction of thinking, that you are discharged by the *unanimous opinion of the Jury and the Court.* I am sure that, although your feelings must have been agitated, you cannot regret that this trial took place; and I am hopeful it will have due effect on the minds of the country, which have been so much and so improperly agitated.[19]

Robertson's *Report* did not pretend to represent the prosecution case in any detailed fashion. It told nothing of the preparations among Sellar's accusers; it gave no interior account of the mind of Robert Mackid, no consideration of the missing witnesses, not even the notes of the prosecuting counsel. It was a patently one-sided version of the formal evidence.

The local newspapers carried only brief and dismissive accounts of the trial, giving the impression that the whole matter had been so much hot air and was no longer contentious. The *Inverness Journal* pointed out that the charges were already twenty-four months old and had been kept alive by 'certain English journals' (meaning the *Military Register* and the *Star*) which had teemed with 'inflammatory statements' for eighteen months. The Inverness newspaper gave the impression that the Lord Advocate had brought the matter forward to get the whole matter ventilated and eliminated once and for all. The case derived from 'misconception, malice and personal hostility'. The first came from the tenantry, who simply misunderstood Lady Stafford's improvement arrangements. The malice belonged to un-named persons against the Sutherland family and against Sellar in particular. And there were, it said, dark figures behind the plot:

> who thought to instigate the deluded people to resistance and misrepresentation while they, the instigators, remained in the background.

This, of course, was precisely Sellar's own conspiracy theory.

The trial, remarked the *Inverness Journal*, had produced total proof of Sellar's innocence, and demonstrated Sellar's capacity 'for moderation, humanity and kindness of disposition'. Sellar had given particular care to the sick and infirm in the very cases cited against him: 'It was the strongest possible defence . . . The tide of prejudice had been completely turned, and upon the best of all grounds, evidence, and the verdict of a jury.'[20]

None of the surviving accounts of Sellar's trial are adequate but several aspects of the case were transparent. The Crown decided against using Mackid's evidence and Cranstoun was not present at the trial. Sellar was not called to the dock. Many of the prosecution and defence witnesses were either not present or not called. Sellar employed distinguished counsel; the Crown case appears to have been assembled hurriedly and without adequate preparation. The jury was entirely male, all gentlemen from outwith the County: from Ross, Caithness and Inverness. Sellar had gathered character references on his own behalf from Moray, though not from Sutherland. The prosecuting counsel had quickly decided that most of the charges against Sellar could not be sustained in the court, and most were immediately dropped, surrendering to the weight of evidence assembled by Sellar's lawyers.

The evidence of the small tenants was poorly attested; the main witnesses were found wanting in reputation and consistency. The prosecution was eventually left with a small number of technical charges relating to the traditional rights of flitting tenants. The arguments mainly concerned the credibility of the prosecution witnesses as against the respectability of Sellar; the court gave credence to the suggestion that a conspiracy had been concocted against Sellar; and the actions of Mackid at the time of the first precognition were heavily criticised. In effect, the weight of evidence against Sellar was much slighter than expected; most of the people involved in the 1814 removals were not presented. Much of the prosecution evidence had evaporated between the time of the Precognitions and the date of the trial. The problem of language may have had its effect; the distance and cost of attendance may have told against the prosecution witnesses.

The Crown case was poorly prepared and poorly supported. The witnesses were not well coordinated and instead of an overwhelming solidarity of testimony against Sellar, supported by many of the common people, the case depended on the evidence of a tinker who was easily blackguarded. The question that emerges is why so little of the head of steam which had propelled the popular campaign against Sellar was not sustained up to the moment of the trial? Why, at the trial, did so little of the original sensational case show its face? Given that many months had been available for preparation and raising support, why was it so slight on the day? These questions were not answered at the time nor subsequently.

On the specific matter of whether Sellar had caused fire to be put to the house before the old woman Mrs Mackay was out, and whether he had ordered the old woman out of the house and into a dangerously bad place which then caused her death, Sellar's accusers did not bring forth adequate witnesses. This was a fundamental weakness in the Crown case. Moreover the Crown prosecutors were not able to persuade the minister of the church, David Mackenzie, to swear to the good character of the tinker, Chisholm. Third, there was no demonstration of sufficient motive for Sellar's alleged offence. The trial, as it was reported, simply confirmed the facts of the evictions: that they had been carried through by fiat; that people were cleared off in large numbers though at differing intervals; that it was certainly a grim business in its execution; that fire was employed; that the people were rattled and some of them were mutinous.

– TRIAL REPORTS –

Direct reaction to the trial was soon supplied by observers to the event. Once more, however, these reports represented Sellar much more than his assailants.

George MacPherson Grant, MP, had

> felt a great desire to attend the trial in order to be enabled to form the most correct opinion of Mr Sellar's whole conduct from the Evidence and Proceedings; but the more I reflected upon it the more I felt that situated as I am, my presence might naturally have been construed as implying an interest on the part of Your Ladyship [Lady Stafford] and Lord Stafford beyond what might be desirable.

He immediately relayed the news of Sellar's acquittal to the anxious Stafford family in the south, describing his conversation with Sellar's senior counsel the day after the trial. Gordon gave him 'the most satisfactory Account of the result of Sellar's trial'. The whole event had been entirely successful and was

> calculated to display the arrangements on the Sutherland Estate and Sellar's own conduct for moderation and humanity in the most favourable light.

The trial was a victory for the landlord's policies as much as for Sellar himself, a view which confirmed the general feeling, despite the clear and consistent efforts made by the Sutherland family to divorce themselves from Sellar's case.

Grant related how Mackid's letter to Lord Stafford had been the first pillar of the defence. Mackid had first denied, and then was forced to admit, that he had said that he was 'Sellar's enemy and that Botany Bay would be too good for him'. Other witnesses also testified that Mackid had uttered 'the most malevolent expressions'. Counsel, on this basis, objected to him as a witness but Pitmilly would not refuse him. Nevertheless, at this critical point, the Crown advocates had decided to discard Mackid's evidence. The Crown had also signally failed to sustain any of the charges except that relating to the burning of barns at the time of the evictions. In this matter, the practice of the country was out of kilter with the law and Sellar was found to be vulnerable.[21]

Grant, reporting the unanimous verdict of the jury and the warm endorsement of Pitmilly, emphasised the point that the Crown lawyer had immediately expressed his concurrence 'and stated that although some of his Witnesses had not been present, yet he was satisfied that had they been examined the result must have been exactly what it was'. Sellar had been completely exculpated and Mackid was made to look as black as possible. The great thing, said Grant, was that it would have

an amazing effect in changing the Current of prejudice which ran against Sellar and had turned out [a] fortunate Circumstance for him contrary to the most sanguine expectations of his friends.

When the judgement was at last announced to the Inverness court, Sellar broke down. As Grant reported the dramatic moment, 'Sellar bore up very well but when the Verdict of acquittal was pronounced, he burst into tears which had a great effect on the Audience.' Tears often flow in dramatic lawsuits, but they had not been expected of the Sutherland sheep-farmer.

Grant's report suggests strongly that the verdict had been far from foregone, that the Crown Counsel had decided that Mackid would be a hazard in the witness box, and that many witnesses had been missing from the trial.[22] He noted that the jury had been composed of five jurymen from each of the counties of Inverness, Ross and Elgin which, in the result, was a benefit because 'the fortunate impression made upon them will be widely circulated.' Grant remarked that 'as the trial terminated, it is much better that Mr Sellar has been left entirely to depend on the Justice of his cause and that his constituents relying on that have given no appearance of any anxiety as to the result, and it must prove more satisfactory to himself.' The proprietor had certainly left her beleaguered tenant and factor to his own devices, and now was the time to make a virtue of this gambit.[23]

MacPherson Grant was in Rothes at the time of the trial and had happened to meet Henry Cockburn, one of Sellar's counsel, on his way home from Inverness. Cockburn related Sellar's acquittal on all the charges:

> After a long and tedious trial, . . . the Crown Lawyers were obliged to abandon every charge but two, in which they persisted but . . . both the Judge and Jury were unanimous in the opinion of Sellar's entire Innocence, and there had been some horrible attempts at false evidence on the part of the Witnesses.

Grant remarked:

> It is most gratifying that the unpleasant business has terminated so favourably and I think Mr Cranstoun must feel rather awkward on the result of his investigation. On perusing the Indictment I was clearly of opinion that it was exaggerated and strained and likely by its extent to defeat its own purpose.

In the British Library's copy of Robertson's *Trial Report* there survives a handwritten note by Henry Cockburn which offered his retrospective opinion:

> The only importance of his trial consists of its being connected with the introduction of the new system of management into Sutherland, which was a matter of intense local interest. Those who were for retaining the old tennantry [*sic*] with all their bad habits were clear for hanging Sellars [*sic*] who they said had burned them out. Those who were for getting them out anyhow were against this; and this trial became a criterion between the two factions. The real truth is that he was not guilty of the crimes charged against him. H.C.

As Cockburn said, this was a trial for the future of the improvement system and Sellar was the focal point of the contest. Cockburn's private opinion is valuable because it confirmed the unanimity of legal opinion at the time.[24]

Another report of Sellar's triumph was sent by William Mackenzie (writing from Edinburgh) and contained notes by Sellar's counsel Gordon, penned in great haste, immediately after the trial. He declared:

> We beat them by *facts* as well as arguments. I have never seen a more thorough victory and I think Mr S is thoroughly whitewashed. The object seems to have been to oppose Lady Stafford's Improvements at all hazards – and to plant a thorn in her side, by the sacrifice of Sellar if nothing better could be done. I did my best to expose this infamous conspiracy – and I hope the audience at least are satisfied by what was proved and shewn that there had been much [wrong done?].[25]

Mackenzie received the report of another friend who had attended the trial which he quoted thus:

Sellar's trial lasted until past 1 o'clock this morning when he was acquitted on all the Charges by a unanimous verdict which was in perfect accord with the judge's opinion and that of I believe almost every unprejudiced person who heard the evidence. The public prosecutor not only failed in establishing the charges of homicide or of oppression but it was distinctly proved that Mr Sellar had given orders not only to spare houses where he had been informed sick persons were but to take care not to injure furniture. There was indeed as is usual in such cases some contrariety in the evidence, but the appearance of the witnesses, the style of their testimony and mode of giving it convinced me that truth was on Sellar's side.

Mackenzie congratulated Lady Stafford on the victory for all 'those who feel interested in the Sutherland Estate.' He said that he had long thought that the calumnies experienced by Sellar 'have been occasioned less by personal [pique?] than by a spirit of opposition to the *System* he was carrying on.' Mackid's punishment and dismissal, he predicted, would follow as a consequence.[26]

A day later Mackenzie gathered his more considered thoughts on the happy outcome of the trial. It was gratifying in every way, but especially to all improvers. It was:

not only a triumph over those in the Country who by every means opposed the new system but will operate as a deathblow to the opposition and so enable the persons in the management to proceed in all matters with much greater ease and advantage than they have hitherto been able to do thwarted on all sides as they have been.

Mackenzie's triumphant account was confirmation that the landlords' thinking had fully assimilated the crucial central proposition bruited about by the *Military Register* in the previous two years. Both sides in the contest explicitly came to regard the trial of Patrick Sellar as a climacteric in the history of the Highlands.

Mackenzie commented specifically on the role of the prosecution in the trial:

Counsel and Agents for the Crown cut a very awkward figure in this business, to have presented a Jury an Indictment with such a tragic narrative every point of which was falsified was really very improper – the only excuse they can offer is that the precognition (which I presume was well manufactured by Mackid) contained this statement but before the trial they should have satisfied themselves as to its truth or falsity.

This added to the impression that the Crown was poorly prepared and lacked conviction in the case they presented. How much of this was the consequence of Mackid's professional incompetence is impossible to say.

Mackenzie concluded that, 'of course', Sellar would soon prosecute Mackid for damages, 'in which the secret history of the Conspiracy will transpire'. Cranstoun would now have to dismiss Mackid. Mackenzie repeated that it was best that he had not attended the trial because it demonstrated that 'Sellar's acquittal was procured without any aid except through the truth and the exertions of his counsel.' Everyone agreed that Sellar had been treated oppressively and that he had incurred great expense in his defence.[27] Mackenzie reported, from another friend, that Pitmilly (in private) had said 'how much he was satisfied of the justice of Sellar's acquittal and how evident it was of a Conspiracy against him'. Moreover Pitmilly had 'averred it was easy to perceive Mackid was at the bottom of the whole'.[28]

William Young, Sellar's closest colleague and most nervous of the implications of the Strathnaver debacle, also reported the acquittal in great excitement. He found himself with only half a page of paper to transmit his immediate account of the long ordeal. He told Lady Stafford that all the charges had been 'confuted'. Sellar had been honourably acquitted by unanimous verdict. He pointed out that

> the greater part was given up as hopeless and the charges confined to the Barns and the Tinker's wife's mother. In the former it was found that Sellar had legal authority as his guide, in the latter that the woman was actually removed before he came to the place, the Tinker and his wife confuted each other while three distinct witnesses deponed in Mr Sellar's favour, the Jury did not hesitate ten minutes.

Young exulted in the verdict: 'Mackid got a most complete thrashing. My own opinion is that he cannot show his face in the north and that Mr Cranstoun *must* instantly dismiss him, *I am quite sure of it*, the trial will be published on Friday.' He noted that Sellar had been supported by two Sutherland farmers throughout the fourteen hours of the trial. Now, said Young, thought must be given to 'Mr Sutherland and the Military Register' in terms of what they had done in the past, and what they might do in the future. He said that no one of consequence read the newspaper, though it was 'read by all Highlanders and Highland Regiments. I daresay he expected to produce rebellion.'[29]

Equally elated was James Loch, who received the news of Sellar's acquittal in Lilleshall, the Shropshire seat of the Stafford family. Loch, in private correspondence with his uncle, Chief Commissioner Adam, was privy to further inside information about the legal reaction to the

Inverness proceedings which had exculpated Sellar. Adam conveyed, confidentially, the gist of 'a most satisfactory conversation' with Lord Pitmilly about Sellar's trial:

> He says it came out clear and satisfactory that no guilt was to be ascribed to him – and very creditable and Honourable as far as the family transactions respecting Sutherland before the public. It may be agreeable to Lord and Lady Stafford to know this immediately from the Judge and I am happy to be the Channel of any communication that is gratifying to them.

Adam was extremely pleased to report this particular *imprimatur* for the Stafford family. It was certainly gratifying: they had been seen to be doing more for the people they removed than other landlords, and they were being seen to follow the protocols of the law. Their vindication in respectable society was now complete.[30]

Loch was able to say triumphantly to Lady Stafford that 'the neck of resistance is broken'. Loch himself certainly interpreted the trial as a vital signal for further clearances and comprehensive change. It was a victory for rationality, improvement and the rights of property.[31] He told the Rev. David Mackenzie that Lady Stafford was delighted with the result of the trial, which demonstrated Sellar's 'complete innocence.' He asked Mackenzie to tell his parishioners the 'absolute necessity of their remaining quiet in their new habitations and behaving well and obediently to the laws.' He asked the Rev. Donald Sage to do likewise.[32]

There may have been a green light for further progress on the estate, but there were other lessons from the trial. Slower, more gradual, progress was essential: this now became the emphatic message in the management which Loch soon moved decisively to reform.[33] Young also advocated extreme caution and harboured grave doubt about immediate new removals. Falconer's leases were, in any case, still causing delay. But the pressure and insistence exerted by the sheep-farmers continued to create a tension in the ranks of the estate managers.[34]

– SELLAR GIRDS HIMSELF –

On the day of his acquittal Sellar reported his success to Lord Stafford. He wrote formally, as a man exhausted by his ordeal. He chose first to acknowledge the critical importance for his defence of Stafford's release of the Mackid letter. He expected that his acquittal would be well regarded by the Stafford family, and he commented, 'I trust its effect may be to afford us more time in future to attend to the <u>real business</u> of the Estate.'[35]

Later on the same day, Sellar wrote to Lady Stafford, though now with more passion:

> By one o'clock this morning the whole accursed plot, under which I have, for the last two years, suffered, was brought to light. The Jury, one half of which were <u>highland gentlemen Freeholders</u>, unanimously acquitted me; the Judge and Advocate depute were pleased both to compliment me; and the [pieces?] concluded with a General ruff [Scots: applause] of approbation, which was truly gratifying to my feelings.

Sellar said that it ended thus 'the last act of a Comedy. But it has been a very serious comedy; and one from which many useful lessons may be drawn.' He had been perfectly aware, at all times, of his own rectitude and 'entire innocence both in intention and commissions [and therefore] I cheerfully put my Confidence in the supreme disposer of all human affairs.' He had known this since the first allegations against him, in 1814. Throughout he had experienced 'the uncommon strength I have felt in mind and body, on every <u>change</u> and <u>turn</u> of this afflicting struggle, and the manner in which every piece of villainy had been brought to light.' He expressed gratitude for the noble patience of the Stafford family as he had laboured under such 'monstrous accusations'; it had been a sign of their great confidence in him.[36] Sellar did not tarnish the moment of his deliverance with any recollection of the actual coolness and distancing with which he had been treated in the months before his trial.

Sellar's euphoria, on the day of his acquittal, did not deter him from returning to his duties; for too long he had devoted half his time to 'unravelling plotts, intrigues, lies and nonsense'.[37] He immediately moved to convert his deliverance into a rout of his enemies: soon his tears and his joy would be turned to serious thoughts of vengeance and reparation.

The effect of the trial on public opinion was music to Sellar's ears. For example, George Tollet, the agriculturist, said that he had never doubted the result. It was utterly impossible that such a man could be guilty of the crimes imputed to him:

> It had been a malicious conspiracy of ignorance and sloth against intelligence and enterprise and I hope all Scotland will be made acquainted with Mr Sellar's merits. He is in my estimation one of the best Agriculturalists in the Empire and an honour to his country. Sutherland I hope in all *time coming* will feel the benefit of his successful labours.[38]

The immediate reaction to the news of Sellar's acquittal among the people of Strathnaver, Sutherland, and the Highlands at large was not recorded. There appear to have been no displays of public feeling or disorder (save for a series of small-scale attacks on sheep stock, mentioned below). The solitary discordant note to Sellar's vindication in the months after the verdict was sounded by the *Military Register*, which still claimed to speak on behalf of the people of Sutherland. The London newspaper first received the news of Sellar's acquittal from the Scottish newspapers and was stunned by the outcome.[39] Its first reaction was relatively muted. Its correspondent rejected Pitmilly's reported comments that the newspaper had influenced the people. The complaints of the people of Strathnaver had required no artificial stimulation. Their case had been overwhelmingly just and they had 'wearied heaven and earth' to bring Sellar to trial over eighteen months. They had been repeatedly bamboozled by legal proceedings, and had received contradictory advice from the King's Advocate, Mackid, Cranstoun and a Ross-shire lawyer. Now Mackid's evidence had been declared inadmissible because of his personal hostility, yet he was a fine citizen.

A week later the *Military Register's* correspondent began his own re-construction of the turn of events. Sellar's acquittal was achieved by several factors which worked against the people of Strathnaver. First, his defence counsel possessed 'zeal, ingenuity and ability' which gave him a clear advantage. The defence had called upon three of the most eminent advocates in Scotland, and Sellar himself was a lawyer. Second, the judge, who was the brother-in-law of Lady Stafford's law agent in Edinburgh, had demonstrated obvious partiality and, indeed, had publicly flaunted his prejudice in favour of the sheep-farmer. Third, the Crown lawyer was utterly ignorant of the people and their customs, and the case had been foisted upon him at the last moment. He had received no assistance, not even that of the Sheriff.

In the fourth place, and most fundamentally for the *Military Register*, most of the key prosecution evidence was not brought before the court. It was not a full investigation because most of the material witnesses were disqualified by the court. Some witnesses did not attend; five or six were refused because their identities could not be estab-lished. Others had been threatened with eviction if they appeared for the prosecution. As for Chisholm, the tinker, his evidence had been ignored because his certificate of good behaviour from the Rev. David Mackenzie had been torn up. And, on the other side, Sellar's ex-culpatory witnesses had been improperly entertained at Sellar's own house at Culmaily *en route* to the trial, which should have disqualified them. These witnesses were 'completely under Sellar's paw'. One of them had been decked out in a new suit of clothes for the occasion. They had perjured themselves because they expected to be hanged if Sellar lost his case. Sellar, himself, had been forced to gather his own character references outside Sutherland because no Sutherland person would provide one, not even the Rev. David Mackenzie. The people had been mesmerised by the legal forms, then confused by legal theatre and legal magic. The trial had been a farce.[40]

Sellar, disregarding the pinpricks of the *Military Register*, quickly swung into a new mood. He sought proper compensation. It was due to him, both legally and morally. This was anticipated in Young's report soon after the trial. Young spoke feelingly of 'the unpleasant situation' under which the estate had suffered for the past two years and, indeed, from the start of the improvements. The trial result had produced great satisfaction but Young now pleaded for the Stafford family to come north to make its presence felt. He also asked that its legal adviser, William Mackenzie, attend at Dunrobin 'to investigate the business, and see who really are culprits in the background – the lower class of people have certainly been much misled and they will never speak out.' While Young urged legal redress against the enemies of the Sutherland estate, he exulted in the current prospects for its fishing, its salt works and coal mines, all of which were now presenting a 'very promising aspect'.

As for Mackid, Young reported that he seemed decidedly unabashed at the recent defeat in Inverness. Cranstoun had, at last, decided to part with Mackid, so that 'we shall instantly get clear of him'. But meanwhile Mackid was still in local circulation.[41] In fact Mackid, against expectations, now apparently refused to resign his position as Sheriff-Substitute. Yet Pitmilly had stated publicly that he had been perfectly satisfied with Sellar's acquittal, having realised 'how evident it was [there existed a . . .] combination against him' and acknowledged that Mackid 'had been at the bottom of it.'[42] His dismissal was, therefore, virtually unavoidable, according to William Mackenzie.[43]

– SELLAR'S ANGER –

Sellar believed that he had been fortunate to escape the potentially fatal consequences of a radical conspiracy in Sutherland. The campaign which brought him to trial in Inverness had been designed to use him as a vehicle for the destruction of the entire improvement movement in the county, and even beyond. The conspiracy was composed of vested interests who were being displaced in the system and who employed their old influence to mislead a naive native population. In the aftermath of his trial he indulged an increasingly shrill rehearsal of this interpretation of his recent experience. He planned the final destruction of his enemies, most particularly his *bête noire*, Robert Mackid.

When Sellar had arrived in Sutherland in 1809 he had adopted a view of the Highlanders which was essentially benign, even if profoundly condescending. They were an ancient people caught in antiquated ways and kept in poverty by an ignorant system which he termed 'feudalism'. By the time of his trial, Sellar's views had become much more virulent. The people were debased and uncivilised, and could not reform without radical policies. His benevolence had turned into transparent hatred; there was now no concealing his loathing and contempt for the society out of which the conspirators had emerged to do him violence. His attitude, understandably provoked by his trial, was an extreme form of the anti-Highland sentiment, a part of which even the most romantic Scotophile absorbed at this time.[44]

Two weeks after his acquittal Sellar provided his fullest interpretation of the events which had led to his trial. Having thanked the Staffords and James Loch for their 'sympathy and kindness', he alluded to his 'past sufferings' and his 'forebodings' for the 'future'. His thesis was now an implicit condemnation of previous estate laxity in its treatment of resistance, and a demand for greater punishment and vigilance for the future. A dangerous conspiracy had been allowed to circulate in Sutherland for several years, unchecked for lack of strong measures. He now warned again that, unless the enemies of progress were rooted out, the county would be given up 'to the highland Captains and sergeants at what they please to give us. This I assure you is no dream.' He claimed that the actual ownership of the county was at stake: there was, in reality, a double proprietorship of the county, namely the lawful proprietors and the customary one of the tacksmen, the latter creaming off the profits of the land from the profits of meat, wool and whisky production. He claimed, in effect, that a 'black economy' operated beneath the formal control of the estate. He declared that the public had not expected Lord Stafford to prevail in 'this crisis' and that the sheep-farmers would soon be ruined. As ever, Sellar's instinct was to polarise the issues facing the owner and the factors.

Sellar based this dramatic view on the events since 1812, when he first sensed the darkness of the conspiracy. His trial was the culmination of a long crisis in the Highlands. By March 1813 he had seen the new shepherds being hounded all over Kildonan and Bighouse, and 'a day had been appointed for driving every South Countryman out of the County.' A message had been delivered to Mrs Reed, wife of a sheep-farmer, that her expected child, if a male, would be killed (a daughter would be unharmed because her mother was a Highlander). The riots and resistance of 1813 had been quelled by the intervention of the military; but in the *dénouement* William Young had foolishly feasted the ringleaders at Rhives, and the estate had naively believed that the trouble had been terminated, and Lord Gower had reassured Sellar. In the early phase, it was already clear that the ministers of the church, though they were sustained by patronage of the Stafford family, were complicit in the resistance. Not one of the ministers had stirred himself against the rioters. When a new minister from Nairn was posted to Assynt in late 1813, having refused to comply with the demands of the conspirators, he and Young had been assaulted. Once more the riots were settled by military force and two prisoners taken but, Sellar added sarcastically, all were let off Scot free as before.

The next manifestation of the conspiracy had been the attack on Sellar himself, a plot using law and perjury 'to take the life of the other Agent of the Estate who happened to be an entering tenant.' 'They swore Plumb in the face of fact, reason and common sense – but their story being fabricated they swore in each other's teeth. And the agent most fortunately had had the precaution to keep, while doing his duty, six men in attendance [whose] connected dispositions convinced the Jury, and he was not hanged or sent to Botany Bay.' Sellar, seeing the sequence of events so clearly, predicted that resistance would again erupt. It was a contest for the control of the Highlands.[45] In the teeth of the orchestrated lies of the common people, Sellar had escaped. He warned, unambiguously, that any soft settlement at this stage would inevitably be followed by an even worse conspiracy to overturn the rights of property in the county. Decisive measures were now imperative. Sellar, in effect, regarded the entire sorry history of the past five years as one of weakness and irresolution, which had simply encouraged the conspirators. It was his way of blaming his superiors for his own awful experience, and was a clarion call for future firmness. The conspirators must be routed.[46]

As Sellar regained his strength after the trial, his indignation redoubled. It burst into tirades against his enemies. He believed that his

triumph in Inverness now gave his views total licence. He denounced
the society which had brought him such grief and anxiety. The
victorious Sellar was utterly confident of his negative views of the
society which he had been employed to change.[47] Among the Highlanders with whom he was forced to deal there was

> an absence of every principle of truth and candour from a population of
> several hundred thousand souls, the sad remnant of a people who once
> covered a great part of Europe, and who so long and bravely withstood the
> invading strength of the Roman Empire.

His long perspective on the decline of the Celts was manifested among
the Highlanders by 'Their obstinate adherence to the barbarous
jargon of the times when Europe <u>was possessed by savages</u>'.

This was the opposite construction of the Celts in romantic form: the
Celts had rejected the languages of civilised Europe which were 'drawn
from the greatest nations of antiquity' and embodied 'the collected
wisdom of all ages, and have raised their possessors to the most
astonishing <u>eminence</u> and <u>power</u>.' In this way, the Highlanders had
placed themselves in the same relationship to European civilisation as
the 'Aborigines of North America were to the colonists'. The Highlanders were 'the Aborigines of Britain shut out from the general
stream of knowledge and cultivation flowing in upon the Common-
wealth of Europe from the remotest fountain of antiquity'. The
Highlanders were, in effect, anachronisms in the civilised world. In
parallel with the American Indians, they lived in turf cabins, with their
animals ('the brutes') and were 'singular for [their] patience, courage,
cunning and address. Both are most virtuous where least in contact
with men in a civilised State.' Sellar expressed himself with awful
clarity, much fuelled by his accumulated rage and his recent triumph.
He was, in his own words, living among savages, who, in common with
the American Indians, were 'fast sinking under the <u>baneful effects of
ardent spirits</u>'. The government, in the meantime, was robbed of
enormous revenues.[48]

Sellar believed that illicit distilling was one of the most evil problems
in the Highlands. He provided a clever economic analysis of the trade
to demonstrate that everyone benefited from this 'nefarious and
abominable trade' except the taxman. It corrupted the entire society
but especially the poor smuggler: 'His life becomes a continual
struggle, how by lies, chicanery, perjury, midnight journeys, the midnight watching of his wife and family, debasing artifices and sneaking
to his superior, he can obtain through theft a miserable livelihood.'

Debauchery and deceit were essential and this was ingrained 'in the children who exceeded parents in that turpitude'. And so 'the virtue of a Scotch Highlander is exchanged for the vices of the Irish peasantry . . . the rapid demoralisation of a brave people.' It was the responsibility of Lord and Lady Stafford to eradicate the trade, which had been accomplished in Banff. Sellar knew how to achieve such a cleansing and it would be consistent with the general policy of improvement.

The answer to the debauching effect of smuggling was to remove the people from the inaccessible regions of the interior to the coast where they would receive alternative employment. For instance, the people of Rogart, which was 'entirely packed and crammed with Whisky Smugglers', should be cleared to Brora and the straths converted to sheep. Everyone would be better off and 'those who live here 50 years [from now] . . . will be at a loss to see how we have got forward under so many disadvantages as at present oppress us.' Sellar said that a great number, more than a thousand families, should be shifted. He entertained no qualms about such a scale of removals, but his associates were less confident. MacPherson Grant remarked, 'I confess my nerves are hardly equal to the contemplation of removing 1056 Families at once even supposing you could find the Means of their Accommodation.'[49]

Sellar, indeed, drew up a precise and rational timetable for these removals. It would be 'a prudent and considerate plan' by which the people would be brought to 'rational pursuits' and their children educated in honest and useful tasks, raised to become 'knit together in the bond of one Society'. Here Sellar spoke of 'the medicines of the mind . . . necessary to change the sentiments and feelings' of the people and induce them willingly to bend to this new state of things. But these things could not be left to people of the old school:

> I venture to say that what we have seen among the people during the last four years could not have happened had the Teachers of Youth, an the Ministers of the several Parishes been men brought from an industrious Country the sons of industrious Parents, and with a passion for industry in them.

The existing ministers were men 'bred in a country of sloth and idleness, the sons of highland tenants and whisky smugglers, and with a tone imbibed from earliest infancy of detestation of every introduction to industry or innovation in the ancient language and manner of the Gael.' The Staffords should replace the ministers and schoolmasters with men from Aberdeen and Kincardineshire 'where the people are extremely industrious'. Their lack of Gaelic was a minor matter because the young now increasingly knew English.

Sellar's detestation of traditional Highland *mores* was obviously reinforced by the hurt he had suffered in recent events, but it also echoed the influence of his own upbringing. Most of all, he attributed the poverty and decadence of the Highlanders to their failure to divide their labour, consistent with the Smithian gospel. Sutherlanders each did all the jobs and were poor, whereas English people concentrated on one task and were prosperous. 'Witness those who live by the twentieth part of the business of a Scotch weaver, or the one tenth part of the making of a pin.' Sellar quoted long sections of *The Wealth of Nations*, archly referring to Adam Smith as 'the old Gentleman to whom I promised to introduce you . . . a Gentleman of great worth and erudition.' His solution was the removal of the people to the coast and the introduction of the vital division of labour. He said that:

> Every man is a quarrier, mason, turff cutter, woodman, carrier, thatcher, wood destroyer, currier, tanner, shoemaker, saddler, shepherd, wool comber, spinner, farmer, cattle dealer, distiller, poacher, and God knows what, and yet with will this bountiful provision for everyman of them, are they not de facto (but as Lord and Lady Stafford well know) de jure beggars.

The people should not be scattered across the inland estate in their hovels but, instead, should be concentrated along the coast where their labour could be divided, each applied to an individual trade, exchanging his 'own surplus labour' with that of his neighbours.

Sellar acknowledged that such changes created transitional trouble and thus there existed 'a spirit of warfare' in the minds of the people. But change was inevitable to eradicate the 'smuggling, indolence, malice, canting hypocrisy, envy, jack-pudding mass of confusion', all causing the 'poverty and begging of a savage Country'. It should be replaced by the virtues deriving from the division of labour in the manner prescribed by 'Mr Smith'. And, as a consequence, civilisation and decent rents would accrue. Sellar quoted Burke approvingly also:

> How preferable are the overflowings of a prosperous country to all the miserable trash that can be expressed from the dry husks of poverty by the most dexterous management and chicanery.

Sellar was, in a phrase, hell-bent on breaking the back of the old Gaelic society. Half measures were futile and contemptible. There would be trouble, even tears, but this was the price of progress. The old Highland world was corrupt: it should be dismantled.[50]

– MACKID IN RETREAT, AUTUMN 1816 –

Sellar's comprehensive condemnation of Highland life became more precisely focused in his determination to destroy his own enemies. Robert Mackid had made a hell of Sellar's life in the previous twenty-four months. Sellar's retribution took several forms. One was the elimination of Mackid from the legal establishment in Sutherland. The next was to remove him from the Sutherland estate. The last was to extract legal penalties. Sellar was eventually successful on all these scores, which completed the victory contained in his trial. Mackid was humiliated in the process. But there were a number of twists in the tale.

In the immediate aftermath of Sellar's trial there was a rash of attacks on sheep on the Sutherland estate; in addition, Lady Stafford's prize Tibetan goat had its throat cut. Sellar lost twenty of his own merinos. James Loch described it as wanton cruelty and pure barbarism.[51] Sellar, fully indignant, announced a reward of £40 for the capture of the perpetrators of 'the death of the Goat and Sheep', but it produced no result.

Sellar announced his appetite for more land, implying that he would expand his production as much as the disposition of the landlord and the interior people would allow.[52] He became vociferous and aggressive in his triumph. The sheepfarmers could only be safe if the country were rendered peaceful enough to allow improving tenants to do their duty. This required more removals and ejections by which process the estate would become more efficient and would also eliminate its enemies. Sellar declared that he had been involved in removals for four years, during which time there had not been a jot of evidence of any harshness in his dealings with the people. Nevertheless the people had 'insinuated and sneaked and whispered Calumnies' against him. The people were led from above and it was now imperative 'to find out and punish the leaders of the people.' By this he meant especially Mackid and the Sutherlands, since fresh libels were again appearing in the *Military Register.*

Sellar was undoubtedly in confident mood, ready to make the most of his legal victory, while also shaping his future as possessor of the lands of Strathnaver. Even in May 1816, within a few weeks of his trial, Sellar ridded from his lands in Strathnaver various people who had spoken against him in the recent events. But some stayed, notably Chisholm the tinker. Sellar reported that 'the tinker is still in his fastness and I suppose military power may be necessary to send him off.' Sellar proceeded to evict other individuals, and drew up lists of ringleaders for similar treatment by the estate.[53] In August 1816, Sellar was pleased to tell Lady Stafford that he was 'removing a few of the leaders of the late conspiracy'. It was a sharp exercise in private retribution, meted out by the victor.[54] He regarded this as a prelude to his forthcoming assault on Mackid and the *Military Register*.

Before Sellar initiated his own legal steps, Mackid had already been removed from his farm at Kirkton. In less than a fortnight after the trial, the Kirkton property was being valued in advance of Mackid's exit from the estate.[55] Sellar identified this as an opportunity for expansion of his Culmaily operations, and therefore entered bids for Mackid's land at Kirkton, Ironhill and Craigton. Sellar believed that the lands would bring 'safety to the merino flocks'. Some of the land was currently occupied, he declared, by some 'very troublesome people', presumably sub-tenants. Sellar was prepared to pay much more than their current rent to be rid of them. In the same correspondence, he told Lady Stafford that he was about to inaugurate his attack on Mackid:

> I shall make a point of having Mackid well trounced, but the rest of the battle I must leave to your Ladyship.

Sellar anticipated large damages from Mackid: his bid for Kirkton would give him possession of the large house that Mackid had built on the farm, and Sellar remarked that he wished 'to give Mackid the honour of building one for me, whereby £1000 may be saved to me'. Sellar would make Kirkton the best farm in Scotland and 'somewhere interesting to the traveller if he is an admirer of good tillage.'[56]

When Sellar applied for Mackid's farm at Kirkton, James Loch regarded his importuning, in the wake of recent events, as tasteless. Sellar had again demonstrated his total lack of diplomacy: his bid for Mackid's farm was rejected out of hand. Loch declared unambiguously, 'In every point of view this would have been quite ruinous to the Estate and the future management.' Sellar had enough land already: 'It shews much too greedy a disposition upon Sellar's part.' It would look bad in the public mind and help to 'keep up this . . . irritation of these men's minds.'[57] Nevertheless Loch said that Sellar should have additional land 'because no man would do so much for it'. But Kirkton, which he described as one of the finest farms in the north, should not be leased to Sellar but to some other man 'of skill and capital'. Thus Sellar was not to be rewarded in so conspicuous a fashion.[58] Mackid surrendered his lease of Kirkton for £1,352 to the Sutherland estate.

Ousted from his farm at Kirkton, Mackid was also pressed to resign his position as Sheriff-Substitute. This had been arranged even before the trial, but Mackid clung on. He refused to resign in July 1816, even though it was clear both Mackid and Cranstoun were on the way out.[59] Mackid eventually delivered his formal resignation on 29 November 1816, at which point he left the county. Cranstoun resigned soon after, in December 1816. Lady Stafford said that most of the trouble in Sutherland had been attributable to the want of a proper law officer. This was about to be changed. She was aware that she had to keep a distance from the choice of replacements.

It was another indication of Sellar's failure of judgement that he applied to succeed Mackid as Sheriff-Substitute in Sutherland. Sellar was certainly highly qualified for the position and he had experience in Moray. Yet everyone except Sellar could see the crudity of his move. Loch was aghast at the idea, and immediately declared that it could not possibly happen.[60] MacPherson Grant agreed that the very idea was madness and that 'it would be a foundation for insinuating that Mackid was sacrificed to Sellar's accommodation, and the present impression of Mackid's undermining *him* would revert upon himself.'[61]

– SELLAR VERSUS MACKID –

Sellar's final quarry was Mackid himself; he vowed to make Mackid pay for the trauma that he had endured since the Strathnaver removals. He therefore initiated legal proceedings against Mackid. Sellar hoped to extract heavy damages from Mackid unless he was bankrupted within sixty days.[62] Though Mackid expected to suffer a damages case at the hands of Sellar, he managed to resist its formal resolution for more than a year. Sellar clearly wanted to ruin Mackid, both morally and financially, and he pursued Mackid with great vigour. With the assistance of his lawyer, James Robertson, Sellar drew up a substantial and detailed case in a document of twenty-five pages against Mackid, seeking compensation.

Sellar alleged that, 'under the colour of law, and by the prostitution of judicial authority and offences of a heinous nature', Mackid had subjected him to 'cruel oppression' and claimed exemplary damages. Much of the case was devoted to the law of imprisonment and bail, invoking the various Acts of Parliament. Mackid's proceedings, it was alleged, were irregular and illegal. Eventually the case turned into an attack on Mackid himself:

Having several years ago, conceived causeless ill will and malice against the pursuer who is a gentleman by birth and education, settled in a respectable situation in the County of Sutherland and the son and heir apparent of a freeholder in the County of Moray.

Mackid was animated by 'revenge and hostility', 'saying that he would do everything in his power to injure hurt or ruin him and lose no opportunity of doing him an ill turn.' Sellar had been defamed and Mackid had spread calumny against him, and had circulated stories that Sellar would be leaving the county for good.

Mackid's malevolence, Sellar declared, originated in Sellar's action against him over the matter of poaching. This had created an 'unreasonable spirit of hostility' in Mackid who then misrepresented all Sellar's conduct as 'tyrannical and oppressive' and had encouraged petitions from Strathnaver, being 'actuated by the strongest and most inveterate ill will and malice'. His precognition in 1815 had been conducted in a 'secret irregular and clandestine manner'. Sellar claimed that Mackid had used 'a spy-glass at the adjoining eminence, that he might enjoy the spectacle of seeing the pursuer conveyed to Jail.' He had refused Sellar bail and deprived him of his legal capacities. Eight days in jail had greatly hurt his health, character and reputation.

Sellar's *coup de grâce* was Mackid's letter, written to Lord Stafford on 30 May 1815, which had been grossly improper and 'a shameful breach of official trust'. Mackid had meant to destroy Sellar and 'take advantage of the temporary clamour which he himself had created.' As a consequence Sellar had been represented as 'the very worst of human beings'. Sellar cited the *Military Register* which used the precognition as the authority for its remarks. Sellar alleged that Mackid had been in direct communication with the authors, as well as the original petitioners, and had advised them to seek subscriptions to bring Sellar to trial. Mackid had made public the contents and told everyone that Sellar would be hanged or transported. The trial had been essential for Sellar to allow him to clear his name. He was 'the most innocent man' and his character had been 'suspended for a period of twelve months and upwards as an object for the gratification of malignity and the detestation of the credulous.' The trial had been his total vindication, but he had incurred heavy costs in combating Mackid's 'private malevolent resentment and insatiable and inveterate revenge, joining a conspiracy of persons to ruin the prisoner.' Sellar sought damages of £5,000 as a '*solatium*'.

Mackid made a spirited response to Sellar's allegations. He denied personal hostility to Sellar, pointing out that he had received 'his professional education' in Sellar's father's own office in Elgin. He made no reference to the poaching matter between them. He claimed, somewhat improbably in the circumstances, that he entertained 'no other feelings towards the pursuer or his family but those of friendship'. He denied all expression of hatred, and regarded the issue as irrelevant in any case. He had circulated no stories about Sellar. He was not responsible for the Strathnaver petitions, and had been involved in no instigation of protest. The precognition had been ordered by Cranstoun, and Mackid had merely followed his duty 'which he did without any undue warmth, irregularity or unfairness'. The evidence had been signed by the private parties, and he had been assisted by proper legal officers and the evidence 'contained a just and true account of what was stated by the witnesses without exaggeration or addition'. The interpreter was a sworn official.

Mackid declared that he had never violated his duty and did not communicate the information. He denied that the key letter he wrote to Lord Stafford had claimed that Sellar had actually committed the crimes; the letter could not be construed in that way. And in any case the letter to Stafford was confidential. Sellar himself had been properly precognosced; the story of the spy-glass was 'palpably absurd', and demonstrated Sellar's pursuit of the most trivial matters to colour his allegations. Mackid had not possessed the power to give the prisoner bail, and did not judge the offences bailable in law. He denied that he had made abusive remarks to William Young at the time of the arrest.

Mackid also declared that it had been vital at that time to 'convince the people that the same law would be impartially applied to illegal conduct on the part of their superiors as had been applied to the lower class on the recent previous occasions of the riots in the parishes of Assynt and Kildonan', when there had been arrests and a military presence. He had shewn the people that the law could be fair and impartial. He denied all connection with the newspaper the *Military Register.*

Mackid pointed out that it was the second precognition (employing the same clerk) which eventually brought Sellar to trial. This, he asserted, confirmed the accuracy of the original precognition. Then Mackid referred to the trial in a passage of striking defiance of the court verdict:

> That the proof afterwards fell short and that the prisoner was acquitted is perfectly true, but this circumstance can infer no damages against a

magistrate who acted *bona fide* and the result of a precognition impartially taken. Moreover, when it is said that the pursuer was acquitted, it ought to be stated that it was not upon a full hearing of the evidence examined in the precognition, but after the rejection (upon objections made by the pursuer's counsel in point of form) of seven material witnesses out of the small number precognosed [*sic*] who had been brought forward to be examined.

Mackid believed the only relevant issue was whether he had 'fabricated or falsified the precognition'. He was adamant that he had not. Mackid denied that he was in any way responsible for the trial or the costs incurred in that event.[63]

Thus Mackid fought back and rejected all Sellar's allegations. He left a nice question about the conduct of the trial and the elimination of so many of the Crown witnesses. His denial of all enmity against Sellar was the least persuasive element in his account.

– MACKID CONCEDES –

Mackid's vigorous defence came to an abrupt conclusion in late 1817 when he suddenly agreed to sign a humiliating apology and to pay damages to Sellar as well as the costs of Sellar's action against him. Sellar stipulated the costs of the libel suit, plus £200 towards his costs of the trial; in return he would drop the action for libel.[64] The final resolution was a compromise on Sellar's part: he explained that he dropped the full action in response to his dying father's wishes for peace and quiet. Sellar's father, on his death bed, apparently asked his son to drop his suit against Mackid, saying his reputation had already been vindicated by the court case. In another version, Sellar stated that he settled with Mackid because he did not wish to ruin the man's family. As he put it, 'I found the miserable man in such difficulties on all hands; and his family of I believed 9 or 10 young Children so certainly about to be beggared by my bringing him to trial that I was well pleased to wash my hands of them.'[65] It is not clear how close Mackid was to bankruptcy. He was, however, already living in Caithness and trying to rescue his career and feed his family.

Sellar eventually decided to settle for the unambiguous confession and apology (a 'humble' letter) extracted from Robert Mackid. The legal document was drawn up in terms of 'the said Robert apologising for his injurious statements about the said Patrick's discharge of his duties as factor for the Marchioness of Stafford and the Sutherland estate, and the said Patrick withdrawing his lawsuit thereunder'.[66] Sellar's moment of triumph thus yielded two letters which became the basis of all his future pronouncements whenever the trial was questioned.[67]

The first letter read:

Robert Mackid to Patrick Sellar, Drummuie, 22 September 1817.
Sir,
Being impressed with the perfect conviction and belief that the statements to your prejudice contained in the precognition which I took in Strathnaver in May 1815, were to such an extent exaggerations as to amount to absolute falsehood, I am free to admit that led away by the clamour excited against you on account of the discharge of the duties of your office as Factor for the Marchioness of Stafford, in introducing a new system of Management on the Sutherland Estate, I gave a degree of Credit to those mis-statements of which I am now thoroughly ashamed, and which I most sincerely and deeply regret.

From the aspersions therein on your character I trust that you need not doubt that you are already fully acquitted in the eyes of the world. That you would be entitled to exemplary damages from me for my participation in the injury done to you, I am most sensible, and I shall therefore not only acknowledge it as a most important obligation conferred on me and on my innocent family, if you will have the goodness to drop your law suit against me, but I shall also pay the expenses of their suit, and place at your disposal towards the reimbursement of the previous expenses which this most unfortunate business has occasioned to you any sum you may exact when made acquainted with the state of my affairs, trusting to your generosity to have consideration for the heavy expense my defence has cost me, and that my connection with the unfortunate affair has induced me to resign the office of Sheriff-Substitute of Sutherland. I beg further that in case of your compliance with my wish here expressed, you are to be at liberty to make any use you lease of this letter except publishing it in the Newspapers which I doubt not you will see the propriety of my objecting to.

I am, Sir, your mt obt sevt Rob. Mackid.

Sellar responded, on the same day, to Joseph Gordon, Mackid's agent:

Dear Sir,
I have instantly received thro' your hands Mr Mackid's letter to me of this date, and have heard from you an explanation of the state of his affairs, which (as he is no longer possessed of the power, illegally to deprive a British subject of his liberty and otherwise to oppress him under form of law) induce me from compassion for Mr Mackid's family to drop my suit against him, on his paying the whole expenses of the said suit and placing at my disposal Two hundred pounds sterling – and having just now received your obligation as security for Mr Mackid's performing this, I cheerfully give this authority for dismissing the process.

From the moderation with which I have acted towards your client in this affair, you will believe I am sure that I have no wish to distress Mrs Mackid

The young Sellar (courtesy of Christopher and Valerie Lang of Titanga, Victoria).

Sellar in his prime. From a painting by Sir David Macnee, 1851 in E. M. Sellar, Recollections and Impressions *(Edinburgh and London 1907). Print courtesy of the Trustees of the National Library of Scotland.*

Mrs Sellar (1793-1875) (courtesy of Christopher and Valerie Lang of Titanga, Victoria).

William Young Sellar (1825-1890), son of Patrick Sellar (courtesy of Christopher and Valerie Lang of Titanga, Victoria).

Patrick Plenderleath Sellar (1823-1892), son of Patrick Sellar (courtesy of Christopher and Valerie Lang of Titanga, Victoria).

Thomas Sellar (1820-1885), son of Patrick Sellar (courtesy of Christopher and Valerie Lang of Titanga, Victoria).

Elizabeth Leveson-Gower, de jure Countess of Sutherland, Duchess/ Countess of Sutherland (1765-1839) by George Romney (with permission from the National Portrait Gallery, London).

George Granville Leveson-Gower, First Duke of Sutherland (1758-1833) by Thomas Phillips (with permission from the National Portrait Gallery, London).

Sir Paul Edmund de Strzelecki (1797-1873) (by permission of the State Library of Victoria).

James Loch (1780-1855) (with permission from the National Portrait Gallery, London).

Stewart of Garth, Major General (1772-1829) by S. W. Reynolds after J. M. Scrymgeour (with permission from the Scottish National Portrait Gallery, Edinburgh).

Dunrobin Castle (with permission from Lord Strathnaver, Dunrobin Castle Limited).
Print courtesy of the National Library of Scotland.

Photograph of Patrick Sellar towards the end of his life (courtesy of Christopher and Valerie Lang of Titanga, Victoria).

Portrait of Patrick Sellar (courtesy of Justice Robert Fisher of Hahndorf).

and her family, and her connections by any publication on the subject in the newspapers; at same time I have explained to you that such publication may happen in the course of the trial of the other participators in the affair without my being able to prevent it.

Sellar, in his victory, distributed Mackid's statement to all his acquaintances though, as agreed, he refrained from its immediate publication. He had been advised to settle by MacPherson Grant, as well as by his ailing father. Naturally enough Sellar put his own private gloss on the outcome. Referring to Mackid's 'confession', he noted:

> He says the people told falsehoods. The people per contra will say distinctly that the Military Register and he led them to falsehood. I have the whole at length in complete arrangement for bringing all concerned in that print to condign punishment, if the noble Family will take half concern; which, I very humbly think, they should, in justice to themselves and to me do – could I Sue it at my instance without the Noble family being heard of in the business?

The suggestion was not taken up by the Stafford family and Sellar did not pursue the *Military Register*.[68]

– THE LATER MACKID –

Mackid's confession looked like a catastrophe for the former Sheriff of Sutherland. He had already been forced out of the county; his finances were threadbare and his reputation had been exploded. Yet his subsequent career showed extraordinary resilience. He moved to Caithness and set up as a legal writer, and was admitted to practice immediately. He soon built up a clientele which included his own brother, who was tacksman to Sir Robert Anstruther of Balcaskie; he also served the Earl of Caithness and Sinclair of Ulbster. This was remarkable for a man only recently destroyed in the neighbouring county. Mackid was obviously clever and professional in his work: his clients, including John Mitchell, gave him warm thanks for his legal work. He became Procurator-Fiscal in Caithness in May 1818. He was regarded as a successful and up-to-date legal adviser.[69]

Mackid may have been subjected by Sellar to severe public and private humiliation, but he was not utterly demolished. He was not, for example, ostracised by the landowning community in the north. In October 1819, he was still in legal business, contracting negotiations between Messrs Freswick and Jolly in Caithness, conducting his affairs as 'Writer in Thurso'. He also became involved in a salmon-fishing enterprise in Thurso, though without financial success, and in 1820 he was indeed bankrupted and his property sequestrated. But once more Mackid's legal business bounced back, and he continued to receive clients. In 1825, he moved back to Fortrose where he again continued his legal work until 1834, and was a tax collector through to 1836. In 1833 he applied to the Duke of Sutherland for patronage. Loch declared that Mackid deserved no favour from the Sutherland estate but he nevertheless instructed that he be given £20. He was still alive in 1842, though he was evidently experiencing financial difficulties. Thus Mackid, like many of the people of northern Sutherland, appears to have migrated to an adjacent county, and at least partially re-established himself. Somehow he had survived the devastation of Sellar's revenge.[70]

– HIGHLAND JUSTICE –

At the Inverness circuit trial on 24 April there were three other cases which attracted far less attention than the ordeal of Patrick Sellar. Mary MacPherson of Snizort, Skye, was tried for child murder and the concealment of a pregnancy. She was committed for a future trial. Isabella McRae of Durness was tried for a similar crime and sentenced to eight months in Dornoch Jail. David Fraser was found guilty of the violent theft of a silver watch, and was given seven years' transportation.[71]

Not only had Sellar escaped both the noose and Botany Bay, he and his philosophy, by virtue of his trial, were seen to triumph. The policy he personified had been given the unequivocal *imprimatur* of the law itself. Sellar's enemies had been dispersed and popular resistance broken. The future for clearance and social reformation had become a clear horizon.

CHAPTER 11

The Dismissal

In 1816, Sellar was thirty-five years old, still a bachelor and at the mid-point in his life. He had wreaked his revenge on Mackid and many of his enemies. His life returned to normal, and he now concentrated his energies on his farms at Culmaily and in Strathnaver, where he was becoming a great sheep-farmer. But he also resumed his duties as factor, still heavily involved again in rent-collection and in the continuing bustle of improvements over which William Young presided. Their greatest challenge was the construction of the massive engineering work at the Mound at Strathfleet. This was an enormous earth dam across the estuarial waterway: it was designed to create farms, as well as being a prime contribution to the dramatically improved road route to the north. The Mound was a spectacular edifice and its construction reached its tense finale in June 1816. Sellar was himself engaged in the enterprise to the last moments and reported being on his legs for almost twenty-four hours in a day, 'very earnestly and actively employed'.[1] When, for the first time, the Mound held the waters of the Fleet, he was excited and jubilant.[2] Here, indeed, was palpable progress.

Though he returned to his duties as a factor immediately after his trial, Sellar received a salutary lecture from James Loch, who warned him, in the frankest terms, about his behaviour towards the ordinary people on the Sutherland estate:

> Let your orders be given directly and distinctly in firm but moderate language, without Taunt or Joke and whenever you can, let them be in writing which will avoid any danger of mistake which is particularly desirable where two languages are in use.[3]

– 213 –

This was a prelude to a much sharper evaluation of both Sellar and Young in the following months. Loch took the view that, whatever his faults, Young was 'a very good hearted man.'[4] But Sellar was too opinionated, and his views had conspicuously hardened in the heat of his trial. When Sellar urged further rapid removals and the promotion of emigration, Loch recoiled, even though the general lines of policy remained intact. Sellar advocated a scale and pace of change in Sutherland which, by their implications, thoroughly alarmed Loch. Sellar's recommendations were not acceptable because they would run rough-shod over the people. His ideas, Loch told him, were impossible, unless

> the Marquis and Lady Stafford depart from their present wise system of not to turn out a single inhabitant against whom crimes have not been proven until a situation on the coast is pointed out.[5]

The other senior adviser to the Stafford family, MacPherson Grant, also reacted negatively to Sellar's overemphatic letters of persuasion. Sellar's advice simply carried too 'much very extraneous matter and his remarks upon many things shew that satirical turn which does him so much harm.'[6]

Sellar, however, was now inflated with confidence, reinvigorated and full of lawyer's vim. In July 1816, he undertook a survey of the woods on the estate. Bursting with improvement energy he redoubled his determination to eliminate all vestiges of the recent troublemakers. He quickly evicted 'four men concerned in the Strathnaver Combination'. This was part of Sellar's continuing retribution against his enemies. In August 1816, he asked that two other tenants be turned off the estate, specifically because they had been 'connected with the late occurrences'.[7] Trees and tenants could not coexist: the timber was 'the prey of the tenants and their cattle and horses'. Sellar had caught a number of depredators running off with loads of bark. He would pursue such miscreants to be 'set down for prosecution and removal'. This became his recurrent recommendation as he toured the estate, and Sellar treated all backsliders equally. Thus Major Clunes, a fellow-sheep-farmer, was observed to have damaged trees. Reporting this encounter in the third person, Sellar said 'a pretty sharp correspondence passed betwixt Mr Sellar and the Major'. Bark-cutters were also singled out for 'prosecution and removal'.[8] The state of the woods demonstrated yet again that sub-tenants were incompatible with the rational and profitable utilisation of the resources of the estate. Only when the people were cleared, could further progress be entertained.

While Sellar proceeded unabashedly about his factorial business, no doubt making new enemies in his travails, there were far-reaching developments in the management framework of the Sutherland estate. These changes came into much sharper focus in the summer of 1816. The Stafford family, and their Commissioner, James Loch, arrived at Dunrobin to spend much of that summer reconsidering all aspects of estate policy, and its administration. It was a grand reappraisal, partly precipitated by the great consternation generated by Sellar's trial. It was also prompted by James Loch's transparent determination to take firmer control over the northern empire. Loch was especially critical of Young's financial management, but he was also deeply concerned with Sellar's methods among the common people.

Lady Stafford arrived in Sutherland six weeks after the Inverness trial, in advance of Loch who had already been charged with the reconstruction of the management of the estates. In late June 1816, she dined with Sellar and Young. She noted, approvingly, that Robertson's account of Sellar's trial had just been published. She now took the view that the trial had been of 'service in putting down that whole opposition'.

The Sutherland proprietrix, surveying all aspects of estate policy, noted that Mackid was quitting Kirkton. She reported that Mackid's character was now 'quite blown'. Cranstoun had done all he could to rescue Mackid but it had become clear that for three years he 'had been exciting the people against us,' preying on 'the democratic feeling all these people have in spite of themselves'. Mackid had believed that the Staffords supported his outrageous attempt to oust Sellar, and 'he thought he was safe'. Lady Stafford expected Sellar to get large damages from Mackid and she also believed that Sutherland of Scibbercross, 'who had been tampering with and exciting the people', would also face action from Sellar. She remarked that Young had been receiving 'requests for forgiveness' from various of the tenantry, and it was expected that they would provide evidence of the conspiracy.[9] Sellar's earlier *cri de coeur* beseeching the Staffords to make their opinions and support clear, must now have echoed in her mind. She found it odd that Cranstoun was allowing Mackid to retain his office until December.[10]

While Lady Stafford was able to celebrate Sellar's victory at the trial (despite her own ambivalent part in the course of his defence), her review of conditions on the estate was less agreeable. She had already surveyed many aspects of policy when Loch arrived at Dunrobin to conduct his own root and branch investigation of the management.

This, therefore, was the moment of truth for the Young/Sellar regime after six years' control over the great Sutherland plan. Loch conducted his *post-mortem* in the aftermath of the trial, keenly aware of the recent explosive growth of Young's expenditures.[11]

Loch quickly diagnosed a malaise in the affairs of the estate. He had no hesitation in sheeting responsibility to the current management in a manner reminiscent of the earlier demolition of Falconer's administration by Sellar and Young.[12] Loch wrote:

> Much discontent exists (and it is well founded) in these districts and especially in Strathnaver in consequence of the people who have been removed to the valley, [from] their various habitations in the hills, having been thrown into one common lot, without any division having been made.

This was direct acknowledgement that the resettlement arrangements in 1814 had been inadequate, if not actually botched, and that public criticism had been well-founded. As Loch put it, 'This state of things must have tended to keep alive that feeling of regret and disquietude which that sudden and not well digested removal from the hills in the first instance produced'. It was a damning internal, and therefore private, indictment.

Loch, in truth, was no less dedicated to the continuing progress of removal and resettlement than Lady Stafford, William Young or indeed Patrick Sellar.[13] In 1816, Loch's critique was not of the policy but of the manner of its execution. He conceded that the implementation of the 'improvements' was intensely difficult. Greater care was required in dealing with the people and 'their present irritations', and to 'repress all disputes'. Loch expressed direct criticism of Sellar's methods, especially in his rent-collecting. He acknowledged that it was arduous work which sometimes gave the people hardship, and it was always difficult to distinguish

> between the man who cannot pay owing to temporary difficulties and he [*sic*] who is incorrigibly lax and behind hand in arrears. Severity and strictness in the collection of Rents can only be effectual when it is executed with judgement and distinction.

Loch said, candidly, that there had been 'a want of this in many cases', in part because no one man could know all the people in detail, and this had produced much complaint. Loch recommended that, in future, local ground officers should collect small rents which would then be forwarded to Sellar, who would concentrate on the large rent payers on the estate. This would keep Sellar at a distance from the people.[14]

Lord Stafford's senior adviser, George MacPherson Grant, who enjoyed Loch's close confidence, was asked by Loch to tour the estate at this time, taking special note of the resettlement arrangements. As an MP, Grant was sensitive to the political vibrations given out by the Sutherland estate policies. Loch repeatedly emphasised that the family wanted above all else

> the improvement and happiness of the people, and that in inducing them to adopt more industrious habits as well, as little as possible should be done to hurt their feelings, both for their sakes and the success of the measures themselves.

This, in a nutshell, was the central contradiction of the Sutherland policies and it was beyond resolution.

Grant toured the estate in August 1816 and found that some of the resettlements had worked well. In other places, however, the small tenantry felt so 'unsettled and uncertain of their Tenures that they were not renovating themselves whatsoever'. He was especially concerned about the large remnant of the population of Strathnaver whose land had still to be incorporated into Sellar's sheep-farm. The district was thickly populated, and Grant recommended that the small tenants remain undisturbed, and that the land be properly lotted out to the anxious people. Strathnaver, he remarked, was 'a most interesting and beautiful portion of the property', and ought to be served by a local factor. To leave these people *in situ*, of course, was contrary to estate policy, and diametrically opposed to Sellar's sheepfarming requirements. The last thing that Sellar wanted was the continuance of a dense small tenantry on his lands. Grant reported that the people were certainly very poor in Strathnaver; cattle prices were so low that they could not realistically pay their rents. Strathnaver would undoubtedly be better utilised under sheep were it not for the 'difficulty . . . of finding a situation for the present occupants'. This, too, was a defining problem of the Sutherland improvements.

Grant was highly critical of many of the existing lotting arrangements. There had been serious misunderstandings among the people about which lands they would receive. The estate managers, 'in neglecting to have the allotments intended for the dispossessed Tenants divided and pointed out to them in proper time', had thereby created some of the causes of the agitation in Strathnaver. Referring yet again to the events of Sellar's removals in 1814, he noted that the people should have gone by 26 May but were not actually told where to go until mid-June, during which delay Sellar had 'indulged' them at

Young's request. Then Sellar had allowed them a further fortnight. Grant had talked among the people who told him that, after the time had expired, Sellar's shepherds had refused them access to timber for their houses. None of this had been revealed in Sellar's trial. Grant reported that John Munro had been an 'active instigator in pressing the other Tenants to proceed by Criminal prosecution', and had been advised by Captain Sutherland in London, and by Mackid. John Mackay, one of the main complainants, had admitted to him that he had been misled by Munro, Mackid and Sutherland of Scibbercross to produce an account of the injury done to his wife. Grant advised their removal from the estate as an example to the community.[15] Enemies and troublemakers were thus weeded out.[16]

Grant was greatly impressed with Young's east coast improvements but he declared that they had been pressed on with 'too much rapidity'. They had been extravagantly expensive and the entire plan should have been followed much more gradually. He believed that the time had come for 'the native Peasantry' to carry the improvements forward, following the models which had been demonstrated to them by the incoming improvers. The natives, indeed, needed more encouragement. He concluded that William Young was indispensable but his expenditures must now be restrained. There was obvious jealousy between Sellar and Young. This was confirmed by William Mackenzie who remarked of William Young: 'I do believe he has even more than a Jealousy of Sellar, he dislikes the manner of his occasional (as he conceives) interference.'[17]

James Loch absorbed this disturbing advice, and pursued his own investigations in a period of intensive activity. He agreed that 'the great sinews of improvement' had been established and that advance should now proceed at a different pace. He was also aware that Young was anxious to resign from the management. He had said so as early as July 1815, and repeated the request in July 1816. As Young said, he had spent five years in the operations and the lands were now all arranged:

> I have seen peace and quiet restored and many of the poor people who were led on by knaves are ashamed of their conduct. We now only want a resident Sheriff with proper officers in different parts of the Country to keep all quiet.

He had also finished his work in Moray, and was looking for a new challenge, a new 'improvable place', perhaps in Kintail. He repeated his request to tender his resignation, couched in typically graceful style.

By this time Loch had already reached decided opinions about the management and policies on the Sutherland estate, after three weeks of 'extreme employment'. He determined on new brooms for the estate management, though the timing of his changes created problems of synchronisation (indeed Loch was worried that Young would resign too soon for his plans to mature). Loch decided on a new general system of accountability over which he would be able to exert direct control. William Young was generally too fidgety, and impatient of delay, and unable effectively to delegate responsibility. Young only trusted men from Moray, though he did not trust Sellar. Expenditures had run out of control and there had been gross planning errors at The Mound. No further large sums would be sanctioned without Loch's *imprimatur*. As for Sellar, Loch felt great apprehension and expected his old jealousies of Young to re-erupt at any time.

Loch announced his reforms, in late August 1816, in a series of memoranda. Young's resignation had now been accepted as from Martinmas 1816, and this would be followed by Sellar's 'removal at Whitsunday' 1817. They would be replaced by Francis Suther, a Scottish agent, who had served very ably on Lord Stafford's English estate at Trentham. Suther would be paid £400 per annum.[18] He was given the general supervision of the estate along with much more clearly specified lines of policy as enunciated by Loch. They included a more sensitive approach to the small tenantry and far better financial control, with particular restraints on expenditure on capital works. Young's astronomically large outlays would cease (and with them some of their employment-generating expenditures). The small tenantry would no longer be subjected to double removals; the emphasis was now that of 'carrying the people along with you.' So far, the removals had been executed by strangers without proper cooperation. Suther would ensure that 'the *honour* and *interests* of the proprietors will not be prejudiced to the interest and as little offensive as possible to the feelings, of the people.'[19] Loch's general verdict on the estate was to reaffirm his commitment to the broad lines of policy, but to state frankly that the expenditures had been reckless.[20]

Loch's grand reappraisal included particular consideration of the amount of land, and latitude, that would be given to Patrick Sellar. This hinged on the timing of Sellar's leases and whether he had the capital to undertake his rental obligations to the estate. In September 1816, Loch pointed out that Sellar had 'derived great advantage from the rise in rents'. Patrick Sellar was probably financing his operations into Sutherland from his father's capital, though the latter was still heavily involved in the Burghead and Westfield ventures in Moray. The younger Sellar had committed capital to both, and to his great sheep stocks. He was paying substantial interest on works undertaken by Lord Stafford.

MacPherson Grant, in August 1816, concurred with Loch's efforts to engineer 'the resignation of Young and the removal of Sellar'. He said it was a *coup* to secure Suther, 'the treasure from Trentham', in their place. He told Commissioner Adam:

> It is well over and I am glad it is done for you have no idea either of the inaccuracy and unsteadiness of execution, the total want of plan, the lavish expenditure, or the total disregard of Justice and regard for the people's feelings that characterised the whole management.

This was a further devastating commentary on the Young/Sellar management, especially in its last remark.[21] Grant was greatly surprised, in October, that Lady Stafford spoke so well of Sellar that he thought he might be retained. Grant told her, unambiguously, that Sellar was 'quite a person when in daily communication with, [and] very apt to make you forget the great and irremediable defects of his character'. He could not have spoken more plainly.[22]

Lady Stafford visited Ballindalloch *en route* south from Sutherland, having sorted out her management. She remarked that 'Young behaves well and with good humour'. She realised that Young had been too frenetic in his work, 'and he flies about a good deal leaving one thing and beginning another'. Yet she evidently continued in her good opinion of him. Meanwhile, she added, 'Sellar goes on at business and we are much satisfied with his conduct.' But he, too, would be replaced by the new manager and new leases would be delayed until the new man arrived: 'It is best for the present to let all remain as it is, carrying things on in the best way to keep the people to Industry, and to avoid the evils of the times.'[23]

Within a few months of his triumphant acquittal in Inverness, therefore, plans were set in motion to oust Patrick Sellar from the Sutherland management. Sellar was desperate to continue as factor, but the estate advisers were adamant. The reappraisal of estate administration had exposed Sellar to withering analysis: Loch and his lieutenants were united in their condemnation. William Mackenzie, already on the coolest terms with Sellar, said that everything Sellar did was suspect:

> Where ever taste temper or feeling is required or even ordinary discretion he is deficient beyond what I ever met with in any man, so that I dont know

one in the whole circle of my acquaintance so ill calculated as him to fill the office of a factor and in such a county as Sutherland.[24]

Loch's final report to Lady Stafford was utterly damning. Sellar was a man 'possessing less discrimination than it is easy to believe, [and] was really guilty of many very oppressive and cruel acts.' Sellar was wonderfully accurate in his work, but:

> In whatever related . . . to the intercourse or management of men [or] to the knowledge or conduct of the world or above all to a gentlemanly feeling of understanding, he is deficient beyond measure . . . He is the most unfit person from these defects to be intrusted with the management and therefore with the character of any ancient and distinguished family.

This was a penetrating private assessment of Sellar's character. Sellar was not a gentleman and was guilty of oppression. Yet Loch was prepared to keep him in the management until Suther arrived in Sutherland.[25]

When he learned of the impending changes, Patrick Sellar asked to be kept on in the management until the end of 1817 to avoid the public drawing adverse conclusions about the changes.[26] Loch quickly vetoed the idea, saying that Sellar would produce 'continual interference and insinuations to supplant the new management'.[27] Loch was utterly clear in the matter: Sellar possessed deep flaws in his personality, and everyone in the management concurred in the assessment.

The removal of Sellar was presented to the public as a resignation and not a dismissal, but the correspondent of the *Military Register* fathomed the true meaning of these internal changes to the Sutherland management. As the London newspaper said, Sellar had been forced out of the management.[28]

– SELLAR BRANDED –

Loch was urgent to wield his new broom, but he faced an immediate difficulty. Young's hurried departure from the management left an awkward interim period before the installation of Francis Suther.[29] Much against Loch's better judgement, Sellar was employed, with increased authority, as a stop-gap until Whitsunday 1817. Loch, caught in a bind by Young's early resignation, regretted the temporary continuance of Sellar, but found no alternative. He explained his predicament with some feeling:

> I have . . . told every body that it is only a temporary measure. It is all Sellar deserves at Lord and Lady Stafford's hand for [the] much injury he has done them in disposing the minds of the people against all reasonable change. From the kindness they have shewn me there is nothing they ask I would not do for them, except engage in the same management and embark my character in the same vessel as him.

This was a further savage characterisation of Sellar, and indicated that he was blamed for the turmoil on the estate since 1813. Sellar had become the scapegoat for all the estate problems, rather than merely those of his own making. Loch's denunciation of his factor carried the implication that the removals could be made acceptable to the people if they were implemented by managers with greater sensitivity. Suther from Trentham had been chosen for the task.[30]

Though Sellar was derided by his associates and, implicitly and explicitly, blamed for the embarrassment of the estate, none of Lady Stafford's advisers (apart from Grant) looked for a reversal or discontinuance of the basic policy. The Stafford family and its managers remained intent on mass removals, though they now acknowledged the constraints of public opinion on the arm of the estate. Thus, in November 1816, Loch was entirely clear when he told Lady Stafford:

> I see the state of Sutherland just as your Ladyship does . . . but I am afraid both from the temper of the people at large as well as the feeling of Government we must get them out of the hills gradually though the other course would be most for their own happiness and comfort.

Sellar meanwhile had lost none of his great appetite for dispute. In late 1816, for example, he began an argument with the Sutherland estate about expenses of £621 which he incurred 'in connection with his imprisonment and trial'. This was a delicate matter, since the estate was thereby required, in some manner, to accept part of the financial responsibility for Sellar's conflict with the people of Strathnaver.[31] Sellar was still pressing for indemnification from the estate eight years after the trial. This demonstrated the persistence and stamina with which Sellar was prepared to pursue his rights, even against his own landlord. It also typified his relations with the estate from 1817 onwards, when he assumed the position of farmer *extraordinaire*, without any further status as factor.

Another source of internal conflict with the estate concerned the terms of Patrick Sellar's leases. William Mackenzie said that Sellar continued to be 'very absurd about his lease' and was squabbling about the future of Mackid's land at Kirkton which Sellar believed he had secured in February before his trial. He exasperated Mackenzie, who said that Sellar was behaving 'like a spoilt child'.[32] In September 1816, Sellar suddenly declared that he wanted to give up his Strathnaver lease because of the conditions imposed upon him.[33] He remarked that he had borrowed a great deal of money from his father, and this had left him somewhat 'pinched'.[34]

Sellar was by no means an easy tenant, and throughout his long association with the Sutherland estate he was given to threats of resignation, sometimes as a device to increase his bargaining power in his negotiation of rents, conditions and leases. In 1816, Loch was extremely critical and declared that Sellar was behaving badly.[35] It was at the same time that Sellar was jockeying for Kirkton and Morvich as Mackid and Young relinquished their farms in Sutherland. In the outcome Sellar lost the struggle for Kirkton but gained Morvich, which included the house that had once been considered for the private use of Lord Stafford.[36] Sellar withdrew his threat to throw up his Strathnaver lease.

Despite his recurrent disagreements about rents and conditions, Sellar remained optimistic about prospects for stock-farmers and reassured Lady Stafford that peace, after Waterloo, would increase the value of Highland estates and increase the rate of conversion to stock as well as the removal of the people to fishing stations.[37] Sellar, who now had a very large interest in the matter, was more confident of wool prices because the postwar glut in the southern woollen mills had been much diminished and demand was therefore set to rise again.[38] But he would not devote his entire energies to the sheep-farms until he served out the last days of his ever-controversial factorship.

CHAPTER 12

Famine and the Final Clearances

– FOOD CRISIS, 1816–17 –

Sellar had been effectively dismissed from the Sutherland management in 1816, though his exit was delayed until the following year. This arrangement, curiously enough, now left him with greater responsibility than ever in the interim. He was caretaker for the estate at a critical time. Through late 1816 and into 1817 Sutherland, in common with many parts of western Europe, experienced a freakishly disastrous season which some commentators attribute to the colossal volcanic explosion of Krakatoa in the East Indies. It was a dire winter and spring, and there were severe food shortages, approaching famine, across the north of Scotland. Sellar was much involved in the administration of relief on the estate during the subsistence crisis. Simultaneously he continued collecting rents (at a time of sharply falling stock prices) and controlling, as always, smuggling and woods.

During Sellar's management he fielded many petitions to the Sutherland estate for rent abatements which flooded in from the inland tenantry. Sellar was sympathetic. He believed that the people could not sustain their rents. He also pointed out that their rents were now a much smaller proportion of the total income of the estate because the sheep-farms had taken over their lands, and paid much higher rents. He remarked that the rising arrears and hunger of the interior tenantry afforded an opportunity to remove them altogether. He added, however, that there were other factors to be taken into account:

> There are considerations of pity and of respect for public opinion, which moderate the effect of this principle.[1]

He followed instructions from James Loch, who needed no reminder of the dangers of adverse public opinion.

In September 1816, Sellar noted that the small tenantry paid their rents primarily out of the proceeds of cattle and illicit distilling and, as he pointed out, these 'two <u>sources</u> [are] now extremely diminished, and of course unequal to the rent'. He predicted that his successor as rent collector would have great difficulty. The people were in a hopeless condition:

> The remedy . . . is to bring the people to ground where, like the poor people of Loth, they may easily take their rents from the sea – that is, to do so, in such <u>prudent manner</u> as to Lord Stafford and your Ladyship may seem best. In the <u>meantime</u> you cannot help submitting (like other proprietors of highland <u>estates under people</u>) to the nature of this burden. It is considerably diminished on this Estate, and must bear much harder on almost every highland proprietor than on your Ladyship.[2]

Sellar said that he had seen the trouble brewing since 1814: 'I could never pay the rent of Culmaily if I grew couch [a type of grass] in place of wheat, barley and turnips; neither can these people pay for Stock land under improper management.' Hence, the people must go to the coast. It was common sense.[3]

Towards the end of his term as factor, Sellar reiterated his views about the condition of the estate. By January 1817, cattle prices had fallen catastrophically and the people were extremely poor. Sellar collected his worst rental. He was not surprised:

> Here is ye cause and ye effect. They cannot be mistaken . . . The people have no money, and they have no meal. But they cannot starve, while any thing, convertible into food, remains in their hands. The cattle, therefore, by which the rents have been paid will be sent to ye pot. Many thousand families in the highlands of Scotland are now living on the cattle which ought to cover the English pasture seasons 1817 and 1818 – and, before harvest 1817 the slaughter will be prodigious.

The people of the interior were eating the means by which they were meant to pay future rents, namely the cattle reared for the English market. It was utterly hopeless: 'If Emigration dont happen, nobody can predict the consequences.' Sellar recommended urgent relief, while rents fell to nothing. He warned of disaster unless 'a vent be not given to let the people out, to some country more suitable to their occupation . . . It applies generally to the <u>whole Highlands</u>, so far as the <u>interior</u> is possessed by people.'

Sellar had been reading *The Times* and recommended a letter there 'on the causes of the present distress, which points to Emigration as a final remedy.' Sellar's remarks were also, of course, the gospel of sheep-farmers whose interests were directly benefited by any plan for the evacuation of the Highlands. Emigration had rapidly become a panacea for the times.[4]

– RELIEF AND EMIGRATION –

Sellar's last months in the Sutherland factorship were, therefore, overshadowed by the subsistence crisis of the winter 1816–17. As he grappled with the emergency, he interpreted the crisis as definitive confirmation of his most fundamental opinion. The old system of dense population of the Highlands simply could not continue.

The inland populations could neither support themselves nor pay their rents. As Sellar relentlessly pointed out, ten years before these people had paid all the rent of the estate. Now they were responsible for only 25 per cent of the estate's income, about £6,000, per annum, 'which sum, I honestly think is fully 25 to 30 per cent more than, with present prices and present mismanagement they can pay.' Of course, the less the small tenants were able to pay, the greater was the case for their final removal and displacement by sheep-farmers. Sellar pointed out that 'Proprietors, in bad times, support and relieve improving tenants lest the Estate lose its tenants. But here it is for the Good of the Estate to lose the petitioners, Ergo you will say, Refuse the abatement.' The landlord could not refuse temporary relief to the tenantry, but the true solution was simple. The common people should be brought to the coast and stock introduced to their lands, and then a rent rise would follow.[5]

The failure of the crops in the interior of Sutherland had become clear in the early autumn of 1816. The potatoes were ruined and meal was in very short supply. Almost the entire Sutherland harvest had been lost, and the famine alarm was sounded. (Sellar was the only farmer, by his own good farming and management, to secure his crops. He claimed that 'By working night and day my people have saved my crop about 15 acres yet . . . But we are quite exhausted and my hand shakes so much I fear you will scarcely make me out.'[6]) In January 1817, Sellar reported that the people simply could not pay rents – the cattle had lost their value and they now had no meal. All this proved that they should not be there at all.[7]

The people were panic-stricken but, according to Sellar, 'They do nothing to save themselves.' Sellar made elaborate and expensive plans to secure relief supplies of meal imports. Indeed, Sellar hoped to use the crisis to the estate's advantage to demonstrate, by its relief measures, how much better Sutherland was treated than the rest of the Highlands. This would set to flight the libellers in the *Military Register* and disperse the allegations of inhumanity made by Mackid and the Sutherlands.[8] It was also an opportunity to make the people provide labour for relief under threat of eviction.[9] But Sellar's relief plans were regarded as grandiose. In mid-December 1816, he had devised what he called a 'well-digested and excellent plan' for relief, a comprehensive scheme to cover the entire emergency. The only problem, as Lady Stafford caustically pointed out, was that it would require 200 overseers and an outlay of £25,000. 'Very characteristic of him', she added, drolly. Sellar's suggestion that relief labour be used to construct a road to Thurso at a likely cost of £8,000 was instantly scotched by Lady Stafford as a wild idea.[10]

The previous famine of 1812 had proved for Sellar the impolicy of keeping the people in the interior, which was really fit only for stock. The 'mildew' of 1816 should now satisfy everyone of this fundamental truth. Resettlement to the coast or emigration were the obvious and inevitable solutions. New Holland or the Cape of Good Hope were the answers.[11] Sellar said that, in the current conditions, 'you must be prepared . . . to let the rents down to nothing (God knows they are the lowest in Scotland at this day), or dispossess a great many miserable beggars. If you are forced to dispossess, then, what is to become of them?'[12] He predicted another mildew by 1821.[13]

The distress in some parts of Sutherland was unmistakable. There were reports in the winter of 1816–17 that people were reduced to eating cockles and pawning their blankets to fishermen, and were sleeping on the shores. Sellar described the state of the

> poor creatures in the interior [who] having begun to [consume] their potatoes before they were ripe and having had their Corn again affected by mildew live in squalid misery and wretchedness, and if Lord Stafford do not again Supply them with meal God only knows what the consequence is to be.

It was the land of these people in the interior that Sellar intended to occupy in the next twenty-four months. Some of the people were down to their last firlots, and some to their last peck, of meal. Sellar had heard that the Stafford family were 'not disposed to do anything for them' and he thought his employers simply did not comprehend the scale of the problem.

The relief measures eventually undertaken by the Sutherland estate, though not on the scale proposed by Sellar, were extensive but distributed on a highly selective basis. Any person who had resisted authority in the recent past was denied support. If they were also in arrears they were likely to be evicted. Moreover, no relief was accorded unless work was given in exchange. No sub-tenants were assisted. Famine became an adjunct to the removal policy.

In late 1816, Sellar was reprimanded for excessive haste in buying up relief supplies. In December 1816, there were still £400 outstanding debts from the earlier crisis in 1814–15. James Loch determined that the people should work on the roads for any relief supplies. But it was expected that there would be large losses in the new crisis. Loch adamantly agreed with Lady Stafford that, 'if they are supplied, they will never feel the inconvenience of their situation, so as to desire a change'. Sellar presided over a large importation of relief supplies to the very people whose existence in the interior glens he regarded as inimical to economic rationality and common good sense.

Relief, therefore, should never be provided gratuitously,[14] but Sellar accumulated great expenditures on relief supplies and these constituted debts by the tenantry to the estate. There was little prospect of their repayment, which left Loch depressed at the financial consequences for which he mainly blamed Sellar. Arrears, Loch said, would never be collected from such people:

> [I] wish they were <u>safely</u> in that beautiful country in New Holland, they are now so busy in discovering. When the present exceeding irritation of men's minds is somewhat composed I really think some plan must be thought of and considered with the King's Government.[15]

This was Loch's first unambiguous advocacy of emigration in place of resettlement, registering the shift in Highland opinion at large about the possibility and utility of emigration from the Highlands. (The context was set by the collapse of kelp and cattle prices and the evidence of rapid population growth revealed in the first official censuses). Sellar had reached the same opinion earlier, and in more robust form. Loch himself was concerned about the state of the entire country, conscious of the radical mobs in London and the steps towards their repression being undertaken by the government. Some of the mob would be hanged, and though they were 'a vast idle hungry body of people now in London', there was 'but one way of keeping them in order'.[16]

– SELLAR AND THE NEW MANAGEMENT –

Francis Suther, promoted from the Trentham estate, took over the management of the estate in mid-1817. Sellar described him as 'a most excellent person'. In the new regime, Lieutenant George Gunn became resident under-factor in Assynt and Capt. John Mackay in Strathnaver.[17] The clearances, of course, were by no means completed, and the next round was subject to precise and emphatic planning. Sellar was no longer directly involved except as a sheep-farmer waiting for further lands to be cleared for his own sheep. He was not a patient man and now became an inexhaustible font of gratuitous advice throughout the intervening period. His interventions were not always well received by the new management.

For Loch and Suther, the agreed cardinal priority was the avoidance of popular disturbance which would attract the attention of Parliament to the events in the northern Highlands. James Loch was a new MP and now held direct responsibility for landlord policy on the Sutherland estate. He had no wish to face the collective criticism of his political friends and foes. He reassured Lady Stafford that she would be spared any further disasters, implying that they had been the result of previous poor management. He had no wish to repeat the catastrophic turmoil of Sellar's removals in Strathnaver, which was still only half cleared. As Loch told Lady Stafford in November 1817:

> Your Ladyship's instructions on the subject of the Strathnaver removals shall be most strictly attended to. It contains everything that is a wise and prudent consideration, for the benefit of the estate, coupled with a due regard to the feelings and interest of the people.[18]

Loch defined the purposes of the anticipated removals. They were essentially designed for 'the clearing of the upper part of Strathnaver and settling the people in the lower district.' He pointed out that the land would be added to 'Mr Sellar's farm . . . it was part of the bargain with him that these lands should be converted into a sheep walk before now. It was postponed but the serious losses which [he] experienced during the last summer can [now be?] the only effective remedy the case admits of, the complete removal of the people from the vicinity of this and every other farm.'

It is apparent, therefore, that Patrick Sellar had already suffered serious financial losses by the events in Strathnaver since he took possession in 1814. His entry into a large part of the lands had been delayed, partly because Young's resettlement arrangements had been fumbled, and because he had agreed to delay his access to these lands. This materially affected the return on his capital, which was determined largely by the sheer scale of his operations. His financial disadvantage was greatly exacerbated by the loss of stock by theft, attributed to the communities still remaining in the straths. 'Depredations' against sheep stock were a substantial problem, and the thefts looked like a concerted, but primitive, attempt by the old residents of the straths to undermine the sheep-farmers. Sellar wanted the people out of the interior because they 'preyed upon' his sheep.[19]

The year 1817 was one of critical consolidation for Sellar. His grasp on the lands of Strathnaver was reasserted and the arrangements for the evacuation of the remaining small tenants was confirmed. Meanwhile the continuing presence of the people of Strathnaver jeopardised the efficiency and profitability of his sheep-farming operations. He was keen to remove more of them, preferably completely out of the country. His convictions about the Highland question hardened further in the early months of 1817. Emigration was the answer. The people would fare better in Canada than in Sutherland, and then the stock-farmers could truly benefit the landlord and the nation. These opinions were not exclusive to Sellar, but others expressed them more guardedly, and Sellar's betters moved to promote emigration while cloaking their objects in continuing secrecy.

Sellar, following his entrepreneurial instincts, pressed for his rights of access at the very time when Loch and Suther repeatedly reassured Lady Stafford that her wishes would be fulfilled. She demanded that the removals would be executed with as little inconvenience to the old occupiers 'as the nature of the change will admit of'.[20] The management was extremely nervous of removals and delayed until 1819, despite Sellar's pressure. There were emerging problems of congestion in the reception areas on the north coast, and Loch was adamant that no removals should occur until proper arrangements were ready.[21] There was evidently no reduction in the determination of the estate to press on with the evictions, but the timetable was lengthened and the preparations made more thorough than in the past.

Released from factorial duties, Sellar became involved in other public roles, now as a great farmer in the county. He made enthusiastic experiments as a stock-farmer, always searching for more profitable stock and methods. By 1817 he had accumulated 530 merinos in the hope of technical improvement.[22] In 1816, Sellar had told the local Committee devoted to the reduction of stock losses that his fellow sheep-farmers had lost 1,400 sheep. In 1817 he became prominent in the Sutherland Association of Farmers, which was part of the effort to create a more efficient wool marketing system for the northern Highlands. Until 1817, wool was traded through Fort William, which was an inconvenient location for many of the Sutherland sheep-farmers.[23] In that year the first annual Inverness Great Sheep and Wool Fair was inaugurated. Sellar announced the meeting which henceforward brought together the 'Highland Gentlemen Farmers', the Inverness merchants and the great manufacturers of Huddersfield, Wakefield, Halifax, Burnley, Aberdeen and Elgin. It was an important moment for the dynamic advance of the northern economy and its integration into the great new national market. Sellar, of course, was right at its centre.[24]

At the same time, Sellar kept up his petty disputation with the small tenantry of the estate. In July 1817, for example, a boy called Alexander Sutherland, of Strathlandye, was jailed on the charge of clipping wool from Sellar's sheep.[25] The record of petty, even trivial, offences runs through the local jail record. Thus, in 1818, three young boys were incarcerated for stealing fruit from Sellar's garden in Morvich. This was one of many cases of minor theft, especially in Criech parish, which ranged from potatoes to turnips and sheep. The record suggests that Sellar was repeatedly at odds with his neighbours, and had recourse to the law on many occasions.[26] Francis Suther had soon taken a measure of Sellar's personality: 'you know his Nickety-Nackety particularity', he said to a fellow estate agent.[27]

The great sheep-farmers did not regard as petty 'the depredations' of the common people on their stock, crops and property. They had experienced great difficulty in identifying and apprehending the culprits, and the estate commissioner ordered that 'bad characters' be dismissed from the estate: 'give them no lot on any part of the estate.' This was an attempt to appease the angry sheep-farmers. But Suther, the new factor of the estate, was told confidentially, by Loch, to keep a wary eye on the shepherds also. As Loch put it, 'I cannot help suspecting, to use a phrase of Sellar's, [they] like good mutton as well as the Highlanders.'[28]

Sellar was also heavily involved in a campaign to preserve access to the drove roads which passed through the Highlands to the southern markets. New road construction and turnpikes were changing the face of Highland transport and threatened the free passage of stock. In May 1818, Sellar wrote on behalf of Sutherland stockmen (called the Committee of the Sutherlandshire Association against Felonry), to the Convener of the County of Stirling, complaining of the encroachments 'on ancient rights of the people of the Highlands'. This showed a surprising respect for anachronistic traditions. The new arrangements, said Sellar, were exceedingly vexatious, and the roads had been 'rendered incommodious', thus retarding the movement of stock to markets. He emphasised the central importance of the drove roads for the prosperity of all concerned, and pointed out that the new market at Inverness would reinforce the necessity of open access of sheep and other stock to the country roads of the south.[29]

– SELLAR MARRIED –

In 1817 and 1818 Sellar's personal circumstances changed. His finances improved significantly when his father died. As he explained, in August 1817, 'My poor father has left me a clear rental of about £1,000, enough to make me an efficient farmer, a more comfortable thing than being a poor Laird'.[30] Sellar was always intensely conscious of status as between lairds and tenants, and also the social nuances within those categories. Then, in November 1818, Sellar married Anne Craig (1793–1875), daughter of Thomas Craig of Barmuckity in Moray and niece of William Young (who never married). The Craigs, like the Sellars, derived from farming stock in Banffshire. Mrs Sellar had been brought up in the school of 'Presbyterian Moderation', and her daughter later said that 'her piety was cheerful, humble and reserved, and drew its strength from certain chapters in the New Testament and its emotion from the beloved Scottish Paraphrases.' She became a steadying influence on Sellar, and bore nine children in the following seventeen years, all delivered in Morvich House. At much the same time Anne's brother, Alexander Craig, obtained the lease of Craigton and Kirkton (which Sellar himself had coveted in 1816) and, as M. W. Grant puts it, 'all was set up for peaceful co-operation.'[31] These events completed Sellar's triumph over his enemy, Robert Mackid. Sellar had humiliated him, hounded him out of the county, practically bankrupted him, and now his brother-in-law occupied Mackid's own house at Kirkton.[32]

Sellar's concern for his sheep stocks continued to mount at this time. His Northumbrian shepherds, 'surrounded by thieves and vagabonds', experienced the greatest aggravation. It was impossible to prevent the theft of up to one-fifth of the sheep stock. As Sellar put it, 'Notwithstanding we pay them double the Northumbrian wages, and there is not a more sober careful race anywhere, they are all poor men.' As far as he was concerned, all the small tenants in the interior were implicated in the thefts, and they were impossible to punish since their crimes were perpetrated under the cover of night, and then concealed by the people at large. Sellar warned the estate managers that the thefts were bound to depress rents and profits. The stockmen had hazarded thousands of pounds, 'speculating on these wastes'. They had 'braved every Toil, and [caused] some nay most of us personal danger in prosecuting our enterprise.' But the farmers could not prevent wholesale theft. Four solitary shepherds were pitted against 'the tricks of 500 thieves – all idle and with little or nothing in such a country to do, but Steal.' The only solution, of course, was to remove the people altogether from Strathnaver, and Sellar appealed to his original agreement of 1813: 'It was on that understanding that I embarked in that country, and I leave the rest to Lord and Lady Stafford and your Justice and generosity.'[33]

Sellar plied the newly arrived Suther with advice about the resettlement arrangements for the people to be removed from his Strathnaver lands. He insisted that he be given access at the scheduled and agreed date in 1819, and that the plans be adhered to 'with concentrated force'. He said that the people must be instructed that from

> now on their own industry, not on meal to be imported by Lord Stafford, or sheep bred by the Stockfarmers, are they to live. If you give them these lots for 1/- each or for nothing for a time you will save yourself much trouble and much good paper and ink in writing such arrear lists.

There was iron in Sellar's remarks. He said that unless the people were cleared from his boundaries, 'you force me to give up, I assure you, or to Suffer ruin.' He repeated that he had already lost £1,000. He warned Loch:

> If you cannot enable me to farm in peace in that district you will Set me free from it. I should rather you did not set me free from it, for I have done, as well as suffered much for the improvement of Rhiloisk farm.[34]

It was thus that market forces were transmitted by the sheep-farmers to the landlords, and the engine of the clearances thus forced its way forward into the remotest straths of the northern Highlands.

– SELLAR AND MALTHUS –

Sellar was already a Malthusian and held decided views on population theory. In 1815, he drew James Loch's attention to

> something of a very fine passage in Malthus . . . After a detail from the history of various of the most barbarous and most civilised, the most slaved and the most free countries, he shews irresistibly how the increase of population is independent of every other circumstance except the increase of food . . . What I have required two pages to Explain, he expresses in two lines.[35]

For Sellar, the situation had become crystal clear. Emigration was the best solution for the people in the interior who were starving. The straths were 'erroneously possessed'. He suggested that the Stafford family should purchase land in Nova Scotia (it could be called 'New Sutherland') to which they could assist the emigrants. He argued that such people be given their last quarter as rent free and, in the colony, 100 acres per family rent free for fifty years. The land on the estate could then be turned over to stock, employing a few shepherds, sustaining the national interest, and yield 'a legitimate return to the owner'. An annual cargo of people from the '<u>mildewed</u> land' could be cleared in this way. Without emigration, said Sellar, the prospect was decidedly Malthusian: 'I doubt not but a few years will diminish the population by Grief, poverty and distress. But it is heart breaking to reflect on the <u>causes</u> which must produce such effect. Malthus shews it clearly – shews what kind of thing it is and how much it is to be avoided.' Sellar's perception was profoundly influenced by two factors on his mind. One was his hunger for sheep lands and the elimination of the incompatible people. The other was his first-hand knowledge of recurrent famine in the interior of Sutherland which had caused crises in food supplies, as well as the outlay of large sums by the landlord, to meet the needs of the small tenantry.[36]

Sellar was excited at the prospect of mass emigration from Sutherland. But he cautioned Loch that 'We must not be too sanguine', in part because the people continued to believe statements in the *Military Register* which had recently assured them that their rents were about to be reduced by 25 per cent. He also believed that the expense of the passage was too great because of the unreasonable victualling requirements of the Act of Parliament. The Act (which, indeed, had been devised precisely to staunch Highland emigration in 1803) specified exacting food provisions for passengers (including pork, beef and flour), when, as Sellar put it, everyone knew that six stones of oatmeal and barley would suffice as 'equal to 12 weeks maintenance to a highlander'. Such a change in shipping regulations would reduce the passage to £3 per adult. Sellar was careful to maintain confidentiality on the emigration question, but emphasised that an emigration would 'take off our hands what formerly supplied the war; we see clearly now, how the property may be infinitely bettered, and the proprietor and farmers as well as the people without any very terrible difficulty.'[37]

The problem with the emigration solution was precisely the poverty of the people. When Scarth, a shipper's agent, toured Sutherland in the spring of 1817, he reported from Brora that 'from all I could see the people are in such a state of poverty that were they to dispose of all they are possessed of they could not realise one half of what the passage would be.' Inevitably, the question then revolved about the possibility of assistance from the landlord or the government.[38]

Sellar received strong signals from the Stafford family that emigration was an increasing possibility. The Countess of Sutherland was already in contact with Lord Bathurst in the Colonial Office, clarifying government policy regarding access to landfall in the colonies and the likelihood of subsidy. She was perfectly prepared to promote emigration, though she knew that the landlord would be best advised not to appear to be pushing emigration in any overt fashion.[39] Sellar, while still factor, had been instructed to evict from the estate all woodstealers, poachers and thieves and the secondary motivation was 'for diminishing the burthen of population'. Sellar, as well as his employers, was convinced by Malthus and knew the population theorist's prescriptions: emigration was beneficial only so long as the place vacated was not filled by more people. It fitted perfectly Sellar's conception of the removal policy. He argued that the population of the interior could only be diminished

> by clearing a certain district annually and laying it under stock; unless the Family were to say, who ever is picked out and ejected, his possession shall lay unoccupied.

This was an unambiguous use of the term 'clearing', and Sellar's meaning was transparent. So, too, was his diagnosis of the changed situation in the county. Lord Stafford's great expenditures on infrastructure were winding down, and the end of the war had also reduced radically the employment opportunities in the county. The population was rising and men were returning from the army. According to Sellar, they 'speedily sett up a turff hutt under shelter of a brother or father, and go into family with their friends'. They had no capital to support themselves, and 'they create nothing to export to other countries in exchange for the supply of these needs.' The value of their cattle had collapsed, and in the current season the cattle were being killed for immediate subsistence. Arrears were mounting and 'By Law we ought to distress and recover – which would certainly produce cleared districts.' But any space left would be refilled, unless action were taken to prevent it. The inland people were redundant and James Loch increasingly agreed with this diagnosis.[40]

– THE NEW TIMETABLE FOR CLEARANCES –

By late 1817, Francis Suther had established the timetable for the forthcoming clearances, which included the relocation of people from Strathnaver to the north coast, between the kirk of Farr and Bighouse. The increasingly impatient Sellar would be a prominent beneficiary, but he was quarantined from involvement in the actual removals. Loch continued to emphasise that it was a policy 'as much for happiness of the people themselves as the advantage of the landlord'. He pointed out that one year in three saw the failure of the inland crops. Despite Lord Stafford's massive relief expenditures in the previous year, 'the misery they endured was beyond belief.' Loch was able to quote a petition, of February 1817, in which the people had pleaded for assistance.

In the forthcoming removals every precaution would be taken. The fullest notice was given, resettlement sites were established prior to the event and Sellar was kept out of the business of removal. Sellar, indeed, was treated with great caution. Lady Stafford was deeply suspicious of her overmighty subject: 'Sellar is too sly and refining upon his plans by concealing half – he is however surprisingly active in doing things on a great scale.'[41] Francis Suther, by contrast, commanded wide respect and was expected to carry through the removals without the sort of explosion of resistance and adverse publicity which had disfigured the previous clearances.[42]

In the planning for the new removals from Strathnaver (and other parts of the estate, including Assynt),[43] it is striking that the managers repeatedly reassured each other and, indeed, the Countess of the humanity and necessity of their plans. Loch took great pains to induct Suther into the agreed policy regarding the clearances.[44] Loch said that the temper of the people made slow progress unavoidable, even though faster progress would be better. Though Sellar was no longer directly involved in the management, in January 1818 he assisted Suther in Armadale where, along twenty miles of coast, lots were being laid out for the people to be removed. The district already contained people cleared from the interior by the previous owner, Lord Armadale, twenty-one years before. Sellar said that they were in comfort, already exporting fish to the London markets. Their condition was to be contrasted with the famished state of the people in Strathnaver in recent years.

Sellar was more optimistic about wool prices which, at the end of the war, had fallen by 50 per cent. He sold £300 of wool as his first clip. The fall in prices 'and some other little accidents' had delayed his regular rent payments, but his accounts were now in good order. He said that the fall in wool prices would certainly eliminate the native sheep-farmers from the business.[45] By this time, Sellar was also selling barley to distillers in Ross-shire, once more demonstrating the competitive edge of large legal production over the illegal commerce of small producers in the region.

Sellar bought 2,000 sheep in anticipation of his entry into his lands in Strathnaver, and had to feed them on turnips till Whitsunday 1819. He was, meanwhile, happy at the display of resolution in the new estate management. The removals had been announced and, said Sellar, the effect in the straths was salutary. It had induced

> already a most astonishing effect on the minds of the aborigines. Several – I believe most of the half-pay captains are meditating or have already planned their flight, and the common people are so effectively cowed that, since Martinmas, here, to the wonder of all my people, [we have not] lost one Sheep by theft! . . . We shall move steadily forward at Whitsunday, and shall make your Clearance of the hill . . . once and for all.

This was the triumphant Sellar, ready for the *coup de grâce*.[46]

Sellar was certainly hungry for expansion and for land. He had taken the lease of the lands of Syre, Kenedale, Gruby and Grubmore with entry at Whitsunday 1819 and the lease specified that they were 'to be cleared of the present possessors', with access to burn the heath in 1819. The rent was set at £200, rising to £250. All the old houses were to be cleared off before entry.[47] In April 1818, his offer for Morvich was accepted and this agreement also contained a clause that required all sub-tenants to be removed. At this time, too, Sellar took over Wester Scibbercross for nineteen years and he surrounded the grounds with 'a Mound to prevent it being affected by the river floods and proposes either burning or floating away the moss lying upon a rich alluvial clay which will produce a most abundant crop.'[48]

In 1819, Sellar also initiated an arrangement with Lord Reay to use part of the Reay Estate for his sheep-farming operations. This entailed the removal of sub-tenants from land vital for wintering. Unhappily for Sellar, the arrangement was not fully executed, and he wrote angrily to Lord Reay that 'if the banditti' continued to keep possession the agreement would lapse. He declared that he could not use 'such stormy ground without the wintering'. No stockman, he said angrily, could succeed 'with flocks mixed among sheep-stealers and their dogs'. This was a typically aggressive letter in which Sellar saw no reason to defer to his social betters. It expressed the recurrent frustration of a man impeded in his rational pursuit of commercial arrangements.[49]

On the Sutherland estate, the new round of removals planned for 1819–20 approached. In that year almost the whole of Strathnaver was to be cleared from Mudale to Invernaver, together with other districts across the estate. These clearances were on a scale greater than ever before in an attempt to finalise the restructuring of the estate. Sellar would gain full possession of his great new sheep-farms. In total, 425 families were to be moved in 1819, and another 475 in 1820. In the outcome more than 1,000 families were cleared in those years. It was calculated that there were five to each family, so that the total affected was well in excess of 4,000 in a little more than twelve months.[50] The number was awe-inspiring, even to the managers. Some of the common people of the inland straths still thought that Lady Stafford would intervene to prevent their removal. The ministers were acting coolly. Sellar was to take all of Upper Naver. He was confident as the price of stock was rising once more. There was frenetic activity in the coastal development.[51]

Loch was extremely anxious about the removals (particularly those demanded by Sellar) and he advised Suther to be especially careful: 'Sellar is so strict a Lawyer that he will adhere to the Letter of any promise from us.' Consequently no precise promise of entry to the lands in question should be made, and the removals must be made 'without cruelty to the inhabitants'. It was utterly vital. Sellar would simply have to accept the delay.[52] To Francis Suther, Loch said, 'let us I beseech you dont do it in to [sic] great a hurry.' Absolute care was crucial.[53]

The people were given many inducements and incentives to go peacefully; sweeteners were offered. Particularly early notice was offered (in November 1817), rent and meal arrears were abandoned, and many of the small tenantry were given rent-free occupation for twelve months before their flittings, on condition that they removed without delay. This did not prevent a great deal of foot-dragging among the removees.[54] Meanwhile the Rev. David Mackenzie interceded to say that the coastal lots were already congested and the people very poor. Mackenzie, much abused by later commentators, exerted his modicum of moral authority to lessen the severity of the removals, but was overruled by the imperatives of estate policy.[55]

– THE LAST GREAT REMOVALS, 1819–20 –

The great Sutherland removals of 1819–21 were the largest such events in the entire history of the Highland clearances and large by any British standard. They entailed extensions of sheep-farms in Assynt, two new farms in Strathnaver and new steadings in Kildonan. John Hall of Roxburghshire was accommodated with grazings, and Patrick Sellar obtained more territory at Morvich in eastern Sutherland (which required the removal of fifty-two families). The changes included two new sheep-farms (Skelpick to John Paterson and Langdale to Sellar) and the removal of sub-tenants from the 'Great Sheep Tenement'. In this round 195 families were removed from Strathnaver in 1819 and 1820 and many of Sellar's sub-tenants were also removed. A few others were cleared in 1821 and 1822. Of the families shifted out of Strathnaver, some were being moved for the second and third times. In all, several thousands of the interior peasantry were shifted to resettlement zones on the coasts; some went to adjoining estates and counties, others to the south of Scotland and unknown numbers emigrated, usually after some prior step-like movements to the ports, usually over several years. After 1821, however, there were few evictions or removals. The main work of clearance in Sutherland was, therefore, accomplished between 1811 and 1821.

The clearances through the seasons of 1819 and 1820 were largely not resisted. There was no violence by the people, nor even much passive resistance or recalcitrance. Sellar's triumph at his trial may have discouraged further collective action among a people who had only recently passed through another severe food crisis. Most of them moved off in advance of the removal parties. But the process was neither gentle nor clinical. The practical requirements entailed in the displacement of hundreds of people were ugly and inevitably caused scenes of pathos and anger. The people were moved off their lands, willingly or otherwise, and they trudged with their dependents, their stock and their possessions to the coast and beyond. Their houses had to be rendered uninhabitable and this produced scenes of demolition, destruction and burning. It was never a pretty sight.[56]

In 1819, as before, the constables who accompanied the clearing parties set fire to the houses after the people had been ejected. This prevented their repossession by the former inhabitants, who were normally paid compensation for their particular effects. Loch was aghast when he heard that Suther had sanctioned 'burnings' once more. The unsavoury news travelled rapidly and even the Lord

Advocate commented adversely that 'it was a matter of great regret that the Engine of fire had ever been resorted to – to pull down the houses was nothing.' There was yet more clamour and bad publicity about the firing of the people's houses. In a confidential note to Suther, Loch chastised him in the strongest terms, and also warned him about the consequences of any cruelty during the removals:

> Depend upon it . . . no one shall ever hear of this but yourself, and even you never again. I trust no acts of cruelty have been committed, they cannot be passed over if they have, and the punishment of them will be a triumph to the Highlanders, and make the next years movings more difficult.[57]

Suther defended himself as Sellar had done five years before. He pointed out that the sheepfarmers, especially Gabriel Reid, had experienced great annoyance from the obstinate people of the Heights of Kildonan who had rapidly rebuilt their huts from their old timber. Reed said that they simply drove their cattle out of sight when the clearing parties approached and then returned the stock to their old pastures when the constables departed.[58] Suther said that the people were unwilling to relinquish their houses and usually stayed until the very last moment. In Strathbrora, for instance, 'had I not sent a party with Brander . . . [to] eject them and pull down their houses they would not have budged of themselves. On Saturday the party had cleared all that were to be removed on the Strathbrora.' These were the realities of Highland clearings. Loch conceded part of this argument but absolutely forbade Suther to employ fire on any future occasion.

In the western clearances in 1819 there were reports that the people had actively cooperated in their own removal: 'Most of them assisted the Ground Officer when he was going through the ceremony of putting out their fires, and such as go to Rhue Stoir are now busied in building houses on their lots.' The minister, Mackenzie, had accompanied the removal parties 'to the several towns and used all [his] influence and arguments with the people to submit with cheerfulness to the proprietors'. The people were, however, generally hostile to the idea of taking up a career of fishing on the coast.[59] Opposition remained mute or dormant; some left the inland without word, others hung on sullenly to the last moment until the arrival of the removal posses.

Reports from the land agents on the clearances in 1819 were unanimous. One wrote:

It is gratifying to me having to report that my poor countrymen have acted in submission to the Laws and defference [sic] to the rights of their superiors. Many are going to America – as many to Caithness, and several to Glasgow.

There was an exception to the general submission of the people in the removals – a report came in from Brora that 'a spirit of determined resistance was evidenced'. About forty people had assembled close to Colonel Sutherland's house, intent 'resolutely on stopping the progress of the party'. But the removals and demolition work had proceeded, and when Suther confronted the resisters he, by his own account, 'scolded and threatened them heartily – they all of course denied all mention of opposing us and promised to behave as they ought to do when the party came.'[60] This indeed was a case in which resistance to clearances had begun to form but which failed to erupt into action. The clearances of 1819 in Kildonan, Strathnaver and Assynt were accomplished without violence from the people.

Loch told Lady Stafford that the renewed burnings had

> created a good deal of observation and reflection. It is very provoking that a measure which had been conducted with temper and moderation should be liable to the misrepresentations which such a circumstance may give rise to.[61]

Ten years later Beriah Botfield, the literary tourist, came across some of the burnt-out remains of the old houses and wrote that 'all was silent and dead; no token of its once peaceful and happy inhabitants remained, save the blackened ruins of their humble dwellings.'[62] In later years, the stories of burning houses in Sutherland were the subject of much scepticism, but the contemporary evidence is indisputable. Burned-out houses provided the most tangible and emotional proof of the act of eviction, and such scenes never failed to stir the passions of the enemies of the Highland landlords.

– Residual Clamour –

In July 1819, Suther's removals produced an outburst of public anger, news of which quickly reached London. Loch was enraged and told Suther:

> I wish to God you had only asked my opinion on the subject. In point of fact the impression is as bad as in Sellar's time.

All Loch's hopes of improving the reputation of the Sutherland management had been cast away.[63] Lady Stafford received a volley of anonymous hate-letters which referred to her as 'a damned old Cat', and her husband as a 'Butcher' and a 'Hyena' and a 'monster'. One such letter said that the day was 'coming when she will tremble'.[64] Loch was worried sick that the question would be raised in the House of Commons again.[65] He warned Suther to avoid the use of fire by anyone, including the stock-farmers:

> I do not believe that there is a single individual not connected with us, and not all of them, but what believe thoroughly in the people having been burned out of their houses; pray caution Sellar well about this.

In mid-1819, Sellar observed that some of the removed people, instead of accepting resettlement sites, left the estate for adjacent places. He advised Loch not to be apprehensive and told him that Skibo and Caithness were 'two receptacles' which had 'unloaded you a great deal of trash, of which you are well rid'.[66]

By July 1819, there were reports in the prominent newspapers of 'violent ejections' on the estate of Sutherland, and the fear of concerted resistance once more.[67] Among the estate managers there was a rising fear of radicalism, either home-grown or spreading in from the south of Scotland. This was given substance by the creation of the quasi-subversive Transatlantic Emigration Association in Dornoch, under the leadership of Thomas Dudgeon.[68] This was, ostensibly, a cooperative society promoting and assisting the emigration of evicted tenants. It raised subscriptions and organised large meetings of the common people. These plans alarmed the local landowners and sheep-farmers who detected a potential for mass protest and opposition. They attempted to scotch the Association and Sellar was one of the signatories to a document of 'respectable gentlemen in Sutherland' designed to outlaw Dudgeon's meetings.[69] Sellar said that any one involved in the Association should be summarily evicted: their names were available on a public list.

The publicity generated by Dudgeon reinforced the public outcry created by the use of fire in the frenetic work of eviction. The officers had fallen into methods which echoed those employed by Sellar himself in 1814. Once more, there were serious allegations of atrocities and premature deaths among the many hundreds evicted from the hills. National attention was again attracted by the sensational news from the remote Scottish Highlands. Once more, too, the landlord was acutely embarrassed and Loch attempted to counter the adverse publicity with public statements in defence of the improvements.[70]

Sellar himself was immune to the state of public opinion, and advised the estate to push on with the necessary removals. In November 1819, against a background of mounting protest and petitions, he urged more clearances, saying that it was 'necessary to wall out the people as bargained' so that the stock-farmers could 'possess in peace'. He pointed out that he was now paying more than £1,000 per annum in rent and had embarked capital between £8,000 and £9,000 (not counting his sheep stock): 'My success depends on the safety and propriety of my proceedings.'[71]

The eruption of controversy in 1819–20 did not entail any direct involvement of Patrick Sellar, whose role was essentially that of one of the beneficiaries of the removals. In any case, Sellar had his own separate arrangements to complete. This entailed forty-five 'subtenants to be removed by Mr Sellar in May 1820'. It was a small part of the total removals at the time, and involved people who were under notice to quit and probably required no physical ejectment by either Sellar or the estate managers.[72]

The outrage at the final great round of clearances in Sutherland of 1819–21 was loud and disturbing but they were eventually accomplished without the popular rebellion which, at several moments, seemed not unlikely. Indeed, while Suther finalised the rearrangements without further spasms of revolt, neighbouring landowners were seriously obstructed by their recalcitrant tenantries. There was, for instance, serious rioting on adjacent estates. At Gruids between 1818 and 1820 clearances were implemented without the provision of alternative settlement for the tenantry. Indeed most estates in the Highlands made little or no alternative provision for the people dislodged in favour of the incoming sheep. At Gruids there was substantial popular resistance which was not pacified until 1821 with the aid of troops.

At Achness and Mudale, in March and April 1821, the Sutherland estate conducted a final series of ejectments. In these cases there was an eruption of popular hostility and turmoil, probably influenced by anti-clearance violence at Gruids. At Mudale in Sutherland, the local factor faced a defiant community of about thirty families when he attempted to execute his warrants of ejectment. He reported:

> I intend to send a party to eject them and to demolish their houses, by cutting the timbers. I am not aware that there will be any resistance offered, but if there should be . . . I will myself with a second party effect the business completely.[73]

At Achness and Ascoilmore the physical obstruction of the clearance in 1821 was far greater than anything witnessed on the estate in the previous two years of mass clearance. Loch described the events in the north at this time as 'a regular and organised system of resistance to civil power'; it required the intervention of fusiliers to bring the Achness people to heel.[74] This was the last spasm of protest on the Sutherland estate for several decades. The main clearances were finished and all parties breathed a sigh of relief. The revolution was at rest, and most of the straths were empty.

Though there was alarming public outcry within and beyond the estate in 1820–1, the last great Sutherland clearances were now mainly completed and the sheep-farmers were in possession of the grazing lands. The former tenantry were reestablished around the coasts or else scattered across Scotland and beyond. Estate statistics suggest that, for the short run at least, most stayed on the estate.[75] The original policy of retaining the cleared population had broken down; the people were leaving and the landlord no longer opposed their departures.

The central message of the events on the Sutherland estate in 1819–21 was that, despite every precaution and the provision of the most elaborate alternative accommodation for the people removed, the business of clearance was, in the last resort, essentially coercive. The people had not been reconciled to the changes. They detested this revolution of their lives. Nor had it been possible to shift hundreds of peasant families without creating fear, panic and indelible loathing in the minds of the people. And, for Patrick Sellar, it proved that, even with the best, the most tender-hearted and the most prepared managers that salaries could buy, there was no avoiding the trauma and the tearing of the social fabric that such 'improvements' entailed. The price of economic progress was heard in the protests of the people wrenched from the straths. But Patrick Sellar, though he demanded their ejection from his land, had stood aside from the action. If there was blame to be distributed, it was not his to own.

The stock-farmers had won the battle for the land. In the coming years they faced a war of prices. Industrialisation had awakened the productive potential of Highland wool production, but then prices sagged and the sheepfarmers were compelled into fierce competition in order to reduce their costs so that they could pay the rents which had effectively destroyed the peasant producers before them. Some of the farmers, including Sellar, had invested hugely. Atkinson and Marshall alone had laid out £20,000 in their stock.[76] In the new context Sellar (whose merino experiments failed) began to betray the Smithian principles of free trade and open competition that had originally fuelled the policy of clearance. In the next decade, he became a strident advocate of a continuing tax on foreign wool. He argued for continuing protection of the sheep-farmers on the grounds that British producers were now so progressive, and so competitive against each other, that the woollen manufacturers were guaranteed the lowest prices for their raw materials.

But there would be no protection for the displaced people of the Highlands.

CHAPTER 13

Heir to the Straths in the 1820s

– PEACE AND SOLITUDE –

Progress and melancholy settled together uneasily in Sutherland after the great removals. Sellar could measure the benefits of improvement in the extraordinary productivity of his fellow sheep-farmers, notwithstanding the difficult economic times they faced in the 1820s. Others saw only desolation and depression in the old communities, now dislodged and dispersed. A touring writer in 1825, Alexander Sutherland, observed the changes on the Sutherland estate in critical style, invoking 'tears' once more. The great 'improvements' constituted, he said

> a vast speculative scheme, which embraced an attempt to revolutionise the habits and prejudices of a whole people, and which, however beneficent in intent, has brought down more tears, and swallowed more gold than any similar experiment ever made in the British Isles.

Alexander Sutherland captured the eternal ambiguities of the recent events, and he did not understate the antipathy of the people.[1]

In June 1821, James Loch told Lord Stafford, 'I am happy to say that the Sutherland Removals are entirely completed.'[2] The great rounds of 'formal' clearances which had aroused public outcry were over. Loch allowed himself the luxury of some criticism of parallel removals on the nearby Novar Estate, which had given rise to the riots at Gruids. The Novar people, he said, were 'turned out without home or habitation', which he contrasted negatively with the recent proceedings in Sutherland, where resettlement was always offered to the removees.[3] In 1820 the second and much extended edition of Loch's *Account* of the improvements on the various Stafford estates was published and was well received among his friends. It was an *apologia* for Lord Stafford's policies (with a long, well-written appendix by Patrick Sellar, recently recovered from influenza). But even the most sympathetic reader knew it could not erase the stories of 'particular acts of hardship alleged against the managers of the Sutherland improvements.'[4]

After the drama of the clearances, the estate looked for a calmer time of consolidation, peace and progress. The outcry had been great and the estate held its breath for the return of a new normality. There was hope that the *Sturm und Drang* of recent events would quickly subside, and the estate would enter a period of quietude. In reality the perennial contest for the control of the land continued.

Patrick Sellar was now in his forties, married and with a growing family into which he channelled much of his ambition. In 1820, his wife gave birth to his first child, a son, and Sellar proudly announced that this was 'the 32nd child of south country parents on both sides which I have been the means of bringing to the Estate.' He quickly explained that, by this, he meant 'the lawful children of Roxburghshire, Berwickshire, Northumberland and Morayshire men and women imported by me into Sutherland'.[5] Sellar indeed believed that the introduction of sheep-farming into the county may have caused a few score families of Sutherlanders to emigrate, but that five score southern families had simultaneously entered the county.[6]

Sellar, by 1821, had two reputations. He had become a great farmer in the north of Scotland, contributing the largest rents to the reshaped Sutherland estate. He successfully coordinated the arable and pasture sectors of his farms in Sutherland, while also continuously improving operations on his farm at Westfield in Moray which he had inherited from his father. He was the complete agricultural entrepreneur, always seeking new economies in his operations, searching new intelligence about agricultural methods and innovation, testing new markets, assaying technical experiments, poring over the latest manuals, keeping at the forefront of new rotations, machinery and breeding possibilities. His status in the county rose apace. In 1825 he was appointed Clerk of Supply. Sellar also lived with a second reputation which derived from the raw memories kept alive from his evictions in 1814. These hatreds were now deeply set in the psyche of the Highland community. Over the following decades, Sellar's notoriety as the harshest Highland evictor was repeatedly revived and reinforced in the collective memory. It was the burden he carried, a hair-shirt he was never allowed to discard.

Throughout the 1820s, Highland wool clips rose prodigiously, but prices sagged and fluctuated around generally low levels. These conditions eventually created severe problems for all farmers, even the largest. Recurrent depression in industry and oscillating foreign markets for British manufactures, especially in the United States, caused hardship among producers. The extravagant expectations generated in the wartime inflation of prices and profits were much flattened by the 1820s. Less efficient producers were weeded out. A greater premium than ever was placed on high productivity and technical advance, in which Sellar excelled.[7] But his own prospects were duller, and he strove with difficulty to maintain his optimism. In the summer of 1820 he reiterated the sheep-farming credo:

> The country being now opened up by roads and part of it under Stock – part not, they [i.e. the world at large] will Judge whether Stock farming be fitt for their country or not – and whether the people who have been sent to the Shore be healthier, more cheerful and industrious, and wealthy, than those in the Status quo ante bellum. I am sure, that if her Ladyship [Stafford] dont chuse to raise a regiment next war she may man a line of battle ships or two with the hardiest fellows possible.[8]

In the late summer of 1820 Lady Stafford journeyed north once more. Like most landed proprietors in the Highlands, she was nervous of the spread of radical thinking among a population already agitated by the clearances. She was intensely aware of the disturbed condition of many Highland estates alarmingly close to her own. There were riots and resistance to removals all about the north eastern shoulder of the Highlands. On her way north, at Ardgay, she passed through 'more wild country and about a dozen black hills the abode of Novar's tenants who rebelled lately'. Such thoughts preyed on her mind as she approached her own estate which had so recently engineered the greatest of all the Highland clearances.

Sellar dined with Lady Stafford at Dunrobin Castle and typically his conversation was commercial. Lady Stafford told her husband that 'Sellar makes a great deal of money by a herd of swine and he has got 80 in number.' He was conveying pigs from Elgin to Sutherland, where they were then cured for the London market. They were selling better than cattle, and Lady Stafford decided to try the experiment on her own account.[9] Sheep and wool prices were low, but Sellar's merinos had 'done wonders'.[10]

Lady Stafford remained no less enthusiastic about the much larger experiment of the clearances. She believed that her estate been lucky in 'getting Strathnaver settled without a riot, though the people are now all quiet and well disposed.' Her view was that 'where there has been dissatisfaction it chiefly arose from ignorance and mistrust of the Factors.' Most of the people had been very well treated, and it was only the use of 'burnings' that had raised a hue and cry. She accepted the theory that the reputation of the factors (almost certainly a reference to Sellar's time) had created a climate of fear and distrust on her estate. When she discovered harsh behaviour by one of her estate officials he was dismissed in a manner reminiscent of her treatment of Sellar five years earlier.[11]

Lady Stafford's attitude swung between benevolent care and angry frustration. In 1822, for example, she insisted on the 'gentle management' of 'the Strathnaver tenants' who were now re-settled on the coast.[12] Two years later, when she faced yet another rash of petitions from people in Sutherland, her tone sharpened. She fulminated that the tenants 'expect that the estate should be given away to them and at the same time without any prospect of profit to themselves'. She remarked that it would be a positive gain 'to get rid of this inefficient people'. Meantime the pertinaciously efficient Sellar began yet another experiment, that of exporting cattle to the English market by sea.[13]

Thus the revolution had been forced through; the common people had been relocated to the coasts. Many of the disgruntled had left the estate altogether. The inland straths had been given over to the great capitalist sheep-farmers, the greatest of whom was Sellar himself. Another of the sheep-farmers, Gabriel Reed, told Lady Stafford that Sutherland would soon be the richest part of the kingdom, and that Lord Stafford would be surprised at the change. Lord Stafford, in fact, was increasingly incapacitated and in 1820 suffered a stroke which impeded his mobility in the next decade, and gave his active wife even more initiative than before.[14]

– PROSPECTS IN THE 1820s –

The commercial sector of the Sutherland estate economy yielded measurable gains in its contribution to regional and national income. This was, of course, the essential justification of the upheavals of the clearances. Already, by 1820, wool production had increased from 140 m lb in 1815 to 480 m lb.[15] Sellar quoted figures showing that the output of the east Sutherland fisheries had increased from 2,400 barrels in 1813, to 30,000 barrels in 1825.[16] Though the human population of the county had been radically dislocated in the removals, a comparison of population between 1815 and 1845 showed Sutherland with a small increase of population, unlike other pastoral counties such as Dumfries, Haddington, Inverness, Kirkcudbright and Wigton which all registered net losses. An increase in population in Sutherland was achieved, despite substantial net outmigration, because births exceeded deaths to an even greater degree. Emigration was not sufficient, until mid-century, to siphon off the increment of population growth in the age of the clearances.

Sellar always contrasted the new achievements in the improved economy of Sutherland with the squalor of the old ways. He held a poor opinion of the distant past. For instance, he believed that in the seventeenth century 'no export [had derived] from the mountains of England and Scotland. They were a nest of outlaws who paid no rent' and their inhabitants lived by plunder on the low countries.[17] Sellar freely quoted statistics to demonstrate the benefits of the changes with which he was so closely associated:

> We formerly used to import some thousands Bolls of meal, taking it from the mouths of more industrious persons, to support an idle population among our mountains, now, we export, by means of our new industry, Skill and Capital from the thirty to Forty thousand Barrels per annum, part of our surplus food, to our neighbours.[18]

When he looked back on his work at Culmaily, he emphasised that in 1810 it was 'in the greatest possible state of Barrenness and at a time when no Sutherland man would do any work, and people of every description required, were to be bribed away from other countries.' The returns to production were slow to increase and he had spent £7,343 at Culmaily since 1810, not counting rents.[19]

Rising aggregate output of wool, meat and fish did not guarantee higher profits, any more than it ensured greater employment. Commodity prices were the critical regulator, and a decade of low returns created tensions at every level of the Highland economy. In 1821 Patrick Sellar remained sufficiently confident to seek the expansion of his operations in eastern Sutherland. He made a bid for a nineteen–year lease of the flood-prone 100-acre farm of Kinnauld, close to Morvich. He explained that any other tenant would require the landlord to spend £2,000 on houses and mills, which he already possessed at Morvich. Sellar declared that Kinnauld was currently barren (the previous tenant had failed) and he hated the thought of 'looking out [on] this Waste all my days.' He would convert it into a beautiful farm, which no other farmer could achieve.[20]

Within a few months Sellar's tone altered totally. Suddenly he fell into deep pessimism about the future of his farming operations, and he begged his landlord for relief from the rent burden which, of course, had been contracted during the time of inflated wartime commodity prices. The impact of the subsequent deflation was now severe and caused panic from which Sellar was himself not immune. In April 1822, he pleaded for an immediate rent abatement, at least on a temporary basis. He said he had been as efficient as anyone possibly could be, but current prices were ruinous: 'A few years sales similar to 1820 and 1821 must compel me to stop short and to sell out at any loss.' He had embarked more capital than any other tenant, and was still paying Lord Stafford 6 per cent on his borrowed capital.

Sellar took to begging his landlord, in a manner reminiscent of the petitions of the old tenantry in hard times, 'that you do not insist on the ruin of my wife and family.'[21] His could only repay his debts, 'while my wound was within the reach of medicine'. But, he asked plaintively, 'What can a man's whining avail his Lordship, when he has once been sucked dry, and has involved himself in Bankruptcy?' He continued in this strain, saying that though he did not 'yet abate any of my industry, or my improvements, or of my confidence in my landlord . . . I am weakened but not reduced.'[22] Lord Stafford was highly critical of Sellar's importuning, and told Loch that he was trying to 'pervert his neighbour's minds as well as his own.'

Sellar's ill-advised rhetoric evidently irritated Lord Stafford and so did his assumption that this landlord would prove aristocratically generous towards the tenantry. But, asked Sellar,

> will they part with their last farthing? Are they prepared to submitt to surrender up to the public creditor their entire fortunes and the property of a loyal and attached tenantry?

He pointed out that wool prices had fallen 60 per cent, and corn, sheep and cattle prices had plunged 55 per cent since 1815. 'With the receipts of 1786 we are subjected to the burthens of 1822.' Sellar blamed Parliament for what he called 'legal robbery', and he railed against foreign imports of agricultural produce. There was a massive crisis looming, he declared, which would unseat Parliament and the Monarchy: 'The people will take the power; and however they may End, they will, most certainly begin by cutting the throats of the upper classes of Society.' The crisis would cause an end to 'all ideas of nobility, gentry and family. The stocks can be transferred in an instant.' Sellar's threatening alarmism and dire predictions received no welcome in the Stafford family.[23]

The Staffords were intensely wary of Sellar's tactics in the struggle over rents and lands.[24] Sellar certainly regarded his negotiations with his landlord as part of his maximising calculus. By late 1822, and despite scepticism about Sellar's claims of dire poverty,[25] economic conditions were so grim that a general rent abatement was instituted to 'keep the Sutherland tenants afloat'.[26] It was an acknowledgement of the dreadful drift of prices. All Highland prices fell badly after 1815, including those of fish. But James Loch maintained that the ordinary people in the new economy were actually much better off.

Sellar applauded Lord Stafford's rent abatement. The tenantry had been saved from ruin. He had improved his own lands without stinting, to the advantage of the landlord and future generations. He had executed almost 400 miles of drains and he would now continue his improvements. He pointed out that he began his farm at Culmaily, in 1810, 'at the very top of the high water'. Having extracted a rent reduction, he next asked to be rescued from the infestation of rabbits. Sellar had conducted a lifelong crusade against vermin, though he respected the preservation of game for sporting tenants of appropriate rank. A neighbouring tenant was promoting rabbits and hares for felt manufacture. The rabbits were devouring Sellar's turnips: 'In the name of the departed Spirit of British Agriculture, I beseech you to save me from ruin,' he expostulated. His choicest sheep, 'those I have improved to beat almost all my neighbours', were threatened by the needs of felt.[27]

Prices stabilised in the mid-1820s and then worsened again. The cycle of complaint and relief was repeated, but each downturn eliminated large and small players in the commodity markets. Even Gabriel Reed, another of the great sheep-farmers, begged for rent reductions while others simply fell bankrupt. In mid-1827 Sellar pleaded for another rent abatement: 'If you do not Strengthen us some way or other you will get our families to keep very soon', he told James Loch.[28] The year 1828 was especially awful for prices and weather.[29] The great sheep-farmers now faced the sorts of difficulties experienced by the small cattle producers in the old economy, the very people they had ousted from the inland pastures in the previous decade. Atkinson and Marshall said that they had lost 50 per cent of the value of their stock during the course of their lease, and the remainder of their capital was rapidly draining away. Wool production no longer even paid their expenses: 'Without your aid and assistance we can see nothing before us but utter and irretrievable ruin.' They were overwhelmed by financial difficulties and could not go on.[30]

– SELLAR AND COMPETITION –

Sellar met the blizzard of depressed prices in three ways. The first was to force the landlord to share the fall; the second was to increase efficiency and lower costs; the third was to protect the conditions of his productivity. All three consumed much of his energy through these difficult years and each transmitted pressure onto the remains of the old society.

Sellar's efficiency depended on the scale of his productions. It was also related to his costs of transport and the security of his flocks. This made him acutely sensitive to the preservation of the ancient droving rights which were threatened by the advent of sealed roads in the north. The issue became a source of friction. In 1819 Sellar was in conflict with road interests in Ardross where his cattle were impounded *en route* between Westfield and Culmaily. He reacted angrily, and eventually extracted 'a letter of apology promising never to molest me in time to come'. Ironically he required the testimony of previously evicted tenants: he was successful in this contest because he had 'ferreted out witnesses' to the old customs of free passage.[31]

The encroachments on drove roads and free passage, and the imposition of tolls, had been worsening since 1792. The hard surfaces of the new turnpikes had no use to stock farmers and in 1823 Sellar undertook to investigate the ancient rules governing Scottish drove roads. He accepted that Parliament had ultimate sovereignty, but argued fiercely that roads were like rivers, and passage along them should never be impeded. He warned James Loch, an MP, that if the danger was not averted the interior of Sutherland would revert to its state in the days of the tacksmen. The drove roads were 'a thing of significance to the northern Counties as well as the Towns which they supply with Beef and Mutton in England'. The campaign had been precipitated by the Duke of Atholl's imposition of tolls in the southern Highlands. Sellar told Loch:

> Parliament is Omnipotent, I grant you; but if this public servitude of thoroughfare were a servitude on a river . . . I think Parliament would not shutt up our navigation.

Sheep from the northern Highlands often travelled 300 to 400 miles to Yorkshire. As Sellar pointed out, 'These creatures, when collected in the mountains, will scarcely let a man within 55 yards of them, without flying from him in all directions.' His campaign to preserve the drove roads continued through the 1820s.[32] In March 1827, he complained:

'If not <u>checked</u> by some means or other the thing will soon come to this pass, that Stock must be sent by sea or not at all. Small black faced Ewes that fetch 5/- to 6/- in the Yorkshire markets are scarcely worth driving or will be so in a short time.'[33]

Sellar believed that road tolls were 'insanity' and he bombarded the newspapers with his protests, trying to create united opinion among Highland interests.[34] But he was scornful of the Highland lairds who were riven with 'pitiful Jealousies', did not understand the danger and had no collective sense whatever.[35] The ineffectual Inverness lairds languished in a 'slough of despond'.[36]

Sellar had higher hopes for steam shipping and suggested prizes for the transport of sheep along the east coast. He began his own experiments to break the transport impasse. If successful, he said, sea transport might double Highland rents, 'although the landlords (excepting a very few) are so stone blind as to see no part of it.'[37] He hoped that the threat of new competition would also serve to alarm the toll-holders, and cause them to adopt more reasonable rates on their roads.[38] In September 1824, Lady Stafford was glad to know of Sellar's 'trial of sending cattle by sea to England which I have often been surprized shd not have before been attempted.'[39] Sellar believed that, 'The time is not far distant when Steam will be the universal conveyance for sheep and cattle.'[40]

Sellar told Loch as early as 1822 that 'sixty miles of land carriage was <u>ruinous to me as well as to your roads</u>'. He wanted access to the sea at Invernaver but this required the eviction of a number of small subtenants from the district, people from whom he had suffered 'by loss and theft'. At Invernaver, Sellar's lands were 'coterminous with several families of highlanders' who, he believed, were responsible for many sheep thefts. 'Moreover, in catching one sheep the highlanders generally drown several in the bog holes.' He referred, contemptuously, to these people as 'inmates' and 'turfcutters' rather than as 'neighbours', and their depredations were bound to increase in times of dearth. If sheep thefts continued, then the district would revert 'to the aborigines'.[41] If, on the other hand, the people were ejected, Sellar would be more secure and he could gain access to the sea. Poor prices, therefore, simply added urgency to his demands for land and its rights.

Sellar expressed himself with crystal clarity on this very issue:

I cant keep my stores in that remote country among highland tenants, cant bring my flocks down to clip among such people. I can get no decent south country man to live among them – nor can I afford his meal costs, cows, wages, and interest on buildings, unless he herd, as well as keep stores; but I can't keep Sheep on Torresdale while you keep highlanders in Invernaver.[42]

His war against sheep-thieves never faltered. As Sellar told Loch:

> As this is the season for Serving notices I hope you will not forget me. Prices are so ruinously low for every thing which our farms produce, that with all that can be done to add to our produce and diminish charges, we shall have enough ado I assure you, and I expect my good landlord and their agent will now stop an evil which injures their tenant without in the smallest degree benefiting their property.

Thus Sellar associated better transport with the elimination of more of the small tenantry, and also with his fight against low prices. It was part of the continuing, though scarcely visible, clearance of pockets of peasantry from the estate which occurred in practically every 'season for serving notices'. These quiet episodes of removal often eliminated the marginal people of the Highlands, people who were subject to less dramatic, but no less thorough, ejectment than those involved in the great set-pieces in the history of the clearances. One of the Sutherland factors said that the estate knew nothing of sub-tenants. Their fate was not part of official estate business.[43]

While Sellar demanded a positively Smithian freedom of trade for his flocks, he argued simultaneously, with equal passion, in favour of taxes on foreign wool imports, thus establishing the limits to his free trade creed. The duty on foreign wool in the early 1820s was as high as 6d. in the pound but fell to 1d. by 1825.[44] English wool imports were running at about 300,000 stone in 1820 (mainly from Spain, Germany and Ireland). Sellar pointed out that Sutherland alone was producing 20,000 stone (it had been 2,000 in 1810) and other Highland counties were now able to produce at least 160,000 stone; a new Scottish supply of wool had arisen within the past twenty years and the supply was advancing rapidly. Consequently, Sellar argued, the need to import was greatly reduced. The British sheep-farmers had beaten down the price of wool by increasing its supply, and further expansion was bound to come from Inverness-shire and Aberdeenshire between the Spey and the Dee; 'all plainly intended by Nature for Stock and all of it fitted to give more rent in Grass than in Corn.' All of this argued against unrestricted foreign imports. Wool imports were simply unnecessary.[45] Sellar wanted protection but received no solace from Loch who was a full-blooded free trader[46] and believed that *laissez-faire* would always be for the best in the long run.[47] Loch was not moved by Sellar's neo-mercantilism.[48]

– SELLAR AND WHISKY –

Sellar, always alert to entrepreneurial opportunity,[49] was aware of the possibilities for legal large-scale distilling in eastern Sutherland when the 'English market was opened to Scotch Spirits.' He had seen whisky produced in Highland bothies, and could 'expect an article quite superior to any thing we have yet seen from the legal distillery.'[50] For more than a decade, of course, Sellar had been the scourge of whisky smugglers. But times had changed. The Sutherland estate acceded to his idea of a distillery to take advantage of the opening of the English market and the introduction of steam navigations at Little Ferry.[51] Sellar said he would be the best distiller in the north:

> I am determined to do what I do well. I have not yet been beat in Sheep and I shall try to beat what I have yet seen in Whisky. If a man could fairly tickle your London gentlemen's pallets [that is, palates], I think you would be inclined to pay him for his skill and attention.[52]

An unbending critic of the illegal sector of the industry, Sellar saw no moral objection to this new enterprise.[53] He was no teetotaller; he enjoyed wines and understood his toddy.

Soon Sellar began preparations for his new distillery, commissioning and quarrying materials, buying up fir logs, and working at the technical details of the project.[54] He also required a good young distiller from the south, being unable to recruit such skills in the Highlands. This prompted Sellar to reflect on the need for strangers:

> Did it not strike you that there was a cause of why Sutherland has at all times imported Strangers to do her duties, and still needed new importation? The sons of these very Strangers invariably turning out ciphers! I have in my eye at the moment many descendants of such strangers incorporated in the mass of your people and indistinguishable from them except in name . . . your schoolmasters are a set of lazy dolts put in by the Clergy. The schoolmasters, instead of the enthusiasm of teachers, have their minds intent upon preaching dull sermons in barbarous Gaelic, to which end, they leave the school in winter months for the divinity Hall; and by the time the teacher is stupid in the pulpit, the Scholars of the last 30 years compose his Sleepy audience. In such a Reign of Stupidity, people are dozed over asleep.

In effect, assimilation to Highland ways neutralised all the benefits of education.

Sellar was full of enthusiasm for his distillery venture but, in the outcome, was extremely lucky not to burn his fingers in the process. Within six months of its initiation, and before he had incurred much expenditure, the entire project was suddenly aborted. The demand for the whisky had collapsed. A similar concern at Helmsdale had sunk £6,000 in a rival distillery, and now faced catastrophic losses. Sellar escaped by the skin of his teeth, and Loch reported that 'Mr Sellar is in high spirits at his narrow escape from being so involved.'[55] While the new legal distillery failed, the older illegal variety continued its controversial existence, sometimes erupting into violence. In late 1827 thirty women assaulted, with volleys of stones, the excise men who attempted to suppress a distilling venture at Torboll. Three of the women were jailed.[56] Sellar continued to supply barley to the southern distillers.

In 1826, Sellar suggested that the tenantry of Sutherland should contribute to a public subscription to thank the Stafford family for the rent abatements and the much improved character of the county. They had been delivered from inevitable 'beggary' by this act of grace in 'a country just emerging from a state of nature'. It was a great privilege, declared Sellar, to be tenant to a family which could boast unbroken succession for 800 years.[57] Loch favoured this idea; the tenants could testify to the fact that their rents were better paid than elsewhere in the Highlands and that the rents paid by small tenantry were much lower than they had been under the old tacksmen system.[58] Loch instructed Gunn (successor to Francis Suther, who died in office in November 1824) that if the tenants 'desire to give Lord Stafford any expression of their gratitude don't let Sellar be too prominent'.[59] In the outcome, Sellar's suggestion lapsed temporarily for want of support, which he described as 'a very Stupid thing.'[60] In his view, the entire proceedings had been surrounded by 'too much Cant and subserviency'.[61] Whatever his standing within Sutherland, his reputation beyond was rising swiftly. He was certainly proud to supply wethers to Lord Harewood and ewes to Lincolnshire, and to extend the range of the Inverness wool market.

– STEWART OF GARTH –

Patrick Sellar's improving equanimity was badly jolted in 1822 by the publication of an influential book by one of the lesser Highland lairds, General David Stewart of Garth. The first edition of his two-volume *Sketches of the Scottish Highlanders* became a much-consulted compendium of the 'romantic' interpretation of Highland history. It was a sustained and eloquent exposition of the tragic view of the recent past and, notably, a loud blast against the clearances. For Sellar it became a particular infuriation by its highly critical account of the events in Sutherland in 1814 and 1819–20. Stewart implied, as clearly as could be without defamation, that Sellar's trial in Inverness in 1816 had been a travesty of justice. Stewart's publication struck Sellar deeply, and he resolved to demolish his traducer.[62]

There was no better juxtaposition of the rival views of the Highland world than those of Sellar and Stewart. Nor could their respective fates have been more symbolic. Stewart took upon himself to represent the old Highlands, or at least his particular version of that world. He voiced a yearning for the pre-improvement world, somewhat tinged with a Jacobitical romanticism. He was totally opposed to the commercialisation of the Highlands. He most of all honoured the patriarchal and military traditions. Stewart wanted to stop the clock of change, even to turn it back. In 1821, he declared that, 'The soil in the Highlands should be improved by the labour of the occupier – fed and clothed and supported in all necessary expenses by the produce.' He believed that the Highlands could be self-sufficient.[63] He regarded Sellar, not improbably, as the personification of the opposite conception of the world. Sellar and Stewart perfectly epitomised the polar versions of the modern Highlands.[64]

Through his mother Stewart was grandson of 'the doughty Jacobite, David Stewart, who died at Culloden'. Less satisfactorily for his Highland *persona*, the Garth Stewarts had served with the Hanoverians at Culloden. His mother raised him in her own tongue, Gaelic, and he was said to have possessed 'from his infancy an insatiable appetite for the Gaelic songs and stories'. Stewart's military career consumed the greater part of his life and he served in many theatres of the French Wars with injuries and distinctions. He had been a relatively liberal leader of his troops, and had found it necessary to have only two shot and one hanged in his entire time with his Regiment. He retired on half pay in 1815 (when he began collecting data for his book).

A late Victorian memorial to Stewart claimed:

> He was not an admirer of large sheep-farms, and on his own land the old system was continued. But he saw the attractions of the towns were telling on the rural population, and he also deplored that so many of the men so . . . fitted for being soldiers were voluntarily emigrating. If he had his wish he would keep them at any sacrifice in the glens and islands, for he was not a political economist but a Highland warrior.[65]

Stewart claimed the glamour and the glory of the Highland warrior. He was also a laird with his own estate in Perthshire. In the wider world, he took upon himself the task of restoring the tradition. He was personally credited with the reconstruction of 'the myth of the Highlands' at the end of the French Wars. After his military service, Stewart devoted great efforts to building up the membership of the Highland Society in London. In 1817 he invited landowners across Scotland and elsewhere to join the Highland Society of London. For a fee, the Society offered a claim on posterity for all members and their respective families. By joining 'this respectable and patriotic Body' they would be able 'to have your name enrolled in this character of a chieftain'. The prospective member was invited to indicate if 'the family entered the field under any particular banner, and distinguishing mark . . . such as a leaf or heather, fur or the like, and if so can a drawing of it be provided for the society – and had they a war cry, to rally or call them.'[66]

In effect, Stewart became guardian and promoter of the idea of Highland culture. He offered like-minded proprietors symbols of prestige to differentiate their families within the pantheon of their Highland identity, conferring a degree of status based on heredity and tradition. Stewart helped manufacture 'the tartan tradition' and was instrumental in the successful organisation of the great pageant for the famous visit of George IV to Edinburgh in 1822. This was the grand culmination of his efforts to rekindle the spirit of the old Highlands and to generate a new sense of identity among its leaders. Stewart was creating, or perhaps recreating, the sense of Highland identity, the very spectre of which Sellar was so urgent to expel from the north of Britain. A collision between the two was likely.[67]

Stewart lived by a set of beliefs which Sellar had come to detest. To add piquancy to the difference, Stewart's own economic fortunes proceeded in the opposite direction to those of his enemy. Stewart was a small Perthshire proprietor who, in common with many of his class, found his postwar finances in crisis, and was reduced to extreme measures to keep his estate together. Between Sellar and Stewart there were, therefore, tensions at every turn in this encounter of opposites.

The collision with Sellar derived directly from Stewart's attempt to write a history of the Highlanders which was designed to turn back the tide of change in the Highlands. He was totally opposed to the transformation of the north into a sheep economy. His indictment of these changes was comprehensive. A review in the *Scots Magazine* said that Stewart had exposed the awful cupidity of the landlords by whose 'insane operations' the people had been reduced to a degree of poverty and wretchedness, incredible to those who have witnessed it, and equalled only by the squalid and desperate misery of the Irish peasant.

Stewart made the familiar case that 'the great curse of the Highlands has been the introduction among the higher classes of Sassenach manners.'[68]

Racial assumptions underpinned Stewart's ideology. The Highlanders, he averred, were derived from pure stock which had produced a particular style of life in an insulated community. They could not adapt to the world of industry. 'Donald' simply could not become a manufacturer: it was against his nature and breeding. Stewart's views were fundamentalist and, though diametrically opposed in their corollary, had a great deal in common with Sellar's own caricature of the Highlanders as the impediment to civilisation. Stewart, like Sellar, was perfectly prepared to depict the entire problem in terms of Saxonism against the Celts.[69]

Stewart said that the Highlanders did not blame their 'honourable superiors, who had hitherto been kind, and to whom they themselves had ever been attached and faithful.' He absolved the landlords and loaded the blame upon their agents, persons 'cast in a coarser mould, and generally strangers to the country'. The agents detested the people and were

> ignorant of their character, capability and language. They quickly surmounted every obstacle, and hurried on the change, without reflecting on the distress of which it might be productive, or allowing the kindliest feelings of the landlords to operate in favour of their Ancient tenantry.[70]

Stewart denounced the 'mode of ejectment, happily long obsolete, by setting their houses on fire', and made reference to such scenes movingly depicted in Walter Scott's *Guy Mannering*. He also noted that the popular reaction against eviction was sometimes so obstinate that force had been required.[71] His book was a passionate condemnation of the philosophy of improvement, its 'cold-hearted spirit of calculation, from before which humanity, and every better feeling, shrink, that induced men to set up for sale the loyalty, honourable fidelity, and affection, which, as they cannot be purchased, are above all price.'[72]

Stewart had been privately critical of events in Sutherland as early as 1817. He said that the 'old and faithful adherents' had given Lady Stafford 'repeated proofs' of their 'attachment', yet they had been 'cruelly oppressed by a factor'. When her factor was 'tried for his life', she had exerted all her influence to 'screen him from the punishment which he so richly deserved.'[73] He acknowledged that Sellar was exculpated:

> The trial ended (as was expected by every person who understood the circumstances) in the acquittal of the acting agent, the verdict of the jury proceeding on the principle that he acted under legal authority. This acquittal, however, did by no means diminish the general feeling of culpability; it only transferred the offence from the agent to a quarter too high and too distant to be directly affected by public indignation, if indeed, there be any station so elevated, or so distant, that public indignation, justly excited, will not, sooner or later, reach, so as to touch the feeling, however obtuse, of the transgressor of the law of humanity written on every upright mind, and deeply engraved on every kind and generous heart.[74]

This was a clever and blistering attack on Sellar and all he stood for, yet it kept within the law. Stewart declared that the Sutherland experiment ruined the country and transformed the people into beggars. Moreover the detested policy had been unnecessary because comparable rent increases could have been obtained from small tenants, given time and patience. Hence the indictment of Sellar in Stewart's account was part of a broader denunciation which trenched on the great underlying question of the economics of land use in the Highlands.[75]

For Sellar, Stewart's book was a red rag to a bull. It aroused all the ire in Sellar's soul and provoked him into renewed torrents of disdain for the world that Stewart claimed to represent. In the years 1822 to 1826, Sellar pursued Stewart as an enemy requiring public correction. Advised by Henry Cockburn that Stewart had committed no actual libel in the *Sketches*, Sellar prepared his own *Statement* of defence aimed at Stewart and 'these pitiful Babblers'. He took care to avoid involving the Stafford family, but intended to ensure that the calumniations did not 'go unanswered to posterity.'[76] His defence was based largely on Mackid's confession of 1817 (which he had not previously publicised to the world at large).[77] He also asserted the economic rationale of the clearance policies, pointing out that Edinburgh, Glasgow and Paisley currently received a weekly supply of 25,000 sheep which would have been utterly impossible if the Highlands still existed in the same condition as in 1725. He posed the central proposition: 'The question is whether Ladies and Gentlemen prefer to want half their necessities, to starve the lower classes, by doubling the summation of their Butcher's Bills.' Sellar's response to Stewart and the 'despicable romancers', was circulated widely to his friends. He urged James Loch to represent the case to the world at large in London.

Sellar also corresponded with Stewart directly and challenged every point in his attack. Sellar wanted to force Stewart into a public apology.[78] Sending a copy of his *Statement,* he told Stewart that he would have taken him to court but for the 'peculiar manner in which the [offensive] paragraph is worded'.[79] He reiterated that he had always been willing

> from first to last to be Judged by Truth. This Goddess, under whose chaste protection it is, that the British press, and British sentiments hold their present influence in the world.[80]

Stewart eventually replied to Sellar. He did not dispute the contents of Sellar's *Statement,* but declared that the Sutherland experiment had been a terrible waste of the Staffords' capital. He claimed that Lady Stafford 'would have been much richer' if she had put her money in the funds and left the estate as it was. His own tenants of the old sort paid very good rents and better than those in Sutherland.

Sellar refused to believe any of this and quoted figures at Stewart proving, for instance, that the output of Sutherland fisheries had increased from nothing in 1813 to 30,000 barrels in 1825.[81] Stewart had used Mackid's Precognition as the basis for his writing. Sellar pointed out to him that Mackid had retracted it all, and that he had been found entirely innocent. Sellar declared that he was deeply offended by Stewart's account and bristled at Stewart's reference to divine judgement, and retorted that he should read *Exodus* XX: 16 – 'Thou shalt not bear false witness against thy neighbour.' According to Sellar the letter was 'quite puerile', and full of the bad passions of

> a selfish petty highland Laird who sees no further than the limits of the little sovereignty where Donald approaches him with fear and trembling – hunger in his face – a tattered philibeg of Stewart Tartan on his other end.

Sellar declared that Stewart was 'an ignorant, intermeddling impertinent man' who merely wanted to turned the landlord against her tenants. He exclaimed, 'with what flimsy drapery does he conceal the illiberal bad passions in his breast'.[82]

Between the second and third editions of Stewart's book, between 1822 and 1825, all references to Sellar, William Young and the Inverness trial were excised. The central offending paragraph was removed, as well as reference to the 'conviction of culpability'. This was a clear concession by Stewart to the opposing account and perhaps to fear of legal action against him. Instead, he extended his broad denunciation of the policies of clearance. He had visited Sutherland in the autumn of 1823 to check his earlier findings, examining the 'improved' and the depopulated districts. He was impressed by the scale of expenditure and the exemplary encouragement that had been given, as well as a liberal abatement of rent to the 'tenants of capital.' The new rents had been reduced to levels not much greater than before the removals. More than £210,000 had been spent on a fallacious system. He hoped that the sour and disaffected people would recover their loyalty. There was, therefore, little recantation in Stewart's account. He had bowed to Sellar's threats without diminishing his broad attack on the system at large. He reinforced his assault on the manner in which the old Highland society had been vilified. In the violent changes, he said, 'all feeling of former kindness towards the native tenantry had ceased to exist.' And though large expenditures had been made, the people had been reduced to the condition of the peasantry of Ireland.[83]

There was a subplot to Stewart's publishing enterprise. Stewart was in desperate financial straits at the time and had hoped for relief to his estate from the royalties of his publication.[84] His problems related to his own Highland estate, which he had inherited burdened with heavy debts accumulated by his father. Stewart first sought cross-funding from his family's West Indian slave-plantations; he subsequently begged for assistance from other family members in Scotland. Neither course produced any alleviation. His personal financial crises therefore invested his criticism of other proprietors with special edge. His own affairs demonstrated the uphill battle his romantic views faced in the postwar world of the Highland laird.

Stewart had referred to emigration from the Highlands as 'the WHITE SLAVE TRADE!' He personally opposed the slave trade but, like other plantation owners, he favoured delaying the abolition of slavery and remained an anti-abolitionist to the end. Since his Highland estate could not survive without external support, he continued to press for extra income from his own slave estates.[85] He became extremely angry when profits from his plantations proved disappointing in the mid-1820s. In 1821, Stewart slaveholdings included thirty-one Negroes valued at £3,195 and he said that his 'only hope of relief is from the West Indies'. But the estates were in a great mess which he blamed on his father (a kind man, with a filthy temper) and his incompetent brother who managed the West Indian property. In the mid-20s Stewart's debts reached £26,375 with rents of less than £1,000 per annum, 'even if they were paid which is not the case'. Stewart relied on regular remittances from Trinidad but was grievously disappointed and accused his brother of failing him: he did not know how to meet the demands upon him. The properties were already fully mortgaged and he could not raise money on his personal security. He eventually willed his stock of Negroes in the Island of St Vincent to his sister.[86]

Stewart's Highland estate was in the same confusion and he was unable to extract rents and profits sufficient to his outlays and dependents.[87] In the manner repeated across virtually all Highland estates, Stewart soon found himself abetting emigration among his own small tenantry. This was, of course, a policy which he found totally anathema to the true spirit of the Highlands. In November 1821, he observed that his Highland tenants, who could not pay rent, were going to America. He said that he wanted to promote voluntary emigration to produce a thinning of the population which had become 'absolutely necessary'. He declared that he was 'hostile to the desolating system of turning out and extirpating a whole race – but without emigration to America as to the Lowlands, how can a man in this country provide for four or five sons when he has so many?'[88]

In 1827 Stewart described himself as 'an old Soldier', now even further burdened with the claims of impecunious relatives. He had a natural son, Neil, whose future was a further financial worry and was left in the hands of relatives. Stewart's sister had fallen into dependence, and was also depleting the family inheritance. Stewart was reduced to begging favours of his own friends. He explained that his sister had married twenty years previously

> a man with more learning in his head, than money in his pocket, and when he died left five sons, with little means for their education and support. I have therefore taken them in charge but with a family estate overwhelmed with debt I cannot do what I wish and must as a consequence . . . encroach on the indulgence of my friends.

In his final years, in the late 1820s, Stewart made pathetic efforts to keep his estates financially afloat from afar. His final stratagem was to seek a colonial governorship to buttress his failed finances. It was in this frame of mind that he was appointed Governor of St Lucia which was one of the unhealthiest spots in the Empire.[89] In 1827, reportedly 'with all the spirit and gaiety of a youthful veteran', he sailed to his new posting. He jested of his eventual return and marriage at the end of a few years. But soon there was bad news:

Very recently, in a letter from him, he contrasted the healthy state of the island with what it was when he visited it as a subaltern; but, alas! for the prospect of human life, in how short a time the tidings have arrived that this excellent man is no more.[90]

Major-General David Stewart died as Governor of St Lucia of 'West India Fever' in 1829. Sellar had thereby lost one of his most prominent and damaging opponents. But many others rose in Stewart's place in the succeeding decades, often enough drawing upon Stewart's words for new denunciations.[91]

– IN THE MOUNTAINS –

While Sellar grappled with his assailants, he literally strode the great pastoral lands over which he now ruled as champion sheep-farmer of the north. He took periodic tours among his flocks, by foot and alone, or with his much esteemed and prolific shepherds. Sellar was a practical farmer whose physical energies would have done proud any colonist of the age. Thus in spring 1828 he apologised to James Loch, explaining, 'I am just come back from a fagging tour among the Strathnaver wastes and my hand shakes so much you will hardly make it out.'[92] He covered great distances, during which journeys he often indulged his passion for geology.[93] In July 1828, Sellar boasted that he had bathed in Loch Inchard and walked to Altnaharra:

> I have threaded nearly every Glen in the North of Scotland, but such a mass of barren Quartz and mica Schist as nearly the whole of Edrachyllis Coast exhibits I never saw. There is no such land of poverty and desolation in Scotland. The mountains of the interior are very Sublime and entertain beautiful pasture.[94]

Sellar was fully familiar with the rigours and needs of the country. When Loch toured Strathnaver in 1822, Sellar advised him that his own men were always equipped with 'great worsted stockings 4 feet long and good usquebae [sic], both of which I recommend to your special notice.'[95] On another occasion, when Loch entered the pathless wastes of the Reay Country, Sellar advised 'a hair mattress and firm light blankets and hair Pillow [. . . which . . .] you will find a valuable accompaniment to this Savage Country which you are about to visit.' Thus equipped, Loch would rise refreshed and vigorous each morning.[96]

Sellar's own geographical world was relatively circumscribed. Until 1828 he had never been to England or Ireland. In that year Sellar was commissioned to prepare a farming treatise which he regarded as a mark of honour. But he was nervous in writing such a work and felt a need to widen his experience, and was especially keen to visit southern breeders.[97] When he 'penetrated' the borders country, he found that there had been great changes, but 'My old Friends are nearly altogether failed or dead and gone. Their fine flocks are sadly dilapidated.'[98] He then toured through all the sheep-producing regions of northern England and visited the great manufacturing centres of Yorkshire. He was confident of expanding demand for Highland wool, but was keen especially to market his coarsest wool 'which is a great drug in the Clothing market'. He explored the technical details of new chemical treatments, notably for the old problem of stains in the wool; he believed that a good chemist could raise the value of the wool by 50 per cent; he was a constant advocate of prizes and incentives for innovators.[99]

Sellar was a firm believer in democratic education, favouring the establishment of London University, and he spiced his correspondence with references to Cicero, Cato, Caesar *et al.* To Sellar, education was the engine of progress and, in that spirit, he prepared his treatise of stock rearing. He reflected that:

> Such foolish prejudices exist against sheep-farming, that I have tried (without professing that intention) to shew, that it is the beneficial and necessary effect of the increased and increasing prosperity of the country. As the multitude of consumers, and, with them, the Consumption has increased, and does increase, so must increase the supply for the Consumption. If the country go on at the rate it has done, during the last century, every part of the highlands will assuredly be put under stock, although General Stewart and Ballindalloch may not live to see it, which I should much regret.[100]

Sellar laboured lengthily on his farming tract, which was not published until 1831.[101]

– NEW CONFLICTS, 1827–8 –

Sellar, though he complained loudly, responded to economic adversity by expanding his scale of operations. This indeed was the economic logic of Highland stock farming, and the ultimate cause of the elimination of small producers and inefficient landowners (for example, Stewart of Garth). Lands at Letterbeg in Farr were let to Sellar for ten years in 1825, at a rent of 3/- per sheep.[102] He also looked beyond the Sutherland estate. When Matthew Culley, the great sheep-farmer on the Balnagowan estate, threw in the towel, Sellar offered £950 p.a. for a ten-year lease of Invercassely. It would carry 6,000 sheep and represent a substantial extension of his operations. Culley believed that the sheepfarmers had 'built up our little fortunes' on 'the unnatural heights to which prices had been forced.' But now the good times were over and he held 'very desponding views as to the future' though he thought Sellar might make a profit.

Sellar, offering the highest bid and the best credentials,[103] said that he would bring in his own flocks and shepherds, 'and above all, a clever fox and Eagle hunter and dogs to lay on, for a concern where a full tythe is drawn by vermin among rocks 3,000 feet above the level of the sea.' He implored the landlord, and the outgoing tenant, whatever they did, not to divide up the great sheep-farm, 'as I am sure I can do more for the farm and the landlord than any three Lotters can'. Sellar said he had been in business for thirty years and had never been behind with his rent. During that time, he explained, he had never had a single transaction tested: 'Where I do not make a plain Straightforward bargain, I make none at all.' He had forgotten his dire conflicts in the previous decade.[104]

Eventually Sellar's negotiation with the Balnagowan estate was disappointed, partly over the question of sporting rights. Sellar made it clear that he would have no truck with special sporting rights on his land. He always believed that sheep alone should possess the land without interference from either inefficient small tenants or frivolous and socially inferior sportsmen. He wanted to place his capital and flocks with a

> Family of such great wealth and standing in the Country, [where] there was no chance of their selling their Game, and thereby exposing their tenants' flocks, to disturbance from Cocknies and other strangers, devoid of courtesy and kindly feeling, which we expect and will receive from our Landlord, and his friends shooting with his permission.

He simply could not stomach the idea of sportsmen buying rights which interfered with sheep-farming.

The needs of sport were beginning to challenge the near monopoly of the stock-farmers even in Sutherland. Just before Christmas 1827, Sellar was reported by a Sutherland estate official, Bantock, for shooting hares and partridge on his own Culmaily farm. This caused Sellar acute embarrassment, partly because Mackid's shadow hung over this issue. It was a sensitive issue since sporting rights marked the limits of social status and Sellar was also angry about the failure of the estate to suppress vermin.[105] His pride was hurt:

> As I am the most unobtrusive person possible, these things do not at all molest me; *unless* they have been the result of any attempt with the Noble Family to filch from me my Good Name.

He clearly suspected the antagonism of Gunn the new factor.[106] Sellar took the incident very badly and remarked to Loch:

> If you had been as nearly hanged, as I was [in 1816], by highland Cunning; and knew, as I do, how perfectly harmless and within the permission given, my conduct has been, and had made the same discoveries when I have done, in other things, you would feel, as I do, vigilant against such practices.

In the same breath, Sellar said how grateful all the tenantry of Sutherland were to the Stafford family. 'We are almost the sole exception from the General State of Bankruptcy existing over all the highlands' which he attributed to 'the bad times' as well as 'the truckling and short sighted management of the Lairds and Knock-dunders' whom they employed.[107]

Patrick Sellar's instincts always drove him in the direction of expansion and conflict. These propensities were again fully displayed, in 1828, in an unsavoury episode concerning the lands of a near neighbour, Polson of Easter Abercross. Sellar described Polson as a relic of past times, the only old-style middleman left in Sutherland. Polson occupied adjacent land in eastern Sutherland much coveted by Sellar, who sought ways of easing him out before his lease expired in 1828: 'His stock of both Sheep and Cattle are so starved that he is making nothing of the farm but the trouble of managing it.'[108] The main Sutherland factor, Gunn, depicted Polson's operations at Abercross as living proof of the squalid farming methods of thirty years before. The Polsons had occupied the land from time immemorial. He paid £60 rent; he had some arable acres and pasture, but 'not one yard of road or of enclosure or drain on the Farm.' Polson used twenty-two horses to work the land, carrying manure and peats in creels. Not a single cart was employed on his lands. Gunn predicted that when Sellar took over he would manage with one pair of horses, and 'the only outlay which this change will call for is about half a mile of Road from Strathfleet to the House.'[109] Sellar took over Easter Abercross in mid-1828.

The acquisition of Polson's lands, it transpired, was a mere prelude to a severe conflict about the Abercross boundaries between Sellar and his own brother-in-law Alexander Craig who had taken over Mackid's old farm at Kirkton ten years before. The original dispute concerned evidence of the traditional marches of the disputed lands between

Sellar and his wife's brother. Sellar said he wanted his wife spared the turmoil of the dispute, but this did not diminish the bitterness with which he contested the case.[110] The controversy soon ballooned into an extraordinarily vituperative dispute. The new factor, George Gunn, tried to arbitrate the question but Sellar immediately accused him of bad motives and worse manners. Gunn, exploded Sellar, had canvassed witnesses against him as to the disputed boundaries: 'he has contrived to make me feel his <u>Influence</u>.'[111] Craig and Sellar rejected each other's witnesses. Gunn suggested another witness who, Sellar claimed, was 'the only man in Morayshire with whom I have had a difference.' An arbitration meeting at Golspie was arranged and twenty witnesses were called, but Sellar walked out, breaking off all negotiations and appealing to James Loch to intervene.

Gunn was desperate to unload the responsibility of the Abercross dispute onto James Loch. Sellar found himself again employing the evidence of people who had been cleared from the same district. They knew the history of the land, and Sellar now needed their testimony: 'I am driven to the evidence of Removed tenants, who are mostly employed in the Herring fishing.'[112] The dispute was eventually settled to Sellar's apparently minor disadvantage. Thereafter, for two decades, Sellar simply refused to deal with George Gunn and this made estate relations exceedingly frosty.

In the middle of the Abercross dispute Sellar declared: 'If Lord and Lady Stafford have one tenant more industrious and improving, or one more dutiful and loyal to them – one who in twice the time has expended, of his own capital, one half of my outlays on such a place, I shall be silent.'[113] It all ended as another controversy in which Sellar made permanent enemies and alienated even his own family.

– THE REAY PURCHASE –

The pace of improvement on the Sutherland estate slackened in 1820s. Small removals were regularly executed, now with little fuss, even though factors were always nervous of publicity. For example, in 1828, George Gunn rearranged groups of tenantry in Kildonan and Loth at Rovie and Craigton, and was pleased to report that they had 'gone without a murmur . . . we have avoided a hue and cry which would have been occasioned by so many families being cast off without any shelter.' He was governed by an explicit estate policy that no one was to be disturbed unless alternative accommodation was provided.[114]

The Sutherland estate remained cautious about the promotion of emigration and did not at this time intervene in the outflows which continued at a modest level. Emigration was unpredictable both in its causes and its effects. Thus, in 1829, Sellar reported that American emigration agents had again been active in his district, and had persuaded forty families of Highlanders to depart, as well as three of Sellar's own shepherds, 'the latter very much against my interests and the men's, I believe.'[115] In 1829, Loch told Sellar that the estate had no wish or intention to facilitate emigration from Sutherland.[116]

In 1827 the Sutherland managers conducted a periodic reappraisal of estate policy and finances which demonstrated that the large sheepfarms were easily the most productive and remunerative parts of the estate. The idea of breaking up some of them for cattle producers was rejected because they yielded less rent and would damage adjacent sheep-farms by trespass and dogs. The economics of sheep-farming remained triumphant, and the dominance of the great tenant farmers, of whom Sellar was the most prominent and successful, was confirmed.[117]

The depression of prices created special opportunities for the Stafford family to increase its landholdings in the county as neighbouring owners fell victim to their own mismanagement and ill fortune. In fact, the Sutherland estate in the mid-1820s made preparations to expand its empire greatly by the acquisition of the Reay Country in the extreme northwest of the county. Sellar had noted in 1826 that Lord Reay had already left his house in Tongue, and Bighouse was also vacated, so that in the north of Sutherland 'there was not one person of common education within 30 to 50 miles of Bettyhill.' Among other things, it meant that no surgeon would serve the district unless a subsidy could be provided.[118] Lord Reay was already up to his eyes in debt to Lord Stafford, whose wife was enthusiastic for a takeover of his estate, which comprised about 400,000 acres. Eventually Reay quit his ancestral lands and the Sutherland estate swallowed it in a single giant's gulp, at the cost of £300,000. Reay went to live in the London suburbs. In 1829, the Stafford family's empire in the county had expanded to 1,122,500 acres, the greatest territorial aggregation in the country.[119] The acquisition confirmed the commitment of the Staffords to sheep-farming, and soon gave Sellar extra employment as consultant for the new estate.

Sellar was always generous with his professional advice. At the time of the Reay purchase he engaged in a warm debate with Joseph Mitchell, the road engineer, about the benefits of road construction in Reay where, said Sellar, peat bogs would never become wheat fields and where cattle would inevitably give way to sheep. Amid these exchanges Sellar painted a vivid picture of the old economy in Sutherland and Caithness:

> This country imported corn and meal in return for the small value of highland kyloes which formed its almost sole export. The people lay scattered in inaccessible straths and spots, among the mountains; where they lived in family with their piggs and kyloes, in turf cabins of the most miserable description; spoke Gaelic only, and spent their time, chiefly, in winter converting potatoes and a little oatmeal into this manure; and in summer converting this manure again into potatoes. Thus, they had gone on, with little change, father to son, excepting what evil was introduced by illicit distillation, and making a little or no export from the country beyond a few lean kyloes, which paid the rent, and the price of oatmeal imported. But about this time the country was begun to be opened up by the parliamentary roads.

The new roads had certainly opened up trade to the north. 'Now the country exports from a barren district 80,000 fleeces and 20,000 cheviots, several cargoes of grain for 3 highland distilleries and still many droves of cattle plus 30 to 40,000 barrels of fish as well as cod and ling.'

Sellar agreed that many of the people had been brought by compulsion to the coast while others came willingly. In his pungent fashion he characterised the impact of the great changes on the people of the estate. Now:

> The piggs and cattle are treated to a separate table. The dunghill is turned to the outside of the house. The tartan tatters have given place to the produce of Huddersfield, Manchester, Glasgow and Paisley. The Gaelic to English; and few young persons are to be found who cannot read and write. And here come the proud export of a poor country – "Men and Steel" – of these young persons, so educated, there is begun an annual voluntary emigration to every part of the Empire of a set of hardy spirited young fellows possessed of industry and daring, to maintain their own and their country's interest wherever fortune may set them down. If the same Tide begin to run from every shore by the roads . . . efforts will follow.

The Empire was the ultimate strength of the country 'and by whose commerce it is chiefly enriched.'[120] Sellar, as ever, was the apostle of economic transformation.

CHAPTER 14

Sellar in his Prime

By 1830, Patrick Sellar was at the peak of his career as a Highland sheep-farmer. He possessed substantial assets in both Moray and Sutherland and was 'by far the greatest Stock Farmer in the Country . . . Mr Sellar's stock is well known all over the North of England, Yorkshire, and Wales.'[1] Sellar commanded the technical and commercial knowledge of the industry in which he had been manifestly successful. He was, consequently, much sought after for advice.

Sellar grazed 10,000 sheep in vast flocks across the lands in Sutherland once employed by a handful of tacksmen and hundreds of sub-tenants with their cattle. He was a large employer in eastern Sutherland. He was wealthy, and still ambitious to extend his lands and raise his social status. He had become indispensable as the largest source of rental income in the great northern empire of the Sutherland family. He had weathered the times of low prices by introducing economies which made him extraordinarily efficient and competitive. His farms represented the finest example of the economies of scale to be derived from the new uses of Highland territory.

Sellar's relations with his landlord were cordial, if not intimate. Lord Stafford was raised to the Sutherland dukedom in 1833. His family was always wary of Sellar's heavy-handed opinions and his clumsy responses. During the 1830s, the estates came into the hands of the second Duke of Sutherland who was never fully convinced that his estate was properly disposed as huge sheep-farms. The legacy of the clearances hung upon the Sutherland family, and this affected its attitude to Sellar who was a living reminder of those events.

At several moments in this decade, the entire conceptual basis of the clearances was held up for inspection and reconsideration. These exercises were strictly for internal purposes only. All the assumptions about the clearances were questioned. The Sellar philosophy, of maximum rationalisation, faced several challenges in an intermittent debate about the revealed consequences of the great Sutherland removals. Sellar, of course, regarded the entire question as settled and inviolable. Having led the revolution which had transformed the Highlands, Sellar, in the 1830s, was caused to defend that revolution.

– SELLAR AND THE POLISH COUNT –

Sellar's agricultural influence extended in some remarkable directions. In 1830, for instance, he was visited in Sutherland by Count Strzelecki, the Polish exile and traveller. Strzelecki possessed a small private income and a passion for geology, mineralogy and languages. He was also intensely interested in the pastoral agriculture of his homelands of Silesia and Poznan, where he was connected with major improvement projects. Strzelecki sought expert advice on the 'correct management of sheep, pastures and shepherds', in order to convey best practice to Poland. He was also involved in debates over the social consequences and ethics of such improvement in Poland.[2]

Strzelecki came to hear of Sellar whom he immediately adopted as his model of pastoral improvement. He toured the north of Scotland in 1830, visiting Tongue and the great Strathnaver sheep farm as well as Sellar's east coast operations. Strathnaver reminded Strzelecki irresistibly of Silesia. Pastoral innovations in the two places were following similar objectives. The 'great lands' were being divided into winter and summer runs for the flocks, the sheep being sorted into their various categories by age, sex and condition for breeding or for the market. Sellar had taken these principles to their highest refinement. As Strzelecki observed:

> I witnessed at Morvich, of every ram and ewe, before being put in a proper herding together, being handled and well examined by Mr Sellar himself, who weighed the ewes in his hands, noticed their general size and proportions, then particularly examined the head, neck, breast, shoulder, rib, back and tail, looked at the quality of the wool, and decided upon the ram, under the number by which he was designated and booked, which should be most noticed to counteract the defect found, or still further to ennoble the blood of the future progeny.

This was a glimpse of Sellar, the practical farmer, prepared to handle and evaluate each sheep in his huge flock. He was equally rigorous with the sorting of his lambs at spleening time.[3] Sellar had an earthy respect for all aspects of his business.

The results of Sellar's scientific breeding methods, reported by Strzelecki, were 'immense'. He measured this by the fact that the original cheviot fleece from Roxburgh had yielded two and a half to three and a half pounds of wool, but in Sutherland the same animal now produced four to five pounds. Within two decades, the average yield in mutton had increased from between twelve pounds and eighteen pounds to more than twenty pounds. According to Strzelecki, Sellar had almost doubled the size of the cheviot fleece while simultaneously halving the number of shepherds. This was a precise measure of Sellar's extraordinary efficiency, of the leap in productivity attaching to his Highland revolution in pastoral management. It explained his successful survival and expansion through the long years of tumbling sheep prices. His scientific methods 'ennobled' the sheep stock under a superb regime of pasture management.

Strzelecki eventually travelled to Australia where he became a well-known explorer and in 1840 ascended and named Mount Kosciusko, the highest mountain of the southern continent. He befriended some of the great colonial graziers, including the Macarthur family at Tumut, New South Wales.[4] Strzelecki was highly critical of colonial flock management, which produced very poor quality sheep, and too little wool per animal from too many sheep. He observed that nine million sheep were grazed on the great inland tracts of New South Wales but were badly managed and bred with total ignorance of best practice. He took pains to recall his observations in the Scottish Highlands a decade before. The pastoralists needed a 'true system of breeding and rearing', that is the 'assortment, division, infusion of the best blood, and what may be termed rotation of pasture ground'. The colonial graziers and shepherds were deficient in expertise and education. Here Strzelecki drew on his experience on his estate at Wartenberg in Silesia, and in Scotland:

> None can be more strongly recommended to the imitation of the Australian wool-growers, than the farm of Patrick Sellar Esq. in the County of Sutherland (Scotland). From its extensive flock (10,000 sheep), and the range of the run, the farm is able to exhibit the best principles in the management both of the flock and food.

Strzelecki, extolling Sellar further, observed that his fleeces and carcasses were managed with great care. The annual increase in sheep numbers was a secondary consideration: 'while the range for pasture is locked up, not so much as affording the means of *numerically extending the flock*, as of *raising the valuable qualities higher and higher.*'[5] Sellar, he said, was the definitive model for sheep-farming:

> Such a splendid success, combining as it does, all the most vital conditions of pastoral industry, is likely to answer best of all the exigencies of an Australian grazier.

Strzelecki rhapsodised, finally, on the social and aristocratic system which had combined with men such as Sellar to produce such a scientific and progressive outcome:

> The highest nobility lead the way to a new national glory – the glory of the perfection of agriculture! The Dukes of Richmond, Rutland, Portland, Buccleugh, and Sutherland . . . are at the head of the movement, and identifying themselves with that noble profession *'upon which the welfare and development of the whole human species, the richness of states, and all commerce depends'.*

This paean of praise might well have been written by Sellar himself and presented the relationship between aristocracy and enterprise in a manner which would have given pause to the Duke of Sutherland.

The oddity of Strzelecki's connection with Sellar was later remarked on by H. M. E. Heney:

> The recommendation of Patrick Sellar comes as a surprise to those who regarded Strzelecki as a humanitarian, since Sellar left in his own country an unenviable reputation for the cruelty with which he evicted crofters and enclosed more land for grazing. But perhaps it was only his agriculture, not his treatment of human beings which was discussed.[6]

Another irony was that the introduction of sheep-farming in Australia wreaked even more savage cost upon the host society than the clearances in Scotland itself. It was perpetrated by immigrants, prominent among them many from the Scottish Highlands, graziers and shepherds alike.[7]

– SELLAR'S FARM REPORT, 1831 –

At home, Sellar exerted his agricultural influence locally in Sutherland. But he also cultivated wide connections in the wool trade as far south as Yorkshire and East Anglia. The new *cadre* of sheep-farmers, though small in number, were not cohesive. The typical member of this class tended to behave like the atomistic unit in the economist's fictional world of perfect competition, as *homo economicus*. Sellar himself tried to encourage a greater sense of camaraderie through the local Farmers Clubs, designed to disseminate technical knowledge and control the depredations of dogs and crofters on the sheep stock. He was a passionate advocate of Highland sheep-farming, and believed that collective improvement was good for the individual producer as well as the nation at large. Sellar mainly persuaded by the excellence of his example, which was most impressive, but in 1829–30 he was given an opportunity to spread his technical mastery to a wider audience, through the commission of the so-called 'Steam Intellect Society', that is the Society for the Diffusion of Useful Knowledge.

Sellar was invited to prepare a *Farm Report* for the *Library of Useful Knowledge,* almost certainly at the instigation of James Loch, who was closely associated with Henry Brougham in the movement for the extension of education and in the eventual formation of London University.[8] Sellar's paper was published in 1831, and required him to explain in detail, for the benefit of fellow farmers, his operations on his farms in Sutherland. It was a characteristic contribution to the mutual education system of the day, and was an opportunity which Sellar seized. It allowed him to describe his methods and his extraordinary efficiency. Indirectly, it was also a precise justification for all the turmoil associated with the removals with which he was indelibly associated. Sellar's *Report* was written in crisp and untypically cool tones, with remarkably little of his usual overblown rhetoric. In twenty pages he was able to explain his life's work employing some colourful Scotticisms to which his editor in London took exception. Loch rose to Sellar's defence, and said that they were 'excellent sheep breeding terms and well understood as far south as Peterborough and Chester at the least.' Indeed Loch, a Scot himself, rejected the very idea that there existed 'any single criterion being pure English', saying that Sellar was a 'scholar and a gentleman'.[9]

The *Farm Report* was Sellar's considered public answer to his critics, his personal balance sheet of the ovine revolution in the Highlands. He presented the new *status quo*, the results of the great changes as seen from his own farm office. It was his accounting of the productivity gains then being reaped in the north, the classic case for radical change in terms of a more efficient use of scarce resources. Arraigned against it, of course, was the assertion, then and since, that the changes had been unnecessary, accomplished with brutal haste and achieved against the interests of the people of the region. Sellar had first eliminated the people and then, in his relentless search for further economy he had dispensed with half his shepherds. He was never less than efficient.

Sellar's account began with the geology and geography of the region which established that Sutherland was intrinsically a pastoral country with strictly limited adaptability to tillage. In the south-east Sellar's two farms of Culmaily and Morvich had carved out new tillage acres from 'moor, moss and pasture', helped by favourable leases and capital loans from the Stafford family. Sellar described his *modus operandi* as a series of 'numerous little experiments' which had brought him to ultimate perfection in farm management. It had allowed him to get through difficult times. As he put it: 'Farmers' books are not such agreeable companions now, as they were before the battle of Water-loo.' He, of course, had embarked on his Sutherland operations at the zenith of wool prices. He left the image of a man browsing agricultural magazines while the straths were decanted of their people.

At the centre of his system was the interdependence of his arable and pasture farms. Sellar's pastoral operations required the support of the tillage farms. This indeed was the imperative which, at the end of the day, determined that small occupiers in the Highlands were incompatible with sheep-farming, not merely because their dogs harassed the sheep, but because their lower pastures were necessary for the seasonal grazing and breeding arrangements.

Sellar's system was simple. The great sheep flocks were bred and reared in Strathnaver. The lowland pasturage at Morvich was used for the 'refuge of the weak end of his ewe stock' and for the purposes of preparing his sale ewes for market. Culmaily was used for the weaker wether stock. They were centres which sorted the sheep for breeding and dispatch to the ewe flocks in Strathnaver, and also for the annual markets. Hence, the system hinged on a careful internal division of function.

The tillage farms at Morvich and Culmaily were divided into twenty-one enclosures, and were fenced by Sellar to provide a sequence of special rotation regimes. He grew potatoes only for the local consumption of his employees. He operated several mills, including a water-powered threshing mill. He used six pairs of horses and a grieve, together with six ploughmen and a spadesman. Another bailiff super-intended the millwright, as well as sixteen women in two threshing mills. Sellar employed between fourteen and twenty boys and girls in cleaning green crops. At harvest he used ten bandwins (groups of reapers), constituting sixty to sixty-six workers. The grieve and plough-men, married men with houses and gardens, were paid £10 per annum and received also sixteen cwt of oatmeal, three cartloads of potatoes and some English coals. Sellar was thus a very large local employer, with about ten adult workers, thirty-five youths, and sixty to eighty seasonal workers too. He employed eight additional families on the fringe of the arable farm, people who held small plots and offered day labour. These were probably people removed from the interior to make way for Sellar's sheep. Sellar offered a vivid and precise account of the conversion of an inland peasantry, where they were lucky, into a coastal proletariat.

Sellar's account also provided a rare sense of the texture of life on a Highland improvement farm. The workday in winter began, with the help of lamplight, at 8 a.m. and finished at 4 p.m. In high summer, under the eye of the grieve, the workers began at 4 or 5 a.m. and continued, with breaks, until 8 p.m. Sellar warmed to his task as he described his rotations, using attractive turns of phrase: 'At the time of sowing green crops in Sutherland, the dusk or twilight of the evening glides into that of the morning, without passing into night.' He was a strong advocate of the 'Scotch farmer', and the use of drill husbandry for the cultivation of turnips. Much of his tillage was devoted to new crops, swedes and mangel-wurzels for his stock, as well as barley for the newly legalised distillers on the east coast.

In one of few references to the small tenantry, and to the people who had been dislodged from the interior, Sellar noted that he commonly received cattle 'from the people who are settled round the shores of Sutherland, in small plots of land, for the prosecution of the herring fishing'. They had two or three cows each and sold them at nine months to the tillage farmers, to be fed further for the southern markets. Sellar took 160 to 180 of them in April and grazed them on his '*superabundance* of deer hair', and then on to Morvich or Culmaily through the following winter in preparation for sale to the south. These were Norland kyloes crossed with the Dunrobin breed, which had been provided to improve stock by the Marquis of Stafford. But, for Sellar, there had been too little selective breeding and the small tenants' cattle were poor specimens because they possessed too much inferior Caithness blood.

The centrepiece of Sellar's farming consisted of his sheep flocks, which occupied with others nine-tenths of the county and were the only appropriate animals for the territory. Moreover, sheep-farming was only feasible if the sheep had full access to all places of refuge. They required sheltered zones without which stock losses became impossibly high and their quality sank below marketable acceptability.[10] Sellar used cheviots which had been naturalised from the highest districts in England. Employing almost Darwinian language, Sellar enthused about the breeding of the best survivors of his flocks, having obtained his basic stock from Messrs Robins and Belford, Samuston and Philogar in Roxburghshire. He had followed in the pioneering footsteps of the 'spirited and intelligent border farmers' in the days of the 1790s. Since then there had been a revolution in yields of the sort that had so impressed Strzelecki.[11] In rough terms there was an almost 50 per cent increase in yields in thirty years, though this did not take account of the fall in prices, which was partly caused by the very fact of improved yields. The sheep had become bigger and better in every dimension except price.

Sellar produced his sheep for markets in Leeds, Manchester and Liverpool. His shepherds were recruited in the south, mainly young men, married and from the eastern border region. He had settled them in cottages on wages considerably higher than the best plough-men. The shepherds were the aristocrats of the new labour force, the key personnel of a high-technology industry. They were also frontiers-men: 'If a shepherd does his duty, he must exercise a deal of con-sideration, and undergo much hardship.' In return, the shepherd received a cottage and garden, thirteen bolls of meal, grass for three cows and a pony, as well as the profit from seventy cheviot sheep kept among his master's sheep. All this was in addition to wages. It was surprising that the modern employer used quasi-feudal payments in kind, though they were no doubt an effective incentive to the hiree. As Sellar observed, the shepherds entered 'something like a partnership', which 'tacitly exists between master and servant', giving them a clear interest in the flocks. Sellar employed eleven married shepherds and eight younger men.

Sellar rotated his flocks through his nine 'herdings' in Strathnaver (see map); he stimulated his shepherds with competitions and prizes, and he synchronised his pastoral and tillage operations for maximum effect. He still endured a 7 per cent loss among his lambs, mainly through the braxy (an internal inflammation leading to death). His great belief was scientific breeding and he regarded the apathy of his fellow stock masters on the subject as incredible. Selective breeding made all the commercial difference in his own operations.[12] The well-bred Cheviot was the only answer, selected from the elite of each flock.

The great Highland farmers, he pointed out, met at the 'great animal market' in Inverness in the second week of July, where they converged with the wool staplers and sheep buyers from the south of Scotland and Yorkshire. At the market, everything ultimately de-pended on 'the character held in the market by the owner and his goods'. Sellar noted how the farmers lingered on after the end of business. They lived in beautiful but solitary places, so when 'congregated with the brethren of their profession, under agreeable circumstances, can seldom be induced to separate before the conclusion of the week.'[13] The Inverness market revealed a fleeting glimpse of Sellar in 1830: Loch advised his factor Gunn to avoid drinking claret at the time of the market, and Gunn explained that Sellar had won ten guineas for his prize tups, and had 'treated the company to a dozen Claret', and told Loch that the episode was harmless.[14]

Sellar was a man of precision:

> When a farmer's accounts betray confusion or sloth, his servants become indifferent to their duty; faithful servants quit, worse take their places, and pillage begins. A rogue is shy to engage with a master who pays punctually and liberally, with a professed intention fearlessly to send the thief to justice.

This was Sellar in tendentious mode.

He also described the community about him, noting that the censuses proved that the population was 'more dense than ever existed in any former period of time'. There were no tithes, poor rates, drunkards or beggars. All he would concede was that the district was disfigured by the presence of a few squalid men from the south, especially gypsies. Otherwise, the common people looked after each other; they were 'in a sense *their mutual* but sole dependence', saving each other from the shame of beggary. 'By reciprocal good offices, by joint industry, sobriety and prudence, they get on wonderfully.' It was a Christian and humane community. The cottars lived on oatmeal, porridge, potatoes, bread and milk, some fish and a little pork. Their only luxury was tobacco, which Sellar believed was necessary in the northern climate. The people were gaining more comforts but were essentially 'a simple, industrious and virtuous class of men'.[15]

Sellar's *Farm Report* was his apotheosis as a stock farmer, a man at the top of his profession, displaying his technical mastery. Sellar made the case that sheep-farming was fundamentally highly capitalistic, and had required all the land available to see him through the difficult years of the 1820s. This was the territorial imperative of sheep-farming. Though Sellar's account was, in its nature, an exercise in self-congratulation, his usual dogmas were kept well under leash. It was a restrained performance in which was located the fundamental proposition that the sheep clearances had been a great boon to the nation and to all those who followed the logic of economic rationality.

– INVESTIGATING REAY –

Soon after Sellar had produced his *Farm Report* in 1831, he was commissioned by James Loch to undertake an internal review of the newly acquired territory of the Sutherland family in the Reay Country. This was a measure of Loch's respect for Sellar's professional expertise. It was a confidential exercise in which Sellar gave full rein to the most robust lines of his thinking on the entire question of Highland improvement and the consequences of the clearances. It was also an important moment in the internal dialogue on the Sutherland estate, which had continued through all the years of the removals. The estate debate was marked by a seriousness of discussion and a respect for process and reason, which always contrasted with the cacophony of abuse which greeted the measures as they had been introduced into the Highlands. Sellar's report on Reay became the basis for a vital discourse on the past and present of the Sutherland plan. Sellar predictably offered the most rigorous case for further radical change.

The purchase of the Reay Country by Lord Stafford in 1829 was a classic transaction by an English aristocrat made rich by the profits of the industrial revolution, buying out an incompetent and spendthrift Highland family unable to cope with the economic pressures of the times. In 1832, after the purchase, Lady Stafford dined with Lord Reay and reported: 'I think he looks much older than when I saw him last but not however from any regrets about Tongue [his former seat in Reay], of which I suspect he was heartily tired and disgusted.' She remarked that Reay had bought a villa in Ealing, which had been furnished by Soames the architect – an excellent house, with thirty acres of land, for £5,000. Reay was a shade deaf, but otherwise well and happy. And thus was a Highland *grandee* brought to suburbia.[16]

The Reay Country, though vast and mostly already cleared, had not been properly arranged according to the lights of Highland improvement. Its 'backward tenantry' had not experienced the advantages of development as instituted in the main Sutherland estate. Thus the Reay Country presented a parallel case to juxtapose with the Sutherland policies, for the past and the future. It prompted a full reconsideration of all the original propositions which had fuelled the Sutherland policies. Sellar's involvement invested the discussion with a special personal and intellectual edge.

Loch asked Sellar to conduct the investigation in the first week of January 1831. Sellar then toured the entire region, made his own map, identified the approximate geology of the region and reported back in mid-May.[17] The manner in which he approached the task typified his focused energy. His subsequent report demonstrated the fierceness of his opinions and assumptions in starker form than any of his published views. He also displayed his breadth of knowledge, for example invoking *Travels in Turkey* to draw a favourite lesson that even the most despotic governments could not extract wealth 'from the dry husks of misgoverned poverty'.

Sellar's report on the Reay Country was, not surprisingly, highly critical. He announced his finding immediately, and then argued it in rich detail:

> I find in the Reay Country, the pastures better, [a] good part of the Tillage land of finer staple, and the fish of higher quality and more abundant, than in this part of Sutherland [Strathnaver?]; yet the stock inferior, the Rents Lower, and the . . . people in comparative indigence.

Not a single tenant was truly thriving. They all lacked skill in the use of the land and possessed little or no capital. Consequently the country did not realise its potential, 'for exportation'. The prevailing tillage system was 'inconvenient' and the tools were 'miserable'. The farm roads were very poor. The people were reduced 'to the condition of beasts of burden'. Sellar calculated that forty families in Durness produced less value that one man and a pair of horses could achieve. Moreover, that man with a pair of horses would be

> better fed, and better lodged, more quietly wrought, and more highly remunerated; because by substituting skill and [tools?], and the division of labour, in the place of brute force, irregularly employed, and misapplied to the most absurd purposes, he produces a great surplus to enrich himself, the landlord, and the Country of which he is subject.

Sellar, of course, was engaged in an exercise ultimately designed to prove that the clearance and resettlement system had been a great boon to humanity. His 'agreeable subject of Enquiry' was to raise up the people of Reay to the level of the rest of Sutherland.

The common people of Sutherland now understood the necessity of change and there had been a moral improvement, 'which must incline the minds of the tenantry there, to yield themselves more readily, up to his Lordship's disposal, and must tend to facilitate your progress.' This encapsulated the essence of Sellar's approach. It was progress induced from above, with the obeisance of the people to the needs of the landlord and the nation.

In the Reay Country the landlord had already 'thoroughly ejected the people from the sheep walks, and settled them along the Shores of the Estate'. Consequently the sheepwalks simply needed to be better managed to 'produce the greatest value of Sheep and Wool.' The main task was to 'convert the people from the bad and unprofitable tillage' on which they currently depended, towards 'scientific and successful prosecution of the fisheries'. Here he stressed that the change must be 'prudent and gradual', but it meant further pressure upon the people to force them to the ocean. Sheep and fish were the two mainstays of the country, and Sellar could not contain his rhetoric on the subject:

> The words 'Kelp' and 'Cattle' rise up in Judgment before me, for my contempt of them, in discussing the management of the highland estate . . . [and it is] *barbarous*, to compel the poor creatures to burn the manure which providence has given for their Ground.

Kelp (the harvesting of seaweed for southern glass and soap manufacture) kept the people 'in abject poverty from Generation to Generation'. (Kelp was also, from the effects of further industrialisation in the chemical industry, in terminal decline.) Cattle production was not profitable, having been destroyed by the long sagging of prices which had relegated the small farmers to total poverty.[18] As Sellar put it, recent prices would not 'recompense for the milk used in bringing up the calf!' The kyloe trade was about to expire; the only hope was for the introduction of improved short-horned cattle for the Smithfield market, a specialised development beyond the reach of small Highland farmers.

Sellar's analysis, of course, reinforced the case for sheep and fishing in Reay, and elsewhere. The fishing was impeded by the indolence of the local curers in Reay. As for sheep, he thought the potential was irresistible, and he joked that his enthusiasm would get him dubbed 'Prosperity Sellar'. Dunlop and Scobie, the current occupiers of a farm at Durness, produced 'the very worst and lowest priced sheep in the country'. Their stock was badly housed, shepherded and equally badly maintained, drained and rotated. If Sellar took it over, 'I should top the market'. He was ultra-critical of the incompetence of the current stock-farmers and consequently advocated a comprehensive reorganisation. This would entail the amalgamation of the sheep-farms and a 33 per cent increase of rents. Typically, he volunteered to take on the lands himself, if no one else would accept such 'modest' terms. In this recommendation, Sellar understood nothing of the confusion of such self-interested advice which became entangled with his role as impartial professional adviser. He simply applied his own personal standard to the task. Unabashedly, he advocated another clearance, in this case the removal of the first wave of sheep-farmers, whose performance was under par, to make way for Sellar himself who could reap much better returns.

As for the fishing, Sellar observed that the mouth of the Polla River was 'quite Choked up with herrings'. It was, however, remote from the main fishing centres, and he suggested that Lord Stafford take the lead in the operations. This was predictably vetoed by James Loch who thought the landlord's role should be strictly limited to the bare infrastructure, sufficient to encourage genuine entrepreneurial curers. Loch also rejected Sellar's idea that Tongue House be retained for the Staffords' residence. Sellar enthused about the prospect of a new village in the same vicinity:

> In such a place as Tongue – the smile of Comfort – the neatness simplicity and modesty in the operations of man, bring to the foreground, the savage Grandeur of nature, and produce a scene, to my mind of singular beauty.

Lord Stafford found this an 'entertaining passage in Sellar's report'. In other parts of Reay, Sellar was critical of the presence of any people whatsoever, it being too stormy and remote for fishing. After twenty years, little progress had been made at Annandale and the rents were far less than the value of the land; the people were in greater poverty than ever.

Sellar believed that the newly acquired territory of Reay could easily, under proper management, carry several thousand more sheep and yield substantially more rent. This would require the removal of many small tenantry, which itself would reduce the costs of 'factorage'. He realised the sensitivity of this recommendation and admitted, 'I feel very sorry to report the unpleasant fact, but I cannot change the nature of truth.' He added:

> But, if I be correct, then, whatever my Lord and Lady's good feelings may prompt during their time, and whatever their immediate successor in his time, yet, in the nature of things, it can scarcely continue to be, that, besides trouble, deterioration of Ground, and expense of different Sort, 50 p. cent of the annual value of the Ground should continue to be sacrificed, on purpose to keep a mass of population from Generation to Generation in a state of beggary.

This was another Sellarian imperative with which he confronted his landlord and, within its terms, constituted the essence of the Highland problem as he saw it. The conspicuous omission from Sellar's implicit equation was the volition of the people. Sellar's assumptions simply denied them control or influence over their own destiny. He undoubtedly believed that it would be kinder to remove the people; the territory would also be much more profitable.

At Armadale, the small tenants were better off, but it would be a mistake to give them more hill ground for their cattle because kyloes did not pay. At Portskerra, however, he said, 'do not I beseech you leave them in the middle of the sheep, to marr a fine Concern, without doing any Good to themselves or to the proprietor.'

Sellar, as wordy as ever, offered his personal manifesto for which his commission had given licence:

> I shall now State Shortly what I have to say with respect to the Gradual abstraction of the people from the imperfect and unremunerating tillage, on which they at present depend, to the great field of the fishing for their subsistence. No man who has, during the last 30 years attended to the progress of civilization, must be satisfied; that, in spite of every prejudice, the rise of proper Roads, tools, and other Conveniences, and the division of labour gradually throw their Ground into the Shape of fields to be wrought by a wise rotation; in a word, into tillage farms, where one man and pair shall create the value produced by 30 Savages with their peat spades and carscrombs; and, in like manner, if Ground be unsuited for tillage, it is wrested from the possession of 50 ignorant persons, who keep upon it, God's plants in a state of decay, and His creatures in the most abject and pitiable state of misery; and it is put into the possession of one man; who, if he mean to pay his increased rent, must, and he will guide the whole, to health, happiness and prosperity – the former rude occupants draining together into villages, and they and their descendants prosecuting those branches of industry, for which this particular district or country where they happen to be situated, is best adapted.

This was Sellar's recurrent rationale of the clearances, in typically forceful form and language. He regularly used expressions such as, 'savages', 'rude occupants', 'ignorant persons' to describe the people of the Highlands. Even his most sympathetic readers shuddered from such terminology. Yet he gave the whole project of removal and improvement a mystical quality too:

> Thus, under the Great fountain of Goodness and benevolence, is the march of mankind in a well regulated country. Where tyranny, corruption, and dishonest practice, bad laws, ignorance, prejudice retard this march, all classes suffer the poverty and misery due to their sins, in diminished Rent Rolls, diminished comforts, famine, disease, and death. Where liberty, honour, justice, education, liberal Landlords [which Loch annotated and added 'fine soil, fair climate etc']. And a manly people advance the natural order of things, all parties are rewarded with health, cheerfulness and opulence.

Sellar invoked the inexorable forces of 'Improvement' for this great Enlightenment project, all for the furtherance of human civilisation. It was a gospel, the logic of which had sanctioned and ordained the clearances, and Sellar merely articulated its truth and beauty. It required the destruction of the last vestiges of the old feudal world, the liquidation of the old society.

Sellar, as we have seen, was fond of painting vivid pictures of the old world before the resettlement schemes had worked their benevolent effect. For example, the people of Golspie were now settled in the thriving village in beautiful and well regulated farms. Before the removals, they had starved in the interior and their 'harvest-clipped sheep, hobbled ponies and starved cattle would have melted a heart of stone'. He recollected how the previous factor, Falconer, who had resigned in 1810, had received famished people at the close in front of his house which 'was choke full of applicants':

> He turned to me, with a face as red as that of a Turkey cock just jilted by his mate, and exclaimed, 'It is sic a country this Sutherland, that my airn grows age could, Mr Sellar, before I can get a chap on it.' Now Sutherland exports food and clothing to other Countries; and the factor had nothing to do with us, except to receive our rents, on the <u>Rent day</u>, twice a year.

Where to set a new village was no more possible to say 'than it can be foretold on what special Bush in a Garden, a swarm of Bees are to settle', but the landlord could set a harbour going and to such a place

> people might Gradually withdraw themselves from their Lotts. Above all, keep the 'Schoolmaster and his primer' among them the only cure for the prejudice and ignorance which Checks emigration, and for that implicit obedience to the passions which, inducing, among the highlanders, the Irish, the illiterate manufacturers all barbarians professing Christianity, premature and Reckless marriages, reduce the mass of the people, to abject poverty, by the increase of their numbers beyond the means of subsistence.

Sellar's most important recommendation in his report on Reay was to extend the clearance system further towards its logical culmination, though he now employed the word 'gradual' more often. He told James Loch and the Staffords that more sheep and fewer people constituted an imperative. The people should now be restricted to places exclusively devoted to fishing.

Sellar's remarkable document of 1831, provocative, intelligent, technical, colourful and highly rhetorical, was the signal for a fundamental debate in the ranks of the Sutherland managers about the past, present and future of the management system which had caused controversy outside the estate since its inception in the first decade of the century. It required a *post-mortem* on the clearances, and defined Sellar's own views in relation to those of his peers.

– SELLAR OPPOSED –

James Loch's response to Sellar's report demonstrated how far his opinion now diverged from Sellar's, which had only hardened in the past twenty years. There followed a robust exchange of differences. Thus Loch agreed that kelp was no longer of any use except for manure. But the idea that kyloes could be eliminated was unpalatable. The small tenantry needed their cattle: 'The day is yet far off before they can rely entirely upon the resources of the Ocean for their only means of support.' Fishing could not employ the people throughout the year, and the herring was, in any case, too capricious a creature on which to depend solely. Just as important was Loch's insistence that the sheep-farms were already too large. Here he admitted that the removals had produced poor social consequences: it was vital 'to keep up that gradation of ranks, so necessary in all countries, and which perhaps in Sutherland prevails too little.' He was prepared to say, in contrast to Sellar, that the poor condition of the common people (in Farr and Strathy, in particular) was related to problems of distance, too many sub-tenants, poor roads, and too little land for either tillage or grazing. Poverty was not simply a measure of indolence and ignorance.

Loch therefore opposed Sellar's basic premises. Loch in 1831 was prepared to concede privately that large-scale sheep-farming had gone too far and that the small tenants needed more land and grazing. Entrepreneurs had not come forward to employ them. The social consequences had not been good:

> Mere profit upon a small scale can never be the sole object with any landlord, and still less with a person in the Marquis of Stafford's situation than with a lesser Proprietor, and a further reason in this case operates from this being a property lately acquired by him where none of that attachment can exist to restore the good feeling, which such a change even when continued in the kindest manner, and upon the most benevolent and liberal principles must for a time interrupt.

Loch had no appetite for further removals. In Moray, he pointed out, it had taken a hundred years to create fishing communities. The 'strict rules of Political Economy' could not be applied to 'such people as our Lotters', because 'there is something in the nature of man that attaches him to the improvement of land though you may prove it to him over and over again to demonstrate that he is doing so at a great loss of capital and expenditure of time.' Here too, Loch observed, even on the east coast, the crofts were still more important than the fishing, 'which was the course we theorists to that extent had chalked out for them'.

The exercise of internal estate criticism, prompted by the Reay acquisition, produced the fundamental concession from Loch, though not from Sellar, that one of the key requirements of the system had failed. The resettlement facilities had not prospered according to the original design. This was a defining moment in the debate. Sellar continued to believe that removals were the answer; a full programme of evacuation was in everyone's best interest. James Loch had retreated, and now gave most emphasis to the practical and political obstacles to such radical ideas.

Loch did not depend solely on Sellar's advice. He had also commissioned Robert Horsburgh, a local factor, to survey Reay, Farr and Assynt. Horsburgh confirmed that the small tenantry (he omitted mention of the squatters) had been relocated by the previous owner, on the coast on plots of two to three acres, and were living reasonably well. He recommended an expansion of grazing for their animals which could be achieved without damage to the sheep-farms. He also set himself diametrically against Sellar's philosophy. Similarly on the other side of the estate Gunn, the local factor (whose disagreements with Sellar were well-known) also said that the small tenantry were too restricted in their landholding. There had developed a clear rift between Sellar, the sheep-farmer, and the new generation of factors on the estate. Gunn observed that the people had no access to shielings, noting:

> I am aware that the whole body of Shepherds will combat this opinion, as high and low they have an abhorrence of the neighbourhood of small tenants, and it is of no use to ask them for advice.

The target of this remark was obviously Sellar. But Gunn had asked several of the great sheep-farmers, who occupied the lion's share of the county, to point out places suitable for grazing for the small tenants: 'They reported that there was not one spot they could recommend.' Yet when Gunn eventually carved out an extent of grazing for the small tenantry there was no complaint, and it became 'of infinite advantage to the people of Loth and Clyne who were before wretchedly ill off and while it is such an accommodation to them, Lord Stafford received a grass-mail of £70 instead of £40 the former rent of it.' He advised the extension of grazing to the small tenants of Lairg and Rogart. Gunn had, indeed, uttered a heresy, at least as far as Sellar was concerned, and implied a minor but authentic unwinding of some of the original removal policy.

It is clear that there had been a significant turn in the direction of policy. Sellar may have been a great success as a sheep-farmer, but his technical excellence failed to convince his peers that the thinking and policy of clearance, which had installed him in Strathnaver, should be taken to its logical conclusion. It might even be reversed.

– SELLAR'S RETORT –

The debate continued. Loch responded to Sellar's original report, and then Sellar rejoined in typically robust and astringent style. In June 1832, he sent Loch another fifteen pages of decisive opinion. He began in high philosophical mode:

> Truth is defined, by a single line, drawn thro the Bounds of Space. Every other line is Error. How likely, that both of us shall miss the first, and stumble into the second, in many particulars; and, how careful and dispassionate the search should be, in questions, involving, like the present, the well-being of tens of thousands of God's creatures, confined by the Creator, to the Guidance of this Great Family.

Sellar was exaggerating the numbers involved (though he probably regarded his precepts as appropriate to the world at large) and declared his pride in being 'summoned to the Council' of the Sutherland estate. Reiterating his commitment to the naked truth, he said that thousands of Highlanders, generation upon generation, had been kept as beasts of burden, for example as kelp producers, retarding the permanent improvement of the land and their own welfare. The kyloe regime was hopeless, and 'to plant Cottars without a view to fishing, is to sow paupers'. It would be ridiculous to break up the great sheep-farms because the geography of Sutherland made large scale operations inevitable. Instead, Sellar declared:

> Lay our farms out according to nature; Let them at full rents to active people, who must use Stock well, to be enabled to fulfil their conditions; and you shall have thriving stock, comfortably kept herds, improving grounds, well paid rent, and neither Law Suits nor Lawyers.

He described Sutherland as 'a magnificent yet compact Province' and gave his final rationale of improvement:

Nature points out to you the Realization, without trouble, of the annual value of its whole <u>pastures, through the</u> medium of from 20 to 30 men of some Education, worth from six to ten thousand pounds each; who shall, in one hour, deposit in the Bank each half years rent, with scarcely the intervention of a factor. There is no man in the Kingdom can have such a tenantry as the Marquis of Stafford; for no man has an Estate so Constituted by nature. The sons of such a tenantry should improve upon whatever practical knowledge came to them by their fathers – <u>that is</u> provided you be pleased to shew confidence to those young men who <u>affect only to be men of business</u> – that you discourage Greyhounds, Galloping horses, Livery servants, and the company of idle and bankrupt Lairds; who abound in, and corrupt the youth of every County – <u>Sutherland hitherto excepted</u>.

This was Sellar's creed, stretched to its logical limit, and it described his own ideal. He contrasted the sensible capitalist sheep-farmer with the effete, ambling aristocrat, alluding to a noble duke in Moray who had wasted away two generations of his family by hunting. All that the Sutherland managers were required to do was to make sensible arrangements of the lands, to install skilled men, particularly 'smiling on young men of promising and industrious habits'. The full value of the land could then be extracted with little trouble, so long as its resources were rationally disposed.

Sellar, of course, was talking mainly of himself. He had once been the 'young man of promising and industrious habits' when he entered the county in 1809. He expected some of his own sons to take over his lands and assets within twenty years – to become

> respectably settled, as numbers of such a Yeomanry, under such an illus-
> trious Family . . . I have always been a man, with perfect confidence in the
> Good providence that ever rules us; and fearless, to go, where my duty calls,
> I dont think that I am blinded by my pitiful views of Self-interest . . . and am
> satisfied of this, the common sense of what I advocate.

Sellar became especially animated and indignant when he encountered the opinions of William Lewis, Lord Stafford's agent from the English estate in Trentham. Lewis, an outsider, made a brief tour of the northern estates and offered some incisive and critical opinions on estate management and rural affairs.[19] Sellar was stung, and retorted that English conditions were quite different from those in the Highlands, and the gradations of society advocated by Lewis did not suit local conditions. Lewis, said Sellar, had

> been in the practice of working among those tillage farmers who feed for
> the Butcher, and Eat Bacon and Guzzle ale with him, and with their

servants. We are Scotchmen; our Table is different; and I am writing of the Reay Country.

Sellar pointed out that he paid £1,700 per annum in rent and asked 'where do you Get the same sum with less outlay and trouble, I mean in England? Where do you see better working people more Civil, or the Game more thoroughly protected?' He added that 'John Bull is a good fellow; but we are Sister Peg.'

Sellar's gospel was that 'Nature' was an imperative force. Limestone conditions in Sutherland had produced a beautiful sward for stock. On the Reay estate the previous owner had made mistakes. Sellar condemned the line of the parliamentary road to Tongue as 'the work of some Charlatan who knew nothing of his business'. Moreover, the common people had been neglected. Sellar believed that education and apprenticeship was the best way to promote new enterprise across the estate. Encouragement 'by a thousand little means, and civilities, and Corrections, and attentions, and selections, and distinctions. By holding and letting go, by joking and being serious, *but* – but never losing sight of your purpose.' Now the Sutherland managers should train a few of the young people in skills, 'to Pull up a few, from this well, at the bottom of which the whole are placed.' He recommended the introduction of a few coopers into the communities. It would be like pouring 'a few drops of oil' on the creaking axle and the whole would be blessed with new endeavour: 'Bye and bye, they will "Birl" on without foreign assistance.'

Sellar finished with one final flourish, saying that persuasion was required to motivate the people:

> By honest acts of kindness, satisfy them, that you are their friend; and, in place of feudal dependence long since Gone bye, in reality, every part of the highlands, you will have the blythe face to shield you from danger. The people know right from wrong. They know their friends; they speak English; they cannot be deluded by the old Tacksmen, who fattened on them, when we came to Sutherland. In fact, people of this stamp have nothing to Say with them.

But the young should be encouraged to emigrate. Sellar had a particular perception of the historical conflict between the forces of retrogression and conservatism: he remarked that it was perfectly possible 'to smile at the tricks of those who affect to be in 1832, men of 1745'. He was a prophet of 'Improvement' still battling the anachronisms of his day.

The great internal estate debate of 1832 was a watershed for Sellar.

His views had rigidified and sharpened, while the opinions of his fellow clearance theorists, who had lived through the changes with him, had shifted and softened. While Sellar remained rock-solid for the original thinking and for its logical implementation, James Loch and his other advisers had revisited the old certitudes and found them wanting. They retreated from the full rigour of improvement theory and trembled at the prospect of more public outrage. They admitted, in private at least, the partial error of their previous ways. They now conceded that the sheep-farms were too big. Loch and his agents thereby conceded half the case of their opponents. Sellar was left ideologically isolated. It was an isolation increased by the passages within the Stafford family. In 1833, Lord Stafford became the first Duke of Sutherland, only months before his death. His heir had less stomach for Highland improvement, though his mother continued to hold the reins of the estate until her own death in 1839.

Beyond the estate management, opinion on the clearances and the subsequent condition of the displaced people was far less constrained. The Rev. David Mackenzie, the minister of Farr, was regarded as a friend by the Sutherland family, but as a turncoat by many critics of the clearances. He was responsible for the parish entry in the *New Statistical Account of Scotland,* and he published a thoughtful and damaging report on the nature of the changes in Sutherland in the late 1830s. He contrasted the old and new systems, as viewed from his manse in Farr:

> A considerable number of tacksmen of the parish occupied extensive farms in different parts of it, a dense population of subtenants resided in the interior straths and glens. Now, however, all the lands, both hill and dale, which they possessed, are held in lease by a few large sheep-farmers, or non-resident gentlemen – some of them living in Caithness, some on the south coast of the county, and some in England, and the straths, in which hundreds of families lived comfortably, are now tenanted by about twenty-four families of herds. In place of scores of Highland cattle, horses, sheep and goats, which formerly were brought to market, or used for domestic purposes, now thousands of fleeces of Cheviot wool, wedders, and ewes, are annually exported. The people who had been removed from the interior in 1818 and 1819, when these great changes took place, are thickly settled along the sea coast of the parish – in some instance about thirty lotters occupying the land in the possession of twelve, and some of them placed on ground which had been formerly uncultivated.

Mackenzie clearly believed that the people were now less well placed and less moral in character. The loss of tacksmen had been devastating but, on the other hand, there had been no extensive failure of crops since 1816. Other ministers, for instance in Rogart, also testified to an improvement in material conditions in the new settlements.[20]

– Sellar on class –

The unending debate, informal and formal, on the ownership, control and use of the land in the Highlands reverberated in many directions. For instance, anonymous attacks on the Sutherland estate continued. In November 1832 'A Highlander' told Lord Stafford to remember 'as a roaring Lyon, and a Raging Bear so is a wicked ruler over the poor people.' The unknown correspondent added, threateningly, that 'Such were the Scourgers your Lordship employed to remove the Brave Sutherland people to make room for sheep, but Revolution will soon take place.'[21]

Meanwhile Lady Stafford had toured in the West Highlands and Islands and she too concluded that it was desirable to enlarge the grazings of the small tenants in Sutherland. Loch concurred with this view, but only where it was practicable. In some parts, he said, the small holders already had too much land. Thus Loch equivocated on the central question and continued to affirm that the improvement system was better than the old.[22] Lady Stafford, despite her earlier leadership in the changes, remarked in 1833 that she simply could not understand how the net income of Sutherland was so small and not hugely greater than it had been before the improvements. James Loch, indeed, calculated on various occasions that Lord Stafford had spent the equivalent of all the Sutherland rents for the period 1811 to 1833, as well as a further £60,000 which brought his low-yielding investment close to a total of £500,000.[23] Lady Stafford's perplexity reflected the relatively modest returns which accrued to the removals and the improvements under the regime of lower prices which continued for so many years after the war.[24]

The economic consequences of the Sutherland policies were certainly circumscribed by the course of commodity prices. In May 1830, Sellar was more optimistic. He believed that prices were recovering and he had 'never seen the land in finer order', and a new tide of trade had begun to flow. He had been delivered a good crop of lambs, and was supplying border farmers with breeding stock. Sutherland was rivalling Dumfries-shire for the finest sheep stock.[25] But Sellar was acutely aware of the malaise among most other farmers. His own methods were, he claimed, virtually perfect, yet even he experienced great difficulties:

> I keep my Books, and balance all my matters, once a year. I have the best selling stock, the best land, the best landlord, and the best servants, and I may venture to think, about the best directed concern in Scotland, at least I know no man, who, with the same capital and other advantages, does, to exclusively devote himself to his business, or have thoroughly and econom- ically realised the produce of his farm. Still I find it difficult to make any progress. Comparing my own concerns with the facts which I have noted, in other people, in various counties, I am persuaded, that, of the Bulk of Scottish farmers, the property is melting down in the great national Crucible, and Joining the Great Stream of Taxes which conveys it, silently and swiftly, to the Public Creditor!

He blamed the government for the lack of profit in all concerns.[26]

At the time of the Swing riots in southern England, Sellar rejoiced that the farmers of Sutherland were blessed by the healthy distance between them and the agitation. But, in the middle of the Reform debate, in December 1830, he said that the King and the aristocracy had much to answer for to the country:

> Tens of thousands of ruined merchants, manufacturers and farmers see no hope but in anarchy, and every year adds to the number, while many of your best citizens have for years been crossing the Atlantic to save from impend- ing ruin.

Sellar thought the country was in a terrible mess.[27]

Sellar's view of the failure of the ruling classes in the capital was of a piece with his broader attitude to class in British society. He was loyal and respectful to the aristocratic system in general, but was vehemently critical when their leisure activities affected the rational use of pastoral land. Eventually, Sellar had to confront the infiltration of the High- lands by sportsmen, the Nimrods who added a new and awkward dimension to the perpetual contest for the land of the Highlands.

In the early phases of this impending invasion, Sellar essayed his own social analysis. Sportsmen came in two sorts:

> The one class consists of encumbered Lairds, half-pay Captains, and retired subordinate Civilians, who, in parties or individually, and with assistants of a Certain stamp, furnish out the shops of the London poulterers . . . I tell you, I would not mix up such persons, with the innocent families, which I have settled on my farm, for the Fee simple of the Ground.

The other class consisted of:

> Noblemen and Gentlemen of respectability, in the South, who take furn- ished Quarters, spend one or two months of summer, respectably among our valleys, fish and shoot like gentlemen and leave money, cheerfully

behind them, in return for the well braced nerves, which they carry back to their avocations. On a common lease I should be . . . happy to make preparation suitable for visitors of the south, from whose acquittance I might profit in many ways.[28]

Sellar was offered leasing rights for trout fishing, grouse, ptarmigan and red deer in Strathnaver, but chose to restrict himself to his own expertise.

Between the encroaching sportsmen, the incompetent statesmen, the demanding crofters, the heretical clergy and a doubting landlord, Sellar found himself increasingly out of sorts in his world of sheep and profits. So far, however, none of these factors had impeded the onward march of his efficiency and the progress of his family.

CHAPTER 15

Rational Principles

– SELLAR'S AMBITIONS –

Well-fed farmers and merchants thronged the Inverness wool market. Patrick Sellar had become a dominant figure among the regulars, men from across the northern Highlands, from the Borders and from the north of England. Between them, these men had revolutionised the production of sheep and wool and achieved economic miracles in textile manufacture. They perfectly represented two key aspects of British industrialisation which, on one definition, exactly coincided with Sellar's lifespan. A thousand people often attended the Inverness market. No animals were in evidence because the buyers already knew the stock on every farm. Sometimes £400,000 changed hands in a week. The road-engineer Joseph Mitchell painted a picture of the scene before the railways changed the system in its entirety. He assembled the cast and picked out several figures, one of them, possibly, Patrick Sellar:

> This meeting is unique. Here you see the portly figure of a wool stapler of Huddersfield and Leeds; besides him the quick and intelligent Liverpool merchant, or the shrewd, broadspeaking woollen manufacturer of Aberdeen or Bannockburn. The burly south country feeder stands at the street corner in deep conversation, and about to strike a bargain with that sharp, lynx-eyed, red-haired little man, who is the largest farmer in the North, and counts his flocks by 40,000 or 50,000.[1]

Sellar grew prosperous, especially in the 1830s when wool prices began their long, slow revival.[2] From his energetic efforts to expand his sheep-farming operations with new leases, as well as his new ventures in Argyllshire in the late 1830s, it is clear that he was phenomenally successful.[3] This was reflected equally in his family, in which he inculcated a hunger for achievement among his sons.

Sellar, however, continued to find cause for contention in every corner of his life. He rubbed abrasively against everyone with whom he came into contact. Moreover, his mind had become set by middle age, his opinions hardened into concrete. On many issues he was now left stranded, defending and advocating ideas from the 1800s, when most of his associates shrank from further radical change in the Highlands. Sellar, throughout his life, drove each principle to its furthest logical destination.

Sellar claimed: 'I am a person little ambitious of public notice, and more sensitive than is Good for me.'[4] He was utterly forthright on agricultural methods, a total believer in the new school of rural science. He esteemed in particular Sir John Sinclair's work on improvement, and was a keen follower of George Culley and Sir George Mackenzie in their efforts to improve technical knowledge of sheep-rearing. From his own student days he had collected 'anatomical plates of . . . the Stomach and other viscera, explaining the purposes of each part, the origins of certain diseases and the cures most approved of etc.' He brought scientific pamphlets to Sutherland in 1814, and furnished his shepherds with copies. He praised 'the clever Norfolk tillage farmers', and the 'most intelligent Gentlemen who have improved the breed of Short horned Cattle':

> The improved short horns are a piece of 'animal machinery' which manufacture (if I may use the word) more value out of an acre of Ground than any other animal of the species. They are not suitable to this remote Country, but, if the principles of the discovery were explained to us, they might lead us to important truths in our branch of Rural Economy.[5]

Sellar found his own literary productions of 1831 and 1832 a testing time, and he searched far and wide for literary ornament to embellish his prose. He thought Virgil not quite appropriate, but had been keen to quote Alexander Pope to his farming readers:

> Look round the world; behold the Charm of Love
> Combining all below and all above.

Sellar was aware of his prolixity and, eventually, his *Farm Report* was shorn of its excesses.[6] He expected 'to put an extinguisher on Stewart of Garth and all the ante [*sic*] improvers.'[7]

After his labours with the pen, Sellar thought of travelling abroad. Instead, he went to the south of Scotland and England. He called at Blair Adam (where James Loch had spent most of his childhood) and felt deeply privileged to meet Lord Chief Commissioner Adam. He visited Liverpool, where he knew many commercial connections, and admired the Stafford family's main country residence at Trentham, in Staffordshire, observing : 'This is truly a residence for Princes.' In April 1831, he returned to Sutherland via the Burghead packet after taking three weeks with 'my <u>Brethren</u> in Northumberland, Roxburgh, Angus'. He reported farmers' reactions to the Reform debate and he declared that most people wanted moderate change to the political foundations, leaving further advance to later generations. He also reported better prices for wool which would happily turn farmers' thoughts away from politics: 'we are all beginning to turn with pleasure from "<u>the State</u>", to the contemplation of our own affairs and firesides.' At Elgin, he witnessed 'a very clever Gentlemanlike man' who had been imported from Cambridge as a teacher of elocution, Sellar noting that 'English Grammar did not dwell there in my day.'[8] His own letters were strewn with vivid Scotticisms and full of the seasonal round of farming detail. In May of 1831, he went into Strathnaver to examine a 'fine Crop of Lambs'.

Back in Sutherland, Sellar offered a rare glimpse of his domestic life:

> I got home just in Time to shake hands with my three boys before they crossed the Frith [they were being educated in Elgin], and to superintend harvest which we began on Monday. We have uncommonly warm weather and the finest crop I ever saw in Scotland.[9]

In 1831 his wife gave birth to their fifth son, and Sellar marked the occasion, saying, 'so I must keep moving.'[10] His wide range of intellectual pursuits included a surprising interest in the etymology of Gaelic words. More characteristically he experimented with a new salve, employing olive oil which, he thought, caused less staining of the wool, to keep his sheep drier in winter. He was equally busy with new methods of producing rape, turnips and barley. He claimed that his intense attention to detail allowed him 'to keep the Top of the market', for his sheep and wool.[11] At this time, he was supplying some of his wool to Patons near Stirling for manufacture into shawls for export.

In February 1831, Sellar again referred to the emigration of some more of his shepherds, which he blamed on the government: 'Lower Taxes and higher profits will stop this Tide; but nothing Else I believe. A new Swarm is preparing to move off at Whitsunday first.' Sellar observed that only the better sort emigrated, leaving behind the less desirable. He reminded James Loch that he had promised 'to Ridd me' of a group of sub-tenants at Bracachy whom Sellar blamed for his stock losses. 'My loss by theft from Martm 1829 to [Oct?] 1830 on his march is 3 hogs, 3 wethers, and 21 Ewes – total 27. I know you will do me the favour to make me free of them by Whitsunday.' It was a minor recrudescence of the removal strategy of the sort which was pervasive in the Highlands in these years. These were small clearances, dislodging small groups of families on the awkward margins of the sheep-farms.[12]

Sellar's mind was crowded with thoughts of taxes and Reform. New road tolls in Inverness-shire continued to threaten the overland stock trade from the northern Highlands, and Sellar earnestly encouraged Lord Stafford to invest in his own new steam navigation link between Sutherland and the south. Joseph Mitchell said that Sellar knew more about stock traffic 'than any other gentlemen in the Highlands'. Sellar told him that about 34,000 sheep left Sutherland each year, usually travelling by way of Bonar Bridge to Beauly, through Forfar, Dalwhinnie, Stirling and Falkirk. The wethers went to be fattened in Northumberland, Cumberland, Durham, Westmorland and Yorkshire; the ewes were delivered further south to York, Cheshire, Lancashire, Staffordshire, Derbyshire and other southern counties. Sellar warned that steam navigation could inaugurate serious competition for the road owners.[13]

Sellar maintained his rage for the abolition of tolls. The Stafford family had spent (with government subsidy) large amounts on road construction but, unlike other proprietors, did not exact tolls. Sellar told Loch that this was one of Lord Stafford's greatest acts 'of his Good Life', for which he was lavished with praise throughout the country:

> I have heard, in Edinburgh, Perth and on the outside and inside of Coaches, [travellers] except his Lordship from the General anathemas against Noblemen and Landed Proprietors, on this sole Ground, 'I knew he must have the heart of a Gentleman, for he will allow no person, high or low, to be interrupted or pay toll on any road in his country'. Nothing, be it, Good or bad, travels so far or so fast, as that which is done, upon, and with respect to, the thorough fare roads of a country.[14]

Within Sutherland, the purchase of the Reay Country by Lord Stafford encouraged Sellar to believed that he could expand his operations and, as we have seen, his bid for the Edderachyllis farm precipitated an internal debate about the future of the clearance policies. Sellar's enthusiasm for expansion revived personal memories:

> In Lord Reay's time I have slept upon the Forest hills, and threaded the Glens that communicate with the Chain of Lochs, while the Shepherds were snoring in their beds; and I then caught the passion which is not yet

> Subdued, of attempting, on rational principles, an improvement there, similar to what I attempted, with Success, in Strathnaver. But I could not venture all the rent that would satisfy Lord Reay.

Lord Reay, of course, had gone into financial free-fall, while Sellar's appetite for expansion was unsated. He had long brooded over these farms, and wanted to know if it would be worthwhile making proposals which 'in my <u>humble</u> opinion may be fair and safe for Landlord and tenant'.

In his exchanges with James Loch, Sellar agreed that an 'uninitiated person' would say that the territory to which he 'aspired'

> was too extensive – and that all our farms here are too large. I never was more convinced of any thing, than that, as you diminish, you <u>diminish every thing with it excepting</u> the trouble to man . . . and sheep – <u>nature</u> had given us things on a great Scale; and she is <u>a Lady</u> to be wooed and won, but not to be crossed with impunity. I could write you pages in illustration.

He explained the complicated division of lands: 'Strathnaver consists entirely of Ewe and Hog land'; Edderachyllis was best for wethers and for wether hogs. All the land was required, in perfect complementarity, for the correct management of sheep. He was, after seven years, still searching for 'a wether hill' and had experienced much financial loss in the process: 'In 10 years more, I shall be like Asop's [*sic*] dog that had lost his teeth and shall see younger men "herry the Bike" [Scots for plundering the pot over the fire] which I discovered.'[15]

The critical moment in the negotiations came in the autumn of 1831. The estate had to decided whether to accept Sellar's logic and his higher rent or to halt the process of clearance. After much agonising, Sellar was told that though Lord Stafford would certainly prefer him as tenant, there was an objection: '. . . he thinks that your getting it would be throwing too much land into one hand' and the reasons were 'various, and formed of general policy as well as circumstances of his own Estate.'[16]

Sellar was furious at this rebuff. Estate policy, in his eyes, had become irrational and Lord Stafford was being ill-advised. Stafford, however, was tired, old and sick, and had no taste for controversy. Nor did his advisers think Sellar's own empire in Sutherland should be extended. He was already too big, and the social fabric of the district had been damaged. For his part, Sellar wanted the clearance policy to be completed to rational perfection but the Sutherland estate drew back. For the next two decades Sellar persistently chafed at this policy. He now personified the monopolising flock-master who, at least in

Strathnaver, had created a social void. He was stymied by the Sutherland estate and began to look beyond to satisfy his territorial ambitions.

– REFORM –

As a Member of Parliament and close adviser to Lord Grey, James Loch was deeply embroiled in the great Reform Debate. Sellar, inevitably, plied him with gratuitous advice. Sellar believed that there was a danger of revolution and told Loch, with a fine metaphor:

> I fervently pray God to bring you to a wise conclusion on a Grave and momentous Question. In every point, except its sad expense, the existing constitution, by the admirable balance it creates, excels whatever man has devised, since the days of Adam and Eve – on so beautiful a Statue let the mallet lightly and cautiously touch the Chisel.

Sellar spoke of 'our overwhelming tendency to Democracy', and was anxious about the sudden extension of the franchise to people without

> the stake in the country, the pride of British ancestry, the acquirement, and the honour of which we expect to attend a nobleman's influence! You can increase your number of voters immensely down to £300 a year and still continue among well-informed Gentlemen. But what can a £10 Smith, Tailor or weaver Judge on such a new Question?[17]

As the political temperature rose, so did the vehemence of Sellar's opinions. By March 1831, he was consumed by 'the all ingrossing subject of Reform'. He again said that he could see no sense in extending the vote to

> persons who almost without an exception, sustain themselves by manual and not by mental labour; or if they think of persons at all, and not of their hourly labour, it is how they can [chaffer?] about some little bargain, to increase their daily earnings. These sapient 'Judges of Mankind' chusing our Legislators! virtuous counsels, wise measures and prosperous times follow.

This, of course, was Sellar in his most mocking, ironical style against which his associates had long warned him.

In Sellar's view, wise judgement related to responsibility: 'below 120 acres or £150 to £200 a year you dip more into physical, less into, moral energy – the thing wanted for ensuring good and virtuous choice of a fit person to serve in Parliament.' He asked himself, 'how are the interests of these millions unrepresented and unrepresentable to be protected?' He answered that their employers would be best served as well as 'by the <u>Great Stake</u> held by the Aristocracy who balance betwixt the employees of and Employed in the welfare, the honour, or Glory of their Country. There are so many weak men among them. Modify your Entail Laws and these will drop out.'[18] Sellar, though at the sharpest edge of *laissez-faire* thinking, the modern entrepreneur *par excellence*, remained politically conservative. He was a paternalist at heart, retaining a remarkable faith in the aristocracy, even though he held many of their class in the utmost contempt.

Sellar bombarded Loch with political advice. To give the vote to brute and physical force was to 'deform' and not reform the constituencies. He now thought that a Revolution was likely, and when it came it would consume many *châteaux* in the conflagration.[19] He was wrong and in April 1835, long after the Reform excitement had passed, Sellar remarked on the more promising political horizon: now 'the Great mass of the people are Reformers, and will have confidence to <u>do more business [under?] a Genuine</u> Reform Government.'[20]

– CHOLERA AND LOCAL AFFAIRS –

William Lewis, the highly respected principal agent from Lord Stafford's English estates, visited the north in autumn 1831 and reported candidly on the Sutherland estate arrangements:

> the farms in general are too large and admit of no medium between the higher and lower classes – evidently a link is wanting to unite a society that would entertain proper feeling towards each other, the reverse being the case at present.

Lewis infuriated Sellar but put his finger on the central social consequence of the removals, namely the destruction of the communal cement and the creation of a social vacuum.[21]

As though responding to such criticism of the sheep-farming fraternity for making no contribution to Sutherland society, Sellar in early 1832 involved himself in local affairs to a new degree. He announced that he had been 'more among the poor people of Rogart . . . than I had been for 16 years preceding.' Although new roads and houses were in progress, he recognised that

> there is a great deal of poverty and Silent suffering among the sort of farmers who inhabit there. I dont know what I would do if I were Landlord over such a population – very likely I would furnish the means of 3/4 of them to emigrate, and make each small farm four or six times its present size. This, with decent tillage, and decent arrangement of farms, would

double the produce, and increase, not only the Comforts of the Tenants, but the rents payable to the Landlord.

But Sellar knew that the Stafford family would not find it expedient to follow his emigration advice. Meanwhile, he suggested that a few dozen pairs of blankets, and some bolls of meal be given to each parish by the estate factor, to relieve 'human suffering' and 'the return of popularity which it behoved to call for on behalf of the donors'.

Sellar regarded the continuing existence of poverty as the residue of the old problem of the Highlands caused by the failure to carry through the full logic of the removals. He asked rhetorically: 'What would have been your case today had the whole vale of Golspie, and Abercross, Kildonan, Strathbrora and Strathnaver been filled with "palmers" of the same sort?'[22] The removals had been incomplete and therefore poverty survived; without the clearances, poverty would have been much worse.

In November 1831, Sellar returned from a journey to the south of Scotland where he had contracted cholera. He held to the theory that the disease had originated in the consumption of unripe grain in northern Europe in the season of 1830. Sellar was lucky to get back to his home at Morvich, despite 'a desperate cholera upon me (not Asiatic however)'. His doctor required him to bind his entire body within 'a huge Roller of flannel'. He wrote to Loch, saying, 'I hope you will not think it necessary to fumigate this letter, [and] to send me to any of the houses of reception.'[23]

Sellar made light of his brush with one of the nineteenth-century's greatest killers, but he derived a clear social lesson from the outbreak of cholera and other diseases as they visited the north. He noted 'a very Great Evil . . . exists in the highlands, I mean the want of police with regard to vagrants', whom Sellar regarded as the essential carriers of fever. He argued:

> the sober people of this country are Generally healthy. The Typhus fever, which occasionally breaks out in the Beggar's Hotels shews the fountain from which such disease springs – the Squalid vagabonds which wander in among us, from the dissipated dregs of the south country population.

He recommended that the local officers at Bonar Bridge, Helmsdale and Meikle Ferry refuse entry to vagabonds whose 'squalid families' he asserted spread vermin and disease in the community.[24] He believed that the northern counties should shoulder a collective duty to provide a 'joint House of Correction', preferably at Inverness, 'and to hold out such other terrors as may keep vagrants at a distance'. Meanwhile, vagrants or not, Sutherland was experiencing the severest winter since 1809.

Sellar became involved with local precautions against the cholera outbreak and accused the local authorities of timidity: 'I find the Gentlemen, nearly one and all, [have been] afraid to touch this subject.' He also calculated that 324 families were in need of relief in the district, and the Sutherland estate issued supplies of meal for relief. He could not resist adding that here was

> a spectacle for the anti-improvers, if the effect of that which they have so much striven to put down – a country which in 1810 was a nest of paupers does in 1832 (by consequence of improvement) place every individual in competence. What a contrast to the unimproved estates.

But the problem was exacerbated by the seasonal movement of very poor people from the west coast to the east, where the local gentlemen would be required to 'grapple with' the consequences, coping with 'heart-rending Scenes', with the poor people 'to a certain extent starving'.

Sellar, in typically practical fashion, devised a plan. He consulted the clergy and the local Boards of Supervision across the county, and calculated that the 324 indigent families would need 8 lb of meal per week for twenty-two weeks. He assumed that the local landowners would bear the responsibility equally. In the course of this planning, Sellar had not let the opportunity slip to observe again the distribution of poverty:

> I was curious to observe how much the condition of the people depended on the nature of the improvement made. In the whole parish of Golspie, where tillage and labour is more perfect, I think they made all 10 families. In Rogart where the arrangement is imperfect 45. On Mr Dempster's Estate which reposes as in 1810, Forbes (his Factor) said repeatedly (for I tried him two or three times in different shapes) there every fourth man was a pauper!

Sellar declared that his relief scheme would be 'a piece of christian brotherly kindness', but in 'a selfish point of view' it would also work 'to unite all classes among us in good-will to each other; and, I see no signs in the times, to render this of little account.' He also predicted that, for the five months of relief, all begging would cease and that this should be counted in the calculus of relief.[25]

But Sellar insisted that the campaign – 'to place us cap a pie agt Cholera' – should be combined with the eradication of the whisky shops which he described as 'poison stores'. He opined that it was 'in vain that we give meal to feed the hungry, if such an agency of poverty, disease and death be let in <u>full</u> employment against us.' At that very time he was supplying commercial barley to the great legal distilleries in the east.[26]

Patrick Sellar regarded the management of the local population as an integral part of social engineering in the new age of progress, and all his observations were premised on this broad conception. He insisted, improbably, that he was not 'a Growler about other people',[27] but repeatedly demanded the expulsion of intruders from his land though he 'hated being placed in warfare with such people.'[28] In truculent mood he often appealed to Loch to intercede over the heads of the local managers.

In 1837, Sellar himself interceded in the case of a man threatened with removal from the Sutherland estate. This was an unusual role for Sellar. The man in question, Angus Sinclair, had come to Sutherland with a very large family, but had been accused of smuggling which, if true, would guarantee his ejection, as well as the instant destitution of his wife and family. Sellar received several testimonials on behalf of Sinclair, all declaring him totally innocent and pleading for his exoneration. Sellar recommended that the family not be evicted, and reported that Sinclair had said that if he were allowed to remain he would 'remember you [the factor] in his prayers (which I suppose are not the shortest) and, he adds that in two years when his family shall be a <u>little older</u> he will go to America.' Despite Sellar's intercession, and the evidence of his exemplary character, and his prayers, Sinclair was given notice to quit in June 1837. Sellar then made the case for humanitarian aid for the woman and her eight children.[29]

– Monumental controversy –

At the other end of Sutherland society, wealth and progress were richly rewarded in 1833, when Lord Stafford was created first Duke of Sutherland. He enjoyed his elevation only briefly, for he died in the same year. His body was transported to Sutherland for a great funeral, and burial at Dornoch. The spectacle was watched by one of the largest crowds of local people ever to be congregated in the county. Their quiet, respectful demeanour was a matter for comment. It was, perhaps, convenient that Patrick Sellar was away in Moray on business at the time and was unable to attend the ceremony. Sellar's attendance might have been an embarrassment to the family of the Duke, for it is clear that most of the unpopularity of their clearances had been conveniently focussed upon Sellar in person. Instead, Sellar sent his condolences and declared, 'I am humbly of opinion that not one Jot or tittle should be, by his tenants, left undone, that may satisfy our passion to testify our sincere respect for his memory that is Gone.'[30]

Sellar wished to influence posterity no less than the present, and was enthusiastic for a great monument to be erected by the Sutherland tenantry for the late Duke of Sutherland. Sellar thought that it should be erected in the middle of the estate, and not on Ben Bhraggie overlooking Dunrobin. A great monument placed in the centre of the dukedom, he reasoned, would make it suitably difficult for any future Duke to relinquish any part of the estate. As for Ben Bhraggie, there were aesthetic objections: 'To surmount it with any of the works of <u>man</u> would be to diminish the natural <u>Grandeur</u> of the Scene, from which it is but one step to the ridiculous.' Sellar was heavily engaged in the fund-raising for the monument (which yielded £1,000), and he also offered an inscription:

> This spot, Her Grace Elisabeth the 1st Duchess of Sutherland, permitted to the Tenantry of the Estate of Sutherland, to consecrate to the memory of George Granville Leveson Gower, her husband, the much beloved Father of His People.[31]

Sellar thought that the question of taste was vital and remarked: 'What monuments I have seen in Scotland seem to be very poor productions, each resembling some Butter Churn, negligently left by some Giantess, after her mornings work.'[32] Eventually, despite Sellar's advice, a spectacular monument was erected on Ben Bhraggie and remained as a symbol of the thinking which created the improvement and clearance policies of the first Duke of Sutherland. Equally, it functioned as a monumental provocation to those in future generations who yearned for the innocent days before the clearances.[33]

– FAMILY MATTERS –

The passage of the years caused Sellar to ruminate on his own health and his robust physical life in the northern Highlands. He recollected, nostalgically, a journey he made in 1829 to the west:

> I slept in a Smoky hut at a place called, I think [Achlyne?] on Loch Inchard. I shall never forget the transport with which I rushed out of <u>suffocating</u> heat, about 6 o'clock on the friday morning, and plunged into the Sea. Well started on foot, about 7 o'clock, all tasting of salt water.

He eventually reached Altnaharrie and Morvich, next morning, 'before the family were out of bed.' He reflected to Loch that:

I have now got in among the "fiftys" which are, decidedly bad things for these recreations, and I suspect the sixties will not improve; but, if you proceed with these roads (which, by the way, curtail the <u>magnificence</u> of such Rambles much) it is hard to say, with Good Guiding, what the 70s may not be up to.[34]

When Loch asked Sellar to report on the Reay Country, Sellar's first reaction, knowing the rigours of the region, was that his wife would resist the idea: 'I suspect, as I got myself overstrained, when in the South, Mrs Sellar will object to my undertaking the Job.' In the event, Sellar spent three weeks on his grand tour of the new territories, and when he submitted his report remarked: 'I have honestly and fearlessly given you the picture that was thrown up, at each turn of the subject, in the kaleidoscope of my mind, and left you, to make of it, what you will.'[35] Sellar's reaction to the regions about Loch Eribol was of astonishment: 'I cannot <u>Surmise</u>, how it has, with such advantages, lain, <u>thro so many Centuries</u> in such a state of neglect.' The Reay Country was in the same primitive condition as Sutherland had been in 1810, before the great clearances.[36]

Much later in the century, long after his death, Sellar's daughter-in-law recollected him as a fine man but a

> man of iron will, and was determined not only that his sons should have the best education, but that they should excel, and be at the head of their classes.[37]

Her words particularly marked the manner in which he raised his large family. His wife was evidently a woman of character and much revered in the household. She eventually outlived her husband by many years and emerged strongly as the centre of the family. But, during the long life of Patrick Sellar, she seems loyally to have served her husband's needs. When he visited Edinburgh, Sellar stayed at his mother's family's, Mrs Plenderleath's, in Hope Crescent. His wife sent hams to Mrs Loch, and socialised modestly in Morvich, without leaving much trace. The Sellars' lives became focused on the future of their offspring. In the long succession of sons, each was sent to school at Elgin Academy and then on to Edinburgh, and some of them on to the university.

Sellar enrolled his sons at the new Edinburgh Academy.[38] William Young Sellar was dux of the school in 1839, and later Professor of Humanity at Edinburgh, and his younger brother, Alexander Craig Sellar, was dux in the 1844–50 period. Patrick Sellar exulted at their success at the Academy. In 1839, he was invited to a dinner of the

Directors of the Academy at the Hopetoun Rooms, as 'parent of the dux'. He told the Duke of Sutherland that many of the pupils had entered the House of Commons, and that a fellowship at Oxford was likely for his brilliant son William. Patrick Sellar made a panegyric speech at the occasion, praising the school and its educational principles. The Academy, he said, sought the love of truth without compromise, and treasured the independence of mind

> that will permit no fear, to interpose betwixt it and the straightforward discharge of duty – that industry which despises repose, and that concentration of the soul, to one single purpose without which not one great deed can be achieved.

William, he remarked, had won the gold medal at one of the best schools in Scotland, and was the youngest dux they had ever had. It was, said his father, an intoxicating thing for a humble man like himself, a mere tenant. Sellar, in his paternal pride, promised to send four more boys to the Academy.[39]

Patrick Sellar encouraged and drove his sons to high achievement, and attempted to stir their ambition in every way. Mostly, he was remarkably successful, though some of his sons felt themselves oppressed by his expectations. At least one broke down under the strain. Much of the correspondence of Sellar's middle years extolled the scholastic and business success of his sons. Patrick Sellar was highly geared to the imperatives of mid-Victorian achievement.

Sellar *père* began to reckon his future in terms of his sons and their likely involvement in his enterprises in Sutherland. But they were not necessarily interested in Highland sheep-farming. In early 1836 his eldest son became first clerk at the rising Glasgow merchant house of Dennistoun in their Liverpool office; his second son was finishing at a school run by Thomas Chalmers' brother, in Edinburgh, and was thirty points ahead of his class in the competition for the medal to New College. Sellar said: 'I have some comfort in my toil, at any rate.' But his son's scholastic success would not necessarily help his sheep operations. He could make 3 per cent on his investments, 'but if one of my chaps will Join me, I will make it [his capital] do better. Time will shew.'[40]

Patrick Sellar wanted at least one of his sons to become a sheep-farmer in Sutherland. It was vital to make the proposition attractive and economic and this led Sellar to request special conditions in his new leases for Strathnaver. One was a full access to the sea on the north coast, so that his son might engage in the fishing, as well as sheep-farming. He claimed that the occupation of sheepfarming, without some respite, rendered a man a 'stupid fellow.'[41]

Two years later, Sellar said that his sons had not been able to wait further on a decision about his leases. Now his two eldest sons had joined Dennistouns, and another had been placed in 'a foreign house'. They were lost to Sutherland sheep-farming 'because every trial to settle [them] in Sutherland had been defeated.' Typically Sellar left the impression that the estate was to blame. He told Loch:

> You have not attended, my good sir, to this truth, that a country like Sutherland, which can only be employed to advantage, in great masses (with each of which the shifts essential for the health of Stock as practicable) requires a 'marriage' of the strength and agility of youth and the sagacity of riper years.

He stressed that a young man could not cope with the 'tricks' of the Yorkshire dealers, while 'An old man again is brought to beggary by the knavery, the tyranny and the laziness of his servants.' Sellar could not hold the interest of his sons in sheep-farming without proper security of leases; they would become merchants unless he could establish them in sheep-farming.[42]

Sellar was widely read and remarkably eclectic, for instance enthusing over *Guy Mannering*, a novel in which, as Stewart of Garth had noted, Scott depicted vivid and affecting 'scenes of eviction (Highland style)'.[43] Sellar sent Lady Sutherland and Mrs Loch copies of Chalmers' latest *Edinburgh Journal*. He had pronounced views on language, and allowed himself a tirade against 'Trashy Latin Poetry', which he oddly likened to the kilt. Latin had little practical value in the modern world, an irony in view of his son's distinguished career as a classicist. Sellar, of course, regarded the survival of Gaelic as an extreme anachronism which, he asserted, held back the rational advance of the region and its benighted people. He was also an accomplished writer with an excellent, if acerbic, turn of phrase. Nevertheless he tended to be self-conscious about his learning, and, when he remarked on literary matters, he would say, 'but I forget that I am but a man of ploughs and harrows.'[44]

He was also an intrepid traveller, and had been warned about his frequent recourse to small boats. In spring 1839, he came close to drowning when returning from Westfield and Inverness, travelling in a small fishing boat which, according to his version of the event, an incompetent and cowardly fisherman had wrecked. He was rescued by a French sailor who swam to Sellar and pulled him through the surf to the shore, saving his life. It caused him to reflect on his close escape and his great good luck.[45]

Sellar observed the passing seasons with bucolic delight. In early 1835, he reported to the Duchess/Countess:

> We have a season in Sutherland of uncommon comfort and plenty. The Granaries cannot be made to contain the crop. Could the working man see the children's "parritch" wet, in winter, with a little brick home brewed beer, in the place of "drinking his dram" at the Whisky Shop, we would be very complete I think.[46]

The 1836 season was severe, and possibly the worst winter since 1816. His own barley crop had been good, mainly on account of his use of bone manure.[47] Sellar, who was suffering rheumatism, described it as a sad season for people with frail constitutions: 'It has swept them off every where, in Great numbers, leaving persons and animals of sound health, untouched.' He was much impressed by his relative Miss Young who, at seventy, travelled by packet from Burghead and got about in an open gig.[48] The winter of 1837/8 was also severe, and Sellar declared in late February, possibly with some satisfaction, that if it did not thaw in 'a very few days, there [would] be very few deer alive in Sutherland. They are much softer than sheep and they are on their last legs.' It was extraordinary weather in which partridge froze to death beneath Sellar's parlour window, and when he lost many hundreds of sheep, despite their superior hardiness.[49]

In April 1837, Sellar was pleased to read a passage in the *Mark Lane Express* which was extraordinarily close to his own opinions on the state of the west Highlands, parts of which region had again descended into near-famine. The journal urged Highlanders to migrate to the seats of industry. They were, it said, the rural equivalents of the handloom weavers, and it was vital that they should avoid repeating their miserable experience, that is of hanging on in a dying trade and suffering extended distress by their own immobility. The Highlanders were 'a forlorn people' and it was absurd to encourage them to grow up 'in idleness and misery on their native soil, when they might do much better elsewhere.' They were a people too much under the influence of sentiment rather than that of reason. Thus 'a large population clings to a country in which there is no use for their services (being now chiefly devoted to pasture) and which refuses them, even in ordinary seasons, a proper sustenance.'[50] Sellar could not have expressed it more clearly himself.

– EXPERIMENTING IN THE MID-1830s –

Most of Sellar's intellectual energy was poured into agricultural improvement and he was forever experimenting with new methods. In 1832, for instance, he imported large quantities of bone manure, costing £388, for his farms in Sutherland and Moray. 'The use of Bone manure has begun a new era in agriculture,' he announced. 'Our maritime greatness (which has condensed so mightily a population within the limits of these islands) coming to the aid of agriculture with this new assistance, [and] doubles the produce of the soil.' In that year he celebrated 'an extraordinary bulk of crop', only slightly marred by intervening poorer weather.

Each year Sellar now made a tour of southern counties and, in early 1834, he was greatly concerned about the poor state of the tillage farmers, particularly in contrast with the highly progressive and flourishing state of manufacturers. He believed that the arable farmers were old-fashioned in their methods and outlook, expensive and imperfect in their farming techniques. They had fallen behind manufacturers in the application of science to their methods.

Sellar observed the brilliant new technology of the railways in Lancashire and was profoundly impressed with the vista of improvement it now revealed. 'No one who has seen 100 tons of Iron and Coal take to flight from Manchester to Liverpool [can] doubt that ten tons of [coal?] may be made to cart manure, to plough, sow and harrow on all alluvial and flat lying tillage land.' Agriculture needed steam-powered machines to do the work of horses and 'that, mark, without the mischievous trampling of horses in damp weather, and with such dispatch as to defy bad seasons.' He calculated that his six pairs of horses, at Morvich, cost him £450 each year. 'One machine, such as I describe', he said, would do all their work and more, 'and much more perfectly.' He would be able to pay more rent and sell his corn more cheaply. He suggested to James Loch, and 'you Parliamentary Gentlemen', that they encourage such an invention. It would settle the Corn Laws question in the best possible way.[51]

Sellar believed that steam machinery in agriculture possessed an even greater potential, beyond its benefit to the market. The extension of the new technology to agriculture would put an end to 'the dangerous jealousy which at present exists on the part of the commercial, towards the Landed interest, on account of the Corn Laws'.[52] Sellar's enthusiasm approached rapture. Science would solve the greatest single problem facing the nation; it would raise agriculture to the level of industry and the nation would march forward as one. He proclaimed his essential philosophy thus: 'People must change and conform to each improvement, as it comes to be discovered.'[53]

Sellar was intensely conscious of rural costs and prices, and the lottery of each season.[54] Despite the vagaries of the seasons, it was clear, at least until the threat of the Repeal of the Corn Laws, that farmers were generally more prosperous. James Loch told the dowager Duchess of Sutherland, in 1836, of the good condition of the stock-farmers of the county: 'There must be a very considerable accumulation of Capital and Wealth among the Stock farmers', which should tide them over any future difficulties.[55]

Sellar enjoyed comparing stock in the north of Scotland and in the Borders. He was scornful of certain Border breeding practices which produced mis-shapen sheep:

> Sheep with Gigantic head and length of Ear, flat neck, narrow shoulder, flat rib, deep narrow chest, long side, and high loin and rump, out of all proportion to the Steam power that is to feed these gigantic hind Quarters, all very well for the butcher, but utterly losing sight of the Safety and interest of the breeder and feeder.

Sellar wanted 'machines for converting highland pastures into wool and mutton'. He experimented, always looking for 'a change of blood' to bring perfection.[56]

Sellar was convinced that arable farmers must increase productivity radically if they were to survive. Mechanisation would make the Corn Laws a dead letter,[57] and in 1839, Sellar again suggested that a prize be offered for 'the discovery of machinery, to enable us to produce corn cheaper than foreigners'. This, he believed, was the only way British farmers could confront the growing competition from abroad.[58] He continued, 'depend upon it, it is a thing quite within the compass of human skill.' Invention was the 'only thing that, without a sponge to the debt', could 'save us'. He was also seriously exercised about the growth of the national debt and the divisions between agriculturists and manufacturers were desperately damaging to the nation. The country could not continue to pay 40 per cent more for food than was available elsewhere. His answer was technology, and Parliament should provide a premium of £20,000 for the invention of scientific remedies.[59]

– FRUSTRATIONS –

Throughout the 1830s, Sellar searched for ways to extend the scale of his sheep-farming operations in the north.[60] He particularly coveted the Durness farm in Reay. He portrayed the current occupant Dunlop as an incompetent, his farm full of 'Ruined hovels, indifferent Shepherds, sheep misgoverned, masters deep in debt.' He discovered 'some thousand acres of plants in decay, and creatures in misery'. He therefore offered to 'redd-up' [i.e. set in order] and 'Sellarise' the Durness farm to 'realise its natural value'.[61]

Sellar was confident of his bid for the Durness farm, though he claimed that he would 'not the less feel the kindness of the Noble Family's present intention whether the transaction came to a maturity or not.'[62] In the outcome Dunlop demanded £10,000 for his stock which Sellar valued at only £6,000, and eventually the transaction collapsed. Sellar became irritable. He explained to his landlord that his main intention was

> to have enticed one of my boys to my own profession, in the hope that, with his better education and his vigour of youth, backed by my experience, and that of the faithful servants who have so long hung by me, he might have exceeded whatever I have done.

With a great display of deference, Sellar thanked his landlord effusively for his consideration. Sellar was plainly burdening his sons with his own ambition.[63]

Sellar's attempt to oust Dunlop was frustrated by the tenant and the estate managers. The local agents pointed out that 'the number of resident respectable Tenants would thus be diminished, which the District can ill-afford'. They advised that Lord Stafford make a rental sacrifice to avoid this loss.[64] Sellar, thus blocked, became truculent and complained bitterly that his efforts in Sutherland had never been properly appreciated. Thus he recollected the painful years of 1812 to 1816, in the time of William Young:

> When chained to Mr Young's chariot wheels and, when the tripping [i.e. dancing] of that clever man, and his Surveyor Roy, were, for a time, shifted to my shoulders, I certainly until investigation, suffered under great and unmerited obloquy; but I think it will be seen on a close scrutiny of my last 21 years conduct as a farmer, that I have not committed many very Capital Errors in my business; and I never was more confident of the probability of Success, and of the consequences of that success, in any piece of business, than, I am, in this case presently under consideration.

This was characteristically elliptical Sellar prose, asserting that his farming successes made him the ideal tenant for any vacant sheep-farm in the north of Scotland.

Success in sheep-farming was bought at a price and in 1833 there was another eruption of public criticism of the Sutherland clearance policies, this time from the formidable pen of William Cobbett, who toured the north of Britain and whose reports were eventually incorporated in his *Rural Rides*. Sellar received an anonymous letter anticipating Cobbett's onslaught. Sellar was informed that 'there were Gentlemen in the "Reformed Parliament" who would shortly bring "the atrocities perpetrated in Sutherland" before the House.' Sellar regarded Cobbett as 'The most radical of all Republican Bablers'. Cobbett, indeed, lectured on Sutherland subjects to a Glasgow audience, and Sellar thought of legal retribution:

> What an error it was, not to have pounded [Alexander] Sutherland, the first defamer in 1816 and at once have settled and silenced these hornets. The 'path of the Just' has, however, conducted the one party to Wealth and honour; while, of the opposite side, the two Sutherlands, McKid, Carrol, Clunes, Stewart of Garth and [others?], all, are or were before death, ruined Bankrupts, and others, whom I know, are fast tending to the same misfortune – which is a matter of Regret.

It was thus that Sellar listed his enemies, and established his criteria and his ultimate defence.

The distance between James Loch and Patrick Sellar widened further. In 1833 Loch conducted yet another tour of the Sutherland properties and, in internal documents, conceded that the original clearance plans had been partially miscalculated. For instance, he visited the northwest district, just south of Cape Wrath (at Oldshores and Shegra), and saw the results of the extreme version of the removal system. The coastal zones had been settled

> for the purpose of fishing for which they are well situated, their lots were made small in order that they might become Fishermen only, and so that they might depend upon their lots for maintenance. The principle was good in the Abstract, but it has succeeded as little in this instance as it has done upon the Sutherland coast.

He noticed, to be sure, that in some places the settlers on the coast had done extremely well, and 'confirming an observation that has always been striking, that it is only necessary to move the people from the lands . . . in order to excite industry and improvement.' Loch recognised that since it was impossible to furnish all the people with good arable lands, 'and as they have been shewing a tendency to go to Canada,' they should be given more encouragement to emigrate. Absolutely clear in Loch's thinking, was the necessity for cautious change. Too much had been asked of the people during the removals. These were great concessions and self-criticisms in which Sellar simply refused to partake.[65]

– HARD BARGAINS –

Tension between Sellar and the Sutherland estate frequently related to his use of the land, his muir-burning and his dogs. This was a variation on the perennial struggle for control of the land in the Highlands. Having wrested possession from the cattle-raising regime of small producers dominant in the previous century, the sheep-farmers now began to confront new competitors for Highland territory. Muir-burning damaged the sport of the owners, their friends and then the new breed of big-spending sporting tenants, but muir control was a vital part of sheep-farming and, without it, there would always be a substantial deterioration of the sheep stock.[66] But Sellar's demands were insatiable, and his equal insistence on the eradication of vermin also collided with the new culture of sport in the Highlands. Thus, in 1833, when he was asked ('commanded', he said) by the estate to remove his sheep dogs and the guns of his employees from a certain part of the estate, he was inflamed. It would 'disarm our Shepherds of those guns . . . which, in every pastoral country where I have been, are used by the shepherds in defence of the creatures under their Charge.' Sellar appealed directly to Lord Stafford, assuring him that his game would always pass unmolested. He had dismissed two of his men he suspected of poaching, and he could always guarantee the landlord's game.

Allegations of poaching among his own shepherds caused Sellar to react heatedly, and he unwisely chose to draw a comparison between this relatively trivial case and his own sensational trial and its precognition back in 1815–16. Then, as now, he claimed, Lord Stafford had half-believed the allegations against Sellar and his men. Picking at this old sore, Sellar recalled that Mackid's Precognition of 1815 had

> cost your Graces, by your partial belief, in it, at the time, many thousand pounds, and many measures of false policy, which may not easily be put right.

Such was Sellar's most outspoken indictment of his landlord masters for the events of 1816. In this outburst, Sellar openly asserted that the

Staffords had failed to believe in the innocence of their factor at that immensely contentious time in the clearances. He had thus been taken to trial and, despite his exculpation, the sensation had crippled the estate. The rational rearrangement of the estate had been seriously impeded. The landlord had failed the tenant and had hamstrung its only sensible policy. The problem had all stemmed from the weakness of the owners. It was a devastating and unwelcome thought for Lord Stafford, himself then approaching the end of his life. The Staffords had paid dearly for their mistake. Sellar had been vindicated, and he was fully prepared to tell them so.

In the same mood, Sellar also reminisced about the early days of Strathnaver and its vermin, before he took it over in 1813. At that time 'the people of that country confined their Lambs in house to save them from vermin. After considerable losses and pains and expense, we rendered the farm comparatively safe, Atkinson and Marshall, Mr Reid and I employed a fox hunter and a small pack <u>which were kept in Strathnaver</u>.' In 1830, James Loch had interceded and decreed that the estate management would take over the control of vermin. This had been a spectacular failure so far as the sheep-farmers were concerned. Eagles and other vermin were at large all over Sutherland. The factors were responsible to George Gunn, the main factor, 'whom Mr Loch well knows to be towards me personally hostile!!' Yet Gunn was supposed to protect his flocks. Sellar had found it essential to employ some dogs in the previous year; they did not attack the Staffords' deer: one was a greyhound, and was employed for hare-coursing and was in any case now lame. The general tone of Sellar's letter was a combination of unctuous deference and blatant truculence.[67]

Sellar dealt with estate managers further down the chain of command with less decorum. When he wrote to the local factor, Horsburgh, about the irritation he felt from the competing sporting uses of the land, he was starkly candid. He had been 'an active improving tenant all my life', and he could not tolerate the restraints placed on him. His frustration was almost flammable. In November 1838, he ranted at Loch, saying that the deer should be sent back to 'their own place' – 'I (and not the deer) should possess Strathnaver'.[68]

On the question of the sheep-farms and their conditions, James Loch believed that the sheep-farmers were now well established, 'with houses, fences, folds, etc., in complete order'. They farmed in a thoroughly modernised system, and their rents had been sensibly set so that the fall in wool prices had not pressed heavily upon them.

Rents were regulated according to wool prices, and consequently 'their capital was let entire and their spirits were kept up. The result is that they are now wealthy and contented, with superior flocks and increased capital.' The system had worked well.[69]

Sellar was not so easily pleased. In the mid-1830s, his original leases were approaching their terms and their renegotiation became a fertile source of aggravation between Sellar and his masters. In October 1835, Sellar had already stipulated conditions which included complete access to the sea, so that he could import meal and stores directly and also export his wool. Currently he was forced to drive his flocks fifty miles overland to port. Moreover, he repeated the needs of his sons: 'I should be very sorry to see any boy of mine left with nothing to employ his mind besides the ennui of sheep, toddy, courting, and the Justice of the Peace Courts.' He also sought the authority to sub-set his lands to his descendants. His main consideration was to sustain at least one of his sons in stock farming in Sutherland.[70]

The Duchess/Countess of Sutherland, now an aged widow, retained close control of her estates and was irritated by Sellar's sinuous manoeuvrings and complained of his 'troublesome letters'. When, in November 1835,[71] Sellar threatened to quit Sutherland she remained cool and told Loch:

> I do not think it would be right to give him the extent of Country he wishes, unless one cd have ensured a resident Gentleman there as it is a great object to get decent people of a better sort to those parts, and it would not do to dispossess those settled on the coast to make way for his objects.

But she still needed Sellar: 'I hope he will end by staying.' She knew he was testing the management by his shifts. It was typical of Sellar, she complained, to imply that the estate wanted him to quit.[72] The new Duke wanted Sellar to be told that 'it would be a very great loss certainly' if he departed, but that there were limits to the concessions the estate was prepared to make.[73]

As the tenancy negotiations tightened, the Dowager Duchess communicated directly with her difficult but expert and valuable tenant. She told him that she and her son, the second Duke, 'both regard and value you, of which I believe you are well convinced, both as a friend and a Tenant.' But she shared a duty to the county, 'to place some resident Gentlemen Tenants in the northern part of the estate.' Equally important, however, she did not want 'to disturb the population now settled on the shores, and all the Estate in general. I mean the Lotters, who as long as they behave well and exert themselves, I feel myself bound to protect.' She agreed that Sellar needed to protect his flocks but, she remarked, 'upon that comparison you will not think me less bound to protect <u>my</u> flock.' This tart exchange indicated that Sellar wanted to pursue aggressive changes in his lands, including the removal of small tenants. The Dowager Duchess regarded this as inimical to the social equilibrium.[74]

In mid-1836, the estate gave serious consideration to breaking up Sellar's great sheep-farms. There was a meeting in Ramsgate in England with the Duke, who was willing to divest Sellar of his lower Strathnaver farm and to let it to resident tacksmen. Sellar was provoked by this line of thinking which he countered with the opposite suggestion, that he should be permitted to extend his farm to the sea to absorb and clear an area currently occupied by small tenants.[75] Loch discussed, with the Duchess/Countess, the possibility of Sellar's withdrawal from his leases and said that 'the best thing for the district would be to have more resident tacksmen, but even this advantage may be purchased too dear, for Sellar's meliorations will be very large.'[76] Sellar had already broached the possibility of quitting. In such circumstances he would need two years to arrange his herdings. The prospect of Sellar's defection was a serious matter to the estate management particularly since he contributed such a large share to the total rental of the estate. It was also a negotiating tactic which Sellar used to the best effect. He pointed out that his great draining work in the straths had allowed him to increase the sheep numbers greatly, and so also to enhance the capital value of the farms. At Rhiloisk, he had spent £750 on drainage and increased the stock capacity from 2,250 to 3,000, but this had been achieved with great difficulty among the people he employed. This had been 'a good transaction for her Ladyship but <u>a decidedly bad one for me</u>.' Sellar put her choice bluntly: 'If I can afford your bargain I will take it; if not, I will wish you a better tenant.'[77] But, he warned, he would demand very large compensation.[78]

In November 1837, terms were prepared for Sellar's continuing possession of Strathnaver.[79] Once more the negotiations were marked by repeated threats by Sellar to leave the estate. By now, the conflict between sheep-grazing interests and those of the sporting tenants had sharpened further. Sporting rents had emerged quickly as a swelling additional source of income to Highland estates, competing with the contributions of the sheep-farmers. To Sellar, sheep-farming and sporting tenants were not compatible. Sellar, indeed, refused to renew his nineteen-year lease 'if the restrictive clauses regarding burning were insisted upon', because the restrictions would be bound to deteriorate the number and value of his stock. Moreover, the game-keepers, the sportsmen and their dogs 'disturbed the sheep from feeding and give them wandering habits.' The sportsmen demoralised the shepherds (who were given gratuities by the sporting tenants for little effort) and divided their loyalties against those of their masters.[80]

In reality, Sellar's losses were always substantially fewer than those of other farmers, which once more demonstrated the extraordinary superiority of his management. Loch posed a counter-argument when he claimed that Sellar had underestimated the damage done to the quality of the land caused by sheep. Loch made a clear historical point, amid these thorny negotiations, that 'Mr Sellar has not . . . allowed for the regular and permanent deterioration of such lands as were formerly cultivated by the people, a deterioration common to the whole of the Highland Sheep Farms.' It was an admission that negative environmental effects were beginning to undermine the profitability of sheep-farming. This was part of the final calculus of the clearances, rarely admitted publicly by the estate.[81]

The problem, at the end of the day, was that grouse and deer reduced the sheep-carrying capacity of the land, and a reduction of rent was suggested by Loch as part of the approaching compromise.[82] Sellar eventually concluded his new lease with the second Duke of Sutherland, for lands in Kildonan, Farr, and Tongue as well as Morvich, in October 1839.[83]

– SPORT AND SHEEP –

Throughout the 1830s, Patrick Sellar was engaged in intermittent but bitter conflict with the estate administration, which eventually led to the partial diversion of his great investments in stock-farming. It derived from his strained relations with George Gunn, the main factor at Dunrobin, towards whom Sellar cultivated extreme dislike and distrust. It also derived from Sellar's failure to gain scope to expand his operations in the estate. He believed deeply in the logical con-sequences of economies of scale in sheep-farming. In the pursuit of this ultimate efficiency, which, of course, had begun with the original removals, he confronted the opposition of the Duke and his succes-sors. This was a matter of acute irritation to Sellar. He could not understand their obscurantism.

Sellar came to the wider conclusion that the entire estate manage-ment was attempting to obstruct and diminish his operations. As each new issue emerged, his exasperation increased and his complaints became more splenetic. Thus, in October 1833, he commented angrily, 'several years experience assures me that nothing but treachery and injustice are to be expected in some quarters as far as I am concerned.'[84]

The situation worsened when Gunn alleged that Sellar's shepherds were implicated in smuggling, and suggested a precognition. Sellar immediately took this as part of Gunn's campaign to make his life impossible. Gunn, he declared, was full of injustice towards him, which 'he takes every opportunity to inflict upon me'. Sellar had spent fourteen years successfully eradicating foxes to protect the 10,000 'innocent creatures which are under me'. The attack upon his shepherds was, he said, part of Gunn's plan to wrest control of Strathnaver from him. Sellar hated poaching as much as anyone: 'I would seize, convict and transport a poacher to the last man.' But the idea of a Precognition was anathema to him ('I am very sick of precognitions'), and he likened them to the Star Chamber. Indeed, for Sellar, the whole thing smacked of the awful experience he had suffered with Mackid in 'the second Strathnaver Conspiracy and precognition' in 1815–16. He had been indecisive at that time, and had suffered dearly by what he called 'my submission'. He believed Gunn was directing a comparable conspiracy against him, this time from within the very heart of the Sutherland estate management.

In 1836 another incident intruded to sour relations. In this instance, one of Sellar's shepherds had misunderstood the limits of permissible burning and had committed an illegal burning. Sellar moved to dismiss the offending parties, and told the Countess that it was inexcusable despite the circumstances; nor did he wish to say that the estate officers were exaggerating. Nevertheless Sellar went on to make a much more damaging claim against them:

> But, <u>since</u> the officers are men who have been themselves dispossessed to make room for sheep, the descendants and relatives of them so situated; <u>and</u> my experience, in McKid's conspiracy, the deer stealing affair [and the subsequent burning affair] has been enough to alarm any reasonable person.

Sellar believed that there were enemies from the old order deep within the estate management, and he was almost certainly alluding to Gunn, the main factor who had served in the regiment.

Sellar pointed out that the muir-burning had done no harm: 'There was not a Muirfowl's Egg in Sutherland . . . not a feather was damaged.' Sellar told the Countess/Duchess bluntly that, in effect, the rich benefits which had accrued to the estate were the result of scientific sheep-farming, and these, he heavily implied, were being subverted by pettifogging estate regulations and the adverse attitudes in the management. And on the question of muir-burning, he believed that the London gentlemen had no conception of what was at stake in the question.[85] There was, of course, supreme irony in the way in which Sellar faced competition for the land resources of Strathnaver. He could no more understand why the world would wish to place a higher value on shooting deer and grouse than on the farming of sheep, than the people he had cleared could understand the priority of sheep over their own subsistence.

By October 1837, Sellar pleaded with James Loch for a decision on his leases: 'Do anything you like, but do not, I pray you, keep me longer in suspense. Such a sum of property as I have, exposed, on these farms, to the chapter of accidents, with six months of a term of removal, is too much for a man with nine bairns.'[86]

But the negotiating difficulties ran on, and in August 1838 Sellar made further severe animadversions on estate policy when he said to Loch: 'If your pleasure be to turn these pastures into a Forest, do so, my good sir, by all means, but do not insist on bleeding us to death while the change proceeds.' This, of course, was the language of a bitter man, frustrated by unpalatable change.[87] And, when the possibility of a new leaseholder was bruited, Sellar was loudly sceptical that there was anyone who could match his skills as a sheep-farmer: 'I am a prosperous man, and produce about the best sheep and wool in Scotland.'[88] It was also a question of who should possess Strathnaver, Sellar or the deer.[89]

Sellar eventually agreed new terms for Strathnaver which curbed his muir-burning activities. But he conceded this much with singularly bad grace. He remarked, 'to Grow cheviot sheep without Burning heath and without washing the animals once a year, but mixed with Sportsmen, their dogs and servants' would be 'a period of Purgatory' and he wanted it to be no more than a brief 'Experiment'. He said that he expected to be dead by 1845, and certainly by 1859. He would soon be 'too old to travel the hills. So, it must be for one of my sons that I must wish to renew and I cannot think of tying a youth, neck and heel, to what at present, appear to me, to be most dangerous conditions.'[90]

Sellar continued this argument when he told the Duchess/Countess that his sheep-farming system in Sutherland had increased effective rents sixfold since the conversion of the lands from cattle. She should recollect also, he said, that the old system had been 'dependent on great periodical imports of meal to keep the people, and great periodical irrecoverable arrears.' These enormous gains to the estate, the landlord and the nation were now being jeopardised by the new policy which, he implied, was harassing the most productive farmer in Scotland. He told her plainly:

> They who attempt to molest Your Grace with exaggerated reports against the Shepherds and their masters, or who strive to excite a policy destructive of the Staple produce, for which these Alpine plants are by Nature given to us, do not know, or do not Consult your Grace's interest.

This was plain speaking, even for Sellar. He alleged that the Duchess/ Countess's advisers were traducing the interests of the estate.[91] His operations in the Sutherland estate were greater than those of the next four largest sheep-farmers taken together, and further restrictive conditions, he threatened, would force his departure.[92] Sellar's attitude to sportsmen was hardly in doubt, and he evidently disapproved of the Sutherland family's own enjoyment of sport in the straths. His prickliness was transparent when he declined to attend a dinner given by the estate for 'shooting Gentlemen and farmers', in September 1837.[93]

– Laird Sellar –

Sellar's expansionary ambitions in Sutherland had been thwarted, and he began to look beyond the county to fulfil his aspirations. He, more than anyone, was aware of dilapidated and inefficient properties throughout the Highlands, and his acquisitive gaze turned to the west coast. In 1838, the year of the death of the Duchess/Countess of Sutherland, Sellar chose to invest at Morvern, in Argyll, in the West Highlands. It was his first entry into the ranks of Highland landownership. His decision was driven by commercial considerations, but he was also intensely aware of the social status conferred by lairdship. Moreover, despite his eloquent denunciation of sportsmen, he was not immune from the attractions of the sporting life in the Highlands and the pleasures of hospitality. His new property gave him unambiguous fishing and shooting rights. He also knew a bargain, and his first purchase in Morvern was primarily another sheep enterprise. He did not gain a mansion for several years after his first venture in the district.

Sellar's purchase in Morvern was a defining moment for himself and also for his relations with the Sutherland estate. He had reached the limits of improvement in Sutherland. He was the greatest sheep-farmer in Scotland and the most efficient. The logic of the removals and the improvements was not allowed to take its full course. Sellar had been denied and the cause was political. Sellar regarded the restraints placed upon him in Sutherland as a victory of his enemies over the best interests of the Sutherland family. Much of this angry reasoning was transparent in the letter that Sellar wrote to Lady Sutherland at the time of his deflection into Argyllshire. He wrote:

> As not a mouse stirs in Sutherland, without Your Grace hearing of it, with many additions of which the poor mouse little dreams, it had occurred to me, that I should myself tell you, that I have bought a small place in Argyllshire, adjoining the Steam Navigation.

He was careful to stress that the capital did not come from large gains he had made in Sutherland: 'In fact, I have now employed the very capital, which I, some years ago tried to invest in Durness; that is, 20 years accumulation of the Westfield rents; which exist in consequence of my toiling like a farmer.' His plans to expand operation in Sutherland had been blocked and he made no bones about the ultimate cause of this re-direction into Argyll – there had been 'political reasons inducing to smaller rather than larger farms, here.' He realised that it was futile to petition further against 'the Line of policy chalked out, for your Grace.' He added, in his most refined tendentious fashion, 'I could not but see, that, for the last few years, your Grace's good wishes towards me (which I always found the same) were thwarted by some cause or other, that retarded and finally prevented the settlement of my affairs on the basis of progressive improvement.'[94]

Thus, after thirty years, Sellar now channelled his capital to another Highland county. It was a letter full of insinuations by a man of many frustrations.

CHAPTER 16

The Frame of Society

– THE 1840s –

Patrick Sellar, with some extravagance, announced that he would be dead by 1845. His thoughts of mortality were a consideration in the way he planned the renewal of his farm leases in Sutherland. In the outcome, he lived a year longer than the biblical span, and died in the year of the Great Exhibition. In his last decade he had certainly out-grown the territory which the Sutherland estate was prepared to make available to him. Having reached into Argyllshire at Morvern, he established himself as a laird. Aided by the charm of his wife and daughters and the manifest talents of his clever sons, his social world expanded. He rose in society and capped his career with wealth and connections, into social strata well above those of his original family. As always, however, his success was dogged by eruptions of controversy which invariably harked back to the events of 1814–16, and to his role in the clearances. There was no escaping his 'enemies'. Even at his death they were at his heels. And in his grave, he was given no peace. Patrick Sellar, no less than Captain Boycott of later agrarian infamy, became synonymous with an agrarian crime, the Clearances.

In the 1840s, Sellar used his declining, but still substantial, energies to extend his acres and improvements on his new estate in Morvern, to argue with his neighbours, and to combat his enemies as they reached above the parapet and let off volleys of criticism against him.

– AGRICULTURAL INVESTMENT –

In January 1840, Sellar duly celebrated, 'by favour of our Little Queen', the new penny post. A recognised authority on Highland property, he was consulted by prospective investors. A wealthy Liverpool merchant became interested in the island of Barra and, wanting to know the likely return on capital on such Hebridean property, sought Sellar's advice on its purchase price. Sellar remarked that he was 'not quite sure about Speculations at present, on Highland land, Stocked with Tenantry'. His attitude towards small tenants was predictably negative; but there was now a new hazard. There was a growing danger that new Poor Laws would be imposed on Scottish estates which would require estate owners to provide systematic (rather than charitable) relief to paupers. It was a prospect which sent shivers through all estate owners, some expecting it to be the final straw on their finances. Sellar calculated that if passed they would cost the prospective owner of Barra an extra £500 or £600 per annum. He noted that another recent buyer was already sick of his acquisition in Uist,[1] 'and, contemplating such a prospect, I dont doubt it.' As always, Sellar could see only disadvantage where the common people were still attached to land in the Highlands.

At home, in Sutherland, Sellar had cultivated warm relations with the factor on the west coast at Scourie, Alexander Stewart, who favoured the prospective purchase of Barra. He explained to Sellar, who no doubt approved, that the original idea of the current owner, Colonel MacNeill, had been 'to remove the *hordes* of small Tenants from the West and East side, so as to get at the most valuable of the pasture for stock, and to put down Fishing settlements, on the south and east, for the purpose of putting employment in fishing Ling and Cod, within the greater part of the population.' But MacNeill possessed neither the capital nor the perseverance for this grand plan and, instead, had instituted soda chemical works, which had fallen into 'a hideous disorder'. Stewart agreed with Sellar that it was most desirable 'to send the Highlanders to Upper Canada':

> But how is this to be done? A landlord of moderate means cannot do it and many who would have Barra would do a wise thing, perhaps to follow any plan – simply to put all the good lands under cheviots and remove many of the people into fishing settlements, giving each family potato land, and pasture for Cow. The superabundance of superior Ling and Cod, at the door will never allow them want of anything.

Given the assistance of a good factor to implement the plan, the island of Barra would be worth at least £40,000. Moreover, for the affluent proprietor, concerned with commuting and leisure, 'His ladies would have beautiful sea-bathing, and could be down from Liverpool in 48 hours.' Barra was a perfect example of the tension between the current interests of the resident population and the logic of economic max-imisation.

Sellar agreed that the fear of impending poor rates was enough to clog the sale of Barra. The threat of poor rates was damaging the value of all Highland property stocked with small tenantry. The people were too distant from productive employment and, in any case, 'many of them were so indolently disposed as not to avail themselves of it'. If poor law assessment became compulsory it would severely affect the value of Barra. The landlord therefore should promote emigration and:

> Upper Canada presents itself as the field most acceptable for general relief, and the sooner government and the landed interests hand in hand concert measures for having the redundant population of the Highlands sent thither, the better for all classes.

The striking candour in these exchanges encouraged Sellar to offer his observations on the concurrent upsurge of Chartism in the south. He felt that a few of the Chartists should be hanged in the same ruthless way that Governor Seaton had recently dealt with radicals in Canada. It would be salutary and would bring swift silence and order to the country: 'God forbid that Blood should be shed, but a few should suffer – than that lives and property of the many should be continually in jeopardy.'[2]

Sellar visited Glasgow, Perth and Liverpool in 1840, over a period of a month, and was 'by no means favourably impressed with the appearance of things'. Economic conditions in the manufacturing districts made him anxious. Supplies of cotton and wool were both scarce, and prices had been driven too high. Nevertheless, he noted, money was flooding in, and interest rates were bound to fall. This, he predicted, would help trade to recover its strength.[3] Within twelve months the entire economy was engulfed in one of the worst cyclical contractions of the century.

Sellar's reaction to all economic and social problems, short-term and long, was that efficiency and productivity should be increased. Technical excellence had brought the country forward wonderfully, in both agriculture and industry, and innovation was the secret of success. Sellar continued to be enthralled with the nicest details of agricultural practice, well able to rhapsodise on the joys of a good tilth. Morvich remained the centre of his experiments, and in 1840 he made special application to introduce a new rotation regime, negotiated through his lease. There was, indeed, no end to his improvisation in farming methods, and it was by his record as an innovator that, in the final analysis, Sellar wished to be judged.[4]

Sellar admired success. Sporting tenants were not generally favoured by Sellar but, in the autumn of 1840, he was intrigued by the appearance of a new sporting tenant, a 'great Brazilian merchant' who was 'a married man about 30, <u>without a family</u>, and is the eldest son which accounts for his passion for Sport.' Sellar had an instrumental view of sport: it channelled unspent energies. In this case, the applicant could be recommended as a 'nice Gentlemanly man'. But sportsmen, in his view, did not contribute to the productivity of the land.

Progress and eating habits were also connected in Sellar's view of social improvement. As a stock-farmer, in June 1842, he heartily extolled his own production:

> I wish to see cheap Beef and mutton, a <u>universal</u> consumption of both, by all classes of Her Majesty's subjects, male and female; because all history attests the indomitable courage of Shepherds, Britons and other such carnivorous animals; the cause why one Englishman, by Sea or Land, fighting two Frenchmen, being, that he consumes twice the quantity of animal food.[5]

Sellar continued to press the inevitability of large-scale operations in Highland farming. Thus, in 1840, when the leases of the Skibo lands (in southeastern Sutherland) were due to fall in, he declared that the land would best be added to his own farm at Morvich. It was presently used to raise kyloes for the Banffshire dealers. But, for efficiency, it ought to be amalgamated with Morvich. 'This will happen, because it is <u>according to nature</u>, whether you or I be in the Kirk yard or no', he told Loch. As a clinching argument, he added: 'I appeal to the fertility of my farms in comparison with the neighbouring farms.'[6] Few farmers could match his level of efficiency, and this gave Sellar special bargaining power on the estate. In the autumn of 1841, Sellar was again threatening to relinquish his leases in Kildonan, Farr and Tongue, and made similar threats about his lands in Morvich and Culmaily in the following year. Each warning was employed to extract more favourable conditions for his current operations, and those of his sons in the future. The estate itself was continuously torn between the wish to appease public opinion by breaking up the sheep-farms, and the need to maintain rent-income, of which Sellar always yielded the lion's share.

Sellar's progress depended on innovation and in 1842, he again became seriously animated about the virtues and possibilities of guano. He experimented with lime, and kept an eagle eye on new methods, recruiting his son Tom (in business in the United States) to send him the latest intelligence. By 1846 Sellar was convinced that Peruvian guano was the farmers' answer to the anticipated repeal of the Corn Laws. He calculated relative costs of bone and guano; he had spent £7,834 on permanent improvements at Culmaily farm and his expenses on cultivation at Culmaily and Morvich amounted to £1,443 each year. Sellar's farms were, of course, part of a sophisticated, heavily capitalised and integrated system which matched his pastoral and arable outputs to optimal effect.[7]

At Morvich, Sellar tested Peruvian and African guano, and concluded that guano was 'the greatest discovery in Agriculture that ever was made. The Atlantic and Pacific Oceans, you observe will, forever, produce the fishes etc, on which these Penguins feed.' Between them, they would produce an inexhaustible supply:

> I shall manure my land for 12/6 p. acre = 1/4 the price of fold manure! We shall positively make the Corn Laws a dead letter – that is, if Sir R. Peel will only seize possession of these African Islands, which are ours by priority of discovery, and will prevent the foreign traders from damaging the Birds, and establish regulations to put our people on their good Behaviour; and that promptly and without delay. There should not be a day lost. The Torrid Zone should be rummaged; the British flag hoisted on every treasure as it shall be discovered, and no mistake. It is a perennial benefit, which, with any prudence, we cannot exhaust; and if we miss the opportunity, we shall deserve all the ills that silliness and misgovernment fail not, wherever they exist, to Bring upon men and Empire. If only we secure these treasures to this United Kingdom we shall make it fit to maintain 50 to 100 millions of people – for fertility is progressive. Our ships will save us and foreign countries may buy from us but cannot sell to us corn so cheaply as we can produce it. The Ball is at our feet, if we will only kick it.

This was Sellar's personal gospel of Imperialism.[8] In some ways he was prescient: 'High Farming', fully modernised and capitalised, was to prove a vital contribution to three decades of progress and prosperity in British farming after 1848.[9] But, in 1847, Sellar nevertheless complained bitterly about the reduction of tariffs on foreign wheat.[10]

– THE DEMOCRATICAL PRESS –

In 1841, Sellar once again found himself the object of public vilification relating to the events of the clearances thirty years before. This recrudescence of hostility came in the form of a series of letters by a stonemason, Donald Macleod, in an Edinburgh newspaper. Macleod had lived through the Sutherland evictions and was named in Sellar's list of defence witnesses for his trial in 1816. At that time Macleod's evidence was not used. But, in 1841, he told a sensational story of atrocities alleged against Sellar in the events of Whitsunday 1814. His articles were republished in book form, and eventually constituted one of the key sources in the anti-Sellar tradition.

Sellar was again roused to instant indignation, and he fulminated at this revival of what he called 'Mackid's conspiracy of the years 1814–15 and 1816' in 'a radical newspaper in Edinburgh'. The *Edinburgh Evening Chronicle* carried 'an attack on the Sutherland Family' under the title of 'Destitution in Sutherland'. It was MacLeod who now recreated the original scene in Strathnaver during which he alleged that Sellar had uttered the infamous words to the aged Mrs Mackay (which had never been reported at the time): 'Damn her, the old witch, she has lived too long; let her burn.'[11]

Sellar was angry that the articles chose to 're-assert <u>as truth</u>, all that the Jury found to be fiction, and that Mackid acknowledged . . . "to amount to <u>absolute falsehoods</u>".' Sellar quickly disinterred his old *Statement* which he had printed and circulated at the time of the Stewart of Garth eruption in 1825. Sellar regarded the new outburst as contemptible. It nevertheless 'in these times, calls for cool reflection'. Sellar summoned his legal adviser in Edinburgh, and asked for James Loch's advice. He thought it might 'be in my power to put these men to Silence and to punishment too, without reference to any question as betwixt them and the Noble Family.'

The attack in the Edinburgh newspaper naturally caused Sellar to rake over the old story again. He recollected that, at his trial in 1816, Lord Pitmilly had presided over the investigation 'in minute detail for <u>15 hours</u>'. Moreover the case had been presented before

> a Jury of Highland Gentlemen; Lord Cockburn who then, as Counsel, interrogated the witnesses and Culbackie the foreman of the Jury are still alive. So is . . . Drummond, the King's Counsel – they can tell how the case was [Sifted?] and how clearly the villainous nature of the Conspiracy was made out.

He added that, 'during the whole struggle, from 1810 downward . . . I have done without flinching, and without fear, what I thought incumbent upon me, to the best of my knowledge; and I will not fall back in these latter days.' He would forever follow the course of 'Truth and Justice'.[12]

Sellar regarded the *Edinburgh Chronicle* articles as

villainous libels . . . against the noble family and their agents, past and present! that Lord Pitmilly and the fifteen highland gentlemen of the Jury, did falsely acquit me from the charges made, and that McKid does not tell the truth, when he says that these charges amount to absolute falsehoods, of which he (bless the mark) is thoroughly ashamed'.

Sellar noted that Loch's own *Account* of 1820, which outlined the 'distress, famine and disease' which the great changes were designed to remedy, had now been transposed by the *Chronicle* into 'the *consequences*' of the changes. It was all part of the *Chronicle*'s campaign

to stir up the unwashed part of mankind against those who shave and wear a clean shirt. If passed over in silence these libels must have weight with a great mass of the people, who elect members for cities and boroughs, and even on respectable farmers who vote in counties, both in Scotland and England.[13]

The 'libels', with each week, became 'more villainously false and pointed than before'. Sellar identified the author, Donald Macleod, as a tenant removed from Strathy by Horsburgh 'some years ago'. Sellar wondered if the Duke of Sutherland, 'so high and fine on his pedestal, ought to do something about the profanum vulgus', and whether he could 'safely allow the uneducated classes to imbibe such prejudices against you [the Duke].' He declared that, in the twenty-six years that had passed since his trial a new generation had arisen which must be 'disabused of such misrepresentations'. He believed that such radical libels exerted 'a most deadly and fatal quality' among the populace. He admitted that he found it impossible to remain cool under the new provocation. But in the outcome no legal action was taken against Macleod, and his words became remarkably influential in the popular account of the clearances though they possessed no contemporaneous validation.[14]

Sellar was watchful for further outbreaks of public criticism. In Sutherland itself there was a spectacular outbreak of anti-clearance protest in 1841, in Durness in the Reay Country, and the management was on high alert.[15] In December 1841, Sellar noticed that 'these Reay Country Highlanders [are] I see still pelting at the management here in the Newspapers and, who, certainly are the most lying, psalm-singing peasantry in the Queen's dominions.'[16] With a weary sense of inevitability, Sellar found himself recirculating his 1825 *Statement* in mid-July 1845 in response to further critical articles, on this occasion in *The Times*. Once more he was confronted by 'villainous statements' in a further assault on the Sutherland estate. Sellar told Loch's son and successor in the Sutherland management (George Loch) that general public opinion simply did not understand. Even 'good and candid men complain of the unremitting Celerity, with which our measures were carried through' back in the 1810s. 'But', said Sellar,

> they do not Consider, that the same leaders who conducted the villainous Conspiracy which the kind communication of Mr David Ross the fiscal, enabled me to defeat, were directing hostilities of another kind against sheep-farmers, some of whom lost from 600 to 1,000 sheep by theft in a single year; and, that the new tenants would have been ruined by the smallest delay on our part to expel the people from the marches, all to involve the masses so removed in a necessity to occupy themselves in a different and more honest Employment.[17]

Sellar thus sustained his view of the conspiratorial elements in the old events, as well as the notion that the evictions had been totally confrontational. It had been a contest for the land in which only the most efficient could survive.

Again in September 1847, Sellar was inflamed by what he termed an 'unprovoked' attack on him in *The Times* and in *Tait's Magazine*. He responded to the latter by invoking the record of the censuses showing that there had been no depopulation in the Sutherland clearances, and that it was simply untrue that 500 hearths had been extinguished in the process. The facts were totally at odds with the popular claims made against himself and the estate.[18] Sellar denounced *The Times* as part of 'the most democratical part of the Press'. He was particularly irritated by exaggerated reports of his own finances in the *Edinburgh Weekly Register:* 'What the press means by attributing to me such wealth as it speaks to, it beats me to find out.' He took a faintly wry attitude to the latest outburst about the Sutherland events of so many years before: 'I fain hope that as the light of truth is beginning to dawn upon them, these ghosts of thirty years old fabrications will now be pleased to return to their coffins.'[19]

The immediate consequence of these recurrent eruptions of public criticism was to render the Sutherland family even more nervous of controversy. The second Duke, in particular, thought the time had come to appease the British public by breaking up his infamous sheep-farms. The idea of reversing the removals, of course, was totally opposed by Sellar who, in his final years, came to be disappointed with his masters.

– PARENTAL AMBITION –

In his own household, at Morvich and Morvern, Sellar was his own master. Through the winter of 1839–40, his eldest son Tom was ill in Elgin. This caused anxiety to the family. It was decided to find the best spa in the south for his recovery. In early 1840, Sellar's wife also fell ill and needed convalescence. This caused Sellar inconvenience in his domestic arrangements, and he said to the factor at Scourie: 'I find this sort of widowhood very irksome, you mind if you come down to the coast, you must come and see me.' It was a rare scene in Sellar's home life and his wife apparently recuperated without further alarm.

The most brilliant of the Sellar sons was William Young Sellar, a precocious boy who was sent off to Elgin Academy where he and his brothers boarded with a clergyman. Sellar's daughter-in-law later recalled the 'iron' regime which Sellar senior imposed on his sons to succeed at school. They were generally successful. At fourteen, William was Gold Medallist and head of the school: 'But he never looked back to this time with pleasure; and his father afterwards said that he had made a great mistake in spurring the willing horse, and that the full participation in the games which was denied him would have been a better preparation for the battle of life than the over-stimulating so young and fine a brain.'[20]

Patrick Sellar monitored his offspring closely, and continued to celebrate their success. In December 1843, he mentioned to James Loch that *The Times* had announced '[Willy?] Sellar's name' as Balliol Scholar, remarking proudly:

> If the fellow dont subside into 'Port and Prejudice' which they pay on Oxford 'fruits' the Study necessary for the King must have done him good. But I mention his name, remembering what he and I owe to Lord Dunfermline and yourself.[21]

Sellar, indeed, had recruited all the influence he could muster to promote his sons' careers. But the pressure was oppressive, and one of Sellar's younger sons fell ill under the strain. The son had also been dux at his school, but overworked himself. Sellar referred to him as 'My little manny' and attributed his son's collapse to excessive studies. He was brought home 'greatly to his and our disappointment . . . If it be God's good pleasure, we shall restore him thoroughly, and bye and by, return him to the Contest.' But even as he convalesced, he was starting his studies at 6 a.m., for this was the contest of life. Overweening ambition, in the father or the son, was bought at a price.[22]

In May 1848 Sellar was able to report with the greatest pride that his son William, who had been helped by the good word of both the Duke of Sutherland and Lord Bathurst, had succeeded brilliantly at Balliol.

> The consequence was, that he won the . . . scholarship, afterwards took a 'first', and this morning's post Brought me advice that he has just been elected to an open Oriel Fellowship that happened to come into competition altho, for the last year, his health had been so weak, [from] over much study, that he scarcely dared to hope for success, We shall now insist on his letting his mind lay [*sic*] fallow for a time until it shall thoroughly recover its tone.

In the meantime, his eldest son had succeeded with the merchant house, Dennistouns: 'He climbed to the highest place at the disposal of his Employers, which he now retains. Neither of the two had the slightest introduction or patronage beyond what I have here mentioned.'[23]

From these years a few fragments of the correspondence of Sellar's elder daughter have survived in a private Australian archive. Written just before and after her marriage in 1842, the light-hearted letters of Jane Sellar display a personality full of exuberance and flirtation. They are a tiny domestic window but hardly suggest that Jane Sellar was the suppressed offspring of a tyrant or a Gradgrind.[24] Sellar *père* may have mellowed in his middle years. As time passed, he seemed to grow closer to the Duke's Commissioner, James Loch, despite Sellar's provocative attitude to leasing and the future of the Highlands in general. When Loch's first wife died, in early 1842, Sellar was full of condolences and remarked, 'That Grim fellow has taken off four of my friends within the past four days! We must just strive to do our duties well and kindly, and Let him take his course, for also there is no other course for us.'[25]

Both Sellar and Loch were fathers to remarkable Victorian dynasties, considerably more distinguished than the offspring of the Leveson-Gowers, the aristocratic family they served respectively as tenant and commissioner. The contrast may have irritated the Leveson-Gowers who were endlessly reminded of the triumphs of the Sellar children. In 1851, Patrick Sellar told the Duke of the success of his sons. His

> Eldest . . . is greatly intrusted by Messrs Dennistoun and his Co partners and has proved himself worthy of Trust. Including my second son, in the management here [Morvich], my young men are off hand now except three – one surviving us, as an apprentice in Stock and crop farming here –

one an apprentice to Littledale of the Great Broker in Liverpool, and my youngest at Rugby school. William, my Oxford son, would have him sent there but, cui Bono, I have not yet discovered.[26]

It was a father's ambition rewarded.

– Poverty and Religion –

Apart from his farms and his newspaper enemies, two issues consumed Sellar in the 1840s and both threatened the established order in the Highlands. One was the Disruption of the Church which, in Sutherland in particular, drove an irreversible wedge between the landlord and the people. Most of the population deserted the established Church, whose ministers subsisted on payments from the Duke. The Sutherland estate tried to resist the tide of revolt, and refused to provide sites for the Free Church. In his obstinate policy of refusal, the Duke of Sutherland 'rendered himself obnoxious to the supporters of the Free Church.'[27] It was a time of passionate division. The second issue concerned the introduction of a systematic and compulsory Poor Law which would require (rather than exhort) landlords and farmers to support paupers across the country. In both debates, Sellar joined the most conservative stream.

In September 1843, Sellar observed that there were 3,000 families of small tenants and cottars in Sutherland and the local Savings Banks showed an average of £3 6s 8d each, which, he thought, was a marvellous indication of their material improvement. He attributed their betterment to the fact that the Duke rented his property to them at 'less than half its value (this I know is true)', which allowed them to accumulate savings, and proved that the talk of poverty was so much nonsense. Sellar's confidence on the question of rents was based on a figure that he would have been prepared to pay for the land, if he took it over, out of the hands of the small tenantry.

Sellar's views on the problem of Highland poverty had been sharpened over four decades. He was scornful of the advocates of a new Poor Law since they evidently believed that 'where people are placed when they cannot live by the sweat of their own Brows, they should live by the sweat of the landlords.' This assumption was entirely anathema to Sellar. Referring to the Highlands, he told Loch, in almost apoplectic terms:

> In this country, you have a vast lot of people, whom you should have, long since, settled in Caithness or Canada – settled them, at a great profit to

themselves and you. You had the power or the capital to do it with comfort and profit to every body; but, you wanted the pluck, the moral courage, to refute and dispatch such [puppies?], as Stewart of Garth and Co, and to do your duty thoroughly; and now, at the distance of seven and twenty years, the consequence comes.

It was a devastating proposition to put to Loch, and carried the fire of Sellar's conviction to its logical conclusion. The clearances had been right, and the men who directed the policy had simply lacked the fortitude and courage to execute the policy properly. They had been afraid of men such as Stewart of Garth. The Sutherland estate had been spineless. All the people should have been cleared from the land long ago.

For Sellar (who originally opposed emigration), the main point now was to minimise the consequences of that earlier damage by 'in every way promoting Emigration', and 'to that end, taking thorough means to promote Education – for boys when educated rightly will <u>insist</u> on going abroad to push their fortunes.' The most important principle, in any provision for the residual poor, was 'not to give a <u>Bonus</u> in favour of laziness, improvidence and dissipation.' Poverty, Sellar insisted, arose from two causes, namely 'impotence' and 'idleness and vice'. The first deserved his warmest sympathy, the second he detested. He therefore advocated a General Poor House for the County of Sutherland, with proper governors together with a housekeeper, and a public school for the children of paupers. The school should be located at twenty miles distance from the parents, so that 'they may get away from the influence and contagion of ill-doing parents.' The local authorities should be empowered to determine eligibility for indoor relief.[28]

The discussion of the oncoming Poor Law reignited Sellar's passionate denunciation of past faults. In October 1845, he summarised his objections to the new Act. It would allow the 'leaders of the Free Church, and other discontented persons, to stir up the lower classes against their superiors'. In consequence, 'the superiors, to avoid this evil, will offer a premium for mendicity, to the monstrous injury of the whole frame of society, of the prosperity and well being of all classes of the people.' To escape these consequences, he advocated one Grand Union with an assemblage of cottages as the Poor House. Each pauper recipient would be required to give up all personal property and holdings, and then would be maintained by the Board of Guardians. 'We shall also take charge of your children and educate them at school, where they may be untainted by the bad example of persons who have done nothing for their child in this life.' It would act as a deterrent to dependence, and it would break the passage of poverty from one generation to the next.

In Sellar's plan, the poor would be encouraged to maintain their private independence. Incurables would be kept in check by the board of management. Meanwhile, by 'the separate education of the children', they would be sensibly 'cut off in a great measure from the fountain from which the tide of poverty springs and threatens to overflow the country.' The chains of inter-generational poverty would be snapped.[29]

Sellar railed not only against the Poor Laws but against democracy itself. The new Poor Laws were

> the most desperate and cowardly concession to democratic tyranny that I can imagine – and this by a conservative Government! It brings you to this, that you must either put our country into farms of useful size, and establish a class of yeomanry whose interests will lead them to support the landlord (subject always to the Control of the Superintendiary Board and inspector) or lay your necks under the feet of the Populace and their leaders of the Free Kirk. The worst feature of it is that it puts the power into the hands of the populace – this dishonest power – to spoil them, and induce them to trust not to industry but to pillage, for their support in old age and infirmity.

He knew exactly how the Highlands should be arranged. In a rational world, the Highlands would be thoroughly cleared:

> If you had your Country in farms of £5,000 to £1,000 a year, as it naturally should be, you would have none of these troubles which keep you in a perpetual worry; the landlord and the rate payer would stand by each other, to what they felt to be Just; the inspector and Board of control would see that they did what was Just, and all would go about – one man (such as I was 20 years ago) would collect your whole rent in three days, more than you do at present. Lacking however the mass of Lies and intrigue which we have.

Sellar's ideal frame of society consisted of large farmers, and few, if any, people to impede rural efficiency.

He exclaimed, 'thank heaven that I have taken my last lease, so that I am personally less anxious than I should be.'[30] Sellar was jaundiced about progress in Sutherland in the past decade. Little had been achieved

> except that it has Gone on under Easy Sail, rents paid with punctuality and tenants, in consequence of previous improvements growing richer, and by the lapse of times, having become independent without Education, they poured out their savings, into the coffers of the Free Church – in recompense for its having taught them that they are an oppressed people.

Sellar certainly understood the radical and subversive consequences of the rise of the Free Church which set the people against the landlords and their religion.[31]

As the controversy over the Disruption and Church sites reached higher temperatures, Sellar found himself equally roused on the side of the landlord. He told the Duke that the Dissenters wanted to 'offer up the Nobleman – an Aristocrat! . . . as victim on the altar of democracy'.[32]

> It seems to be the opinion of every person in Scotland who had thought on the subject, that the late secession has purged the Church of a great many silly fellows, and ill-tempered fanatics; in place of whom, their successors make a good exchange for the country.

There was simply no 'common honesty in the Free Church', and its demagoguery was worthless.[33]

– FAMINE IN THE 1840s –

When the 'Great Famine' fell upon the West Highlands in 1846, Sellar believed that all his views on Highland welfare were now vindicated. He painted his own caricatured portrait of West Highland life before the famine of the late 1840s:

> The Highland people, cultivating potatoes on which they while away the winter, squabbling about Church politics, petitioning the Laird, or leading before the Sheriff, catching a few fish on a 'good day'. These habits will be overturned [only] by the establishment of a fishery.

In Sutherland, especially in the east, conditions were superior: 'There is no doubt, that the Sutherland highlanders of this Generation, exceed in industry, everything that has gone before them, and every other clan now existing. It is when one mixes with others that the difference is seen.'[34]

When Sellar heard of the total failure of the potato crop in 1846, he was quick to point out that good American flour was selling at 1/- per pound in Glasgow, and therefore 'Donald must go South and win the 1/-.'[35] He believed now that the Repeal of the Corn Laws was inevitable. He predicted that the potato shortage, in 1847, would be even worse because there were 'so little seed potatoes'. Therefore, he argued:

> Whatever can be done to diminish the number of unprofitable consumers, should be set about directly while the whole summer season is before us.

> Instead of employing a host of ships during next <u>winter and spring</u> to import supplies for the poor potato cultivator, would it not be well to consider, whether the same ships and money employed in <u>summer</u> to convey the redundant population to locations of various sizes in Canada and kindly and paternally settling them there <u>where provisions are comparatively cheap</u> would not be better?

Famine made emigration inescapable and he advocated Canada as the best destination because it would ' "stand as a wall of Fire" betwixt you and the Yankees'. Sellar embellished his argument by a historical analogy, pointing out that 'Scotland was never free from the Sword of the English, until Malcolm Canmore gave the waters of the Tweed to the expelled Saxons – settle a similar colony of men who love you, on the frontiers, of which the Great Lakes form a part, and a seeming calamity, you will convert into a Great Benefit to the Country.' Emigration would solve the Famine and the American problem at one fell swoop.

James Loch had access to the centres of government, and Sellar regarded him as a conduit for his own views. In the west Highlands, the crofters lived off potatoes for three months every year and in 1847 again no potatoes had been planted. He recommended an emigration scheme in which the emigrants would eventually repay the passage costs. He thought that landlords could make advances to prospective emigrants. He warned: 'If nothing be done, the distress of 1848 will exceed that of 1847. The expense of 1848 will exceed that of 1847 and nothing done to remedy the misgovernment,' which had brought it all about from the start.

Indeed Sellar's opinions of emigration had not changed since 1816. He did not mince words:

> If facilities were given for emigration, there would be a General wish to go abroad. The <u>difference of Cost</u> of eating Indian meal in America, besides eating it at home would pay the expense of their transport. 10 millions applied, merely to pass through the Bowels of a misgoverned people, is worse than thrown away. It destroys their self reliance. Makes a mistletoe on the British oak.

Without emigration the 'most serious consequences must await us.' He was unlikely to persuade anyone with this turn of phrase.

– Sellar in Morvern –

Sellar directly confronted West Highland conditions as a laird on his newly acquired property in Argyll. During the famine years, he was chairman of the parochial board at Ardtornish, in Morvern, and spoke for his parish: 'I believe an offer by government to locate emigrants in Upper Canada, would be <u>greedily embraced</u>.' But the benefits of emigration would be wasted unless the land relinquished was resettled in farms of the size of at least five moderately sized fields, 'to be cultivated according to the Rules of Good Husbandry.'[36]

Sellar's entree to Morvern had begun in 1838 when he bought the Archan estate, for £11,250, from an unsuccessful non-resident proprietor, Alexander Fraser of London, £4,400 less than had been paid for it in 1825, reflecting the poor times through which the region had passed in the previous twenty years. Philip Gaskell suggested that when Sellar entered Morvern in 1838 he may well have been 'the most widely hated man in the Highlands still'. Morvern already had a record of removal and migration and was already dominated by sheep-farming as early as the 1790s[37] and there were later recollections of clearances in the district by means of 'the crowbar and the faggott'.[38] In the nineteenth century about 3,250 people left the parish and at least 750 people were evicted by its new owners.

Sellar probably required his new lands to be cleared before his entry but he also revived his own career as an evictor, of which he had had little direct experience since the events of 1814.[39] A flock of blackfaced sheep were driven from Sutherland to restock his new Argyllshire property. But his operations required the disposal of forty-four families from the lands, about 230 people, a greater number than those involved in his more infamous eviction in Strathnaver in 1814. But at Arachan and Archan there was no resistance, and no force was required to effect the clearance. But nor did Sellar make provision for the people, and nothing is known of their subsequent fate, either collectively or individually. One source claimed that Sellar acted the part of 'the ruthless evictor,' even though the people 'owed not a single penny of rent'.[40]

Three years after his first land purchase in Morvern, Sellar expanded his investment, buying a nearby property of 4,794 acres at Clounlaid and Uladail, from John Sinclair, at a price of £7,500, together with the remainder of the fishing rights for the River Aline. By 1841, he possessed a good compact sheep-farm, but without a decent residence for his family. In 1844, he acquired the Ardtornish estate, 9,965 acres for £11,100 with arable land and a good mansion included.[41] He was now well established, with added rental land: 32,000 acres in all, enough in the 1850s for 8,250 sheep. In the early days of his new status, Sellar attended an event in Argyllshire which would soon draw him away annually. He told James Loch that he had joined a 'meeting of the Morvern Lairds, who are forming an "association" like our old Sutherland one, and have placed me unworthily, at the head of it.' This was Sellar's triumph: he was now the laird and social leader.[42]

Sellar's arrival at Morvern was noted by the traveller James Wilson in 1842. He reported that the man, famous in the Sutherland improvements, was stocking his new lands with cheviot sheep. He remarked, 'Morvern is still altogether without roads, no modern improvements have been attempted, the population is considerable, and the people are ill-off for want of work.'[43] It was a little feudal principality, ready to be dragged by Sellar into the ninetenth century. The new laird set about the task with his customary energy and capital. He was at this time as heavily involved at Ardtornish as he had been in Culmaily three decades before. He was effectively commuting between the two places, despite the distance involved, returning north to Sutherland and Moray each year in October.

As landowner in Morvern, Sellar had greater latitude to follow his own principles, and he did not fail to proclaim this fact. He told Loch, at the end of 1845, that he had a flock of 8,000 sheep in Argyll:

> I am busy accomplishing . . . in one year, what I took ten years to do in Sutherland, and I have such a lot of new shepherds, drainers, trenchers, quarryers, dykeleaders, and dyke builders, and stonemasons building piers, that I have been obliged for this year to devote myself entirely to this concern; and lucky it is that I shape my course in this manner and made all my bargains in 1844, for there is every prospect, if half the railways contemplated be proceeded with, that wages will be too extravagant for a man of common prudence.

In October 1844 he declared, 'Next season will conclude my Toils in that Country, after which I must seek more comfort I think.' In fact he had just set up construction work on two new quays at Morvern, 'from which to walk Sheep into the Steam Boat.'[44] Describing himself now as 'so small a proprietor', he thought the railway would bring great benefit to the west coast and especially to the wool and fish trades.[45] It was all practical progress and a relief from the cacophony of the Disruption. In all, it was 'A Better employment this – supplying of food for the industrious, than is unravelling the Canting lies and humbug of an idle population.'[46]

For Sellar, perhaps inevitably, there was a critical problem with his Morvern properties, and it was full of the promise of conflict. Sellar's lands were divided into two parcels, split by an intervening property, Achranich. To pass from one part of his property to the other, he, his friends and his flocks required the concurrence of his neighbour, Octavius Smith, the highly successful Pimlico entrepreneur. Smith was of a more benevolent cast than Sellar, and did not sweep the small tenantry from his estate. He was the only local owner to be praised in the Napier Commission on crofting in 1886.

The convergence, from opposite ends of the great British economy, of Sellar and Smith, titans of Victorian enterprise, did not excite charity in either man. They chose to fall out over two issues which became connected and corrosive. Sellar, on the one hand, held the fishing rights on the River Aline and prohibited Smith from fishing even from his own river banks. Reciprocally, Smith refused Sellar permission to move his flocks across Achranich. Their fury and obstinacy were perfectly balanced, and they refused to speak to each other for two years.[47] As Sellar's daughter-in-law recollected: 'both men [were] accustomed to have their own way, and very much disliking to be thwarted; so for a time, a modern Montague and Capulet drama was enacted.' Eventually a distinguished lawyer mediated a meeting, 'on the hill', and the matter was settled in October 1850. Smith bought half the fishing rights for £400, and, as part of the settlement, Sellar's rights of access were clarified. Honours were evenly divided, and a time of great rapport now enveloped the two families at Ardtornish. This Victorian melodrama was later crowned by the marriage of Sellar's youngest son, Alexander Craig, to Smith's daughter Gertrude.[48]

Sellar and his family visited Ardtornish each summer and early autumn. They became part of what Philip Gaskell characterised as a new class of gentry in the Highlands: 'Rich, cultured foreigners who had no professional interest in the land but who migrated to the West Highlands for lengthy holidays to walk and shoot and fish and relax in a country of insidious beauty utterly removed from their usual environment.'[49] They spent many happy summers there. Ardtornish was Tennyson's idea of heaven[50] yet, though he wrote about Morvern, he said little of the life of the place, and certainly nothing about the *traumas* of the clearance years. Herbert Spencer, was similarly rhapsodic about Ardtornish in his *Autobiography* but no less blinkered about the social system in which his West Highland heaven was set.[51]

According to Iain Thornber, the real story is found 'in the homely verses of the local bards and songwriters'. For instance, Duncan MacPherson who left Morvern to become a sheepfarmer in Otago,

New Zealand, carried with him all the anger and hatred of the evicted, some of which attached to Sellar directly.[52] Another account described a Morvern eviction, involving 'the poor half-naked widow, with the house smoking about her head; Sellar and his vile companions laughing at her loss.' The memorialist chided the people for their 'dumb and inactive' response to the landlords. Sellar's role in the Morvern evictions remains confused, the oral record at odds with the benign picture drawn by Gaskell, and no contemporary documentation survives to settle the matter.[53]

– EVER THE CLEARER –

Back in Sutherland Sellar increasingly devolved responsibilities on his young son, also named Patrick, who already supervised the lambing season in Strathnaver in May 1844. In the following year Sellar asked for an extension of his lease: 'I have given my son a share of it, and wish, in so great a concern, to make everything clear for him without the possibility of misunderstanding.' The main source of 'misunderstanding' remained the conflict over heather eradication and sporting rights and Sellar's permanent feud with the factor George Gunn. Sellar defined his attitude to the landlord:

> You know my anxiety, during the last 30 years, to do all things correctly that are becoming of a tenant, and especially to preserve the woods, which are, in their place, so Beneficial to our Stock, and I think you can discover no change in my conduct, beyond that [which] time inflicts upon us all.

The muir-burning was a recurrent issue of the sort that inevitably set Sellar against his landlord.[54]

Age was taking its toll of Sellar; his handwriting deteriorated and he complained of 'shaking hands'.[55] Nevertheless, he agreed to help James Loch prepare a second edition of the *Account* (which, in the outcome, was never produced). Prompted by Loch's book, Sellar looked back to the time when 'you found the country [in 1812] in the most grievous state of feudal tyranny and mismanagement, the landlord receiving nothing out of it and the population ground to dust, by the exactions of the middlemen and the grievous manner in which these exactions were levied.' He enumerated the old exactions. They included rent, labour, victuals, hens, eggs, work services for the harvest and thrashing corn, manufacturing peats, repairing peat roads, thatching houses, making and cutting hay and various other impositions. These dues were paid to a middleman who owned a £800 mortgage (in the form of a wadset), and paid no rent to the landlord. Under this old system the same lands were relet at £150, and rented again to the people for £229, plus the services of sixty-eight tenants. 'Well!' exclaimed Sellar to Loch:

> You dismissed the middlemen; set the tenants free from thraldom; expended vast sums of money on making roads through the country, building houses and fences, establishing the various means of communication, with comfort, introducing every sort of improvement applicable to the country; contriving, in an especial manner, that the Alpine herbage of the mountains should be converted to wool and mutton.

Clearly, the 'people formerly employing themselves in preventing the above improvements' ought to enter 'the fisheries which surround the coast'. Since the great changes, the tenantry now paid three times the former rent, and had 'passed into easy circumstances, the cottars in Rogart actually enjoying more comfort than did the Lieutenants Colonel of the Local Militia and Volunteers, when I went to Sutherland.'

Sellar's pent up anger and frustration knew no bounds as he looked back on the story, and the failure of the full logic of improvement to take its course. All remaining poverty and incompetence was a simple consequence of that failure. Any contemporary criticism was derived from deluded and malicious sections of society.[56] Sellar was fully satisfied that Loch's *Account* had been 'a complete . . . refutation of all that has been said against the Sutherland improvements. If a man will read it and not be convinced neither would he believe (I have told him) although one rose from the dead.' Sellar identified the problem precisely. Neither before nor after his death, would people at large accept the logic of his case, regardless of what they read.

In 1846, Sellar again found himself in acrimonious debate with his landlord over the terms of his lease. He claimed that his rents were too high, that he was forced to collect cottar rents, and that the Duke should pay for improvements to cottages on his farm. Sellar gave the impression that he was threatening, once more, to resign his farms in Sutherland. The Duke, thoroughly irritated, was prepared to call Sellar's bluff and remarked: 'I therefore offer to him to take his farms off his hands . . . that in making him the offer of taking his farms I must say that after the long connexion it must be a subject of regret that it should cease.' He continued that 'if he [Sellar] will stay when free to go he has not right to complain and the sooner we can make new arrangements the better for the public and private good.' Thus the

Duke took a robust attitude to his argumentative tenant, having been especially annoyed about Sellar's description of his arrangements as rack-rented.[57]

Sellar was paying a rent of £2,200 p.a. He blamed George Gunn for the embarrassing quarrel with the Duke. 'I have no doubt either that it is easier for Mr Gunn to receive from you the £2,200 yearly, than it would be to collect the same amount from 2 or 3 others – and that in a pecuniary point of view it is an advantage for me, but other considerations are involved in this concern.'[58] Gunn and Sellar had been adversaries since the year 1827 when Sellar declared that 'while Mr Gunn represented your Grace', he would confine himself to private matters in Sutherland. Sellar also claimed, 'I have spent more money in draining, levelling, fencing, liming, etc manuring your Grace's estate, than all you Scotch Tacks men put together.'[59] He regarded Gunn as a man tarred with the old system, and therefore a natural enemy. The bargaining became frostier. Sellar maintained that he had 'seven boys to get on in the world', which forced him to stipulate precise requirements for his retreat, especially in terms of the evaluation of his stock. He said that he had no wish 'to unsettle my son, in a business, for which by honesty, zeal . . . and good conduct, he is so eminently qualified.' He scoffed at the idea of reducing the size of the farms. It would return the estate to 'hand loom' arrangements, 'at the very point of time when the profession is discovering the impossibility of competing against the untaxed Growers of foreign provisions, unless on the factory system; you would greatly lose by doing so; for the concern is worth greatly more to us than to your Grace.'

William Lewis, the Trentham agent, advised the Duke that there was little prospect of an equitable settlement with Sellar. Moreover, he agreed firmly with the Duke that the property would be much enhanced if the large farms were reduced in size 'and a more happy and prosperous population will be the consequence'. All this remained anathema to Sellar.[60]

In the upshot Sellar soon settled the issue after the Duke chose to intervene. Sellar explained that the phrase 'rack-rent' was a technical term for a non-ameliorating lease, and had no connection with being 'racked or tortured'. Once more, therefore, he rescinded his threat to withdraw. He had no intention of leaving, and the Golspie farm was indispensable for his operations in Farr. He told Loch, 'You have known me 35 years and are sensible, that I am not a Sulky nor a discontented man, tho' I was always prone to wrestle for what I thought was right too keenly. Sixty six modifies such success.' The truth was that

Sellar was a hard man in negotiations, and by no stretch of the imagination was he an easy tenant in his dealings with the Sutherland estate.[61]

His lease at Morvich was extended to 1859, and he embarked on new drainage work with the help of his landlord. He said that the prospect of Repeal would not deter him, though he emphasised the need for thrift and industry:

> To enable our manufacturers to compete against all the world, then I am sure that we shall now beat the cheap land on the continent by poaching and like old fashioned hand loom weavers. We must go the whole hog and, if we do so, and the guano islands be placed under the British Flag (for that is an important condition) take care, after they have emptied an island of its stuff, that the birds be protected, then we shall beat foreigners in perpetuity and we shall give employment to such a fleet of merchantmen as will add something to the strength of the country.[62]

– OPPOSING THE DUKE, 1847–8 –

In September 1847, another round of 'unprovoked abuse' in *The Times* brought Sellar to the boil. He told the Duke of Sutherland that he was a self-made man, and had never been guilty of any malpractice. At Ardtornish he had replaced the blackfaced sheep with cheviots, and made substantial improvements:

> And in the course of that speculation I divide more money among work people than all the proprietors in the district put together. In this year, I have kept on a squad of men, who otherwise must have been fed from public charity, and I furnished them with what meal they wanted, 6/- per Boll, under constant prices. In this, I know, I fall short of your Grace and Mr Matheson's charities, but I toppled over most men of my own humble calibre.

In the light of his good works, he thought it outrageous that he should be subjected 'to the worst of all tyrannies, that of an unprincipled and democratical press!' He asked the Duke to make his case known to his aristocratic friends.[63] The Duke responded with calming words, and told Sellar not to be despondent. He also received Sellar's advice that a change in the system of his farms would be financial foolishness.[64]

The famine in the Highlands had caused serious heart-searchings in the Sutherland family, partly precipitated by the investigation made by Captain Elliot into the condition of the West Highlands, in March 1848. Elliot's report announced that the Duke of Sutherland was contemplating some important relaxation connected with the great sheep-farms, that will enable him to carry out his own views, which are not in accordance with the opinions of those who consider that sheep and men are incompatible, and the former should have precedence over the latter.

In essence, the second Duke questioned some of the original principles to which Loch and Sellar had been attached for forty years.[65] Sellar himself regarded the size of sheep-farms as irrelevant to the condition of the people.

By August 1848, the Duke, in correspondence with Sellar, was adamant that 'we differ in his views of sheep'. He had been rereading Sellar's report on Reay in 1831, and said that he entirely opposed the idea of removing the people, though he agreed with Sellar's old recommendation for a north-coast harbour. Referring to the need to promote fishing, however, the Duke remarked, 'it was rather late for him to state this after having had so much to do with the removing them to the coast.' The Duke evidently associated Sellar directly with the removals in Sutherland, and wanted to distance himself from that inheritance.

The second Duke of Sutherland was moving further from the creed of his forbears. He had become, in Sellar's perception, a reactionary. The Duke pointed out that in 1832 the factor Gunn had been in favour of extending pasture land to the small tenantry in Rogart, but had known that 'the Sheep Farmers would oppose it'. The Duke was in the mood to change the assumptions of estate policy, in the teeth of Sellar's profound scepticism.[66] Sellar continued to resist all suggestion that he should relinquish even small amounts of land, though he gave way on the question of some hill ground at Culmaily, even when it would reduce his sheep-carrying capacity by 1,500.[67]

For all his laboured social deference Sellar expressed his irritation clearly enough when he remarked to Loch that, 'Noblemen and landed Gentlemen will manage their Estates according to their Tastes and passions.' If they wanted profits, they could not avoid progressive methods. As for tenants, said Sellar, 'to each generation I would give a fair opportunity to outstrip those who went before them.'

His disagreement with the Duke about estate policy prompted Sellar to voice his opinion on crofting. 'I object to crofters, because they are in a false position,' he declared. The crofters were

'hand loom' agriculturists, who cannot stand competition with Science, skill and capital – men who being constantly turning from one job to another, do nothing perfectly. If half-rented, they are paupers struggling against hope, and who, through all time, are succeeded by favourites, of whom those individuals only rise in comfort, usefulness, importance, should abandon crofting, and get into some circle of useful skilful, well-directed labour calculated to pay each party employed in it. The poor defeated cottar or crofter loses hope; if more than half rented, and being in a false position, should be set free from it.

In effect they should be evicted for their own sakes, and the sooner the better.

Sellar said that, ideally, the Sutherland estate should have no arable farms of less than 100 acres. Employing euphemistic terms, he said:

those set free by such an arrangement I would assist to emigrate, and those who did not emigrate I would gather round a Mill [seat?], and have them taught whatever manufacture was most likely to pay in that particular locality – their children educated and sent into the world, so as to [drive?] away any undue increase at home.

He was advocating a new northern Galashiels, to be built at Inverbrora where there was a good head of water. Sellar would give no leases to crofters: 'I would entice them by every means in my power to more useful profitable pursuits.' His entire view required the disengagement of the people from the land.[68] He had been much influenced by the towns of the Scottish borders, which he believed could be replicated in the Highlands. His thinking was the same as the plans of William Young three decades before: 'my 35 years handling among the Rogart Lads and Lasses' convinced him of their adaptability.[69]

Surprisingly, relations between Sellar and the Sutherland family were not permanently chilled by these differences. In the autumn of 1848, for instance, the Duke, to Sellar's unbounded delight, visited his Argyllshire seat at Ardtornish. 'I need not say,' he gushed, 'how honoured we felt ourselves here by his Grace's short visit which I considered a very great act of kindness on his part.'

The second Duke, responding to public opinion, was shifting estate policy against the system which had created the huge sheep-farms. He appeared bent on the reversal of the original scheme, to reduce the size of sheep-farms and provide more land for the small tenants, while also promoting emigration. Sellar found this turn of policy highly unpalatable and complained loudly, at least to Loch. He spoke warmly 'of the Duke's present desire to expel Capital . . . from his Estates.' He questioned the wisdom of the policy: 'I want to cultivate with all my Skill what I hold; Fear God, honour the Queen and my Landlord, have my neighbours, and Let the world take its Fling.' This was his creed.[70]

By 1848, Sellar's son Patrick was in charge of operations at Morvich; he was a man of less fire and opinion than his father and gave James Loch, and the Duke, far less aggravation. Improvements at Morvich continued through the mid-century, the landlord taking advantage of government loans to counter the effects of the repeal of protection. Sellar himself was still obsessed with every detail of his property. Thus, for example, he complained sourly about the unsatisfactory appearance of a pauper's house which was too conspicuous on his property. He was still rubbing against estate restrictions and was still cold-shouldering the main Sutherland factor, George Gunn, though Loch regarded neither as blameless in their mutual antagonism.[71]

– KICKING THE HEELS, 1849–51 –

Frictions marked the last two years of Sellar's life, as they had most of those before. Gunn, who was scarcely impartial, hinted at Sellar's heavy-handed methods with his neighbours, saying that he 'knew so well how to keep other Tenants in Strict order when he had to'.[72] They clashed again over shooting rights.[73] Sellar had benefited from the provisions of the Drainage Act, but the improvements entailed the provision of capital by the landlord at special rates.[74] The Duke declared in March 1849 that he would advance no more money to his tenants at 5 per cent. He particularly noted that he had always thought that 'too much had been done for Mr Sellar on such terms. I have not the money & cannot afford it.'[75]

Sellar's self-justificatory style led him to tell the Duke that 'during the last 39 years I have studied not only to be the most profitable tenant to you and your rent-roll, but he who gives least trouble to the management.' This was his way of introducing another request for compensation for his improvements in Sutherland. At the same time, he was finalising his work at Ardtornish:

> One Season more will complete my improvements here, after which I will try for a Border tenant, if spared until then. After the 70s begin [he would be 70 in 1850] one feels entitled to kick one's heels in a park, or at least, more fit for that than travelling on the precipitous cliffs of this Country.

Even so, Sellar found the energy to disagree with the estate on several questions in his final year. There was a damaging fire at Drumrunie which was thought to have been arson, and Sellar pursued the investigations with vigour. He was keen to absolve his own employees from suspicion. His investigation even involved 'the little boys at

School.' The case naturally attracted Sellar's forensic skills. He offered a reward for information, but without success.[76] A servant was dismissed for dishonesty and appealed against his eviction. Curiously, therefore, Sellar's final year in Sutherland was marked by episodes of burning, eviction and precognition. All were on a scale far smaller than in 1814–16. But Sellar could not suppress such memories before his death and entered his final year as a man bent on conflict on virtually every level. His was a troubled mind.[77]

Late in 1850, not long before Sellar died, there was yet another outburst of public vituperation in the northern newspapers. On this occasion the *Northern Ensign* in Wick again attacked Sellar and made specific allegations about brutality during evictions at Abercross in 1818–20. The younger Sellar, jealous for his father's reputation, chose to interview those involved in the events thirty years before. It was a salutory exercise in the oral history of the clearances.

It became clear that there had been, in reality, two episodes of clearance. The first was conducted by Francis Suther in 1818 (at Wester Abercross) and another ten years later by George Gunn (at Easter Abercross), both to give Sellar clear occupation of lands located above Morvich. The elder Sellar recollected that in neither case had force been necessary to effect the removal: there was no dispute and no resistance, and therefore little attention was generated at the time. As he remembered the events, the tenants had been treated very kindly by the Stafford family, being allowed twelve months rent-free accommodation before they were required to flit. They were also offered lots elsewhere. 'They were removed from the ground one morning in May 1819, without the presence of a sheriff's officer, and were, he thinks, put into lots on the Dornoch Muirs.' Gunn, Suther's successor (and long-standing foe of Sellar), intervened in this exchange, prompted by what he described as 'the vile article in that most vile newspaper'. However, he told Loch that Sellar's account was true only 'as far as it went', but he had not stated 'all that took place at the removals from Wester Abercross' notably that 'the houses were set fire to and all consumed'. In all, fifteen families had been removed. But Gunn confirmed that there was no opposition and no military force employed – 'the whole was done by Brander and the Sheriff Officers from the County.'

Easter Abercross had been cleared ten years later and neither the estate nor Sellar had been involved. The out-going tenant, Polson, had removed all the sub-tenants himself and, by 1828, he took his few servants, a shepherd and two or three cottars from the land as he vacated: 'Mr Polson removed without any interference of any person, so far as my father knows.' Polson took them, 'of their own accord', to his new tenancy at Rorie Craigton. Gunn was able to confirm that they had 'flitted themselves . . . without a word of dissatisfaction being uttered by any party.'

The Abercross story demonstrated the fallibility of memory (which had sanitised the account significantly), and showed that Sellar's recollection had minimised all suggestion of disruption. But it also confirmed that Sellar had no direct role in either clearance. The first had been accomplished by the estate; the second was the work of the previous tenant. The case illustrated the different forms of evacuation and ejection that were employed across the Highlands during the age of the clearances. In both cases Sellar was the beneficiary, but by 1819 he was insulated from the business of eviction, even though his name was forever indelibly linked with such events. In neither Gunn's nor Sellar's version of the episodes at Abercross did the cottars and squatters warrant any prominence, though it is likely that they were the main casualties of the rearrangements.[78] The burnings had passed quietly; only the ashes remained to be raked over by the 'Radicals'.

– THE FINAL POST-MORTEM –

The Duke of Sutherland had sympathised with Sellar over the attacks upon him in the newspapers. He also seemed to accept that Sellar's farming system could not succeed on a smaller size of holding. He agreed that 'you can make them [i.e. farms] yield the highest profit, and with the greatest economy, in consequence of the great scale of your superior business, and also let me add, by your superior knowledge of the surest ways of making the most of what you have to deal with.' The Duke acknowledged that he, too, would be a loser if this were changed and he could not afford that. He went on, more decisively:

> If you had continued, as in my Mother's time a resident Tacksman giving personal attention to your own concerns, and farther than that, ready as I at least had conceived you to have been, to cooperate undesirable and useful concerns, even tho' not immediately advantageous to yourself, I should probably never have felt, the least wish to have disturbed you, tho' I believe it would be generally thought better that you as Tacksman, & it may perhaps also be thought it would be better that I as proprietor, held less extent of land.

The Duke thus ordered his own priorities. It was essential to have 'resident gentlemen' in the district

> to act as magistrates, to give assistance in supporting the poor, in attending to concerns of those who require their assistance in 1,000 ways, and not merely to attend to private affairs for their own immediate gain – and what part of the country can require such gentlemen more than Sutherland?

The Duke implied, as directly as possible, that Sellar had not performed his proper role as tenant. Sellar would not even renovate an old cottage because his lease did not required it of him. The Duke, discounting Sellar's endless complaints about rent, said he had his farms on a good bargain. He accused Sellar of using his quarrel with Gunn 'as a reason for refusing to attend to anything in Sutherland but your private affairs.' It was an 'insuperable hostility' which had not softened. Sellar paid £2,200 yearly in rent, and the Duke admitted that it would be more difficult to collect the same figure from smaller tenants, but there was more at stake than rents alone.[79] In the heat of these negotiations the Duke had delivered a powerful indictment against Sellar.

James Loch seconded the view of the Duke, and told Sellar that he had had the benefit of excellent times. The estate, as presently divided, created a 'monopoly in favour of a few rich capitalists, men to whom, I am happy to think the country owes much, but who on the other hand have no reason to complain of their want of success. They fully deserve it.' Now the estate was shifting its priorities. The Duke wanted gradations of holdings for men of different levels of capital. He believed it would create more employment. The existing arrangement, the result of the clearances, was not perfect and the time had come to administer a salutary correction. This would widen the benefits of 'Improvement'.[80] Loch, therefore, made it unambiguously clear that Sellar had failed to consider the welfare of the people in his calculations of the 'improvements' in Sutherland. In this final *post-mortem*, Loch had encapsulated the essence of the problem of economic growth in the Highlands.

The Duke and Duchess themselves harboured heretical notions of the sort which frequently occurred to travellers who ventured into the Sutherland estates. When the Duke toured through Strathnaver in 1850 he felt the emptiness of the place, and thought that the conspicuous greenery of the land should support many more people. George Loch had to warn him that 'such [an] impression cannot be safely trusted'.[81]

CHAPTER 17

Death, Denunciation and Posterity

Towards the end of Patrick Sellar's life, probably in 1850, there was a grand meeting of two Farmers' Clubs in Sutherland. It was an unprecedented display of solidarity between landlords and the large sheep-farmers. There had been a competition for the best cheviot sheep, and a great deal of mutual congratulation about the progress of the industry in the county. The stock on display offered proof 'of what could be achieved by an energetic tenantry under a liberal landlord.' Sutherland, it was claimed, was the best place in the British Isles for sheep production. Moreover, the sheep-farmers were all currently making very good profits[1] and even Patrick Sellar admitted, 'free trade has not done harm here yet.'[2]

The Duke of Sutherland sponsored a dinner for the clubs attended by most of the large tenant farmers, together with a number of the great landowners and their senior factors. In addition to the Duke of Sutherland, there were the Duke of Argyll, Alexander Matheson (returned with his amazing fortune from the Orient), the Marquess of Stafford, Lord Grosvenor and others. After the loyal toasts, came a series of speeches which captured the mid-century spirit of the philosophy of improvement. Amid the platitudes were a number of surprisingly introspective *post-mortems* on the impact of the new order on the Highlands.

The Duke of Argyll, already well-flattered by his hosts, spoke warmly of ancient Scottish allegiances and the arrival in the northern Highlands of farmers who were not natives to the place. They had brought skill, industry and prosperity to the Highlands and

> to those gentlemen feelings of personal affection had fully supplied the place of ancient hereditary attachment.

He spoke directly of Patrick Sellar (who was not present, but was represented by his sheepfarmer son). He noted that *The Times'* reporters, 'those implacable enemies of the sheep-farmers', expressed horror at Sellar's acquisition of Ardtornish, 'one of the ancient seats of the Lords of the Isles'. Argyll joked that the Lords of the Isles might have preferred Sellar to the Campbells. Now 'Good clips of Sutherland wool had stormed and taken the castle of Ardtornish' and the present generation fully approved:

> They did not grudge Mr Sellar possession of Ardtornish, first, on the general ground that they were always glad to see industry, skill and intelligence meeting with their due reward; and, secondly, on the minor ground that they were glad to have him. They hoped that he might introduce with the sheep-farming of their county, some of that enterprise and skill which had made the sheep-farming of Sutherland the best in Scotland. His grace then proposed the health of Mr Sellar and the Sheep-farmers of Scotland. (Cheers).

This was the best and most public aristocratic recognition: Sellar was welcome as a new pillar of Argyllshire society. Patrick Sellar junior expressed 'his grateful thanks to the noble Duke and the company for the honour they had done his father.'[3]

When James Loch rose, he chose to ventilate views which reflected the distance he, and the Duke of Sutherland, had moved from the original rigorous version of Highland improvement at the start of the century. Loch began with the expected eulogy of his fellow improvers. In his thirty-five years, Sutherland had done wonderfully well:

> It was impossible for any one to come into the country from year to year . . . and not be struck with the vast improvements everywhere manifesting themselves. That their land was admirably cultivated, and that they had brought sheep-farming to a degree of excellence unequalled in any other part of Scotland, were facts admitted by all.

Having praised the stock-farmers, Loch then delivered a sharp lecture to the company on the problem of the small tenantry in the Highlands. He dwelt on a theme which penetrated to the moral core of the farmers who sat sipping their good wines after dinner. This was 'the condition and welfare of the poorer working classes', which was the question of the day but which was seriously neglected by the gentlemen of Sutherland:

> Those whom he was addressing were men of wealth, of education, and intelligence; they were able to stand for themselves, and take care of themselves, but the case was far different with those whom he was recommending

to their protection and care – they required looking after in many ways, and assistance and advice from those above them must necessarily be of great advantage to them . . . If they and their families would but take an interest in the poor people living in their neighbourhood, would visit them, and would see that they kept their cottages clean, and themselves and the children tidy, and would, above all things, impress upon them the great, the very great advantage, that their children would derive from being properly educated.

Predictably Gabriel Reid, the most venerable of the sheep-farmers, got up and said that nowhere in Britain were the poor better treated than in Sutherland. Another, Gilchrist, made no reference to Loch's larger message. And the meeting ended without further debate.[4]

Loch's remarks, on the surface, were a bromide for a relaxed and self-contented gathering of the sheep-farming fraternity. In reality, he uttered a radical message to the assembled tenantry. For this was a rare moment in Sutherland: the sheep-farmers were not a natural collectivity. They had little by way of a sense of solidarity. They knew each other mainly as competitors in the nearly perfect market for wool and stock and land. Their political visibility was slight, and they rarely gathered together. It was, therefore, highly uncommon for Loch to address them *en masse*. Despite the constraints of the social gathering, Loch elected to admonish the great tenants for a profound failing in their role in northern society.

Loch's words were deeply critical of the role of the larger tenantry in Highland society. The great sheepfarmers had failed to provide the leadership and the implied paternalism, even the simple humanity, which could be expected of their status in society. They had not succoured the poor. They had not provided the common people with the care and protection they might decently expect. The sheepfarming tenantry did not fulfil their social function, and expected the landlord to provide all the social cement. Loch had come close to the very position of many of the opponents of the new order in the Highlands, personified, in many ways, by Patrick Sellar himself.

Patrick Sellar was the most obvious target of Loch's indictment. Loch saw the great clearances in Sutherland as following a grand design. The sheep-farmers now dominated the territory, as planned, but were separated from the society in which they made their money. A social vacuum had been created in Sutherland. The sheep-farmers were rational, economic men but they interpreted their role too literally, and lived out their lives entirely divorced from the people – people who, as Loch oddly stressed, could be 'useful' to them. In reality, of course, the common people were of little use to the farmers, who saw them as impediments to the full rationalisation of land use in the region. The sheep-farmers may indeed have been bemused by Loch preachifying to them about the remnants of the old world now so alien to them.

– The Last Breath –

In his final year Patrick Sellar's health began to fail and he required medical treatment in Edinburgh. In the winter of 1850–1 Sellar continued to wear himself out in unceasing disputes with the estate management, and complained of 'a good deal of fatigue' relating to a contested fire insurance case. In February 1851 Sellar fell ill and took several weeks to recover enough 'to read over the papers'. After forty years, he continued to argue about the smallest details of improvement.[5]

By early September 1851, Sellar's health was fragile. He told the Duke of Sutherland that he was receiving treatment in Edinburgh for a 'severe sickness, brought on they say by too close application to business . . . which has obliged me to put myself under the care of the most skilful practitioners here.' He could not be in Sutherland that summer, because 'My health is so very delicate at present that I could scarcely bear the removal.' He now dictated his letters, but was able to attach his own wobbly signature.[6]

The Duke had asked Sellar for his vote regarding the distribution of seats in a Sutherland church, still a profoundly controversial issue in the county. Sellar answered with typically tendentious, but deferential, remarks, pointing out that he was 'only a Tenant (though the principal Tenant in the Parish)' and consequently he possessed no vote in the disposition of seats in the church. On the other hand, had he possessed such a privilege, he could not have denied himself 'the pleasure of falling in with what would be most agreeable to your Grace.' Sellar hoped for more sweeping changes in the Church so that 'each person would get his number of square feet in proportion to the amount of rent he pays'. Thus the seating in the church would be allocated 'accordingly . . . in proportion to the size of his farm in relation to the whole rent of the parish'. The church would become a map of the social hierarchy. At the end of his life, Sellar's priorities were unchanged.

Loch was conscious of Sellar's decline, and expressed warm sympathy. He noted that they were almost exact contemporaries. Both were born in 1780, they were 'years bairns.' Loch advised Sellar to do less work and

> let the youngsters take the labouring oar, which you have so long and so successfully pulled.

He noted that he also had been obliged to curtail his own labours at Christmas: 'indeed I had no choice, for my illness, occasioned by a chill, was so suddenly effective in taking away all my strength that I was obliged to so', and all his papers were withheld from him. After a while, Loch found the recuperative regime relaxing and not only 'useful but pleasant'. His daughter-in-law had provided him with complete nursing, and Sellar was lucky to get similar care from his own wife.

Loch told Sellar that the Queen was likely to visit Dunrobin in the following year, 'but as we used to say at the High School, "Seeing is believing."' Loch was anxious about how the Queen would be entertained, and recommended a steam trip up the coast from Loch Inver. Having enticed the Queen to Sutherland, Loch would show her the great improvements which he and Sellar (among others) had wrought on the estate in the past half century. Loch knew this would strike a happy chord with the sick and declining Sellar. They could both look back over their lifetimes' achievements. But Loch also offered a deeply held valediction:

> Although these matters are objects of wonder and delight to us who saw it all otherwise, it is impossible to convey to strangers those feelings even if able to tell what was the condition of things before 1812.

Loch referred to the stagnant lochs, the birch woods, the black peats which used to cover the land, now transformed into the fine fields of Culmaily. The final irony was that the Queen, and everyone else, including posterity, would never be able to understand what the likes of Sellar had done for the country and for progress. 'I wish I had the means of telling this', remarked Loch, sadly.

This was Loch's last lament for the dying Sellar. The improvers' dilemma was that they could not convince the world that they had wrought an economic miracle. The evidence was invisible, and they were condemned to almost universal misunderstanding. This was the final irony of improvement, and a forlorn despair in the minds of the great improvers as they approached their ends.

The kindliness of Loch's feeling for his fellow improver, in his last hour, was unmistakable. He ended, 'If you should like it, I will come by Elgin on my way south and be most happy to see you. Who is the oldest man about the place who could tell me about Culmaily?' There was pathos in Loch's notion that the *status quo ante* could find witness only in the memory of an ancient of east Sutherland, from someone who could remember not only the turmoil of the Sellar revolution, but also the condition of the place before that revolution.[7] This was Loch's last communication with Sellar.

At the beginning of October 1851, Patrick Sellar junior helped his sick father journey from Edinburgh north to Maryhill, at Elgin, where he had hired a house to be close to his local practitioner, Dr Stephen. He was 'very frail'.[8] In the event, old Sellar was too sick to respond to Loch's solace or his doctor's care. He was fast sinking, and Thomas Sellar correctly predicted that he would not survive many days more. 'Though very feeble in body, his mind is as clear and acute as ever and though restless, and not easy, he suffers no severe pain.' His wife kept a close vigil on her departing husband, who received the 'unremitting and kindest care from his old schoolfellow and friend, Dr Stephen.' Sellar was dying 'in the midst of his own and my mother's oldest and dearest friends.' Sellar's other sons arrived (though Robert was in Australia), gathering at Maryhill for the final farewell.[9]

As the family awaited the inevitable the eldest son, Thomas, mused on the nature of the loss they were about to confront:

> Our loss we will not know till after he is gone and his warning voice and energetic will are quiet forever. But we, his sons, and particularly his eldest sons should be thankful that he had been preserved so long – to implant in us a spirit of well-doing and industry, which may enable us, I hope, to pass through life as useful and contented members of society, doing our duty.[10]

Seven days later Patrick Sellar died. Thomas Sellar's remarks were, of course, sobered by the event and the circumstances, but they conveyed the ambience of the Sellar household, its stern understanding of duty and industry, its energy and vigilance invested in the pursuit of what was good for society, and its commitment to improvement. In the coming decades, Thomas Sellar was required to defend his father's reputation precisely by these very criteria.[11]

For Sellar's widow, it was a time of great affliction, as she recorded in her personal almanac:

> On the 28th October my dearest Mr Sellar died calmly. I saw his last breath and he passed away without a struggle.

Mrs Sellar's daughter Helen died the following year, in February 1852. The shock to her mother was 'almost too much for her frail body'.[12]

The cleverest of the Sellar sons, William Young Sellar, was also the most sensitive, and he was deeply affected by his father's death. He had passed from Glasgow University to Balliol, and then to a Fellowship at Oriel, always straining to fulfil his father's ambitions for a brilliant son. But he was subject to nervous collapse. His mentor was Benjamin Jowett, who comforted him, saying that he did 'not doubt that it is well with your father after his long and honourable life.' Jowett told his old pupil, 'You need only a small portion of his energy and decision of character to give you success in life.' He hoped that Sellar would

> feel it to be a duty you owe to your father to nerve yourself for your new post. Could he live to see it, there is nothing that would give him so much pleasure as your success in it. I was very much struck more than a year ago with what your father told Harvey, 'that he had lain awake at night thinking of your illness, because he fancied that he had encouraged you to overwork at Glasgow'.[13]

– CONTESTED OBITUARIES –

Sellar's death became a matter for lively discussion in the northern newspapers. The obituarist in the *Elgin Courier* declared that Sellar's life was 'illustrative of his remarkable shrewdness, energy, and successful career as a farmer and proprietor in the north.'[14] The *Aberdeen Journal* respectfully outlined Sellar's career, noting that his enterprising spirit had made him 'one of the most extensive rearers of Cheviot sheep in Great Britain'. He was described as, 'a most intelligent and active man of business, and amidst his numerous and important transactions and the various calls on his time, he contrived to keep pace with most of the discoveries of science, and was well informed on the literature and public questions of the day.'[15] No reference was made to the controversies with which Sellar's life was associated.

The *John O'Groat's Journal* followed by the *Inverness Courier* also celebrated Sellar as a great and successful breeder of cheviot sheep:

> No one who ever met, even accidentally, with the deceased, in his various steamboat journies . . . or while travelling to the southern markets, or attending the great Inverness Fair (of which he was one of the original founders and promoters) could fail to be struck with the vigour and originality of his mind, and with the ardour and perseverance which he carried in all his pursuits . . . His intelligence, shrewdness, and energy gave him great influence among his brother farmers, and made him distinguished in every cause in which he embarked.

The obituary recollected Sellar's association with William Young and their fateful journey to Sutherland in 1809. Sellar became the great sheep-farmer. 'Whatever could be accomplished by talent and incessant care was done by the deceased. Difficulties vanished before him, and as other able sheep-farmers and spirited natives of the district followed in the same tract, Sutherlandshire rose to be the first pastoral county in the kingdom.' Sellar had made the Highlands productive. The obituarist added, 'In personal life the deceased was a highly agreeable companion, ever lively and acute; and in affection for his family or anxiety to promote their education and improvement, he has rarely been equalled.'[16]

These encomia from the conservative press were predictable, but there was a simultaneous, radical current running through the political life of the northern Highlands. Sellar died at a time of renewed agitation and further evictions in Sutherland and elsewhere, and the dead Sellar was not spared in the columns of the fire-eating *Northern Ensign*. The Wick newspaper carried a debate prompted by the eulogistic obituaries in the other newspapers. In a letter signed by 'A Celt' Sellar was described as 'the well-known Sutherlandshire sheep-farmer, whose name had long been associated with the notorious Sutherland clearances.' He concentrated on the evictions in Strathnaver, once occupied by the Mackays, now 'cruelly laid waste' by the late Sellar. 'Celt' continued:

> I do not deny the talent of Mr Sellar. He certainly led the way to an improved system of sheep-breeding; but his talents were ever and anon employed in gratifying an inordinate selfishness, which was fed, unhappily, from the moment he planted his foot on the devoted soil of Sutherland. In contriving these things, he certainly displayed great talent, and his talents produced good results for himself; but his large fortune has been acquired by means never to be forgotten by the descendants of those who suffered by his policy, whether these be now on the face of broad Scotland, or in the wilds of Canada. It was Mr Sellar's advice, suited to his own views, which tended to fix eternal obloquy on the great proprietrix of the day, and to destroy a highly moral and respectable population [which] with honest counsel, given in the same direction, would have placed in enviable circumstances, having their capabilities improved to meet the resources of their native country.

One week later, the *Northern Ensign* printed another attack on Sellar, by 'A Sutherland Highlander in Glasgow,' who adopted an ironic tone, noting also the 'the high eulogium passed upon' Sellar in the Glasgow newspapers:

I am put to a loss to know who the deceased may have been, not having resided in the north for many years . . . I almost take it for granted that the individual who is thus made the subject of such unbounded praise cannot be the notorious Patrick Sellar, who . . . drove away the poor Highlanders of Sutherlandshire to the wilds of America, and to the already too-much-crowded towns of the south of Scotland – burning their houses to ashes, and converted a happy county into a wilderness.

The case against Sellar was reinforced by another correspondent who declared the indictment as 'no fiction':

I saw the pleasant straths of Sutherland darkened with the smoke, as the houses of the once happy natives were being consumed to ashes. Ah! I saw Sutherland a happy county – a happy county it indeed was before the names of Roy, Young and Sellar were ever heard of; but, alas! how changed. How changed when I visited the county of my birth some five years ago – ah how altered are these once beautiful straths and glens! Instead of the voice of praise to which in my younger days I have often listened, I heard nothing but the bleating of sheep, and instead of the dwellings of these brave and worthy men, whose forefathers well showed themselves to be their country's stay, I saw the cots of a few border shepherds, cowering in the distance. Surely, then, this Mr Sellar, who is thus held up to such praise, cannot be the same person who was the principal instrument of bringing about such revolting changes, and whose name will be remembered with sadness in Sutherland as long as it is a county.

Sellar, so recently dead, now resided in an unquiet grave.

– INHERITANCES –

Patrick Sellar left considerable personal stock in Sutherland and Ardtornish to which was added the capital value properties in Morvern and Westfield and his investments in Sutherland.[17] It amounted to a substantial but not a princely fortune, and James Loch (who outlived Sellar by four years) reported pointedly, 'I have heard that he has not died so rich as was expected – his *Lairdship* having been less profitable than his leaseholds.' Loch was quietly satisfied by this intelligence since it provided final evidence of the greater profitability of Sellar's Sutherland farms over his purchase in Argyll. It also confirmed Loch's deep-seated principles of the rural division of function and status. He believed, throughout his life, that tenant farmers ought to confine their energies and capital to their farms; they should not engage in social climbing, out of their class.[18]

Before his death Patrick Sellar indicated that he wanted to leave

Ardtornish and Westfield to his eldest son, Tom, alone. Tom begged his father to reconsider the decision, and to share the whole among the brothers, saying, 'If you do not do this, I shall as soon as it is mine.' The old Sellar reluctantly agreed. 'Tom was a man of great abilities and chivalry and it was an act of great self-denial'. His sister said, 'I have always thought of it as one of those deeds that makes one think highly of human nature.'[19] The Morvern properties were administered by his sons with a farm manager.

The family was held together mainly by Sellar's widow, though she found the early days of her widowhood difficult to bear. In 1852 she confided to a friend that she regretted the passage of 'bye gone days that can never return', and confessed that she could take 'little interest in the world or what belongs to it'. She was certainly proud of her sons and their wives.[20] Westfield was put up for sale in mid-1854.[21] Morvich and Ardtornish remained, though the latter was bought by Octavius Smith in 1859 and he built a new house.[22] The marriage of the youngest Sellar to Gert Smith eventually ensured that Ardtornish remained a place of fond memories for the Sellar family, and for their friends. Old Mrs Sellar possessed great charm and character, a love of literature and learning, and encouraged annual family visits to the Argyllshire house. She died in 1875, with all her family about her, except Robert Sellar, who was in Melbourne.[23] The family members were friends of Tennyson, Palgrave, Herbert Spencer, Tennant of Rollox and Jowett, and were, more generally, familiar with Froude, Huxley, Carlyle, Kelvin, George Eliot, Ruskin and R. L. Stevenson.

Patrick Sellar had achieved much of his ambition in the lives of his children. The Sellar family was large and successful in the Victorian world and fulfilled the aspirations of the previous age. In Benjamin Jowett's oddly apt phrase, there were 'Seven sons, and not a black sheep among them.'[24] Two of the sons rose to eminence, the others were substantial men of business, and all lived lives of respectability and achievement. His nine children were a veritable dynasty of talented and aspiring Sellars, and they made their mark in the later nineteenth century at home and abroad. Despite their remarkable talents, the logic of Sellar's economic revolution in the Highlands meant, inevitably, that they had little future in Sutherland. They too were part of the Highland diaspora, all but one dispersing to new pastures in every distant direction.[25] Nevertheless, however far they removed themselves from the scene of the clearances, they could not avoid the incubus of their father's reputation. The Sellars were remarkably successful and adventurous, but the mark of Patrick Sellar remained upon them.

In Sutherland Patrick Sellar's leases were placed in the hands of Patrick Plenderleath Sellar 'being bound to his father's trustees for the proceeds.'[26] The only son to follow in his father's footsteps, he was born in 1823, educated in Edinburgh, but left school at fifteen to join a large mercantile house in Liverpool. After three years he re-joined his father at Morvich. P. P. Sellar eventually became one of the most widely known and most enterprising agriculturalists in the north of Scotland. Like his father, he was a familiar figure at wool markets for nearly fifty years. He held extensive tracts of land in Sutherland, Ross and Lewis, and lived through some of the best and worst days of sheep-farming of the nineteenth century. The Sellars' relations with the Sutherland estate management remained cordial. In 1852, one of Sellar's sons, John, was involved in discussions for a lease of a Sutherland farm, and Loch told the Duke, 'If he turns out well I am very glad that one of the family has got the farm.'[27]

Nevertheless, by the time of Sellar's death, the framework of rural economy in the Highlands was in transition. Free trade, for the moment, had lost its menace.[28] But the Sutherland estate was not significantly lucrative. In mid-1853, a review of the estate finances revealed that its three districts yielded a total revenue of £36,936; expenditure came to £34,912, leaving the small surplus of £2,024. In 1853, as for all the years before, it is evident that the Sutherland family depended utterly on its English income to sustain its finances.[29] In the second Duke's own obituary in 1861, the *John O'Groat's Journal* pointed out that his Highland rental of nearly £40,000 per annum 'is hardly self-supporting and had not infrequently become a burden on the Duke's English estates.' The second Duke had maintained a high level of expenditure on the estate.[30]

Already in 1851 the revenues derived from the new competitors for the Highlands, the sporting tenants whom Sellar had despised, were beginning to figure prominently in the rentals of the Sutherland estate. This income was increasing by annual leaps towards £5,000 per annum. By 1870, the sportsmen contributed £8,280 to the Sutherland estate finances.[31] The sheep-farms were under critical scrutiny even within the estate structures. In 1856, the Sellar leases were reconsidered, and the 'quiet principle' of dividing up the great sheep-farms was invoked. In any case, the Strathnaver farm was so enormous that it required a massive level of capitalisation which very few tenants could command.[32]

By 1861, the great days of the Sellars in Sutherland were numbered. George Loch had succeeded his father as Commissioner to the Sutherland estates, and he was glad to see a turnover of talent among the sheep-farming tenancies. Letting lands on the north coast, George Loch told the Duke that he was exceedingly glad of this importation of new blood into the country, and especially that it 'comes from the pastoral districts of the South of Scotland – it is itself as valuable as the increased rent you receive.' The old generation was moved aside and, as a faint echo of the 1810s, a new shift in Sutherland was in train.[33]

The crofters nevertheless remained on the margins and did not regain the interior. The clock was not turned back. The Sellar revolution in Sutherland, despite the soul-searchings of the latter-day Loch and the second Duke of Sutherland, remained intact. By contrast, Sellar's ill-fame in the Highlands and beyond continued to compound after his death, and eventually lived on to serve the symbolic needs of modern posterity.

– VICTORIAN OPPONENTS –

The demonisation of Patrick Sellar had begun, even before Mackid's precognition in 1815, in the angry pages of the *Military Register*. It was then fed generously by David Stewart of Garth in the 1820s and by Donald Macleod two decades later. It grew further when the question of the Highland clearances reached the attention of economists (including Lavergne and Sismondi), and was then, especially in the 1880s, fully politicised in the debate about the land laws and the plight of the crofters. Karl Marx, in *Das Capital*, employed the Sutherland case as his best example of the capitalist expropriation of the peasantry. Hugh Miller was another effective voice, as was Donald Ross, in the 1850s. Macleod's writings were reissued and widely quoted, forming the core of the case against Sellar and the clearances. Later reminiscences by the Rev. Donald Sage were published, and they, too, reinforced the story of exploitation and ruin.[34]

Eventually, the growth of Sellar's notoriety began to take on a life of its own, inflating with each generation. In the middle decades of the twentieth century the account was heavily compounded with fictional extrapolation and invention. A succession of novels, plays and television dramatisations of the clearance stories kept the level of indignation simmering in a manner comparable with the role of the Great Famine in Irish history and tradition.

The anti-Sellar tradition grew powerfully, even though the documentary basis of the account had changed little since the time of David Stewart of Garth. The first generation of Sellar's family attempted to resist the tide. Thereafter the resistance ceased while the indictment continued to swell. Eventually some historians believed that the Sellar story had become an interesting phenomenon in its own right, a manifestation of a special need in the Scottish psyche and long divorced from the realities of Highland life. Philip Gaskell spoke warmly of the 'absurdity of the Sellar folklore which persists in Scotland', and Rosalind Mitchison believed that the entire account had become grossly exaggerated.[35]

The literary record gave little expression to the more subterranean traditions which inhabited the common culture of the people of the Highlands, notably those abroad. The folk memory accommodated much of the accumulated, collective, mental attitudes of Highland society. It also shaped the mentality itself. For historians, as for others, it is difficult to interpret the content of the oral tradition except where it can be juxtaposed with some contemporary written record. Donald Meek has subjected the *genre* to thorough scrutiny.[36] Meek acknowledges that much of the Gaelic narrative is largely inaccessible and preserved mainly in the oral tradition, often outside Scotland. He speaks of the 'transmissional pressures and prejudices' which affect the passage of songs down to the present day. This tradition of poetry, he says, shows 'anger, and most of all, one powered by a deep desire for vengeance' against 'wrongful rulers whose tyranny ruined the land'. Moreover, 'the pre-1874 poems are valuable if only in dispelling the view that Highlanders reacted tamely to the evictions and territorial engineering of the period.'

Only one song directed against Sellar by name survives, a 'Satire on Patrick Sellar' by Donald Baillie, an unknown Highlander said to have been alive at the time of the clearances: it was probably composed soon after the Inverness trial in 1816. A highly vituperative version is preserved among the expatriate communities in Prince Edward Island. It does not mince words: Sellar had been guided by the devil, and should have been burned for his crimes. As Meek points out, Sellar is portrayed as a 'grotesque hybrid with animal characteristics, [which] drives home the view that he does not belong to the human race. The song opens with the vision of a great fire in which Sellar's henchmen have been placed.' In the song, Sellar is referred to as 'the black rogue':

> like a wolf
> catching and oppressing
> everything that comes within his range.

The song emits profound hatred, wishing Sellar in irons to be burned 'in the big fire':

> When death comes upon you you will not be placed in the ground, but your dung-like carcase will be spread like manure on the field's surface.[37]

In the year of Sellar's death, the Andersons' *Guide to the Highlands*[38] noted the great changes in Sutherland and claimed that the current Duke had come to regret the manner in which the clearances (by which term the changes had come to be called) had been executed:

> Ignorant of the habits, attachment, and even the language of the Celtic tribes, the advisers of those measures hurried on the improvements and arrangements which should have been extended over many years.

They had roused the pride and indignation of a people who were broken-hearted by the changes. By this time, the obloquy for the clearances, now twenty years previous, was almost entirely imputed to the factors, among whom Sellar's name was always most prominent.[39]

While Sellar's descendants prospered in Victorian society, their tranquillity was severely jolted in the early 1880s by the agitation which soon led to the Crofter Commission. The strength and extent of contemporary anti-Sellar feeling among the Highlanders was attested in 1883 in the evidence uttered to the Commission. At the head of the successful agitation was the rallying work of Alexander Mackenzie, who generated widespread interest in the plight of the common people. Among a series of books, he published his *History of the Highland Clearances* (1883).[40] This was mainly an anthology of earlier writings about the clearances across the entire Highlands over the past century. It included much recycled material about Sutherland. Mackenzie's book was noticed in the *Athenaeum*, which pointed out that the land question had become a matter of vehement debate. The reviewer quoted Mackenzie's account of the 'atrocious barbarities directed against a peaceful and inoffensive population' which claimed that:

> There are few tales more pathetic than that of the thousands of Sutherland crofters who were driven from their native soil and turned out of the homes to which they had a better claim than those who expelled them. The blame of these evictions attaches not so much to the countess-duchess who ordered them as to those at whose instigation they were undertaken.

Mackenzie inevitably focused on the old stories about Sellar and 'the brutality practised by the land agents of the time'. His compendium merely quoted one side of the story, namely the work of Macleod, Ross, and Stewart of Garth. His case was supported by the widely read Professor of Greek, John Stuart Blackie, who wrote his own trenchant reconstruction of the Highland ethos in *Altavona,* published in 1882. All these works assumed Sellar's guilt in the events of 1814.[41]

Eventually the eldest Sellar son, Thomas, was roused to respond to these outpourings. He prepared an able and powerful defence of his father which contested every attack since 1816. His defence was entirely based on Robertson's *Report* of the trial, and he rejected all other evidence as ill-informed and prejudicial. He republished his father's own defence of 1825, which included the trial *Report,* and Mackid's 'confession' of 1817. He made the point that his father

> was not a fool or a madman – as such acts, if committed, would show him to have been – but an experienced, able, and energetic man of business, who did his duty justly, faithfully, and fearlessly, through his whole life.[42]

Thomas Sellar engaged Mackenzie in an chilly exchange of letters during which Mackenzie agreed to include Mackid's 'confession' in future editions of his *History of the Highland Clearances* as well as the result of Sellar's trial.[43] Thomas Sellar also successfully challenged Blackie, who modified his attack on Patrick Sellar in the subsequent editions of his book.[44] It was the last attempt by the Sellar family to defend its father, an exercise which Alexander Mackenzie said was 'as futile as an attempt to turn the ocean into dry land'.[45]

In 1885, the Marquis of Stafford, eldest son of the Duke of Sutherland, contested an election in the county and found himself currying favour with the new voters by denouncing the landlord policies of his own family. 'I do not approve of the evictions . . . I have nothing to do with the management of the estates.' He specifically denounced what he called the Loch/Sellar policy as wrong, though he conceded that most of 'the county had been in a bad state at the time.' The people had been removed to the seashore 'because it was thought they would do better there,' – a remark which drew laughter at the meeting.[46] Appearing in the ranks of the landowners, Stafford clearly carried the weight of the past on his shoulders, but he took care to attribute the main fault of history to the factors rather than to his own family. In reality Patrick Sellar, became the all-purpose scapegoat for the clearances and for the state of the Highlands.

– FICTIONS –

The reach of Patrick Sellar's reputation was phenomenal, both in place and time. The bitterness was conveyed to the most distant colonies and even erupted in the Victorian Parliament in Australia in 1891 when Robert Sellar became the butt of public abuse simply for being the son of Patrick Sellar.[47]

In the new century, Patrick Sellar remained the target of the accumulated and ritualised indignation of posterity against the clearances. The most effective evocation was Neil Gunn's *Butcher's Broom* (1934), which satirised Sellar in the figure of Heller and argued that the community and culture of the Highlanders was destroyed by the clearances. Fionna MacColla's *And the Cock Crew* (1945) was a passionate criticism of the Calvinist ideology and attitudes which left the people vulnerable to landlord policy. Sellar became the personification of factorial evil and avarice in the children's story, by Kathleen Fidler, *The Desperate Journey* (Edinburgh, 1964). Iain Crichton Smith's *Consider the Lilies*[48] was a more substantial and convincing novel, but did not pretend to historical accuracy as such. It dealt with the clearances through the eyes of an old woman confronting an eviction and depicted Sellar as an outsider, 'a short fat man with piercing eyes and thin lips [*sic*], working for the Duke whom he despises.' Sellar conformed to racial type too, for 'His head wasn't Highland.' The novel notably attacked Scottish Presbyterianism and the role of the ministers, particularly their falsity and hypocrisy during the removals. Crichton Smith also wrote a play about the trial of Sellar, though he chose to set the events in Hell. He wrote a poem on 'The Clearances' in which he uses an 'uncharacteristically harsh voice', to denounce Sellar:

> Though hate is evil we cannot
> but hope your courtier's heels in hell
> are burning.[49]

The savagery of the writing against Sellar was reinforced by the work of Ian Grimble who, like Alexander Mackenzie a century before, built his case on the succession of anti-Sellar polemics from Stewart of Garth onwards. Grimble heightened his case against Sellar by drawing a specific modern parallel. Sellar's crimes against the people of Strathnaver, he said, were to be ranked with those of Heydrich, the man who conducted unspeakable acts against the Jews in Prague in the Second World War. Grimble's contribution was, therefore, to make Sellar the centrepiece of the popular account of the clearances, which brought the events into comparison with the Holocaust and serious talk of the 'genocide' of the Highland people.[50]

By the 1990s, the entire Highland story, in one influential view, could be rendered into 'a war between two Scotlands. It was the mercantile, Protestant, Scots-speaking Lowlanders who wanted to destroy their feudal, cattle-rearing, Catholic Gaelic-speaking neighbours and helped the English to do so.'[51] Sellar's reputation expanded so that, in 1996, it was claimed that he moved 8,000 people out of Britain's largest county to make way for sheep, leaving it 'the deathly desert it is today.' John Macleod described Sellar's tactics in *Highlanders*, his published history of the Gaels: 'Violent assault: men, women and children beaten with staves, young women kicked in the genitals. Wanton destruction: the burning of houses and effects. Grand larceny: the seizing of cattle and other livestock. And murder.'[52]

Only a few doubts remained. Between the same covers of the *New Companion to Scottish Culture* (1993) the Sellar episode in 1814 was represented by one contributor as 'one of the most emotive and searing moments in the history of Gaelic Scotland', while another pointed out that the accusations of brutality were not proved in court, though they had certainly entered the popular image of the clearances. A further entry in the same volume, on 'Supernatural Beliefs', established that Sellar, in tradition, would have been 'eaten alive by worms' on account of his crimes.[53]

Public opinion in Scotland and elsewhere was primed by such writings. In 1994 there was considerable agitation to topple the statue of the first Duke of Sutherland from his place on Ben Bragghie. And Patrick Sellar's grave in Elgin Cathedral became 'the perennial target for mucus, divots and paint – and much worse when to hand.'[54] Before the end of the twentieth century, the global mail system was abuzz with electronic graffiti directed against the hated clearer.

The folkloric and the literary evocations of Patrick Sellar have evidently travelled a great distance from the known substance of his life. He has become the most potent symbol of the Highland Clearances, an inverted pyramid of hatred balanced on a fragile base of evidence. After almost two centuries, we know more of the man and his times and a new, though no less critical, perspective is now possible.

CHAPTER 18

The Tears of Progress

– THE MAN –

Patrick Sellar was well able to speak for himself to his contemporaries and even to posterity. But, after almost two centuries, how does he emerge beyond the clamour of his reputation? What indeed was the nature of his crime? What formed his cast of mind? What was his function in the new Highlands and in industrialising Britain? And what, finally, was the meaning of his tears in 1816?

– SELLAR'S GUILT –

To invoke Sellar's name in the same breath as the Holocaust, or genocide, or Heydrich, is inappropriate. He was not involved in mass murder; he had not set about the killing of people in Strathnaver. There is no firm evidence that he killed anyone. Perhaps the worst that can be said of him is that, in his zeal and impatience for improvement, he hurried a reluctant community to resettle thirty or so miles away from their usual homes. The numbers involved in the particular episode in Strathnaver which led to his trial were relatively small, probably no more than 150 people. In his haste, though, he had allowed them to stay beyond the normal time of flitting, and he may have accelerated the death of one or two very elderly people. But this much was not proved. Sellar's unambiguous crime was vaguer and broader in its implications. He was the instrument of a detested policy of economic change. He became the target of a concerted campaign to stop him, and to stop the policy.

There were much larger clearances in Sutherland, before and after 1816, and they were implemented by other estate officials, though several of them were directly beneficial to Sellar's own farming purposes and to other stock-farmers in the county. He was certainly central in the clearance of the Sutherland estate, but he was not the executer of the greater part of the programme. He was responsible for the direct removal of rather more tenants when he acquired territory in Argyll in the early 1840s. Strathnaver had been the most populous part of Sutherland which in 1806 was inhabited by 338 families, about 2,028 people, who occupied about 1,600 acres of arable, each family with 12 head of cattle, 6 small horses, 15–20 sheep and a few goats.[1] Most of their land was taken over by Sellar, but he removed only about 27 families, together with Chisholm the tinker.[2] Mostly, they were cleared by Francis Suther five years later. The majority left peacefully, even if tearfully.

Given the central place of the trial in Sellar's life, it is difficult to avoid rendering his life as a detective story about his guilt or innocence in the events of 1814. Disappointingly, there can be no final judgement, merely a balancing of different categories of evidence. He was not accused of murder but of culpable homicide. Mackid's original precognition was an impressive document which strongly suggests that Sellar encouraged harassment and coercion in the Strathnaver removals. Some of the very old people died after the clearance, but it could not be demonstrated that Sellar's specific actions accelerated their deaths. Mackid's precognition gathered the preliminary testimonies of a large number of witnesses to the ugly process of eviction. They, no doubt, believed that such procedures should be deemed illegal and punished at law. But it was almost equally remarkable that so large a body of witnesses could not sustain a single specific unlawful charge against Sellar. Their complaint was against the crudity and inhumanity of the process; they did not maintain their solidarity when it came to the charge of homicide. Even sympathetic observers thought that this allegation was a gross inflation.

Many of the witnesses evaporated after the first precognition, but there was sufficient confirmatory testimony to persuade the Lord Advocate to take the matter to trial. There is no evidence that the trial was rigged and Sellar was never fully confident of the judge, the jury or the result. He gained little aid from his landlord/employer or his colleagues. But Sellar was vastly better prepared than his adversaries. He employed the best counsel. The verdict was unanimously 'not guilty'. Scottish law allowed for a majority verdict, as also for a verdict of 'not proven'. Though Sellar's colleagues and associates knew that Sellar's was a flawed personality, none of them believed that he was reckless enough to cause death in his evictions.

But they thought he was perfectly capable of harsh and ill-judged behaviour.

The cleared people of Strathnaver, as far as can be determined, were outraged at the summary termination of the entire bases of their livelihoods, all in the name of progress. Sellar had clashed with practically everyone he dealt with, and his conflict with the Strathnaver people pre-dated the actual evictions. He was a natural quarreller (though he specifically denied this charge) and his life can be charted as a series of such quarrels. Among the Strathnaver people, it is likely that he goaded and was goaded in return. His activities in Strathnaver did not amount to genocide or extermination, nor even homicide. It is more certain that the people themselves reacted negatively to coerced economic change. They were bloody-mindedly uncooperative and dragged their feet at any proposal to move. They attempted to resist the transformation of the Highland economy by pre-industrial methods. Sellar faced a cauldron of frightened and angry people.

The people were encouraged by previous efforts at resistance in Sutherland (in Assynt) and by the covert assistance of other losers in the transformation, notably among some of the old tacksman class. Of the latter, some were passively complicit in the resistance, and then in the attack on Sellar; others more actively supported the campaign. The assault on Sellar assumed remarkable sophistication for its time when the attack reached the London newspapers and then Parliament itself.

The tenacity of the campaign and its recourse to the law itself was a stunning achievement for a remote peasant society, assisted by the profoundly ambiguous figure of Mackid. The fact that Sellar feared for his life was a measure of the cohesion of the campaign. That the coordination of the people finally broke apart before the trial and the assault ultimately failed should not diminish the scale of the resistance that they mounted through 1814 to 1816.

Within this collision was the personality of Sellar, which attracted trouble like a highly-charged magnet. He undoubtedly possessed an extraordinary intellectual energy that fuelled economic change. But his relentless pursuit of rationality and efficiency exposed other sides of his personality. Always seeking opportunity, he trod an awkward line between avarice and humanity. As well as quarrelsome, he was often aggressive, unyielding, dogmatic and opinionated. His flawed mental balance swung between cloying deference and sneering cynicism. He had an irrepressible taste for sarcasm, and was often unctuous and obsequious. In political opinion, he was extremely conservative, and he expressed himself in rhetorical and rancorous terms. His quest for improvement made him tenacious and didactic, but he was also combative, argumentative, finicky, pedantic, litigious, paranoiac, indignant, arrogant, short-tempered and abrasive. When the world about him failed to respond to his rationality he whipped himself into a frenzy of frustration. He consoled himself with economic doctrine and religious rectitude. He had an overwhelming belief in progress; rationalism had become a civic duty.

Sellar took great pride in his own family story, risen from Banff cottars, demonstrating the just rewards to effort, virtue, application, intelligence and efficiency. He sincerely believed that the act of eviction was the best thing that had happened to his own forebears. Outside his own family, he was a man who inspired fear and loathing; people did not warm to him, though he certainly inspired professional respect.

That Sellar's was a combative personality does not demonstrate that he was capable of murder. In the pressurised events of 1814, Sellar had every reason, as well as legal sanction, to force through the clearance of his lands. But he had no reason to commit murder or manslaughter. His legal training warned him against such stupidity. He was impatient and, on his own admission, impetuous. His cold fury no doubt increased as each day of delay devoured his profits and increased his debts. He may have reached the edge of patience, but he was not a man to overstep the law in front of a large number of heterogeneous witnesses.

– THE ENLIGHTENED SELLAR –

Sellar's compulsive drive for improvement derived from his origins and his times. He was the product of three of the most important sectors of Scottish life – law, religion and estate management. He was also a man of the Enlightenment, formed in the Edinburgh of the 1790s when certain intellectual priorities were pervasive. Within a handful of decades, the foundations of Scottish life were shifted and a model of change was created for the world beyond. Many Scots, including Sellar's own progeny, carried the ideology beyond Scotland to England, the United States, Canada and Australasia. It was part of the intellectual and moral imperialism which Sellar learned at his father's hearth in Elgin and among the sages of Enlightenment Edinburgh.

From this particular well sprang several sources of social and economic reform. They took different forms, including a stream of socio-medico reformers (e.g. Kay, Gaskell, Perceval and Ferrier) and one of civil servants who devoted much of their life's energies to factory, health and educational reform (e.g. Horner, Steuart, Gilroy, Garvin and Morell). James Loch was part of this generation and so was Patrick Sellar. Sellar embraced the passion to change the world. These men demonstrated a complex and kaleidoscopic set of responses to the challenges of improvement, and Sellar's was a particular variant. Most of all, it gave a special confidence to their mission.[3]

The belief in a programme of betterment for society commanded general adherence, and so did the faith in reason and education and the responsibility to enlighten from above. All were essential to the Enlightenment mentality which Sellar absorbed in its totality. Specifically, he believed that the change with which he was associated in the Highlands represented a long overdue liberation from the shackles of feudalism, the ending of serfdom. He adopted an explicit set of values which were modern, liberal and capitalist in form. They were pitted against traditional and feudal values. Yet Sellar was also deeply conservative with an attachment to older notions of *noblesse oblige*. He was the prototypical man of the Enlightenment, who absorbed its precepts in a highly pragmatic and literal form. Most of all he believed in progress.[4]

Patrick Sellar bears comparison with another 'Child of the Enlightenment', to use the phrase of Nicholas Phillipson. Hugh Cleghorn (1752–1837) was older than Sellar, but passed through a similar moulding in Edinburgh and then a wider career in London, North America, the Caribbean and India. As Phillipson puts it:

> Enlightened culture was providing Scotland with a new national identity and its young men with practical and marketable skills which were in demand in a world being transformed by war, commerce and the growth of empire.[5]

Specifically, Cleghorn was taught that true liberty was the product of good laws and regular government. In India he confronted 'all the things he had been taught to distrust and abhor – a vast decaying oriental despotism, which was riddled with superstition and corruption.' In his everyday work, he employed the enlightenment virtues: he was markedly intelligent, observant, pragmatic, and methodical. Through men such as Cleghorn and Sellar, the ideas of the Enlightenment were transmitted to a wider world and were eventually manifested at the workface of British society. Sometimes, of course, the ideas mutated into extremes of *laissez-faire* and gross individualism;

sometimes they went in the opposite direction. But the intellectual confidence was rarely in doubt.

Sellar found support and re-inforcement from Adam Smith and Thomas Malthus: they possessed almost biblical significance for him. He would also invoke the Bible itself, together with Benjamin Franklin and Robert Burns. He respected Thomas Chalmers. But, beyond individual influences, Sellar believed in the application of legal rules to the world about him; and, even more, he believed that rigorous economic rationality was the guide to all action, especially when it faced the forces of tradition and custom.

It was a commonplace of Scottish Enlightenment thinking that the Highlands required 'civilising'. It was an explicit agenda. The Enlightenment was a lowland phenomenon which sought to assimilate the Highlands into the improvement ideology. Sellar was heir to this thinking and its most obvious propagandist and implementer in the north. He carried the message from Edinburgh to Elgin, and to Sutherland. The longer the change was delayed in the Highlands, the greater was the tension and urgency of the mission.[6]

Sellar was the centrepiece of a great conflict in the Highlands. It was between the society on the retreat and its thrusting, aggressive successor, a technologically more advanced economy responding to the needs of a wider market. Sellar was the very point of collision, the aggressor and the victim of these larger circumstances at the same time. He was the man leading the revolution which required the demolition of the old world, the *ancien régime* of the Highlands. He then became the target of resistance by a society which attempted, in poorly organised ways, to stand its ground and stop the invasion. The 'aborigines' – as Sellar called them on many occasions – possessed, ostensibly, only 'the weapons of the weak'. Such people are usually set to flight, and are commonly regarded as passive in the face of the demolition of their societies. Sellar discovered that his antagonists were prepared to employ extra-legal methods: rioting, threats of personal violence, intimidation and delaying tactics of all sorts – as well as appeals to distant authority and the newspapers. His trial was the ultimate act of resistance. Sellar's life, and his tears, were testimony not only of the turmoil of these events, but also of the efficacy of the popular resistance. Sellar's ordeal represented one of the last stands of the Highlanders against the new world.

– THE ENTREPRENEUR –

A long tradition in economic history displays the entrepreneur as hero, the great innovator carrying advanced techniques and new methods of production. Sellar demonstrated these functions as one of the most successful innovators of his generation of pastoralists, increasing the productivity of the Highland economy by a quantum leap in the years 1810 to 1850. Sellar himself trumpeted his success whenever he could. In the process, of course, he poured endless scorn on the feudal squalor of the old economy which he and others replaced. They reaped massive increases in productivity to land, labour and capital as part of the critical success of British agriculture in meeting the rapid increase in demand for food and raw materials in the vital years of industrialisation. Sellar performed the role of entrepreneur as risk-taker, always searching for cheaper methods of production, questing for new market opportunities, reinvesting, maximising economies of scale and thinking about every point in the productive process. But his quest for progress and profits ran roughshod across the old world.

His farming methods and his innovations were remarkable: the introduction of cheviot sheepfarming into the Highlands was a technological innovation as revolutionary as the impact of machinery in the textile industry or steam propulsion in transport. Sellar was an agrarian captain of industry. He improved transport and markets in the north of Scotland, connected the region with the rest of the national economy and literally created new markets, making more efficient the exchange of trade and of credit. He was heavily involved in the institutional base of the economy, namely the legal structures of trade and tenure, the imposition of new wage regimes, the import of cheaper fuels, the preservation of drove roads, the institution of steam shipping and railways, the introduction of fertilisers and new machinery.

Sellar was, therefore, an exemplary entrepreneur whose life spanned the classic years of industrialisation, and his bourgeois family exhibited the aspirations, networks, and ladders of Victorian society. Sellar coped with the imperatives of technical change, and the rigours of economic fluctuations, which damaged so many of his contemporaries. He was a genuine shaper of events, a maker of the new economic order in the north. His life was consciously devoted to the pursuit of economic and social progress, both for himself, and the world at large. R. H. Campbell has remarked that:

> In the later eighteenth and much of the nineteenth centuries at least it was possible for an individual to believe in all good faith that in following the maximisation of his own profit he was promoting the welfare of society at the same time.[7]

Sellar followed this dictum with ceaseless enthusiasm. He made this explicit on a thousand occasions.

His combative personality ensured that he would do battle against the forces of conservatism and resistance. His self-chosen role as the agent of 'improvement' in the northern Highlands, on perhaps the most resistant frontier of economic backwardness, guaranteed enduring conflict. For fifty years, amid the great transformation of the national economy, Sellar propounded his philosophy and promoted, in the most muscular way, the accelerated restructuring of Highland life. His career sharply focused the issues, moral and economic, which were inextricably caught in the imperatives of economic growth and the larger calculus of the benefits and costs of the process.

Sellar's economic biography crystallises some of these central questions which modern economic analysts commonly render in abstracted terms. Economic historians mockingly refer to, 'The ghosts of grasping capitalists, expropriated small farmers and exploited factory workers [who] still haunt economics and politics.'[8] Sellar, no wraith, provides an exemplary case of entrepreneurial initiative on the distant periphery at a critical moment in British industrialisation. He was instrumental in creating the 'special ingredients' for growth in the Highlands, those conditions which economists describe as the 'institutions conducive to individualism'. Sellar, and his landlord's *apparatchiks*, were committed to such matters as 'stable government, legalised contract, [and] double entry book keeping'.[9]

Patrick Sellar was 'Improvement Man', armed with the ideology of his times, passionately embracing 'the necessary pre-conditions of modern economic growth'. Sellar came from the world of 'the austere, turbulent, democratic universities of Calvinist Scotland which sent out a stream of brilliant, career-seeking and rationalist young men to the south country', men such as James Watt, Thomas Telford, Loudon McAdam and James Mill.[10] He was the perfect specimen of economic leadership, the very embodiment of 'entrepreneurial flair, technological inventiveness, mercantile ruthlessness' in a new industry which required swift structural change in a hostile environment.[11] The change required the liberation of men such as Sellar from the bonds of custom, freeing their entrepreneurial energy in the interests of

economic advance. No one was ever more insistent on the requirement for the freedom of action than Sellar himself.

Sellar's rationalising capitalistic ethic was pitted against the forces of
resistance and inertia in the Highlands. This was the ultimate source of
his tears, a man frustrated by the essential unreasonableness of the
world to the improvement of which he devoted his life. Sheep farming
in the Highlands was certainly a capitalistic activity, but was set in an
aristocratic framework which, though hell-bent on improvement,
continued to make gestures to the old and withering feudal contract
(for instance, during military recruitment in the French Wars). These
persisting contradictions were part of Sellar's intense frustration with
the world. He fought the inertia of older society and its infuriating
refusal to bend to the needs of rapid change. Sellar believed that the
backwardness of feudal society in the Highlands stood as obstacles to
the requirements of economic change, to the demands of a growing
population, to the opportunities of rapid financial gains.

Sellar would have agreed vehemently with modern economic historians that producers must respond to the dictates of the market,[12]
and that technical progress determines efficiency and survival. Had the
British Isles followed the model of the old Highlands, Britain could not
have led the way to industrialisation.[13] Few knew better than Sellar (to
use the words of the economic historians, James and Thomas) that
'Institutional rigidities will . . . generate market failure by preventing
continually efficient allocation of resources.' This was Sellar's life work:
'to respond to economic imperatives'. No one was more emphatic
about the impossibility of the old ways of thinking, nor of the problems
where 'custom and culture are slow to respond to economic challenges.'[14]

Sellar was the *epitome* of the market opportunist, at a vital moment
when the response times of traditional economic leaders in the
Highlands were notoriously slow. Sellar's life brings into the sharpest
focus the problem that his sort of achievement creates. He was the best
model of entrepreneurial endeavour which brought great benefits to
the British economy, by providing cheap, high-quality wool and
mutton to the industrial populations of Great Britain. Sellar was
technically a mere tenant farmer, a class which performed most of
the practical tasks of transforming British agriculture after 1800. In the
course of industrialisation, the resources of the Highlands were
radically revalued under a different mode of production. Sellar, with
his own sense of urgency, was a powerful agent in compelling the
change.

The language of modern development economics captures the practical realities with which Sellar, and the Highlanders at large, wrestled at the time of the clearances. Progress and efficiency simply required the 'instantaneous reaction of economic agents to price signals'.[15] In the Highlands, in the early nineteenth century, the price signals were perfectly clear. They blazoned out a stark message: the population should disperse to other regions where the returns to labour were greater, and living standards and opportunities were more secure; new capital and technology should enter and radically change land use to the large-scale production of wool and mutton. This was the message of the market which, by implication, voiced the national interest.

In the Highlands, as Sellar discovered to his peril in 1815, the price signals were seriously questioned and, indeed, resisted by the old society. He faced the coordinated obstruction of those sections of local society whose traditional ways of life had quite suddenly been rendered obsolete by the new economy. Some of the Highland reactions were monumentally negative, and brought great turmoil to the process of economic growth. In economists' terms, non-market forces fought a rearguard action against the power of technology to shift the bases of society. Nevertheless, the resistance, though it did great damage to Sellar in particular, was broken, and the imperative of economic development did its work. It took on the shape of an inexorable force with the power of increasing returns in an entirely new scale of operations.

Long passages of Sellar's life took the form of a collision between the forces of reaction and the dictates of the market. Conflict attached itself to Sellar at every turn, so that his life came to illustrate the frictions which, in reality, often impede the smooth adjustment of societies to economic rationality as defined in economic theory. An eloquent modern analyst, Joel Mokyr, points out that 'technological progress inevitably involves losers,' and these were often easily mobilised into opposition, often in 'non-market' formation, creating great friction and rigidity in the course of progress. He conjures up an economic dream-world in which 'labourers have no fear of being made redundant by labour-saving innovations, because a worker replaced by a machine can always find an equivalent job elsewhere.'[16]

In the nightmare reality of the Highlands in the early nineteeth century, the worker was replaced by sheep, and alternative employment was both unacceptable and geographically distant. In the Highlands, technological change generated severe frictions, and Patrick Sellar was at the centre of its greatest collision. Across the Highlands, conservative interests from almost every stratum of Highland society gathered against the change and Sellar confronted their full fury. The people of Strathnaver, in particular, accurately understood their fate: 'their specific assets and skills' were devalued in the spate of progress. They faced a lesser life and they recognised their fate. In the process they improvised a series of efforts to resist. They even made gestures to assimilate the technological change into the traditional framework of their lives (that is, by offering higher rents in competition with Sellar and other sheep-farmers). As Mokyr hypothesised, resistance generally arose from interested parties 'defending their turf and skills against the inexorable obsolescence that new techniques will bring about.' But they were also abetted by intellectual forces which often 'express genuine concern for some social values'. Sellar came face to face with both sorts of resistance. He spent much of his life attempting to counter what Mokyr denotes as 'technophobic writers', and he added his own measure of intellectual energy to the dialogue.[17]

Opposition to great economic changes was not unique to the Scottish Highlands and much of the history of British industrialisation is marked by such resistance. But, as Mokyr notes, the British government generally decided not to support 'reactionary forces'.[18] Despite the record of riot and obstruction to economic change, most active resistance proved 'impotent'. It became a story of 'unstoppable change': 'when violence erupted, the government sent soldiers who smothered the rebellions'.[19] The new technologies were victorious across the board despite recurrent violence, partly because the opposition forces lacked unity. Mokyr draws attention to the romantic reaction against industrialism, through Blake and Wordsworth to Ruskin and Morris. But the decisions about technical progress were effectively left to the market.

Sellar was, therefore, fully conscious of the issues which are accorded central significance in modern economic history. He lived in recurrent frustration at the failure of the world about him to adjust smoothly and uncomplainingly to the requirements of rational economic growth. The clamour which arose in the Highlands was part of the universal tension set at the heart of industrialisation. The problem faced by Sellar in the Highlands was essentially a particularly vivid instance of the general phenomenon.

– TEARS AND TEARS –

Modern historians, influenced by the triumphalism of the market in the late twentieth century, have tended to turn away from the negative consequences of industrialisation. In this context, the case of Patrick Sellar is emblematic. As Sellar built up his flocks and his productivity, as he perfected his system and established his family in the comfort of achievement, as he fed and clothed the nation in the south, there was a cost to be counted in the tears of the people ousted from the straths and glens of Sutherland and Morvern. That the quantitative accounting of such changes is extremely difficult, and ambiguous does not diminish the rupturing that accompanied Sellar's achievement. Herbert Heaton long ago suggested that the entire history of the Industrial Revolution could be better understood if it were written from the point to view of those who failed.[20]

The imposition of radical new methods of production on the Highlands between 1780 and 1850 was not dissimilar to many cases of contemporary economic change determined from above, usually driven by the market demands from the industrial world, which have dislocated indigenous peoples. From the introduction of commercial sugar production in the Philippines in the nineteenth century to the construction of dams in India and Indonesia in recent times, economic growth has commonly wreaked devastating effects on local people, not at all unlike the effects of the clearances on the Highlanders.[21] Economic history and the modern world are replete with such examples because they are problems integral to modern economic change in which the burdens are often carried disproportionately by the least able in society.

Some historians vehemently object to reference to 'the disasters of the industrial revolution', denying that 'the technical and economic changes were themselves the source of the calamity', even regarding the very idea as 'perverse'. As T. S. Ashton eloquently stated the case in 1948, the great national problem of the first industrial age was 'how to feed and clothe and employ the generations of children outnumbering by far those of any earlier time'. Without industrialisation the consequences would have been cataclysmic, as the case of Ireland tragically demonstrated, as well as the 'unmentioned horrors' to which so much of Asia continued to be condemned.[22] These are arguments which Sellar anticipated and used to justify the radical changes with which he was involved in Sutherland. In effect, the problems faced by the displaced Highlanders, in this view, were the unavoidable transitional costs required in the achievement of the greater benefits to the national economy as a whole.

Climatic metaphors recur in the economic literature. Joseph Schumpeter, the great theorist of capitalist development, referred to the social costs of innovation, and spoke of the gale of 'Creative Destruction' which blew much good into the economy as well as eliminating the obsolescent. Schumpeter declared that progress depends upon the unsuccessful being driven 'to the wall' which is 'the price a society pays for sustained progress'. Economic development requires 'the extinction of the inefficient',[23] and 'the continuous obsolescence of specific, non-malleable assets, both physical and human'.[24] Sellar was the agent for this process as well as a direct beneficiary. The old Highland society, its entire fabric and population, was the 'non-malleable asset' driven to the wall.

The English historian, George Kitson Clark, also thought that the moral issue could be illuminated in a climatic metaphor. Industrialisation, he declared, was a vast force beyond the control of humanity. There was, he said, little point in contemplating its moral content nor the perils of economic development. The Industrial Revolution was

> as nearly void of moral significance as a change in the weather which happens to produce in some years a good harvest; probably the human agents who promoted it were in many cases as innocent of any far-sighted visions for humanity as the human agents who caused the increase in population. It was in fact morally neutral . . . It might bring good and might bring evil.[25]

Yet, in the Highlands, few people regarded the process as inexorable or neutral. Even Sellar, who believed in the inevitability of progress, always emphasised the role of volition, as well as the virtue of individual enterprise. Sellar's intervention in the Highlands was clearly not void of moral significance, even beyond the climacteric events of 1814. The view from the Highlands, it is true, accentuated the dislocating effects of modernisation and the stream of casualties in the process.

There is a distinction to be made. Some changes are engineered by a particular and identifiable agency – such as the construction of a dam, the liquidation of slums for a new road or a railway line, the eviction of peasants for commercial enterprise. Other changes are part of a broader process such as the gradual elimination of an industry (like handloom-weaving, nail-making or kelp manufacture) which succumb to a fall of prices and employment under the cool logic of the market. Where the course of economic change was accelerated by an agency or a proprietor, the identifiable individual becomes the focus of obloquy. Yet the two processes interweave, and it was in such circumstances in the Highlands that Patrick Sellar became irretrievably ensnared.

Sellar's conflict was part of the logic of industrialisation, and this was the ultimate source of the tears in his story, his own and those of the Highlanders. Sellar's case focused the matter in extreme form, and he did nothing to lessen it. When the people were shunted off their lands, the impact to them was cataclysmic. They became the casualties in the long march of progress.

This is a universal theme in modern history, of rural populations migrating freely, or under coercion, as modern economic growth commences. Across the world, peasantries have departed the land, usually seeping away as better opportunities come within their reach, a percolation until the rural population settles at a lower level. Land-lords and capitalists, invested with power and authority, have behaved like ordinary mortals and pursued their self-interest and accelerated the changes. But the tragedy was wider: the very process of change causes intense turmoil and imposes the burden of adjustment upon the poorest in society. The price of progress is great, and the costs are borne on the shoulders of the weakest. That the people affected responded with suspicion, misunderstanding, despair, loathing and malice is hardly surprising. It was an eternal tragedy, and carried through by men such as Sellar, their resolve stiffened by the needs and ideologies of their time.

Philip Gaskell was critical of the customary overemphasis on the 'misfortunes of the Highland peasantry' which has produced 'a ritualistic condemnation of the landlords, most of whom were reasonable men, as good and as bad as people generally are.'[26] Yet every sound that can be heard from the Highland population was opposed to the clearances, often voicing total incredulity at the forced changes. The tragic proportions cannot be avoided, for this was demolition of the lives of thousands of people.

Sellar's life was of a piece with this tragic aspect of economic progress. It entails the inescapable price of progress, the permanent tension that exists at the centre of economic change, in the turmoil and dislocation which resided in the kind of revolution in which Sellar had been instrumental. The benefits were palpable, but the costs were large, even though difficult to calculate. At the time of the clearances, the costs seemed to be appalling and the cause of endless bitterness and despair. Such costs were recurrent in the annals of economic history. Modern economic historians are extraordinarily quiet, if not dumb, about these matters. Rarely is the collision of interests captured so dramatically as in the life of Sellar.

There were tears at the trial of Patrick Sellar, and tears were shed throughout the story; they were shed at Sellar's own death, thirty-five years after his acquittal in Inverness. Tears recurred through the clearances when people were wrenched from their inland communities, and there were tears of anger at the loss of old loyalties and certainties. There were tears when the factor Falconer was dismissed for his lack of resolution and energy in bringing the changes to Sutherland. There were tears of shame when Sutherlanders were forced to plead for favours in the middle of the evictions. But the dislocation, the uncertainty and the fear and the insecurity brought by the removals in Sutherland were not new. Security was not an apt word for the condition of the people before the clearances. The insecurity of the food supply, the arbitrary exactions of the landlord and the tacksmen, the lottery of the harvest and the looming dangers of demographic growth as well as the demands of seasonal labour and military recruitment, all made that pre-clearance life much less than idyllic.

The upheavals of the Sutherland clearances were cataclysmic but were, at least in part, designed to diminish the ageless insecurity of old Highland life. Nevertheless, the clearances represented a tearing of the social fabric, rending the Highland world apart. Ultimately the tears of Patrick Sellar were the tears of forced economic change and his frustration with society's failure to understand the imperatives of that change.

Notes

The following abbreviations have been used throughout the notes (see also the bibliography which follows):

HMC   Historical Manuscripts Commission
NLS   National Library of Scotland
NRA   National Register of Archives
NSA   *New Statistical Account of Scotland, 1835–1845*
SDUK Society for the Diffusion of Useful Knowledge, 1826–48
SRO   Scottish Record Office

– EPIGRAPH –

1. Referring to General Haig, in *London Review of Books,* 2 January 1997, p.7.

– PREFACE –

1. R. J. Adam (ed.), *Sutherland Estate Papers,* 2 vols (Edinburgh, 1972).

– CHAPTER 1   THE TEARS OF PATRICK SELLAR –

1. *The Trial of Patrick Sellar* (Edinburgh, 1816), prepared by P. Robertson, Sellar's junior counsel.
2. See Eric Richards, 'The *Military Register* and the pursuit of Patrick Sellar', *Scottish Economic and Social History,* 16 (1996), pp. 38–60.
3. See *The Trial of Patrick Sellar,* op. cit., reporting Pitmilly's remarks.
4. NLS Dep. 313/1587 MacPherson Grant to Lady Stafford, 27 April 1816.
5. See, for instance, the account of such a scene in Morvern in 1824, recalled later in the century, in P. Gaskell, *Morvern Transformed* (Cambridge, 1968), p. 34.

6. *Saturday Review*, 8 September 1883, p. 313. Thomas Sellar, *The Sutherland Evictions of 1814* (1883), p. 27, fn. 1.
7. Auslan Cramb, *Who Owns Scotland Now?* (Edinburgh, 1996), p. 162; *Radical Scotland*, 25 and 26 (1987).
8. *Listener*, 5 March 1964. See also Charles W. J. Withers, 'Place, memory, monument: memorialising the past in contemporary Highland Scotland', *Ecumen*, 3 (1996), pp. 325–44.
9. See R. J. Adam (ed.) *Sutherland Estate Papers*, 2 vols (Edinburgh, 1972), I, pp. xiv-xv.

– CHAPTER 2   ELGIN DAYS, 1780–1809 –

1. Donald McCloskey, in Roderick Floud and Donald McCloskey (eds), *The Economic History of Britain since 1700*, vol. 1, *1700–1860* (Cambridge, 1981), p. 104.
2. See R. A. Houston, 'Scottish education and literacy, 1600–1800: an international perspective', in T. M. Devine (ed.), *Improvement and Enlightenment* (Edinburgh, 1989), pp. 47–50.
3. Patrick Lang Selkirk, *The Langs of Selkirk* (Melbourne, 1910), pp. 60–1; see also Robert Young, *Annals of the Parish and Burgh of Elgin* (Elgin, 1879), p. 580.
4. Her father was the Rev. David Plenderleath, minister of the College Church, Edinburgh. Being a Wesleyan in Scotland was unusual but not rare: it may have indicated a mildly 'outsider' mentality, though it does not seem to have inhibited the rise of the Sellars in Morayshire society.
5. See *Journal of Rev. John Wesley*, 4 vols (London, 1906), IV, pp. 201–3, III, pp. 184, 404, and Selkirk, op. cit., pp. 60–1.
6. I owe this point to Mr G. A. Dixon of the Central Archives of Stirling. On local Sellars see Herbert B. Mackintosh, *Elgin, Past and Present* (Edinburgh, 1914), p. 260; William Cramond, *The Records of Elgin* (Aberdeen, 1903), p. 205.
7. In 1816, Sellar referred to the case of Sir William Grant (1753–1832), Master of the Rolls (1801–17), whose own father had been a very small farmer in Elchies in Banff; Sir William Garrow (1760–1840), Baron of Exchequer, was another product of a very modest north-east connection in an improving society in which agrarian change had catapulted people into the wider world. See R. J. Adam (ed.) *Sutherland Estate Paspers*, 2 vols (Edinburgh, 1972), I, p. 177, fn. 1 and 2. Compare Elizabeth Grant of Rothiemurchus, *Memoirs of a Highland Lady* (Edinburgh, 1988, reprint edition), I, p. 131.
8. D. G. Lockhart, 'Patterns of migration and movement of labour to the planned villages of north east Scotland', *Scottish Geographical Magazine*, 96 (1983), pp. 141–157; and D. Turnock, 'Stages of agricultural improvement in the uplands of Scotland's Grampian Region', *Journal of Historical*

Geography, 3 (1977), pp. 327–47. and T. C. Smout, 'The landowner and the planned village in Scotland, 1730–1830', in N. T. Phillipson and Rosalind Mitchison (eds), *Scotland in the Age of Improvement* (Edinburgh, 1970).

9. I have received generous assistance from Dr Douglas Lockhart and his unpublished PhD thesis, 'The evolution of the planned villages of north east Scotland: studies in settlement geography, c.1700 to c. 1900', Dundee University, 1974.

10. The 1798 class included Francis Horner and Thomas Dudgeon. In 1800 Sellar's contemporaries included Andrew Clephane; a year ahead of his class was another group which included James Loch, Henry Cockburn and Robert Gourlay. His colleague of later years, James Loch, was regarded at that time as one of the young men most likely to blaze a trail in the highest ranks of political and intellectual life. Sellar was never mentioned in quite this light. *Edinburgh University Matriculation Roll*, University of Edinburgh Library, II, pp. 596, 611.

11. SDUK, 32 Sellar to Baldwin, 2 December 1831.

12. SRO GD 248/3417/2 Seafield Muniments, letter of 12 February 1799.

13. I owe this point to Mr G. A. Dixon.

14. See SRO Seafield Muniments, GD 248/3373/2 Sellar to Garth, 29 November 1815 and related documents.

15. See Lachlan Shaw, *History of the Province of Moray*, 3 vols (Glasgow, 1882), II, p. 124; and *Survey of the Province of Moray* (Aberdeen, 1790), p. 123.

16. NLS Dep. 313/1227 Sellar to Lord Gower, 13 August 1810.

17. Robert Young, *Annals*, op. cit., p. 580. Young reported that Thomas Sellar retired from business in 1809 to devote himself to the further improvement of Westfield. Nevertheless Thomas Sellar (with J. Ritchie) continued to conduct business as a writer in Elgin. In 1812, for instance, he was negotiating feus at Lossiemouth, as well as at Westfield. See the *Inverness Journal*, 10 April 1812.

18. *Aberdeen Journal*, 31 December, 1816.

19. Young, *Annals*, op. cit., p. 581.

20. Robert Young, *The Parish of Spynie* (Elgin, 1871), p. 77.

21. *Inverness Journal*, 29 May 1812.

22. See J. and W. Watson, *Morayshire Described* (Elgin, 1868), passim.

23. *Aberdeen Journal*, 30 March, 1842.

24. Information of G. A. Dixon. Young died at Maryhill, Elgin, aged seventy-eight.

25. *Survey of the Province of Moray* (Aberdeen, 1798), p. 126.

26. Rev. William Leslie, A *General View of the Agriculture of the Counties of Nairn and Moray* (London, 1813), p. 276.

27. At Hopeman he reclaimed 113 acres of land which had been 'formerly blown over with sand, now reclaimed by being trenched, limed, and partly enclosed'. Young's fishing village prospered as one of a group of

new villages along the adjacent coast including Cummingstown, Duffus and Covesea. Inverugie became the centre of Young's own improvement operations and its rapid expansion between 1806 and 1811. See the *Inverness Journal*, 4 December 1807, 7 August 1807. Obituary of Young, *Aberdeen Journal*, 30 March 1842 and Leslie, op. cit., pp. 406–10, 256. Young, *Spynie*, op. cit., p. 29.

28. Lockhart, thesis, op. cit., vol. 2, pp. 17–19. Advertisements relating to Hopeman are in the *Inverness Journal*, 17 November 1813, and the *Aberdeen Journal*, 15 October 1806.

29. NLS Dep. 313, Box 19, Young to Gower, 30 January 1813.

30. *Aberdeen Journal*, 31 March 1842.

31. *NSA*, XIII (April 1835), pp. 43, 155, 96, 29. The Spynie scheme was then described as a failure.

32. William Young's brother, Robert Young, was land steward to Sir William Gordon Cumming. In 1811 Cumming embarked on sheep clearances in the Dallas Hills, associated with the creation of a reception village. It is likely that Cumming was influenced by the concurrent work of William Young in Sutherland. See Lockhart, thesis, op. cit., vol. 2, p. 13.

33. There is a description of Burghead in *Inverness Courier*, 8 July 1808.

34. *Survey of The Province of Moray*, op. cit., p. 126.

35. Lockhart, op. cit., p. 7, quoting a letter from Telford to Dunbar, 19 March 1803.

36. *Notes on Burghead, Ancient and Modern* (Elgin, 1868), pp. 12–13, 28–33; G. A. Dixon, 'In the dawn of every improvement', *Northern Scot*, Christmas number, 1978, Elgin, passim.

37. Telford's *Report on the Coasts of the Central Highlands of Scotland in April 1803* and Report of the *Committee on the Funds arising from the Forfeited Estates of Scotland* (1806), App. 6.

38. Robert Young, *Notes*, op. cit.

39. SRO Seafield Muniments, GD 248/623/1: Conveyances and Deeds, relating to Burghead. Memorial of Proprietors of Burghead to Hon. Committee of the House of Commons, 27 May 1806. The coordination of local grain markets was made vivid in the meal riots of 1817 in Inverness and elsewhere. Even as late as 1847 food riots rocked the wider region – see Eric Richards, *The Last Scottish Food Riots* (Oxford, 1982).

40. *Aberdeen Journal*, 20 May 1808. Feus were advertised in the *Inverness Journal*, 20 May 1808, 1 July 1808, and completion was announced on 6 January 1809.

41. HMC 17173, NRA (Scotland), Papers of Sir Ewan MacPherson Grant, Ballindalloch, Banff, Bundle 729, Sellar to Grant, 4 March 1809.

42. J. and W. Watson, op. cit., pp. 288–9.

43. Ibid., pp. 288–9.

44. In 1818, Young sold his property at Hopeman (to William Stuart, a plantation owner in the West Indies), which suggests a switch of assets.

See Lockhart, op. cit., p.20. Thereafter he was styled 'Young of Maryhill', ibid., p. 9. In 1819 Young advertised for corn dealers and fishermen to utilise his facilities at Burghead. *Aberdeen Journal,* 17 November 1819.

45. See *Aberdeen Journal,* 14 Febuary 1827, 18 October 1827.
46. *NSA,* XVIII (1845), p. 41; *Elgin Courant,* 18 October 1839. For its subsequent history see *Elgin Courant,* 7 July 1868. Burghead was evoked in Richard Ayton, *A Voyage Round Great Britain* (1814), vol. V, pp. 34–5.
47. *Aberdeen Journal,* 30 March 1842, derived from the *Elgin Courier.* See also Joseph Mitchell, *Reminiscences of my Life in the Highlands,* 2 vols (originally published privately in 1883 and 1884, reprinted in Newton Abbot, 1971), I, p. 149.
48. She was daughter of Thomas Craig and Helen Young, who was daughter of William Young's sister Helen. See Selkirk, op. cit., p. 63, and E.M. Sellar, *Recollections and Impressions* (Edinburgh, 1907), p.23.
49. He had bequeathed Burghead to William Young, eldest surviving son of his brother Robert: Selkirk, op. cit., p. 63, E. M. Sellar, op. cit., p. 23; Robert Young, *Notes,* op. cit., pp. 13–14.
50. Brown was a factor for the Seafield and Novar estates and later described by Mitchell, op. cit., I, p. 142, as exceptionally upright and honest.
51. See letter of Brown to Anderson, 19 October 1818, quoted by Lockhart, op. cit., p. 9.
52. Burghead was advertised for sale by public roup in the *Aberdeen Journal,* 29 April 1818.
53. New work at Burghead, which entailed harbour deepening, was announced in the names of both Sellar and Young in the *Aberdeen Journal,* 2 December 1818.
54. According to Sellar, at the original auction, Burghead had been offered at £10,000; Brown's brother-in-law had offered the absurdly low figure of £5,000 and this figure had prompted Sellar's own larger offer which he had made on the spur of the moment. The exchange is located in SRO Seafield Muniments, GD 248/623, Brown to Sellar, 4 Nov. 1818, 27 Nov. 1818, Sellar to Brown,16 Nov. 1818, Sellar to Grant, 7 Jan. 1819.
55. Grant (1781–1846), MP for Sutherlandshire 1809–12 and 1816–21. Adam, op. cit., I, p. xvii, fn. and II, p. 93.
56. Ballindalloch Papers, Ballindalloch Castle, Bundle 729, Sellar to Grant, 28 Febuary 1809.
57. Patrick Sellar, Appendix to James Loch, *Account of the Improvements on the Estates of the Marquess of Stafford* (1820), p. 51. Dixon, op. cit.

– CHAPTER 3   COLONISING SUTHERLAND AND THE DAZZLING PLANS OF 1809 –

1. Patrick Sellar, *Statement of Patrick Sellar* (privately printed, n.d. [*c.*1825]), in Thomas Sellar, *The Sutherland Evictions of 1814* (1883), p. 24, originally

in James Loch, *Account of the Improvements on the Estates of the Marquess of Stafford* (1820), Appendix, p. 54.

2. D593/K/1/3/38, Horsburgh to James Loch, 27 September 1850.

3. The population of a district in Assynt rose from 535 in 1774 to 856 in 1811. See Malcolm Bangor-Jones, *The Assynt Clearances* (Dundee, 1998), p. 11.

4. Wool prices increased sixfold by 1809, the year which saw severe distress among the West Highland population. For improvers this was the most compelling conjunction of conditions justifying structural changes. See the *Inverness Journal*, 17 Febuary 1809.

5. D593/K/Grant to James Loch, 11 June 1845.

6. NLS Dep. 313, II, Household and Personal, Box 30, Lady Stafford to Lord Stafford, 14 July 1808.

7. R. J. Adam (ed.), *Sutherland Estate Papers*, 2 vols. (Edinburgh, 1972), I, pp. 16–27.

8. See Eric Richards, *The Leviathan of Wealth* (London and Toronto, 1973), ch. 1.

9. Wadsets (see note 18 below) were still being issued as late as 1789. See Adam, op. cit., I, p. xxiii.

10. See *The Bee*, 14 December 1791, reprinting an essay dated 1785. See Hugh Rose's plan of 1786 for the improvement of the Sutherland estate in 1786 in John Henderson, *General View of the Agriculture of the County of Sutherland* (1812), Appendix VIII.

11. D593/K/1/3/38, R. S. Taylor to James Loch, 23 September 1850.

12. See Bangor-Jones, op. cit., pp. 5–6.

13. See Adam, op. cit., I, p. xxix.

14. In 1759, within nine days, the Earl of Sutherland was able to assemble on the lawns of Dunrobin Castle a Fencible Regiment of 1,100 men. Lord Reay raised 800 men in 1792. In 1800 600 men were raised in Sutherland which was then increased to 1,000 under General Wymess. See Joseph Mitchell, *Reminiscences of my Life in the Highlands*, 2 vols (originally published privately in 1883 and 1884, reprinted in Newton Abbot, 1971), II, pp. 89–90.

15. Adam, op. cit., I, p. xxx, fn. 4. In the outcome the estate gave strictly limited promises of security to the families of the recruits to the regiments. Ibid., I, xxvii-iii. See also Bangor-Jones, op. cit., p. 7.

16. Adam, I, op. cit., p. 55.

17. See B. Falk, *The Bridgewater Millions* (London, 1942), ch. VIII.

18. Wadsets are defined by the *Chambers Scots Dictionary* as a deed from a debtor to a creditor assigning the rents of land until the debt was repaid. They were a means by which a landlord could raise money from a tenant, a reverse mortgage. 'Tacks' were the lease agreements held by 'tacksmen' or leaseholders.

19. See Adam, op. cit., I, p. 6.

20. Ibid., II, p. 9.
21. Lady Stafford to Lord Stafford, 16 July 1805, in ibid., II, pp. 40–1.
22. See M. W. Grant, *Golspie's Story* (Golspie, 1983), p. 107.
23. D593/K/1/3/38, Horsburgh to Loch, 27 September 1850
24. Grant, op. cit., p. 112. Many left for America in a ship that was wrecked off Newfoundland. See Henderson, op. cit., p. 24.
25. See Henderson, quoted in Grant, op. cit., p. 107.
26. Adam, op. cit., II, p. 28.
27. Ibid., II, p. 38
28. See ibid., II, pp. 7–8
29. Mackenzie had been making secret inquiries about the exactions of the tacksmen. The role of the tacksman in the old Highlands is discussed in Eric Richards, *A History of the Highland Clearances: Vol. I. Agrarian Transformation and the Evictions 1745–1886* (London, 1982), pp. 60ff.
30. NLS Dep. 313, II, Household and Personal, Box 30, Lady Stafford to Lord Stafford, 23 July 1805, 1 August 1805, 3 August 1805, 6 August 1805, 9 August 1805.
31. Quoted in Grant, op. cit., p.112; see also Adam, op.cit., I, p. xiii et seq.
32. Ibid., II, p. 66.
33. The question of rents and dependency was further complicated by the unofficial population of the Sutherland estate, which was large. James Loch recalled the 1812, 1813 and 1817 famines 'when it was found that there were 408 families comprising 2,000 persons who had squatted on the estate and paid no rent. They were chiefly from the adjoining estates of Ross and Sutherland where sheep-farming had been previously and extensively introduced.' D593K/1/5/65, Loch to Sir John MacNeill, 22 February 1851.
34. Adam, op. cit., II, p. 59. NLS Dep. 313, III, Estate Management, Box 19, Colin Mackenzie to Lady Stafford, 24 January 1806.
35. NLS Dep. 313, III, Estate Management, Box 19, William Mackenzie to Lady Stafford, 20 July 1807.
36. NLS Dep. 313, III, Estate Management, Box 19, Colin Mackenzie to Lady Stafford, 3 February 1808.
37. NLS Dep. 313, III, Estate Management, Box 19, Advertisements, 1809.
38. Adam, op. cit., II, p. 63.
39. Ibid., II, p. 64.
40. Ibid., II, p. 95.
41. See NRA 1454/2/2/21, Loch to Adam, 28 September 1813; NRA/63/1822A, Loch to Adam, 11 September 1822.
42. At the beginning of August 1809 Lord Gower travelled by the new Burghead packet and probably met Young and Sellar.
43. NLS, Dep. 313, Letters to George, Lord Gower, Box 26; Lady Stafford to Lord Gower, 13 July 1809.
44. NLS, Dep. 313, Box 26, Lady Stafford to Lord Gower, 13 July 1809.

45. Grant, op. cit., p. 114.
46. D593/K/P/22/1/2, Minute of Lease, 1809.
47. Adam, op. cit., II, p. 113, Young and Sellar, 16 April 1810.
48. Ibid., II, p. 144, Young to Lady Stafford, 5 May 1811.
49. Ibid., I, p. 36.
50. Grant, op. cit., p. 172.
51. Ibid., p.117
52. NLS Dep. 313 III, Estate Management Box 19, Sellar and Young to Lady Stafford, 19 August 1809.
53. See Henderson, op. cit., passim.
54. NLS Dep. 313, Box 19, Young to Lord Gower, 12 January 1810.
55. NLS Dep. 313, III, Estate Management, Box 19, Sellar to Gower, 4 November 1809.
56. NLS Dep. 313/1127, Sellar to Gower, 4 November 1809, 18 November 1809. He quoted Burns at length in support of his views. But he opposed seasonal migration of wives and daughters to the Lothian harvest because they returned little improved in either money or morals.
57. Quoted in Eric Richards, 'The prospect of economic growth in Sutherland at the time of the clearances', *Scottish Historical Review*, XCIV, 148 (1970), pp. 159. fn. 4.
58. See Adam, op. cit., II, p. 7.
59. NLS, Dep. 313, III, Estate Management, Box 19, Young to Gower, 19 August 1809.
60. See Richards, 'Prospect', op. cit.
61. Adam, op. cit., I, p. xliv.
62. NLS Dep. 313, III, Estate Management, Box 19, Sellar and Young to Lady Stafford, 23 November 1809.
63. Their thinking was underpinned by an optimistic assumption: they believed that the economic progress achieved so spectacularly in Lancashire and Lanarkshire could be replicated practically anywhere, given expertise, cooperation and capital. See Richards, 'Prospect', op. cit., passim.
64. Quoted in ibid.
65. NLS Dep. 313 III, Estate Mangement, Box 19, Sellar to Lady Stafford, 31 August 1809.
66. See Richards, 'Prospect', op. cit. *passim*.
67. NLS Dep. 313, III, Estate Management, Box, 19, Falconer to Gower, 4 September 1809
68. NLS Dep. 313, III, Estate Management. Box 19, Falconer to Gower, 29 October 1809.
69. NLS Dep. 313/1127, Sellar to Gower, 13 August 1810.
70. NLS Dep. 313/1127, Sellar to Gower, 13 August 1810.
71. NLS MS 3881 (1811), f. 89, Lady Stafford to Walter Scott, 22 October 1811.
72. See Richards, 'Prospect', op. cit., passim.

– CHAPTER 4   THE INSTALLATION –

1. He was at this time styled as 'Patrick Sellar of Elgin'.
2. MacPherson Grant Papers, Ballindalloch Castle, Bundle 739; Sellar to MacPherson Grant, 29 March 1810, 31 March 1810.
3. Young and Sellar to the Marchioness of Stafford, 2 November 1809, in R. J. Adam, II (ed.), *Sutherland Estate Papers*, 2 vols (Edinburgh, 1972), p. 40.
4. D593/K/P/22/1/2 Sellar to Gower, 13 August 1810.
5. NLS Dep. 313, Box 25, Lady to Lord Stafford, 6 July 1810.
6. Adam, op. cit., II, p. 117.
7. Ibid., II, p. 106.
8. Ibid.
9. D593/P/22/1/2, Young to Lady Stafford, 27 July 1810. The estate had certainly been geared to such a change for a decade by then. In the late summer of 1810, the Stafford family, Sellar, Young and the engineer Thomas Telford (who had also condemned the wholesale introduction of sheep into the Highlands) toured the entire Sutherland estate. They examined and planned the coastal settlement schemes, and looked at Strathnaver in particular. It was a time when the building activity was putting a strain on the local labour supply. D593/K/P/22/1/2, Young to Gower, 12 August 1810.
10. Adam, op. cit., II, p. 126.
11. Ibid., II, p. 128.
12. Ibid., I, pp. xiv-xv.
13. Ibid., I, p. xiv, fn. 3.
14. NLS Dep. 313, Estate Management, Box 7, 'Document of Agreement between the most noble the Marquis and Marchioness of Stafford and William Young and Patrick Sellar'. See also Adam, op. cit., I, pp. 43–5.
15. Other law business was conducted by legal advisers in Edinburgh and London.
16. D593/K/P/22/1/2 Young to Lady Stafford, 3 August 1809,
17. Adam, op. cit., I, p. xvii.
18. Ibid., I, pp. 42–3.
19. See ibid., I, p. xcvi.
20. Ibid., II, p. 242 and I, pp. 96–7; I, p. xcv, II, p. 242 and information from Dr Malcolm Bangor-Jones.
21. NLS Dep. 313, Box 19, Young to Gower, 29 October 1812, and Young to Gower, 29 April 1812.
22. Adam, op. cit., II, p. 149.
23. See ibid., I, p. xx.
24. Ibid., pp. 153–2, 149–50.
25. NLS Dep. 313, Box 36, Wm Mackenzie to Lord Stafford, 28 November 1811.
26. Adam, op. cit., II, p.169.

27. NLS Dep. 313, Sellar to Gower, 13 August 1810. In August 1810 Sellar was unctuously grateful for the role in the county with which he had been entrusted. NLS Dep. 313/1127/16, Sellar to Gower, 13 August 1810.
28. Adam, op. cit., I, p. 34.
29. Ibid.
30. Sellar regarded Henderson's Report as pompous and premature. NLS Sutherland Collection, Dep. 313, Sellar to Gower, 27 May 1812.
31. NLS MS 3881 (1811) f. 89, Lady Stafford to Walter Scott, 22 October 1811.
32. NLS Dep. 313, Sellar to Gower, 28 February 1811.
33. NLS Dep. 313/1127/18, Sellar to Gower, 15 January 1811.
34. NLS Dep. 313/1127/19, Sellar to Gower, 5 February 1811.
35. NLS Dep. 313/1127/21, Sellar to Gower, 11 February 1811.
36. NLS Dep. 313/1127/22, Sellar to Gower, 11 February 1811.
37. NLS Dep. 313, Sellar to Gower, 25 February 1811, 26 February 1811.
38. NLS Dep. 313/1127/26, Sellar to Gower, 27 February 1811.
39. NLS Dep. 313/Box 19, Sellar to Gower 8 January 1811.
40. See Eric Richards, 'The *Military Register* and the pursuit of Patrick Sellar', *Scottish Economic and Social History*, 16 (1996), pp. 38–60, passim.
41. Adam, op. cit., II, p. 146.
42. See above Chapter 3.
43. In his Appendix VII to James Loch, *Account of the Improvements on the Estates of the Marquess of Stafford* (1820).
44. NLS Loch Muniments, GD 268/216, Lady Stafford to Loch, 27 December 1812.
45. SRO SC/1/3, Dornoch Sheriff Court Minute Book, 22 March 1811.
46. See Eric Richards, 'The prospect of economic growth in Sutherland at the time of the clearances', *Scottish Historical Review*, XCIX, 148 (1970), p. 168.
47. See M. W. Grant, *Golspie's Story* (Golspie, 1983), p. 118.
48. See Adam, op. cit., I, pp. 45–118.
49. Ibid., I, p. 119.
50. Ibid., I, pp. 120–6.
51. Ibid., I, p. 126.
52. NLS Dep. 313/1127/19, Sellar to Gower, 16 and 17 April 1811.
53. NLS Dep. 313/1127/48, Sellar to Gower, 21 March 1812.
54. NLS Dep. 313/1127/39, Sellar to Gower, 14 December 1811.
55. NLS Dep. 313/1127/19, Sellar to Gower, 3 April 1811.
56. NLS Dep. 313/1127, Sellar to Gower, 11 February 1812. NLS Dep. 313, Box 19, Sellar to Gower, 3 April 1811.
57. NLS Dep. 313, Sellar to Gower, 2 December 1811.
58. NLS Dep. 313/1127/48, Sellar to Gower, 21 March 1812.
59. NLS Dep. 313/1127/23 Sellar to Gower, 14 February 1811 and 26 February 1811 in which he pressed for a clearer definition of his functions in the estate.

60. NLS Dep. 313, Box 19, Sellar to Gower, 6 February, 1811. Sellar referred to his father as 'a Factor of longstanding'.
61. Adam, op. cit., II, pp. 135–7.
62. NLS Dep. 313/1127/49, Sellar to Gower, 18 April 1812.
63. Adam, op. cit., II, p. 169.
64. NLS Dep. 313/1127/24, Sellar to Gower, 28 February 1811.
65. NLS Dep. 313/1127/48, Sellar to Gower, 4 May 1812, 7 May 1812, 10 May 1812.
66. NLS Dep. 313/1572, Reported by Sellar, 10 March 1811.
67. NLS Dep. 313/1127/27 Sellar to Gower, 11 February 1811. Sellar believed that two or three hundred pounds might be recovered 'if firm measures are used, and firmness will be absolutely necessary'.
68. NLS Dep. 313/1127/29, Sellar to Gower, 19 March 1811.
69. NLS Dep. 313/1127/29, Sellar to Gower, 19 March 1811.
70. Subsequent lists carried the signatures of both Sellar and Mackid, Sellar being responsible for the Sutherland estate in particular. NLS Dep. 313/1127/31, Sellar to Gower, 3 April 1811. But Sellar continued to complain of Mackid's professional dilatoriness and said, 'We shall give him no peace and no rest till we have carried it through.' NLS Dep. 313/1127/38 Sellar to Gower, 2 December 1811.
71. Adam, op. cit., II, p. 133.
72. It included 'Mr McKid', who, of course, was supposed to be on the side of law.
73. Adam, op. cit., II, p. 134.
74. Ibid.
75. NLS Dep. 313, Estate Correspondence, Box 19, Sellar to Gower, 1 April 1811.

– CHAPTER 5 THE NEW CLEARANCES, 1811–12 –

1. I have drawn on M. Bangor-Jones, *The Assynt Clearances* (Dundee, 1998) and also James Loch's *Account of the Improvements on the Estate of the Marquess of Stafford*, (1820), and Eric Richards, *A History of the Highland Clearances* vol. 1, (London, 1982), passim.
2. See Bangor-Jones, op. cit., passim.
3. On the sale of the estate see Angus Mackay, *The Book of Mackay* (Edinburgh, 1904), pp. 232–3, (especially fn. 1) and pp. 236–7, and below Chap. 14.
4. Ibid., p. 229.
5. See Bangor-Jones, op. cit., pp. 17 ff.
6. Young to Lady Stafford, 22 December 1811, in R. J. Adam (ed.), *Sutherland Estate Papers*, 2 vols, II, pp. 159–60.
7. NLS , Dep. 313, III, Estate Management, Box 19, Young to Lord Gower, 26 April 1812.

8. Quoted in M. W. Grant, *Golspie's Story* (Golspie, 1983), p. 125.
9. NLS Dep. 313/1127, Young to Gower, 10 February 1812.
10. NLS Dep. 313/1127/48, Sellar to Gower, 21 March 1812.
11. NLS Dep. 313/1127/48, Sellar to Gower, 29 May 1812.
12. Adam, op. cit., II, 165.
13. NLS Dep. 313, Sellar to Gower, 18 April 1812, 27 May 1812.
14. See Sellar's *Statement* (1825), p. 2. See also Adam, op. cit., I, p. 1.
15. Ibid., I, p. 130.
16. See Eric Richards, *The Leviathan of Wealth* (London and Toronto, 1973), ch. 2.
17. *Letters of Harriet Countess Granville, 1810–1845*, ed. F. Leveson Gower, 2 vols (1894), I, p. 39.
18. Quoted in Richards, *Leviathan*, op. cit., p. 178.
19. Young believed that Lord Stafford's English rents could be raised by 300 per cent. NLS Dep. 313, Box 19, Young to Gower, 29 April 1812.

– CHAPTER 6 'THE PEOPLE'S FOLLY': KILDONAN AND ASSYNT, 1813 –

1. NLS Dep. 313/1584, Sellar to Lady Stafford, 30 March 1813.
2. This section is based on Eric Richards, 'The prospect of economic growth in Sutherland at the time of the clearances', *Scottish Historical Review*, XCIX, 148 (1970).
3. See K. D. Logue, *Popular Disturbances in Scotland 1780–1815* (Edinburgh 1979), pp. 64–72, and M. W. Grant, *Golspie's Story* (Golspie, 1983), p. 126.
4. R. J. Adam (ed.), *Sutherland Estate Papers*, 2 vols (Edinburgh, 1972) I, p. 138.
5. NLS Dep. 313, Box 36, Sellar to Lady Stafford, 29 January 1813, 17 Febuary 1813, 26 February 1813. There was an account, not entirely unsympathetic to the people, in the *Inverness Journal*, 30 April 1813, referring also to correspondence in the *Morning Star*.
6. NLS Dep. 313, Young to Lady Stafford, 17 February 1813.
7. Adam, op. cit., II, p. 177.
8. Ibid., II, p. 178.
9. NLS Dep. 313/1578 Sellar to Lady Stafford, 29 January 1813.
10. NLS Dep. 313/1578, Sellar to Gordon, 4 February 1813.
11. Ibid.
12. NLS Dep. 313, III, Box 36, Melville to Lady Stafford, 12 September 1813.
13. NLS Dep. 313/1578, 17 February 1813.
14. Ibid., Sellar to Lady Stafford, 26 February 1813.
15. NLS Dep. 313/1584, Sellar to Lady Stafford, 26 February 1813.
16. Adam, op. cit., II, p. 181.
17. Adam, op. cit., II, p. 185.

18. Cranstoun significantly declined to accept accommodation at Dunrobin Castle. He explained that the people needed to be persuaded that he was 'an independent judge and magistrate'. He nevertheless described the faith of the common people, in their petitions to Lord Stafford and the Regent, as 'one of the principal delusions.'

19. See Grant, op. cit., p. 127.

20. See Eric Richards, '*The Military Register* and the pursuit of Patrick Sellar', *Scottish Economic and Social History*, 16 (1996), passim.

21. Adam, op. cit., II, p. 188. GD 268/216 Lady Stafford to Loch, 1 April 1813, 5 April 1813. SRO GD 268/216, Lady Stafford to Loch, 25 March 1813. Lady Stafford to Loch, 1 April 1813, 5 April 1813.

22. Adam, op. cit., II, p. 190.

23. NLS Dep. 313/1578, Sellar to Lady Stafford, 29 January 1813 and Sellar to Thomas Gordon, 4 February 1813.

24. NLS, Dep. 313, Young to Gower, 4 April 1813.

25. Adam, op. cit., II, p. 44.

26. NLS, Dep. 313, Young to Gower, 3 May 1813.

27. Macdonald, the people's 'representative', was also involved in Selkirk's plans for the American emigration. Macdonald had been dissuading the people from accepting lots at Strathy. Moreover, the residents of Armadale, aware of the impending influx of people from Kildonan, voiced their opposition to the influx. Young, hearing this response, hoped many of the small tenants would indeed emigrate. GD 268/216, Lady Stafford to Loch, 5 April 1813. NLS, Dep. 313, Young to Gower, 3 May 1813.

28. NLS , Dep. 313, Young to Gower, 27 May 1813.

29. Ibid. Sellar to Lady Stafford, 30 March 1813.

30. NLS Dep. 313/1578, Sellar to Lady Stafford, 14 March 1813.

31. NLS Dep. 313/1578, Sellar to Lady Stafford, 30 March 1813.

32. NLS Dep. 313/1578, Sellar to Lady Stafford, 14 March 1813.

33. NLS Dep. 313/1584, Sellar to Lady Stafford, 14 April 1813. He also observed the role of women among them. The fishermen on the Armadale coast were 'more remarkable for their industry than for any tenderness to their women, whom I saw employed in every menial office, digging the ground, carrying out manure on their backs, and covering in the oatseed by a harrow which three of them generally trailed behind them, while the men were busy dressing and repairing their lines, nets, etc.' NLS Dep. 313/1578, Sellar to Lady Stafford, 14 April 1813.

34. NLS Dep. 313/1578, Sellar to Lady Stafford, 30 March 1813.

35. NLS Dep. 313/1578, Sellar to Lady Stafford, 14 March 1813.

36. Adam, op. cit., I, p. 135. See also Callum Brown, *The Social History of Religion in Scotland since 1730* (London, 1987).

37. See Grant, op. cit., pp. 76–7.

38. See Logue, op. cit., pp. 170–4.

39. Adam, op. cit., II, p. 195.

40. Brown, op. cit., p. 124.
41. Adam, op. cit., II, p. 199.
42. Grant, op. cit., p. 129.
43. GD 268/216, Mackenzie to Lady Stafford, 17 September 1813.
44. NRA 1454/2/21, Loch to Adam, 31 December 1813.
45. Adam, op. cit., II, pp. 200–4.
46. NLS Dep., 313/1584, Sellar to Lady Stafford, 15 October 1813.
47. GD 268/216 Lady Stafford to Loch, 25 September 1813. NLS Dep. 313, Sellar to Gower, 13 August 1813.
48. NLS Dep. 313/1584, Sellar to Lady Stafford, 24 November 1813.
49. NLS Dep. 313, Sellar to Gower, 13 August 1813. In April 1813, Sellar was already in expansive mode when he tried unsuccessfully to persuade Gilchrist to release some of his land to round out his own holdings. SRO Gilchrist of Ospidale Papers, GD 153, Box 19, bundle 5, no. 4, Sellar to Gilchrist, 18 April 1813. I thank Malcolm Bangor-Jones for this data.
50. Adam, op. cit., I, p. lix, fn.
51. Adam, op. cit., II, pp. 144–5.
52. NLS Dep. 313, Estate Management, Box 11, K. Mackay to Young, 18 December 1813.
53. NLS Dep. 313, Box 37, Young to Lady Stafford, 3 January 1813.
54. Adam, op. cit., I, p. lxi.
55. Before his trial Sellar began a legal process to remove the remaining thirty-two families (sixteen each from Rossal and Truderscraig) who had been subset. Mainly these families were resettled on the estate in the strath or at Bettyhill.

– CHAPTER 7 SELLAR AND THE STRATHNAVER REMOVALS, 1814–15 –

1. NLS Dep. 313, Box 37, Young to Lady Stafford, 1 May 1814. R. J. Adam (ed.), *Sutherland Estate Papers*, 2 vols (Edinburgh, 1972), II, p. 226.
2. NLS Dep. 313, Box 37, Young to Lady Stafford, 3 January 1814, 14 February 1814, 9 March 1814, 1 May 1814, 5 May 1814 ; Adam, op cit., II, pp. 204–5.
3. Sellar told Lady Stafford that Mackid had falsely tried to blame his son for his own offence. For other details see NLS Dep. 313, Box 37, dated 31 January 1814, Sellar to Lady Stafford.
4. NLS Dep. 313/1578, Sellar to Lady Stafford, 10 January 1814, in two letters of the same day.
5. D593/K/1/5/3, Sellar to Loch, 3 March 1814.
6. NLS Dep. 313, Box 25, Lady Stafford to Lord Stafford, 3 July 1814.
7. Sellar to Lady Stafford, 31 January 1814.
8. NLS Dep. 313, Box 19, Sellar to Lady Stafford, 27 January 1814.
9. NLS Dep. 313, Box 37, Sellar to Lady Stafford, 16 February 1814.

10. NLS Dep. 313, Sellar to Lady Stafford, 7 April 1814.
11. Sellar pointed out that Mackid's poaching had been reported to Cranstoun in November 1813 and that Mackid had used pressure to persuade the informant, Bannerman, to withdraw his evidence. Eventually Mackid's apology to Lady Stafford was accepted; in Sellar's contemptuous phrase, the matter had been set aside to avoid 'vexing the pigeons'. Sellar concluded, cynically, that the entire episode demonstrated that it would be 'dangerous to prevent a Sheriff from poaching in time to come'.
12. NLS Dep. 313/1578, Sellar to Lady Stafford, 16 February 1814; Adam, op. cit., II, p. 171, fn. 2. NLS Dep. 313/1578, Sellar to Lady Stafford, 24 May 1814.
13. SRO SC 9/1/3, Dornoch Sheriff Court Minute Book, 8 February 1814.
14. D593/K/1/5/3, Young to Loch, 14 May 1814.
15. Adam, op. cit., II, p. 213.
16. Ibid., II, p. 208
17. D593/K/1/5/3, Young to Loch, 3 March 1814.
18. D593/K/1/5/3 Young to Lady Stafford, 8 June 1814.
19. Adam, op. cit., II, p. 217.
20. See ibid., II, p. 217
21. Ibid., II, p. 218.
22. See Eric Richards, *The Leviathan of Wealth* (London and Toronto, 1973), and F. C. Mather, *After the Canal Duke* (Oxford, 1970), passim.
23. Adam, op. cit., II, p. 221.
24. Ibid., II, p. 226.
25. See ibid., I, pp. 16–17 and above ch. 3.
26. Angus Mackay, *The Book of Mackay* (Edinburgh, 1904), pp. 227–8.
27. Horace Fairhurst, 'The surveys for the Sutherland clearances, 1814–1829', *Scottish Studies*, 8 (1964), pp. 1–18.
28. For the most optimistic view of the old society of Strathnaver see Ian Grimble's Introduction to Donald McLeod, *Gloomy Memories in the Highlands of Scotland* (1892 edn reprinted, Bettyhill, 1996).
29. M. W. Grant, *Golspie's Story* (Golspie, 1983), p. 132.
30. NLS Dep. 313/1578, Sellar to Lady Stafford, 27 July 1814.
31. Adam, op. cit., II, p. 229.
32. Ibid., II, 229.
33. See ibid., I, p. 151.
34. D593/K/1/5/3, Young to Lady Stafford, 21 November 1814.
35. D593/K/1/5/3, Sellar to Loch, 1 August 1814.
36. NLS Dep. 313, Sellar to Lady Stafford, 5 January 1815.
37. He was far less optimistic about the corn-lands of the nation: he dreaded 'the collapse of Corn Farms if the Corn Bill is not introduced.' SRO Dep. 313/1584, Young to Lady Stafford, 3 January 1815.
38. SRO Dep. 313/1584, Young to Lady Stafford, 24 February 1815.
39. NLS Dep. 313/1584, Young to Lady Stafford, 3 January 1815.

40. NLS Dep. 313, Sellar to Lady Stafford, 15 February 1815.
41. Adam, op. cit., II, pp. 236–8. Cf. SRO GD 271/124, Loch to Wm Mackenzie, 24 October 1832.
42. Adam, op. cit., I, pp. 151 and 154–5.
43. Ibid., II, p. 240.
44. Ibid.
45. NLS Dep. 313/1586, Sellar to Lady Stafford, 22 March 1815.
46. NLS Dep. 313/1586, Sellar to Lady Stafford, 15 February 1815.
47. The phrase of James C. Scott, *Weapons of the Weak. Everyday Forms of Peasant Resistance* (New Haven, CT, 1985).
48. NLS Dep. 313, Box 19, Young to Gower, 16 February 1815.
49. NLS Dep. 313, Box 19, Grant to Young, 22 March 1815.
50. Adam, op. cit., II, p. 241.
51. This concurs with the account offered in Thomas Sellar, *The Sutherland Evictions of 1814* (1883), p. 16, based on Patrick Sellar's later statements.
52. SRO SC 232/S/23/2, Lady Stafford's answer to the petition, 22 July 1815.
53. See Eric Richards, 'The *Military Register* and the pursuit of Patrick Sellar', *Scottish Economic and Social History*, 16 (1996), pp. 38–60.
54. Eventually it was agreed that the author was Captain Alexander Sutherland, an ex-army man in London, who was supplied with local intelligence by his brother, Scibbercross, in Sutherland. Between them they personified the old social hierarchy of pre-Sellar Sutherland, and they cleverly orchestrated the campaign against Sellar in Sutherland and London.
55. NLS Dep. 313, William Young to Lady Stafford, 17 April 1815, Young to Lady Stafford, 25 May 1815.
56. NLS Dep. 313/1127/59, Sellar to Gower, 18 April 1815.
57. NLS Dep. 313, Young to Lady Stafford, 25 May 1815.
58. NLS Dep. 313/1127/59, Sellar to Gower, 15 April 1815.
59. NLS Dep. 313, Sellar to Gower, 15 April 1815.
60. INLS Dep. 313, Sellar to Lady Stafford, 12 May 1815.
61. Blair Adam Papers, NRA 1454 /2/84, Loch to Adam, 11 June 1816.

– CHAPTER 8 MACKID'S PRECOGNITION IN STRATHNAVER, MAY 1815 –

1. Sheriffs-Depute were required to reside in their county for four months of the year – but in 1814 less than half complied. See David Tidswell, 'Geographical mobility, occupational changes and family relationships in early nineteenth century Scotland (with particular reference to the precognitions of the Lord Advocate's Department, 1812–21)', unpublished PhD thesis, University of Edinburgh, 1993, p. 25.
2. See Tidswell, op. cit., and K. D. Logue, *Popular Disturbances in Scotland 1780–1815* (Edinburgh, 1979), pp. 218–21.

3. The relevant documents have recently been located in SRO Court of Sessions Records, CS 232 and I am extremely grateful to Dr Bangor-Jones for supplying me with the crucial references.

4. SRO CS 232/S/23/2, Gower to the Strathnaver tenants, 8 February 1815.

5. SRO CS 232/S/23/2, Cranstoun to Munro, 30 March 1815.

6. SRO CS 232/S/23/2, Petitions of the tenants of Strathnaver to Lord Gower, 18 January 1815.

7. SRO CS 232/S/23/2, Mackid to Cranstoun, 8 May 1815.

8. SRO CS 232/S/23/2, John Munro to Andrew Clephane, 2 May 1815, 24 May 1815.

9. Further detail was cited in SRO CS 232/S/23/2, Additional complaints of Strathnaver tenants.

10. SRO CS 232/S/23/2, Copy of petition of tenants of Strathnaver and warrant of incarcerating Mr Sellar and others, 30 May 1815.

11. SRO CS 232/S/23/2, ibid.

12. SRO CS 232/S/23/2, Declarations of Kenneth Murray, Alexander Mackenzie, James Fraser and Alexander Sutherland, 29 May 1815.

13. SRO CS 232/S/23/2, Precognition of Mr Patrick Sellar and others, May 1815.

14. R. J. Adam (ed.), *Sutherland Estate Papers*, 2 vols (Edinburgh, 1972), I, pp. 155–161.

15. Ibid., I, p. 161–2.

16. They were Kenneth Murray, of Ironhill, Alexander Mackenzie of Blaremore in Rogart, James Fraser of Golspie, and Alexander Sutherland of Backies in Golspie, all sheriff-officers. They were accused of 'being participators with Mr Sellar in the alleged charges of wilful fire raising and destroying a Mill'. They were lodged in the attic room of the Castle Tower.

17. Adam, op. cit., II, pp. 243–4.

18. SRO CS 232/S/23/2, Mackid to Lord Stafford, 30 May 1815.

19. SRO CS 232/S/23/2, Sellar's instrument of protest for wrongous imprisonment and damages versus Mackid and other abettors, 31 May 1815 and 6 June 1815.

20. *Military Register*, 22 June 1815.

21. *Military Register,* 21 June 1815. The newspaper remarked that it was glad to have been instrumental in the effort 'to rescue the County and indeed the nation at large, from the disgrace of the system of *Colossal Tyranny* with which for years, local agents have bestridden that country and a brave people.' *Military Register,* 28 June 1815.

– CHAPTER 9 SELLAR CONCUSSED –

1. NLS Dep. 313, Sellar to Lady Stafford, 31 May 1815.

2. Ibid.

3. Sellar made an official complaint against Mackid, dated 24 May 1815, claiming that he was concerting against him and that he was 'the silent mover of the business'. NLS Dep. 313, Box 19, Sellar to Cranstoun, 24 May 1815. Sellar alleged that Mackid timed the precognition during Cranstoun's absence from the county and told several people that Sellar would be hanged. William Young was told, for his own reputation, to leave Sellar to his fate.

4. See H. M. Mackay, *Notes on the Successive Buildings used for County, Municipal and Judicial Purposes of the County of Sutherland and Burgh of Dornoch* (Privately published, Edinburgh, 1896), pp. 21–3.

5. SRO cS 9/1/3, Dornoch Sheriff Court Minute Book. My thanks are again due to Dr Bangor-Jones for this reference.

6. Details of the precognition were published before Sellar's arrest. NLS, Dep. 313/1815 (part), Account Patrick Sellar . . . and James Robertson.

7. NLS Dep. 313, Young to Lady Stafford, 31 May 1815.

8. NLS Dep. 313, Young to Lady Stafford, 28 June 1815.

9. D593/K/1/5/3, Loch to Young, 9 June 1815.

10. R. J. Adam (ed.), *Sutherland Estate Papers*, 2 vols (Edinburgh, 1972), II, p. 246.

11. Ibid., II, pp. 243–4.

12. Ibid.

13. Sellar's liberation from jail was ordered by the Lord Justice Clerk 'who declared his astonishment at any such warrant of Imprisonment having been granted. It is thought the arrest (and indeed there seems to be proof of it) was the result of a conspiracy among several of the Sutherland people among who, a high offl. character there, is ranked.' MacPherson Grant Papers, Ballindalloch Castle, Bundle 739, Ritchie to Macpherson Grant, 29 June 1815.

14. Inverness Public Library, Highland Regional Archive, L/S/M/1/2 Record of Prisoners Incarcerated in the Tolbooth or Jail of the Burgh of Dornoch. Murray, Sutherland, Mackenzie and Fraser were released on the following day. I thank Monica Clough for locating this document.

15. NLS Dep. 313/1815 (part), Account Patrick Sellar . . . and James Robertson.

16. D593/K/1/5/3, Sellar to Loch, 28 June 1815.

17. NLS Dep. 313/1584, Young to Lady Stafford, 6 July 1815, encl. copy of letter Young to Cranstoun, 28 June 1815, Dep. 313/1585, Cranstoun to Young, 1 July 1815. D593/K/1/5/3, Loch to Sellar, 25 June 1815, Sellar to Loch, 15 June 1815, Young to Loch, 6 June 1815 (twice).

18. NLS Dep. 313, Sellar to Gower, 3 July 1815.

19. NLS Dep. 313/1586, Sellar to Lady Stafford, 3 July 1815.

20. NLS Dep. 313, Sellar to Lady Stafford, 8 July 1815.

21. NRA 63, Blair Adam Box F, Sellar to Lord Advocate, 24 May 1815.

22. NLS Dep. 313, Sellar to Lady Stafford, 15 July 1815.

23. NLS Dep. 313, Box 37, Mackenzie to Lady Stafford, 5 June 1815.
24. NLS Dep. 313, Box 19, Mackenzie to Lady Stafford, 3 June 1815.
25. NLS Dep. 313, Box 19, Mackenzie to Lady Stafford, 9 June 1815.
26. Blair Adam Papers, 1454/2/84, Sellar to Lady Stafford, 1 July 1815, enclosed in Loch's letter to Adam, 6 July 1815.
27. D593/K/1/5/3, Sellar to Lady Stafford, 28 June 1815.
28. See, for instance, George Rudé, *The Crowd in History* (New York, 1964).
29. NLS Dep. 313, Lady Stafford to Lord Stafford, 14 August 1815, 22 August 1815.
30. Blair Adam Papers, NRA 1454/2/84, Loch to Adam, 7 July 1815.
31. D593/K/1/5/3, Lady Stafford to Loch, 24 July 1815, Adam to Loch, 21 June 1815, Loch to Cranstoun, 30 June 1815.
32. NLS Dep. 313, Box 25, Lady Stafford to Lord Stafford, 8 August 1815.
33. Adam, op. cit., II, p. 255.
34. NLS Dep. 313, Box 25, Lady Stafford to Lord Stafford, 10 August 1815.
35. NLS Dep. 313, Box 25, Lady Stafford to Lord Stafford, 12 August 1815. NLS Dep. 313, Box 19, Mackenzie to Lady Stafford, 12 July 1815.
36. NLS Dep. 313, Lady Stafford to Lord Stafford, 15 August 1815.
37. Blair Adam Papers, 1454, Loch to Adam, 6 July 1815.
38. NLS Dep. 313, Box 38 Loch to Lord Stafford, 12 and 14 August 1815.
39. Adam, op. cit., I, p. xxvii, II, p. 162–3, 163.
40. NLS Dep. 313, Box 19, Lady Stafford to Lord Stafford, 4 August 1815.
41. NLS Dep. 313, Box 19, Lady Stafford to Lord Stafford, 5 August 1815.
42. M. W. Grant, *Golspie's Story* (Golspie, 1983), p. 135.
43. D593/K/1/3/3 Sellar [to Loch?], 14 September 1815.
44. D593/K/1/3/3 Sellar to Loch, 13 September 1815.
45. D593/K/1/3/3 Sellar to Loch, 19 September 1815, and Sellar to Cranstoun, 14 September 1815 (copy). Loch to Lady Stafford, 8 October 1815.
46. See Adam, op. cit., I, p. 163, fn. 2 , and Eric Richards, *The Leviathan of Wealth* (London and Toronto, 1973), pp. 275–6. The citing of Macleod remains a mystery which is only increased by the fact that Macleod was never called upon to give the evidence promised by Sellar.
47. Robert Bell, *A Treatise on Leases* (1803), p. 484.
48. Adam, op. cit., II, p.168.
49. NLS Dep. 313, Lady Stafford to Lord Stafford, 26 August 1815. D593/K/P/18/2, Lady Stafford to Sidmouth, 25 August 1815.
50. Anon. [James Loch], *Account of the Improvements on the Estate of the Marquis of Stafford* (1815).
51. NLS Dep. 313, Sellar to Lady Stafford, 23 October 1815.
52. D593/K/1/3/3, Sellar to Lady Stafford, 28 September 1815.
53. D593/K/1/3/3, Loch to Sellar, 10 and 26 October 1815 and again Loch to Grant, 3 February 1816, in which Loch was concerned how Sellar knew of the letter. It transpired that Young had been shown the letter by Mackid himself.

54. Adam, op. cit., II, p. 259.

55. NLS Dep. 313, Young to Lady Stafford, 6 October 1815.

56. D593/K/P/22/1/28, Young to Gower, 6 October 1815.

57. Adam, op. cit., II, p. 260.

58. Ibid., II, pp. 267–72. Young declared, with a certain acerbity and little sense of fraternal loyalty, 'No poor Highlander ever charged me with cruelty or oppression.' D593/K/1/3/3, Young to Lady Stafford, 8 December 1815.

59. NLS Dep. 313, Young to Lady Stafford, 15 November 1815.

60. NLS Dep. 313, Young to Lady Stafford, 31 December 1815.

61. NLS Dep. 313, Young to Loch 1 November 1815.

62. NLS Dep. 313/1585, Loch to Lady Stafford, 12 November 1815.

63. Adam, op. cit., I, p. 211; Sellar made his complaints known to Lady Stafford on 16 March 1816.

64. On 20 January 1816 Sellar was involved in discussion with his lawyer 'respecting an overture for settlement'.

65. NLS Dep. 313/1589, Young to Lady Stafford, 10 March 1815.

66. See Eric Richards, 'The *Military Register* and the pursuit of Patrick Sellar', *Scottish Economic and Social History*, 16 (1996) passim. Until the news of his trial arrived in mid March 1816 Sellar had been thinking in terms of bringing a suit against Mackid and against the people he termed 'the London libellers'.

67. NLS Dep. 313, Sellar to Lady Stafford, 16 March 1816 and enclosed correspondence between Sellar and Mackenzie. On the ambivalent role of the ministers, especially Mackenzie, see Alexander Mearns, 'The minister and the bailiff: a study of presbyterian clergy in the Northern Highlands during the clearances', *Scottish Church History Society Records*, XXIV (1990), pp. 53–75.

68. D593/K/1/5/5, Sellar to Lady Stafford, 28 January 1816.

69. D593/K/1/5/5, Lady Stafford to Loch, March 1816.

70. MacPherson Grant Papers, Ballindalloch Castle, Bundle 739, Mackenzie to Macpherson Grant, 17 March 1816.

71. NLS Dep. 313, Box 37, MacPherson Grant to Lady Stafford, 11 March 1816.

72. Mackenzie had set out to oust Mackid from the estate and to induce Cranstoun to dismiss him from his official law position. Now Mackid had agreed to resign to avoid his dismissal. Ballindalloch Papers, Bundle 360, Mackenzie to Grant, 17 March 1816. NLS Dep. 313, Box 38, Mackenzie to Lady Stafford, 17 March 1816.

73. NLS Dep. 313/1587, W. Dempster to Lady Stafford, 14 February 1816.

74. Ibid.

75. NLS Dep. 313/1588, Mackenzie to Lady Stafford, 22 March 1816.

76. On 11 March 1816 Sellar received notice from officers of the Crown intimating their 'determination to bring you at trial at next Circuit.' This

is from the lawyers' accounts. Dep. 313/1815 (part), Account Patrick Sellar . . . and James Robertson.

77. SRO GD/1/979. This appears to be a draft of the printed document, since various names are missing.

78. NLS Dep. 313, Box 1588, Sellar to Lady Stafford, 16 March 1816.

79. See Adam, op. cit., I, p. 211, fn.

80. Ibid., II, p. 273.

81. NLS Dep. 313/1588, Sellar to Lady Stafford, 8 April 1816.

– CHAPTER 10   TRIAL AND RETRIBUTION –

1. On the Scottish category of culpable homicide see David M. Walker, *The Oxford Companion to Law* (Oxford, 1980).

2. On Pitmilly see Henry Cockburn, *Circuit Journeys* (Edinburgh, 1888), p. 78. See also, idem, *Letters Chiefly Connected with the Affairs of Scotland* (London, 1874), pp. 55, 201; and idem, *Memorials of His Time* (Edinburgh, 1856), pp. 257–8

3. The main source for the trial was prepared by Sellar's own junior counsel and published soon after: [Patrick Robertson], *Report of the Trial of Patrick Sellar, Esq. Factor of the Most Noble the Marquis and Marchioness of Stafford for the crimes of Culpable Homicide, Real Injury, and Oppression. Before the Circuit Court of Justiciary, held at Inverness, on Tuesday 23 April, 1816* (Edinburgh, 1816), copy in the British Library.

4. See, for example, the anthology of anti-Sellar views in Ian Grimble, *The Trial of Patrick Sellar* (London, 1962).

5. Quoted in NLS Dep. 313/1587, MacPherson Grant to Lady Stafford, 25 April 1816.

6. NLS Dep. 313/1815 (part), Account Patrick Sellar . . . and James Robertson.

7. On Macleod, see above, Ch. 9.

8. NLS Dep. 313/1815 (part), Payments to Witnesses, 24 April 1816.

9. Chisholm had been inconveniently mobile since the 1814 evictions. He had moved to Urqhart on Loch Ness, and finding him entailed a great search after a tip-off had been received at Culmaily. Getting Chisholm to the trial was 'not without great difficulty'. NLS Dep. 313/1815 (part), Account of Messrs Anderson and Shepherd, for which thanks to Dr Bangor-Jones.

10. D593/K/1/5/5, Grant to Lady Stafford, 4 April 1816.

11. D593/K/1/5/5, Mackenzie to Loch, 21 April 1816.

12. D593 K/1/5/5, W. Mackenzie to Lord Stafford, 21 April 1816. The failure of the estate to synchronise the removals with the preparation of the resettlement lots was made apparent in the correspondence of Gabriel Reid, one of the incoming sheep-farmers. Reid was upset when the *Military Register* named him as an oppressor of the people. He explained

to Lady Stafford that, at great disadvantage of his farming operation, he too had allowed many of the people to stay on temporarily until the lots were readied. As a consequence, he was further criticised for hypocrisy in using 'feudal' methods of subletting. Reed's letter showed the failure of the estate to provide resettlement facilities for the removees as well as the financially painful forbearance of the new sheep-farmers who were placed in an exquisite moral dilemma by the leases they had contracted. NLS Dep. 313/1590, Reed to Lady Stafford, 29 August 1816.

13. NLS Dep. 313, Box 19, Sellar to Lord Stafford, 9 April 1816.

14. D593/K/1/5/5, Loch to Sellar, 1 and 8 April 1816.

15. Sellar's counsel Gordon had been alive to the great prejudice of the people and had suggested to Sellar (and his father, with whom Sellar was evidently close at this time) that he should plead for trial in Edinburgh, but Sellar was adamant and resisted the notion.

16. Robertson, *Report*, op. cit.

17. Robertson, *Report*, op. cit., p. 1: NLS Dep. 313, MacPherson Grant to Lady Stafford, 20 May 1816.

18. Ibid., p. 49.

19. Ibid., p. 5. Emphasis added by Sellar.

20. *Inverness Journal*, 26 April 1816, and quoted in M W. Grant, *Golspie's Story* (Golspie, 1983), p. 135. *Edinburgh Evening Courant*, 2 May 1816, noted the lively expectation in the country for the result of the trial. The judge, it reported, gave his 'full and perfect concurrence' to the verdict. The Crown counsel had said distinctly that 'even if the witnesses, whose testimony had been rejected on consequence of objections to their designations, had been examined, it would have made no difference to the result.'

21. NLS Dep. 313, Grant to Lady Stafford, 27 April 1816.

22. NLS Dep. 313/1587, MacPherson Grant to Lady Stafford, 27 April 1816.

23. Ibid., MacPherson Grant, to Lady Stafford, 2 May 1816.

24. Robertson, *Report*, op. cit.

25. NLS Dep. 313/1588, J. Gordon to Mackenzie, 24 April 1816.

26. NLS Dep. 313, Mackenzie to Lady Stafford, 26 April 1816.

27. NLS Dep. 313, William Mackenzie to Lady Stafford, 27 March 1816.

28. NLS Dep. 313, Box 38, Mackenzie to Lady Stafford, 4 May 1816.

29. NLS Dep. 313/1588, Young to Lady Stafford, 24 April 1816.

30. GD 268/28–30, William Adam to Loch, 17 May 1816.

31. D593/K/1/5/5, Loch to Young, 30 April 1816, Grant to Loch, 26 April 1816.

32. D593/K/1/5/5, Loch to Lady Stafford, 15 May 1816.

33. D593/K/1/5/5, Grant to Loch, 10 June 1816.

34. D593/K/1/5/5, Young to Loch, 8 June 1816.

35. NLS Dep. 313, Sellar to Lord Stafford, 24 April 1816.

36. NLS Dep. 313, Box 38, Sellar to Lady Stafford, 24 April 1816.

37. NLS Dep. 313, Sellar to Lady Stafford, 24 April 1816.
38. NLS Dep. 313/1590, Tollet to Lady Stafford, 3 May 1816.
39. See Eric Richards, 'The *Military Register* and the pursuit of Patrick Sellar', *Scottish Economic and Social History*, especially pp. 50–2.
40. Ibid.
41. D593/K/1/5/5, Young to Lady Stafford, 12 May 1816.
42. Loch Muniments, GD 268/28030, Adam to Loch, 17 May 1816.
43. GD 268/28030, Mackenzie to Lady Stafford, 4 May 1816.
44. See for instance, Colin Kidd, 'Teutonic ethnology and Scottish nationalist inhibition, 1780–1880', *Scottish Historical Review*, LXXIV, 1995, pp. 45–8, *passim.*
45. D593/K/1/5/5, Sellar to Loch, 7 May 1816.
46. R. J. Adam (ed.), *Sutherland Estate Papers*, 2 vols (Edinburgh, 1972) II, p. 284.
47. Ibid., pp. 175 ff.
48. NLS Dep. 313, Box 19, Sellar's Notes, 31 May 1816. Cf. Leah Leneman, 'A new role for a lost cause. Lowland romanticisation of the Jacobite Highlander', in Leah Leneman (ed.), *Perspectives in Scottish Social History: Essays in Honour of Rosalind Mitchison* (Aberdeen, 1988), pp. 119–21.
49. Adam, op. cit., II, p. 183.
50. Based on ibid., II, pp. 186, ff.
51. D593/K/1/5/5, Loch to Adam, 21 May 1816. The sheep-farmers, Atkinson and Marshall, attributed losses of 2,783 sheep and 2,000 lambs in a single season to what they described as their natural enemies – dogs, foxes, eagles and the people. The result was further summary evictions in Strathnaver. D593/K/1/5/5, Atkinson and Marshall to Loch, 31 January 1817.
52. D593/K/1/5/5, Sellar to Lady Stafford, 17 May 1816.
53. D593/K/1/5/5, Sellar to Loch, 23 and 27 May 1816.
54. NLS Dep. 313, Box 38, Sellar to Lady Stafford, 27 August 1816.
55. D593/K/1/5/5, Young to Loch, 4 May 1816.
56. NLS Dep. 313, Sellar to Lady Stafford, 1 May 1816.
57. D593/K/1/5/5, Loch to Adam, 31 May 1816.
58. NLS Dep. 313, Box 21, Loch to Sellar, 12 January 1818. Despite Loch's firm opposition, Sellar was offered a lease in late 1816 but failed to agree terms. See Adam, op. cit., II, p. 292, fn. 3.
59. Dep. 313, Box 38, Mackenzie to Lady Stafford, 11 July 1816.
60. Adam, op. cit., II, p. 288.
61. See ibid., II, p. 292. NLS Dep. 313/1015, Sellar to Lady Stafford, 30 August 1816.
62. D593/K/1/5/5, Sellar to Loch, 2 June 1816.
63. SRO CS 232/S23/2, Sellar's Instrument of Protest for wrongous Imprisonment and Damages versus Mackid and other Abettors, 31 May 1815 and 6 June 1815. This document ends abruptly on page 19.

64. Adam, op. cit., I, p. 137.

65. D593/K/1/3/5, Sellar to Grant, 23 September 1817, with copies.

66. SRO, Sinclair of Freswick Papers, GD 136/266, Sheriff Court Books of Sutherland, 13 November 1817. According to M. W. Grant, Mackid implored Sellar to settle out of court and in September 1817 wrote a 'humble' letter which appeared to confess all responsibility. Grant, op. cit., p. 136. There was no evidence of imploring in Mackid's retort to Sellar before the issue of his apology.

67. D593/K/1/3/5, Copies of letters Mackid to Sellar, 22 September 1817, Sellar to Gordon, 22 September 1817, Gordon to Sellar, 22 September 1817.

68. D593/K/1/3/5, Sellar to Loch, 24 September 1817. The Mackid statements are in SRO GD 136/266/1.

69. This information is by favour of Dr Bangor-Jones.

70. SRO, Sinclair of Freswick Papers, GD 136/266 and GD 136/531.

71. *Edinburgh Advertiser*, 3 May 1816.

– CHAPTER 11 THE DISMISSAL –

1. See R. J. Adam (ed.), *Sutherland Estate Papers*, 2 vols (Edinburgh, 1972), II, pp. 288–9, Sellar to Lady Stafford, 5 June 1816.

2. Ibid., II, p. 294; see also M. W. Grant, *Golspie's Story* (Golspie, 1991), pp. 137–8. The Mound eventually cost £9,600 of which Lord Stafford contributed £1,600; it was 2,965 ft long, 180 ft at the base, 20 ft high, with bridge and flood gate.

3. Adam, op. cit., I, p. xciv, Loch to Sellar, 15 May 1816.

4. NLS Dep. 313/1587, Loch to Lady Stafford, 17 December 1816.

5. Adam, op. cit., I, p. xcvii. Public opinion on the fate of the Highlanders was beginning to take form. For instance, a pamphlet argued in 1816 that their sufferings were to be compared to those of Negroes sent to America, but the hardships of the Highlanders had 'excited no sympathy' from those who concerned themselves with the slave question. Joseph Marryat, *Thoughts on the Abolition of the Slave Trade* (1816), p. 97.

6. Adam, op. cit., I, p. xcv.

7. Ibid., I, p. 202, Memo of 19 August 1816.

8. Ibid., I, pp. 202, 189.

9. NLS Dep. 313, Lady Stafford to Lord Gower, 27 June 1816.

10. NLS Dep. 313, Box 26, Lady Stafford to Lord Gower, 27 June 1816.

11. Joseph Mitchell, *Reminiscences of My Life in the Highlands*, 2 vols (1883 and 1884), II, p. 81 misconstrued the lines of control in Sutherland.

12. See above, Ch. 3.

13. His views were elaborated in his anonymous *Account of the Improvements on the Estates of the Marquess of Stafford* (1815).

14. Adam, op. cit., I, p. 19.

15. Ibid., I, pp. 198 ff. NLS Dep. 313, Box 37, Grant to Loch 19–23 August 1816; Grant to Lady Stafford, 18 August 1816, where he said: 'No delay should be taken in communicating to the following persons in Strathnaver, who were connected with the late occurrences, that they be turned off at Whitsunday which ought to be done without fail.' NLS Dep. 313, Estate Management Papers, Box 37, Loch's Report, 18 August 1816.
16. NLS Dep. 313/1587, Loch to Lady Stafford, 1 September 1816.
17. NLS Dep. 313/1588, Mackenzie to Lady Stafford, 16 August 1816.
18. NLS Dep. 313, Box 22, Loch to Suther, 30 August 1816. See also Grant, op. cit., p. 138, and NLS Dep. 313/1588, Young to Lady Stafford, 24 August 1816.
19. Adam, op. cit., II, p. 304.
20. NLS Dep. 313, Loch to Lady Stafford, 1 September 1816.
21. Blair Adam Papers, NRA 1454 /2/84, Grant to Adam, 22 August 1816.
22. Blair Adam Papers, NRA 1454 /2/84, Loch to Adam, 3 October 1816.
23. MacPherson Grant Papers, Ballindalloch Castle, Bundle 739, Lady Stafford to Macpherson Grant, 19 September 1816.
24. Adam, op. cit., I, p. xciv.
25. D593/K/1/5/5 Loch to Lady Stafford, 3 October 1816, Mackenzie to Loch, 19 October 1816; NLS Dep. 313, Loch to Lady Stafford, 20 September 1816.
26. D593/K/1/5/5, Loch to Lady Stafford, 13 May 1817.
27. D593/K/1/5/5, Loch to Lady Stafford, 11 October 1816.
28. See Eric Richards, '*The Military Register* and the pursuit of Patrick Sellar', *Scottish Economic and Social History*, 16 (1996), *passim.* Mitchell, op. cit., II, p. 88 was also well informed on this question.
29. The new arrangements were explained in NLS Dep. 313/1587, Loch to Suther, 30 August 1816.
30. Adam, op. cit., II, p. 304.
31. No settlement was reached and the contention ran on until 1824, when there was still controversy in the management about Sellar's old accounts. But there was a clear reference to 'the Family having paid the Expense of the Trial'. D593/K/1/3/10, Suther to Loch, 22 September 1824, 13 November 1823 .
32. NLS Dep. 313, Box 38, Mackenzie to Lady Stafford, 28 November 1816.
33. NLS Dep. 313, 1588, Sellar to Lady Stafford, 25 September 1816. It had been a fair bargain but now his father's affairs needed assistance partly because Sellar had drawn on him so greatly in the past year during his troubles. He wanted to refund his father by the sale of his sheep stocks. NLS Dep. 313, Box 19, Sellar to Lady Stafford, 14 September 1816.
34. NLS Dep. 313/1588, Sellar to Lady Stafford, 4 August 1816.
35. NLS Dep. 313/1588, Mackenzie to Lady Stafford, 14 December 1816.
36. NLS Dep. 313/1588, Sellar to Lady Stafford, 27 August 1816.
37. NLS Dep. 313/1588, Sellar to Lady Stafford, 4 August 1816.

38. NLS Dep. 313/1591, Sellar to Lady Stafford, 3 January 1817 and 14 January 1817.

– CHAPTER 12 FAMINE AND THE FINAL CLEARANCES –

1. NLS Dep. 313, Sellar to Lady Stafford, 23 September 1816.
2. NLS Dep. 313, Sellar to Lady Stafford, 11 September 1816.
3. NLS Dep. 313, Sellar to Lady Stafford, 11 September 1816.
4. NLS Dep. 313, Sellar to Lady Stafford, 3 January 1817.
5. NLS Dep. 313/1587, Sellar to Lady Stafford, 21 September 1816.
6. NLS Dep. 313, Box 38, Sellar to Lady Stafford, 13 November 1816.
7. NLS Dep. 313, Box 19 Sellar to Lady Stafford, 3 January 1817.
8. D593/K/1/5/5, Sellar to Loch, 2 November 1816.
9. D593/K/1/5/5, Sellar to Loch, 16 November 1816.
10. NLS Dep. 313, Box 26, Lady Stafford to Lord Gower, 12 December 1816.
11. D593/K/1/5/5, Sellar to Loch, 11 December 1816.
12. D593/K/1/5/5, Sellar to Loch, 2 December 1816. Lady Stafford seemed to agree: ibid., 15 January 1817.
13. D593/K/1/5/5, Sellar to Loch, 23 March 1817.
14. NLS Dep. 313/1587, Loch to Lady Stafford, 3 December 1816.
15. NLS Dep. 313/1587, Loch to Lady Stafford, 3 December 1816.
16. Ibid.
17. NLS Dep. 313/Box 38, Sellar to Lady Stafford, 24 August 1817. On Gunn, see Malcolm Bangor-Jones, *The Assynt Clearances* (Dundee, 1998), p. 25.
18. NLS Dep. 313/1591, Loch to Lady Stafford, 3 November 1817.
19. NLS Dep. 313/1015, Loch to Mackay, 27 September 1817. In the autumn of 1817 Sellar pressed for further removals to clear his land at Syre and Grubmore, saying that he was losing £1,000 by the delays. In September 1817, the Staffords specifically 'directed that Syre and Grubmore be cleared for Sellar.' D593/L/2/1, Loch's notes, pp. 28–9.
20. NLS Dep. 313/1051, Loch to Capt Mackay, 27 September 1817.
21. D593/K/1/5/5, Sellar to Loch, 6 September 1817; Loch to Mackay, 27 September 1817; Mackay to Loch, 10 October 1817.
22. NLS Dep. 313, Box 38, Sellar to Lady Stafford, 24 August 1817.
23. NLS Dep. 313, Box 8, Report from Sellar.
24. See C. Fraser-Mackintosh, *Antiquarian Notes*, 2nd edn (Stirling, 1913), pp. 316–20. See also Joseph Mitchell, *Reminiscences of My Life in the Highlands*, 2 vols (1883 and 1884), I, pp. 336–7.
25. There was a more curious incarceration in the Dornoch Tolbooth: Peter Fraser of Strathspey, a vagrant, was alleged to have been travelling about the countryside, 'abusing the name of William Sellar, son of Mr Patrick Sellar, Culmaily'. Sellar appears not to have had a son at this stage. Inverness Archives, L/S/M 1/2, Record Book of Dornoch Tolbooth. I owe this reference to Monica Clough.

26. Ibid.
27. Quoted in Bangor-Jones, op. cit., p. 28.
28. Many sheep were lost in the sheep drains. D5093/Additional/11, Draft letter from Trentham 3 October 1817.
29. NLS. MS 10916 (Airth MS), Sellar to Convener of the County of Stirling, 26 May 1818.
30. In 1817 Sellar was paying £2,000 in rent per annum. D593 P/20, Sellar to Duke of Sutherland, 2 September 1847.
31. M. W. Grant, *Golspie's Story* (Golspie, 1983), quoting E. M. Sellar, p. 145.
32. Alexander Craig took over Kirkton in 1819 at a very substantial rent, rising to £500 p.a. D/593/L/2/1, James Loch's Memorandum Book, 1817–1842, pp. 44–7.
33. D593/K/1/3/5, Sellar to Loch, 12 September 1817.
34. D593/K/1/3/5, Sellar to Loch, 16 September 1817.
35. D593/K, Sellar to Loch, no date [*c.* October 1815].
36. D593/K/1/3/5, Sellar to Loch, 17 April 1817; Scarth to Sellar; NLS Dep. 313/1588, Sellar to Loch, 20 October 1816.
37. D593/K/1/3/5, Scarth to Sellar, 5 May 1817, Sellar to Loch, 10 April 1817; Allan to Loch, 25 November 1817.
38. D593/K/1/3/5, Scarth to Sellar, 14 April, 24 May 1817.
39. D593/K/1/3/5, Lady Stafford to Loch, 15 January 1817; Sellar to Loch, 31 January 1817.
40. D593/K/1/3/5, Loch to Bathurst, 3 December 1817, Suther to Loch ,12 November 1817; Loch to Lady Stafford, 26 October 1817; Loch to Allan, 22 November 1817; D593/K/1/3/6, Loch to Suther, 1 December 1817.
41. D593/K/1/5/5, Lady Stafford to Loch, 11 November 1818. See also *New Edinburgh Review* (April 1822), pp. 289–96.
42. D593/K/1/3/5, Loch to Bathurst, 3 December 1817; Suther to Loch, 6 December 1817.
43. See Bangor-Jones, op. cit., pp. 29–44.
44. D593/K/1/3/5, Loch to Lady Stafford, 3 November 1817.
45. Macpherson Grant Papers, Ballindalloch Castle, Bundle 498, Sellar to MacPherson Grant, 24 January 1818.
46. D593/K/1/5/5, Sellar to Loch, 13 April 1818.
47. D 593/L/2/1, James Loch's Memorandum Book, 1817–1842, pp. 44–7.
48. Simultaneously, one of the old tacksman class, John Polson, took over neighbouring Easter Scibbercross, which Sellar also sought, even though it was among the dearest land in Sutherland.
49. Angus Mackay, *Book of Mackay* (Edinburgh, 1904), p. 466.
50. D593/K/1/5/5, Loch to Suther, 13 November 1818, Suther to Loch, 29 May 1819, Loch to Suther, 8 June 1819.
51. D593/K/1/5/5, Sellar to Loch, 19 June 1818, Loch to Morton, 1 May 1818.
52. D593/K/1/5/5, Loch to Lady Stafford, 31 October 1817.

53. D593/K/1/5/5, Loch to Suther, 7 February 1818.
54. Thomas Sellar, *The Sutherland Evictions of 1814* (1833) p. 14.
55. D593/K/1/5/5, Mackenzie to Loch, 19 March 1818.
56. In Assynt there was no evidence of houses being burnt. See Bangor-Jones, op. cit., p. 36.
57. D593/K, Loch to Suther, 18 July 1819.
58. D593/K, Suther to Loch, 5 June 1819.
59. D593/K, Gunn to Loch, 2 June 1819. See also Bangor-Jones, op. cit., pp. 35–45.
60. D593/K, Suther to Loch, 12, 26 May 1819.
61. D593/K, Mackenzie to Loch, 30 September 1819; Loch to Lady Stafford, May 1819.
62. B. Botfield, *Journal of a Tour Through the Highlands* (published anonymously, Norton Hall, 1830), p.152.
63. D593/K, Loch to Suther, 18 July 1819.
64. NLS Dep. 313/1016, Letters relating to the removals in 1819.
65. NLS Dep. 313/1015, Loch to Suther, 20 March 1820.
66. D593/K/1/5/5, Sellar to Loch, 22 June 1819.
67. *Scotsman*, 10 July 1819.
68. *Inverness Courier*, 13 January 1820.
69. *Inverness Courier*, 13 January 1820.
70. See James Loch, *Account of the Improvements on the Estates of the Marquess of Stafford* (1820); more generally, see Eric Richards, *A History of the Highland Clearances: Vol. I. Agrarian Transformation and the Evictions, 1745–1886* (London, 1982), I. ch. 11. One of the most telling pieces of evidence, from a clearing officer, is quoted by J. Mitchell, *Reminiscences of My Life in the Highlands*, 2 vols (1971), II, p. 91.
71. See Appendix to Loch's *Account*, op. cit., p. 67.
72. NLS Dep. 313/1015, Note of Removals on the Estate of Sutherland in May 1819.
73. D593/K/Mackay to Loch, 13 April 1821.
74. See Eric Richards, 'Patterns of Highland discontent 1790–1860', in Stevenson, J. and Quinault, R. (eds), *Popular Protest and Public Order 1780–1920. Six Studies in British History* (London, 1974), passim.
75. See Richards, *Clearances*, op. cit., I., ch. 11.
76. *New Edinburgh Review* (April 1822), pp. 289–96.

– CHAPTER 13   HEIR TO THE STRATHS IN THE 1820s –

1. [Alexander Sutherland], *A Summer Ramble in the North Highlands* (London, 1825), p. 90.
2. D593/K, Loch to Lord Stafford, 17 June 1821.
3. NLS Dep. 313, Box 21, Loch to Suther, 8 July 1820.
4. D593/K, Smith to Loch, 11 August 1820.

5. D593/K/1/3, Sellar to Loch, 21 January 1820, 18 January 1820.
6. James Loch, *Account of the Improvements on the Estates of the Marquess of Stafford*, Appendix, p. 61.
7. D593/K, Sellar to Loch, 13 May 1820.
8. D593/K, Sellar to Loch, 3 April 1820.
9. NLS Dep. 313, Box 25, Lady Stafford to Lord Stafford, 16 September 1820.
10. NLS Dep. 313, Box 26, Lady Stafford to Lord Gower, 28 January 1820. Sellar's merinos eventually proved uneconomic in the north and he gave up the experiment.
11. GD 268/360, Lady Stafford to Lord Stafford, 2 July [1821?].
12. GD 268/360, Lady Stafford to Loch, 18 July 1822; 20 July 1822.
13. GD 268/361, Lady Stafford to Loch, 24 September 1824.
14. Ibid., Lady Stafford to Lord Stafford, 29 September 1820, 29 September 1820, 24 September 1820, 16 September 1820.
15. D593/K, Loch to Suther, 23 February 1820.
16. D593/K, Copies of letters of Sellar to Stewart, 18 May 1826, 29 April 1826.
17. D593/K/1/3/12, Sellar to Lord Gower, 6 March 1824.
18. D593/K/1/3/11, Sellar to Stewart, 18 May 1826.
19. D593/K/1/3/9, Sellar to Loch, 30 November 1821.
20. D593/K/1/3/9, Sellar to Loch, 6 October 1821.
21. D593 K, Sellar to Loch, 29 April 1822.
22. D593/K/1/3/9, Sellar to Loch, 29 April 1822.
23. D593/K/1/3/9, Sellar to Loch, 16 September 1822.
24. D593/K/1/3/9, Lord Stafford to Loch, 12 March 1822.
25. D593/K, Suther to Loch, 5 April 1822.
26. D593/K/P/22/1/28, Young to Gower, 22 October 1822.
27. D593/K/1/3/9, Sellar to Loch, 23 October 1822. See also Sellar's appendix to Loch, *Account* (1820), op. cit., p. 58.
28. D593/K/1/3/11, Sellar to Loch, 9 June 1827.
29. D593/K, Maxwell to Gunn, 1 July 1828. See wool prices series in B. R. Mitchell and P. Deane, *Abstract of British Historical Statistics* (Cambridge, 1962), p. 495, which show prices in 1829 at one-sixth of their level in 1810.
30. D593/K/1/3/17, Atkinson and Marshall to Loch, 4 August 1829.
31. D593/K/1/3/9, Sellar to Loch, 10 October 1821.
32. NLS Dep. 313/1014, Sellar to Loch, 2 January 1823, 20 January 1820, 25 February 1823, 13 March 1823; Sellar to Rickman, 3 May 1823; Minutes of the AGM of the Sutherland Association for the Protection of Property, 19 May 1824. Presided over by George Gunn, 20 August 1824.
33. GD 271/6/34, Sellar to William Mackenzie, 24 March 1827.
34. D593/K/1/3/11, Sellar to Loch, 25 September 1827.
35. D593/K/1/3/11, Sellar to Loch, 21 October 1827.

36. D593/K/1/3/16, Sellar to Loch, 12 January 1828.
37. D593/K/1/3/16, Sellar to Loch, 16 February 1828.
38. D593/K/1/3/16, Sellar to Loch, 23 May 1828.
39. SRO GD/268/361/13, Lady Stafford to Loch, 24 September 1824.
40. D593/K/1/3/16, Sellar to Loch, 29 Dec 1828.
41. D593/K/1/3/9, Sellar to Loch, 15 March 1822.
42. D593/K/1/3/9, Sellar to Loch, 29 April 1822.
43. D593/K/1/3/16, Gunn to Loch, 1 June 1829.
44. J. H. Clapham, *Economic History of Modern Britain*, 3 vols (Cambridge, 1926–38), I, p. 243.
45. ID593/K/1/3/16, Sellar to Loch, 18 January 1820; Sellar to Loch, 12 March 1826.
46. D593/K, Loch to Mackenzie, 12 Dec 1826.
47. D593/K, Loch to Mackenzie, 12 Dec 1826, 3 April 1820.
48. Sellar was not alone in his selective departure from free trade: Malthus was also 'guilty of the ultimate heresy of his own day' when he supported duties on corn to protect agriculture. See A. J. Taylor, *Laissez-faire and State Intervention in Nineteenth Century Britain* (London, 1972), p. 21.
49. D593/K/1/3/13, Sellar to Loch, 10 January 1825.
50. D593/K/1/3/13, Sellar to Loch, 7 July 1825.
51. D593/K/1/3/13, Sellar to Loch, 20 January 1825.
52. D593/K/1/3/13, Sellar to Loch, 20 January 1825.
53. D593/K, Loch to Gunn, 22 February 1825.
54. D593/K/1/3/11, Sellar to Loch, 4 June 1825.
55. D593/K/1/3/11, Gunn to Loch, 17 April 1826.
56. D593/K/1/3/11, Gunn to Loch, 19 Dec 1825.
57. D593/K/1/3/11, Sellar to Lord and Lady Stafford, 12 April 1823.
58. D593/K/1/3/16, Loch to Sellar, 28 Dec 1825.
59. D593/K/ Loch to Gunn, 22 January 1826.
60. D593/K/1/3/16, Sellar to Loch, 10, 14, January 1826.
61. D593/K/1/3/11, Sellar to Loch, 23 January 1826. In 1826 the Staffords were presented with four large skins of parchment with more than 1,200 signatures, as a blessing for the improvements undertaken by the family. See M. W. Grant, *Golspie's Story* (Golspie, 1991).
62. Colonel David Stewart, *Sketches of the Character, Manners, and Present State of the Highlanders of Scotland with details of the Military Service of the Highland Regiments,* (2 vols, (1822). On Stewart see John Prebble, *The King's Jaunt* (London, 1988), p. 33.
63. Fragment of 1821 document dated 1821, in Irvine-Robertson MS, for which I thank Mr Irvine Robertson of Stirling.
64. Warm endorsement of Stewart is located in Joseph Mitchell, *Reminiscences of My Life in the Highlands,* 2 vols (Newton Abbot, 1971) I. pp. 115–7 and also most pointedly in James Hunter, *A Dance Called America* (Edinburgh, 1994), especially p. 113.

65. Proposed Memorial to General Stewart of Garth, c. 1898, in Irvine-Robertson MS.

66. SRO Maclaine of Lochbuy Letters, GD 174/1639, Stewart of Garth letter dated 29 March 1817.

67. SRO, Maclaine of Lochbuy Papers, GD 174/1639, Stewart to Maclaine, 29 March 1817.

68. *Scots Magazine*, March 1822, pp. 328–30.

69. David Stewart, *Sketches of the characters, Manners and Preset State of the Highlanders of Scotland . . .*, 2 vols, 2nd edn (Edinburgh, 1825), I, pp. 9, 21, 90.

70. Ibid., 1825 edn, I, p. 160.

71. On Scott and his treatment of old Highland evictions in *Guy Mannering* see also Graham McMaster, *Scott and Society* (Cambridge, 1981), pp. 157–60. On Scott's general attitudes to the Highlanders, see David Richards, *Masks of Difference* (Cambridge, 1994), ch. 4. Stewart, op. cit., I, pp. 154, 171 fn.

72. Ibid., I, p.143.

73. 'More about Sellar and the Sutherland Clearances', *Celtic Magazine*, XX (1884), p. 489, quoting letter from Stewart to Duncan MacPherson of Cluny, 9 September 1817.

74. Stewart, op. cit., I, p. 158.

75. Ibid., p. 171.

76. D593/K/1/3/16, Sellar to Loch, 22 December 1825.

77. Patrick Sellar, *Statement* (1825).

78. D593/K, Sellar to Loch, 23 January 1826.

79. D593/K, Sellar to Loch, 2 January 1826; GD 268/360, MacCulloch to Lady Stafford, 3 October 1822.

80. D593/K/1/3/16, Sellar to Loch, 23 January 1826, Sellar to Stewart, 10 January 1826. In the recrudescence of public criticism, Sellar significantly now emphasised Young's 'neglect to lay off the allotments' at the time of the 1814 events. D593/K, Sellar to Loch, 18 February 1826.

81. D593/K, Sellar to Loch, 4 April 1826, 15 April 1826.

82. D593/K/1/3/16, Sellar to Loch, 7 April 1826; D593/K copies of Sellar to Stewart, 18 May 1826, 29 April 1826.

83. Stewart, op. cit., pp. 168–9.

84. NLS MS 571, Constable to Stewart, 26 October 1822. See Duncan Campbell, *The Book of Garth and Fortingall* (privately printed, Inverness, 1888), pp. 235–6; NLS, Constable Letter Book 1820–2, MS791, f.183, 21 May 1824, 11 November 1824, 16 October 1824.

85. Stewart, op. cit., 1822 edn., I p. 136, fn. Stewart ventured several comparisons between conditions in the Highlands and slavery, (p. 144). Stewart contrasted happy slaves with the unhappy serfs. On his own estate it was said 'the old system was continued' (Memorial to General Stewart of Garth, op. cit).

86. Last Will . . . of David Stewart', in Irvine-Robertson MS.
87. David Stewart to John Stewart, 20 July 1827, in Irvine-Robertson MS.
88. Stewart to Irvine, 5 March 1821, in Irvine-Robertson MS.
89. See Sir Alan Burns, *History of the British West Indies,* (London, 1965), pp. 645–6.
90. *Gentleman's Magazine,* vol. 100 (1830), p. 270.
91. Support to the Stewart of Garth line on the clearances emerged in a respectable place in L. Kennedy and T. P. Grainger, *The Present State of the Tenancy of Land* (London, 1829), pp. 213–14.
92. D593/K/1/3/11, Sellar to Loch, 17 May 1828.
93. D593/K/1/3/11, Sellar to Loch, 23 May 1825.
94. D593/K/1/3/16, Sellar to Loch, 12 July 1828.
95. D593/K/1/3/9, Sellar to Loch, 16 September 1822.
96. D593/K/1/3/16, Sellar to Loch, 25 July, 1829.
97. D593/K/1/3/16, Sellar to Loch, 13 August 1828.
98. D593/K/1/3/16, Sellar to Loch, 29 Dec 1828.
99. D593/K/1/3/17, Sellar to Loch, 16 February 1829.
100. D593/K/1/3/16, Sellar to Loch, 30 March 1829.
101. See Ch. 14 below.
102. NLS Dep. 313/1261, Gunn and Sellar to Horsburgh and Reed, 26 May 1828.
103. He cited the opinions of a galaxy of notable farmers in Scotland and England (including Culley, Atkinson, Rennie Craig, Preston and Lamb, as well as Ratcliffe of Huddersfield).
104. SRO GD 129/2/90 (Balnagowan Papers), Sellar to Murray, 3 and 9 November, 10, 15, 16, 24, 22, December 1827, 12 January 1828; Murray to Sellar, 28 December 1827; Culley to Sellar, 26 November 1827, 1 Dec 1827.
105. D593/K/1/3/11, Gunn to Loch, 4 December 1827.
106. D593/K/1/3/16, Sellar to Loch, 22 September 1829.
107. D593/K/1/3/16, Sellar to Loch, 5 October 1829.
108. D593/K/1/3/11, Sellar to Loch, 12 September 1824.
109. D593/K/1/3/16, Gunn to Loch, 12 May 1828.
110. D593/K/1/3/16, Minutes of Submission between Sellar, Tacksman of Morvich and Easter and Wester Abercross and Alexander Craig of Kirkton, Craigton and Ironhill, November 1828.
111. S D593/K/1/3/16, Sellar to Loch, 21 September 1829.
112. D593/K/1/3/16, Sellar to Loch, 27 July 1829.
113. D593/K/1/3/16, Sellar to Loch, 21 September 1829.
114. D593/K/1/3/16, Gunn to Loch, 29 May 1828.
115. D593/K/1/3/16, Sellar to Loch, 19 May 1829.
116. D593/K/1/3/16, Loch to Sellar, 23 May 1829.
117. NLS Dep. 313, Estate Management, Box 11; Report by Mr Horsburgh and Mr Reed on Sheep Farms in Sutherland, 24 August 1827.

118. D593/K/1/3/16, Sellar to Loch, 15 April 1826.
119. NLS Dep. 313, Box 23, Loch to Lady Stafford, 1 February 1829.
120. D593/K/1/3/16, Sellar to Mitchell, 1 March 1828.

– CHAPTER 14   SELLAR IN HIS PRIME –

1. SDUK, Loch to Coates, 7 January [1830?].
2. By Rawson, quoted in Lech Paszkowski, *Sir Paul Edmund de Strzelecki: Reflections on His Life* (Melbourne, 1997), p. 30,
3. P. E. de Strzelecki, *Physical Description of New South Wales and Van Diemen's Land* (London, 1845), p. 372.
4. The Macarthurs assisted his expedition to the western face of the Snowy Mountains and beyond. Strzelecki eventually emerged through Gippsland, and he contested priority of exploration in that region with Angus Macmillan. The latter was a Scottish Highland grazier who did great damage to aboriginal groups in the district, and was left with an unsavoury reputation in colonial history.
5. Strzelecki, op. cit., pp. 371, 433, 365.
6. H. M. E. Heney, *In a Dark Glass* (Sydney, 1961), p. 33. Sellar remarked on Strzelecki's book in D593/K, Sellar to G. Loch, 2 November 1845.
7. See Don Watson, *Caledonia Australis* (Sydney, 1984) p. 117. Strzelecki's *Physical Description*, it should be said, has many humanitarian remarks about the fate of the aborigines, ibid., pp. 345–56.
8. The correspondence is located in the archives of University College, London, Society for the Diffusion of Useful Knowledge, 1826–1848 (SDUK).
9. SDUK, Loch to Coates, 11 March 1831.
10. Ibid., p. 70.
11. Sellar provided these figures: before the turn of the century; the average Cheviot fleece was between 2 1/2 and 3 1/2 lb; now it was 4 to 4 1/2 lb. During the same period the mutton value had increased from 12 to 18 lb to 18 to 26 lb.
12. Patrick Sellar, *Farm Reports III, County of Sutherland. Strathnaver, Morvich and Culmaily Farms, Library of Useful Knowledge* (London 1831); also cited in J. A. Symons, *Scottish Farming, Past and Present* (Edinburgh, 1959), pp. 81, 167, 170–1, 177, 179.
13. Ibid., p. 84. See also Sellar's appendix to James Loch, *Account of the Improvements on the Estates of the Marquess of Stafford* (1820), p. 66.
14. D593/K/1/3/18, Gunn to Loch, 16 June 1830.
15. Sellar, op. cit., p. 87.
16. GD, 268/224, Lady Stafford to Loch, 1 December 1832.
17. D593, Private and Confidential: 'Mr Sellar's Report on certain portions of Durness, Tongue, Farr and Reay' with Mr Loch's answer and Mr Sellar's Reply, May–June 1831.

18. Until 1815 Sellar had bought cattle from the small tenants at from £3 to £5 and fed them for sale at £8 to £10. 'Peace reduced the prices to 40/- to 50/- for re-sale at £5 to £6.' More recently, the imposition of tolls and turnpikes along the route to market, as well as the introduction of steam packets for the import of Irish cattle, had further reduced saleability. Cattle prices had fallen to 15/- to 20/- to the poor Reay farmer, and at resale after fattening they were worth only 55/- to 66/- each.
19. NLS Dep. 313, Box11, Lewis to Loch, 15 September 1831.
20. *New Statistical Account of Scotland*, XV (1845), Sutherland, Farr Parish.
21. D593/K, Anon to Lord Stafford, 24 November 1832.
22. D593/K/1/3/18, Loch to Gunn, 1 October 1831.
23. See, for instance, Thomas Sellar, *The Sutherland Evictions of 1814* (1883), p. 9, fn 4.
24. D593/K, Gunn to Loch, 6 September 1833.
25. D593/K/1/3/18, Sellar to Loch, 1 May 1830.
26. D593/K/1/3/18, Sellar to Loch, 24 February 1830.
27. D593/K/1/3/18, Sellar to Loch, 24 Dec 1830.
28. D593/K, Sellar to Horsburgh, 17 April 1836.

– CHAPTER 15   RATIONAL PRINCIPLES –

1. Quoted by A. R. B. Haldane, *The Drove Roads of Scotland* (Edinburgh, 1968), pp. 195–6. The source is J. Mitchell, *Reminiscences of My Life in the Highlands*, 2 vols (Newton Abbot, 1971), I, pp. 336–7.
2. See J. A. Symon, *Scottish Farming, Past and Present* (Edinburgh, 1959), p. 276.
3. His private papers do not survive and his exact financial history is largely unknown. Some of his papers were destroyed in September 1838, D593/K/1/3/37, and family papers were burned at Ardtornish in 1929: see P. Gaskell, *Morvern Transformed* (Cambridge, 1968) p. 82, fn. 2.
4. SDUK 29, Sellar to Coates, 23 January 1832.
5. SDUK 28, Sellar to Coates, 2 December 1831.
6. D593K/1/3/19, Sellar to Loch, 7 July 1831; Sellar to Loch, 6 January 1831, 7 January 1831.
7. D593/K/1/3/19, Sellar to Coates, 6 August 1831; D593/K/1/3/19, Sellar to Loch, 10 September 1831.
8. D593/K/1/3/19, Sellar to Loch, 20 April 1831.
9. D593/K/1/3/19, Sellar to Lady Stafford, 6 August 1831.
10. D593/K/1/3/19, Sellar to Loch, 16 June 1831.
11. D593/K/1/3/19, Sellar to Loch, 30 May 1831.
12. D593/K/1/3/19, Sellar to Loch, 26 February 1831.
13. D593/K/1/3/19, Mitchell to Sellar, 7 March 1831, Sellar to Mitchell 10 March 1831.
14. D593/K/1/3/21, Sellar to Loch, 2 February 1833.

15. D593/K/1/3/19, Sellar to Loch, 29 September 1831.
16. D593/K/1/3/19, Sellar to Loch, 20 September 1831, Loch to Sellar 23 September 1831. This discussion was specifically about the Glendhu Farm.
17. D593/K/1/3/19, Sellar to Loch, 20 March 1831.
18. D593/K/1/3/19, Sellar to Loch, 12 March 1831.
19. D593/K/1/3/19, Sellar to Loch, 9 May 1831.
20. SDUK 32, Sellar to Baldwin, 22 April 1835.
21. NLS Dep. 313, Box 11, Lewis to Loch, 15 September 1831.
22. D593/K/1/3/20, Sellar to Loch, 4 January 1831.
23. See also M. W. Grant, *Golspie's Story* (Golspie, 1983) pp. 149–50. There were deaths in Golspie and a local Board of Health was established.
24. D593/K/1/3/19, Sellar to Loch, 24 December 1831.
25. D593/K/1/3/20, Sellar to Loch, 16 February 1832.
26. D593/K/1/3/20, Sellar to Loch, 29 February 1832.
27. D593/K/1/3/20, Sellar to Loch, 21 September 1832.
28. D593/K/1/3/20, Sellar to Loch, 22 June 1832.
29. D593/K, Sellar to Loch, 17 March 1837, 31 March 1837.
30. D593/K/1/3/21, Sellar to Loch, 1 August 1833.
31. D593/K, Sellar to Loch, 3 September 1833. There is a list of subscribers in M. W.Grant, op. cit., pp. 172–3. Bhraggie is 1,293 feet.
32. D593/K, Sellar to Loch, 11 January 1834.
33. The modern debate is discussed in Charles W. J. Withers, 'Place, memory, moment, memorialising the 'past in contemporary Highland Scotland', *Ecumen*, 3 (1996) pp. 325–44 and Rob Gibson, *Toppling the Duke – Outrage on Ben Braggie?* (Evanton, IL, 1996).
34. D593/K/1/3/20, Sellar to Loch, 8 January 1832.
35. D593/K/1/3/20, Sellar to Loch, 13 June 1832.
36. D593/K/1/3/20, Sellar to Loch, 28 April 1832.
37. E. M. Sellar, *Recollections and Impressions* (Edinburgh, 1907), p. 24.
38. Founded in 1824 by Horner and Cockburn, who were dissatisfied with the High School. It prided itself on its greater liberality of principles, eschewing flogging and demanding the highest academic standards and the best teachers. See Magnus Magnusson, *The Clacken and the Slate. The Story of the Edinburgh Academy, 1824–1974* (1974), pp. 208, 226.
39. D593/P/20, Sellar to Duke of Sutherland, 10 August 1839.
40. D593/K, Sellar to Loch, 28 January 1836.
41. D593/K, Sellar to Loch, 24 September 1833.
42. NLS Dep. 313, Box 11, Sellar to Loch, 5 March 1838 and 21 March 1838.
43. See Graham McMaster, *Scott and Society*, (Cambridge, 1981), pp. 158–9.
44. D593/K, Sellar to Loch, 5 May 1839.
45. D593/K, Sellar to Loch, 7 May 1838; D593/P/20, Sellar to Duke of Sutherland, 9 August 1839.
46. D593/K, Sellar to Lady Sutherland, 25 February 1835.

47. D593/K, Sellar to Lady Sutherland, 14 March 1836.
48. D593/K, Sellar to Loch, 30 April 1837, Sellar to Lady Sutherland, 19 March 1837.
49. D593/K, Sellar to Loch, 26 February 1838, 2 March 1838.
50. D593/K, Sellar to Loch, 28 April 1837.
51. D593/K, Sellar to Loch, 2 January 1834.
52. D593/K, Sellar to Duke of Sutherland, 3 March 1836.
53. SD593/K, Sellar to Loch, 6 September 1834; D593 /K Sellar to Loch, 21 June 1836.
54. SDUK 32, Sellar to Coates, 20 June 1835.
55. D593/K/P/2/1, Loch to the Countess/Duchess, 20 July 1836.
56. A letter from Sellar to Thomas Scott of Letham, Jedburgh, 22 April 1839, in the possession of Dr Michael Robson, brought to my attention by Dr Malcolm Bangor-Jones.
57. SDUK 34, Sellar to Coates, 26 January 1837.
58. GD 268/180, Sellar to Loch, 2 March 1839.
59. GD 268/180, Sellar to Loch, 2 March 1839.
60. NLS Dep. 313, Sellar to Horsburgh, 17 March 1832.
61. D593K/1/3/20, Sellar to Loch, 28 Aug, 1832.
62. D593K/1/3/20, Sellar to Loch, 29 September 1832.
63. D593K/1/3/20, Sellar to Lord Stafford, 8 January 1832, 29 December 1832.
64. D593K/1/3/20, Sellar to Loch, 2 September 1832; Bairgrie and Horsburgh to Loch, 21 September 1832.
65. D593/N/4/1/1c, Loch's Tour of Inspection, Sutherland and Reay, 1835.
66. Dep. 313, Box 11, Lewis to Loch, 15 September 1831.
67. NLS Dep. 313, Box 11, Sellar to Lord Stafford, 27 May 1833.
68. D593/K, Sellar to Loch, 8 November 1838.
69. NLS Dep. 313, Loch to Lady Sutherland, 15 March 1834
70. D593/K, Sellar to Lady Sutherland, 15 March 1836.
71. GD268/230/27, Countess to Loch, 9 November 1835. My thanks once more are due to Dr Bangor-Jones.
72. GD 268, Lady Sutherland to Sellar, 16 November 1835, and GD 268/230, Lady Sutherland to Loch, 9 November 1835.
73. GD 268/230/28X, Countess to Loch, 9 November 1835, quoting her son the Duke of Sutherland.
74. Ibid.
75. D593/P/20, Loch to Lady Sutherland, 22 August 1836.
76. D593/P/20, Loch to Lady Sutherland, 22 August 1836. D593/K/P/22/ 1/4, Falconer to Gower, 22 October 1809, 8 November 1809.
77. NLS 313, Box 11, Sellar to Horsburgh, 23 February 1832.
78. D593/K/1/3/20, Sellar to Loch, 19 January 1832.
79. NLS 313, Box 11, Sellar to Loch, 15 October 1835.
80. NLS 313, Box 11, Sellar to Loch, 24 May 1838.

81. NLS 313, Loch to Lady Sutherland, 6 September 1838. For a modern account see Alexander Mather, 'The environmental impact of sheep Farming in the Scottish Highlands', in T.C. Smout (ed.), *Scotland Since Pre History* (Aberdeen 1993).

82. GD 268, Loch to Lady Sutherland, 14 September 1838; NLS Dep. 313/II Household and Personal Box 41, Loch to Lady Sutherland, 6 September 1838.

83. D593/K/1/3/29, Sellar to Loch, 30 September 1841.

84. D593/K, Sellar to Gunn, 26 October 1833.

85. D593/K, Sellar to Loch, 5 September 1837.

86. D593/K, Sellar to Loch, 12 October 1838.

87. D593/K, Sellar to Loch, 26 February 1838.

88. D593/K, Sellar to Loch, 31 August 1838.

89. D593/K, Sellar to Loch, 1 Nov. 1838.

90. NLS 313/ Box 11, Sellar to Loch, 24 May 1838; NLS Dep. 313, Sellar to Horsburgh, 24 May 1838.

91. D593/K, Sellar to Lady Sutherland, 25 June 1838.

92. D593/K, Sellar to Lady Sutherland, 16 August 1838.

93. D593/K, Sellar to Loch, August 1838.

94. D593/K, Sellar to Lady Sutherland, 26 January 1838.

– CHAPTER 16   THE FRAME OF SOCIETY –

1. See Eric Richards, *A History of the Highland Clearances: Vol I. Agrarian Trnasformation and the Evictions, 1745–1886* (London, 1982), pp. 402–411.

2. D593/K/1/3/28, Stewart to Sellar, 18 January 1840.

3. D593/K/1/3/28, Sellar to Stewart, 10 January 1840.

4. D593/K/1/3/28, Sellar to Loch, 12 September 1840, 21 September 1840, 25 September 1840.

5. D593/K. Sellar to Loch, 5 June 1842.

6. D593/K/1/3/28, Sellar to Loch, 29 September 1840.

7. D593/K/1/3/30, Sellar to Loch, 29 January 1842.

8. Sellar found himself out of sorts with Loch and the Leveson-Gowers on the question of Repeal and the anti-Corn Laws agitation. The Sutherland family was divided within itself on other issues, but Loch and the second Duke were ideological and political free traders. Sellar hotly contested the views of his landlord. Neither side budged, and once more Sellar simply polarised his position, without gain. See Peter Mandler, *Aristocratic Government in the Age of Reform* (Oxford, 1990), p. 219, fn. 62. I am grateful to Dr Robin Haines for this reference.

9. D593/K/1/3/28, Sellar to Loch, 6 June 1844.

10. In 1842 Sellar had protested against the reduction of duties on foreign cattle, saying that British producers could not 'compete with the prairies

of Central America and pay British Taxes'. D593/P/20, Sellar to Duke of Sutherland, 30 March 1842.

11. See Ian Grimble, 'Introduction' to Donald McLeod, *Gloomy Memories in the Highlands of Scotland* (1892, reprinted Bettyhill, 1996), p. 24.

12. D593/K/1/3/29, Sellar to Loch, 8 January 1841.

13. D593/K/1/3/29, Sellar to Loch, 16 January 1841.

14. Donald Macleod's works were collected in an edition entitled *Donald M'Leod's Gloomy Memories in the Highlands of Scotland versus Mrs Harriet Beecher Stowe's Sunny Memories in (England) a Foreign Land: or a Faithful Picture of the Extirpation of the Celtic Race from the Highlands of Scotland* (Glasgow, 1892). This edition has been reissued in recent times, containing the 1841 letters, entitled 'Destitution in Sutherlandshire' but without publishing details.

15. See Eric Richards, *The Leviathan of Wealth* (London and Toronto, 1973), pp. 250, ff.

16. D593/K/1/3/29, Sellar to Loch, 1 Dec 1841, Sellar to Loch, 22 June 1841, 30 September 1841.

17. D593, Sellar to George Loch, 10 September 1845.

18. D593/K/P/2/1, Sellar to *Tait's*, 20 September 1847, Sellar to Duke, 2 September 1847. There is correspondence in *The Times* about Sellar in October 1847, the controversy having been noted in the *Elgin Courant*, 8 October 1847.

19. D593/K/P/2/1, Sellar to Loch, 19 April 1847.

20. E. M. Sellar, *Recollections and Impressions* (Edinburgh, 1907), p. 26.

21. D593/K/P/2/1, Sellar to Loch, 15 Dec 1843.

22. D593/K/P/2/1, Sellar to Loch, 15 November 1844.

23. D593/K/P/2/1, Sellar to the Duke of Sutherland, 1 May 1848. James Dennistoun of Golfhill was a Glasgow merchant prince who maintained large trading connections with America, Australia and India with large shipping interests too; see S. G. Checkland, *Scottish Banking, A History, 1695–1973* (Glasgow, 1975), p. 169.

24. Letters by Jane Plenderleath Sellar to Helen Brown in 1842 and 1843; by courtesy of Christopher Lang of Titanga in Victoria, Australia.

25. D593/K/1/3/30, Sellar to Loch, 6 February 1842; Sellar to Loch, 25 August 1846. More genererally see Callum Brown, *The Social History of Religion in Scotland since 1730* (London, 1987).

26. NLS Dep. 313, Box 19, Sellar to Duke of Sutherland, 8 February 1851.

27. T. Sellar, *The Sutherland Evictions of 1814* (1833), p. 57. See also J. Mitchell, *Reminiscences of My Life in the Highlands*, 2 vols (Newton Abbot, 1971), II, pp. 97–8.

28. D593/K/P/2/1, Sellar to Loch, 21 April 1845, 5 May 1845.

29. D593/K/P/2/1, Sellar to Loch, 13 October 1845.

30. D593/K/P/2/1, Sellar to Loch, 15 October 1845.

31. D593/K/P/2/1, Sellar to George Loch, 10 September 1845.

32. D593/K/1/3/31, Sellar to Loch, 19 September 1843, 26 September 1843, 5 November 1843, Sellar to Duke of Sutherland, 5 November 1843

33. D593/K/8/20, Sellar to Duke of Sutherland, 23 October 1843

34. D593/K/2/1, Sellar to Loch and the Duke of Sutherland, 4 April 1846.

35. D593/K/2/1, Sellar to Loch, 12 August 1846.

36. D593/K/2/1, Sellar to Loch, 6 March 1847.

37. See A. R. L. Haldane, *The Drove Roads of Scotland* (Edinburgh, 1952), p. 193.

38. P. Gaskell, *Morvern Transfromed* (Cambridge, 1968), p. 220.

39. Ibid., p. 27.

40. Ibid., p. 216.

41. In 1847, *Tait's Magazine* published an article in which Sellar, in his words, was alleged to have extirpated 5,000 families, and from the benefits he derived 'a garrish mansion . . . built by me beside the rock of Ardtornish.' Sellar pointed out that he had not built a house at Ardtornish, but 'dwelt in the old farm house which was held by the Duke of Argyll's factor.' The external appearance of the house had not been altered. He described the so-called 'Venerable Chieftains' at the time of Edward IVth as 'traitors to their country'. He also claimed, 'My possessions in this country I found under black cattle at the time of my entry.' D593/K/8/20, Sellar to Tait's, 20 September 1847.

42. D593/K/P/2/1, Sellar to Loch, 21 March 1840.

43. James Wilson, *A Voyage Round the Coasts of Scotland and the Isles*, 2 vols (Edinburgh, 2v. 1842), I, p.184.

44. D593/K/1/3/31, Sellar to Loch, 4 October 1844.

45. D593/K/1/3/31, Sellar to G. Loch, 2 November 1845.

46. D593/K/1/3/31, Sellar to Loch, 15 October 1845.

47. Herbert Spencer, *An Autobiography*, 2 vols (1904), I, pp. 489, 491; II, pp. 67–9, 370–2.

48. Gaskell, op. cit., pp. 63–5.

49. Ibid., p. 41 from *Oban Times*, 3 March 1883.

50. Gaskell, op. cit., p. 42

51. Spencer, op. cit., I, pp. 489, 491; II, pp. 67–9, 370–2.

52. There was severe commentary on Sellar, in the *Oban Times* in October 1844.

53. Iain Thornber, 'Some Morvern songwriters of the nineteenth century', *Transactions of the Gaelic Society of Inverness*, LIII (1982–4), pp. 1–90.

54. D593/K/1/3/32, Sellar to Duke of Sutherland, 22 May 1844.

55. D593/K/1/3/32, Sellar to Loch, 25 May 1844.

56. D593/K/1/3/32, Sellar to Loch, 27 October 1845.

57. D593/K/1/3/32, Sellar to Loch 23 October 1846, Duke of Sutherland to Loch, 16 November 1846.

58. D593/K, Sellar to Loch, 28 September 1847.

59. D593/P/20, Sellar to Duke of Sutherland, 22 October 1847.

60. D593/K/P/2/1,Sellar to the Duke of Sutherland, 28 September 1847, Lewis to the Duke, 7 Dec 1847.
61. D593/K/1/3/35, Sellar to Loch, 14 January 1847.
62. D/593/K/1/3/34, Sellar to Loch, 18 February 1846.
63. D593/K/8/20, Sellar to Duke of Sutherland, 2 September 1847.
64. D593K/8/20, Sellar to Duke of Sutherland, 6 October 1847. Alexander Matheson, a native of the Sutherland estate, had bought the island of Lewis out of his famous profits from the China trade, and he undertook large relief operations in the ensuing famine.
65. D593/V/10/10, Pamphlet.
66. D593/K/8/20, Duke of Sutherland to Loch, 1 August 1848.
67. D593/K/8/20, Sellar to Loch, 29 September 1848.
68. D593/K/8/20, Sellar to Loch, 18 October 1848.
69. D593/K/8/20 Sellar to Loch, 23 October 1848.
70. D593/K/8/20, Sellar to Loch, 25 October 1847. See also Mitchell, op. cit., II, pp. 86–8, 99–100, 111, 215.
71. D593/K/1/2/36, Sellar to Loch, 26 February 1848.; NLS Dep. 313/1210, Loch to Gunn, 7 February 1849.
72. Dep. 313, Box 41, Gunn to Duke of Sutherland, 13 November 1846.
73. NLS Dep. 313/1258, Horsburgh to Gunn 17 August 1846, 15 and 25 September 1846.
74. NLS Dep. 313/1212, Loch to Gunn, 17 April 1846. The Drainage Act provided financial aid designed to assist improvements by farmers and landlords in compensation for the repeal of protection.
75. NLS Dep. 313/1215, Loch to Gunn, 6 March 1849, including a note from Duke of Sutherland.
76. D593/K/3/39, Sellar to Loch, 17 April 1850.
77. D593/K, Sellar to Loch, 24 September 1849, P. P. Sellar to Loch, 25 March 1850.
78. D593/K/1/3/38, Gunn to Loch, 24 Dec 1850; P.P. Sellar to Alex Craig, 23 Dec 1850.
79. D593/K/P/2/1, Duke to Sellar, 6 October 1847.
80. D593/K/P/2/1, Loch to Sellar, 8 November 1847.
81. D593/K/P/22/1/25, Duke to Lady Stafford, 14 July 1850. This was in response to Donald Ross's recent public criticisms, noting that Ross 'when in Suthd [was] convicted of forgery and imprisoned in Dornoch Jail'.

– CHAPTER 17   DEATH, DENUNCIATION AND POSTERITY –

1. D593/K/1/8/27. This is an undated item in a collection of contemporary newspaper clippings.
2. D593/K/P/28/9, Duke to Lady Stafford, 14 July 1850.
3. D593/K/1/8/27.

4. Ibid.
5. D593/K /1/3/37, P. P. Sellar to Loch, 12 February 1851.
6. D593/K /1/3/37, Patrick Sellar to Duke of Sutherland, 8 September 1851.
7. D593/K /1/3/37, Loch to Patrick Sellar, 17 October 1851.
8. D593/K /1/3/37, P. Sellar, junior, to Loch, 3 October 1851.
9. D593/K /1/3/37, Loch to the Duke of Sutherland, 23 October 1851.
10. D593/K /1/3/37, Thomas Sellar to Loch, 21 October 1851.
11. D593/K /1/3/37, Thomas Sellar to Loch, 21 October 1851.
12. E. M. Sellar, *Recollections and Impressions* (Edinburgh, 1907), p. 38.
13. Jowett to W. Y. Sellar, 26 October 1851, in Evelyn Abbott and Lewis Campbell, *The Life and Letters of Benjamin Jowett*, (1897), I, pp. 125, 140. 222–3; P. Gaskell, *Morvern Transformed* (Cambridge, 1968), p. 39, 204, fn. 4.
14. *Elgin Courier*, 31 October 1851.
15. *Aberdeen Journal*, 12 November 1851 from the *Elgin Courier*, 31 October 1851.
16. I am most grateful to Dr F. W. Robertson of the Caithness County Library in Wick for transcripts of these obituaries, which he made for me in 1969.
17. SRO SC 9/36/4, Inventory of Patrick Sellar's Personal Effects. NLS Dep. 313/118, Loch to Horsburgh, 10 Dec 1851.
18. NLS Dep. 313/1181, James Loch to Duke of Sutherland, 2 November 1851.
19. E. M. Sellar, op. cit., p. 29.
20. Titanga Papers, Ann Sellar to Mrs Brown (undated, 1852).
21. *Elgin Courant*, 30 June 1854.
22. Culmaily remained in the family until May 1901, see M. W. Grant, *Golspie's Story* (Golspie, 1991), p. 145.
23. Her brother Craig, in Sutherland, was highly sociable and would invite people to dinner at the drop of a hat. He badly fell out with Patrick Sellar in 1828. See above Ch. 13.
24. Quoted by E. M. Sellar, op. cit. (1907), p. 41.
25. See Eric Richards, 'The Highland passage to colonial Australia', *Scotlands* (1995), pp. 28–44. On the Sellar family see Gaskell, op. cit., p. 41; NLS MS 10084, A. C. Sellar to Rosebery, 28 September 1885.
26. NLS Dep. 313, James Loch to Horsburgh, 10 December 1851.
27. NLS Dep. 313, James Loch to Duke of Sutherland, 26 November 1852.
28. NLS Dep. 313, Duke to Lady Stafford, 14 July 1850.
29. D 593L/2/29, Memorandum Book. Statement of revenue and expenditure by James Loch for 1852, dated 19 July 1853.
30. *John O'Groats Journal*, 7 March 1861.
31. D593/N/4/1/4, Sporting Rents, 1856–70.
32. D593/K/P/22/1/24, George Loch to Duke of Sutherland, 5 Oct. 1856.
33. D593/K/P/2/1, Loch to the Duke, 7 June 1861.

34. Donald Sage was a witness to many of the events in Sutherland and to the evictions. His account was published posthumously as *Memorabilia Domestica* (Wick, 1889). He was confused as to dates, and suggested incorrectly that Sellar was personally involved in the 1819 removals.

35. See Gaskell, op cit., p. 38, fn. 3. and R. M. Mitchison, 'The Highland Clearances', *Scottish Social and Economic History*, I (1981), pp. 4–24.

36. See Donald Meek (ed.), *Tuath is Tighearna. Tenants and Landlords* (Edinburgh, 1995).

37. Ibid., pp. 190–1, 17–18, respectively.

38. George and Peter Anderson, *Guide to the Highlands and Islands of Scotland*, 3rd edn (Edinburgh, 1851), p. 408.

39. On the Duke's frame of mind at the time, see D593/K/1/5/75, Loch to Shaftesbury, 4 June 1853.

40. See Eric Richards, *A History of the Highland Clearances: Vol. II: Emigration, Protest, Reasons* (London, 1985).

41. *Altavona: Fact and Fiction from my Life in the Highlands,* 1st edn (Edinburgh, 1882) was heavily reliant on Macleod.

42. T. Sellar, *The Sutherland Evictions of 1814* (1883), p. 19.

43. Ibid., p. lxxii. In the outcome, Mackid's 'confession' was not reproduced, and all modern editions also omit this evidence. Mackenzie, however, reproduced the Robertson account of the trial in a new edition in 1883, with his own total rejection of the *Report* which he denounced as a piece of special pleading. *The Trial of Patrick Sellar*, new edition with introductory remarks by Alexander Mackenzie (Inverness, 1883).

44. NLS MS 2644 f.iii, Letters of John Stuart Blackie, Sellar to Douglas, 17 July 1882. See above, Ch. 1.

45. Alexander Mackenzie, *Isle of Skye in 1882–3* (Inverness, 1883), p. lii. Alfred Russel Wallace was another passionate critic of evictions in the Highlands in his *Land Nationalisation* (5th edn, London, 1902). He believed that people should not be 'de-housed', and instanced the history of the Sutherland clearances. Wallace's account went through several editions and, while invoking the writings of Oliver Goldsmith, also used the Sellar story as ammunition for its attack on landlords. His main source was Macleod's book of 1841. Wallace too was challenged by the Sellar family, and his later editions eliminated all references to Sellar.

46. *Inverness Courier*, 15 June 1885.

47. See Richards, 'The Highland passage' op. cit., passim.

48. Iain Crichton Smith, *Consider the Lilies* (reprint of 1st edn, Edinburgh, 1987).

49. Quoted in Lorn Macintyre, 'A rare intelligence', in Colin Nicholson (ed.), *Iain Crichton Smith. Critical Essays* (Edinburgh, 1992), p. 158.

50. Grimble, *The Trial of Patrick Sellar* (London, 1962), passim. Sellar also figures in the well-known play by John McGrath, *The Cheviot, the Stag and the Black Black Oil.*

51. Review of John Prebble in *The Times*, 1996.
52. *Guardian Weekend*, 12 October 1996, p. 36.
53. David Daiches (ed.), *New Companion to Scottish Culture* (Edinburgh, 1993), pp. 54, 318. The folklore view is exemplified by Alexander Campbell, *The Romance of the Highlands* (Aberdeen, 1927), p. 263.
54. Letter of Robert Dryden to *The Scotsman*, 21 October 1994.

– CHAPTER 18 THE TEARS OF PROGRESS –

1. John Henderson, *General View of the agriculture of the County of Sutherland* (1812), pp. 24, 87, 104,
2. Thomas Sellar, *The Sutherland Evictions of 1814* (1883), pp. 12–15.
3. See M. W. Flinn's Introduction to Edwin Chadwick, *The Sanitary Condition of the Labouring Population of Gt. Britain* (1842; Edinburgh, 1965), pp. 22–3. My thanks to Dr Ralph Shlomowitz for reminding me of this passage.
4. Cf. Robert Darnton, 'George Washington's false teeth', *New York Review of Books*, 27 March 1997, pp. 34–8.
5. In the Foreword to Aylwin Clark, *An Enlightened Scot: Hugh Cleghorn* (1752–1837), (Duns, 1992), pp. xiv-xvii.
6. See the examples of Enlightenment thinking towards the Highlands anthologised in Jane Rendall, *The Origins of the Scottish Enlightenment* (London, 1978), pp. 11, *et seq.*
7. In P. Gaskell, *Morvern Transformed* (Cambridge, 1968) p. xiii.
8. D. McCloskey in R. Floud and D. McCloskey (eds), *The Economic History of Britain since 1700*, 2 vols. (1981), I, p. 104.
9. John A. James and Mark Thomas (eds), *Capitalism in Context* (Chicago, 1994); see especially Introduction, pp. 1–6.
10. See E. Hobsbawm, *The Age of Revolution* (London, 1962), p. 47.
11. James and Thomas, op. cit., p. 1.
12. One of the standard indictments of the early twentieth-century British economy is that it 'lacked effective mechanisms to remove inefficient firms and managers.' N. Crafts, 'Managerial decline, 1870–1990?', *History Today*, 44 (1994), p. 40.
13. James and Thomas, op. cit., p. 7.
14. Ibid., p. 8.
15. Jeffrey Williamson, quoted in ibid., p. 9.
16. Joel Mokyr, 'Progress and Inertia in technological change', in ibid., p. 231–5.
17. Ibid., pp. 236–7 and Joel Mokyr, *The Lever of Riches* (New York, 1990), pp. 176–9
18. He says that between 1750 and 1850 'the British political system unflinchingly supported the winners over the losers' in the course of industrialisation. Mokyr, *The Lever of Riches*, op. cit., p. 256.
19. Mokyr in James and Thomas, op. cit., p. 245.

20. Quoted in J. Barzun and H. F. Graff, *The Modern Researcher* (San Diego, CA, 1985), p. 179, fn.
21. See, for example, Kate de Selincourt, 'The Damned', *New Statesman and Society,* 12 March 1993, pp. 29–30.
22. T. S. Ashton, *The Industrial Revolution* (London, 1948), p. 129.
23. Joseph A. Schumpeter, *Capitalism, Socialism and Democracy,* 4th edn (London, 1954), ch. VII, p. 83, and Jonathan Hughes, *Industrialization and Economic History* (New York, 1970), p. 63.
24. J. Mokyr, *Lever of Riches,* op. cit., p. 261.
25. G. Kitson Clark, *The Making of Victorian England* (London, 1962), p. 93. The same metaphor is employed by G. M. Young in *Victorian England, Portrait of an Age* (London, 1953), p. 22. It recurs in Kenneth Clark's *Civilisation* (London, 1969), p. 323.
26. Campbell, in Gaskell, op. cit., p. v.

Bibliography

– ARCHIVAL SOURCES –
– PRIVATE PAPERS –

Titanga Papers, by courtesy of Christopher and Valerie Lang of Titanga, Victoria, Australia.
Irvine-Robertson MS, by courtesy of Mr Irvine Robertson, Stirling.
Blair Adam Papers, Blair Adam, NRA 1454.
Papers of Sir Ewan MacPherson Grant, Ballindalloch Castle, Banff.
Papers of Mr Justice Robert Fisher, Adelaide.

– SCOTTISH RECORD OFFICE –

SRO Gilchrist of Ospidale Papers, GD 153.
SRO Balnagowan Papers, GD 129.
SRO Seafield Muniments, GD 248.
SRO Maclaine of Lochbuy Papers, GD 174.
SRO Dornoch Sheriff Court Minute Book, SC/1/3.
SRO Loch Muniments. GD, 268.
SRO Court of Sessions Records, CS 232.
SRO Sinclair of Freswick Papers, GD 136.

– NATIONAL LIBRARY OF SCOTLAND –

NLS Sutherland Collection, Dep. 313.
NLS Constable Letter Book 1820–2, MS 791.
NLS Letters of John Stuart Blackie, MS 2644.

– STAFFORDSHIRE COUNTY RECORD OFFICE –

Sutherland Collection, D593.

– INVERNESS PUBLIC LIBRARY, HIGHLAND REGIONAL ARCHIVE –

Record of Prisoners Incarcerated in the Tolbooth or Jail of the Burgh of Dornoch, L/S/M/1/2.

- UNIVERSITY COLLEGE, LONDON -

Society for the Diffusion of Useful Knowledge, 1826–48 (SDUK).

- NEWSPAPERS -

Aberdeen Journal
Caledonian Mercury
Edinburgh Evening Courant
Edinburgh Advertiser
Elgin Courant
Elgin Courier
Inverness Journal
John O'Groats Journal
Morning Star
New Edinburgh Review
Oban Times
The Scotsman
The Times

- PUBLISHED WORKS -

Abbott, Evelyn and Campbell, Lewis, *The Life and Letters of Benjamin Jowett* (1897).
Adam, R. J. (ed.), *Sutherland Estate Papers*, 2 vols (Edinburgh, 1972).
Anderson, George and Anderson, Peter, *Guide to the Highlands and Islands of Scotland* 3rd edn (Edinburgh, 1851).
Ashton, T. S., *The Industrial Revolution* (London, 1948).
Bangor-Jones, Malcolm, *The Assynt Clearances* (Dundee, 1998).
Barzun, J. and Graff, H. F., *The Modern Researcher* (San Diego, CA, 1985).
Bell, Robert, *A Treatise on Leases* (1803).
Blackie, J. S., *Altavona, Fact and Fiction from my Life in the Highlands* (Edinburgh, 1882).
Botfield, Benjamin, *Journal of a Tour Through the Highlands* (published anonymously, Norton Hall, 1830).
Breen, Henry, *St Lucia* (1844).
Brooking, Tom, *Lands for the People* (Dunedin, 1996).
Brown, Callum, *The Social History of Religion in Scotland since 1730* (London 1987).
Burns, Sir Alan, *History of the British West Indies* (London, 1965).
Cain, P. J. and Hopkins, A. G., *British Imperialism, 1688–1914* (London, 1993).
Campbell, Alexander, *The Romance of the Highlands* (Aberdeen, 1927).
Campbell, Duncan, *The Book of Garth and Fortingall*, 2 vols (Inverness, 1888).
Chadwick, Edwin, *Report on the Sanitary Condition of the Labouring Population of Gt. Britain* (1842; Edinburgh, 1965).

Checkland, S. G., *Scottish Banking, A History, 1695–1973* (Glasgow, 1975).

Clapham, J. H., *Economic History of Modern Britain*, 3 vols (Cambridge, 1926–38).

Clark, Aylwin, *An Enlightened Scot. Hugh Cleghorn (1752–1837)* (Duns, 1992).

Clark, G. Kitson, *The Making of Victorian England* (London, 1962).

Clark, Kenneth, *Civilisation*, (London, 1969).

Cockburn, Henry, *Memorials of Henry Cockburn* (Edinburgh, 1856).

Cockburn, Henry, *Letters Chiefly Connected with the Affairs of Scotland* (London, 1874).

Cockburn, Henry *Circuit Journeys* (Edinburgh, 1888).

Crafts, N., 'Managerial decline, 1870–1990?', *History Today*, 44 (1994).

Cramb, Auslan, *Who Owns Scotland Now?* (Edinburgh, 1996).

Cramond, William, *The Records of Elgin* (Aberdeen, 1903).

Daiches, David (ed.), *New Companion to Scottish Culture* (Edinburgh, 1993).

de Serville, Paul, *Port Phillip Gentlemen* (Melbourne, 1980).

de Strzelecki, P. E., *Physical Description of New South Wales and Van Diemen's Land* (London, 1845).

Dodgshon, Robert, *A Land and Society in Early Scotland* (Oxford, 1981).

Fairhurst, Horace, 'The surveys for the Sutherland Clearances, 1814–1829', *Scottish Studies*, 8 (1964), pp. 1–16.

Falk, B., *The Bridgewater Millions* (London, 1942).

Floud, Roderick and McCloskey, Donald (eds), *The Economic History of Britain since 1700: 1. 1700–1860* (Cambridge, 1981).

Fraser-Mackintosh, C., *Antiquarian Notes*, 2nd edn (Stirling, 1913).

Gaskell, P., *Morvern Transformed* (Cambridge, 1968).

Gibson, Rob, *Toppling the Duke – Outrage on Ben Braggie?* (Evanston, IL, 1996).

Grant, Elizabeth of Rothiemurchus, *Memoirs of a Highland Lady* (reprint edition Edinburgh, 1988).

Grant, M .W., *Golspie's Story* (Golspie, 1983).

Grant M. W., 'Why always Sutherland?' (Typescript, n.d.).

Grimble, Ian, *The Trial of Patrick Sellar* (London, 1962).

Haldane, A. R. B., *The Drove Roads of Scotland.* (Edinburgh, 1952).

Henderson, John, *General View of the Agriculture of the County of Sutherland* (1812).

Heney, H. M. E., *In a Dark Glass* (Sydney, 1961).

Hobsbawm, E., *The Age of Revolution* (London, 1962).

Houston, R. A., 'Scottish Education and literacy, 1600–1800: an international perspective', in T. M. Devine (ed.), *Improvement and Enlightenment* (Edinburgh, 1989).

Hughes, Jonathan, *Industrialization and Economic History* (New York, 1970).

Hunter, James, *A Dance Called America* (Edinburgh, 1994).

James, John A. J. and Thomas, Mark (eds), *Capitalism in Context* (Chicago, 1994).

The Journal of the Rev. John Wesley, 4 vols (London, 1906).

Kennedy, L. and Grainger, T. P. *The Present State of the Tenancy of Land* (London, 1829).

Kidd, Colin, 'Teutonic ethnology and Scottish nationalist inhibition, 1780–1880', *Scottish Historical Review*, LXXIV, 1995, pp. 45–68.

Lang, Patrick, *The Langs of Selkirk, updated 1910–1992* (Warrnambool, Australia, n.d. [*c.* 1993]).

Leneman, Leah (ed.), *Perspectives on Scottish Social History* (Aberdeen, 1988).

Leslie, William, *General View of the Agriculture of the Counties of Nairn and Moray* (London, 1813).

Leveson-Gower, F. (ed.) *Letters of Harriet Countess Granville, 1810–1845*, 2 vols (1894).

Loch, James, *Account of the Improvements on the Estates of the Marquess of Stafford* (1815; 1820).

Lockhart, Douglas, 'The evolution of the planned Vvillages of north east Scotland: studies in settlement geography, *c.*1700 to *c.*1900', unpublished PhD thesis, Dundee University, 1974.

Lockhart, D. G., 'Patterns of migration and movement of labour to the planned villages of north east Scotland', *Scottish Geographical Magazine*, 98, 1982, pp. 35–49.

Logue, K. D., *Popular Disturbances in Scotland 1780–1815* (Edinburgh, 1979).

Mackay, Angus, *The Book of Mackay* (Edinburgh, 1904).

Mackay, H. M., *Notes on the Successive Buildings used for County, Municipal and Judicial Purposes of the County of Sutherland and Burgh of Dornoch* (Privately published Edinburgh, 1896).

Mackenzie, Alexander, *Isle of Skye in 1882–3* (Inverness, 1883).

Mackenzie, Alexander, *The History of the Highland Clearances* (Inverness, 1883).

Mackintosh, Herbert B., *Elgin, Past and Present* (Edinburgh, 1914).

Donald M'Leod's *Gloomy Memories in the Highlands of Scotland versus Mrs Harriet Beecher Stowes Sunny Memories in (England) a Foreign Land: or a Faithful Picture of the Extirpation of the Celtic Race from the Highlands of Scotland* (Glasgow, 1892).

McLeod, Donald, *Gloomy Memories in the Highlands of Scotland* (1892, reprinted Bettyhill, 1996).

McMaster, Graham, *Scott and Society* (Cambridge, 1981).

Magnusson, Magnus, *The Clacken and the Slate. The Story of the Edinburgh Academy, 1824–1974* (London, 1974).

Mandler, Peter, *Aristocratic Government in the Age of Reform* (Oxford, 1990).

Marryat, Joseph, *Thoughts on the Abolition of the Slave Trade and Civilization of Africa* (1816).

Mather, Alexander, 'The environmental impact of sheep farming in the Scottish Highlands', in T. C. Smout (ed.), *Scotland Since Pre History* (Aberdeen, 1993)

Mather, F. C., *After the Canal Duke* (Oxford, 1970).

Mitchell, B. R. and Deane, P., *Abstract of British Historical Statistics* (Cambridge, 1982).

Mitchison, R. M., 'The Highland Clearances', *Scottish Economic and Social History*, 1 (1981), pp. 4–24.

Mearns, Alexander, 'The minister and the bailiff: A study of Presbyterian clergy in the northern Highlands during the clearances', *Scottish Church History Society Records*, XXIV (1990), pp. 53–75.

Meek, Donald (ed.), *Tuath is Tighearna. Tenants and Landlords* (Edinburgh, 1995).

Mitchell, Joseph, *Reminiscences of My Life in the Highlands*, 2 vols (originally published privately in 1883 and 1884; reprinted Newton Abbot, 1971).

Mokyr, Joel, *The Lever of Riches* (New York, 1990).

New Statistical Account of Scotland, vols XV and XVII (1845).

Nicholson, Colin (ed.), *Iain Crichton Smith. Critical Essays* (Edinburgh, 1992).

Omand, D. (ed.), *The Sutherland Book* (Golspie, 1985).

Paszkowski, Lech, *Sir Paul Edmund de Strzelecki* (Melbourne, 1997).

Phillipson, N. T. and Mitchison, Rosalind, *Scotland in the Age of Improvement* (Edinburgh, 1970).

Prebble, John, *The King's Jaunt* (London, 1988).

Rendall, Jane, *The Origins of the Scottish Enlightenment* (London, 1978).

Richards, David, *Masks of Difference* (Cambridge, 1994).

Richards, Eric, 'The prospect of economic growth in Sutherland at the time of the clearances', *Scottish Historical Review*, XCIX, 148 (1970) pp. 154–71.

Richards, Eric, 'The mind of Patrick Sellar, 1780–1852', *Scottish Studies*, 15 (1971), pp. 1–20.

Richards, Eric, *The Leviathan of Wealth. The Sutherland Fortune in the Industrial Revolution* (London and Toronto, 1973).

Richards, Eric, 'How tame were the Highlanders during the Clearances?', *Scottish Studies*, 17 (1973), pp. 35–50.

Richards, Eric, 'Patterns of Highland discontent 1790–1860', in Stevenson J. and Quinault, R. (eds), *Popular Protest and Public Order 1780–1920. Six studies in British History* (London, 1974).

Richards, Eric, 'The Sutherland clearances: new evidence from Dunrobin', *Northern Scotland*, 2 (1976) pp. 57–75.

Richards, Eric, *A History of the Highland Clearances: Vol. I. Agrarian Transformation and the Evictions, 1745–1886* (London, 1982).

Richards, Eric, *The Last Scottish Food Riots* (Oxford, 1982).

Richards, Eric, 'Australia and the Scottish connection 1788–1914', in R. A. Cage (ed.), *The Scots Abroad* (London, 1984).

Richards, Eric, *A History of the Highland Clearances: Vol. II. Emigration, Protest, Reasons,* (London, 1985).

Richards, Eric, 'Fate and culpability in the Highland clearances', *Yearbook of the Scottish History Teachers' Association* (1989), pp. 17–27.

Richards, Eric, 'The Highland passage to colonial Australia', *Scotlands* (1995), pp. 28–44.

Richards, Eric, 'The *Military Register* and the Pursuit of Patrick Sellar', *Scottish Economic and Social History*, 16 (1996), pp. 38–60.

[Robertson, Patrick] *Report of the Trial of Patrick Sellar, Esq. Factor of the Most Noble the Marquis and Marchioness of Stafford for the crimes of Culpable Homicide, Real Injury, and Oppression. Before the Circuit Court of Justiciary, held at Inverness, on Tuesday 23 April, 1816* (Edinburgh, 1816).

Rudé, George, *The Crowd in History* (New York, 1964).

Smith, Iain Crichton, *Consider the Lilies* (1st edn, London, 1968; reprinted Edinburgh 1987).

Sage, Donald, *Memorabilia Domestica* (Wick, 1889).

Schumpeter, Joseph A., *Capitalism Socialism and Democracy*, 4th edn (London, 1954).

Scott, James C., *Weapons of the Weak. Everyday Forms of Peasant Resistance* (New Haven, CT, 1985).

Scott, Walter, *Guy Mannering* (1957 edition).

Selkirk, Patrick Lang, *The Langs of Selkirk* (Melbourne, 1910).

Sellar, E. M., *Recollections and Impressions* (Edinburgh, 1907).

Sellar, Patrick, *Statement* (1825).

Sellar, Patrick, *Farm Reports III, County of Sutherland. Strathnaver, Morvich and Culmaily Farms, Library of Useful Knowledge* (London, 1831).

Sellar, Thomas, *The Sutherland Evictions of 1814* (1883).

Shaw, Lachlan, *History of the Province of Moray*, 3 vols (Glasgow, 1882).

Smout, T. C., 'The landowner and the planned village in Scotland, 1730–1830', in N. T. Phillipson and Rosalind Mitchison (eds), *Scotland in the Age of Improvement* (Edinburgh, 1970).

Spencer, Herbert, *An Autobiography*, 2 vols (1904).

Stewart, David, *Sketches of the Character, Manners, and Present State of the Highlanders of Scotland with details of the Military Service of the Highland Regiments*. 2 vols, 2nd edn (Edinburgh, 1825).

Survey of the Province of Moray (Aberdeen, 1790).

[Sutherland, Alexander], *A Summer Ramble in the North Highlands* (Edinburgh, 1825).

Sutherland, Alexander, *Victoria and its Metropolis* (Melbourne, 1888).

Symon, J. A., *Scottish Farming, Past and Present* (Edinburgh, 1959).

Taylor, A. J., *Laissez-faire and State Intervention in Nineteenth Century Britain* (London, 1972).

Thornber, Iain, 'Some Morvern songwriters of the nineteenth century', *Transactions of the Gaelic Society of Inverness*, LIII (1982–4), pp. 1–90.

Tidswell, David, 'Geographical mobility, occupational changes and family relationships in early nineteenth century Scotland (with particular reference to the precognitions of the Lord Advocate's department, 1812–21'. Unpublished PhD thesis, Edinburgh University, 1993.

The Trial of Patrick Sellar, new edition with introductory remarks by Alexander Mackenzie (Inverness, 1883).

Turnock, D, 'Stages of agricultural improvement in the Uplands of Scotland's Grampian Region', *Journal of Historical Geography,* 3 (1977), pp. 327–48.

Walker, David M., *The Scottish Jurists* (Edinburgh, 1985).

Walker, David M., *The Oxford Companion to Law* (Oxford, 1980).

Wallace, Alfred Russel, *Land Nationalisation,* 5th edn (London, 1902).

Watson, Don, *Caledonia Australis* (Sydney, 1984).

Watson, J. and Watson, W., *Morayshire Described* (Elgin, 1868).

Wilson, James, *A Voyage round the Coasts of Scotland and the Isles,* 2 vols (Edinburgh, 1842).

Withers, Charles W. J. 'Place, memory, monument: memorialising the past in Contemporary Highland Scotland', *Ecumen,* 3 1996, pp. 325–44.

Young, G. M., *Victorian England, Portrait of an Age* (London, 1953).

Young, Robert, *Notes on Burghead, Ancient and Modern* (Elgin, 1868).

Young, Robert, *The Parish of Spynie in the County of Elgin,* (Elgin, 1871).

Young, Robert, *Annals of the Parish and Burgh of Elgin* (Elgin, 1879).

Index